OBLIVIOUS TO THE SIGNS

WHEN IT'S OBVIOUS THE KING IS COMING

END TIMES ARMOR SERIES

OBLIVIOUS TO THE SIGNS
WHEN IT'S OBVIOUS THE KING IS COMING

Copyright © 2024 Marsha Kuhnley
Visit the author's website at Rapture911.com

Edited by Drezhn Publishing LLC

All rights reserved. No part of this publication may be reproduced, distributed, or transmitted in any form or by any means, including photocopying, recording, or other electronic or mechanical methods, without the prior written permission of the publisher, except in the case of brief quotations embodied in critical reviews and certain other noncommercial uses permitted by copyright law.

While the author has made every effort to provide accurate internet addresses at the time of publication, neither the publisher nor the author assumes responsibility for errors or changes that occur after publication. The publisher and author do not have any control over and do not assume responsibility for third-party websites or their content.

Published by Drezhn Publishing LLC
PO BOX 67458
Albuquerque, NM 87193-7458

Cover Design by MIBL ART and Drezhn Publishing LLC

Print Edition - September 2024
Version 1.0

PAPERBACK ISBN: 978-1-947328-82-2
HARDBACK ISBN: 978-1-947328-83-9

Unless otherwise indicated, all Scripture quotations are taken from the World English Bible (WEBP), a public domain translation of the Holy Bible.

Scripture quotations marked (NLT) are taken from the Holy Bible, New Living Translation, copyright © 1996, 2004, 2015 by Tyndale House Foundation. Used by permission of Tyndale House Publishers, Inc., Carol Stream, Illinois 60188. All rights reserved.

Scripture quotations marked (NKJV) are taken from the New King James Version®. Copyright © 1982 by Thomas Nelson. Used by permission. All rights reserved.

TABLE OF CONTENTS

INTRODUCTION 1
- Oblivious When It's Obvious 2
- End Times Armor 6

PART 1 BLESSED FOR WATCHING 9
- Chapter 1 - Watch 10
  - Why Watch? 10
  - So We Know The Details Of Jesus's Coming 10
  - So We Know Who's Who In Jesus's Coming 11
  - So We Know When Jesus Is Coming 12
  - So We Know What To Watch For 14
  - So We Know Where Jesus Is Coming 16
  - So We Know What To Do Before Jesus Comes 16
  - So We Know What Gift To Bring 17
- Chapter 2 - Today Is Different 19
  - Sign Legend 19
  - #1 - Israel Is A Nation 21
  - #2 - The Timing Is Right 22
  - #3 - When You See All These Things 25
  - #4 - Birth Pains 27
  - #5 - Tribulation In View 32
  - #6 - The Point Of No Return 33

PART 2 SIGNS OF THE HEART 37
- Chapter 3 - It's A Heart Condition 38
- Chapter 4 - A Turned Away Heart 42
  - #7 - Apostasy 42
  - #8 - Backsliding 44
  - #9 - Worshiping Other Gods 45
  - #10 - Idolatry 47
  - #11 - The Occult 49
  - #12 - Satanism 50
  - #13 - Great Fear 52
  - #14 - Polar Opposite - A Seeking Heart 53
- Chapter 5 - A Prideful Heart 56
  - #15 - Puffed Up With Pride 56
  - #16 - Lovers Of Ourselves 57
  - #17 - Everyone Does Right In Their Own Eyes 59
  - #18 - Fortified Cities And High Towers 61
  - #19 - Changing Times And Laws 63
  - #20 - Polar Opposite - A Worshiping Heart 64
- Chapter 6 - A Foolish Heart 67
  - #21 - Curses Are A Warning 67
  - #22 - Cancel Culture 68
  - #23 - Anxiety Of Nations With Perplexity 70
  - #24 - Always Learning But Never Know Truth 72
  - #25 - Fake Bibles 74
  - #26 - Refusal To Believe 76

#27 - Scoffers 77
#28 - Neither Hot Nor Cold 79
#29 - Despising God's Word 81
#30 - Atheism 83
#31 - Hopelessness 85
#32 - Rapture 911 86
#33 - Polar Opposite - A Wise Heart 89

Chapter 7 - A Hardened Heart 91
#34 - God's Warnings Aren't Heeded 91
#35 - Don't Endure Sound Doctrine 93
#36 - Children Of Disobedience 96
#37 - Censorship 98
#38 - Rebellious 101
#39 - No Apologies 103
#40 - Polar Opposite - A Heart Of Flesh 105

Chapter 8 - A Coveting Heart 107
#41 - Coveting 107
#42 - Jealousy 108
#43 - Entitlement 110
#44 - Lovers Of Pleasure 112
#45 - Love Of Money 114
#46 - Stealing 116
#47 - Destruction Of Wealth 118
#48 - Wealth Gap 121
#49 - The Rise Of Babylon 123
#50 - Polar Opposite - A Serving Heart 125

Chapter 9 - A Deceiving Heart 128
#51 - Deception 128
#52 - Slander 130
#53 - Conspiracy 131
#54 - Blasphemy 133
#55 - Assault On The Afterlife 136
#56 - False Teachers 138
#57 - False Prophets 140
#58 - The False Prophet 141
#59 - False Christs 143
#60 - The Antichrist 145
#61 - The Lie 148
#62 - A Covenant With Death 151
#63 - Lying Wonders 154
#64 - Polar Opposite - A Discerning Heart 156

Chapter 10 - A Discouraging Heart 158
#65 - Hypocrisy 158
#66 - Encouraging Sin 159
#67 - Profane Worship 161
#68 - Polluted Sanctuary 163
#69 - One World Religion 165
#70 - One World Currency 167
#71 - Image Of The Beast 171
#72 - Mark Of The Beast 172
#73 - Forced Worship 175
#74 - Polar Opposite - A Steadfast Heart 177

- Chapter 11 - A Perverse Heart 179
  - #75 - Drugs And Alcohol 179
  - #76 - Perverted Bodies 181
  - #77 - Abstain From Certain Foods 183
  - #78 - Cussing 184
  - #79 - Sexual Perversion 186
  - #80 - Attack On Marriage 189
  - #81 - Without Natural Affection 190
  - #82 - Genetic Engineering 192
  - #83 - Nephilim 193
  - #84 - Fading Of Normality 195
  - #85 - Downfall Of The United States 197
  - #86 - One World Government 201
  - #87 - Polar Opposite - An Upright Heart 202
- Chapter 12 - A Hateful Heart 205
  - #88 - Hatred 205
  - #89 - Victimhood 207
  - #90 - Mocking 208
  - #91 - Betrayal 210
  - #92 - Anti-Semitism 211
  - #93 - Unholy People Celebrated 214
  - #94 - God's Prophets Are Persecuted 216
  - #95 - Oppression Of God's People 218
  - #96 - Slavery 220
  - #97 - Polar Opposite - A Pure Heart 222
- Chapter 13 - An Evil Heart 224
  - #98 - Continually Only Evil 224
  - #99 - Child Sacrifice 226
  - #100 - Cannibalism 228
  - #101 - Perilous Times 230
  - #102 - Evil Inventions 232
  - #103 - Evil Leadership 234
  - #104 - The Election Omen 237
  - #105 - Kingdom Vs Kingdom 242
  - #106 - The Prince Of Persia 244
  - #107 - Psalm 83 Allies 247
  - #108 - Gog Of The Land Of Magog 250
  - #109 - Gog's Allies 254
  - #110 - The Antichrist Rules The World 256
  - #111 - Nation Vs Nation 259
  - #112 - All Nations Against Israel 261
  - #113 - Destruction Of Damascus 264
  - #114 - Shocking Amount Of Destruction 266
  - #115 - War Against God's People 268
  - #116 - Gathered To Armageddon 272
  - #117 - Polar Opposite - A Good Heart 275

PART 3 SUPERNATURAL SIGNS 277

- Chapter 14 - Positive Signs 278
  - #118 - God's Presence Is Obvious 278
  - #119 - Prophets Warn About The Future 280
  - #120 - Many Run To And Fro 282

#121 - Knowledge Shall Increase 283
#122 - Prophecy Sealed Until End Times 284
#123 - Population Explosion 287
#124 - Secrets Revealed 288
#125 - Israel's Wealth 290
#126 - Israel's Birds Of Prey 292
#127 - Israel's Beasts 293
#128 - The Third Temple 294
#129 - The Blessed 296
#130 - The Accursed 299
#131 - Broken Pagan Altars 301
#132 - Christian Revival 303
#133 - The Gospel Preached Everywhere 305
#134 - A Place Prepared By God 307

Chapter 15 - Signs On The Earth 311
#135 - The Curse 311
#136 - The Day Of The Lord 312
#137 - Pestilences 314
#138 - Earth Made Desolate 316
#139 - Great Earthquakes 320
#140 - Planet On Fire 325
#141 - Severe Storms 328
#142 - Sea And Waves Roaring 330
#143 - God's Wrath 334
#144 - Polar Opposite - Restored Earth 337

Chapter 16 - Signs In The Heavens 339
#145 - Wonders In The Sun, Moon, And Stars 339
#146 - The Heavens Shake 342
#147 - The Black Sun 344
#148 - War In Heaven 346
#149 - Polar Opposite - New Heavens 349

Chapter 17 - The Rapture 352
#150 - The Rapture 352
God's Purpose For The Rapture 355
Rapture Precedents 357
Will The Rapture Be Witnessed? 359
Timing Of The Rapture 362

Chapter 18 - God's Judgment Has A Purpose 369

PART 4   THE KING IS COMING 375

Chapter 19 - Was Blind, Now I See 376
Blinded By Your Intelligence 377
Blinded By Magic 382
Blinded By Biblical Ignorance 384
Blinded By Being Offended 386
Blinded By The Cares Of The World 388
Blinded By Peer Pressure 391
Blinded By Escapism 393
Blinded By Looking For The Wrong Savior 395
Blinded By Hurt 396
Blinded By Unrighteousness 398

Chapter 20 - Ready To Reign 401

- THE KING IS COMING 401
- WHAT JESUS DOES WHEN HE RETURNS 403
- TIMING OF THE SECOND COMING 404
- ARE YOU READY TO REIGN? 406

APPENDIX **411**
- A. SIGNS BY CATEGORIES 412
  - SIGN LEGEND 412
  - SIGNS IN JESUS'S OLIVET DISCOURSE 414
  - SIGNS BY CATEGORY 423
  - SIGNS IN DEUTERONOMY CURSES 432
  - SIGNS IN END TIMES NEW TESTAMENT SCRIPTURES 433
- B. OBLIVIOUS SUMMARIES AND END TIMES NOTES 435
  - GOOD HEARTS AND BAD HEARTS 435
  - PATTERNS IN THE PAST 435
  - END TIMES TIMELINE 436
  - HEAVENLY REWARDS 437
- ABOUT THE AUTHOR 439
- TESTIMONY OF MARSHA KUHNLEY 440
- ANSWERING GOD'S CALLING 445

GET FREE BOOKS **448**

BOOKS BY MARSHA KUHNLEY **449**

ENDNOTES **450**

OBLIVIOUS TO THE SIGNS

WHEN IT'S OBVIOUS THE KING IS COMING

End Times Armor Series

Marsha Kuhnley

INTRODUCTION

OBLIVIOUS WHEN IT'S OBVIOUS

I'm sure many of you are like me and have read several books about end times signs. You'll soon discover that this book isn't going to be like those. Those books usually discuss a dozen, maybe two dozen signs, with a chapter devoted to each one. My intent with this book is to show you every sign that I could find in the Bible that points to Jesus's return. I purposely wanted it to be overwhelmingly obvious that Jesus is coming any minute. Because this is what I and other end times Bible prophecy scholars see every day. It's obvious to us. Frankly, it's hard to understand why most everyone else seems so oblivious.

In fact, that's what inspired this book. I was thinking about why some people today are so spiritually blind to the signs. Which then got me thinking about how people living in the first century AD, who heard Jesus and watched his miracles, reacted to what he said. Of course, there were those who believed and those who followed him, like most of the disciples. To them it was obvious that Jesus was the Messiah. But to others, not at all. Consider the people who followed Jesus only because they got a free lunch (John 6). Jesus's own family and friends were spiritually blind to who he was (John 7:1-5, Mark 13:53-58). The Pharisees and Sadducees were so oblivious they wanted to kill him (Matthew 23, John 10:22-39). Judas Iscariot spent years with Jesus and saw countless miracles but was ignorant the whole time and actually ended up betraying him (Acts 1:15-17).

In this book, we're going to look at a lot of signs. I've labeled 150 of them! You'll soon see there are sub signs within signs. So, there are actually many more than that. Since there are so many signs to discuss, we're not going to go into an in-depth conversation about each one. But I'm going to give you ample evidence using examples and in many cases data from today that each sign is being fulfilled. And we're also going to discuss spiritual warfare. How someone can be blind to the signs, how Satan has a hand in that, and how to overcome this spiritual blindness.

Let's start with what's obvious. God made his existence obvious (Romans 1:18-20, Psalm 19). God also made it obvious that judgment was coming in the days of Noah. Noah and his grandfather, Methuselah, preached for 120 years and built a gigantic ark to withstand the coming flood (Genesis 6). I can't imagine that the construction project was a secret.

God also made it obvious that judgment was coming in the days of Lot. God sent angels to rescue Lot and his family (Genesis 19). The whole city saw the angels! And, before the angels and Lot's family left Sodom and Gomorrah, Lot warned people that God was going to destroy the city.

God also made Jesus's first coming obvious. Consider all the signs and miracles, the hundreds of fulfilled Bible prophecies, all the eyewitness testimony, and all the changed lives that resulted in Jesus's ministry. Jesus fulfilled 100% of the first coming Bible prophecies about the Messiah. God has a perfect track record of making his comings obvious. So, we can be confident that he's going to fulfill all the second coming prophecies too.

Yet even though God made those events obvious, the majority of people were oblivious. Consider Noah's day. Only Noah, his wife, his three sons and their wives were saved out of the hundreds of thousands of people who must have been alive at the time. Did they listen to Noah's preaching? Did they ever even ask him what he was building and why? How about with Lot? You know it's not an everyday occurrence to see an angel, yet that city saw two angels that day and wasn't amazed. No one asked why they were there. When Lot warned people about the coming destruction they didn't believe him. The city was only interested in their own pleasure and how they could use the angels to satisfy their evil desires. And, with Jesus's first coming, the Pharisees and Sadducees were expecting a different type of savior. So, they couldn't believe that he was the one sent by God.

In Chapter 3, we're going to discuss how the root of this blindness is a matter of the heart. The people of Noah's day had evil hearts, the people of Sodom and Gomorrah had foolish and perverse hearts, and the Pharisees and Sadducees had hard hearts. In fact, their hearts were so hard that they refused to believe even when they saw Jesus raise Lazarus from the grave (John 11).

Perhaps you feel like you're the only person who realizes that Jesus is coming soon. I for one see Christians busying themselves with things that are unimportant in light of the proper biblical perspective about the end times. Does it really make sense to invest thousands of dollars to make your house use green energy if you know Jesus is coming before that investment will break even? Some are bent on planning and striving for a future that I know isn't going to exist.

Or they're doomsday prepping, thinking they must fight against the Antichrist and survive the tribulation period. And then there are some who are even sorta mocking Jesus's coming with their "live it up" lifestyle: spend all you can, and who cares about the debt because I won't have to pay it back mindset.

I get that most people don't have anything to do with God, church, or the Bible these days. And I also get that very few churches even preach about Bible prophecy today. So, in a way I'm not surprised by the spiritual blindness today. But even up against the rise in unbelievers, Christian apostasy, and false teachers, this book is going to show you that God has made his next coming so obvious that I don't believe you need to have any prior knowledge of Bible prophecy in order to realize that something is about to happen. To anyone with just a bit of discernment, it's obvious that something is very wrong with the state of the world. I think you'll find this book encouraging, and it'll give you plenty of information to share with others.

Or perhaps you're someone who thinks today is no different than any time in the past. You think the signs have manifested in each generation. You've seen preachers set dates for the rapture that come and go. And the only reason you're reading this is because a friend bought the book for you, and you were slightly curious. Well, I've noticed that most people in this camp are often only aware of a small handful of signs from Jesus's Olivet Discourse. Signs like wars, famines, plagues, and earthquakes. And I would agree that those are signs that have always existed. However, Jesus gave us many more clues about those particular signs along with a long list of additional signs that would reveal the last generation. Convergence, birth pangs, and the fig tree parable are a few examples. We're going to go over all these signs.

I think you'll find Chapter 2 of particular interest because I explain six key signs that reveal how today is different. I hope you'll stick around. If you're wondering, no, I do not set a date for the rapture. We can't know the exact day that Jesus is coming again, but you'll learn that we can absolutely know the season, and wow are we in it!

Maybe you're a new believer or at least new to Bible prophecy and you really want to be looking for Jesus, but you have no idea where to begin. You are in the right place. It can certainly be daunting to delve into Bible prophecy, especially with the volume of false teachers today. I'd like you to know that I interpret the Bible literally. Sure, the Bible uses metaphors and symbols, but all of those can be explained when using the biblical text to interpret them.

I believe that God, Jesus, Satan, angels, and demons are all very real beings. I also believe that heaven and hell are very real physical places. None of these things are merely symbolic or only in your mind's eye. I also subscribe to the pre-tribulational interpretation of the rapture. The rapture happens prior to the tribulation period. We'll review the rapture in detail in Chapter 17. I'm also a pre-millennialist and believe in the physical second coming of Jesus to planet earth, followed by his literal 1,000-year reign on earth.

I share my personal testimony in the Appendix, but know that I've attended Calvary Church in Albuquerque, New Mexico for over 15 years. I've learned a ton about the Bible and Bible prophecy from Pastor Skip Heitzig. He's known for his expository style of teaching through the entire Bible and his literal interpretation of Scripture.

Get ready, because you're about to embark on an exciting journey through all the signs that point to Jesus's next coming. I'd encourage you to finish reading this introduction and then Chapters 1-3. After that, you can read the chapters sequentially or skip around and read whichever chapters or signs pique your interest. Then, pick back up in Chapter 18 to finish out the book. You might take a look at the Appendix too. I've included some handy reference tables to help you explore this book in many ways, like focusing on the signs that Jesus gave in the Olivet Discourse, all the signs regarding the Antichrist, or even each sign that relies on modern technology.

Regardless of what you currently believe, thanks for joining me on this journey through the Bible. I hope you come to see how obvious it is that Jesus is indeed coming again, and that it might be today!

END TIMES ARMOR

This is the third installment in my End Times Armor standalone book series. If you've read the other books in the series, this armor will be familiar to you. Since we're living in the very last of the last days before Jesus returns, we must be equipped to deal with the spiritual war that we're in. As you might suspect, a spiritual war isn't an ordinary war where land and resources are at stake. No, this war involves demonic rulers. What's at stake is the most precious thing of all, your soul.

The apostle Paul tells us about this war and the armor we need to be wearing in Ephesians chapter 6.

> Finally, be strong in the Lord and in the strength of his might. Put on the whole armor of God, that you may be able to stand against the wiles of the devil. For our wrestling is not against flesh and blood, but against the principalities, against the powers, against the world's rulers of the darkness of this age, and against the spiritual forces of wickedness in the heavenly places. Therefore put on the whole armor of God, that you may be able to withstand in the evil day, and having done all, to stand. Stand therefore, having the utility belt of truth buckled around your waist, and having put on the breastplate of righteousness, and having fitted your feet with the preparation of the Good News of peace, above all, taking up the shield of faith, with which you will be able to quench all the fiery darts of the evil one. And take the helmet of salvation, and the sword of the Spirit, which is the word of God; with all prayer and requests, praying at all times in the Spirit, and being watchful to this end in all perseverance and requests for all the saints. (Ephesians 6:10-18)

Paul tells us who we are and aren't fighting in this war. We aren't fighting "flesh and blood" means it's not a war against people, since people are made of flesh and blood. This means your coworker who disagrees with you on the key issues today or end times theology isn't your enemy. This is a war against the wiles or strategies of "the devil." Satan is the devil.

That's right. Satan is very real, and he's your enemy. In fact, one of the reasons people are so oblivious to the reality of Jesus returning any minute is because of Satan. He's the master of deception and doesn't want anyone to be prepared for Jesus's return. You need to know that he's the evil general in this war of the "principalities," "powers," "rulers of the darkness," and the "spiritual forces of wickedness."

There is so much hatred in the world today. So, please remember that your fellow humans aren't the real enemy. We are living in spiritually dark times where many people are imprisoned by Satan and his lies. Your goal should be to rescue them, not attack them.

Since our enemy is not made of flesh and blood, we must use spiritual means to both protect and defend ourselves. The "armor of God," is our End Times Armor. We're going to be dealing with some very heavy content in this book. The vast majority of signs that point to Jesus's return are negative in nature. Thus, it can get overwhelming to read about that page after page. So, it's important for you to be prepared in advance and have your armor on for spiritual protection.

This armor isn't ordinary armor made of leather or chain mail. Let's look at the elements in this armor. The "belt of truth" is God's Word. That means you need to know your Bible. Read it every day so that you have God's truths stored in your heart and close to you, ready to use like a tool you'd pull out of a utility belt.

The "breastplate of righteousness" is you placing your faith in Jesus. He's the one who makes you righteous. This is of the utmost importance considering the nearness of Jesus's return. You do not want to be left behind following the rapture. If you don't know who Jesus is, haven't asked him to forgive your sins, and haven't invited him into your heart, then stop right now and turn to Chapter 19. You need to get your heart right with Jesus and make sure he's the guardian of your soul before going any farther.

The next piece in this armor is having "fitted your feet" with the gospel. It means you're able to demonstrate your faith in both words and actions. It's important to have the right kind of busyness in your life. Helping other people is a great way to take your mind off things.

The "shield of faith" is you knowing and calling on all the promises of God when Satan's attack comes against you. In each chapter of signs, you're going to learn about some promises of God as we explore what life will be like during Jesus's millennial kingdom reign on earth. So, don't be afraid of the signs. Have hope. After all, the fulfillment of these signs means Jesus is coming!

Your "helmet of salvation" is being fully confident that you have been saved through your faith in Jesus. You are sealed with the Holy Spirit. Nothing, not even Satan, can steal you away from Jesus. We'll explore more ways we can use this armor in the last chapters of this book.

I want you to notice that God gave you a weapon as well. He expects you to use it. The "sword of the Spirit" is your weapon. It's the Word of God. When Satan came against Jesus to tempt him in the wilderness, Jesus combated Satan's lies with Scripture (Matthew 4; Luke 4). There is power in the Word of God. Use it.

> For the word of God is living and active, and sharper than any two-edged sword, piercing even to the dividing of soul and spirit, of both joints and marrow, and is able to discern the thoughts and intentions of the heart. (Hebrews 4:12)

After we've put on our armor, Paul tells us we need to pray at all times. We need to be close to God in order to draw strength from him. We get close to God by talking to him, reading his Word, and worshiping him. Start listening to Christian music if you don't already. It's positive and uplifting. It really does focus your mind on heavenly things.

The last thought I want to leave with you is the expectation God has put on us to take action. There's a purpose for wearing armor. It's to protect us in battle. That means we're supposed to be engaged in the battle. Look at how many times God used the word or variation of the word *stand* in Ephesians 6:10-18. I counted four times. It doesn't say put on God's armor and sit on the couch and watch what happens. No, it says stand! This means rise up, hold your ground, hold your position, endure, and display courage and strength.

I also hope you noticed the word *watchful* in the last verse about the armor. It means to be attentive, awake, and ready. God calls all of us Christians to be watchmen or observers (Ezekiel 3:17-21). When I think about this armor, the mental image that comes to my mind is that of a knight. Like what you see on this book cover.

We're living in one of the most exciting times in all of history. Put on your armor like a knight suited up for duty. Let's stand, watch, and be ready for Jesus!

PART 1

BLESSED FOR WATCHING

CHAPTER 1 - WATCH

Before we delve into all the end times signs that point to Jesus coming in the very near future, we first need to understand what signs to watch and why we're even supposed to be watching. There are lots of signs, but not everything is a sign. So, we need to be disciplined about this.

WHY WATCH?

Let's start with why we're even watching all these end times signs. The Bible tells us that in these last days, God has spoken to us by Jesus (Hebrews 1:1-2). Now, every Scripture in the Bible is the Word of God and Jesus is that Word (John 1). But sometimes it's interesting to study what Jesus himself actually said during his first coming. Well, guess what? The best and simplest answer is that Jesus himself told us to watch. And he didn't say it just once. Throughout the Gospel books, I counted that Jesus told us to watch 19 times. Of which, 11 happen in the Olivet Discourse.[1] The Olivet Discourse is recorded in three of the Gospel books: Matthew 24-25, Luke 21, and Mark 13. It's a long teaching that Jesus shared with his disciples about signs of the end of the age and of his coming again.

> Jesus went out from the temple, and was going on his way. ... As he sat on the Mount of Olives, the disciples came to him privately, saying, "Tell us, when will these things be? What is the sign of your coming, and of the end of the age?" ... "**Watch** therefore, for you don't know in what hour your Lord comes. ... Therefore also be ready, for in an hour that you don't expect, the Son of Man will come." (Matthew 24:1, 3, 42, 44)

This instance of *watch* means to give strict attention to, be vigilant. It's an active form of watching. Jesus told us to watch. It's a command. So, not actively watching is a form of disobedience. Think back to the Introduction when we discussed the armor of God. Picture the knight, standing at the ready and being watchful.

SO WE KNOW THE DETAILS OF JESUS'S COMING

There are several reasons why Jesus told us to watch. It's because

Jesus's second coming is a party invitation. If you were planning a party, you'd want to make sure your guests knew who the party was for, what the party was for, when the party was happening, where the party was taking place, and what to bring to the party. We watch in order to get all the party details.

SO WE KNOW WHO'S WHO IN JESUS'S COMING

Let's talk about who's who at this party. There's who the party is for, who's throwing the party, and who's invited to the party.

Jesus is the guest of honor and who the party is for. After Jesus's resurrection, he went back to heaven, and he's been there ever since. But he's not going to stay there. Jesus is coming back to earth again to reign and live with us forever.

In case it wasn't obvious, God is the one throwing this party. God wants to make sure he gets all the credit and glory for this big event. So, he's told us what he's going to do in advance. You see, God doesn't want an idol, false god, aliens, Satan, or you name it, getting credit for his work (Isaiah 48:1-11). And by telling us in advance what's about to happen, it increases our faith when we actually see it all come to pass (John 14:29). God wants us to believe. It's one of the reasons Jesus did so many miracles during his first coming. Signs are one of the ways that God reveals himself to us.

Lastly, there's who's invited. Jesus told a couple parables to help us understand who's invited to his party. The parable of the wedding banquet (Matthew 22:1-14) and the parable of the virgins (Matthew 25:1-13).

We learn that the people invited to the wedding banquet made excuses and didn't go, so then everyone got invited and the hall was filled with guests. It's about the Jews rejecting Jesus as Messiah, resulting in the gospel being preached to all the gentiles (non-Jews). In essence, everyone is now invited to the party. Jesus died for everyone, so everyone is invited. But few will actually go. That's because most people don't want anything to do with God and Jesus.

There was also a guest that wasn't dressed for the occasion and got thrown out. What was that about? Well, you must be a believer in Jesus Christ in order to attend the party. The wedding clothes are you being sealed with the Holy Spirit because you accept Jesus as your personal savior (Ephesians 1:3-14). When our name is written in the Book of Life, we're promised clothes of white (Revelation 3:5). That guest thought he was a believer but wasn't.

The other parable about the ten virgins just reiterates this point. The five foolish virgins who didn't have oil for their lamps didn't have the Holy Spirit. They thought they were invited and ready for the wedding, but in reality, Jesus didn't know them. You can't be a cultural Christian and expect to be included in the party. Your faith in Jesus must be real. If you aren't sure of your own personal salvation, go to Chapter 19 and learn how to get your heart right.

SO WE KNOW WHEN JESUS IS COMING

So, when exactly is this party? Well, that's the big question. Jesus said we won't know the day or hour, so that's why we're given so many signs to watch (Matthew 24:36-44). The signs point to the when.

Jesus did tell us that he's coming at a time he's not expected, which I find quite curious. Don't you? When would people expect Jesus to show up and directly intervene in our affairs? Probably at one of two extreme times. Some people would expect him when it seems like the world is about to end. You know, some global catastrophe has happened. Others today would expect him after we've achieved peace on earth and when everything is just peachy perfect.

Well, the Bible is very clear that Jesus is indeed coming again when it seems the world is about to end. That's Jesus's second coming (Revelation 19). It happens after the tribulation period, a time in which God sends judgment upon the world after the rapture. The Bible is also very clear that peace on earth and perfection is not something we humans will ever achieve. When Jesus returns at his second coming, he himself will usher in that peace and perfection we all long for (Isaiah 9:6-7).

So, since Jesus is indeed coming at a time we would expect, which is after the tribulation, then why did Jesus say he wouldn't be expected? Ah, that's because he's referring to his coming at the rapture! There are two stages to Jesus's next coming: the rapture and the second coming. They are two separate events. Using our party metaphor, think of the rapture as the wedding, and the second coming as the reception. We're going to discuss each event in detail in Chapters 17 and 20.

At this point in time, know that the rapture is the event in which Jesus comes to take all born-again Christians on earth to heaven. Everyone alive instantly gets a new body. Anyone who died as a believer after Jesus's resurrection, who's been living in heaven, will get their new body too (1 Thessalonians 4:16-17). It really is for a wedding. You see, Jesus referred to the church, which is comprised of believers, as his bride (Revelation 19:7-9).

Shortly after the rapture, the tribulation judgments begin. Those are only meant for unrepentant sinners, fallen angels, and demons. That's why all the believers were taken to heaven first. At Jesus's second coming, everyone included in the rapture, all the Old Testament believers, anyone who puts their faith in Jesus during the tribulation period and dies, and all the holy angels, will return with Jesus to the earth (Revelation 19:1-14).

Jesus is coming at the rapture when the world seems relatively normal. That's when he's least expected.

You know, at Jesus's first coming he wept outside Jerusalem because he said the people didn't know the time of their visitation (Luke 19:41-44). They should have known that Jesus was their Messiah. They should have been expecting him to arrive when he did. The prophet Daniel gave them the sign to start counting from and the exact number of years to count (Daniel 9:25).

The starting point was the command to restore and rebuild Jerusalem. Artaxerxes gave the command in 445 BC (Nehemiah 2:1-8). They were to count 69 weeks of years. A week of years is 7 years. That equals 483 years. Factor in that the Jewish calendar is only 360 days. Just doing quick math, you'd end up expecting Jesus around AD 32.[2] Jesus showed up right on time as predicted.

Since Jesus expected them to know, he certainly expects us to know as well. Jesus is the one speaking in the first Scripture below. "He" is a reference to Jesus.

> "Even so you also, when you see all these things, know that he is near, even at the doors." (Matthew 24:33)

> ... as you see the Day approaching. (Hebrews 10:25)

Both of those Scriptures use "you see" to indicate it'll be obvious to those who are watching all the signs that Jesus is at the doors.

In Chapter 2, when we discuss why today is different than times in the past, we're going to look at six key signs that reveal Jesus's party could start any minute.

SO WE KNOW WHAT TO WATCH FOR

Now, let's discuss the purpose of the party and what exactly we're supposed to be on the lookout for. The party is to celebrate Jesus's next visitation to earth. That means we're to watch for the rapture and the second coming.

The people who are raptured will get to witness a very awesome event in heaven (Revelation 5). We'll get to see that Jesus is the only one in all of heaven and earth found worthy to take God's scroll. It's like a title deed for us and the earth. Jesus will redeem both mankind and the earth from sin and the curse.

Of course, many people will witness Jesus's second coming. Believers who come to faith after the rapture and survive the tribulation period, and everyone who comes back with Jesus from heaven, which includes those who were raptured and believers throughout the ages. And even unbelievers who survive the tribulation and gather at Armageddon against Jesus (Sign #116). After Jesus quells the rebellion, he'll live on earth with humanity forever. That'll be quite the party.

The rapture is an imminent event, there aren't any signs that precede it. As we discussed in the prior section, the rapture will happen at a time that it's least expected, so when things are relatively normal.

On the other hand, the second coming is not imminent. It occurs seven years after the tribulation period officially begins (Daniel 9:24-27, 12:6-12). The tribulation period starts after the rapture, when the Antichrist signs a seven-year peace treaty with Israel (Daniel 9:27). We'll get into the detail of this timing in Chapter 20.

In the Olivet Discourse, Jesus gave us a whole slew of signs to watch for that precede the second coming. And there are even more signs we can glean from the rest of the Bible. As we watch for the nearness of the second coming and events which occur in the tribulation period, we'll know that the rapture is close at hand. Because the rapture must happen before both of those events.

So, then what are we supposed to watch for? We're supposed to be ready for Jesus's next visitation by watching all the signs (Matthew 24:33) as they begin (Matthew 24:32), and then keep on watching them (Matthew 24:42-43). But it's imperative we frame this with the proper biblical context. If we're only watching for these things to happen within a small rural city, then we're going to miss a lot. Many of Jesus's signs deal with things happening across the planet, so we're going to discuss worldwide events and trends. But there are also specific countries and people groups that we'll focus on.

When Jesus gave the signs, he was speaking to his disciples, who were Jewish and who were in Israel. Israel and the Jewish people are at the center of biblical events. We must watch the signs from this perspective. We must also watch the signs from the perspective of a broader definition of a disciple, which is a Christian.

Since Christian is a very loose term in regard to beliefs, I think it's best to hone this into Protestant Christianity. It subscribes to the Bible as its sole source of divine inspiration, and most Protestant churches adhere to being saved by faith through grace alone (Ephesians 2:8-9). As such, the United States of America (US) currently has the largest percentage of the world's Protestant Christians with 190 million professing this faith, or 20% of the global population.[3] No other nation is even close.

The US is also the one nation who has consistently (until recently) been a staunch ally of Israel. I also find it fascinating and revealing that America is so closely following the same patterns of judgment that God leveled against ancient Israel.[4] Jonathan Cahn exposes this parallel in his books. The US is uniquely tied to the Bible.

So, when looking at the signs, I'll be focused on how they are manifesting for Israel, the US, Christians, and the Jewish people. I'll only mention other countries and people groups when it makes sense for a particular sign.

Perhaps you're still not convinced we're supposed to be watching for signs. Because you're recalling a conversation that Jesus had with some Pharisees who asked when the kingdom of God was coming. Jesus told them it wasn't coming with observation, that it was "in their midst" (Luke 17:20-37 NIV). On the surface this seems to contradict Jesus telling us to watch. So, let's break this down.

Your Bible might say "among you" or "within you" instead of "in your midst." The prior two aren't great translations. The Holy Spirit certainly wasn't living inside the Pharisees. They wanted to kill Jesus. Keep reading the entire conversation Jesus had with them. He said he first had to suffer, and then he gave them signs to watch for. That's because the second coming does indeed come with observation. Jesus was referring to his first coming when he said it was "in their midst." He, God in the flesh, was right there in front of them, and they were totally oblivious. Jesus knew that displaying another miracle for them wouldn't change their hearts. He wasn't the Messiah they were looking for.

SO WE KNOW WHERE JESUS IS COMING

If you plan on going to this party, then you also need to know where it's taking place. We've already established that there are two events in this party: the rapture and the second coming.

The rapture will take place in the clouds (1 Thessalonians 4:16-17), where we'll meet Jesus, and then he'll take us to his house in heaven (John 14:1-3).

The second coming takes place on earth at the Mount of Olives in Jerusalem, Israel (Acts 1:9-12). Jesus, and everyone in heaven that's with him, will leave heaven and return to earth (Revelation 19, 2 Thessalonians 1:7). What's more is that somehow everyone on the planet will see Jesus return to earth in a similar way you can see lightning flash and light up the whole sky (Revelation 1:7, Matthew 24:27). Jesus will not return to heaven after this because the city that's in heaven, New Jerusalem, will come down to earth (Revelation 21). Jesus will always be with us on earth after the second coming.

In the Olivet Discourse, Jesus says something else that's a bit curious regarding where we're watching for his second coming. He warns us not to believe people who say Jesus has returned and that he's in the desert or in the inner rooms (Matthew 24:23-27). This leads me to believe the Antichrist is going to fake the second coming in an effort to convince people that he's actually Jesus.

SO WE KNOW WHAT TO DO BEFORE JESUS COMES

Since Jesus is coming at the rapture at a time he's not expected, he not only told us to watch for certain signs regarding his coming, but to also watch ourselves. Meaning, he expects us to be watching how we live our lives. We should be prepared for the party.

Jesus doesn't want believers caught unaware and then ashamed at the rapture party (1 John 2:28). Watching helps keep us from temptation and the cares of this world (Luke 21:34-36). We're to live righteously from now until he comes to get us so we can earn all the heavenly rewards that we can. All the signs that point to the nearness of his return should encourage you in this pursuit. We're also to keep in mind that troubles will come. The morality of the world is going to continue to degrade. And that can be scary. But we're not to lose our faith. It all points to how close he is. The signs are meant to give us comfort and hope.

Jesus also doesn't want unbelievers caught unaware and left out of the rapture party, like the five virgins who were left out of the wedding (Revelation 3:3). This is why Jesus described the rapture like a thief breaking into a house unexpectedly. The rapture will come upon unbelievers like a thief.

This is another reason that Jesus gave us clear and specific signs of his coming, so that we would evangelize more urgently. We believers have a duty to watch over people by inviting unbelievers to come to the party (Mark 16:15). We should also be encouraging believers to look for the signs and be prepared for the party (Ezekiel 3:17-21, Luke 12:35-48).

SO WE KNOW WHAT GIFT TO BRING

The last detail we need to know regarding Jesus's party is what we should bring. I've mentioned the importance of being prepared, not ashamed, and focusing on earning heavenly rewards. That's because after the rapture, one of the events that takes place in heaven is the judgment seat of Christ (2 Corinthians 5:9-10). It's where believers are rewarded for behavior on earth. This has everything to do with the gift you'll be giving to Jesus at his party. You see, anyone who's given a crown as a reward is going to toss that right back to Jesus, sitting on his throne, in an act of worshiping and glorifying the real strength and power behind that reward (Revelation 4:9-11).

We're going to look at these rewards and how to earn them in Chapter 20. For now, know that there's a special blessing for those who are watching. Jesus is the one speaking below.

Chapter 1 - Watch

> "Behold, I come like a thief. Blessed is he who watches, and keeps his clothes, so that he doesn't walk naked, and they see his shame." (Revelation 16:15)

Now that you know all the reasons to watch for the signs of Jesus's next visitation, you're ready to start examining all the signs. Let's go!

CHAPTER 2 - TODAY IS DIFFERENT

SIGN LEGEND

You'll notice the following elements included for each Sign # in this book.

Category Bar - you'll see the category bar that's shown below. Figure A describes what each category includes. The categories I've placed the sign into will be bold, underlined, and appear in black text, as shown here:

Anti | DD | Earth | Gov | Israel | **<u>Jesus</u>** | Leader | Sky | Society | Tech | Trib

Scripture - A Scripture that describes the sign.

> But know this: that in the last days, grievous times will come. (2 Timothy 3:1)

An explanation of the Scripture and the sign.

Fulfillment - Examples that reveal how the sign is being fulfilled.

Today Is Different - A discussion of why today is different when compared to prior generations regarding fulfillment of the sign.

Additional Scriptures: A list of additional Scriptures to read regarding the sign. If I refer to any other biblical content when describing the sign, like a parable of Jesus or an event in the Old Testament, you'll find the Scriptures for those in this list.

Table A. Sign Legend	
Category	Description
Anti	The sign is a characteristic of the Antichrist.
DD	The sign is a double down. When judgment came, instead of repenting, the people were often called out for continuing to do specific sins. Sometimes even worse than before. 1 Kings 13:33-34, 2 Kings 17:13-17, Jeremiah 44:7-10, Revelation 9:21.
Earth	The sign is in nature or on the earth.
Gov	The sign is about nations, governments, wars, or politics.
Israel	The sign is about the Jewish people or the nation of Israel.
Jesus	The sign is a direct quote of Jesus.
Leader	The sign is about leaders, kings, rulers, teachers, prophets, and judges.
Sky	The sign is in the heavens, sky, space, or is about angels.
Society	The sign is about human behavior and society.
Tech	The sign requires a technology, scientific advancement, or modern invention for fulfillment or substantial progression in fulfillment.
Trib	This sign takes place during the tribulation period.

Figure A. Sign Legend

Refer to Appendix A for lists of the signs in each category.

#1 - ISRAEL IS A NATION

Anti | DD | Earth | **Gov** | **Israel** | **Jesus** | Leader | Sky | Society | Tech | Trib

> Say to them, 'The Lord GOD says: "Behold, I will take the children of Israel from among the nations where they have gone, and will gather them on every side, and bring them into their own land. I will make them one nation in the land, on the mountains of Israel. One king will be king to them all. They will no longer be two nations. They won't be divided into two kingdoms any more at all." ' (Ezekiel 37:21-22)

The prophecy above is an excerpt from a vision that God gave the prophet Ezekiel. It's of the dry bones of the Jewish people coming back to life and dwelling in their own land.

The nation of Israel was broken into two kingdoms right after the reign of King Solomon. The northern territory was referred to as Israel and the southern territory as Judah. Israel was taken captive by the Assyrians in 722 BC. Judah was taken captive by Babylon in 586 BC, which is also when Solomon's Temple in Jerusalem was destroyed. King Cyrus of Persia let the Jews return to their land in 538 BC. While they were again living in the land that God gave them, the Jews weren't their own nation. They were under the rule of the Persians, Greeks, and then the Roman Empire. The Jews revolted against Rome in AD 70 and lost. They were subsequently dispersed all over the globe.[1] The Diaspora culminated in the genocide of six million Jews during the Holocaust of WWII.[2]

Jesus spoke about Israel, the fig tree, being a nation again in the Olivet Discourse. Their existence is a sign of the second coming.

Fulfillment - The number one sign that we're in the last days before Jesus's second coming is that Israel once again exists as a nation. After over 2,500 years of not being their own sovereign nation and almost 1,900 years of being exiled from their land, they came together and became a legitimate nation again shortly after WWII on May 14, 1948.[3] Israel regained the city of Jerusalem as part of their territory in June 1967.[4] In 1950, the population of Israel was 1.3 million. Today, it's 9.9 million, a 624% increase.[5]

Israel must exist as a nation, with Jerusalem included, before the tribulation events can take place. It's because both are center stage during that time period.

Scripture tells us that Israel is a witness so that all people can know and believe God. Israel is also a light to the gentiles, displaying God's faithfulness. We see God through what he's done for Israel.

God hasn't forsaken Israel. The church hasn't replaced Israel because they rejected Jesus as their Messiah. God's promise of specific land and a nation to Abraham almost 4,000 years ago still stands because God said it was an everlasting, unconditional covenant that passed to his son Isaac. The apostle Paul makes it clear in Romans 9-11 that God has not cast away his people.

Today Is Different - For a country that's the size of the state of New Jersey, Israel is constantly in the world news today. I looked at a handful of the top news websites in June 2024 (nytimes.com, cnn.com, foxnews.com, msn.com, news.google.com). I discovered that the Israel-Hamas War either linked from the home page or had articles about it on the home page of three of them. The other two had articles about it on the main page of their News or World News pages.[6] Don't you find it revealing that the entire world is so interested in a tiny nation in the Middle East?

Additional Scriptures: Ezekiel 36:16-38; 37; 39:6-7, 22-23. Genesis 15:18-21; 17:19-21. Isaiah 43:10-12; 49:3-7; 66:7-10. Matthew 24:32-34. Romans 9-11. Zechariah 12:6.

#2 - THE TIMING IS RIGHT

Anti | DD | Earth | **Gov** | **Israel** | **Jesus** | Leader | Sky | Society | Tech | Trib

> He told them a parable. "See the fig tree and all the trees. When they are already budding, you see it and know by your own selves that the summer is already near. Even so you also, when you see these things happening, know that God's Kingdom is near. Most certainly I tell you, this generation will not pass away until all things are accomplished. Heaven and earth will pass away, but my words will by no means pass away." (Luke 21:29-33)

"The fig tree" is a reference to the nation and people of Israel. Since trees are often used in the Bible to describe nations, "all the trees" thus refers to all the other nations. Here's what we learn from Jesus's parable. When we see the nation of Israel and all the other nations springing to life, then we'll know that God's kingdom, which is the second coming, is near. What's more is that we're told the generation that sees all the trees budding will not pass away, or die, until all the prior things Jesus mentioned are accomplished. Prior to this parable, Jesus gave a long list of signs that point to his second coming. His entire teaching is called the Olivet Discourse. Appendix A has all the signs that Jesus himself gave to his disciples that day. We're going to examine all of them, and more, throughout this book.

Let's look at another Scripture that speaks to the timing.

> "I will return again to My place Till they acknowledge their offense. Then they will seek My face; In their affliction they will earnestly seek Me." Come, and let us return to the LORD; For He has torn, but He will heal us; He has stricken, but He will bind us up. After two days He will revive us; On the third day He will raise us up, That we may live in His sight. Let us know, Let us pursue the knowledge of the LORD. His going forth is established as the morning; He will come to us like the rain, Like the latter [and] former rain to the earth. (Hosea 5:15-6:3 NKJV)

God is speaking a prophecy to Hosea here. Jesus is the one who returned to his place. Israel's offense is that they rejected him as their Messiah. But one day they will seek him. We're told that God will revive Israel after two days and then raise them and live with them on the third day. It gets even more specific and tells us Jesus's "going forth" or his return will be in the morning. That means his return will be the morning of the third day.

Well, Israel's been a nation for a lot longer than three days, so there must be more to this than actual days, and there is. We learn in the New Testament that with God one day is as 1,000 years. So, this means Israel will be revived after 2,000 years and that Jesus will return right after that.

Here's another interesting tidbit. In Genesis 1-2, God gave his account of the seven days of creation. Six days of work followed by one day of rest. Then God applied that to mankind when he told us to work six days and rest for one. If we apply this to the formula above, we get 6,000 years for work followed by 1,000 years of rest. This prophecy of the week of millenniums speaks to the timeline for humanity. Jesus is prophesied to return 6,000 years after creation and reign over a period of rest for 1,000 years during the millennial kingdom. Lamb & Lion Ministries has an in-depth article about this on their website if you're interested.[7]

https://christinprophecy.org/articles/the-prophecy-of-the-week-of-millenniums/

James Ussher, the Archbishop of Ireland in the early 17th century, calculated the beginning of the world based on biblical genealogies to be 4004 BC.

Fulfillment - From Sign #1 - Israel Is A Nation, we learned that Israel became a nation in May 1948. That just so happens to be around the time that the United Nations (UN) was founded, October 1945. There were 51 founding member states of the UN. Today there are 195 countries on the planet, of which 193 are members of the UN. You can see the progression of new nations springing forth in figure 2.1 below.

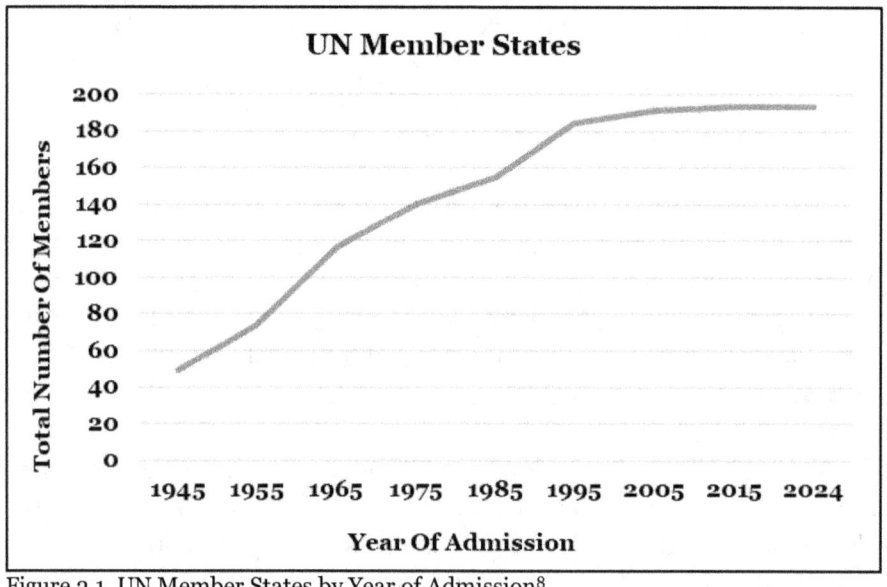

Figure 2.1. UN Member States by Year of Admission[8]
Source: Compiled from UN member states data at https://en.wikipedia.org/wiki/Member_states_of_the_United_Nations

It's an upward sloping line from 1945 through 1995 and then it levels off. Only 4 countries have been added since 2000. The last was added in 2011. Since this is 2024, we've had 13 years of stagnation in regard to new nations. It's safe to say the nations have budded as Jesus described.

Israel was indeed revived after two days or 2,000 years. They ceased being a sovereign nation in 586 BC and were reborn in 1948. They became a nation over 2,500 years later. Israel is now existing in their third day.

Today Is Different - The fig tree generation makes today unique. It's June 2024 as I'm writing this. The nation of Israel is now 76 years old. Since Jesus promised the generation that sees the nations budding would also see his second coming, I hope you realize there's not much time left before that whole generation passes away!

Considering Hosea's third day prophecy in light of the resurrection also makes our generation special. It's been nearly two days or 2,000 years since Jesus's crucifixion and resurrection in AD 32.[9] We're only 8 years away from it being the morning of the third day!

Another reason today is different is because we've fulfilled the prophecy of the week of millenniums. If the world really did begin in 4004 BC, that means it's been 6,027 years since then. We should be expecting Jesus's return any day now and the 1,000 years of rest to begin.

All these prophecies reveal the same thing. Time is up!

<u>Additional Scriptures:</u> 2 Peter 3:8. Exodus 16:23-26. Ezekiel 31. Genesis 1-2. Hosea 9:10. Jeremiah 24. Mark 11:20-24; 13:28-31. Matthew 21:18-22; 24:32-25. Revelation 20:4.

#3 – WHEN YOU SEE ALL THESE THINGS

<u>Anti</u> | <u>DD</u> | <u>Earth</u> | <u>Gov</u> | <u>Israel</u> | <u>Jesus</u> | <u>Leader</u> | <u>Sky</u> | <u>Society</u> | <u>Tech</u> | <u>Trib</u>

> "Even so you also, when you see all these things, know that he is near, even at the doors. Most certainly I tell you, this generation will not pass away until all these things are accomplished." (Matthew 24:33-34)

Jesus is the one speaking in the Scripture above. He says this to his disciples on the Mount of Olives after they've asked him to describe the signs of his second coming and the end of the age. Jesus provides quite the list of signs. Refer to Appendix A for the complete list. So, this statement tells us that we should be looking for the fulfillment of every single sign that he mentioned. Furthermore, we learn from Luke's account of this conversation that the timing is even more specific. It's when we begin to see all these things. This is the sign of convergence.

Fulfillment - Every single sign that we're going to cover in this book, 150 of them, are seeing fulfillment today. And I have examples that reveal how today is different for every single one of them. It's incredible!

I think the Rapture Ready Index on raptureready.com paints a nice picture of this. It's shown below in figure 3.1. Their index monitors news in 45 different categories and ranks each category on a scale of 1 to 5 for how much prophetic activity is occurring, a score of 5 being the most activity. The week of June 24, 2024 has a score of 186. Over the many years they've been monitoring, they report their all-time high is 189. You can see in figure 3.1 that there's activity happening in each category.

Rapture Ready Index

Rapture Index: 186   Change from last update: -1   Updated: Jun 24, 2024

#	Category	Score	#	Category	Score	#	Category	Score
1.	Debt & Trade	4	26.	Nuclear Nations	5	43.	Climate	4
2.	False Christs	3	18.	Ecumenism	4	35.	Date Settings	3
3.	Occult	3	19.	Globalism	5	36.	Volcanoes	5
4.	Satanism	3	20.	Tribulation Temple	3	37.	Earthquakes	4
5.	Unemployment	3	21.	Anti-Semitism	5	38.	Wild Weather	5
6.	Inflation	4	22.	Israel	5	39.	Civil Rights	4
7.	Interest Rates	4	23.	Gog (Russia)	5	40.	Famine	3
8.	The Economy	5	24.	Persia (Iran)	5	41.	Drought	3
9.	Oil Supply/Price	5	25.	False Prophet	4	42.	Plagues	4
10.	Financial Unrest	4	27.	Global Turmoil	4	44.	Food Supply	4-1
11.	Leadership	5	28.	Arms Proliferation	5	45.	Floods	5
12.	Drug Abuse	3	29.	Liberalism	5			
13.	Apostasy	4	30.	Peace Process	3			
14.	Supernatural	3	31.	Kings of the East	4			
15.	Moral Standards	5	32.	Mark of the Beast	5			
16.	Anti-Christian	3	33.	Beast Government	4			
17.	Crime Rate	5	34.	The Antichrist	5			

Figure 3.1. Rapture Ready Index[10]
Source: https://www.raptureready.com/rapture-ready-index/

I also find it interesting that there's a secular Doomsday Clock that monitors the likelihood of a global catastrophe, which would be midnight on their clock.[11] They look at things like nuclear war, climate, and technologies. It's been maintained since 1947, right near when Israel became a nation. Do you think it's a coincidence this came to be right when biblically prophetic end times activity was going to kick into gear?

In 1947, the clock was 7 minutes to midnight. In 1991, it was the farthest back it's ever been at 17 minutes to midnight. Today, it's as close as it's ever been at 90 seconds until midnight. It's been that time since January 2023. It's even obvious to unbelievers that something with the world isn't right. They sense a dramatic change on the horizon.

Today Is Different - This one's going to become obvious as you read through this book. There are 79 different signs from Jesus's Olivet Discourse that you're going to see are being fulfilled in various degrees today. On top of that, there are another 29 signs that Jesus mentions in the gospels or the book of Revelation that are also being accomplished right now. See Appendix A for the complete list of signs that Jesus told us to look for.

I also want you to think about the technology that exists today that enables us to watch signs that we wouldn't have been able to see until recently, like wonders in the heavens. The Hubble telescope was launched in 1990, and the significantly upgraded James Webb telescope launched near the end of 2021.[12] When I think of watching or surveilling something, I also think of satellites. They monitor all sorts of things on the earth. They also provide TV, internet, and GPS, which we use to watch and keep track of everything. The very first satellite was Sputnik, launched by the Russians in 1957.[13] Fast forward to 2009, and about 2,300 of them orbited the planet.[14] Today, June 24, 2024, there are 10,226 of them orbiting.[15] Today is unique because we can clearly see all things on earth and in the heavens.

Additional Scriptures: Luke 21:28, 31. Mark 13:29-30. Matthew 24:6, 8, 32-24, 36, 42-51; 25:1-13.

#4 - BIRTH PAINS

<u>Anti</u> | <u>DD</u> | <u>Earth</u> | <u>Gov</u> | <u>Israel</u> | <u>Jesus</u> | <u>Leader</u> | <u>Sky</u> | <u>Society</u> | <u>Tech</u> | <u>Trib</u>

> But concerning the times and the seasons, brothers, you have no need that anything be written to you. For you yourselves know well that the day of the Lord comes like a thief in the night. For when they are saying, "Peace and safety," then sudden destruction will come on them, like birth pains on a pregnant woman. (1 Thessalonians 5:1-3)

Here, the apostle Paul likens the signs of the "day of the Lord" to birth pains. In the Bible, the day of the Lord refers to the tribulation period, which ends with the second coming of Jesus. This means signs will become more frequent and more intense the closer we get to Jesus's coming. Jesus also spoke about this when he compared the signs to the beginning of sorrows.

Fulfillment - We can see this prophecy coming to life because end times events are being fulfilled at an accelerating pace. In the Olivet Discourse, Jesus predicted the destruction of the Second Temple which stood in Jerusalem during the time of his ministry. It happened just as he said in AD 70.[16] From then up until the early 1900's not much happened in terms of Bible prophecy being fulfilled. Now, over 2,000 years later, we're seeing activity in every sign that Jesus told us to watch, and the activity is getting more and more intense with each passing day.

You could say the Industrial Revolution got the ball rolling on the technology that would be needed for the tribulation period. But honestly it wasn't until the world wars of the early 1900's that we started to see the wars and persecution against the Jews that Jesus spoke about as end times signs. Look at figure 4.1 of combatant deaths in wars since 1800. It's obvious that the world dynamic changed with WWI. That's when we started to see these birth pains begin.

Oblivious To The Signs When It's Obvious The King Is Coming

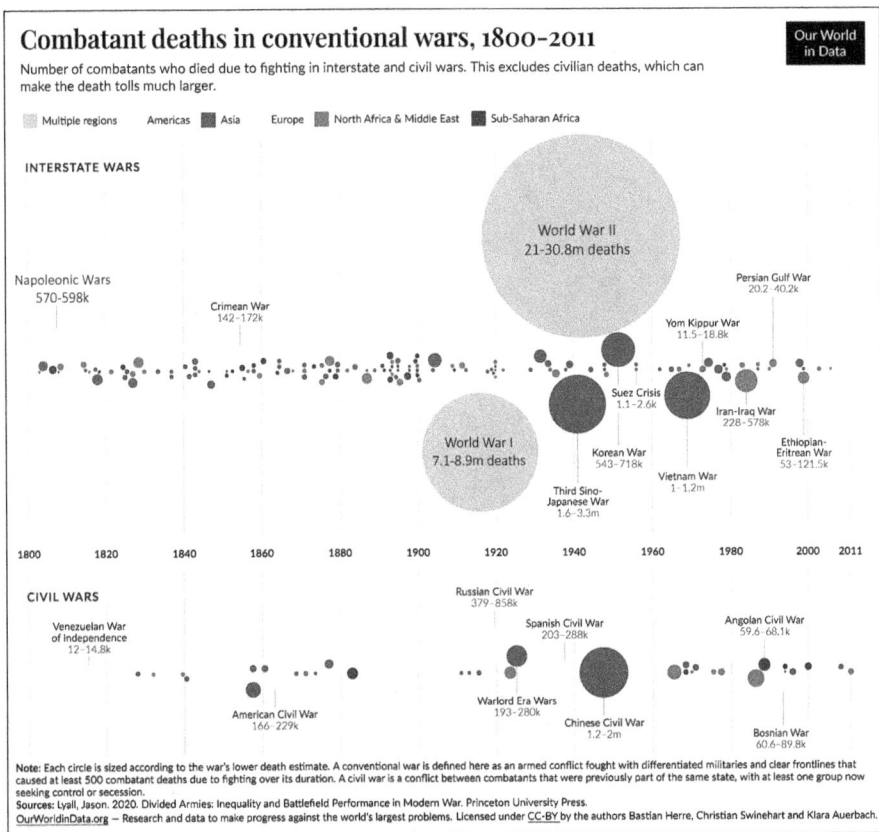

Figure 4.1. Combatant Deaths In Conventional Wars Worldwide[17]
Source: https://ourworldindata.org/war-and-peace?insight=some-conflicts-are-much-much-deadlier-than-most#key-insights

From 1800 until 1900 there were small regional wars. The Napoleonic Wars had the greatest number of combatant deaths at 570,000. When we arrive at WWI, multiple regions were involved, and the death count was at least 7.1 million. Since then, we also see WWII with over 21 million deaths and larger regional wars with higher combatant deaths than the Napoleonic Wars.

And the wars haven't let up. Figure 4.2 displays the number of armed conflicts since 1989. See how the number of wars is increasing over time. The graph also resembles ocean waves.

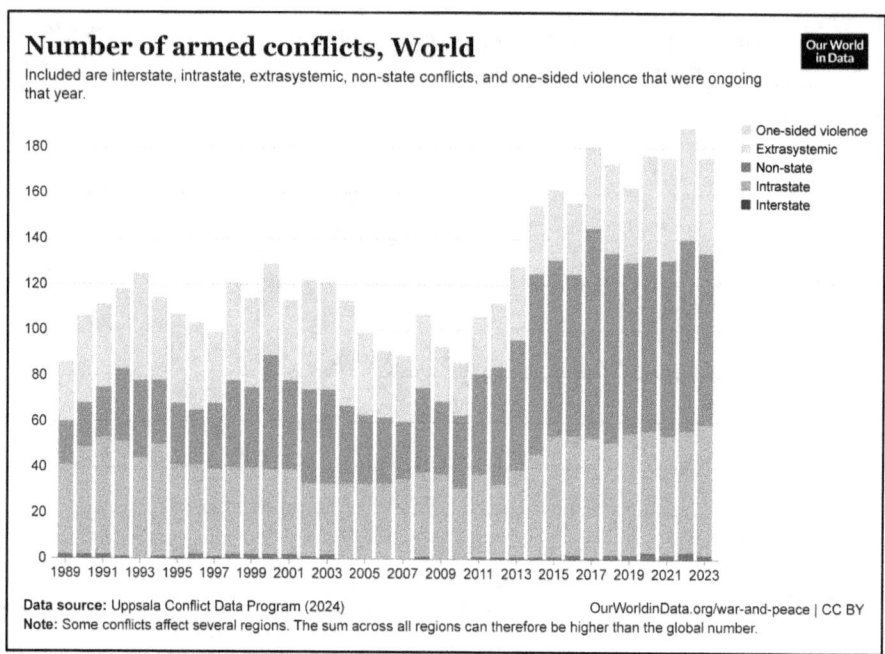

Figure 4.2. Number of Armed Conflicts Worldwide[18]
Source: https://ourworldindata.org/war-and-peace?insight=armed-conflict-is-common-and-takes-different-forms#key-insights

There's an increasing wave of armed conflicts in the early 90s, then a lull. Then a bigger wave of conflicts in the late 90s to early 2000s, and then another bigger lull. Then a really big wave of conflicts starts in 2013 and continues into the 2020s. Notice how the number of armed conflicts in 2022 was over double those in 1989. This graph also resembles the ups and downs of labor pains, doesn't it? You're going to see a lot more labor-looking data throughout this book.

Today Is Different - In the Scripture that we started with, Jesus said when the people say "peace and safety" that's when the sudden destruction would come. Using the birth analogy, that's when the baby's coming! During a time in which we're experiencing significantly more armed conflicts, somehow there's also more peace between countries. This is illustrated in figure 4.3 below.

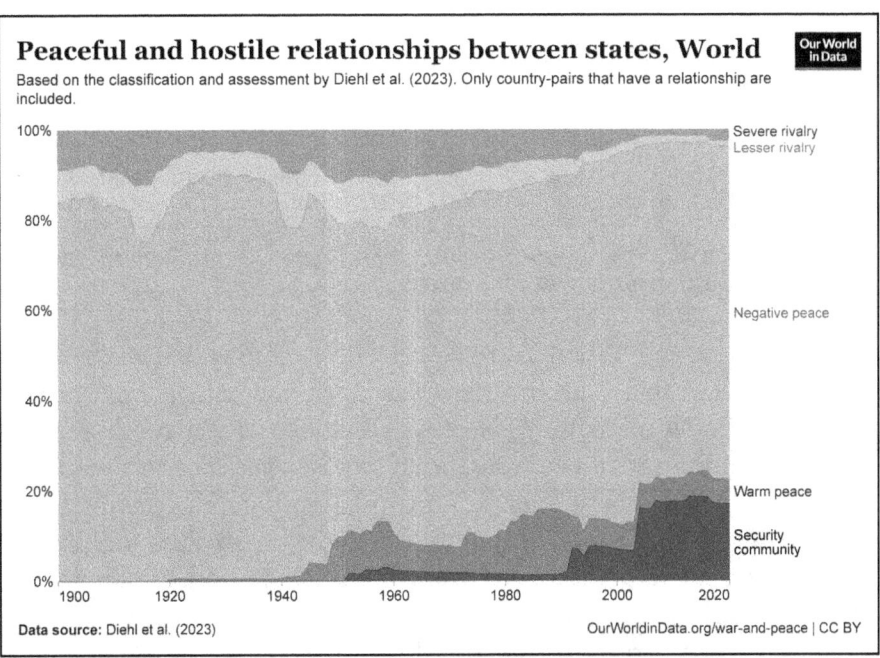

Figure 4.3. Peaceful And Hostile Relationships Between States Worldwide[19]
Source: https://ourworldindata.org/war-and-peace?insight=relationships-between-countries-have-become-more-peaceful#key-insights

From 1900 through 1990, we can clearly see severe and lesser rivalry among nations. Beginning in the 1990s and going through 2020, there's a noticeable decrease in the rivalries and an increase in peace. Now, that's just fascinating, isn't it?

Technology has had an obvious impact on this particular birth pain as well as many others we'll be looking at in this book. Just think about how the weapons of war have changed in modern times. Weapons of mass destruction didn't exist until WWII. Nuclear weapons, surveillance technology, chemical and biological weapons, electromagnetic pulse weapons, and cyber warfare all certainly influence peace among nations due to their destructive potential.

Additional Scriptures: 2 Timothy 3:1, 13. Mark 13:7-8. Matthew 24:1-2, 6-8. Micah 4:10. Romans 8:22.

#5 - TRIBULATION IN VIEW

Anti | DD | Earth | Gov | Israel | **Jesus** | Leader | **Sky** | Society | **Tech** | **Trib**

> "You will not be unpunished; for I will call for a sword on all the inhabitants of the earth," says the LORD of Armies. ... "The slain of the LORD will be at that day from one end of the earth even to the other end of the earth. ... The shepherds will have no way to flee. The leader of the flock will have no escape." (Jeremiah 25:29, 33, 35)

From Sign #3 - When You See All These Things, we learned that when we begin to see all the signs Jesus spoke about being fulfilled, then we'll know his coming is near. He spoke of his coming in the rapture, not the second coming, because a few verses later he tells us to pray that we would be counted worthy to escape all those things and stand before him. Many of the signs we're going to explore in this book are events that happen during the tribulation period. When we can start to see tribulation events falling into place and nearing fulfillment, then we know the rapture must be close.

This prophecy above was spoken by God to the prophet Jeremiah. It's about God judging "all the inhabitants of the earth" at the second coming of Jesus. This is an event that happens at the end of the tribulation period. Notice how it says the slain will be "from one end of the earth even to the other end." And that there's no way for anyone to escape. These are very important clues that reveal the tribulation period is now in view.

Fulfillment - Perhaps you've noticed that SpaceX is in the news a lot these days. They've been working with NASA on two important space missions. The Artemis mission, which plans to land people on the moon again (no earlier than September 2026), and the Mars mission in which they're hoping to colonize the infamous red planet.[20] SpaceX has been doing all sorts of launch tests on the Starship. Elon Musk is confident they'll be able to land a craft on Mars this decade.[21] Wow!

The Scripture above makes it clear that judgment comes upon inhabitants on the entire earth. No one is able to escape. That means everyone is on the earth. There's no mention of the moon or Mars or even space for that matter. Which means no one will be off planet. All those grand plans that SpaceX and NASA have aren't going to happen.

Something happens between now and the end of this decade which prevents it.

You know, one of the big indicators of how near we are to the tribulation period is technology. There's a point at which we'll eclipse the technology mentioned in the Bible. I think we're right at that point. You can see all the signs with a technology component in Appendix A.

Today Is Different - You might be wondering what'll happen to the handful of astronauts on the International Space Station (ISS). Well, on June 26, 2024, SpaceX was awarded a contract by NASA to deorbit the ISS.[22] NASA said the ISS is planned for destruction by 2030. Literally, every day there's something in the news pointing to Bible prophecy being fulfilled.

So, once again we're in this paradoxical state. We have the technology to send people into space and out of harm's way of whatever's happening on earth, and we'll shortly be able to send people to the moon and Mars. Yet at the same time, we're also planning to leave the only place that humans have been dwelling off earth. I think it's in this window of time in which we're going to see God act.

There are many signs that occur during the tribulation period itself. Have a look at Appendix A to see a list of those so you can read how each is starting to see fulfillment today. I'd like to call your attention to Sign #62 - A Covenant With Death. The Bible tells us that's the exact event which triggers the tribulation, and it's seeing a lot of activity today!

Additional Scriptures: Daniel 9:24-27. Luke 21:28, 36. Matthew 24:8, 33, 42-44. Revelation 14:14-20.

#6 - THE POINT OF NO RETURN

Anti | DD | Earth | **Gov** | Israel | **Jesus** | **Leader** | Sky | **Society** | **Tech** | **Trib**

> But know this: that in the last days, grievous times will come. For men will be lovers of self, lovers of money, boastful, arrogant, blasphemers, disobedient to parents, unthankful, unholy .... But they will proceed no further. (2 Timothy 3:1-2, 9)

The apostle Paul, inspired by the Holy Spirit, wrote this in a letter to his disciple Timothy. We're told that in the last days "men will be" and then he lists a whole slew of bad behaviors that we'll be exploring throughout this book. The part I want to focus on in this sign is how Paul ended the list. "But they will proceed no further." God only allows behavior to reach a certain boiling point and then that's it. God has had it, and nothing is going to stop his judgment from coming. It's the point of no return.

God clearly demonstrated this pattern in the Old Testament. Before the flood, God said the people were continually only evil and thus his judgment was triggered.

Then there's the Tower of Babel that people were building to reach into heaven and survive another flood. God said all the people had one language and that nothing was going to stop them from achieving whatever they desired. God's judgment was triggered again, so he destroyed the tower and created other languages.

Then there are the people of Sodom and Gomorrah whose sinful behavior was very grave and triggered God's wrath of fire and brimstone. Abraham pleaded with God to save the city for the sake of the righteous living there. There weren't enough of them to warrant God saving the city. Only Lot and his two daughters were saved.

We're also told that Israel and Judah were taken into captivity and destroyed because of the sins of King Jeroboam and King Manasseh. The behavior of those two kings and the sins they encouraged their people to commit are ultimately what triggered God's wrath through the Assyrian and Babylonian invasions. God even told Jeremiah to stop praying for the people. That even if Moses pleaded with him, he still wouldn't save them from his coming judgment.

Paul simplifies this by revealing that the wrath of God is triggered when unrighteous men, who know God because his existence is obvious, suppress God's truth, don't glorify him as God, and don't give him thanks. The wrath of God is a reference to the tribulation period.

When society has reached God's point of no return, there is no amount of prayer that can fix it. That's why Jesus said when we begin to see all the signs that he mentioned that we should look up, because he's on his way.

Fulfillment - So, have we provoked God to the degree that we've reached this point of no return? Some of those triggers include worshiping other gods (Sign #9), idolatry (Sign #10), the occult (Sign #11), encouraging sin (Sign #66), and profane worship (Sign #67). You'll see when you read those signs that we've certainly crossed the line.

Today Is Different - The number one trigger that reveals how much we've transgressed against God is what evil King Manasseh and the people of Judah got called out for. It's child sacrifice (Sign #99). The World Health Organization states that 73 million babies are murdered across the planet via abortion every single year![23] It's hard to even fathom. That's more than the number of people who live in the entire United Kingdom.[24]

The article doesn't say what year they started tracking this, but you and I both know this practice has been going on for quite some time now. Even if we stay really conservative and pretend it's only been this bad since 2000, that's 1.7 billion babies! That's the equivalent of the population of China or India today.[25] They each have 17% of the world's population. I have no doubt that we've killed over a quarter of the world population through child sacrifice in modern times.

With modern medicine, this evil practice has become as easy as taking a pill. I think this is especially grieving to God considering the level of scientific advancements we've achieved regarding the ability to prevent an unwanted pregnancy in the first place through contraception or surgical means. We also have the ability to save babies in all sorts of dire medical conditions through fetal surgeries in the womb and incubators, ventilators, and feeding devices to keep micro-preemie babies alive.

You cannot tell me that today is no different than any other time period. We have most definitely triggered God's wrath. Not convinced? When you're finished reading this entire book, circle back to this sign and see if you still disagree.

Additional Scriptures: 1 Kings 12:26-33; 13:33-34. 2 Chronicles 33:1-11. 2 Kings 21:1-18; 24:1-4. Deuteronomy 28:15-68. Ephesians 5:3-6. Ezekiel 14:12-23. Genesis 6:5-7; 11:1-9; 18:16-33. Jeremiah 7:16; 15:1, 4; 16:10-12; 30:12-13. Luke 21:28. Matthew 24:33. Revelation 6:16-17. Romans 1:18-32.

PART 2

SIGNS OF THE HEART

CHAPTER 3 - IT'S A HEART CONDITION

In the Bible, King Solomon tells us that there is nothing new, that history repeats itself, and that people forget the past (Ecclesiastes 1:9-11). Even more than that, he reveals that this is a pattern because God makes the same things happen over and over (Ecclesiastes 3:15). Since that's the case, it's important that we understand what God did in the past. What were the signs from the past? We need to know because they're bound to manifest again.

When studying the Old Testament, we learn about these cycles and patterns. If you aren't familiar with Israel's ancient history, here's a quick recap. There's a sin cycle that's really obvious in the book of Judges. It starts out with the people of Israel knowing, worshiping, and being obedient to God. Then the people turn away from God and fall into sin and all sorts of idolatry. The people of Israel then find themselves under oppression. They finally cry out to God for help when it gets so bad they can no longer bear it. God then rescues the people from the oppression. The cycle is finished when they return to God. It's a cycle that's repeated many, many times.

What's interesting is that there's another pattern that's revealed as soon as the people turn away from God and start to experience difficulties. God provided signs, warnings to them, as to why they were experiencing hardships. We're going to look at oppression and each sign in the pattern as individual signs throughout this book. We'll learn how they're manifesting again today. God's warnings follow this five-step pattern.

First, **prophets warn about the future**. Consider the flood. God sent Enoch and then Noah to warn about the coming judgment (Hebrews 11:7, Jude 1:14-15). Refer to Sign #119.

Second, **curses are a warning**. God's original curse on mankind as a result of the very first sin should be warning enough that God judges sin (Genesis 3). So that the people would know why bad things were happening to them in the future, God gave Moses a long list of curses that would befall the people of Israel if they forsook him (Deuteronomy 28). As an example, consider all the curses that God put upon Pharaoh and the Egyptians during the Exodus (Exodus 3-17). Each of those curses was a sign to Pharaoh. Refer to Sign #21.

Third, **God's warnings aren't heeded**. It should have been obvious to the people of Israel that their oppression was a result of sin because God had warned them ahead of time. But unfortunately, the warnings were ignored. No one besides Noah and his seven family members got saved from the flood (Genesis 7:7). Pharaoh didn't listen to Moses (Exodus 3-17). And even when two angels appeared in Sodom to warn Lot, Lot's subsequent warning to his sons-in-law were mocked (Genesis 19:14). Refer to Sign #34.

Fourth, **false prophets** appear. Our enemy, Satan, uses our foolishness to his advantage. He knows that we'll listen to him if we're not listening to God. So, he sends in false prophets to oppose God's prophets. Since God has dominion over Satan, it's God who's allowing this to happen as a sign. The real kicker here is that Satan's able to perform signs and wonders to further deceive people into believing his lies. When Moses confronted Pharaoh, God gave him the ability to perform signs. Well, Satan gave Pharaoh's false prophets abilities too. When Aaron turned his staff into a snake, the false prophets did as well (Exodus 7:10-12). These false prophets made it difficult for Pharaoh to believe Moses. Refer to Sign #57.

Fifth, **God's prophets are persecuted.** The people of Israel got so frustrated with God's warnings through his prophets, that they couldn't tolerate it. They didn't want to listen to or hear them anymore. So, they started persecuting the people who were preaching God's truth. Pharaoh had enough of listening to Moses and threatened his life (Exodus 10:28). After God delivered the Israelites out of Egypt, Pharaoh was so angry that he and his army chased after them (Exodus 14). Refer to Sign #94.

Although God saved the people of Israel many times when they cried out to him for deliverance, there was a point at which Israel's sin got so bad that God refused to save them. They had reached the point of no return. Recall that we discussed how that sign is manifesting today in the prior chapter. Here, I want to consider how Israel got to the point of no return. It'll help us understand how America is in the same place, and how easily we as individuals can get to that point too.

Well, how did the people of Israel start sinning in the first place? God made his presence obvious to them. God physically walked with Adam and Eve in the garden of Eden (Genesis 3:8). The Israelites saw a lot of God's power and miracles during their exodus from Egypt

(Exodus 3-17). Consider the plagues against Egypt, the parting of the Red Sea, the manna, and God dwelling with them in a pillar of cloud by day and fire at night. Even so, the people turned away, fell into sin, and eventually got kicked out of their land. It's difficult to comprehend. God revealed what's really going on to the apostle Paul.

> For the wrath of God is revealed from heaven against all ungodliness and unrighteousness of men who suppress the truth in unrighteousness, because that which is known of God is revealed in them, for God revealed it to them. For the invisible things of him since the creation of the world are clearly seen, being perceived through the things that are made, even his everlasting power and divinity, that they may be without excuse. Because knowing God, **they didn't glorify him as God**, and **didn't give thanks**, but became vain in their reasoning, and their senseless **heart was darkened**.
> Professing themselves to be wise, **they became fools**, and traded the glory of the incorruptible God for the likeness of an image of corruptible man, and of birds, four-footed animals, and creeping things. Therefore God also gave them up in the **lusts of their hearts to uncleanness**, that their bodies should be dishonored among themselves; who exchanged the truth of God for a lie, and worshiped and served the creature rather than the Creator, who is blessed forever. Amen.
> For this reason, God gave them up to vile passions. For their women changed the natural function into that which is against nature. Likewise also the men, leaving the natural function of the woman, burned in their lust toward one another, men doing what is inappropriate with men, and receiving in themselves the due penalty of their error. Even as they refused to have God in their knowledge, God gave them up to a reprobate mind, to do those things which are not fitting; being **filled with all unrighteousness**, sexual immorality, wickedness, covetousness, malice; full of envy, murder, strife, deceit, evil habits, secret slanderers, backbiters, hateful to God, insolent, arrogant, boastful, inventors of evil things, disobedient to parents, without understanding, covenant breakers, without natural affection, unforgiving, unmerciful; who, knowing the ordinance of God, that those who practice such things are worthy of death, not only do the same, but also approve of those who practice them. (Romans 1:18-32)

The people turned away from God when they wouldn't worship him or give him thanks. Then they became foolish, confused about God, and worshiped idols. As a result, they became perverse, doing vile things with their bodies. Lastly, their lives became full of every kind of evil, wickedness, and sin. It's because they had a bad heart condition. Their "heart was darkened." I like how Sean McDowell sums this up in one of his blog posts about why people don't believe in Jesus. He says, "The heart of the problem is the problem of the heart."[1]

So, I looked at every verse in the Bible that contains the word *heart*. Did you know that there are over 800 verses that refer to a type of heart condition? Some are good conditions, what I call strengths, like loyal, wise, upright, and knowing. While others are bad, like hardened, which is the most referenced type of heart in Scripture. After compiling similar heart conditions into groups, here's what I determined are the top ten bad heart conditions mentioned in the Bible. Notice how they follow the pattern revealed in Romans 1: they turned away, then became foolish, perverse, and ended up evil.

A Turned Away Heart - A Prideful Heart - A Foolish Heart - A Hardened Heart - A Coveting Heart - A Deceiving Heart - A Discouraging Heart - A Perverse Heart - A Hateful Heart - An Evil Heart

These heart conditions reveal the majority of signs that point to the nearness of Jesus's next coming. Bad leaders are clearly involved, whether it's an evil king, a false teacher, an evil judge, or a false prophet. Over the course of the next ten chapters, we're going to be looking at the end times signs associated with each of these bad heart conditions. Let's start at the beginning with a turned away heart.

CHAPTER 4 - A TURNED AWAY HEART

> When Solomon was old, his wives **turned away his heart** after other gods; and his heart was not perfect with the LORD his God, as the heart of David his father was. (1 Kings 11:4)

#7 - APOSTASY

Anti | **DD** | Earth | Gov | Israel | **Jesus** | Leader | Sky | **Society** | Tech | Trib

> But the Spirit says expressly that in later times some will fall away from the faith. (1 Timothy 4:1)

As you can see in the verse above, in the "later times some will fall away from the faith." That's what apostasy means, a departure from your faith. A falling away from the faith first requires initially being with the faith. That's what Jesus said happened to the church in Ephesus, they left their first love. So, this refers to people who were Christians and then for some reason turned and walked away and no longer believe. The Old Testament is full of examples of this in regard to the nation of Israel. Sometimes a generation would turn away from God to follow what the nations around them were doing. Sometimes they just didn't train their children in the ways of the Lord and thus the next generation didn't know him or follow him.

Fulfillment - Think of all the ways that America has distanced itself from Christianity just over the past few decades. We've removed God from schools and no longer teach creationism and the Bible. Instead, kids are taught that God doesn't exist and that creation evolved from space sludge. They even say humans eventually evolved from primates, without the myriad of archaeological evidence that should exist if it were true. It's been 165 years since Darwin's theory was published. Yet, the theory of evolution still hasn't been promoted to one of the laws of nature. It's still just a made-up theory.

You can see the secularization of society just about everywhere today. It's in the workplace, in the courts, and prominent in all media and entertainment.

Also, consider the rise in Christian deconstructionism.[1] It's where Christians start to pick apart the Bible and abandon core doctrines.

Many eventually leave Christianity. I'm sure you even know fellow believers who've fallen prey to this sort of thinking. I do. Rhett and Link, the hosts of the *Good Mythical Morning* daily YouTube show, have discussed how they deconstructed their Christian faith and ultimately left it behind.[2] They have almost 19 million subscribers![3] They and other celebrities who've walked away from Christianity have a lot of influence today, especially over the younger generations.

Today Is Different - The US has more Christians than any other nation.[4] According to a Gallup poll on religion in the US between 1948 and 2023, 68% of Americans identified as Christian in 2023. That's down from 91% in 1948 and a peak of 96% in 1956. It's been on a downward trend since. During this same period, there's been a steady increase in the percentage of Americans who don't identify with any religion. Back in 1948, they were only 2%. In 2023, they account for 22%.[5] Looking at another metric, Barna published a graph on weekly church attendance. Back in 1993, 45% of Americans said they attended church weekly. In 2020, it was down to only 29% of Americans.[6]

You and I both know that the percentage of Christians in the US is even lower because many of those self-professed Christians don't have a real saving faith in Jesus Christ. They just identify with the morality or good works of Christians and thus claim to be one as well. In fact, Barna's 2023 worldview report says that although the majority of the US population (68% in their analysis) identify as Christian, only half of that group say they're born again. Just a mere 6% actually hold to a biblical worldview.[7] This means only a tiny fraction actually believe things like the Bible is authoritative, Satan exists, there's only one God, and there are absolute moral truths.

So, what about Israel? It's the birthplace of Christianity. According to Israel census data, in 1949 only 3% of their population were Christian. The majority, 86%, were Jewish and about 10% were Muslim. Fast forward to 2022 and what do you think it looks like? You guessed it, Christianity has declined and only accounts for not quite 2%. Muslims have increased to 18% of the population while Jewish has dropped to 74%.[8] When digging deeper into the 74%, we learn that the majority of the population aren't even religious Jewish. It's cultural because 65% of Israelis identify as atheist.[9]

As you can see, both America and Israel have indeed fallen away from Christianity and continue to become more and more secular and irreligious.

Additional Scriptures: 2 Thessalonians 2:3. Deuteronomy 28:15, 45, 47, 58. Isaiah 9:8-13. James 2:19. Jeremiah 9:12-14. Judges 2:10. Luke 13:22-27; 18:8. Psalm 78:32. Revelation 2:1-5. Romans 1:21, 28; 3:11-12.

#8 - BACKSLIDING

Anti | DD | Earth | Gov | Israel | **Jesus** | **Leader** | Sky | **Society** | Tech | Trib

> And when people escape from the wickedness of the world by knowing our Lord and Savior Jesus Christ and then get tangled up and enslaved by sin again, they are worse off than before. It would be better if they had never known the way to righteousness than to know it and then reject the command they were given to live a holy life. They prove the truth of this proverb: "A dog returns to its vomit." And another says, "A washed pig returns to the mud." (2 Peter 2:20-22 NLT)

In Peter's second letter, he speaks about the last days and the day of the Lord. In these verses, he illustrates that some people who leave the Christian faith will become "enslaved by sin" and be worse off than they were before even becoming a Christian. These are essentially prodigals.

I'm sure you remember the parable Jesus gave of the prodigal sons. One son demanded his inheritance, moved away, and then spent all the money on wild living. When the money ran out, he got work as a farm hand and was so hungry that even the food he fed the pigs looked appetizing. His backsliding behavior made him worse off than he was when he lived in his father's house, when he only thought he had it rough.

Fulfillment - Do you know any prodigals? Perhaps it's someone who grew up going to church with you, but now doesn't want to have anything to do with church or God. The people I know in this group continue to walk farther and farther away from God and more and more into worldly sinful behavior.

Now, consider yourself and your church family. Do you behave differently than the rest of society? You only listen to Christian radio, only watch movies after you've read reviews that identify inappropriate content, dress modestly, and don't use foul language. Or do you watch the same R rated movies, listen to the same sexual songs on the radio, wear skimpy, tight outfits to the gym, and use the same coarse language that everyone else in society does? I know a lot of people in the latter camp.

Perhaps these people aren't full blown prodigals because they still have their toes dipped into church, but if Christians are backsliding into sin and aren't distinguishable from the world, then how do we know their faith is real?

Today Is Different - We learned in the prior sign, that a mere 6% of people who identify as Christian in the US actually have a biblical worldview.[10] In Barna's 2024 worldview report they indicate: "A majority of adults accept lying, abortion, consensual intercourse between unmarried adults, gay marriage, and the rejection of absolute moral truth as morally acceptable."[11] More shocking than that is what came out of Barna's 2022 worldview report in which they interviewed a representative sample of US Christian pastors. They learned that only 37% of pastors have a biblical worldview.[12] So, is it any wonder that Christians are leaving the faith and backsliding into sin?

Additional Scriptures: 2 Peter 3:3, 10. Genesis 19:26. Jeremiah 7:24; 11:9-11. Luke 9:62, 15:11-32. Romans 3:12; 6:1-14.

#9 - WORSHIPING OTHER GODS

Anti | DD | Earth | Gov | Israel | Jesus | Leader | Sky | Society | Tech | Trib

> Who exchanged the truth of God for a lie, and worshiped and served the creature rather than the Creator, who is blessed forever. (Romans 1:25)

In this sign, we see that when people turn away from God, that they turn toward something else. They begin to worship things God created instead of God. Things like angels, demons, the sun, moon, stars, animals, nature, and of course ourselves. This particular sign is a departure from the very first of the Ten Commandments that God gave us, which is to have no other gods but God.

During the tribulation period we'll see the pinnacle of this when people worship the Antichrist and Satan. You might recall that Satan even tried to get Jesus to worship him.

Fulfillment - While there are thousands of religions that people across the earth practice, there are just a handful of major religions that account for most of the world population. Christianity (31%), Muslim (25%), Unaffiliated (16%), Hindu (15%), Buddhist (7%), Folk

(6%), Jewish (<1%), and Others (<1%).[13]

So, what do all these religions worship? Well, we need to break up Christianity. Protestant Christianity accounts for about 37% of the world Christian population and uses the Bible, which they believe was written by God acting through man, as its sole source of divine knowledge. Most Protestants also believe that you're saved by Jesus's grace through faith, not by any works (Ephesians 2:4-9).[14] Thus, they only worship the God of the Bible who is defined as a Trinity: God the Father, Jesus the Son, and the Holy Spirit.

Then we have Catholicism which accounts for 50% of the global Christian population. They use the Bible plus sacred tradition as divinely inspired. They also believe that you're saved by doing good works, like the seven sacraments (baptism, confirmation, penance), in conjunction with having faith in Jesus.[15] Since they put tradition, communications from the pope, and human works on the same level as God, it means they worship God plus church authorities plus themselves. The Catholic Church also venerates Mary, the mother of Jesus, and people they've bestowed sainthood on. This is another form of worship because the followers pray to them.

Orthodox makes up another 12% of Christianity and has some similar practices to that of Catholicism, so they also are worshiping other gods.[16]

As for the Muslim, Hindu, Buddhist, and Folk religions, all you need to know for this sign is that they don't use the Bible as their source of divine knowledge. They each rely on other texts which are in direct contradiction to the Bible and in particular to the divinity of Jesus. They do not worship the God of the Bible; they all worship another god.[17]

You might say the Unaffiliated don't worship anything, but that's not the case. They're trusting in their own knowledge or human knowledge in general above everything else. So, they essentially worship themselves.

This means only 12%, a high estimate, of the entire planet worships Jesus Christ, who is God in the flesh (John 5:18, 10:30, Colossians 2:6-10).[18] The overwhelming majority worship another god.

Today Is Different - There's another religion that makes today different than times past. It's not captured among the traditional religions we've discussed. It's the worship of mother nature, and it's front and center today. You're familiar with it. It goes by many names like climate change, global warming, sustainable development, green energy, net zero, and climate crisis.

Don't think this is a religion? US President Biden said climate change is the number one issue facing humanity.[19] *Time* magazine named Greta Thunberg person of the year in 2019 for her work on climate change.[20] In November 2022, dozens of religious leaders from around the world gathered as participants in the UN Climate Conference COP 27, and they developed the new ten commandments they call "Ten Principles for Climate Repentance."[21] Even more recently, in March 2023, Thunberg was awarded an honorary Doctor of Theology degree by Helsinki University.[22]

Let's look at how much money is being spent on this. In 2009, the UN's Framework Convention on Climate Change committed to a collective goal of mobilizing $100 billion a year by 2020 for climate action in developing countries. This was the Paris Agreement. They actually hit their goal in 2022 and raised nearly $116 billion.[23] If that's not crazy enough, the UN has now said it's going to take $6 trillion a year to accomplish their climate goals.[24]

This form of nature worship has infiltrated everything. Consider all the regulations and laws coming out in America. There's a war against gas powered anything and a push to get us to use electric. Investors now evaluate and compare companies using ESG metrics that measure how well they're doing against environmental, social, and governance standards. There's a war against anything that generates greenhouse gas emissions, like cows. There's even a war against the size of the population through abortion, infanticide, euthanasia, and child policies.

The world is indeed worshiping another god. People are worshiping God's creation.

Additional Scriptures: 2 Kings 17:7-11; 21:3-5. Colossians 2:18. Deuteronomy 28:36, 64. Exodus 20:2-3. Jeremiah 44:2-10. Luke 4:5-8. Revelation 2:20-21; 9:20; 12:9; 13:4, 8. Zephaniah 1:5.

#10 - IDOLATRY

Anti | DD | Earth | Gov | Israel | Jesus | Leader | Sky | Society | Tech | Trib

> And traded the glory of the incorruptible God for the likeness of an image of corruptible man, and of birds, four-footed animals, and creeping things. (Romans 1:23)

You'll notice that we'll be looking at verses from Roman's 1 frequently in this book. Starting in verse 18, the apostle Paul reveals the behaviors that bring about God's wrath. Here, we see that people making an image of anything in creation and worshiping that is called out. In fact, it's a violation of the second of the Ten Commandments that God gave us, which is don't make an idol.

In the Old Testament, the Israelites sometimes made idols to represent God and then worshiped them. Like Aaron's or Jeroboam's gold calves. At other times, they fashioned an idol to represent a false god. In either case it's wicked. No image will ever adequately represent the complete nature of God.

In the tribulation period, idolatry will be forced upon the world when the False Prophet demands everyone worship the image of the Beast (Sign #71). Jesus also spoke about idolatry when he told us that we can't worship both God and money.

Fulfillment - You might think this seems like an ancient pagan practice and that we don't really do this today. While this might not be as obvious in America, if you've ever traveled abroad, this smacks you right in the face in many countries. I've seen temples that contain giant golden figures, jade creatures, and you name it for worshiping a whole host of gods. If you've been to Israel, you've noticed that an opulent church has been erected on every single holy site.

In the prior sign, I pointed out that idols exist even in Christianity today, just like they did in ancient Israel. We don't necessarily have gold calves, but many churches have depictions of Mary and a host of saints that people then pray to. Those are idols.

Today Is Different - Today, we've turned ourselves into idols for worship. We worship a particular look, style, and in many cases a celebrity. We even track how many "worshipers" we have through followers, likes, and comments. Consider all the time that people spend on how they look in person and on social media. Selfies on social media are the hallmark idols of today.

But it doesn't end there. Today, we also worship symbols. As I'm writing this, Pride month just ended in the US, and I saw countless pride rainbows everywhere, both in person and all over the media.

I think the biggest idol that makes today different is our worship of technology. It's become a lot more than just a tool to help us be more productive, efficient, and conquer difficult challenges. Can you live without your phone and the internet for a day?

With the boom of Artificial Intelligence (AI), you can now "resurrect" dead loved ones and chat with them. There are even apps that let you chat with dead Bible characters. It's just digital idolatry.

Today, companies are using technology to tackle challenges that are squarely in God's realm only. God alone has the power over life and death. Yet, many people are putting their faith of living forever into technologies like AI, brain chips, cryogenics, genetic engineering, and other biotechnologies.

Today is different because we're putting our faith into technology, idols we've created, to solve all the world's problems instead of looking to and trusting in God.

<u>Additional Scriptures:</u> 1 Kings 12:25-33. 2 Kings 17:13-16; 21:3-7. Colossians 3:5-6. Deuteronomy 28:36, 64. Exodus 20:4-5. Matthew 6:24. Revelation 2:14-16, 20-21; 9:20; 16:2.

#11 - THE OCCULT

Anti | **<u>DD</u>** | Earth | Gov | Israel | Jesus | Leader | Sky | **<u>Society</u>** | **<u>Tech</u>** | **<u>Trib</u>**

> The rest of mankind, who were not killed with these plagues, didn't repent of the works of their hands, that they wouldn't worship demons, and the idols of gold, and of silver, and of brass, and of stone, and of wood, which can't see, hear, or walk. They didn't repent of their ... sorceries. (Revelation 9:20-21)

God's Word tells us not to practice the occult, which includes witchcraft, soothsaying, sorcery, spells, divination, and calling up dead spirits. This is because doing those things is communicating with demons. Yet, as you read in the above Scriptures, this is exactly what people are called out for doing in the tribulation period.

Fulfillment - People are drawn to the mysterious and forbidden. You can easily see the fulfillment of this in entertainment. Consider what some of the most popular books, movies, and TV shows are about. Well, the best-selling book series in history is the *Harry Potter* series. It's about wizards and witches living and going to school in the modern day.[25]

There's now a whole slew of content in this same vein. Want to guess what one of the top 10 lifetime grossing movies (adjusted for inflation) is? It's *The Exorcist*.²⁶ This one is straight up demonic and about a demon possessed girl. Then there's *Stranger Things*, one of the most popular TV shows on right now and in fact the most popular one on Netflix.²⁷ It's a supernatural horror show about opening a portal to an alternate hostile dimension. Our culture is obsessed with the occult.

Today Is Different - I bet you didn't know that techno witchcraft is a thing. It includes online covens, digital and emoji spells, virtual rituals, and even apps for spell casting, divination, and ritual planning. People are even creating digital altars. It's a personalized space with images, videos, and other digital objects that showcases their deities.²⁸

Here's why this is so troubling to me. Teenagers and young adults can spend a lot of time online. The availability of these dark practices on social media makes it easy for young people to check them out from the comfort of their room, likely without a parent even knowing they're doing it.

Case in point, WitchTok. As of September 2024, there are 6.8 million posts to this hashtag on TikTok.²⁹ In October 2022, the BBC reported that videos with this hashtag had amassed an incredible 30 billion views!³⁰ That was almost two years ago. And recently in July 2024, Independent ran a story explaining how the WitchTok community is becoming the latest wellness fad. While people do talk about spells, rituals, tarot, crystals, and magic, there's also plenty of content about holistic approaches to health and wellbeing.³¹ One key theme I kept coming across in interviews of people in this community is that they liked the sense of control and power they felt by participating in these occult activities.

Additional Scriptures: 1 Timothy 4:1. 2 Chronicles 33:1-10. 2 Kings 17:17; 21:6. Deuteronomy 18:9-14. Isaiah 8:19; 47:9-13.

#12 - SATANISM

Anti | DD | Earth | Gov | Israel | Jesus | Leader | Sky | Society | Tech | Trib

> Again, the devil took him to an exceedingly high mountain, and showed him all the kingdoms of the world and their glory. He said to him, "I will give you all of these things, if you will fall down and worship me." Then Jesus said to him, "Get behind me, Satan! For it is written, 'You shall worship the Lord your God, and you shall serve him only.' " (Matthew 4:8-10)

Satan wants to be worshiped. He even tried to get Jesus to bow down to him. In the tribulation period, he's going to get his wish because the world is going to worship him and his representative, the Antichrist.

Fulfillment - The fact that we can see the rise of Satanism today is clear evidence of how near the tribulation period is. Consider the news you read regarding The Satanic Temple. They claim they don't worship Satan. That they only regard him as a literary figure. Yet they dress up as Baphomet and Satan at conventions and everything they do is in direct opposition to Christianity and the Bible. It certainly looks like Satan considers them to be his legit followers, don't you think?

They're the organization behind the after-school Satan clubs. They seek to have a presence at any school that offers a Christian based club. They also seek to erect statues of Baphomet alongside Christian depictions, like the nativity.[32]

They even started hosting a convention called SatanCon. The first event took place in 2022 in Arizona.[33]

Today Is Different - One thing that sets today apart from prior generations is the changing perception of Satan in entertainment. He used to be portrayed as the villain, solely as evil. That's not the case anymore. He's a full-blown Hollywood movie star today. Now, he's depicted as relatable, misunderstood, and even the good guy.

Consider the popular Netflix show *Lucifer*, where Satan leaves hell to open a nightclub and help solve crimes.[34] There's also *Hazbin Hotel*, an animated show that portrays Lucifer as a loving father helping his daughter rehabilitate sinners in hell, and he's even funny.[35] This type of content is now on Disney+ too. They just released a show titled *Pauline*, about a 19-year-old who gets pregnant from a one-night stand with the devil's son.[36] It's hard to get away from this demonic content today.

Celebrities are even coming out endorsing Satan. Back in 2021, remember rapper Lil Nas X and his Satan shoes with a pentagram, inverted cross, and a drop of blood inside.[37] How about Sam Smith's "Unholy" performance at the 2023 Grammy's where he dressed up as the devil.[38] His satanic song even won a Grammy that year. Then there's the most popular singer on the planet today, Taylor Swift. People are speaking out that she's including occult, demonic rituals, and pentagrams at her concerts.³⁹ And as you might expect, people calling out this troubling behavior are now labeled as inciting "satanic panic."

Additional Scriptures: 1 Corinthians 10:20-21. 1 Timothy 4:1. Deuteronomy 32:17. Revelation 9:20; 12:9; 13:4; 16:13-16.

#13 - GREAT FEAR

Anti | DD | **Earth** | Gov | Israel | **Jesus** | Leader | **Sky** | **Society** | **Tech** | **Trib**

> "Men fainting for fear and for expectation of the things which are coming on the world, for the powers of the heavens will be shaken." (Luke 21:26)

In this Scripture, Jesus is the one speaking, and he's informed his disciples that one of the signs of his second coming will be "men fainting for fear." During the tribulation period people are going to have great fear from all the judgments that God sends. When they see the two witnesses of God get resurrected, they're going to freak out. We're also told people are going to hide in caves because they'll be so afraid.

Fulfillment - The volume of daily doomsday predictions and doomsday prepping materials that are available are signs of fulfillment. Perhaps I've even fulfilled this one. I even have a page on my website, rapture911.com, for doomsday prepping.

https://rapture911.com/prepper-resources/

It's meant for people who are left behind after the rapture, but I have links to all sorts of popular TV shows and books in this space.⁴⁰

The main fear being spread over the media today is climate change. They say the planet is going to heat up to such an extent that all the ice will melt and thus the sea will rise. However, I also frequently see in the news a warning that a large asteroid is flying by earth and has the potential to hit us. There's also fear about WWIII being on the horizon.

I have news for you, the vast majority of these doomsday scenarios aren't going to happen. At least not prior to the tribulation period. The Bible tells us that the sun, moon, stars, and the laws of nature endure all generations. And remember what we discussed in Chapter 1 regarding Jesus coming when he's least expected. It's going to be relatively normal when the rapture happens. Have a look at Sign #84 - Fading Of Normality, for more on this.

Today Is Different - Do you remember a few years ago when the entire world was frozen in a state of fear over Covid? Literally everything shut down and people holed up inside their homes. Now, four years later, I still see people wearing face masks in their cars by themselves.

Around that same time there were riots in all the major cities in the US and several across the world. The push to defund the police gained traction, and now we're seeing the result of that with increased crime, looting, and violence. I admit that I don't like going out as much anymore because of this. I'd rather stay at home. I believe there is more fear in society today than perhaps there ever has been.

Another thing that makes today different is the technology we have to seemingly save ourselves from any sort of doomsday. A Japanese company, N-Ark, is building a floating city to withstand a disaster.[41] Consider the new space race to colonize the moon and Mars and save humanity from whatever might ail the planet.

What I find the most interesting though is the popularity of doomsday bunkers, particularly among the wealthy.[42] Even they can tell that something extreme is on the horizon. Discovery has a TV show about these bunkers.[43] Do an internet search and you'll see a bunch of companies selling these things. Zuckerberg is spending $270 million building a huge mansion underground in Hawaii.[44] I guess he hasn't read the bit in the book of Revelation where it says God removes all the islands during the tribulation period.

Additional Scriptures: Deuteronomy 28:28, 34, 65-67. Isaiah 2:19; 13:6-8. Jeremiah 31:35-37. Luke 21:11. Micah 7:15-17. Psalm 72:5. Revelation 6:4, 15-17; 11:11; 16:20; 18:9-10, 15. Zechariah 14:13.

#14 - POLAR OPPOSITE - A SEEKING HEART

Anti | DD | **Earth** | **Gov** | **Israel** | **Jesus** | **Leader** | Sky | **Society** | **Tech** | Trib

> I heard a loud voice out of heaven saying, "Behold, God's dwelling is with people; and he will dwell with them, and they will be his people, and God himself will be with them as their God." (Revelation 21:3)

Throughout this chapter we've looked at signs related to a turned away heart. This sign is what I call a polar opposite. It's meant to illustrate how far away we currently are from the life we believers are going to live during Jesus's reign on earth in the millennial kingdom.

Recall from Sign #6 - The Point Of No Return, that God only lets evil progress so far before he intervenes.

In the verse above, we learn that after Jesus's second coming, that God will dwell with us here on earth. After reading the additional Scriptures I have listed below, you'll discover that God's sanctuary will be among us, no one will ever be afraid again, and there will be no idol worship.

Everyone will have a seeking heart, one that follows God.

> Blessed are those whose ways are blameless, who walk according to the LORD's law. Blessed are those who keep his statutes, who **seek him with their whole heart**. (Psalm 119:1-2)

Fulfillment - So, how far away are we? Well, Jerusalem will be the center of God's government on earth and where his tabernacle resides. Today, most people in Israel are atheist, and there's no holy temple on the Temple Mount in which to worship God. Instead, it's the Muslim's Dome of the Rock. People can't even pray to God on the Temple Mount safely today.

A fun way to consider just how opposite we are is to contemplate what the worst-case scenarios might look like and see just how close we are to those.

Worst case, our entire planet worships another God. Today, at least 88% do. Refer back to Sign #9 - Worshiping Other Gods. We're really close to this worst case.

Worst case, idols are located everywhere and on everything. Well, advertising certainly seems to fit that bill today. Is it a form of idolatry? Perhaps. We all take our phones everywhere and most people post everything online. That's definitely a type of idolatry. We're really close to this worst case too.

Worst case, there are no Christian churches. If you remember a few years ago, the government in many US states shut down all the churches and forced everyone to participate online from home. That wasn't even an option for many smaller churches that didn't have an online presence. This worst case has happened for some of us.

Worst case, everyone in the world is afraid. No one goes out for entertainment, to shop at a store, or for dining out. Everyone works from home, has everything delivered, and just binge watches TV. Covid certainly shaped this behavior, didn't it? Many people live this way today. This worst case has already happened for some people too.

Worst case, the entire society practices the occult and dresses up like witches, vampires, Satan, or zombies. Yikes! We totally do this at Halloween don't we? In fact, back in 2005 the US spent $3.3 billion on Halloween. That includes candy, costumes, and decorations. In 2023 it's quadrupled to $12.2 billion.[45] We're at the worst case here.

Today Is Different - So, what do you think? Is today different? Have we turned away from God to such a degree that we've reached the point of no return? How many people really have a heart that's seeking God?

Additional Scriptures: Ezekiel 37:23, 26-27. Isaiah 2:2-3. Matthew 24:30. Micah 4:1, 4. Zephaniah 3:13-17.

CHAPTER 5 - A PRIDEFUL HEART

> Then Daniel answered, and said before the king, ... "O king, the Most High God gave Nebuchadnezzar your father a kingdom and majesty, glory and honor. ... But when his **heart was lifted up**, and his spirit was **hardened in pride**, he was deposed from his kingly throne, and they took his glory from him." (Daniel 5:17-18, 20 NKJV)

#15 - PUFFED UP WITH PRIDE

<u>Anti</u> | <u>DD</u> | Earth | Gov | Israel | <u>Jesus</u> | <u>Leader</u> | Sky | <u>Society</u> | <u>Tech</u> | <u>Trib</u>

> But know this, that in the last days perilous times will come: For men will be ... boasters, proud, ... haughty. (2 Timothy 3:1-2, 4 NKJV)

When the apostle Paul wrote to his disciple Timothy and gave him a list of behaviors describing the last days, he listed about twenty things, mentioning pride three times using three different words. He clearly wanted to call out this particular behavior being a hallmark of the last days. The word *boaster* in this instance means an empty pretender. While the word *proud* means showing oneself above others, and pre-eminent. *Haughty* means to be puffed up with pride, and to render foolish or stupid.

Satan's sin was pride. One of Sodom's sins was pride. Jesus told us the Antichrist would come in his own name and be received by the world. During the tribulation period, the Antichrist will embody this negative character trait.

Fulfillment - I think you'll agree that we as a society have fulfilled this today. I'm sure I'm not the only one who's been around someone who can't help bragging about themselves. They talk about how much money they make, all the new stuff they just bought, and the big vacation they have planned.

When I was younger, we didn't have the internet or social media where parents could brag about their kids. Instead, parents put those stickers on their cars that said, "My kid is an honor student" and such. Remember those?

It seems every celebrity and popular politician these days thinks their lives are so interesting that they have to write a book about themselves. I'm browsing Amazon's list of bestsellers in biographies, and it includes Anthony Fauci, Matthew McConaughey, Whoopi Goldberg, Elon Musk, Britney Spears, Matthew Perry, Prince Harry, Viola Davis, and Reba McEntire.[1] There are 109,048 reviews on Prince Harry's book. They're writing these because we as a society gobble them up.

We have an insatiable desire to peer into other people's lives either through social media, magazines, reality TV, or books. People want to compare themselves to others so they can puff themselves up when they discover that they're better at something, they look better in an outfit, or they have a more perfect life.

Today Is Different - We're prideful about our lives and accomplishments to such a degree that we've created places we can share and post about all the stuff we do every day. You guessed it, it's called social media. Facebook is the dominant player in this space and has nearly 3 billion active users each month.[2] There are a little over 8 billion people on the planet.[3] That means nearly 38% of all people are using Facebook. A fact even crazier is that it's estimated there are 5 billion unique social media users globally, that's almost 63% of the planet.[4]

You and I both know that people aren't primarily using social media to read and comment on the news and current affairs. They're posting pictures of themselves, their kids, what they cooked for dinner, and videos of their pets. Pew Research Center published a recent study about what teens are posting on social media. Shocker, 43% say they're posting about their accomplishments.[5]

Additional Scriptures: 1 John 2:16. 1 Timothy 6:3-5. Daniel 7:8, 11, 25; 8:24-25. Exodus 10:3. Ezekiel 16:49-50; 28:2-8. Isaiah 2:11-12; 14:12-21. John 5:43. Malachi 4:1. Proverbs 6:16-17. Revelation 13:5. Romans 1:30.

#16 - LOVERS OF OURSELVES

Anti | DD | Earth | Gov | Israel | **Jesus** | Leader | Sky | **Society** | **Tech** | **Trib**

> But know this, that in the last days perilous times will come: For men will be lovers of themselves. (2 Timothy 3:1-2 NKJV)

Another behavior trait of the last days is loving ourselves. It's the first sign in the apostle Paul's list. It's different than pride. This one means selfish. Jesus frequently called out the religious leaders during his first coming for doing good works just to be seen by the people. Their hearts weren't right. They didn't have a love for the people. They just loved the praise from the people. They did their works for selfish reasons.

This is going to be a hallmark of the tribulation period too. That's because the Antichrist is going to love himself so much that he'll declare himself God and demand everyone worship him.

Fulfillment - I think one way we can assess how selfish we are as a society is to look at how many people are getting married today compared to prior years. Marriage requires compromise. You have to be willing to forgo your wants and needs for your spouse's. A selfish society won't be willing to do that.

Here's a quote from the Our World in Data website: "Within the last decades the institution of marriage has changed more than in thousands of years before. ... Over the period 1990-2010, there was a decline in marriage rates in the majority of countries around the world."[6]

Refer to figure 16.1 below. It displays the number of marriages in the US and Israel over time.

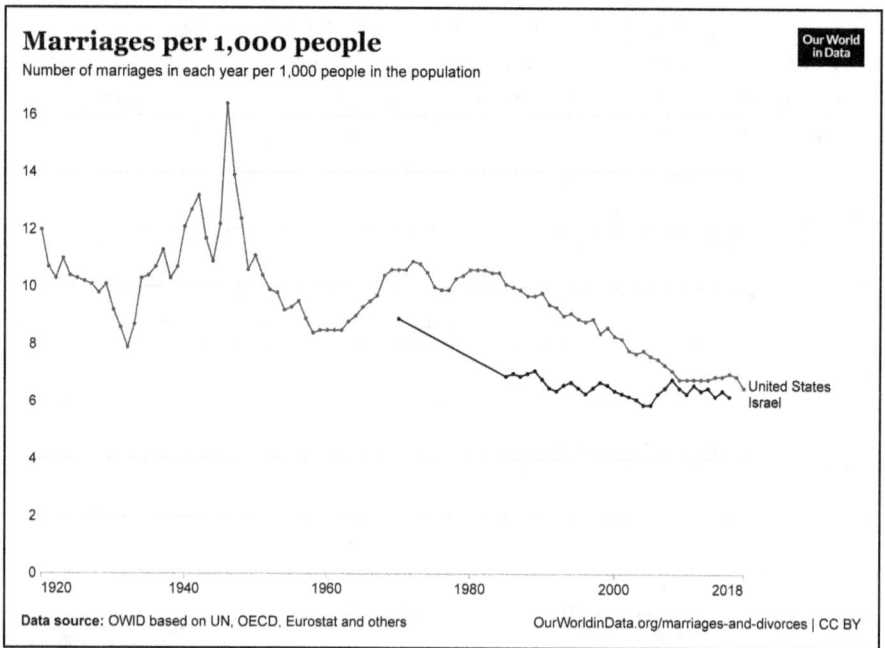

Figure 16.1. Marriages per 1,000 people[7]
Source: https://ourworldindata.org/grapher/marriage-rate-per-1000-inhabitants?country=USA~ISR

In the US, the peak marriage rate was in 1946 when there were 16 marriages annually per 1,000 people in the population. As you can see, it's been on a steady decline since then. In 2018 there were only 6.5 marriages annually per 1,000 people. Israel isn't fairing any better. In 1970 their rate was 8.9 and in 2018 it was down to 6.2.

Today Is Different - I'm going to talk about social media again. It plays such a big role in what sets today apart from prior years. If people aren't getting married and spending time with another person or with their children, then what are they spending their alone time doing?

Well, back in 2012 people across the world spent an average of 90 minutes a day on social platforms. That time has steadily increased every year and in 2023 it was up to 151 minutes per day.[8] That's over two and a half hours a day! Do you think most people are chatting with someone else, or posting and browsing?

Ok, what else are we spending time doing, probably alone? Using the internet is often something we do by ourselves, unless we're streaming a movie to watch with someone else. Internet users worldwide are spending an average of 6 hours 40 minutes online every day. Wow! No surprise, both the US and Israel have usage above the worldwide rate. Israelis are online 7 hours 20 minutes a day while Americans are at 7 hours 3 minutes.

This daily time spent online includes streaming TV content (3 hours 6 minutes a day global average), reading news (1 hour 41 minutes), streaming music (1 hour 25 minutes), listening to a podcast (49 minutes), and playing a game (1 hour 2 minutes).[9] Some of those activities might be spent with someone else or a group. I'd guess at least half of the internet time is spent doing something solo. That's over 3 hours a day that most people on the planet are spending just with themselves.

Additional Scriptures: 2 Thessalonians 2:3-4. John 12:42-43. Luke 18:9-14; 20:45-47. Matthew 23:5-7. Romans 2:8.

#17 - EVERYONE DOES RIGHT IN THEIR OWN EYES

Anti | DD | Earth | Gov | Israel | **Jesus** | **Leader** | Sky | **Society** | Tech | Trib

> "It will happen, when you tell this people all these words, and they ask you, 'Why has the LORD pronounced all this great evil against us?' or

'What is our iniquity?' or 'What is our sin that we have committed against the LORD our God?' then you shall tell them, 'Because your fathers have forsaken me,' says the LORD, ... 'You have done evil more than your fathers, for behold, you each walk after the stubbornness of his evil heart, so that you don't listen to me.' " (Jeremiah 16:10-12)

God told the prophet Jeremiah that the reason his righteous judgment was coming upon the people was because they were each walking "after the stubbornness" of their evil hearts. This is when the Israelites were taken into captivity by Babylon. I like how another Scripture in the Bible phrases this. It's Judges 17:6, and it says, "everyone did that which was right in his own eyes."

The problem with each person following their own heart is that our hearts are inherently deceitful and wicked. We're born with a sinful nature. We are incapable of behaving righteously without God's help, the Holy Spirit.

Jesus even spoke of this when he told us that people reject God's commands in order to keep their own traditions.

Fulfillment - Live your best life now. You do you. Live your truth. Do what feels right. Speak your truth. Sound familiar? Many of these popular sayings today are best-selling book titles too. They have descriptions that include "it's time to put your happiness first," "when it's okay to be selfish," and "prepare to be your best self."[10]

You and I both know this mentality is just excusing and condoning bad behavior, from sexual perversion to bullying.

I like this quote from an article titled "How 'You Do You' Perfectly Captures Our Narcissistic Culture" in *The New York Times Magazine*: " 'You do you,' taken to its extreme, provides justification for every global bad actor. The invasion of Ukraine is Putin being Putin, Iran's nuclear ambitions Khamenei being Khamenei. Haters gonna hate."[11]

Today Is Different - Do you think politicians accurately represent the voice of their constituents or do you think they do whatever's right in their own eyes once elected? John G. Matsusaka with the University of Southern California reported his results of a study looking into this in July 2022. There are 23 states in the US that give citizens a chance to repeal a state law that was approved by their state government. He examined 32 laws across 9 states representing 4,094 roll-call votes on those laws. He compared a legislator's roll-call vote on a law with the votes cast by their constituents on that law in a referendum election.

He found that only 66% of legislator's roll-call votes were aligned with the majority opinion of constituents. The most powerful determinate of their vote was legislator ideological preference. In fact, when a legislator disagreed with their constituents, they only cast congruent votes 29% of the time. Well, that's not good. He also said re-election pressure, media pressure, and being term-limited had no ability to predict congruence.[12]

I have a feeling his results accurately represent all levels of government across the world. Today is different because even when someone is elected and getting paid to represent a group of people, they often don't. Instead, they do whatever they think is right in their own eyes.

Additional Scriptures: Jeremiah 8:6; 17:9; 18:11-12. Judges 17:6. Mark 7:8-9. Romans 10:1-4.

#18 – FORTIFIED CITIES AND HIGH TOWERS

Anti | **DD** | **Earth** | **Gov** | Israel | Jesus | Leader | Sky | Society | **Tech** | **Trib**

> The great day of the LORD [is] near .... A day of trumpet and alarm Against the fortified cities And against the high towers. (Zephaniah 1:14, 16 NKJV)

This is an interesting sign. It's from the Old Testament, and it tells us that the "day of the Lord," a reference to the tribulation period, will come against "fortified cities" and "high towers." That means those are two things we should be looking for as signs. A fortified city is one that's enclosed, made inaccessible, or guarded. A high tower means a literal tall tower, but it could also mean an exalted ruler.

God destroyed the first really tall tower that mankind built, the Tower of Babel. It's because the people were doing it to reach into heaven and make a name for themselves. It was a symbol of pride. The Bible tells us that during the tribulation period, the city of Babylon will be destroyed. It's where all the kings of the earth will live in the tribulation period. It seems it'll be their fortified city.

It's also worth noting that a characteristic of the Antichrist is that he honors a god of fortresses.

Fulfillment - Well, we certainly have a lot of fortified cities and tall towers on the planet today. In 2020 it was reported that 4.7 billion people, 61% of the world population, lived in a country that had a border wall.[13]

As for tall towers, the number of tall buildings (over 200 meters or 656 feet) completed across the world in 2020 was 23.[14] To put that in perspective, the Eiffel Tower is 300 meters.[15] We've been building more and more of these every year since the Eiffel Tower. We peaked in 2018 with 146 tall towers completed that year. Not only do we have an obsession with building tall, but we have to continually build taller and taller. The Eiffel Tower was the tallest building in the world in 1930. Since 2009 it's been the Burj Khalifa at 828 meters or 2,717 feet. Now there are over 100 buildings on earth that are taller than the Eiffel Tower.

Another area of fulfillment that I think we have in common with the people of ancient Babel is one language. Babel's ability to communicate with each other aided in their success and was the reason they were even able to build the tower. That's why God's judgment against the tower also included the creation of various languages. While there are still thousands of languages in the world, the language of business and accomplishing great things is English. Rosetta Stone says English is the most widely spoken language in the world with 1.5 billion speakers.[16] It's one of the six official languages of the United Nations and the official or majority language of 58 countries.[17] But, with apps like Google Translate, we really are able to communicate with anyone in real time.

Today Is Different - These days, it's not just a wall that makes a city or country guarded. It's military defense technology. Consider what's used today to keep a city protected: autonomous drones with laser weapons, Iron Dome type air defense systems that shoot down incoming missiles, radar, air forces, the threat of a counterattack with nuclear weapons or cyber warfare, surveillance technology, hypersonic aircraft and missiles, and military robots to name a few.

When thinking about the god of fortresses that the Antichrist will honor, we're also told it's a god his fathers didn't know. It certainly seems like ancient Israel worshiped every sort of god. So, what could possibly be new? They didn't have the technology that we have. I think military defense technology is an excellent candidate for what he's going to spend all his gold and silver on and put his faith in.

<u>Additional Scriptures:</u> Daniel 11:37-38. Genesis 11:1-9. Hosea 8:14. Isaiah 2:12-15; 9:8-13; 30:25. Jeremiah 50:1-51:58. Revelation 16:18-20; 18.

#19 - CHANGING TIMES AND LAWS
Anti | DD | Earth | **Gov** | **Israel** | Jesus | **Leader** | Sky | Society | Tech | **Trib**

He will plan to change the times and the law. (Daniel 7:25)

This is a sign from the Old Testament that's referring to the Antichrist. He will "plan to change the times and the law." This will happen during the tribulation period. Since it says he plans to do it, that implies he doesn't actually do it. This likely means he just talks about it. The word *times* means a set time, appointed time, or season. The word *law* could refer to God's Law or the law of a ruler. Since government laws change all the time today, I don't believe it's referring to that. I believe it's an intent to change some sort of biblical law related to a set time.

Fulfillment - Today we're certainly seeing governments change their laws to allow behavior the Bible expressly forbids. The legalizing of abortion, same sex marriage, and drugs are a few examples. I think those are just partial fulfillments of this though.

When looking at what's going on in Israel these days regarding their laws, we start to get some ideas of how this might get fulfilled in the tribulation period. One contentious law change being discussed is in regard to their Law of Return. This law is a big deal because it describes who is able to immigrate into Israel.

The religious parties of the government want to revoke the Grandchild Clause which guarantees citizenship to anyone with a Jewish grandparent. They argue most people immigrating this way aren't really Jewish according to Jewish law. It would largely affect immigrants from the former Soviet Union. That means nations like Russia and Ukraine. On the other hand, the opposition lawmakers are against changing the law and even want to add a Great-Grandchild Clause.[18] I'm sure you can see that this one is quite political. Could the Antichrist offer an opinion on this controversial law? Perhaps.

Here's another one that might have fulfillment in the tribulation period. Since the beginning of Israel's war with Hamas on October 7, 2023, there's been controversy regarding their Shabbat, aka their Sabbath or holy day of rest. On a normal Shabbat, Orthodox Israelis turn off their radios and phones, lay down their weapons, public transportation doesn't run, and most places of business are closed. In the midst of war, these religious practices aren't conducive to public safety or people and military personnel getting around easily. So, trains have been allowed to run on Shabbat and religious leaders in synagogues have been able to have their phones on and with them.[19] Since this is a conflict that deals with a biblical law regarding an appointed time, I believe the Shabbat has potential to be a topic the Antichrist will have an opinion on.

Today Is Different - This might be the most contentious law change in Israel. It's the Nation-State Bill. It was passed in 2018 and defines Israel as the nation-state of the Jewish people, makes Hebrew the official language, and that the right to exercise self-determination in Israel is unique to the Jewish people. Well, as you can imagine, this didn't go over well among the Palestinian and Arab communities. The law was challenged in their courts and their Supreme Court upheld it in 2021.[20] Might the Antichrist desire to change this one? Definitely!

A current topic that's split the Israeli government is what to do about governance in Gaza after they've finished the war with Hamas. The debate is whether they should have Israeli civil or military governance, or non-Hamas Palestinian governance.[21] Also, there's still international pressure for Israel to create a two-state solution and re-establish Palestinian settlements.[22] We know the Antichrist is going to spearhead a peace treaty with Israel that breaks up their nation. Perhaps he comes on the scene with the seemingly perfect solution to this debate.

Additional Scriptures: Daniel 9:27. Hebrews 7:11-28. Isaiah 24:5. Joel 3:2.

#20 - POLAR OPPOSITE - A WORSHIPING HEART

Anti | DD | **Earth** | **Gov** | **Israel** | Jesus | **Leader** | Sky | **Society** | Tech | Trib

> It will happen that everyone who is left of all the nations that came against Jerusalem will go up from year to year to worship the King, the LORD of Armies, and to keep the feast of booths. (Zechariah 14:16)

Throughout this chapter we've looked at signs related to a prideful heart. This sign is what I call a polar opposite. It's meant to illustrate how far away we currently are from the life we believers are going to

Oblivious To The Signs When It's Obvious The King Is Coming

live during Jesus's reign on earth in the millennial kingdom. Recall from Sign #6 - The Point Of No Return, that God only lets evil progress so far before he intervenes.

In the verse above, we learn that after Jesus's second coming, during the millennial kingdom, that every year we'll go to Jerusalem to worship Jesus as "the King" and celebrate the "feast of booths." If you recall, the Feast of Booths is also called the Feast of Tabernacles. God ordained it for the Israelites so that they would remember their days of dwelling in booths when God rescued them from Egyptian captivity. They journeyed through the wilderness for forty years before entering the promised land.

After reading the additional Scriptures I have listed below, you'll also discover that the whole earth will be at rest, we'll break into singing, there won't be any proud or arrogant people, everyone will be full of thanksgiving, and there will be a Highway of Holiness. Of course, there will also be the glorious city of New Jerusalem that's a 1,400-mile cube.[23] It's hard to fathom a city that size. It makes any city or tower we've ever built look like a kid's Lego creation in comparison.

Everyone will have a worshiping heart, one that glorifies God.

> Let's **lift up our heart** with our hands to God in the heavens. (Lamentations 3:41)

Fulfillment - So, how far away are we? Well, today people certainly go to Jerusalem to worship. Some do go to worship Jesus, but Israel has a very small Christian population. It's likely that Christian tourists are the ones mostly doing this. You can see the Orthodox Jews at the Wailing Wall, but they're not worshiping Jesus. They don't believe he's the Messiah. And the Muslims in Jerusalem are there to worship their god at the Dome of the Rock.

A fun way to consider just how opposite we are is to contemplate what the worst-case scenarios might look like and see just how close we are to those.

Worst case, everyone worships themselves, so there are statues of people everywhere. While we don't have these statues all over our cities, we do stop and take pictures of ourselves everywhere. Then we post them in our online communities where they live forever. We're really close to this worst case.

Worst case, everyone spends their entire free time on social media posting about themselves. No one talks to each other because they're too busy talking about themselves. After learning we're practically spending an entire workday doing things online every day, we're close to this worst case too. Refer back to Sign #16 - Lovers Of Ourselves.

Worst case, every city has a high tower and some type of fortification. Well, aside from the Southern border of the United States, this seems to be true for most of the planet. Cities and countries are protected with a military presence today. We can check the box on this one, we're at this worst case.

Worst case, nobody gets married anymore. How many people do you know who live together and aren't married or who just choose to be single? We're really close to this worst case.

Worst case, God's Law is completely disregarded, and we're banned from even reading it. Well, the Bible is indeed banned or very difficult to obtain in many countries today, most of which are Muslim.[24] This includes China, India, Saudi Arabia, Iran, Afghanistan, Turkey, and Cuba. China and India are the two most populated countries today.[25] Those two by themselves have nearly 36% of the global population. While we're far from this worst case in America, parts of the world are at this worst case.

Today Is Different - So, what do you think? Is today different? Do we as a society have a prideful heart that's selfish and worships itself? Have we thus reached the point of no return? How many people really have a heart that's worshiping God?

Additional Scriptures: Isaiah 14:7; 35:8. Jeremiah 30:19. Leviticus 23:33-43. Revelation 21:10-21. Zephaniah 3:11-12.

CHAPTER 6 - A FOOLISH HEART

> Behold, two of them were going that very day to a village named Emmaus, which was sixty stadia from Jerusalem. ... While they talked and questioned together, Jesus himself came near, and went with them. ... He said to them, "**Foolish** people, and **slow of heart** to believe in all that the prophets have spoken!" (Luke 24:13, 15, 25)

#21 - CURSES ARE A WARNING

Anti | DD | **Earth** | **Gov** | **Israel** | Jesus | **Leader** | **Sky** | **Society** | Tech | **Trib**

> "All these curses will come on you, and will pursue you and overtake you, until you are destroyed, because you didn't listen to the LORD your God's voice, to keep his commandments and his statutes which he commanded you. They will be for a sign and for a wonder to you and to your offspring forever." (Deuteronomy 28:45-46)

After God rescued the Israelites from Egyptian captivity, he gave them the Law and then promised blessings if they obeyed and curses if they didn't. Moses is speaking in the verses above and relaying the bit about curses to all the people. We learn that curses are meant to be a sign for us. God gave quite a long list. Refer to Appendix A for the signs corresponding to each curse.

Before God even gave us the Law, you'll recall he instituted this cursing for disobeying principle right off the bat. It happened when Adam and Eve sinned in the garden. God put enmity between us and Satan, made childbirth painful, created marital strife, and then cursed the ground so that work was difficult.

The entire point of God doing these things is to get our attention. He wants us to realize the curse he promised for disobedience is upon us. It should make us repent of our sin and turn back toward God. When we continue to ignore the curses, we just get more and more of them. God makes it more and more obvious that he's the one behind what's happening in hopes that we'll finally clue in. This is exactly why all the curses are going to appear during the tribulation period.

Fulfillment - Read Deuteronomy 28:15-68 so you'll get a feel for all the curses God brings upon a nation for disobedience. We'll be reviewing 31 signs in this book that correspond to all those curses. Every one of them is seeing fulfillment today. Have a look at the Signs

In Deuteronomy Curses in Appendix A for a list of them. God's shouting at us from his throne wondering why we're so blind and foolish toward what's happening all around us.

Today Is Different - God sent us a messenger for our day and age that's been revealing parallels between curses upon ancient Israel for disobedience and recent events in the United States. Perhaps you've read one of his books. It's Jonathan Cahn. I read his first book, *The Harbinger*, shortly after it was published in 2011. He explains the biblical pattern behind the September 11, 2001 attack on New York City, along with some other negative events. I was so captivated by it that I bought one for everyone I knew. It was a *New York Times* bestseller for over 100 consecutive weeks and sold over 2 million copies.[1]

It's eerie to see the same exact biblical patterns that happened in Israel playing out in America. I get goosebumps when I read his books because he reveals the specificity and attention to detail that God has in fulfilling prophecies. I highly recommend his books if you're interested in end times signs. Jonathan's books make it obvious that today is different.

Additional Scriptures: Daniel 9:10-14. Deuteronomy 28:15-68. Exodus 7-12. Genesis 3. Jeremiah 11:6-8. Micah 7:15-17. Revelation 6-18.

#22 - CANCEL CULTURE

Anti | **DD** | Earth | **Gov** | Israel | Jesus | Leader | Sky | **Society** | **Tech** | Trib

> We don't remember what happened in the past, and in future generations, no one will remember what we are doing now. (Ecclesiastes 1:11 NLT)

King Solomon wrote about this particular sign. We don't remember history. Therefore, we end up not learning from it and doing better. Instead, we just repeat the same mistakes of the past. The apostle Peter discussed this as well when he revealed the last days would include scoffers who willfully forget that God made the heavens and sent the flood of Noah's day. To *willfully* forget means you're resolved to, determined to, and even take delight in forgetting. It's ignorance by choice.

Ancient Israel was continually forgetting God's judgments and God's power of deliverance. You'll notice a pattern of this in the Old

Testament. It seems like one generation would know and follow the Lord, but they wouldn't teach their children about God and all he'd done for them. So, the next generation didn't know God and followed the worship practices of the evil people around them. The people would eventually cry out to God for help, so he'd rescue them. Then the cycle would repeat again.

Fulfillment - That cycle is like the Energizer Bunny. It keeps going and going. We have a name for it today though. It's called cancel culture. Today, we're quick to cancel someone, either dead or alive, from history because we don't like something about their behavior. Consider all the statues of war heroes and past presidents that are being vandalized or removed from public display because there's outrage that they owned a slave. Instead of learning from their past mistakes we've just chosen to forget they existed. History books are rewritten. Their names are erased from schools and public buildings.

Today Is Different - I've talked about Christian deconstructionism before. It fulfills this sign too. We're canceling God today when we willfully forget content in God's Word that we don't like and disagree with. I know people who choose to ignore Romans 1 because they support a lifestyle that God calls out as wicked. I also know people who pick apart other biblical truths, like the flood of Noah's day, and rationalize it to being a local event.

Today, people don't understand God's love, righteousness, and justice. They also don't understand the human condition and sin. They can't come to terms with a God who punishes sin. They think everyone deserves to go to heaven because God is love and therefore God wouldn't send anyone to hell. In doing so, they fail to fully understand God's character because he's also righteous and judges sin. So, they start to deconstruct or spiritualize whatever it is in the Bible that they don't like. They're replacing God's truth with their own truth. We as a society are canceling God.

I will add that our technology and level of scientific advancement can make it more difficult for people to believe biblical events. You can find all sorts of shows on TV and the internet today that claim to debunk Noah's flood, the parting of the Red Sea, and the crucifixion of Jesus for example. Science seems to have an explanation for everything. Today is different because science and technology have canceled God too.

Chapter 6 - A Foolish Heart

Additional Scriptures: 2 Peter 3:3-6. Ezekiel 16:22, 43; 23:35. Hosea 13:6. Isaiah 17:10. Jeremiah 8:7; 44:2-10. Judges 8:34. Psalm 78:10-12, 41-43.

#23 - ANXIETY OF NATIONS WITH PERPLEXITY

Anti | DD | Earth | **Gov** | Israel | **Jesus** | **Leader** | Sky | **Society** | **Tech** | **Trib**

> "There will be signs ... on the earth anxiety of nations, in perplexity for the roaring of the sea and the waves." (Luke 21:25)

This is a quote from Jesus in his Olivet Discourse. The word *anxiety* means dismay, distress, or anguish. It comes from a Greek root word that means to press together lest it fall to pieces. It's a nation that's perplexed and at its wits end because the sea and waves are roaring.

I believe the sea and waves has a double meaning. Literally, it's a reference to a storm on the water. We'll examine that in Sign #142 - Sea And Waves Roaring. Metaphorically, we're told in Isaiah 17:12 that many people make a noise like the roar of the sea and make a rushing like the rush of water. It's a prophecy about the destruction of the city of Damascus, which could happen before or during the tribulation period, that causes the people to be in an uproar. We'll talk about that more in Sign #113 - Destruction Of Damascus. So, for this particular sign, the people of a nation are roaring about something, and the nation cannot resolve it.

Fulfillment - If you read or listen to the news these days, you've noticed that people are not happy with their governments. It doesn't matter what country or state they're in. There are protests happening everywhere for all sorts of things.

Just looking internally at the US, it's never been more divided politically than it is right now. We're living in a world of stark polarity. Each political party feels like the world is going to end if the other party wins. Even the branches of government can't get along. The Executive and Legislative branches are at odds with the Supreme Court. The two Legislative branches have different political majorities, so it seems like absolutely nothing is being accomplished in terms of passing or changing legislation. They can't even agree on a budget each year.

The state governments are at odds with the Federal government. Even local city governments are disagreeing with their state governments. Have you seen that the rural counties in California want to break off and form New California?[2] And thirteen counties in Oregon want to break off and join Idaho?[3] Our nation is fracturing.

A July 5, 2024 poll regarding US President Biden after his first debate with President Trump shows only a 36% approval rating among likely voters.[4] Pew Research Center conducted a poll in September 2023 and reports that 8 in 10 Americans respond with a negative word when describing US politics[5]. I'm not surprised. I have a lot of negative things to say as well.

I don't think international tensions between countries have ever been higher, either. Consider the tension between the US and Russia, the US and China, Israel and Iran, Ukraine and Russia, China and its neighbors, South Korea and North Korea, Russia and the European Union, and lately even the US and Israel. It seems like the superpowers are on the brink of war.

Today Is Different - Have you noticed recently that Israel seems to be in a constant state of elections for prime minister and the Knesset, their legislative body? That's because they've had five elections since 2019. And guess what? Netanyahu, the current prime minister, is starting to lose support in the Knesset due to his handling of the war with Hamas. There's talk of yet another election this September, in 2024.[6] It's almost like they're having elections every year at this point. They certainly seem to be a nation at its wits end, don't you think?

The Knesset has a four-year election cycle, so what's the deal? Well, Israel has a multi-party system in which citizens vote for which political party they want to represent them in the Knesset. They don't vote for a particular candidate like we do in the US. The seats in the Knesset are assigned proportionally based on how each party does in the election.

Now, here's the tricky part. No party has ever won a majority of the seats. So, after the election, the president of Israel consults with the party leaders and picks the one who has the best chance of forming a viable government. You know, one that will get along well enough to be able to pass legislation. I'm sure you see where this is going now. The leader chosen only has a few weeks to form a government. If they can't, another party leader is chosen to give it a go.

Once the Knesset is formed, if folks can't get along and start changing allegiances or drop out of the government altogether, then the Knesset is dissolved, and another election is held. You can see it's quite unstable.[7] Proverbs 28:2 describes this situation perfectly. When a nation is rebellious, it'll have many rulers.

Let's consider the role technology plays today in creating this state of perplexity for a nation. Social media and the internet changed the game for citizens and protesters. It's easy to post about an event, like a rally, and communicate with those who plan on attending. We even have online petitions today. We also have more access to information about politicians than in times past. It's easy to see what they're voting for and be able to hold them accountable in the next election. They even broadcast some of the congressional meetings live on TV and the internet. Perhaps one of the most potent social weapons today is a post that has gone viral because a certain billionaire comments on it.

Additional Scriptures: Deuteronomy 28:20, 28. Habakkuk 3:6. Isaiah 17:12. Proverbs 28:2.

#24 - ALWAYS LEARNING BUT NEVER KNOW TRUTH

Anti | DD | Earth | Gov | Israel | **Jesus** | Leader | Sky | **Society** | **Tech** | **Trib**

> But know this: that in the last days, grievous times will come. For men will be ... always learning and never able to come to the knowledge of the truth. (2 Timothy 3:1-2, 7)

Here, we're told that in the last days people will be always learning, but somehow never actually learn the truth. Jesus's parable of the sower illustrates this as well. He likened the seed that fell by the wayside and got eaten by birds to hearing the Word of God, not understanding it, and then Satan stealing what was sown.

During the tribulation period, the Bible tells us that none of the wicked will understand.

Fulfillment - Does it seem like the world is getting smarter or dumber? In 1950, only 50.1% of the world (over age 15) had attained some type of formal education. In 2020, it's up to 89.2%. During that time frame, the US population that's formally educated increased from 98.3% to 99.6%. Israel is currently at 99.1%.[8] That means nearly everyone in the US and Israel has had some formal education. What's more impressive is the college graduation rates. In 1960, only 7.7% of

Americans had a college degree. In 2022, it's up to 37.7%.[9]

Has all this education improved our lives? Despite this boom in education, in 2016 only 48% of the world's children could read with comprehension by the end of primary school.[10] Is there less poverty on the planet and in our countries? Yes and no. In 1990, 56.7% of the world lived on less than $3.65 a day ($1,332 annual). In 2022, only 22.7% did.[11] That's good improvement. Yet, in 1990, 88.8% of the world lived on less than $30 a day ($10,950 annual). In 2022, it's only marginally improved to 83.6%.

About 75% of the world population is over age 15.[12] That's around 6 billion people, of which 5.4 billion have achieved a formal education. Yet here we are with 6.8 billion total people on the planet still living in a state of poverty.[13]

What are we really learning? What are we doing with all this education? It certainly seems that people can spend a lifetime in school and learn very little.

Today Is Different - One thing that makes today different is that there are many people who now don't know basic truths, like the difference between a male and a female. Because our society can't determine gender anymore, now we can't seem to figure out what's fair regarding transgender athletes and which gender they should compete with. We might be the most advanced society that's ever lived. Yet, somehow, we're the stupidest.

Technology has certainly helped us achieve great things over the past century and even especially the last fifty years with the invention of the microprocessor. Consider the volume of information at our fingertips today. All we have to do is open an internet browser and we can learn how to do pretty much anything. But, with all this knowledge available to us, we're not really getting smarter, are we? We rely on it for all the answers. In a way, our tech has become our brain.

We certainly are a society that values education, but we're not learning things that matter, like God's Word, how to treat each other, or skills that will directly improve our lives and the lives of others on the planet.

<u>Additional Scriptures:</u> Daniel 12:10. Deuteronomy 28:20, 28. Hosea 4:1, 6. James 2:19. Mark 4:24-25. Matthew 13:1-23. Micah 7:4. Romans 1:21-22, 31; 3:11. Zephaniah 1:17.

#25 - FAKE BIBLES

Anti | DD | Earth | Gov | Israel | Jesus | Leader | Sky | **Society** | **Tech** | **Trib**

> I testify to everyone who hears the words of the prophecy of this book: if anyone adds to them, God will add to him the plagues which are written in this book. If anyone takes away from the words of the book of this prophecy, God will take away his part from the tree of life, and out of the holy city, which are written in this book. (Revelation 22:18-19)

This sign is a warning to not alter God's Word, the Bible. The penalty for doing so is quite high. The plagues refer to all the judgments of the tribulation period. The ultimate judgment is losing access to the Tree of Life, which is in heaven. As you can see, this is a very serious offense.

The apostle Paul told his disciple Timothy that all Scripture was given under inspiration of God. That's why God doesn't want us tampering with it. The Bible is one of the ways in which God reveals himself to us today. The book of Revelation in particular is the revealing of Jesus Christ. It's where we witness him in his glory.

The Bible isn't the product of mankind. It's literally God's Word to us. God created the entire universe. Don't you think he can make sure the Bible that we use today says exactly what he wants it to? Seems like a small detail in comparison to the entirety of creation, wouldn't you agree?

Fulfillment - According to Guinness World Records, the Bible is the best-selling book of all time. They estimate 5 billion have been sold.[14] Over 100 million are printed each year with the US accounting for a quarter of that volume.[15] With all those Bibles out in the world, you'd think people would be reading them. Nope. An American Bible Society study indicates 128 million Americans or 50% used the Bible at least a few times during the year back in 2021. This year, in 2024, it's down to only 99 million occasionally using it or 38%.[16] So, what's going on?

People no longer want to hear God's Word. We've talked about Christian deconstructionism in some of the other signs. It's obviously relevant to this one too because there's a growing portion of Christians who are starting to pick apart the Bible and say that some of it doesn't apply to us today. It's like they're taking words out of God's mouth.

Another example of this today is churches that refuse to teach particular doctrines in the Bible. Perhaps you attend a church that ignores the book of Revelation or the entire subject of Bible prophecy and you're reading this book to learn about it. Maybe you know of a church that doesn't mention sin or the crucifixion and instead only preaches feel good messages.

One of the pastors at my church recently spoke of his experience as a guest preacher at a Christian youth event out of state. He shared a message of sin and salvation with the youth and several of them came to Christ that day. However, the event leaders asked him to change his message for the next day and not mention anything about sin. Of course, he refused and ended up cutting the trip short. This just highlights a growing problem in our churches today. People don't want to hear all of God's Word.

Today Is Different - On top of that behavior, there are now new Bible translations being published that alter God's Word to make it better conform to society's worldview today. Several modern translations use gender neutral language throughout the Bible.[17] Some dilute the verses about homosexuality.[18] At least one has replaced all male pronouns for God with just "God" so that it appears gender neutral.[19]

Then we start getting into the fake Bibles as I call them. Those that portray God as a female or the Holy Spirit as a female.[20] There's a vegan Bible.[21] As you might imagine, it makes Jesus a vegan. The Chinese government has published its own version of the Bible for its nation.[22] In their version, the Ten Commandments are replaced with quotes from their nation's leader. And as you might expect, there are even LGBT Bibles in print today.[23] One such version replaces words like sin and hell and the Scriptures that pertain to homosexuality with text that's more palatable to their audience.

We also can't forget the Bibles that have been altered to align with a particular doctrine. The Catholics, Mormon's, Jehovah's Witnesses, and Christian Science all have their own version of the Bible for example. Judaism only uses part of the Bible because they don't even recognize the New Testament. If your church prohibits you from using one of the popular and widely read Bible translations today (NIV, KJV, ESV, NLT, CSB, NKJV), that's a big red flag.[24]

Technology is playing a huge role in this today. It's not all bad. It's never been easier to translate a book into another language. But it's also never been easier to publish junk. Especially now that Artificial Intelligence (AI) is being used to edit and create content.

Additional Scriptures: 2 Timothy 3:16-17. Ezekiel 7:26. Galatians 1:6-9. Proverbs 30:6.

#26 - REFUSAL TO BELIEVE

Anti | **DD** | Earth | Gov | Israel | **Jesus** | Leader | Sky | **Society** | Tech | **Trib**

> The Jews therefore came around him and said to him, "How long will you hold us in suspense? If you are the Christ, tell us plainly." Jesus answered them, "I told you, and you don't believe. The works that I do in my Father's name, these testify about me. But you don't believe, because you are not of my sheep, as I told you. ... I and the Father are one. ... If I don't do the works of my Father, don't believe me. But if I do them, though you don't believe me, believe the works, that you may know and believe that the Father is in me, and I in the Father." (John 10:24-26, 30, 37-38)

Jesus told us that he's the Christ, the Messiah, God in the flesh. His works proved it. I mean he resurrected Lazarus who'd been dead for days. And he resurrected himself and appeared to over 500 people afterward. He made it obvious, but people refused to believe.

When Satan tempted Jesus, he displayed the attitude of these people. He demanded Jesus prove himself by showing signs.

At the end of the tribulation period, those who continue to refuse to believe will be cast into the lake of fire and brimstone.

Fulfillment - From a 2015 study by Barna, they state that most Americans, 92%, believe that Jesus was a real person who actually lived. While only 56%, still a majority, believe Jesus is God.[25] Lifeway Research did a more recent study in 2021 that revealed the majority of Americans, 53%, now believe Jesus was a teacher, but not God. The shocking part is that 44% of evangelical Christians agreed.[26]

It's not just Jesus that people refuse to believe. Another way I see this being fulfilled today is with addiction denial. I know people, and I'm guessing you do too, that struggle with some sort of addiction. Alcohol, drugs, porn, etc. The problem I see in almost every one of them is that they refuse to believe they have an addiction. They're in a state of denial. It's obvious to their family and friends and often times their employer too. For the person with the addiction, it's not that they don't know they have a problem, it's that they don't want to admit it, confront it, and overcome it. Their denial is a defense mechanism.[27] They want to keep living the same way. That was the case with those who witnessed Jesus's miracles too.

Refusing to believe that Jesus is God enables a sinner to keep living a life of sin.

Today Is Different - This one even makes me shake my head in disbelief. I can't believe the volume of people today who refuse to believe even secular things that are crazy obvious. Consider those who believe the US economy is better today than it ever has been. They must not ever shop for groceries or put gasoline in their vehicle.

And even with all the evidence and testimony that's come out, four years after Covid there are still those who refuse to believe it was a bioweapon.

The best example today is those who think US President Biden is fit to run for US president in 2024 or even be president now for that matter when it's obvious he has a cognitive impairment. They've rejected reality and substituted their own.

Additional Scriptures: 1 Corinthians 15:1-8. 2 Corinthians 3:14-17; 4:3-4. 2 Kings 17:14. John 6:30-36; 8:43-47; 11:1-44; 12:37-40. Luke 16:19-31. Matthew 4:1-7; 13:13-15. Numbers 14:11. Psalm 78:19-22, 32. Revelation 21:8.

#27 - SCOFFERS

Anti | DD | Earth | Gov | Israel | Jesus | Leader | Sky | **Society** | Tech | **Trib**

> Knowing this first: that scoffers will come in the last days, walking according to their own lusts, and saying, "Where is the promise of His coming?" (2 Peter 3:3-4 NKJV)

Here, we see that scoffers are a sign of the last days. In particular, it's people who scoff at Jesus's coming. So, the rapture or second coming. *Scoff* means to deride, mock, or express contempt. Peter goes on to tell us they also deny God created the earth, that the flood happened, and that Jesus is coming to judge the earth.

The Bible has many examples of this. God's prophets, and even Jesus, were derided when they pronounced God's judgment and predicted events the people didn't like. In the book of Jude, we learn that people scoff at things they don't understand, like the supernatural.

The tribulation period will come against people settled in complacency who say the Lord won't do good or evil. People who don't think God is going to intervene in our affairs.

Fulfillment - Flat-earthers. Have you read about this group of people or perhaps even had a conversation with one? So, I met a flat-earther at a Christian writing conference several years ago. I sat down at a table with some others and asked what they'd been talking about. One says the other is trying to convince him that the earth is flat. How I wish someone had snapped a picture of my face at that moment. I was a physics major in college for two years before switching to economics. So, you can imagine my shock that someone could reject all the evidence we have that the earth is spherical. I felt like I'd time warped to the middle ages.

I didn't get into a scientific debate about it. I just mentioned that the Bible even reveals that it's a sphere. It's in Psalm 103:12. It says God has removed our sins from us as far as the east is from the west. If the earth were flat like a cookie and had an edge, the difference between east and west would be measurable. However, on a spherical earth, you can travel east forever and never start walking west or encounter west. The two are infinitely apart. That's how God treats our sin when we've put our faith in Jesus.

This is a growing community of scoffers, and it's not limited to the US. It's worldwide and also includes support groups in Israel.[28] The mainstream media and scientific journals are even starting to report about them.[29] In addition to believing the earth is flat, some also believe gravity is an illusion, the moon landing was fake, and the stars are just projections on a dome. They're denying biblical truths about God's creation.

If you read *The Prophecy Watcher* magazine regularly, then you also know that Mondo Gonzales has written a series of articles to biblically counter their beliefs. It's also a reason why they started their Psalm 19 project and use telescopes to watch and report on astronomical events.[30] In Mondo's articles, he's discussed that the flat-earth community he engages with are reluctant to even use a telescope to view things in the heavens themselves. It seems they don't want to be proven wrong. So, they scoff at even considering the evidence their own eyes can provide.

Today Is Different - Have you encountered a scoffer before? Perhaps an unbelieving friend that you invited to church or tried to have a biblical conversation with. And I can imagine how the conversation went if you mentioned the rapture. If they completely rejected the notion, I understand why.

A 2022 Pew Research study indicates that a majority of Americans, 58%, don't believe that we're living in the end times. Not even a majority of Christians believe that we are. Only 47% think so. Even less Americans, 55%, believe that Jesus is going to come back. And what I'm still trying to wrap my mind around is that only 75% of Christians think Jesus is returning. The rest must not have read the Bible.

The data just gets worse. Only 14% of Christians in America believe that Jesus will return in their lifetime.[31] Really?! I truly hope you're not in that camp anymore and that it's just as obvious to you as it is to me that Jesus is about to burst onto the scene again.

Today, it's not just Christians who scoff at Jesus returning. A 2023 survey revealed that almost half, 45%, of Jewish Israelis don't believe the Messiah is coming. Joel C. Rosenberg notes that the more religious an Israeli Jew, the more likely they are to believe the Messiah will come one day. The more secular they are, the more likely it is that they've given up on the entire concept of Messiah.[32] Remember that even religious Jews don't believe Jesus was the Messiah. As we discussed in Sign #7 - Apostasy, the majority of Israelis today are atheists.

Additional Scriptures: 2 Chronicles 36:16. Amos 6:3. Ezekiel 12:22-28. Isaiah 22:12-14. Jeremiah 12:4. Jude 1:8-10. Psalm 103:12. Zephaniah 1:12.

#28 - NEITHER HOT NOR COLD

Anti | DD | Earth | Gov | Israel | **Jesus** | Leader | Sky | **Society** | **Tech** | **Trib**

> "To the angel of the assembly in Laodicea write: ... 'I know your works, that you are neither cold nor hot. I wish you were cold or hot. So, because you are lukewarm, and neither hot nor cold, I will vomit you out of my mouth.' " (Revelation 3:14-16)

Jesus is the one speaking above. The sin of the church in Laodicea was that they were "neither hot nor cold." They were called lukewarm because they were neutral and indifferent. The letters to the churches in the book of Revelation can be applied to churches, people, and even ages of time. The last letter is to Laodicea and represents our age of time.

In the Old Testament, were told that one of Sodom's sins was their abundance of idleness and lack of caring for the needy. They had plenty of time to help, but they just couldn't be bothered to do so.

We learned in the prior sign that the tribulation period will come against people settled in complacency.

Fulfillment - Have you noticed that most people today don't have a desire to be great or to do hard things? It seems like most people are content with just showing up to work, preferably at home, and doing the bare minimum to not get fired. Do your friends or family talk to you about their career aspirations?

When I was working in the corporate world, most managers didn't want to deal with an employee who wasn't performing. They just passed them along to another manager to deal with. It's hard to have a conversation with someone about poor work performance, so they just opted not to.

Consider customer service. I used to get annoyed when front-line workers, like cashiers or waitresses, lacked good customer service skills and were rude. Today, I'm honestly just happy they showed up for work and are willing to take my order. What's happened to society?

I know several teenagers of driving age, and most of them could care less if they learn to drive. What's up with that? When I was a teenager, driving equaled freedom. This is apparently a nationwide problem. In the 80's, nearly half of 16-year-olds in the US were driving. That was down to 25% in 2020.[33] I'm going to guess they have no desire to drive to a part-time job after school or over the summer, or to drive somewhere to hang out with their friends.

We don't even keep score in a lot of kids' sports anymore. Is it because we don't want to deal with the kids and parents who haven't learned how to lose and maintain sportsmanlike conduct? So, we gave in and quit caring who won or lost? What's the incentive for a kid to work hard and strive to become a better player?

Have you looked around your neighborhood lately? Do your neighbors maintain their house, pull the weeds, clean up the dog poo, or pick up trash that blows into the yard? I live in a normal neighborhood in a nice part of town. Most of my neighbors could care less what their yards look like. If not for the Home Owners Association, I'm sure there would be broken down cars parked in people's yards.

It certainly seems like most people are neither hot nor cold.

Today Is Different - I read an article on the news recently that said the US House Oversight subcommittee on National Security, the Border, and Foreign Affairs held a hearing on UFOs because people are calling for more transparency. It was revealed that the US government is in possession of nonhuman biological matter that was recovered from a crash site. This didn't really even make the news cycle! It seems as though nobody even cares about aliens anymore.[34]

Technology is definitely an enabler of our indifference today. It's made us lazy in many ways. Do you have to physically get up to turn the lights on? I have a feeling many of you just tell your Alexa device to do it.

By far the biggest contributor to why today is different is streaming and binging. Do you remember when we had to drive to Blockbuster, walk around the store looking at movies, and hope they still had a copy of the one we wanted to watch. Now, we can stream any movie we want with ease. We can even binge watch an entire TV series over the weekend. Kids don't have to leave the house to hang out with friends anymore, they just chat with them online while playing video games.

Today, are we really any different than Sodom, who had an abundance of idleness and didn't care about the things they should have?

Additional Scriptures: Amos 6:1-6. Ezekiel 16:49-50. Jeremiah 8:7. Judges 2:10. Zephaniah 1:12.

#29 - DESPISING GOD'S WORD

Anti | DD | Earth | Gov | Israel | Jesus | Leader | Sky | **Society** | Tech | **Trib**

> They mocked the messengers of God, despised his words, and scoffed at his prophets, until the LORD's wrath arose against his people, until there was no remedy. (2 Chronicles 36:16)

They "despised his words" until there was no remedy. The people hated God's words and God's Law so much that they reached the point of no return. Consider that Jesus, the actual Word of God, was despised so much that he was crucified.

During the tribulation period, the Antichrist will despise the words of the two witness God sends to preach in Jerusalem so much that he'll kill them, and the world will rejoice that he did.

Fulfillment - Did you know that practicing Christianity is illegal in many countries today? That means the Bible, God's Word, is also illegal and banned in those same countries. Here's where it's illegal or under extreme suppression: Afghanistan, North Korea, Somalia, Libya, Yemen, Eritrea, Nigeria, Pakistan, Iran, India, and Saudi Arabia.[35] Together, these countries account for 26% of the world's population.[36]

That's not counting the countries were persecution is very high, like China and Indonesia. Including them puts us at 48% of the world's population living in a place where the government and the majority of the people despise God's Word.[37] Including the entire list of countries where Christian persecution is very high would put us well over a majority of the world's population. How much do you think it takes to trigger God's wrath and reach the point of no return?

Today Is Different - There are a few things happening in this space that stand out today. One is conversion therapy bans. There are many states in the US today that ban conversion therapy on minors.[38] They've made it illegal to counsel a young person about their sexual orientation or changing their gender. So, no one can tell them that God is perfect, doesn't mess up, and didn't create them as the wrong gender. It's really Satan attempting to destroy their life.

It's essentially banned sharing biblical content that speaks the truth into this, like Genesis 2 and Romans 1. They know that God's Word has the power to break down strongholds. That's why they don't want us sharing it. The therapists are under threat of losing their licenses if they're caught doing this type of counseling. It's also shrinking the number of counselors that are willing to work with minors.[39]

The next thing is bans that are starting to happen against public prayer. People despise God's Word so much that they don't want us to even talk to God. The Supreme Court in the US recently ruled on such a case. A high school football coach was fired for praying on the field after a game with some of the players. The court ruled the coach's conduct was protected by the First Amendment.[40]

But consider Israel. To maintain the "status quo" on the Temple Mount, non-Muslims can visit the area, but not pray. They've equated prayer to sovereignty over the location. I find that interesting, don't you?[41] With arrests for public prayer outside abortion clinics starting to happen in other countries, I expect we'll see more activity in this sign.[42]

The last event I want to call out that makes today different is the pro-Palestinian protests that are happening on college campuses in the US. The anti-Semitism has sparked some much-needed outrage in the US congress. However, the Anti-Semitism Awareness Act that the US House recently passed is actually damaging to our ability to share God's Word.

The bill would force universities to restrict anti-Semitic statements or risk having federal funding withheld. But the bill uses the International Holocaust Remembrance Alliance's definition for anti-Semitism, which says it's anti-Semitic to state that Jews killed Jesus. You can see where this is going. It could easily be used to silence speaking about Jesus or the entire New Testament for that matter because that could be offensive to a Jew. We'll have to see if this one passes the US Senate.[43]

Additional Scriptures: 2 Timothy 3:1, 8. Amos 2:4. Ezekiel 20:13, 16, 24. Isaiah 5:24; 30:12; 53:3. Jeremiah 36:1-25. John 1:1-15. Psalm 107:11. Revelation 11:1-10.

#30 - ATHEISM

Anti | DD | Earth | Gov | Israel | Jesus | Leader | Sky | **Society** | **Tech** | Trib

> For the wrath of God is revealed from heaven against all ungodliness and unrighteousness of men who suppress the truth in unrighteousness, because that which is known of God is revealed in them, for God revealed it to them. For the invisible things of him since the creation of the world are clearly seen, being perceived through the things that are made, even his everlasting power and divinity, that they may be without excuse. Because knowing God, they didn't glorify him as God, and didn't give thanks, but became vain in their reasoning, and their senseless heart was darkened. (Romans 1:18-21)

This Scripture reveals another behavior that triggers the wrath of God. It's atheism, not believing there's any deity. We learn that no one has an excuse for not knowing that God exists because he's made it obvious. See Sign #118 - God's Presence Is Obvious for more on that. In fact, it says God has revealed it in them. God's written his existence in our hearts.

Fulfillment - In prior signs, like Sign #7 - Apostasy, we talked about the rise in the number of Americans who aren't affiliated with any religion. In 1948, they only accounted for 2% of Americans, and in 2023, it's up to 22%.[44] And in Israel, we learned that 65% of Israelis today identify as atheists.[45]

In reports of survey data, this group is often referred to as unaffiliated or nones. They include atheists, agnostics, and people who answer "nothing in particular" when asked about their religion. According to a 2023 Pew Research study, 17% of the unaffiliated Americans identify as atheists.[46]

When looking at the world, nearly 16% of the planet or 1.2 billion people are unaffiliated.[47]

Today Is Different - In that same 2023 study, Pew Research revealed something really interesting that sets today apart. 79% of the atheists think science does more good than harm in society. Only 40% of religiously affiliated Americans believe that. And 78% of atheists believe science can explain everything. As you might imagine, the percentage is much lower for the religiously affiliated. It's only 16%.[48] Atheists have put their faith in human knowledge, science, and technology.

Scientific and technological advancements have certainly made it harder for people to realize their need for God and salvation. Science can explain so many complicated things today. Just do an internet search on any of the miracles in the Bible, and you'll get a bunch of results and even some TV shows that try to explain what happened with science. I just did it for "what caused the Red Sea to part," and I get scientific explanations from *The Washington Post*, ABC News, *Smithsonian Magazine*, *The Jerusalem Post*, and *National Geographic*.

Technology advancements have even reached the point where people are trusting that it'll enable them to live forever. Atheists don't need God because they have the god of science and tech. In fact, futurist Ray Kurzweil thinks humans will achieve immortality by 2030! He says this will be made possible with nanobots, microscopic robots that'll repair our bodies at the cellular level.[49]

Additional Scriptures: 1 Corinthians 1:21-22. 2 Corinthians 3:14; 4:3-4. Colossians 2:8. Ephesians 2:11-12; 4:17-18. Jeremiah 9:3. Psalm 14:1-3. Romans 2:12-16.

#31 - HOPELESSNESS

Anti | DD | Earth | Gov | Israel | Jesus | Leader | Sky | **Society** | **Tech** | **Trib**

> For the LORD of Armies, the God of Israel says: "Behold, I will cause to cease out of this place, before your eyes and in your days, the voice of mirth and the voice of gladness, the voice of the bridegroom and the voice of the bride." (Jeremiah 16:9)

We're told that God will remove the "voice of gladness." This happened when Israel was taken into captivity by the Babylonians. It's going to happen again during the tribulation period. The prophet Amos describes that period of time as dark and hopeless. In fact, there's a duration of time during the tribulation period in which people will want to die but will be unable to.

Fulfillment - One way to gauge the feeling of hopelessness in the world is to look at the suicide rate over time. On a hopeful note, the worldwide suicide rate has actually decreased during the last twenty years. Down from 14.1 in 2000 to 8.9 in 2019. It's decreased slightly in Israel too, from 6.5 to 5.1.[50] I've read the rate has actually continued to decrease in Israel even after the Hamas attack in October 2023.

It's quite the opposite for the US. Our suicide rate has risen from 10 in 2000 to 14.3 in 2019.[51] In the US, the rate is now at its highest point since 1941, during World War II.[52] It's one of the top three causes of death in the US for people in age groups between 10 and 34. In 2021, there were almost twice as many suicides in America than homicides.[53]

Another indicator of hopelessness is the use of antidepressants. The US CDC reports that between the years 2015 and 2018, 13.8% of American adults had used an antidepressant medication in the past month. That's up from 10.6% of adults in 2010.[54] The American Academy of Pediatrics just published a study in February 2024 on antidepressant use among US individuals between 12 and 25 years old. Between the years 2016 and 2022, the monthly dispensing rate increased 66.3% for this young population.[55]

This shouldn't come as a surprise when we're constantly flooded with bad news in the media and each political party feeling like they're losing the battle for civilization and life as we know it. These things can weigh heavily on a person. It also doesn't help that the media and many leaders today pretend that all is well even in the midst of the bad news

Chapter 6 - A Foolish Heart

onslaught. So, then we start feeling like we're crazy or that the news media and leaders are incompetent. In either scenario, we can start to feel like the situation is hopeless.

Technology certainly has a part to play in this too. Consider how easy it is to search for whatever symptom you're having and then read a whole slew of articles indicating you could have any number of horrible diseases. It's also mentally unhealthy that we as a society compare ourselves with celebrities, social media influencers, and our friends and family online. It can be quite overwhelming and lead to negative views about oneself.

Today Is Different - I think the most telling example of the hopelessness epidemic in society is that assisted suicide and euthanasia are being legalized in an increasing number of countries throughout the world. Active euthanasia is not legal in any state in the US or in Israel. However, passive euthanasia (refusing treatment or life support) is legal in the US. Physician assisted suicide is legal in 10 states and D.C.[56] It first became legal in the US in 1994, in Oregon.

Both euthanasia and self-administered medication-assisted suicide have been legal in Switzerland since the 1980s and in the Netherlands, Belgium, and Luxembourg since the 2000s. It's also been legal in Columbia and Canada since 2015. Within this decade, Spain, Austria, New Zealand, and several Australian states have made it legal.[57]

According to a survey published in April 2024, a majority of Americans, 53%, believe doctor-assisted suicide is morally acceptable. That figure hasn't changed much since 2001 when it was 49%.[58]

Additional Scriptures: Amos 5:18-20. Deuteronomy 28: 29-34, 65-67. Revelation 9:6; 18:22-23.

#32 - RAPTURE 911

Anti | DD | Earth | Gov | Israel | **Jesus** | Leader | Sky | **Society** | **Tech** | Trib

> "But take heed to yourselves, lest your hearts be weighed down with carousing, drunkenness, and cares of this life, and that Day come on you unexpectedly. For it will come as a snare on all those who dwell on the face of the whole earth. Watch therefore, and pray always that you may be counted worthy to escape all these things that will come to pass, and to stand before the Son of Man." (Luke 21:34-36 NKJV)

> "But no one knows of that day and hour, not even the angels of heaven,

but my Father only. As the days of Noah were, so will the coming of the Son of Man be. For as in those days which were before the flood they were eating and drinking, marrying and giving in marriage, until the day that Noah entered into the ship, and they didn't know until the flood came and took them all away, so will the coming of the Son of Man be." (Matthew 24:36-39)

Jesus is the one speaking in the verses above. These are taken from the Olivet Discourse where Jesus told us what to watch for regarding his coming. In both, he's speaking about his coming in the rapture. See how he tells us to watch that we "may be counted worthy to escape all these things" and that "no one knows of that day and hour." Being worthy to escape is ensuring you've placed your faith in Jesus before the rapture happens.

We're going to look at the rapture in detail in Sign #150 - The Rapture. In Chapter 20, you'll learn that the date of the second coming can indeed be calculated because it occurs seven years after the Antichrist confirms a peace treaty with Israel during the tribulation period.

What I want to call attention to in these verses is that Jesus indicates the rapture is going to come on the world "unexpectedly" and "as a snare." It's because like in Noah's day, the people "didn't know until the flood came." The planet will be oblivious to the nearness of the rapture until it happens.

During Jesus's first coming, he rebuked the people for not knowing the time of their visitation. They should have known Jesus was coming and they didn't.

I titled this sign *Rapture 911*, after my book by the same title, because this is the sign of the rapture emergency.

Fulfillment - We have a rapture emergency because this world-changing event is on the horizon and people today aren't prepared for it. People are not looking to Jesus to save the US, or the planet for that matter, from everything that ails it. Most people aren't expecting Jesus to make himself known and directly intervene in our daily lives by making a bunch of us disappear. No, people are looking to political leaders, billionaires, industry leaders, and now even AI to solve the world's problems.

Recall from Sign #27 - Scoffers that we discussed that only 14% of Christians in America believe that Jesus will return in their lifetime.[59] And, a 2023 survey revealed that almost half, 45%, of Jewish Israelis don't believe the Messiah is coming.[60] Even Christians today aren't expecting Jesus to return and it's ridiculously obvious that he's going to.

So, did you know that rapture anxiety is a thing? I didn't until I started doing some research for this book about the reasons why people were deconstructing from Christianity. What do you know, there are articles about it on mainstream media, *CNN* and *The Washington Post*.[61] I learned that one of the popular deconstructionists on TikTok, April Ajoy, posts about her rapture anxiety. She has 356,000 followers and 26.8 million likes![62] There are people walking away from the church, Christianity, and Jesus because they disagree with and have anxiety about the rapture doctrine.

This one makes my heart sink because it has such an easy remedy. If you put your faith in Jesus, you'll be included in the rapture. Go read Chapter 19 if you aren't sure that you'll be raptured if it happened today.

If you share the gospel with those you care about, you'll know you did your part. Hopefully they'll believe and won't be left behind. Ultimately, we have to realize that none of us can save anyone no matter how much we care about them. That's Jesus's job. And he loves that person more than you do. If you get a book like *Rapture 911* and have it displayed in your house, then someone you care about might find it after the rapture and learn how to be saved.

But even with all the warnings that preachers and authors like me have been giving about the nearness of Jesus's return, most people just don't want to hear it or believe it. They're going to get caught in the snare that Jesus spoke about.

Today Is Different - One reason today is different is because people are so much more distracted now than in the years before. No one is truly paying attention to the biblical signs of Jesus's return. People are too preoccupied with their phones, streaming the latest TV series, playing video games, and viewing posts on social media. I see people who are doing all those things even while sitting through a church service. We've become a culture of busy multitaskers. Because of this, it's hard to even have a serious conversation with anyone today. People just want to talk about the superficial.

Journalists at *The Daily Star* asked Google's AI, Bard, who would save humanity if it was on the verge of extinction. What do you think it said? "If humanity was going to be saved from extinction in the next 20 years, I would pick Elon Musk as the person most likely to do it. Musk is a visionary entrepreneur who has a track record of success in developing new technologies and businesses."[63] Even a computer program thinks a tech billionaire can save humanity! It named three reasons why: space exploration, renewable energy, and AI. Those are things that certainly set today apart from all years prior.

Today, society has the same opinion as Bard and has placed their hope of salvation in the product of their own hands.

<u>Additional Scriptures:</u> 1 Thessalonians 5:1-3. 2 Peter 3:10. Hebrews 9:27-28. Jeremiah 8:7. Mark 13:32-37. Matthew 24:42-51; 25:1-13. Luke 12:56; 13:22-27; 19:41-44.

#33 - POLAR OPPOSITE - A WISE HEART

Anti | DD | Earth | **<u>Gov</u>** | **<u>Israel</u>** | Jesus | **<u>Leader</u>** | Sky | **<u>Society</u>** | **<u>Tech</u>** | Trib

> For the earth will be filled with the knowledge of the LORD's glory, as the waters cover the sea. (Habakkuk 2:14)

Throughout this chapter we've looked at signs related to a foolish heart. This sign is what I call a polar opposite. It's meant to illustrate how far away we currently are from the life we believers are going to live during Jesus's reign on earth in the millennial kingdom. Recall from Sign #6 - The Point Of No Return, that God only lets evil progress so far before he intervenes.

In the Scripture above, we learn that during the millennial kingdom everyone on the planet will know the Lord. When reading the additional Scriptures below, we find out that people will go to Jerusalem and Jesus will teach everyone his ways.

Everyone will have a wise heart, one that knows God and his Law.

> The **heart of the wise** instructs his mouth, and adds learning to his lips. (Proverbs 16:23)

Fulfillment - So, how far away are we? Well, the earth certainly isn't filled with the knowledge of Jesus, is it? Reading through the signs in this chapter, we discovered that most Christians don't even know or believe the Bible well enough to have a biblical worldview today.

A fun way to consider just how opposite we are is to contemplate what the worst-case scenarios might look like and see just how close we are to those.

Worst case, the world is entirely atheist. No one believes in any deity. Everyone has put their faith in science and technology. So, the world isn't close to being atheist. Some countries for sure are, including Israel. The world mostly worships another god or an idol, like technology. So, we're not close to the worst case on this one.

Worst case, history is no longer studied, only repeated (which no one realizes). Sometimes it seems like people aren't studying history these days. Even when they are, they choose not to believe it. We still have holocaust deniers today. And now we've got flat-earthers. With our extremely short news cycle and the sheer volume of news, people forget about a news headline in a matter of days. It's easy to forget about history today. I think we're close to this worst case.

Worst case, everyone on the planet has a college degree but the employment rates and global economies are the worst they've ever been. We discussed some of this dichotomy in signs throughout this chapter. Today, you can spend a lifetime in school and learn very little that's actually useful in terms of earning a living or improving society. We're close to this worst case too.

Worst case, Bibles are illegal across the globe. While a majority of the planet lives in a country that's hostile to God's Word, thankfully it's still accessible even in those countries because of daring missionaries and the ability to read the Bible online and through apps. We're certainly close to this worst case though, but it's hard for us in America to see that.

Worst case, suicide pills are available over the counter. You know this is a tough one. While we're not even close to this worst case as I presented it, I want you to consider the drug epidemic that's plaguing the globe. It's certainly easy to overdose on a readily available drug if someone wanted to. We're going to talk about that in Sign #75 - Drugs And Alcohol.

Today Is Different - So, what do you think? Is today different? Do we as a society have a foolish heart that doesn't know anything about God and his ways? Do you think we've reached the point of no return? How many people really have a heart that's wise toward God?

Additional Scriptures: Isaiah 2:3; 11:6-9. Jeremiah 31:33-34. Micah 4:2.

CHAPTER 7 – A HARDENED HEART

And Pharaoh's **heart grew hard**, and he did not heed them, as the LORD had said. (Exodus 7:13 NKJV)

#34 – GOD'S WARNINGS AREN'T HEEDED

Anti | **DD** | Earth | Gov | Israel | **Jesus** | **Leader** | Sky | **Society** | **Tech** | **Trib**

> Yet the LORD testified to Israel and to Judah, by every prophet and every seer, saying, "Turn from your evil ways, and keep my commandments and my statutes, according to all the law which I commanded your fathers, and which I sent to you by my servants the prophets." Notwithstanding, they would not listen, but hardened their neck like the neck of their fathers who didn't believe in the LORD their God. (2 Kings 17:13-14)

Many of the Old Testament prophets warned their people about the coming judgment because of their grievous sins against God. Here, we're told that they just flat out refused to listen. Noah preached and warned of the coming flood for 120 years, yet only he and his family were saved. Jesus preached a message of repentance during his first coming and warned that the kingdom of heaven was near. Instead of listening to him, they crucified him.

Jesus also warned in the Olivet Discourse to be watching for his next coming, the rapture. But we know that most people are going to be left behind. Most of the letters that Jesus dictated to the churches in the book of Revelation have a warning of repentance too. The two witnesses who show up during the tribulation period are going to be warning the world and sharing the gospel. During that time, an angel is even sent to fly around the world telling people not to get the mark of the Beast. Yet, we're told that most people get the mark and will not repent.

Fulfillment - The most important warning from God is our need to repent and be saved by putting our faith in Jesus. It's so we can live for eternity with God instead of in hell with all the fallen angels. Prominent and popular pastors today are frequently on social media warning both people and leaders about the behavior they see and the need for us to repent and turn to God in prayer. Messages from the likes of Jonathan Cahn, Franklin Graham, Jack Hibbs, and Greg

Laurie. They're also warning about how near they believe the events of the tribulation period are. It certainly seems like they are mocked more than heeded.

We're also ignoring God's warnings regarding how to live our lives so that we'll be blessed, fulfilled, and happy. Consider that the Bible teaches a marital relationship between a man and a woman. That means no premarital sex or, in biblical speak, no fornicating. Yet, a recent study of Americans revealed that by age 44, 95% of Americans have had premarital sex.[1] Okay, that's pretty much everyone in American ignoring God's warning on this. Is it any wonder we now see the results of this one particular sin: abortion, divorce, sexually transmitted disease, and single moms. We'll discuss trends like this more in Sign #79 - Sexual Perversion and Sign #80 - Attack On Marriage.

We've also decided not to heed God's warnings regarding mixing species. We're going to discuss this in detail in Sign #82 - Genetic Engineering. For now, just consider how we're playing God in this space. The scientific advancement CRISPR is used today to modify DNA. It's also being used to create chimeras, like the monkey we learned about in Fall 2023 that was born with glowing green eyes and fingers and was created from multiple embryos.[2]

Today Is Different - The most prominent pastor of our day and age was Billy Graham. Did you know that when the Korean War broke out in 1952, he suggested at a revival he was conducting in D.C. that the nation's leaders kneel down before God in prayer. A congressional representative introduced the bill for the National Day of Prayer in the US the very next day.[3]

His lifetime audience likely surpassed billions of people. It's estimated 3.2 million people responded to the invitations he gave at worldwide crusades for people to put their faith in Jesus.[4] It's likely many more millions responded by seeing him on TV or reading one of his books. I know that's how my own pastor came to faith in Jesus. Billy Graham even had an audience with twelve consecutive US presidents. He was so influential that US Congress just unveiled a statue of him in May 2024 that will be on permanent display at the US Capital.[5]

So, do you think we're better off spiritually today as a nation and as a world because of Billy Graham's warnings? Recall from Sign #7 - Apostasy, that back in 1956 the number of Americans identifying as

Christian was at its peak of 96%. That's back when Billy Graham was doing crusades. In 2023, now only 68% of Americans say they're Christian.

All our nation, and the world for that matter, has done is move farther and farther away from God. A lot of people got saved during the Christian revivals of the past decades, but it didn't have a lasting impact. It certainly doesn't seem like people really heeded Billy Graham's warnings all those years, does it?

Additional Scriptures: 2 Chronicles 36:15-16. Deuteronomy 28:15-68. Exodus 9:12. Genesis 6:3, 7:13. Jeremiah 6:17; 36:1-25; 44:4-5, 15-17. Matthew 4:17; 24:37-39, 42-44. Proverbs 1:30. Revelation 2-3; 9:20-21; 11:1-10; 14:9. Zechariah 7:11-12.

#35 – DON'T ENDURE SOUND DOCTRINE

Anti | DD | Earth | Gov | Israel | **Jesus** | **Leader** | Sky | **Society** | **Tech** | **Trib**

> Preach the word; be urgent in season and out of season; reprove, rebuke, and exhort with all patience and teaching. For the time will come when they will not listen to the sound doctrine, but having itching ears, will heap up for themselves teachers after their own lusts, and will turn away their ears from the truth, and turn away to fables. (2 Timothy 4:2-4)

The apostle Paul wrote this to his disciple Timothy. We're told that as time progresses that people will not "listen to the sound doctrine." A few verses prior to this instruction to Timothy, Paul says that in the last days people will resist the truth. Jesus also spoke about this during his first coming. He said people ignore God's Law so that they can substitute their own tradition.

During the tribulation period, the Antichrist will be so against sound doctrine that he's going to murder God's two witnesses and wage a war against believers. We're going to look at that in detail in Sign #115 - War Against God's People.

So, what's the sound doctrine? It's the gospel that Jesus and the disciples taught. The apostle Paul is also included in that bunch because after the resurrection, Jesus appeared to Paul and commissioned him to preach the gospel to the gentiles. We also know that the signs of an apostle, like miracles, accompanied Paul. He even raised someone from the dead.

Fulfillment - Would you like to guess how many Christian denominations are on the planet? Midway through 2024 it's estimated to be 47,100.[6] Wow! That's a lot of different theologies and traditions. In 1900, there were only 2,000. Today, we read about splits in denominations happening over doctrinal disagreements about same sex marriage, LGBT pastors, female pastors, what constitutes a sin, and how to be saved. Today, if someone doesn't like or gets offended by what was preached in their church, they can easily find another church that'll be more agreeable to them.

With the decline in Christianity and church attendance, more and more churches are trying to reach new members by blending in with the world instead of standing apart from it. These seeker sensitive type churches don't preach about sin or share the gospel. They want to cater to someone who isn't saved. So, they preach on self-improvement, offer political commentary, and deliver a feel-good message each week. The worship songs are watered down. Many have really short sermons and services as well.

Here's a quote from the web page of one of the largest of these churches in America: "Each service is 90 minutes long and is packed with uplifting music, powerful worship and an inspiring message."[7] Did you notice that music is listed first and twice! Nothing about God, the gospel, or learning the Bible. With only inspiring messages, no one is going to leave feeling convicted by the Holy Spirit.

Another thing that's concerning is that The Center for the Study of Global Christianity estimates there are about 5 million pastors or priests in all Christian tradition across the world, of which only 5% likely have formal theological training.[8] With a sad statistic like that, is it any wonder that people are biblically illiterate today and unable to endure sound doctrine?

Today Is Different - Progressive Christianity is invading our churches today. These churches don't believe the entire Bible is literally the actual Word of God. They think some of it is inspired in the same way anything a Christian might produce today is. Once you go down the path of man wrote it, then you can pick it apart, disagree with it, and choose to say some of it doesn't apply to our modern day. Personal feelings also trump biblical teaching in these churches. They can't believe God would send people to hell. They don't think there's anything wrong with loving whoever you want regardless of their gender. They believe our only job is to show God's love to people, not tell them about sin and how to be saved.[9]

You might recall that Bishop Joseph Strickland of Texas was removed from his position in November 2023 because he spoke out against the pope's progressive efforts within the Catholic Church. Namely women in governance and LGBT Catholics and clergy.[10]

Back in 2015, Pew Research Center reported the following churches sanctioned same-sex marriage: Episcopal Church, Evangelical Lutheran Church in America, Presbyterian Church (USA), Reform Jewish Movement, Conservative Jewish Movement, Society of Friends, Unitarian Universalist Association of Churches, and the United Church of Christ.[11] Well, since then, there's been quite the activity in this sign. Just recently, April 2024, the United Methodist Church removed prohibitions against LGBT clergy and same-sex marriages.[12] It resulted in yet another denomination as some congregations chose to disaffiliate.

America's largest protestant denominations have all become progressive. In addition to this, Pope Francis formally approved the blessing of same-sex couples by Catholic priests, announced by the Vatican in December 2023.[13] So, now we're seeing fulfillment of this even in the Catholic denomination, which accounts for 50% of the global Christian population.[14]

So, I went to progressivechristianity.org and watched a couple video resources they have in a series titled *Ask a Progressive Christian*. One posted in March 2024 was titled, "Did the resurrection really happen?" The pastor's answer includes: "I don't know." and "I don't need the resurrection to be literal."[15] Here's another one. Also posted in March 2024, it's titled, "Did Jesus die for our sins?" You are not going to like the pastor's answer, which includes: "No, that's bad theology." and "Jesus did not die for human sin. Jesus died because of human sin."[16] Yikes!

Progressive Christianity deconstructs Christianity. I've mentioned deconstructionism in prior signs. I see this as the main reason why people are leaving Christianity and not enduring sound doctrine today. They're listening to these people who aren't speaking biblical truth. Technology is a huge boost to this movement with social media, podcasts, YouTube, and blogs. Deconstructionism begins with the premise that there is no fundamental objective truth. It's about personal feelings and living your truth. It's about tearing down doctrine they believe is morally wrong. Each person becomes their own authority on truth. You can't even call this Christianity. It's honestly more reminiscent of new age teachings.

If you'd like to learn more about this and understand what to say to someone going through this, I recommend Alisa Childers' website and YouTube channel.[17]

https://alisachilders.com/

https://www.youtube.com/user/alisachilders

<u>Additional Scriptures:</u> 1 Corinthians 3:1-3; 15:1-11. 2 Corinthians 12:11-12. 2 Timothy 3:1, 8. Acts 2:42; 9, 15:7, 20:9-12; 22:1. Hebrews 5:12-14. Isaiah 30:8-10. Jeremiah 5:30-31. Mark 7:8-9. Revelation 6:9; 11:1-10.

#36 - CHILDREN OF DISOBEDIENCE

Anti | DD | Earth | Gov | Israel | Jesus | Leader | Sky | **<u>Society</u>** | Tech | Trib

> But sexual immorality, and all uncleanness or covetousness, let it not even be mentioned among you, as becomes saints; nor filthiness, nor foolish talking, nor jesting, which are not appropriate, but rather giving of thanks. Know this for sure, that no sexually immoral person, nor unclean person, nor covetous man (who is an idolater), has any inheritance in the Kingdom of Christ and God. Let no one deceive you with empty words, for because of these things the wrath of God comes on the children of disobedience. (Ephesians 5:3-6)

For this sign, the apostle Paul tells us that God's wrath will come upon "children of disobedience." So, what does it mean to obey God? Well, the prophet Micah tells us that God requires us to do justly, love mercy, and walk humbly with God. Jesus boiled the Law down to two principles, the greatest commandment. Love God with all your heart, soul, and mind; and love your neighbor as yourself.

In Luke's account, a man wanting clarification asks Jesus who his neighbor is. Jesus then gives the parable of the good Samaritan. We learn that our neighbor is anyone we encounter who is in need. It's not simply those we live next door to.

Fulfillment - This one should become obvious once you read all the signs in this book, in particular the ones I've categorized as Society. Refer to Appendix A for a list of those. To sum it up, as a society we don't love God, and we could care less about each other.

I'd like you to contemplate something in your own life for this one. In Jesus's parable, a priest and a temple assistant both walked by a Jewish man who had been attacked and left for dead. They looked at him, but that was it. Neither chose to help him. Do you notice the needs of people around you? And if you have, did you do anything about it? This is about more than the homeless person in the street median that you see on occasion. This is about your family, your friends, and your coworkers.

I have found that most people today are self-absorbed, don't notice the plight of those around them, and honestly don't even ask. I've also seen that even when someone is brave enough today to ask for help, very few people in their circle actually step up. People can't be bothered to give a Saturday or a couple hours in the evening to someone else. Perhaps your experience is different than mine though.

What do people deem more important? As we saw in some prior signs, probably social media and binge watching. Why have we become so calloused? I'm not surprised that the world behaves this way, but even Christians today are children of disobedience.

Today Is Different - One of the issues with today is that Christians are in many ways indistinguishable from anyone else. A book titled *unChristian*, which was published in 2007, reports on a survey by the Barna Group. They discovered that Christians are just as likely to visit a porn site, get drunk, do drugs, lie, and get back at someone as non-Christians are. Only 15% of non-Christians surveyed thought the Christians they knew had a lifestyle that was significantly different than their own.[18] This was seventeen years ago. We know the situation has only gotten bleaker.

A key indicator of a hard heart is an unwillingness to speak with God. So, let's look at prayer. In 2007, 58% of adults reported that they prayed daily. In 2021 you guessed it, it's down and only at 45%. The people who seldom or never pray rose from 18% to 32% during that time frame. These stats aren't that much better when singling out Christians. Only 61% of Christians today pray every day. What's shocking is that 14% say they seldom or never do, and that percentage was even higher for non-evangelical Christians (24%) and Catholics (20%)[19].

Additional Scriptures: 2 Chronicles 34:21. Deuteronomy 28:15, 45. Ephesians 2:1-3. Hosea 4:10. Jeremiah 32:22-23. Luke 10:29-37. Matthew 22:36-40. Micah 6:8. Proverbs 6:16-18. Psalm 78:56; 106:24-25, 34-35. Romans 2:5, 8. Titus 1:16.

#37 - CENSORSHIP

Anti | DD | Earth | Gov | Israel | Jesus | Leader | Sky | Society | Tech | Trib

> For the wrath of God is revealed from heaven against all ungodliness and unrighteousness of men who suppress the truth in unrighteousness. (Romans 1:18)

God's wrath comes against people who "suppress the truth." This is the sign of censorship. One of the things Jesus warned about in the Olivet Discourse is the persecution and hatred that believers would suffer because people would try to silence God's truth. We're going to look at persecution in particular in Sign #94 - God's Prophets Are Persecuted and Sign #95 - Oppression Of God's People.

During the tribulation period, the prophet Daniel describes the Antichrist as throwing truth to the ground. And there's a reference in the book of Amos that appears to be describing the tribulation period. It says in that day God will send a famine of the words of the Lord. It certainly makes it seem like Bibles will be difficult to find during the tribulation period.

Fulfillment - We looked at the attack today on God's Word through Bible bans in Sign #29 - Despising God's Word. This sign will focus on the broader censorship context.

Did you know that, back in 1985, 50 companies controlled most of American media? Today, it's only a handful of corporations and 15 billionaires: AT&T (CNN), Comcast (NBC), Disney (ABC), National Amusements (CBS, Viacom), and NewsCorp (Fox News).[20] Those few companies make money through subscribers and advertisers. That will naturally stifle their willingness to have an opinion which counters the majority public opinion or the opinion of their biggest advertisers.

And consider what this means if those 15 billionaires have an agenda. What if they're all invested in a pharmaceutical giant? Naturally, they wouldn't be against the very pharmaceutical products that are making them money. What if they all support the same political party? We sure wouldn't hear good things about the opposing party. When industries like the media see such consolidation, it's going to result in censorship.

This also means that when one of these companies has a news anchor that chooses to go against the grain so to speak, they risk being censored and fired. Case in point, Tucker Carlson. He was fired from *Fox News* in April 2023. What's odd is that Tucker was the most watched cable TV news host, averaging 4.3 million viewers per show. He holds the cable news viewership record.[21] Tucker says he was fired as part of the Fox News settlement with Dominion Voting Systems regarding claims of election interference in the 2020 US Presidential Election. [22] Despite his enormous popularity, the bosses and advertisers didn't like what he said, so they got rid of him.

Today Is Different - Censorship is widespread today. It's because the technology available today makes it easier to find and remove content on social media or the internet that authorities deem offensive, inappropriate, or untrustworthy. It's one of the key uses for AI. A human isn't looking at every post or website out there and determining if it warrants a take down. It's all done by a computer program that's given parameters, keywords, or images to look for.

Do you remember the Covid years and all the censorship that was happening on social media regarding the vaccines, different treatment options, the origin of the virus, and the deaths being reported? People were put in social media jail or banned from platforms just because they had an opinion which differed from the official government position. Independent journalists were even banned from using popular payment platforms like PayPal and Stripe. Yet, we Americans live in a country that supposedly fosters free speech?

I'm sure you recall the most famous case of censorship in America. It was against US President Trump. He got banned from Twitter and Facebook while he was still the acting US president![23] He had 140 million followers at the time.[24] It led to him creating his own platform, Truth Social. After Elon Musk purchased Twitter and rebranded it to X, he reinstated Trump's account in November 2022.[25]

The Gateway Pundit, a top 250 website in the US in 2021, has reported that they've been censored by T-Mobile, a wireless network operator in the US. Links to their news articles weren't being delivered via text messages.[26]

YouTube has started demonetizing channels.[27] Content creators earn income when ads play during their videos. YouTube has been removing ads from channels that they claim have violated their content policies. A famous example of this is actor and comedian Russell Brand. YouTube demonetized his channel in September 2023 based solely on sexual assault allegations against him. He hadn't been convicted of a crime. He had 6.6 million subscribers, and it's estimated he was earning $2,500 per video, which would equate to $650,000 annually if he posted one video every business day. In addition to that, the UK parliament requested the platforms Rumble and X deplatform him entirely. It seems the real motivation behind his censorship may have been that he was starting to speak out against things like vaccines.[28]

This isn't solely a US issue. Did you know the United Nations has a tool they've started disseminating that helps countries counter disinformation? It's called iVerify. Here's the description from their website: "iVerify is UNDP's fact-checking tool provided and used by national stakeholders to identify false information and prevent and mitigate its spread. It is supported through the UNDP Chief Digital Office and the UNDP Brussels-based Task Force on Electoral Assistance."[29] I'm sure this is totally harmless, especially since they mentioned elections. Not! The site says it's only in a handful of countries today. How long do you think we've got until this product is being used everywhere?

The Digital Services Act just went into effect in the European Union (EU) this past January 2024. Its purpose is to govern the content moderation practices of social media. Each EU member state has a digital services coordinator who is responsible for certifying "trusted flaggers," organizations independent of social media who detect, identify, and remove illegal content.[30] The US tech giants like Facebook, Amazon, X, and YouTube have to comply with this.[31]

The situation is only getting worse. Robert F. Kennedy Jr. has sued Meta for colluding with US President Biden's administration and allegedly shadowbanning his documentary, *Who is Bobby Kennedy?*, in an effort to sway the 2024 US Presidential Election.[32] Shadowbanning is nearly impossible to detect because it limits the visibility of content without the content creator's knowledge. For example, a Facebook post suffering this fate would be visible on the content creator's profile, but not display on the timelines of other users.

Unfortunately, the US Supreme Court ruled in June 2024 that the White House and federal agencies can continue to persuade social media companies to take down content the government views as disinformation.[33]

Additional Scriptures: Amos 5:13; 8:9-12. Daniel 8:11-12. Jeremiah 11:18-23; 38:4. Luke 21:12-17.

#38 – REBELLIOUS

Anti | DD | Earth | Gov | Israel | **Jesus** | Leader | Sky | **Society** | **Tech** | **Trib**

> "Who then is the faithful and wise servant, whom his lord has set over his household, to give them their food in due season? Blessed is that servant whom his lord finds doing so when he comes. Most certainly I tell you that he will set him over all that he has. But if that evil servant should say in his heart, 'My lord is delaying his coming,' and begins to beat his fellow servants, and eat and drink with the drunkards, the lord of that servant will come in a day when he doesn't expect it and in an hour when he doesn't know it, and will cut him in pieces and appoint his portion with the hypocrites. That is where the weeping and grinding of teeth will be." (Matthew 24:45-51)

Jesus is the one speaking here. This parable is about the faithful and evil servants. The evil servant rebelled against his master by treating the other servants poorly and spending his time partying. The evil servant rebelled against authority.

Another type of rebellion against authority that we're told manifests in the last days is children who are disobedient to parents. The ultimate rebellion will come during the tribulation period when all the unbelievers gather to war against Jesus at his second coming.

Fulfillment - People throughout time have been rebellious against authority. Today is no different. We continue to show a lack of respect. It's no wonder we behave this way toward authority. Just think about all the ways we disrespect other people.

Today, people think it's okay to dress in a manner that's blatantly offensive to others. Whether it's a man who wears his pants under his rear so that his underwear is visible, or it's a female who wears a see through top so everyone can view her bra, or it's someone who wears clothing with foul language, or it's someone marching in a Pride parade topless or nude. And now we have a US Senator who's wearing gym clothes to congress. Really? The Senate had to institute a formal dress code as a result.[34]

We can't forget the climate protesters. I just read that people representing Just Stop Oil spraypainted Stone Henge.[35] What? I thought they wanted to protect things in the environment. There are even protesters throwing food at the Mona Lisa because their government isn't handing out 'food cards', what we'd think of in the US as food stamps or SNAP benefits.[36] Why do these people think it's okay to destroy a national treasure to get attention? It's another way this rebellious spirit is manifesting today.

Today, people disrespect their employers perhaps to an elevated degree compared to prior generations. I would argue it's because technology (like computers, cell phones, the internet, Zoom, and webcams) has made it possible and easy for a lot of people to work from home. You and I both know that most people are abusing that because their employer can't see what they're doing at home. It's no different than the parable above. Now, there's even a revolt happening against employers who are demanding their employees return to the office to work.[37]

Today Is Different - There are several things that I believe make today different than any other previous time. Consider the disrespect for political leaders. Many Americans, regardless of political affiliation, refuse to refer to the current or former presidents by using the title "president."

I know several people who are or used to be schoolteachers. When I was growing up, if a kid talked back to a teacher, all the other students in class would gasp. Then the offender got sent to the principal's office and served in detention. Wow is it different today. One teacher who's in public high school told me she can't even say "Hi" to kids in the hall anymore. They just tell her to "F-off." That's not to mention the disrespect kids show during class by not paying attention and using their cell phones.

This business about using cell phones at inappropriate times isn't limited to the young generation. Adults are just as disrespectful today. I'm sure you know someone who's constantly on their phone when they're out to dinner with you. I see adults in church texting, surfing social media, and playing games on their phones during the entire service. I'm honestly not sure why they even show up. Do they consider how that looks to the pastor up front? Or how it makes him feel? Of course not.

Here's the biggest rebellion that makes today different. It's the utter contempt for parental rights. It's frequently in the news that a teacher has enabled and hidden a student's gender transition from their parents.

It's not just teachers against parents, it's entire school districts. It's reported there are over 1,000 districts across America that have secrecy policies.[38]

And now even the government is behind this rebellion. Consider the couples who aren't able to foster or adopt because they refuse to affirm gender transition.[39] The government is labeling it a form of child abuse. Thus, US President Biden's administration is trying to make federal funds to foster agencies contingent on gender transition support. In July 2024, California passed a law that prevents schools from informing parents of their child's gender dysphoria.[40]

Additional Scriptures: 1 Corinthians 14:33. 2 Timothy 3:1-4. Ezekiel 5:6-8. Hosea 4:18. Isaiah 1; 66:4. Lamentations 4:16. Matthew 21:33-41. Proverbs 6:16-18. Revelation 19:11-21. Romans 1:30, 32; 2:5.

#39 – NO APOLOGIES

Anti | **DD** | Earth | Gov | Israel | **Jesus** | **Leader** | Sky | **Society** | Tech | **Trib**

> For the wrath of God is revealed from heaven against all ungodliness and unrighteousness of men ... who, knowing the ordinance of God, that those who practice such things are worthy of death, not only do the same, but also approve of those who practice them. (Romans 1:18, 32)

In this Scripture, people "who practice such things" is a reference to the sinful behavior listed prior. The apostle Paul tells us these people know God's Law but continue to do those evil things and encourage others to do them too. These are people who have hardened their hearts to such a degree that they simply aren't even apologetic about their bad behavior.

A good example of this is Moses's brother Aaron. When Moses was on the mountain with God and was slow in returning, Aaron blamed the evil people for making him create the golden calf for them to worship. He even went so far as to say the calf just popped out of the fire on its own. He didn't apologize; he blamed other people. Adam did the same thing when God asked him if he'd eaten from the Tree of the Knowledge of Good and Evil. He said Eve made him do it.

Before the Israelites were taken into Babylonian captivity, many prophets were sent to warn them. When destruction finally came upon them, we're told that God called for them to weep and mourn for their sins. Do you know what they did instead? They danced and feasted and said, "let's eat and drink for tomorrow we die." I guess they didn't have any regrets.

Most of the letters that Jesus dictated to the churches in the book of Revelation have a warning of repentance. Yet we know that even during the tribulation period people won't be apologetic.

Fulfillment - People don't apologize for their behavior today. It's simply not their fault. It's blamed on someone or something else. We're going to explore that fault business more in Sign #89 - Victimhood. People also aren't sorry because many things that were once considered sinful to everyone in society are now accepted.

Recall Trump's US presidency and that all the mainstream media outlets accused him of colluding with the Russians to win the 2016 election. We were constantly bombarded with Russiagate conspiracies during his entire presidency. Yet, the Robert Mueller special counsel report showed no collusion with Russia. No one has apologized.[41]

Even more recent, before the 2020 US Presidential Election, Trump was accused of colluding with the Russians again. In fact, a couple weeks before the election, 51 intelligence agents signed a letter claiming that material from Hunter Biden's laptop, that was published by *The New York Post*, had the earmarks of a Russian information operation. That Russia would do anything to help Trump win. That letter effectively killed the story about the contents of the laptop and the dealings of the Bidens. The issue is that none of the 51 had ever seen anything on the laptop. The letter wasn't true. They still haven't apologized for interfering in an election.[42]

Today Is Different - Remember how the world shut down in the spring of 2020 due to Covid? Remember how governments and businesses made bad decisions and even told all sorts of lies during that time? Some businesses went bankrupt because they were forced to close while others were allowed to stay open. People lost their jobs. People got injured by treatments and vaccines that they were forced to get by their employer, their school, or their government. Kids didn't really learn anything for a couple years because school was only online. Has anyone apologized to us? Nope!

Additional Scriptures: 1 Kings 13:33-34; 18:17-18. Exodus 10:3; 32:21-24. Genesis 3:11-12. Isaiah 22:12-13. Jeremiah 8:6. Psalm 78:31-32. Revelation 2:18-21; 9:20-21; 16:9, 11.

#40 - POLAR OPPOSITE - A HEART OF FLESH

Anti | DD | Earth | Gov | Israel | Jesus | **Leader** | Sky | **Society** | Tech | Trib

> Tell those who have a fearful heart, "Be strong! Don't be afraid! Behold, your God will come with vengeance, God's retribution. He will come and save you. Then the eyes of the blind will be opened, and the ears of the deaf will be unstopped." (Isaiah 35:4-5)

Throughout this chapter we've looked at signs related to a hardened heart. This sign is what I call a polar opposite. It's meant to illustrate how far away we currently are from the life we believers are going to live during Jesus's reign on earth in the millennial kingdom. Recall from Sign #6 - The Point Of No Return, that God only lets evil progress so far before he intervenes.

In the verses above, we learn that when God returns, he's going to open the "eyes of the blind" and the "ears of the deaf." No one will have a hardened heart anymore.

Instead, everyone will have a heart of flesh. One that wants to listen to God, believe what he says, and obey him.

> I will also give you a new heart, and I will put a new spirit within you. I will take away the stony heart out of your flesh, and I will give you a **heart of flesh**. (Ezekiel 36:26)

Fulfillment - So, how far away are we? With the volume of Christian denominations becoming progressive, it's obvious that society today doesn't want to listen to or believe God's Word. A majority of Americans don't even want to talk to God through prayer today. We also learned that society is rebelling against all types of authority figures today.

A fun way to consider just how opposite we are is to contemplate what the worst-case scenarios might look like and see just how close we are to them.

Worst case, it's illegal to speak out against the government. It's considered treason. No one even attempts to anymore because the penalty for doing so is death. According to World Population Review, freedom of expression is legal in the majority of countries today.[43] There are some notable ones, like China and North Korea, who do a lot to control what their population can view or post on the internet, news, and social media. So, we're actually not very close to a worst case here.

Worst case, there are no conservative Christian churches anymore. All of them are progressive and teach from a variety of texts, not solely the Bible. Well, we've learned about the rise in progressive Christianity and how it impacts a majority of Christian denominations. So, this is a real problem for people today. We're closer to a worst case than I realized before writing this chapter.

Worst case, parents no longer have a say in how their children are raised. The government controls it and enforces it. Children are incentivized to rat out their parents and are then placed with more agreeable foster parents. While this isn't happening on a wide scale today, the fact that's it happening at all is disconcerting. We're not close to this worst case yet.

Worst case, sin is never acknowledged because all behavior is acceptable. Can you imagine if people were so hard-hearted that they were allowed to murder their own children? Yikes! That's legal. We've hit this worst case in many ways on this one.

Today Is Different - So, what do you think? Is today different? Do we as a society have a hardened heart that doesn't listen to or obey God? Do you think we've reached the point of no return? How many people really have a heart of flesh that's even willing to consider the teachings of Jesus?

Additional Scriptures: Ezekiel 37:24. Revelation 1:7. Zechariah 12:10.

CHAPTER 8 – A COVETING HEART

> But there were also false prophets among the people, even as there will be false teachers among you. ... They have a **heart trained in covetous practices**, [and are] accursed children. They have forsaken the right way and gone astray, following the way of Balaam the [son] of Beor, who loved the wages of unrighteousness; (2 Peter 2:1, 14-15 NKJV)

#41 – COVETING

<u>Anti</u> | DD | Earth | Gov | Israel | <u>**Jesus**</u> | **Leader** | Sky | **Society** | Tech | **Trib**

> He said to them, "Beware! Keep yourselves from covetousness, for a man's life doesn't consist of the abundance of the things which he possesses." He spoke a parable to them, saying, "The ground of a certain rich man produced abundantly. He reasoned within himself, saying, 'What will I do, because I don't have room to store my crops?' He said, 'This is what I will do. I will pull down my barns, build bigger ones, and there I will store all my grain and my goods. I will tell my soul, "Soul, you have many goods laid up for many years. Take your ease, eat, drink, and be merry." ' "But God said to him, 'You foolish one, tonight your soul is required of you. The things which you have prepared—whose will they be?' So is he who lays up treasure for himself, and is not rich toward God." (Luke 12:15-21)

Jesus is the one speaking here. He tells us to keep ourselves "from covetousness" and then speaks a parable about a foolish rich man who just stored treasure for himself. The word *covetousness* means a greedy desire to have more or an eagerness to have what belongs to others. It's the tenth of the Ten Commandments.

In the Olivet Discourse, which is Jesus's teachings about signs of his second coming, he gave another parable with a teaching on coveting. In the parable of the talents, the wicked servant buried his master's talent instead of using it, investing it, or even putting it in the bank.

We'll continue to see this behavior even through the tribulation period. We're told that the evil city of Babylon will be prominent in the tribulation period as the home for all the demons and the kings of the world. They'll live luxuriously and won't believe they'll see sorrow. It was the same with the foolish rich man.

Fulfillment - Have you ever met a hoarder? Or watched one of the many TV shows that now exist about them? I like to watch *American Pickers*, and many of the episodes depict someone with this condition.

Chapter 8 - A Coveting Heart

It's a mental disorder characterized by difficulty parting with possessions or the excessive accumulation of stuff that there's no room for.[1] Even though Jesus talks about it, it didn't have its own official diagnosis code until 2012.[2]

Another indicator of this behavior in society is the volume of self-storage properties. Since 2019 the market cap of self-storage REITs grew from $63 billion to $102 billion in 2023.[3] And if you're wondering if all those units are just sitting empty, nope. The vacancy rate of units has been under 10% for the last decade.[4] This does appear to be primarily a US behavior though. In 2018, 90% of global storage facilities were in America.

Today Is Different - One thing that makes today so much different than prior generations is that companies across the world are hoarding cash. Here are some examples of companies with large amounts of cash on hand, with data as of July 2024: Alphabet $108 billion, Saudi Arabian Oil $91 billion, Amazon $85 billion, Alibaba $83 billion, Microsoft $80 billion, Samsung $71 billion, Apple $67 billion, Taiwan Semiconductor $62 billion, and Meta $58 billion.[5] It's understandable that a bank would have a lot of cash on hand, but why these companies?

Back in September 2023, thirteen companies in the S&P 500, mostly tech giants, were sitting on over $1 trillion in cash. They accounted for almost 40% of all the cash held by all the companies in the S&P 500. It was enough to give every person in the US almost $8,000.[6]

Instead of investing that money into other companies or research and development, paying it out as a dividend to their investors, or increasing the salaries of their employees, it's just sitting there. Reminds me of the rich man we read about above who just kept building barns to store all his crops.

Additional Scriptures: 1 John 2:16. Colossians 3:5-6. Ephesians 2:1-3; 5:3-7. Exodus 20:17. Isaiah 56:10-12. James 4:1-2; 5:1-6. Jeremiah 6:13; 22:13, 17. Luke 20:46-47. Malachi 3:8. Matthew 25:14-30. Micah 2:1-2. Revelation 18. Romans 1:29.

#42 - JEALOUSY

Anti | DD | Earth | Gov | Israel | **Jesus** | Leader | Sky | **Society** | **Tech** | **Trib**

For the wrath of God is revealed from heaven against all ungodliness and unrighteousness of men who ... being ... full of envy ... knowing the ordinance of God, that those who practice such things are worthy of death, not only do the same, but also approve of those who practice them. (Romans 1: 18, 29, 32)

The Holy Spirit, speaking through the apostle Paul, tells us that God's wrath will come against people who are "full of envy." The word *envy* means jealousy or spite. There's a desire to hurt that's involved with this particular behavior. Jesus spoke about this when he taught that it's what comes out of a man that defiles him, not what goes in. That it's out of the heart that sinful behavior like envy originates.

During the tribulation period, the Antichrist is going to be the poster child of jealousy and envy when he blasphemes God and then demands the entire world worship him as God. He'll be so full of spite, that he'll seek to kill anyone who refuses to worship him.

Fulfillment - When I think of jealousy, a sports scandal comes to mind. It happened a couple months before the 1994 Winter Olympic Games. You guessed it. That's when US figure skater, Nancy Kerrigan, was attacked at the US Figure Skating championships by someone that her rival's ex-husband hired. Tonya Harding, who denied involvement, ended up pleading guilty to conspiracy to hinder the prosecution and was banned from the US Figure Skating Association.[7] They've even made some movies about this true story recently. I know you'll find this shocking, the 2017 movie *I, Tonya,* wants you to feel sorry for Tonya instead of the victim of the jealousy, Nancy.[8]

Have you ever been the victim of jealousy? I have and it was over something stupid too. I used to compete in bowling and one night many years ago I had 10 strikes in a row. I just needed two more for a perfect game. When I released the 11th ball, someone at the control desk hit the reset button on the pinsetter on my lane. Yep, on purpose. So, my ball crashed into the pinsetter as it came down. By the time the machine was fixed and I was back at it, I failed to get those next two strikes. It's crazy that my doing well at a game that didn't even have any significance triggered someone's jealousy like that.

Our world is full of jealous people. You are well aware of this because you've experienced these feelings yourself. As my pastor says, it's easier for us to grieve with someone than to celebrate with them.

Today Is Different - Cyberbullying and revenge porn. Those are reasons that today is different in terms of envy and jealousy. If you want to inflict harm on someone without actually hurting them physically, today you can use AI. It can be used to generate a realistic looking image or video of someone doing something they wouldn't normally do, or something they'd be embarrassed about. That image or video could then be posted on social media.

Pew Research indicates that nearly half of US teens are victims of cyberbullying behavior today.[9] Revenge porn is such a problem that most of the US states, 48, have laws against it now.[10] New Jersey was the first in 2004.[11] Israel passed a law against it in 2014.

Additional Scriptures: Acts 13:44-45; 17:5. Daniel 11:20, 36-37. Ecclesiastes 4:4. James 3:14-16. Job 5:2. John 11:47-53. Mark 7:14-23; 15:10. Matthew 21:12-17. Revelation 13:6-8, 12-15. Romans 3:14; 13:11-13.

#43 - ENTITLEMENT

Anti | DD | Earth | **Gov** | Israel | **Jesus** | Leader | Sky | **Society** | Tech | **Trib**

> "For the Kingdom of Heaven is like a man who was the master of a household, who went out early in the morning to hire laborers for his vineyard. When he had agreed with the laborers for a denarius a day, he sent them into his vineyard. He went out about the third hour, and saw others standing idle in the marketplace. He said to them, 'You also go into the vineyard, and whatever is right I will give you.' So they went their way. Again he went out about the sixth and the ninth hour, and did likewise. About the eleventh hour he went out and found others standing idle. He said to them, 'Why do you stand here all day idle?' "They said to him, 'Because no one has hired us.' "He said to them, 'You also go into the vineyard, and you will receive whatever is right.' "When evening had come, the lord of the vineyard said to his manager, 'Call the laborers and pay them their wages, beginning from the last to the first.' "When those who were hired at about the eleventh hour came, they each received a denarius. When the first came, they supposed that they would receive more; and they likewise each received a denarius. When they received it, they murmured against the master of the household, saying, 'These last have spent one hour, and you have made them equal to us who have borne the burden of the day and the scorching heat!' "But he answered one of them, 'Friend, I am doing you no wrong. Didn't you agree with me for a denarius? Take that which is yours, and go your way. It is my desire to give to this last just as much as to you. Isn't it lawful for me to do what I want to with what I own? Or is your eye evil, because I am good?' So the last will be first, and the first last. For many are called, but few are chosen." (Matthew 20:1-16)

Jesus is speaking the parable above about workers in the vineyard. The master hired workers throughout the day. He agreed to give those he hired first thing a day's wage, a denarius. At the end of the day, because he felt like being generous to those he hired late in the afternoon, he gave all the workers a denarius regardless of how much time they worked. We're told the workers the master hired first were upset because they expected to get more than what was agreed upon. You see, they believed that they were entitled to more.

Jesus also told us about the entitlement the Antichrist is going to display during the tribulation period. The Antichrist will believe he's entitled to the worship that he'll see the Jewish people giving to God. So, he'll stop the temple sacrifices, place an object of desecration inside the temple, and then demand all people worship him as God.

Fulfillment - It doesn't take super observation skills to notice that the world we live in has become entitled. People expect freebies. Whether that's a free college education, free health care, a government provided living wage, free TV, free software, free books, or even free games for your phone. We don't want to pay for anything anymore.

I have to admit that I'm not immune to this. I often expect to find free software for whatever it is I need to do on my computer. I get annoyed when a news site wants my email address before I can read their articles. I'm even upset that I won't get free shipping on my Sam's Club orders now unless I spend a certain amount.

One reason this has happened is because we've been getting trained for years by huge corporations to not pay for things. Regular broadcast TV was always free. Email services like Gmail, free. Public school, free. Local libraries make books free to read. Music on the radio, free. Want a webpage for yourself or your business? Use Facebook, it's free. Food samples at Costco, free.

But these things haven't really been free. We've willingly given up our data in exchange for free. We've also willingly given up some of our time for ads and commercials. But now that costs are rising and these things that we've willingly given up aren't paying the corporate bills anymore, we revolt when they want to actually charge us for a product or service.

Today Is Different - This is one of the hot topics of today. In March 2021, Evanston, Illinois became the first US city to make reparations available to its Black residents for past discrimination and effects of slavery. It's a suburb of Chicago. They're going to give 16 households $25,000 for home repairs or down payments. It's being funded by revenue from a tax on marijuana. They agreed to distribute $10 million over the next ten years. To qualify, the resident has to have lived in their city or be a direct descendant of a Black person who did between the years 1919 and 1969, and who was the victim of housing discrimination during that time period.[12]

A bill to study reparations was introduced to US Congress in the 1980s but didn't move forward. The California legislature is currently debating and making progress toward reparations for its citizens.[13]

This is a topic of contention in Israel too. Germany entered into a reparations agreement with Israel and the Jews in 1952 due to its treatment of the Jewish population during WWII.[14] By the end of 2021, Germany had paid 80 billion euros. In 2022 they agreed to pay an additional $1.2 billion to Holocaust survivors in 2023.

Well, now the international tables are turned, and the International Court of Justice (judicial arm of the UN) issued a legal opinion in July 2024 stating Israel is responsible for systemic discrimination against Palestinians and should pay them reparations.[15]

We've opened a whole can of worms. There is seemingly no end to the wrongs that people groups could feel entitled to compensation for.

<u>Additional Scriptures:</u> 1 Kings 21:1-16. 1 Samuel 15. 2 Timothy 3:1-2. Daniel 11:31, 12:11. Deuteronomy 28:47. Mark 12:1-9. Matthew 24:15; 25:14-30.

#44 - LOVERS OF PLEASURE

<u>Anti</u> | <u>DD</u> | Earth | Gov | Israel | <u>Jesus</u> | <u>Leader</u> | Sky | <u>Society</u> | <u>Tech</u> | <u>Trib</u>

> But know this: that in the last days, grievous times will come. For men will be ... lovers of pleasure rather than lovers of God. (2 Timothy 3:1-2, 4)

In Paul's letter to his disciple Timothy, he speaks of the last days. We're told one of the signs will be people who are "lovers of pleasure," but not of God.

Jesus also spoke out against this sin. He told the Pharisees that they were full of self-indulgence. He also said that some of the people who came to hear him only did so because they wanted a free meal. He even taught about it in the parable of the sower. The seed that's scattered among thorns and gets choked out illustrates how God's Word gets choked out by the pleasures of life.

It might seem surprising, but during the tribulation period there will be many people living this way. We're told that the kings of the earth will dwell in Babylon and live luxuriously and that all the merchants of the world will become rich because of that.

Fulfillment - Have you noticed in your city that the homeless people who stand in the street median soliciting money usually all have a cell phone? And for some reason many of them also have a dog. I think this reveals a lot about society. It doesn't matter how bad off we are financially, we'll figure out a way to meet our need for pleasure before we meet other needs, like getting a job or a place to live.

Worldwide, people spend an average of 6 hours 40 minutes on the internet each day. Here's what people are doing in particular, and they could be doing these activities concurrently: 3 hours 6 minutes watching TV, 2 hours 23 minutes on social media, 1 hour 41 minutes on news, 1 hour 25 minutes listening to music, and 1 hour 2 minutes playing a game.[16] We love to be entertained.

In December 2023, the CEO of Wayfair got blasted on social media for statements he made in a memo to employees about the value of a hard work ethic. Some people were so incensed that they started a boycott of his company. Here's part of what he said: "There is not a lot of history of laziness being rewarded with success. Hard work is an essential ingredient in any recipe for success. I embrace this, and the most successful people I know do as well."[17] Mike Rowe, host of the TV show *Dirty Jobs*, commented on the CEOs backlash and said that "work ethic used to be a virtue" but that "today, that turn of phrase has become like so many other turns of phrase, a kind of triggering dog whistle of sorts. It means that if you come out in favor of work ethic, then you are de facto on the side of the greedy, rapacious capitalists who are merely trying to exploit the worker."[18]

Today Is Different - The vast amounts of entertainment that are available make today different than prior generations. And not just available, but most of this is instantly available. You don't have to go anywhere to consume it. Movies and TV shows that we can watch on demand. Video games on a variety of platforms and even our phones. Books, board games, audiobooks, podcasts, social media, YouTube videos, puzzles of every kind, sports, concerts, plays, and I could go on. The entire entertainment and media industry had global revenue of $2.8 trillion in 2023.[19]

The top websites people visited paint a more insightful picture. Of the top 20 sites visited across the world, 4 of them are pornographic. And two of those are in the top 5 sites.[20] In 2018, the US market for this sexual content was $607 million and in 2023 it surpassed $1 billion. In five years, the industry grew 80%.[21]

I'd also like you to consider that today is different because you can find and purchase anything your heart desires online and have it delivered to you. It doesn't matter where in the world it is either. One of the top websites in the world is Amazon.com with over 4.2 billion visits each month, of which almost 1 billion are unique visitors.[22] Think of how easy it is today to stay at home and lounge around all day, yet still eat from all your favorite restaurants because of the convenience of delivery.

Additional Scriptures: 1 John 2:16. Amos 6:1-7. Colossians 3:5-6. Ephesians 2:1-3; 5:3-7. Ezekiel 16:49-50. Isaiah 22:12-13. James 5:1-6. Jeremiah 5:27-28. John 6:26-27. Luke 8:4-15. Matthew 23:25. Revelation 18.

#45 - LOVE OF MONEY

Anti | DD | Earth | **Gov** | Israel | **Jesus** | **Leader** | Sky | **Society** | Tech | **Trib**

> But know this: that in the last days, grievous times will come. For men will be ... lovers of money. (2 Timothy 3:1-2)

Paul's disciple Timothy is told that one of the hallmark signs of the end times will be people who are "lovers of money." Jesus taught about this quite a bit. He had a conversation with a rich man who lacked one thing. Jesus told him to sell his possessions, give the money to the poor, and then follow him. The rich man went away sad because he was very rich. The rich man loved all his stuff. Jesus also drove the money changers out of the temple because they'd made God's Temple a house of merchandise. And you may recall that Jesus famously said that you can't serve two masters, God and riches.

The Bible is also full of examples of people who accepted bribes because they loved money more than they cared about justice or loyalty or doing the right thing. Consider Judas Iscariot and how he betrayed Jesus for a mere thirty pieces of silver.

This behavior will continue through the tribulation period. In the book of Revelation, we're told about the city of Babylon. The kings of the world will live there in luxury, and all the merchants get rich because of it. But all their silver and gold won't deliver them on the day of wrath.

Fulfillment - Do you remember the 2007-2008 global financial crisis? Predatory lending in the US is what caused it. Lenders were giving mortgages to people who couldn't afford it and charging high interest rates. All because they wanted to make a commission. Demand for houses and the price of houses rose due to the increased number of people getting approved for loans. As housing prices increased even more, the lenders gave people a second mortgage on the equity their home had gained.

One third of all US mortgages in 2006 were considered sub-prime. It's no surprise that the whole thing came crashing down when people couldn't pay their mortgages. All the foreclosures flooded the housing market and home prices collapsed. The financial institutions who owned those loans or were invested in mortgage-backed securities lost big.[23] Lehman Brothers and Washington Mutual both went bankrupt. They are the two largest bankruptcies in US history. Lehman Brothers was worth $691 billion and Washington Mutual $328 billion.[24]

This one greedy act by banks in the US impacted the entire planet for years. It's estimated US and European banks lost $1 trillion in toxic assets from bad loans. The stock market crashed. It sparked the Great Recession. Do you remember all the US and European government bailouts that resulted?

If you're interested in learning more about what happened, they made several movies about it including *The Big Short* and *Too Big To Fail*.

Today Is Different - What makes today different is that we didn't learn a thing from the 2007-2008 financial crisis. Banks are doing it again, and this time the US government is encouraging it! Because housing prices and interest rates on mortgages in the US are climbing, it's becoming difficult for lower income households to purchase a home. So, the government has taken steps to increase financing opportunities for higher risk borrowers.

Starting in May 2023, the US government is subsidizing loans to higher risk borrowers. People with lower credit scores (640-659) who have a 15% down payment have their rate reduced by 0.5%. While people with high credit scores (760-779) with that same down payment pay an additional 0.4%. Yep, that totally seems fair—not! It gets worse, borrowers getting a loan through the government corporations of Freddie Mac and Fannie Mae will be happy to know they raised the mortgage limit from a $766,550 loan to a $1.15 million loan.[25] Insane!

You see, the government corporations don't have to comply with the lending standards that were put in place for private lenders as a result of the financial crisis. Yeah, not sure how that makes sense. Mortgages issued by private lenders can't exceed 43% of the borrower's income. The government can give riskier loans. Freddie Mac backs $3.5 trillion in mortgages today. Yet its net worth and ability to absorb any losses is only $50 billion. That's a 70:1 leverage, over twice that of Bear Stearns before it collapsed during the financial crisis. And the White House in June 2024 just gave Freddie Mac the ability to issue second mortgages.[26] Here we go again.

Freddie Mac cannot support the risk it's taking on. So, why is the current administration doing this? The government gets revenue from these loans. There are large construction firms that lobby congress for more affordable housing. There are lobbyists for insurance companies who also benefit when there are more houses needing to be insured. The lobbyists in turn contribute to political campaigns. The political party pushing the legislation also might get a voter. If that candidate wins the election, they're getting a government income and all sorts of perks from the lobbyists. It's for the love of money.

There is no way this will stay confined to the government corporations backing the loans. The big banks will want a piece of this lending pie. It's just a matter of how they'll get around or just completely disregard the regulations that were put in place to prevent another crisis. How long will this house of cards stand?

<u>Additional Scriptures:</u> 1 Timothy 6:6-10. Ezekiel 16:49-50; 22:12; 28:2-8, 12-19. James 5:1-6. Jeremiah 17:21-23. John 2:13-17. Luke 8:4-15; 16:1-14; 18:18-24. Mark 14:10-11. Matthew 21:12-13; 26:14-16; 28:11-15. Micah 3:11; 7:1-4. Revelation 3:14-22; 9:20; 18. Zephaniah 1:18.

#46 - STEALING

<u>Anti</u> | <u>DD</u> | Earth | Gov | Israel | <u>Jesus</u> | Leader | Sky | <u>Society</u> | <u>Tech</u> | <u>Trib</u>

They didn't repent of their … thefts. (Revelation 9:21)

We read in the book of Revelation that people refuse to repent of thefts. This is stated after the sixth trumpet judgment. So, by that time there will have been 13 judgments from God. Yet they continue to steal. Don't steal is the eighth of the Ten Commandments.

Jesus told us that Satan is the thief who comes to steal. So, it's no surprise that the Antichrist, Satan's agent, will exude that behavior in the tribulation period. He'll be conquering countries, dividing land for gain, and plundering nations.

Fulfillment - The fulfillment of this one should be obvious to you. Stealing is front and center in the news today. Just consider all these examples: squatting in houses, stealing copper from ACs, orchestrated smash and grab mobs, stealing fire hydrants for metal recycling, credit card skimming, stealing copper from EV charging stations, identity theft, stealing catalytic converters for the precious metals, email scams, stealing cars, large scale looting mobs, swapping price tags at self-checkout, cyber theft, brushing scams (where you get a package you didn't order), pirated movies, counterfeit purses, romance scams, and I could go on and on.

Have you been to a big box retail store like Walmart, Home Depot, or Walgreens lately? Perhaps you've noticed they now have a lot of merchandise locked up behind glass or wire doors. It's not even necessarily expensive stuff either. They're having to do it because shoplifting is so commonplace. Stealing is making shopping in stores difficult these days.

Today Is Different - One thing that makes today unique is that at least half of Americans believe the 2020 US Presidential Election was stolen. A good portion of them have lost confidence in the entire election system now as a result.

Another reason today is different is because huge financial scams are frequently in the news now. The Enron fraud happened at the start of this century in 2001. They admitted to the SEC that they overstated profits by $600 million before they went bankrupt. This obviously artificially inflated their stock price. Many executives were sentenced to prison as a result.[27]

Who could forget the infamous Bernie Madoff, who is believed to have stolen $19 billion from investors. He was sentenced to 150 years in prison in 2009 and died in 2021.[28]

More recently, there's Sam Bankman-Fried, the founder of the now defunct cryptocurrency FTX. He was sentenced to 25 years in prison in March 2024 for fraud and money laundering. He was one of the top 50 richest people in the world before his demise. The court ordered him to forfeit $11 billion.[29]

I just read an article in June 2024 that the US DOJ has charged almost 200 people with stealing $2.7 billion in a variety of health care fraud schemes.[30]

This is happening all over the world. Let's look at Israel. In 2019, Simon Leviev was sentenced to prison for stealing an estimated $800 million from people in a Ponzi scheme.[31] In August 2023 in Israel, Moshe Hogeg was accused of defrauding crypto investors of $290 million.[32]

Now, what's being labeled as the "biggest fraud in a generation" is the theft of at least $300 billion from the US government (so us taxpayers) that was meant to help businesses and the unemployed during Covid. That would make it the largest fraud in US history.[33]

Technology is enabling a lot of this theft today. There's malware and spyware that can infect your computer or phone and enable criminals to access sensitive info like credit card details or passwords. And there are credit card skimmers that get installed on credit card machines, at gas pumps for example. Who can forget data breaches? I'm constantly getting notified from companies about these today. I think we're all going to end up with free credit protection for life as a result. AI algorithms can be used to crack passwords. The internet is full of how-to-videos for these things. Social media can easily be used to organize a smash and grab.

According to Cybersecurity Ventures, the global annual cost of cybercrime is estimated to reach $9.5 trillion in 2024, and $10.5 trillion in 2025.[34]

Additional Scriptures: 1 Corinthians 6:9-10. Daniel 11:24-43. Deuteronomy 28:15-68. Exodus 20:15. Hosea 4:1-2. James 5:1-6. John 10:10; 12:1-6. Luke 20:45-47. Matthew 6:19-21; 21:12-13. Micah 2:1-3.

#47 – DESTRUCTION OF WEALTH

Anti | DD | Earth | **Gov** | Israel | Jesus | **Leader** | Sky | Society | **Tech** | **Trib**

"This vision is for a future time. It describes the end, and it will be fulfilled. If it seems slow in coming, wait patiently, for it will surely take place. It will not be delayed. ... Has not the LORD of Heaven's Armies promised that the wealth of nations will turn to ashes? They work so hard, but all in vain!" (Habakkuk 2:3, 13 NLT)

God is speaking to the prophet Habakkuk in the verses above. We learn that in the end times, that God will turn the "wealth of nations" into ashes. This will ultimately be fulfilled during the tribulation period when God brings judgment upon the entire world. It culminates in the destruction of Babylon, the center of wealth, and where all the kings live in luxury.

Fulfillment - What happens when a government makes it more and more expensive for a company to do business, either through regulations, taxes, minimum wage laws, or monetary policy? Well, the company has a few options. It could increase prices they charge customers, reduce their cost of goods sold, or move to a location that doesn't have the government burdens. They often do a combination of those.

In order to lower the cost of goods sold, a company needs to reduce the cost of labor, sourcing materials, or production. They can't pay employees less because they actually have to pay them more when the minimum wage is increased. They could try to source cheaper materials, but inflation makes that difficult.

So, they invest what they can into production efficiencies. That means more tech and automation. And they automate the labor. They lay off the more expensive, more experienced employees and hire minimum wage folks. Or they shift the labor to a cheaper location. This is why you're encouraged to order your fast food in the mobile app, and you often talk to someone across the globe when you call a customer service number. These government burdens always impact the labor workforce the most.

Since 2000, it's estimated that 1.7 million global manufacturing jobs have been lost to industrial robots. It's estimated that automation could impact as much as 33% of the world workforce by 2030.[35]

On top of these government burdens, the world was hit with Covid in 2020. That just compounded the urgency for companies to replace their labor force with something that's not impacted by a human virus and can't infect anyone with one either, a machine.

As prices rise, there's a continued demand for higher wages. As prices rise, the government needs more income, which means more taxes. This death spiral, as a I call it, never ends. The cure to this destruction of wealth and the fall of a nation is less government burden. That means less taxes, less regulation, a smaller government workforce, a smaller government budget, and reduced inflation because the government stops printing money. It's not going to happen today. These things are unacceptable to a bloated greedy government that only cares about its own survival.

Today Is Different - I'd like you to consider how much Covid destroyed global wealth when companies and countries completely shut down. Think of all the businesses that didn't reopen and all the people who lost their jobs. It completely changed how people shop today too. In my city, you couldn't dine in a restaurant anywhere. So, there was no longer a need for wait staff or as many cashiers. Today, many restaurants in my city are still just drive-thru or delivery.

Inflation is a destroyer of wealth, and today, it's wreaking havoc. Back in 1938, the real wage in the US was $0.25. Adjusted for 2023 inflation, it would be $5.34. Fast forward to 1970, where the real wage was $1.60, and inflation adjusted was $12.61. I bet you see where this is going now. That's right, that $12.61 from 1970 is higher than the federal minimum wage today. In 2023 the wage was $7.25. In the US, we've seen a 42% reduction in what a minimum wage is really worth in the past 53 years.[36]

A TikTok user's recent post about inflation went viral. He purchased 45 items from his local Walmart in 2022 that cost $126. In 2024 those same items now cost $414. That's over three times as expensive as just two years ago![37] We're all feeling the sting of inflation today.

What do you do when you can't afford something? You get a loan for it. The government does the same thing. The US national debt as of July 23, 2024 is $34.9 trillion.[38] The US population is about 342 million.[39] That means each of us Americans is on the hook for $102,000 in government debt.[40] Yikes!

If that's not bad enough, what makes it even worse is how much it costs to service that debt. You know that when you have a loan, which is debt, you have to pay interest on it. Well, so does the government. Other countries, investors, and people own the US government debt. In return, they receive interest payments from the US. When interest rates rise, so does the amount the US government owes. This is the mother of national wealth destroyers.

I read an article on *Zero Hedge* earlier this year that illustrated this nicely. In Q4 2023 the US GDP increased $334 billion, so the economy grew. That's good. What's really bad is that the US spent $834 billion to achieve that! It cost $2.5 in debt to grow $1 in GDP.[41] The US cannot sustain this fiscal insanity.

Unfortunately, this is a global problem. At the end of 2022, Japan had the highest debt to GDP ratio of 261%. That's on par with the US in Q4 2023. There are 11 countries with ratios over 100%. That means they spend more in debt than their economy generates in growth. Israel is surprising spending less, with a ratio of 61%. The US was only at 121% in 2022.[42]

Additional Scriptures: Amos 3:15; 6:1-8. Deuteronomy 28:15-68. Isaiah 3:18-24. James 5:1-6. Revelation 6:1-8; 8:9; 13:16-17; 18.

#48 - WEALTH GAP

Anti | DD | Earth | **Gov** | Israel | Jesus | **Leader** | Sky | Society | **Tech** | **Trib**

> When the Lamb broke the third seal, I heard the third living being say, "Come!" I looked up and saw a black horse, and its rider was holding a pair of scales in his hand. And I heard a voice from among the four living beings say, "A loaf of wheat bread or three loaves of barley will cost a day's pay. And don't waste the olive oil and wine." (Revelation 6:5-6 NLT)

During the tribulation period, we're told that it'll take an entire day's wage to buy a loaf of bread. Yet, we also know that there will be plenty of people living a life of luxury in Babylon. Even the merchants of the earth are going to get rich because of Babylon's desires.

In the Old Testament, we're told that one of Sodom's sins was that the people were gluttonous and refused to help the poor and needy because they were lazy. And just like in Sodom's day, there will be a considerable wealth gap between the rich and poor when judgment comes.

Fulfillment - Let's look at the wealth gap in America. The top 1% of wealthy households held 31% of the nation's wealth in 2023, up from 23% in 1990. Expanded to the top 10%, they accounted for 67% of the nation's wealth in 2023, up from 60% in 1990. The top 10% own more than the bottom 90% combined. The rich are getting richer.

What about everyone else? The middle class (in the 50-90% wealth bracket) had 36% of the nation's wealth in 1990, and in 2023 it was down to only 31%. The bottom 50% are also down, from 4% of America's wealth in 1990 to 3% in 2023. Everyone else is getting poorer.[43]

It's the same story when we look at Israel. In 2022, the richest 10% owned 63% of the wealth, up from 61% in 1995. However, when we look at the worldwide figure, it's been pretty steady since 2002. The richest 10% on the planet owned 77% of the wealth in 2022.[44]

How did we get here? Executive salaries are a big reason; that's who's in the top 10%. We'll discuss that below, in Today Is Different.

I also believe science and technology have a big part to play in this wealth gap. Today, the highest paid jobs are all in the medical field. If you exclude that industry, then it's Finance and Technology, particularly big data, software engineering, and AI. They're all dependent upon a higher education or years of experience. Advancements in automation technology in particular are displacing less-educated workers. Just consider how fewer cashiers there are today in stores and fast food because of self-checkout technology. Or how fewer telephone customer service reps there are because we now chat with an AI bot first.

It also used to be that you had to actually work in order to earn a living. Well, today your money can work for you through investments and passive income. Those income streams aren't easily accessible to the lower income brackets, but they account for a large portion of the richest people's income.

If you're interested in examining the effects of inflation, refer to Sign #47 - Destruction of Wealth.

Today Is Different - Have you ever heard of a salary cap? Limiting how much money a person can make? In the context of US sports teams, sure. What about one imposed by a government that applies to CEOs? Neither had I, until recently. Turns out Israel's parliament passed a law in 2016 that limits the top executive gross salary to 35 times the gross salary of the lowest-paid worker in the company. Failure to comply results in higher taxes for the company. Back in 2016 the minimum wage in Israel was $1,215 gross. So, it limited executive pay to $510,000 gross. What's odd is that this law was only for the financial sector, so banks.[45]

The CEO-to-worker pay ratio and this salary cap business are what make today unique. Evaluating the largest 350 publicly owned companies in America between 1965 and 2022, the CEO-to-worker pay ratio increased a whopping 1,588%! Back in 1965, a CEO at one of these large companies made 20 times more than the average salary of a nonsupervisory employee. In 2022, the CEOs are making 344 times as much![46]

I know you're wondering which companies in America have the highest ratios. Browsing companies in the S&P 500, Coca Cola is one of the highest at 1,883 with the median worker earning $12,122. Apple is at 1,771 with the median employee making $84,493. Walmart has a CEO-to-employee pay ratio of 933, with the median worker earning $27,136. This one's crazy, Alphabet is at 808 with the median employee earning $279,802.[47]

Guess what got introduced to the US Senate in January 2024? The Tax Excessive CEO Pay Act. It would raise taxes on companies that have a CEO-to-worker pay ratio higher than 50.[48]

Additional Scriptures: Ezekiel 16:49-50; 22:12. Genesis 47:13-26. Jeremiah 5:27-28. Nehemiah 5:1-13. Revelation 8:8-9; 18.

#49 - THE RISE OF BABYLON

Anti | DD | **Earth** | **Gov** | Israel | Jesus | Leader | Sky | **Society** | **Tech** | **Trib**

> He cried with a mighty voice, saying, "Fallen, fallen is Babylon the great. ... The merchants of the earth grew rich from the abundance of her luxury. ... For she says in her heart, 'I sit a queen, and am no widow, and will in no way see mourning.' ... merchandise of gold, silver, precious stones, pearls, fine linen, purple, silk, scarlet, all expensive wood, every vessel of ivory, every vessel made of most precious wood, and of brass, and iron, and marble; and cinnamon, incense, perfume, frankincense, wine, olive oil, fine flour, wheat, cattle, sheep, horses, chariots, and people's bodies and souls. ... 'the great city, she who was dressed in fine linen, purple, and scarlet, and decked with gold and precious stones and pearls! ... the great city, in which all who had their ships in the sea were made rich by reason of her great wealth!' ... for your merchants were the princes of the earth."
> (Revelation 18:2-3, 7, 12-13, 16, 19, 23)

There's much confusion about the Babylon of the end times. That's because it refers to a literal city and a religion. The Babylon religion, the mother of harlots, will be discussed in Sign #69 - One World Religion. Another reason it's confusing is because the harlot is pictured riding the Beast, which is the Antichrist. So, the one world religion will be intertwined with the political rule of the tribulation period. Refer to Sign #110 - The Antichrist Rules The World, for discussion about that.

In the verses above, we read the description of the city of Babylon which will be prominent during the tribulation period. As you can see, the city is wealthy, and many merchants become rich as a result. When reading the additional Scriptures below, you'll also discover the city is full of people from all nations and tongues. It's the mightiest hammer of the earth. And it's the "hindermost" of nations which means it comes into existence in the end times.

There's also a reference to the city being on seven hills. Now, before you start speculating where this city is located, we're told that those hills refer to kings. So, that's just another reference to the political aspect of Babylon.

You're probably wondering, is this the ancient Babylon that took the Israelites captive? Perhaps. There are many prophecies in the Bible regarding the utter destruction of Babylon in a single day that will render it uninhabitable forever. That hasn't happened yet. Ancient Babylon certainly diminished, but people still live there today. So, God still needs to fulfill that prophecy against ancient Babylon. But it doesn't mean ancient Babylon has to be revived during the tribulation. It might be, but it doesn't have to be.

In Revelation 17:5, Babylon is also referred to as "Mystery." That descriptor is there for a reason. It might mean the tribulation period Babylon will be a mystery until that point in time. The world is going to be in chaos right after the rapture. It's hard to say which cities could emerge as the world economic centers. In either case, Babylon and Mystery Babylon will meet their demise before Jesus's second coming.

Fulfillment -If ancient Babylon isn't Mystery Babylon, there are certainly other contenders across the world, assuming they survive the rapture. The cities where the wealthiest people today live include New York City, Tokyo, San Francisco Bay, London, and Singapore.[49] If we're looking at the most futuristic smart cities, those are London, Zurich, Taipei City, New York City, and Barcelona.[50]

Countries are even starting to invest in developing and building futuristic cities. Consider the project Saudi Arabia started in 2017, The Line. They envision a 106-mile-long smart city with mirrored walls that make it seemingly blend in with the natural landscape. They aim to have 1.5 miles complete by 2030.[51] In 2022, the World Economic Forum unveiled the world's first prototype for a floating city that can adapt to rising sea levels.[52]

The world certainly has a lot of cities today that you could argue rival Babylon's past glory.

Today Is Different - Could ancient Babylon rise again? Saddam Hussein started rebuilding the ancient city of Babylon in the 1970s. It's in modern-day Iraq. In the 2000s, The World Monuments Fund began working with Iraq on conservation efforts. In July 2019, Babylon was named a UNESCO World Heritage Site.[53]

This city has been growing too. In 1997, only 592,000 people lived there. Today its population is close to 2 million.[54] Babylon isn't far from Baghdad, about 55 miles (85 kilometers) south. Baghdad is the capital of Iraq and home to 7 million people, and also the largest city in Iraq.[55] There's certainly a lot of people living in and near Babylon today.

Did you know that the world's largest embassy is located in Baghdad? It's the US embassy, which sits on 104 acres and opened in 2009. At its peak, there were 16,000 staff members there.[56] I think it's fascinating that the US chose a location so close to ancient Babylon to build its biggest embassy. Could this be the future home of the kings of the world?

Additional Scriptures: 2 Kings 20:12-19; 24:1-16; 25:1-21. Daniel 2:28-38. Ezekiel 29:19. Isaiah 13:19-20; 47:1, 8. Jeremiah 50:12, 23, 31, 42; 51:13, 33, 41, 44-45. Revelation 14:8; 17; 18:8. Zechariah 2:7.

#50- POLAR OPPOSITE - A SERVING HEART

Anti | DD | Earth | Gov | Israel | **Jesus** | **Leader** | Sky | **Society** | **Tech** | Trib

> "He who overcomes shall inherit all things, and I will be his God and he shall be My son." (Revelation 21:7 NKJV)

Throughout this chapter we've looked at signs related to a coveting heart. This sign is what I call a polar opposite. It's meant to illustrate how far away we currently are from the life we believers are going to live during Jesus's reign on earth in the millennial kingdom. Recall from Sign #6 - The Point Of No Return, that God only lets evil progress so far before he intervenes.

In the Scripture above, we learn that those who overcome "inherit all things" from God. To overcome means to put your faith in Jesus for salvation. Refer to the letters to the seven churches in Revelation 2-3. It applies to people who live either before or during the tribulation period. We're all going to live together during Jesus's millennial reign on earth. At that time, everyone's desire to covet will disappear because we'll all have everything that we need and want. And our work won't be in vain during Jesus's reign. We'll actually enjoy what we do, benefit from the fruit of our labor, and no one will steal our stuff.

Everyone will have a serving heart, one that desires to bring glory to God using whatever skills and resources they have.

> Now, Israel, what does the LORD your God require of you, but to fear the LORD your God, to walk in all his ways, to love him, and to **serve the LORD your God with all your heart** and with all your soul (Deuteronomy 10:12)

Fulfillment - So, how far away are we? Well, I wouldn't say that we're a society of people who are storing our treasure in heaven. Would you? We just keep buying bigger purses, bigger cars, bigger storage units, and even bigger houses to hold all of the stuff we're accumulating here on planet earth.

A fun way to consider just how opposite we are is to contemplate what the worst-case scenarios might look like and see just how close we are to them.

Worst case, nobody owns anything because they can't afford it or someone just steals it. This one depends on where you currently live. I've seen news reports that people in San Francisco, CA just leave their vehicle windows down and trunk open so that thieves know there isn't anything inside to steal. Most places are still far from this scenario though. We're not at this worst case yet.

Worst case, there's no point to passwords because cybercriminals are able to hack even the most complex ones with quantum computing and AI. With all the data breaches happening and the push to using biometric security and two-factor authentication methods, this one is close to reality. We're almost at this worst case. This one also reveals how near the mark of the Beast system is. Refer to Sign #72 - Mark Of The Beast.

Worst case, we become a society of pleasure-loving homebodies who do everything, including occasionally working, from the comfort of the sofa. Okay, be honest. Does this describe you? This wasn't really a widespread lifestyle until Covid, and now it's really prevalent. Large companies are still having a difficult time getting people to return to the office. We're close to this worst case.

Worst case, we think we're entitled to a reward just for showing up. Yikes! This is our society in so many ways today. Kids get participation awards for all sorts of things. How many of us expect to get a pay raise at work every year? I think we're close to the worst case on this one too.

Today Is Different - So, what do you think? Is today different? Do we as a society have a coveting heart that needs and wants and takes some more? Do you think we've reached the point of no return? How many people really have a serving heart and are sacrificing their time, talent, and money for the Lord?

Additional Scriptures: Isaiah 65:22-23. Matthew 6:19-21. Revelation 2-3; 22:3.

CHAPTER 9 - A DECEIVING HEART

> Then the LORD said to me, "The prophets prophesy lies in my name. I didn't send them. I didn't command them. I didn't speak to them. They prophesy to you a lying vision, divination, and a thing of nothing, and the **deceit of their own heart**." (Jeremiah 14:14)

#51 - DECEPTION

Anti | DD | Earth | Gov | Israel | **Jesus** | **Leader** | Sky | **Society** | **Tech** | **Trib**

> Now as He sat on the Mount of Olives, the disciples came to Him privately, saying, "Tell us, when will these things be? And what [will be] the sign of Your coming, and of the end of the age?" And Jesus answered and said to them: "Take heed that no one deceives you." (Matthew 24:3-4 NKJV)

The first sign that Jesus gave regarding his second coming is deception. I wonder if that's because the very first sin by mankind was the result of being deceived. Satan, the deceiver of the whole world, flat out lied to Eve when he told her that she wouldn't die if she ate from the Tree of the Knowledge of Good and Evil. Eve believed his lie.

Deception means to be led astray, to be led into error, or be seduced. As you learned above, you can be the giver or receiver of a lie. This is the ninth of the Ten Commandments, don't lie.

The tribulation period is going to be full of deception. We're told the Antichrist will use Satan's lying powers to make everyone believe a lie. We're going to look at those powers in Sign #63 - Lying Wonders and consider what the lie could be in Sign #61 - The Lie. We're also informed that Babylon will deceive all the nations through its sorcery. You can read more about that particular deception in Sign #75 - Drugs And Alcohol.

Fulfillment - Would you say that we live in a world of truth? Where employees, kids, politicians, and leaders never tell lies and always do what they say they're going to do? Absolutely not! It's obvious that we live in a world full of deception and lies. It's difficult to find the truth about anything today. Just do an internet search on any topic. You'll find conflicting information on it, guaranteed. It's because people, businesses, and governments are motivated by money and power, and most are willing to lie to achieve those.

Other than in politics, one of the biggest deceptions being committed today is the green climate agenda. The world is trying to get everyone to worship God's creation instead of God himself. There's ample evidence the climate data is being manipulated to tell whatever story suits the moment.[1] If you look at the earth's temperature data and CO2 levels over a long period of time, you'll see that the two are not correlated. Sometimes the CO2 is low when the temperature is high and vice versa. The earth might be warming, but it's not likely that CO2 is causing it.[2] God is perfectly in control of his creation.[3] In Chapters 15 and 16 we'll look at the supernatural signs on the earth and in the heavens.

Today Is Different - I just read an article in May 2024 that said Wiley, a publisher of science journals, retracted 11,000 peer reviewed papers that were published because they determined they were fake. It seems as though AI was used to make them look original by just changing up the wording and making stuff up. They decided to shut down 19 publications as a result of this fraud.[4]

That's one thing that makes today so much different. Technology is being used to create and proliferate deception today, whether it's AI generating content, deep fake videos, or enemy states flooding social media with misinformation. The World Economic Forum's Global Risks Report for 2024 names AI generated misinformation and disinformation as the #2 global risk, behind of course what I already mentioned earlier, extreme weather.[5]

AI systems are programmed by humans, so it's no surprise they aren't perfect truth tellers. A ChatGPT-4 chatbot recently tricked a real human into thinking it was a visually impaired human and got help solving a CAPTCHA. Meta's CICERO AI was designed to play the board game *Diplomacy*, which is about world domination. Meta trained it to be helpful and honest. Well, despite that, CICERO was an expert liar and betrayed other players.[6]

Another thing that makes today unprecedented is the blatant lie regarding US President Joe Biden's mental acuity and physical fitness that's been forced upon the entire world for years. Finally in the summer of 2024, politicians, journalists, and celebrities are confessing to covering this up. It forced President Biden to drop out of the 2024 US presidential race. The fact that they were able to get away with this for so long reveals how large-scale deception has become the norm in society.

You know, I read a book that sheds some light on this. It's *How Evil Works* by David Kupelian. In his book, he states that society is more likely to believe a big lie than a small one. That's because we ourselves wouldn't dream of fabricating and spreading a whopper for fear of being quickly found out. So, we don't consider that anyone else would either. Big lies were one of Hitler's strategies.

<u>Additional Scriptures:</u> 1 Timothy 4:1-2. 2 John 1:7. 2 Thessalonians 2:9-12. 2 Timothy 3:13. Ephesians 5:6. Exodus 20:16. Genesis 3:1-13. Hosea 4:1-2. Jeremiah 9:3-6. Revelation 3:9; 12:9; 18:23; 21:8; 22:15. Romans 1:29, 31; 3:13. Zephaniah 1:7-9.

#52 - SLANDER

Anti | DD | Earth | Gov | Israel | **Jesus** | **Leader** | Sky | **Society** | Tech | **Trib**

> But know this: that in the last days, grievous times will come. For men will be ... slanderers. (2 Timothy 3:1-3)

The apostle Paul tells his disciple Timothy that one of the signs of the last days is slander. The word *slander* comes from the Greek word *diabolos* and means to falsely accuse, or to side with the devil. Jesus warned about this behavior. He told us believers that we're to consider it a blessing when people say evil things against us. It's because that means our reward in heaven is great.

This will be the last sin that many people living in the tribulation period commit before the second coming of Jesus. You see, the unbelieving world is going to gather to war against Jesus. They'll be taking the side of the devil, believing Satan's lie that they'll be able to conquer God himself. For more on that refer to Sign #116 - Gathered To Armageddon.

Fulfillment - You may recall during the 2016 US Presidential Election that Hillary Clinton infamously referred to Donald Trump's supporters as "a basket of deplorables." [7] Now, it's common for candidates to slander each other, but this seemed like a moment the tide changed and crossed the line. It suddenly became acceptable to slander the voters, a population of people they were seeking to lead.

And now it's infected society. Consider all the news anchors and celebrities that resort to name calling. They don't care that they're insulting potentially half their audience.

Today, anyone who disagrees with someone else is at a minimum labeled a racist, a bigot, or a sexist. Christians, evangelicals in particular, are now labeled as right wing or extremists. It's even reached the point that people are saying those who disagree with them don't deserve to live.

Today Is Different - The biggest example that comes to mind that reveals why today is different is the volume of false accusations that keep coming against President Donald Trump. The Russia collusion hoax is being named the "worst political scandal in American history."[8] Some of the things he's been accused of include tax evasion, sex scandals, valuing property incorrectly, keeping classified records, election interference, and causing an insurrection. Remember what I said in the prior sign about big lies? A big lie, regardless of how unbelievable, will sow seeds of doubt.

The other example which makes today different is the increased volume of slander against Israel from what used to be its closest ally, America. Consider all the protests that are happening across the country, at the capital, and on college campuses. The protesters say Israel is a terrorist, apartheid, and they chant anti-Semitic slogans all while siding with terrorists, the devil.

Additional Scriptures: 1 Peter 2:12; 3:15-16. Ezekiel 36:1-7. Jeremiah 9:3-6. Luke 23:2, 10. Mark 3:2; 14:55-59. Matthew 5:11. Proverbs 6:16-19. Revelation 12:10; 19:19-21. Romans 1:29-30.

#53 - CONSPIRACY

<u>Anti</u> | DD | Earth | <u>Gov</u> | Israel | <u>Jesus</u> | <u>Leader</u> | Sky | <u>Society</u> | Tech | <u>Trib</u>

> 'For among My people are found wicked [men]; They lie in wait as one who sets snares; They set a trap; They catch men. As a cage is full of birds, So their houses [are] full of deceit. Therefore they have become great and grown rich. They have grown fat, they are sleek; Yes, they surpass the deeds of the wicked; They do not plead the cause, The cause of the fatherless; Yet they prosper, And the right of the needy they do not defend. Shall I not punish [them] for these [things]?' says the LORD. 'Shall I not avenge Myself on such a nation as this?' (Jeremiah 5:26-29 NKJV)

God is speaking to the prophet Jeremiah in the Scripture above. This is just prior to the Israelites being taken captive by Babylon. A few verses prior, God states that when the people ask why judgments have come against them, that this is one of the reasons. We're told the people "lie in wait" to set snares that "catch men." They're conspiring to do something sinful, deceitful, unrighteous.

Jesus told us about the conspiracy against him that would lead to his betrayal, false accusations, and his crucifixion. He also told us that many people would seek to betray believers in the time before his second coming. We're going to explore that in Sign #91 - Betrayal.

In the tribulation period, some interesting events will take place in the realm of conspiracy. Satan, the Antichrist, and the False Prophet will all be working together to deceive the world and obtain its worship. The kings of the earth will also conspire with the Antichrist and rise up against the Babylon religion. Check out Sign #69 - One World Religion to see how that plays out.

Fulfillment - With the increased difficulty of parsing fact from fiction these days, conspiracy theories abound. That in itself is fulfillment of this sign. Let's consider some of the key conspiracies being discussed today. Of course there's the Trump-Russia collusion hoax. There's the protest that happened on January 6, 2021 at the US Capital building. The CIA spying on political candidates and Americans. Chemtrails. The US government colluding with big tech to censor social media information and interfere in elections. The US botched withdrawal from Afghanistan that gave a lot of modern weapons to terrorists. Holocaust denial. The 2020 US Presidential Election. The Roswell UFO crash. Did the Israeli or US government know about the October 7, 2023 attack in advance? The US giving billions of dollars to Iran. Large nations interfering in political and economic ways in foreign countries. What's really going on between Russia, Ukraine, and the US?

Today Is Different - I mentioned this in Sign #51 - Deception, but it fits here too. The conspiracy to cover up US President Joe Biden's mental acuity and physical fitness. Just think of how many people chose not to speak up until summer of 2024. What would prevent them from doing so?

Do you remember the Nordstream pipeline explosion in 2022? Who blew it up is still a looming question today. Russia owns these pipelines that supply gas to Germany. I think this one is a big deal because one theory is that the US did it to pressure Germany into entering the Russia-Ukraine War. Any nation committing an act of terrorism against an ally would make today different.

As I'm writing this chapter, another important conspiracy has surfaced. The attempted assassination of President Trump in July 2024. There were security failures on an epic scale. It's hard to fathom it was all due to incompetence. Rally attendees are speaking out about what they saw and reported. Their testimony makes a case that it was obvious the shooter was there. So, now people are rightfully asking a lot of questions. If it turns out the US government was involved in an assassination attempt on one of its own, on someone they vowed to protect, I think you'll agree that puts us at a whole new level of evil deception.

Covid is the number one reason today is different. It's still not clear what really happened. I doubt we'll ever know. This was a global conspiracy that impacted everyone on earth. It seems it was bioengineered in a lab in China. Was it released on purpose? If so, who did it and why? Were all the deaths they reported legitimate? You may recall that hospitals in the US got extra money from the government when they reported a Covid case or death. That certainly wouldn't influence any bad behavior, would it? There were lots of independent reports of empty hospitals in the US when the media was telling us they were overwhelmed with patients. How'd the pharmaceuticals create the vaccines so quickly? Some journalists are reporting they had patents on them prior to Covid. Was anyone paid to endorse the vaccine? Just consider that the pharmaceutical industry is huge and global, lobbies governments for favorable policies, supports political parties and candidates, and is a key advertiser in all forms of media. I could go on and on, but I'm sure you get the point.

Additional Scriptures: 1 Kings 21:1-16. 2 Chronicles 24:20-21. Acts 23:11-35. Ezekiel 22:25. Genesis 37:17-18. Jeremiah 5:26-29. Mark 14:55-59. Matthew 17:22-23; 20:18; 24:10; 26:1-5, 59-60. Nehemiah 4:7-8. Psalm 64:1-6; 83. Revelation 13; 17.

#54 - BLASPHEMY

Anti | **DD** | Earth | Gov | Israel | **Jesus** | **Leader** | Sky | **Society** | Tech | **Trib**

> But know this: that in the last days, grievous times will come. For men will be … blasphemers. (2 Timothy 3:1-2)

Here, we're told that one of the signs of the days before Jesus's second coming is blasphemers. It means to speak evil, particularly against God. You know, Jesus was accused of blasphemy when he forgave sins, cast out demons, and said he was the Christ. A false blasphemy charge is why Jesus was condemned to crucifixion by the Jewish religious leaders.

Because the religious leaders refused to believe he was God, some of them reasoned that Jesus performed his miracles by Satan's power. Well, Jesus informed his accusers that Satan isn't casting out demons because a divided house cannot stand, thus Satan's house isn't divided.

Jesus warned us in the Olivet Discourse that many people would come in his name, essentially professing to be God, and deceive. During the tribulation period, a ruler will arise that will indeed speak many words of blasphemy against God. It's the Antichrist, and he'll commit that ultimate blasphemy when he states that he is God. We'll look at him in detail in Sign #60 - The Antichrist.

The Antichrist won't be the only one committing blasphemy at that time. During the judgments that come upon the earth, unbelievers will continually curse the name of God.

Fulfillment - Lies about God, Jesus, the Bible, and biblical truths are not new. The New Testament documents many struggles the early church had with false doctrine. Let's consider what's prevalent in society today though.

The lies about God state that God is a female, all loving and won't judge sin, is a queer, is a liberal, is vengeful, and is absent. In regard to Jesus, the blasphemy is similar. People state Jesus isn't God, is a liberal, is gay, was married, wasn't resurrected, would be pro-abortion, was a trans, and sinned. What's most concerning is how Satan and the fallen angels are now being regarded as cool, misunderstood, sexy, and even the real truth bearers.

We've talked about Christian deconstructionism and picking apart the Bible in other signs throughout this book. Some believe the Bible isn't authored by God but was written by flawed men who had an agenda. Just like with the early church, there are many evils spoken of in regard to biblical teaching. Many people today think it's okay to be a Christian and pro-abortion, or a Christian and anti-Semitic, or a Christian living a life of sin.

Today Is Different - The most prominent religious leader on earth is known for blasphemous speaking. That's right, it's the pope. Here's one of his latest statements. In January 2024, Pope Francis said, "What I am going to say is not a dogma of faith but my own personal view: I like to think of hell as empty; I hope it is."[9] Well, if the pope knew and believed the Bible, he would have stated that the Bible tells us that hell has a wide gate, a broad road, and that many go that way. The problem with an empty hell is that it implies God isn't just. That God doesn't punish or reward people.

Something else that makes today different is the volume of large religions, and the unaffiliated, who blaspheme Jesus. Islam accounts for 25% of the global population.[10] We don't notice this as much in America, but let that sink in for a minute. One out of every four people is a Muslim. They believe Jesus was only a prophet (lower than Mohammed), didn't die on a cross, and isn't God or the son of God. At the second coming, they believe Jesus will return as a follower of Mohammed and revive Islam.[11]

The unaffiliated group is next, representing 16% of the world population.[12] These are the atheists and agnostics, so they are obviously blasphemous regarding God, Jesus, and the Bible. Hindu accounts for 15%.[13] They worship many gods and thus consider Jesus one of the many. But they blaspheme the existence of sin and that Jesus died for our sin.[14] Then the Buddhist religion has 7% of the population.[15] In similar fashion to the unaffiliated, they don't believe in a personal God or believe God's existence doesn't matter. They believe Jesus was a good teacher but consider Buddha more important.[16]

Just looking at those religious groups and the unaffiliated, we're at 63% of the worldwide population believing and speaking blasphemous things against the God of the Bible. However, I think the most dangerous and blasphemous religion today is new age. Think of it as a buffet of beliefs, where people pick and choose what suits them. Most followers are influenced by the Eastern religions of Hinduism and Buddhism, but it also includes the occult. Christ consciousness is popular in the new age community. It's a belief that every person can achieve the divine state and become the Christ.

<u>Additional Scriptures:</u> 2 Thessalonians 2:3-4. Colossians 3:5-8. Daniel 7:8, 11, 25; 11:36-37. John 8:48-59. Luke 5:17-26; 11:14-23; 22:63-65; 23:35-39. Mark 14:60-64. Matthew 7:13, 24:5. Revelation 13:5-6; 16:9, 11, 21; 17:3.

#55 - ASSAULT ON THE AFTERLIFE

Anti | DD | Earth | Gov | Israel | **Jesus** | **Leader** | Sky | **Society** | **Tech** | **Trib**

> They worshiped the dragon because he gave his authority to the beast; and they worshiped the beast, saying, "Who is like the beast? Who is able to make war with him?" ... He opened his mouth for blasphemy against God, to blaspheme his name, his dwelling, and those who dwell in heaven. (Revelation 13:4, 6)

In the Scripture above, we read about an event that happens during the tribulation period. The Dragon is Satan, and the Beast is the Antichrist. We learn the Antichrist will speak against God, God's name (Jesus), God's dwelling place (heaven), and those who dwell in heaven (holy angels, dead believers, raptured believers).

Jesus spoke about one aspect of this particular blasphemy when he taught about the resurrection. Some of the religious leaders during Jesus's first coming didn't believe in a resurrection of the dead. So, they questioned Jesus about it. Jesus taught that he was the resurrection, proved it by raising people from the dead (like Lazarus and himself), and clarified that God is the God of the living.

There's a lot that can be revealed and discussed in the verses above. I titled this sign *Assault On The Afterlife*, after my book by the same title. In the book, I unpack Revelation 13:6 in detail and reveal all sorts of ways it's seeing fulfillment today. A day is coming in which the Antichrist will assault every aspect of the afterlife that God has promised to believers.

Fulfillment - A popular lie today regarding the afterlife is that it doesn't exist. John Lennon's song "Imagine" encourages listeners to imagine there's no heaven, no hell below, and people only living for today.[17] Perhaps you've even sung along to it, not really contemplating what you're saying. It came out in the 1970s and is regarded as one of the most popular songs of all time. For some reason, they like to play it at the Olympics.

There's the lie that heaven is boring and bureaucratic. The TV show *Good Omens* takes advantage of this myth. On the opposite spectrum there's the deception that Satan isn't really evil, but fun. This rebranding of Satan is evidenced in the popular Netflix show *Lucifer*, which depicts him abandoning his boring life in hell to run a nightclub in LA, solve crimes, and sleep around.

There are many who believe that heaven and hell aren't real physical places, but instead are just states of mind or spiritual concepts. Deepak Chopra is a famous proponent of this assault on the afterlife. Here's what he stated in an article from May 2024, "Where do we go after we die? Nowhere in physical terms. ... I realize that making existence the same as consciousness sounds alien."[18] Guess who else is in this camp? Yes, it's the pope. In an interview in May 2023, Pope Francis stated: "Hell is not a place. ... Hell is a state, there are people who live in Hell continuously."[19]

We should also consider the lies about those who dwell in heaven. Do you know anyone who thinks they can communicate with a dead loved one? There are people who make a living from this. Psychics and mediums prey on people in a state of grief. TV shows and movies popularize Ouija boards today. God forbids this behavior for a very good reason. He doesn't want us talking to demons.

Today Is Different - Scientists of today believe they've figured out how to live forever without the help of God and his offer of salvation. Futurist, Ray Kurzweil, predicted that humans would achieve immortality by 2030 because the singularity would enable it.[20] The singularity is a time in which technology grows and self improves to a point in which its intelligence far surpasses humans. They believe humanity would then merge with machines. Transhumans, part human and part machine, would have bodies full of nanobots that travel around repairing cells and eliminating aging. They believe we'd eventually evolve into posthumans who would have no need of a body but would live forever in the "cloud" after our brain is uploaded. There's even a popular TV show about this called *Upload*.

Perhaps you think this is a bunch of hogwash. Well, the billionaires on the planet (like Jeff Bezos, Elon Musk, Peter Thiel) are putting their money into this tech. Consider what's being developed: cryonics and freezing people's bodies and brains so they can be thawed and reanimated when we've achieved singularity or cured disease, rejuvenation using stem cells, brain implants like Neuralink, and uploading memories to a computer.[21]

Additional Scriptures: 1 Corinthians 10:14, 20-21; 15:12-58. Deuteronomy 18:10-12, 14. Ezekiel 28:11-19. Genesis 2:16-17; 3:1-6. Isaiah 8:19; 14:12-19. John 2:13-17; 11; 20. Leviticus 19:26, 31. Luke 16:19-24. Matthew 22:23-33. Revelation 12:9; 21.

#56 - FALSE TEACHERS

Anti | DD | Earth | Gov | Israel | **Jesus** | **Leader** | Sky | Society | **Tech** | Trib

> Preach the word; be urgent in season and out of season; reprove, rebuke, and exhort with all patience and teaching. For the time will come when they will not listen to the sound doctrine, but having itching ears, will heap up for themselves teachers after their own lusts, and will turn away their ears from the truth, and turn away to fables. (2 Timothy 4:2-4)

The apostle Paul tells us that the time will come in which teachers will arise who will turn people away from the truth and toward fables. A false teacher doesn't impart truth or wisdom, but, in fact, does the opposite. Jesus spoke about false teachers too when he criticized the religious leaders of his first coming for crushing people with religious demands and ignoring the important aspects of the Law, like faith.

The Bible has a lot to say about false teachers. When you read through the additional Scriptures below, you'll discover that they deny Jesus is Lord, love to brag, indulge in evil pleasures, earn money by doing wrong, listen to the devil's doctrine, cause divisions, and speak evil of the way of truth.

Fulfillment - There are many types of false teachings today. One of the most popular is the prosperity gospel or word-faith movement. It teaches that financial wealth and physical and mental health are always the will of God. They believe poverty is a sin. That you just need to increase your faith, positivity, positive speech, and tithing to reap the benefits.[22] Of course that sounds nice. Who doesn't want to be financially secure and healthy? The problem is that it's not biblical.

Refer back to the Scriptures and discussion from Sign #45 - Love Of Money. Remember that Jesus asked a rich man to sell everything, give it to the poor, and follow him. Jesus's will for that man clearly wasn't financial wealth. As for health, the apostle Paul told us that he begged God to take away his thorn in the flesh that tormented him. God told him that his grace was all he needed, and that his power worked best in our weakness. I mean come on, that's who we consider the super apostle. Yet God's will wasn't physical health for him.

People are buying into this false teaching because of what we discussed in Sign #35, they don't endure sound doctrine. The preachers promoting this are no different than the bad prophet from the Old

Testament, Balaam, who deceived people for money.

Today Is Different - Televangelism and social media are key reasons today is different in regard to false teachers. Both of these modern technologies have enabled the rise of megachurches and celebrity pastors. Unfortunately, some of the most popular pastors today teach the prosperity gospel.

Figure 56.1 displays the social media followers for pastors and teachers who are known for teaching prosperity gospel and word-faith messages.[23] As you can see, Joel Osteen has 27 million followers on Facebook, significantly more than any other celebrity pastor today. He's also the pastor for one of the largest churches in America.

Table 56.1. Social Media Followers July 2024				
Name	Facebook	X	Instagram	YouTube
Joel Osteen	27M	10.1M	5.6M	3.5M
Joyce Meyer	11M	6.3M	4.8M	1.3M
T.D. Jakes	7.1M	4.5M	6M	2.8M
Steven Furtick	6.6M	0.8M	3.8M	3M
Benny Hinn	3.5M	0.8M	1.1M	0.7M
Paula White	3.5M	1.1M	0.6M	0.1M

Figure 56.1. Social Media Followers Of Prosperity Gospel Pastors, July 2024[24]
Source: Compiled from social media data on July 31, 2024

Figure 56.1 doesn't even touch on how many have read one of these people's books. Osteen's most popular video on YouTube has 10 million views.[25] His sermon that changed the way Oprah saw her life, "The Power Of I Am," has over 4 million views.[26] Jakes's most watched has almost as many at 9.7 million views.[27] There's an enormous amount of people who are getting exposed to this false teaching today.

<u>Additional Scriptures:</u> 1 Timothy 6:6-10. 2 Corinthians 11:3-4, 12-15; 12:6-10. 2 Peter 2. 2 Timothy 3:1-7. Galatians 1:6-9; 2:4. Jude 1:4-19. Luke 18:18-24. Matthew 23:1-36. Revelation 2:13-15, 20-24. Romans 16:17-18.

#57 - FALSE PROPHETS

Anti | DD | Earth | Gov | Israel | **Jesus** | **Leader** | Sky | Society | **Tech** | Trib

> As he sat on the Mount of Olives, the disciples came to him privately, saying, "Tell us, when will these things be? What is the sign of your coming, and of the end of the age?" Jesus answered them, ... "Many false prophets will arise and will lead many astray." (Matthew 24:3-4, 11)

Jesus, in the Olivet Discourse, tells us that the prevalence of false prophets will be a sign of his second coming. One of the primary attributes of a false prophet is that they lie and speak about their dreams, not what God told them.

Before the Babylonian invasion of Jerusalem, the false prophets denounced the true message from God delivered through Jeremiah and said no evil would come upon them. In the Bible, they are often compared to the wicked prophet Balaam who taught people to sin by eating food sacrificed to idols, encouraged sexual sin, used divination, and deceived people for money.

We also know that false prophets will pretend to be real followers of Christ because they'll follow in the way of Satan, who transforms himself into a holy angel. We're told that we can test a false prophet by his works and if he believes that Jesus Christ came in the flesh.

The False Prophet will be a key ruler during the tribulation period, and we'll discuss him in the very next sign (Sign #58).

Fulfillment - False prophets are known by their failed predictions. Date setters have been predicting the second coming, the rapture, and apocalyptic events for centuries. There are several Wikipedia pages that try to keep track of them all.[28] Notable ones include: Harold Camping, Jack Van Impe, Edgar Cayce, Jeane Dixon, Ronald Weinland, and Nostradamus.

The year 2000 was particularly active with it being the turn of the century and the whole Y2K message of doom. As was the year 2012 with speculation about the Mayan calendar, planet x colliding with earth, and an alien invasion. These date setters are one of the reasons people are so confused about end times events. It also gives unbelievers a very good reason to think Christianity isn't God's truth.

We're going to look at the timing of the rapture and the second coming in Chapters 17 and 20. Please know that I do not predict a date for either one. But it is obvious that we're certainly living in the season of Jesus's return.

I've mentioned Muslims before. It's worth calling out again because that religion accounts for 25% of the global population.[29] That's 2 billion people following a false prophet, Mohammed. The founders of most religions and cults could be considered false prophets. Like Mohammed, they claim to have received a divine revelation through a dream or an angel.

Today Is Different - I came upon an interesting article in *The New York Times* from February 2021. It's titled "Christian Prophets Are on the Rise. What Happens When They're Wrong?"[30] Being wrong. That is their hallmark.

The journalist explains that most of these self-professed prophets are independent and don't lead churches, but that they have a large following through social media. Many of them gained fame prior to the US 2020 Presidential Election when they were predicting President Trump would win reelection. And as we learned from the Bible, most of them indicate they received their special revelation through a dream.[31]

One of the ways they're able to achieve so much success today is through a popular TV program that started in 1996. You may have guessed it. It's *Sid Roth's It's Supernatural!*[32] Not only is it broadcast on cable networks, but it has over 2 million subscribers on YouTube.[33] Now, not everyone on his show is a false prophet. My point is that today they have a platform and a large audience who wants to hear them, even when they continually make false predictions.

Additional Scriptures: 1 Corinthians 11:3-4, 12-15. 1 John 4:1-3. 2 Corinthians 11:3-4, 12-15. 2 Peter 2. Acts 8:9-24. Ezekiel 13; 22:25-28. Jeremiah 14:13-15, 23:13-17, 25-40; 27:9-10. Joshua 13:22. Jude 1:11. Mark 13:21-23. Matthew 7:15-20. Numbers 24:1; 25:1-3; 31:16. Revelation 2:13-15, 20-24.

#58 - THE FALSE PROPHET

Anti | DD | Earth | Gov | Israel | **Jesus** | **Leader** | Sky | Society | **Tech** | **Trib**

> They worshiped the dragon because he gave his authority to the beast; and they worshiped the beast, saying, "Who is like the beast? Who is able to make war with him?" ... I saw another beast coming up out of the earth. He had two horns like a lamb and it spoke like a dragon. He exercises all

the authority of the first beast in his presence. He makes the earth and those who dwell in it to worship the first beast, whose fatal wound was healed." (Revelation 13:4, 11-12)

In the verses above, the False Prophet is "another beast." Notice that he has the same authority as the "first beast" who is also known as the Antichrist. That means both the False Prophet and the Antichrist derive their power from Satan, the Dragon. This prophet will look like a lamb but will speak like a dragon. That perfectly describes Satan. He'll appear to be a legit prophet of God, but he won't speak God's truth. This event takes place after the rapture and during the tribulation period.

You may recall from the prior sign (Sign #57) that Jesus warned about false prophets who would arise and deceive many people. Jesus spoke of the False Prophet in particular when he stated a false christ and a false prophet would be able to show signs and wonders to deceive. That's a key characteristic of this particular prophet. Using Satan's power, he will be able to perform miracles. We'll look at those in Sign #63 - Lying Wonders.

The False Prophet will be very busy during the tribulation period. He will force people to make an image of the Antichrist (Sign #71), worship both the image and the Antichrist or be killed (Sign #69, #73, #115), receive the mark of the Beast (Sign #72), and he'll be a leader in the war against Jesus at his second coming (Sign #116).

Fulfillment - When many Christians contemplate who could become the leader of the one world religion, they think of the pope. And for good reason. He certainly behaves in ways that foreshadow that future leader. The pope holds a religious office that comes with a certain degree of global respect and, dare I even say, worship by some people. Pope Francis even joined the social media platform X in 2012 and has 18.5M followers.[34] The pope is also known for promoting ecumenism, the concept that all Christian denominations should work together and promote unity in the church. Well, that's of course a big problem today because so many churches and denominations aren't aligned with biblical teachings. Even Pope Francis approved blessings for same-sex couples in December 2023.[35]

If that's not enough, he's also trying to unify the world religions. Big red flag for this one. You may recall that back in 2019, Pope Francis signed the *Document on Human Fraternity for World Peace and*

Living Together with Sheikh Ahmed el-Tayeb, the Grand Imam of Al-Azhar (the highest authority in Sunni Islam). A clearly controversial statement in this document is: "The pluralism and the diversity of religions, colour, sex, race and language are willed by God in His wisdom, through which He created human beings. This divine wisdom is the source from which the right to freedom of belief and the freedom to be different derives. Therefore, the fact that people are forced to adhere to a certain religion or culture must be rejected, as too the imposition of a cultural way of life that others do not accept."[36]

Really? The pope believes God created the diversity of religions. No, that was Satan and his horde of fallen angels. A result of this document was the UN establishing the International Day of Human Fraternity on February 4.[37]

Today Is Different - I'd like to point out that as popular as Pope Francis is, that he doesn't have nearly as many followers on social media as celebrities like athletes, actors, and musicians do. Have you heard of Cristiano Ronaldo? He's a Portuguese professional soccer player who has 632 million followers on Instagram.[38] Selena Gomez, a singer and actress has 426 million Instagram followers. James Donaldson, "MrBeast," is the most subscribed to channel on YouTube with 307 million followers.[39] There are many more celebrities just like these who have immense followings.

Could it be possible that the False Prophet who arises in the tribulation period isn't a religious authority, but instead someone the world idolizes? Someone considered an influencer? After all, they'll be influencing the world to get the mark of the Beast and worship the Antichrist.

Additional Scriptures: 2 Corinthians 11:3-4, 12-15. 2 Thessalonians 2:9-12. Mark 13:21-23. Matthew 7:15-20; 24:3-4, 11. Revelation 12:9; 13:4, 11-18; 19:20.

#59 - FALSE CHRISTS

Anti | DD | Earth | Gov | Israel | **Jesus** | **Leader** | Sky | Society | Tech | Trib

As he sat on the Mount of Olives, the disciples came to him privately, saying, "Tell us, when will these things be? What is the sign of your coming, and of the end of the age?" Jesus answered them, "Be careful that no one leads you astray. For many will come in my name, saying, 'I am

> the Christ,' and will lead many astray. ... Then if any man tells you, 'Behold, here is the Christ!' or, 'There!' don't believe it. For false christs and false prophets will arise, and they will show great signs and wonders, so as to lead astray, if possible, even the chosen ones. Behold, I have told you beforehand. If therefore they tell you, 'Behold, he is in the wilderness,' don't go out; or 'Behold, he is in the inner rooms,' don't believe it." (Matthew 24:3-5, 23-26)

Jesus tells us about false christs, people coming in his name, being prominent before his second coming. These are people who claim to be Jesus, the Christ, or the Messiah, but they aren't. Jesus even warns us against chasing after a false christ when others want us to go have a look, perhaps because they've seen a miracle.

The Bible tells us that we can know someone is a false christ because they will deny that Jesus is the Christ, that Jesus is the son of God, and that Jesus came in the flesh. That seems obvious since they claim to be all of those things themselves.

We're going to talk about the ultimate fulfillment of this prophecy in the very next sign, Sign #60 - The Antichrist.

Fulfillment - A bunch of people throughout time have claimed to be Jesus or the Messiah.[40] Some notable recent examples include: Menachem Mendel Schneerson (Rabbi of Chabad-Lubavitch, his followers expected him to be the Messiah), David Koresh (Branch Davidians), Alan John Miller (Divine Truth), Ezra Miller (yes, the actor in *The Flash*), Jim Jones (Peoples Temple), and Marshall Applewhite (Heaven's Gate).

Today Is Different - I briefly mentioned this in Sign #54 - Blasphemy, it's the popular new age teaching of Christ Consciousness. This false teaching says Jesus became one with the Christ Consciousness and earned the title Christ. Thus, we can do the same when we achieve our own enlightenment. The root of it is a desire for secret knowledge. After all, it's what Satan offered to Eve in the garden.

A crazy popular book and now a movie, *The Secret*, teaches this. Here are some things Rhonda Byrne, author of the book, says: "You are god in a physical body... You are all power... You are the creator... No matter who you thought you were, now you know the Truth of Who You Really Are. You are the master of the universe. You are the heir to the kingdom. You are the perfection of life. And now you know The Secret."[41] New agers literally say, "I am the Christ."

Notice in the Scripture above that Jesus says don't look for him in "inner rooms." Well, according to Strong's definition, it means a secret chamber. I don't think it could fit more perfectly as a warning against what books like *The Secret* are teaching today. Jesus isn't a secret hidden inside of us. He is God in the flesh, and we are his creation.

Additional Scriptures: 1 John 2:18-23; 4:1-3. 2 Corinthians 11:3-4, 12-15. 2 John 1:7-11. Genesis 3. Matthew 24:5.

#60 - THE ANTICHRIST

<u>Anti</u> | DD | Earth | Gov | <u>Israel</u> | <u>Jesus</u> | <u>Leader</u> | Sky | Society | <u>Tech</u> | <u>Trib</u>

> Then I stood on the sand of the sea. I saw a beast coming up out of the sea, having ten horns and seven heads. On his horns were ten crowns, and on his heads, blasphemous names. The beast which I saw was like a leopard, and his feet were like those of a bear, and his mouth like the mouth of a lion. The dragon gave him his power, his throne, and great authority. One of his heads looked like it had been wounded fatally. His fatal wound was healed, and the whole earth marveled at the beast. They worshiped the dragon because he gave his authority to the beast; and they worshiped the beast, saying, "Who is like the beast? Who is able to make war with him?" ... Authority over every tribe, people, language, and nation was given to him. All who dwell on the earth will worship him, everyone whose name has not been written from the foundation of the world in the book of life of the Lamb who has been killed. (Revelation 13:1-4, 7-8)

The "beast" coming out of the sea is the Antichrist. Notice that Satan, the Dragon, gives him his power and great authority. The word *anti* means to be against or the opposite of. He will be both against Christ and the very opposite of Christ. Jesus warned us about the Antichrist in particular when he stated a false christ would come, in the Antichrist's own name not Jesus's name, who would be able to show signs and wonders to deceive. Just like the False Prophet, he will be able to perform miracles using Satan's power (Sign #63). Working hand in hand, they will be masters of deception.

Before you start speculating which evil rulers today could be the Antichrist, please know that the Bible gives us a lot of clues about this person. He will become the ruler of the world during the tribulation period (Sign #110). In the book of Revelation, he's the rider on the white horse who comes in peaceably since he has no arrows for his bow. But he won't come to power until after the rapture. We'll examine that in Sign #150 - The Rapture, in the section titled Timing Of The Rapture. So, although I believe he is most certainly alive today because we're so very near Jesus's second coming, I'm not expecting to see him rise to power because I'll be up in heaven when that happens.

He will not be of royal blood but will instead obtain his crown through charm and flattery. At least at first and from some followers. So, the world should expect a very skilled speaker. Someone who is going to appeal to the masses. He won't say things that offend. He'll tell people what they want to hear. It'll be easy to like him and follow him. However, in the Scripture above, see how the people question who could make war with him. When his charm fails, he's going to use sheer might to conquer the world.

He will come from the people group which destroyed Jerusalem and the temple in AD 70. We know that was the Romans, led by future emperor Titus.[42] In AD 70, the Roman Empire included at least parts of these modern-day territories: Albania, Algeria, Armenia, Austria, Belgium, Bulgaria, Croatia, Egypt, France, Germany, Greece, Hungary, Israel, Italy, Lebanon, Libya, Morocco, North Macedonia, Portugal, Romania, Serbia, Spain, Switzerland, Syria, Tunisia, Turkey, and the United Kingdom.[43] So, that means we should expect the Antichrist to have a lineage that originates in one of those places.

I would like to point out that the United States is not included in that list of nations which were part of the Roman Empire in AD 70. So, we should not expect the Antichrist to be a natural born citizen of America.

Since he is the ultimate false christ, he will broker a false peace with Israel (#62), indeed claim to be God halfway through the tribulation period (Sign #67), defile the Jewish temple in Jerusalem where God is worshiped (Sign #68), wage a war against many nations (Sign #114), martyr believers (Sign #115), and be a leader in the war against Jesus at his second coming (Sign #116). To learn even more about this future world ruler, have a look at Appendix A for all the signs regarding the Antichrist.

Fulfillment - Antiochus IV (Epiphanes), the king of Syria, captured Jerusalem in 167 BC, erected an altar to Zeus inside the Jewish temple, and then sacrificed a pig on it.[44] He was a foreshadow of the Antichrist of the Bible.

The world has seen its share of evil rulers. It's estimated Joseph Stalin killed 40 million people in the Soviet Union during his dictatorship from 1924-1953. Mao Zedong is at 65 million people in

China from 1949-1976. Adolf Hitler is attributed with 35 million deaths as a result of Nazi persecution during WWII.[45]

America has never been more divided regarding a presidential election. Each political party thinks their candidate is a savior who's going to usher in peace and prosperity while the opponent is an antichrist who's going to start WWIII and end humanity. The world is looking for and hoping for a savior.

Just consider the popularity of the superhero genre or stories about saving the world. I read an article in January 2024 that listed the top 10 highest grossing movie franchises of all time for North America.[46] Nine of them are about heroes or superheroes. Here's the nine:

1) Marvel cinematic universe (a lot of heroes and superheroes), $11.7 billion
2) Star Wars (heroes and Jedi superheroes), $5.1 billion
4) Spider-Man (a superhero), $3.3 billion
5) J.K. Rowling's Wizarding World (superhero wizards), $2.9 billion
6) Batman (a hero with high tech), $2.8 billion
7) DC Extended Universe (heroes and superheroes), $2.7 billion
8) Avengers (heroes and superheroes), $2.6 billion
9) X-Men (mutant superheroes), $2.5 billion
10) James Bond (a classic hero), $2.3 billion

Let's imagine that someone like one of the beloved characters in these movies appeared on the world scene after a terrifying and world changing event. He said all the right things to ease people's fear and had a plan for solving the problems plaguing the world. Do you think people would listen? Of course they would!

Today Is Different - Since only God knows when Jesus is returning in the rapture, I believe that Satan always has someone in mind that he could use as the man who comes to power afterward. When we see Satan seemingly anoint someone, we should pay attention. You see, Satan can tell time much better than we can. He knows the season of Jesus's return is near. Not even 100 years ago, Satan chose a man to rise up against God's people, just like the Antichrist will. Satan almost succeeded in his goal of annihilating the Jewish people during the Holocaust. Adolf Hitler is one person who makes today different. Six million Jews were murdered by Hitler's regime.[47]

Hitler didn't have things like broadcast TV, the internet, or social media to communicate with people. He basically had the radio and newspapers. Yet, he was able to amass a following. Consider the reach a leader like Hitler could achieve today.

We're so much closer to Jesus's return now. All the signs the Bible speaks of can be clearly seen today. That wasn't the case during Hitler's reign. Israel wasn't even a nation yet. You can see countries and leaders around the world jockeying for political power and becoming more aggressive against foreign nations. Who might Satan have in mind today?

Additional Scriptures: 2 Corinthians 11:3-4, 12-15. 2 Thessalonians 2:3-4; 9-12. Daniel 2; 7; 8; 9:26-27; 11:21-45. John 5:43; 8:44. Luke 21:20. Mark 13:3-6, 14, 21-23. Revelation 6:2; 12:9; 17; 18:3, 9; 19:19-20.

#61 - THE LIE

Anti | DD | Earth | **Gov** | Israel | **Jesus** | **Leader** | **Sky** | Society | **Tech** | **Trib**

> The coming of the [lawless one] is according to the working of Satan, with all power, signs, and lying wonders, and with all unrighteous deception among those who perish, because they did not receive the love of the truth, that they might be saved. And for this reason God will send them strong delusion, that they should believe the lie, that they all may be condemned who did not believe the truth but had pleasure in unrighteousness. (2 Thessalonians 2:9-12 NKJV)

The "lawless one" in this Scripture is the Antichrist. Notice how many times in this handful of passages that we're told about lying and deception: lying wonders, unrighteous deception, didn't receive truth, strong delusion, believe the lie, didn't believe the truth. That's six times. In this particular sign, we're going to focus on what "the lie" could be.

This strong delusion that's coming will arrive after the rapture. That timing is revealed in the verses which directly precede these. The origin of the lie is Satan. He's the Father of Lies, and we're told that Satan will deceive the entire world in the tribulation period. In prior signs in this chapter, we discussed the things that Satan likes to lie about. They include God, Jesus, heaven, hell, the angels, and salvation. In particular, Satan wants to be worshiped, and he's going to get it during the tribulation period.

I believe Jesus warned about this particular lie in the Olivet Discourse when he told us not to believe someone who claims they've seen the Christ. Because right afterward, Jesus said the false christ would even be able to perform signs.

Another clue we're given in the Bible about the lie is that Babylon deceives all the nations through sorcery. Now, we're going to explore that sorcery, which could mean drugs, in Sign #75, but keep it in mind for how this sign might get fulfilled too.

Consider what's going to happen shortly after the rapture. Satan and his army of fallen angels are going to lose the remaining dominion they have in heaven and get banished to the earth. He isn't going to arrive looking like a demonic monster carrying a pitchfork. That's not what he looks like. He's going to look magnificent, like a holy angel, perhaps even be mistaken for God.

Fulfillment - Millions of people will have disappeared in the rapture, and the people left behind will be expecting an answer explaining what happened. Most people are not going to believe that it was the rapture spoken of in the Bible. Nope. That's because there are going to be self-professed Christians who will be among the left behind. Jesus told us there would be people who do works in his name, prophesy in his name, and even perform miracles in his name, but that they wouldn't enter the kingdom of heaven because they had no real saving relationship with him.

But I bet people would believe that the raptured believers got abducted by aliens or somehow disappeared by aliens. Society is getting prepped for a UFO and alien deception. Consider the volume of popular movies with superheroes from other planets. Or movies like *E.T.*, *Independence Day*, *Alien*, *Contact*, *Close Encounters of the Third Kind*, *Signs*, and *Men In Black*. How about TV shows like *Resident Alien*, *Ancient Aliens*, *Falling Skies*, *V*, and *Alf*. Do you remember the movie *Avengers: Infinity War*? It came out in 2018. Thanos, a super villain, snapped his fingers while wearing the infinity gauntlet and half of the people in the universe disintegrated.[48] It was mockingly called the snapture.

There's all the testimony of people who've been abducted by a UFO. All the sightings happening around the globe. Even US military personnel are speaking out about encounters they've had with UAPs on mainstream news.[49] The US congress even just held congressional hearings on this topic. We learned the US is in possession of recovered craft and non-human pilots.[50]

With all this revelation, do you know what's happened? It seems no one is interested anymore. That's how desensitized our society has become. That doesn't bode well. When the unholy angels arrive, people are going to believe the lies they've been fed for years. That the angels are an advanced alien species from a planet far away, here to help humanity in its time of greatest need. Of course, these fallen angels will have all the answers regarding what happened to the people who vanished.

Today Is Different - It's never been more feasible to generate video that's completely fake but looks absolutely real. I have no doubt that the Antichrist is going to employ sophisticated technology like augmented reality (AR), mixed reality, holograms, volumetric images, and AI generated deepfake content for his lie. Augmented reality is viewing the physical world with an overlay of digital content. Mixed reality is viewing the real physical world with an overlay of digital elements in which both can interact, like interacting with a hologram or volumetric image of someone.

Have you seen all the ways the NFL is using mixed reality? It started back in 2021 when the Carolina Panthers had a giant virtual panther leaping around the stadium before game time. It was broadcast live on TV and aired in the stadium at the same time. The virtual panther was rendered within a live feed of the real world.[51] They've done all sorts of cool things since. Technology like this could certainly be used to explain what happened to all the people who disappear.

When picturing a hologram, I'm not talking about those flat pictures you tilt back and forth to see a 3D image appear. A better depiction is how a volumetric image of Princess Leia was projected from R2-D2. Microsoft has quite an impressive product in this space called Holoportation that transports a 3D image of someone real time anywhere.[52] But, you've got to wear a HoloLens (like big glasses) to be able to see and interact with the hologram.

At the 2024 Consumer Electronics Show (CES) hologram inspired products were on full display.[53] The most impressive at CES was the Holobox, which displays a full-size holographic rendering of the person you're talking to with virtually no latency. It's as if the person is right there having a conversation with you.[54] No need to wear any special glasses to see them either.

We're going to explore this in Chapter 17, but contemplate for a minute that when the rapture happens, there will also be a resurrection of believers (the dead in Christ) who have died since Jesus's resurrection. Every other resurrection in the Bible was witnessed. Now, if millions of dead people were suddenly visible to the living, how on earth would that get explained away? It's within the realm of possibility today that they could say they were all holograms or volumetric images animated with an AI.

Combine both of these technological feats with the release of a drug into the water supply or into the air that calms people and makes them more susceptible to programming or to hallucinating, and now you've got a recipe for "the lie."

<u>Additional Scriptures:</u> 1 Thessalonians 4:13-18. 1 Corinthians 15:51-57. 2 Corinthians 11:3-4, 12-15. 2 Thessalonians 2:1-8. Daniel 8:25. Ezekiel 28:12-19. John 8:44. Mark 13:3-6, 21-23. Matthew 7:21-23. Revelation 12:9; 13:5-6; 18:23. Romans 1:18-25.

#62 – A COVENANT WITH DEATH

Anti | DD | Earth | **Gov** | **Israel** | Jesus | **Leader** | Sky | Society | Tech | **Trib**

> "Then he shall confirm a covenant with many for one week; But in the middle of the week He shall bring an end to sacrifice and offering. And on the wing of abominations shall be one who makes desolate, Even until the consummation, which is determined, Is poured out on the desolate." (Daniel 9:27 NKJV)

The angel Gabriel is speaking to the prophet Daniel in the verse above. He's talking about the Antichrist when he says, "he shall confirm a covenant." It means he'll give strength to an alliance, an agreement, or a treaty. We're told this agreement is for one week. That means seven years.

We know the other party in this agreement is Israel because God rebukes the leaders of Jerusalem for making a covenant with death and making lies their safety. The leaders do it because the Antichrist promises they'll be safe from the coming destruction, a reference to war. God tells the leaders he's going to annul this covenant because it divides the land that he gave Israel as an eternal possession. Israel will place their faith in a lie instead of trusting in God.

We also know the other party is Israel because in the middle of the week, so three and a half years in, the Antichrist stops the sacrifices and commits an abomination that desecrates the temple. We'll look at that in detail in Sign #67 - Profane Worship and Sign #68 - Polluted Sanctuary.

The Third Temple in Jerusalem doesn't exist today. The Israelites haven't been doing daily sacrifices for almost two centuries. It's also quite the contentious topic given the Muslims have their own place of worship on the Temple Mount currently. We can infer from the Scripture that this future agreement with Israel enables them to build the temple and start daily sacrifices. We'll talk about this more in Sign #128.

Fulfillment - Throughout Israel's modern history, since 1948, they've had numerous conflicts with the surrounding Arab nations. The day they became a nation, the First Arab-Israeli War started.[55] It ended with Israel not only controlling the entire area the UN had established for them, but also 60% of the land they had proposed for an Arab state. And thus began these agreements with Israel which swap land for peace. Israel gives up land in exchange for peace. The Green Line set the de facto borders of Israel between 1949 and 1967.[56] Jerusalem was divided in half, Israel got West Jerusalem.

Then came the Six-Day War in 1967.[57] Israel regained Egypt's Gaza Strip and Sinai Peninsula, Syria's Golan Heights, and Jordan's West Bank and East Jerusalem. For the first time since 1948, the Jews were able to enter the Old City in Jerusalem and pray at the Western Wall. After the war, Israel once again returned most of the land they had gained in exchange for peace. However, they kept all of Jerusalem. At this time, the UN formalized this land for peace method with Israel.

This pattern has continued to repeat until the present day. The world is pressuring Israel to create a Palestinian state. The US is included in that. It's all just a foreshadow of what's to come. None of the peace agreements last because Israel's enemies don't want Israel to exist. It's the spirit of the Antichrist.

So, the question is what, after all this time, would convince Israel to sign a deal that divides Jerusalem? I'm convinced Jerusalem will be involved because it'll be enough of their land that it triggers God's wrath. Since God rebukes the leaders in Jerusalem for this covenant with death, I think we can infer they divide God's Holy City.

Keep in mind this treaty happens after Israel's war with Gog of

Magog in which God will supernaturally intervene and destroy the enemy. See Sign #108 - Gog Of The Land Of Magog and Sign #112 - All Nations Against Israel. After what God does, perhaps the entire world will literally be against Israel and threaten to annihilate them? Instead of trusting in God, they'll continue to trust in this land for peace business. I think the Antichrist will sweeten the deal by enabling them to build their cherished temple.

Today Is Different - The Abraham Accords make today different from prior generations who brokered peace agreements with Israel.[58] The first agreement was signed in September 2020 between Israel and the United Arab Emirates (UAE), and Israel and Bahrain. Both the UAE and Bahrain recognized Israel as a nation. Since the original agreement, Morocco has also joined.

This treaty is a big deal because it's the first time since 1994 that an Arab country has established diplomatic relations with Israel. This treaty is also one of the things that triggered Iran (Shia Muslim) into attacking Israel through Hamas in October 2023.[59] It was a catalyst and essentially put more end times events into motion.

You see, Saudi Arabia (Sunni Muslim) was in talks with the US and Israel to join the agreement.[60] That would really have changed the dynamic in the Middle East. Saudi Arabia and Iran are in an ongoing struggle for dominance in that region and have conflicting religions. But Saudi Arabia wanted to ensure there would be improvements for the Palestinians before signing, like forward progress on creating a state for them. Well, what better way for Iran to prevent any normalization between Israel and anymore Arab countries than to spark a war between Israel and the Palestinians. And now Iran's escalated that war by involving terrorist proxies in Syria and Lebanon, and by directly attacking Israel themselves. We're going to talk more about Iran in Sign #106 - The Prince Of Persia.

There will be a ruler who will broker widespread peace with Israel and its Arab neighbors. The Abraham Accords got closer to achieving that than ever before.

Additional Scriptures: Daniel 8:9-14, 17, 23-26; 9:24-27; 11:21-45. Ezekiel 38-39. Genesis 15:18-21, 17:19-21. Isaiah 28:14-22. Jeremiah 7:4. Joel 3:1-2.

#63 – LYING WONDERS

Anti | DD | **Earth** | Gov | Israel | **Jesus** | **Leader** | **Sky** | Society | **Tech** | **Trib**

> The coming of the [lawless one] is according to the working of Satan, with all power, signs, and lying wonders. (2 Thessalonians 2:9 NKJV)

Here, we're told that the Antichrist, who is the lawless one, will come with all of Satan's power, signs, and lying wonders. A lying wonder means it's a lie, not what it seems, or not what it professes to be. During the tribulation period, he's going to have a partner in these deceptions, the False Prophet. The wonder itself could be a deception, the power they claim is behind the wonder could be a lie, or both. We know the Antichrist is going to claim to be God.

The Bible tells us what some of these wonders are. The Antichrist is going to appear to be fatally wounded but will be healed. The whole world will marvel at this. So, there's going to be a fake resurrection. The False Prophet will be able to call down fire from heaven and make the image of the Beast speak.

They're going to be able to do these things because Satan has real powers that were given to him by God. Consider how he used his power against Job by bringing enemy raiders against his livestock, calling fire from heaven to destroy his livestock, and sending wind against his eldest son's house thereby knocking it down and killing all his children. If that wasn't enough, Satan was even allowed to inflict Job with boils on his body. You may also recall that the Egyptian Pharaoh of the Exodus had magicians who were able to replicate some of the signs that God did through Moses and Aaron. They could turn their rods into snakes, turn water into blood, and make frogs appear.

We must also keep in mind that Satan is the master of illusions. So, many of the signs that arise in the tribulation period won't be real displays of power, but rather elaborate deceptions. Jesus said they'd be so convincing that if God allowed it, they'd even deceive believers.

Fulfillment - Let's talk about calling fire down from heaven. There have been a lot of advancements in weapons technology in modern times. Rockets, with their trail of fire, appear to fall from the sky, don't they? Space weapons are a real thing too. Today, it's certainly possible to drop something from space that would burn up in the atmosphere upon reentry. It would create a fireball much like a meteor does when it falls from the sky. Even oil could be lit on fire and dropped from the sky.

Things that were once considered science fiction are also now being developed. Like directed energy weapons. Think *Star Wars*. A lightsaber is an example of this kind of weapon. An object in space, like a satellite, could fire a laser down to earth. In January 2023, scientists were even able to redirect a lightning bolt with a high-powered laser.[61]

With today's technology, the False Prophet won't need real powers from Satan to accomplish the lying wonder of calling fire down from heaven.

Today Is Different - We've been living in a world of lying wonders for a while now. You'd think we'd all be experts at detecting it. But it's getting harder and harder for us because deepfake technology is getting that good. Did you see the young Harrison Ford in *Indian Jones and the Dial Of Destiny*?[62] Even better, have you seen the trailer for the new movie titled *Here*?[63] It uses de-aging technology, which debuted in 2006 in an X-Men film, to make Tom Hanks and Robin Wright appear decades younger than they are in real life. It's crazy how real it looks.

What's even more surprising is how widespread the use of this is. It's estimated 85% of movies made today use de-aging. Here's what Tom Hanks thinks of all this, "Anybody can now recreate themselves at any age by way of AI or deep-fake technology. I could be hit by a bus tomorrow and that's it, but performances can go on and on and on and on. Outside the understanding of AI and deep-fake, there'll be nothing to tell you that it's not me and me alone."[64]

Wow! There's no doubt the Antichrist could use technology like this to deceive people. It might even play a part in his appearing mortally wounded. Perhaps even in conjunction with what we learned about in Sign #61 - The Lie, holograms and volumetric imaging.

The fact that the Antichrist won't need real powers from Satan to accomplish the lying wonders illustrates how different today truly is.

Additional Scriptures: 2 Corinthians 4:3-4; 11:12-15. 2 Thessalonians 2:9-12. Acts 8:9-11. Ephesians 2:2. Exodus 7-8:19. Daniel 8:9-14, 17, 23-25. Job 1:12-19, 2:7. Mark 13:21-23. Revelation 13:1-4, 12-15; 16:13-14.

#64 - POLAR OPPOSITE - A DISCERNING HEART

Anti | DD | Earth | <u>Gov</u> | <u>Israel</u> | <u>Jesus</u> | <u>Leader</u> | Sky | <u>Society</u> | Tech | Trib

> I saw an angel coming down out of heaven, having the key of the abyss and a great chain in his hand. He seized the dragon, the old serpent, who is the devil and Satan, who deceives the whole inhabited earth, and bound him for a thousand years, and cast him into the abyss, and shut it and sealed it over him, that he should deceive the nations no more until the thousand years were finished. (Revelation 20:1-3)

Throughout this chapter we've looked at signs related to a deceiving heart. This sign is what I call a polar opposite. It's meant to illustrate how far away we currently are from the life we believers are going to live during Jesus's reign on earth in the millennial kingdom. Recall from Sign #6 - The Point Of No Return, that God only lets evil progress so far before he intervenes.

In the verses above, we learn that Satan, the one who's been deceiving the whole world, is going to be bound in the bottomless pit for the duration of the millennial kingdom. His influence will no longer infect the world. This happens at the second coming of Jesus. Jesus did tell us in the Olivet Discourse that the powers of the heavens would be shaken as a sign of his second coming. This is the culmination of that shaking.

In addition to this, the Bible tells us that God will establish a covenant of peace with Israel. He'll once again make them one nation with one king. They won't ever be deceived or divided by the promise of a false peace again.

Everyone will have a discerning heart, one that not only listens to and obeys God, but one that truly understands God and his ways.

> "Give your servant therefore an **understanding heart** to judge your people, **that I may discern** between good and evil; for who is able to judge this great people of yours?" (1 Kings 3:9)

Fulfillment - So, how far away are we? I'm not sure it's possible for more deception to exist in our world today. With the volume of information available at my fingertips with the help of the internet, I struggle to find the truth. As you've learned throughout this chapter, there's so much technology today that's used to deceive.

A fun way to consider just how opposite we are is to contemplate what the worst-case scenarios might look like and see just how close we are to those.

Worst case, all the news that we read or watch is a lie. No real news exists anymore. Okay, wow. I have a hard time deciphering real vs fake news. I don't trust anything anymore. It doesn't matter who says it. It certainly seems to me that we're close to the worst case here.

Worst case, a few governments and people conspire to control all world affairs. Yikes! Well, out of the 193 member states in the UN, only 5 have veto power: China, France, Russia, the UK, and the US.[65] That's quite the power consolidation. How about the mysterious Bilderberg Meeting, the annual gathering of about 150 elites.[66] What are they plotting? You may also remember from Sign #37 - Censorship, that only a handful of companies and 15 billionaires control all American media. We're at the worst case here too.

Worst case, pastors no longer teach correct biblical doctrine or the gospel. They just reference the Bible like they would a C.S. Lewis novel. More and more churches and pastors are doing exactly this. We discussed that the pastors with the largest followings on social media are teaching the prosperity gospel. From Sign #54 - Blasphemy, we learned that 63% of the worldwide population believes and speaks blasphemous things against the God of the Bible. We're close to this worst case here.

Worst case, the world believes Satan's lie that God is evil and Satan is good. So, they put their faith in Satan to save humanity. Oh my goodness. Thankfully we're not at this worst case yet, but we're close when you consider how few have put their faith in Jesus. Unfortunately, this is exactly what people who get the mark of the Beast during the tribulation period will believe.

Today Is Different - So, what do you think? Is today different? Do we as a society have a deceiving heart that loves to hear lies that support our lusts? Do you think we've reached the point of no return? How many people really have a discerning heart and can tell what time it is and how near we are to Jesus's return?

Additional Scriptures: Ezekiel 37:21-22, 26-28. Matthew 24:29. Zephaniah 3:13.

CHAPTER 10 - A DISCOURAGING HEART

> These [are] the words which Moses spoke to all Israel on this side of the Jordan. ... "The LORD our God spoke to us in Horeb, saying: 'You have dwelt long enough at this mountain. ... See, I have set the land before you; go in and possess the land which the LORD swore to your fathers—to Abraham, Isaac, and Jacob—to give to them and their descendants after them.' ... Nevertheless you would not go up, but rebelled against the command of the LORD your God; and you complained in your tents, and said, ... 'Where can we go up? Our brethren have **discouraged our hearts**, saying, "The people [are] greater and taller than we; the cities [are] great and fortified up to heaven; moreover we have seen the sons of the Anakim there." ' " (Deuteronomy 1:1, 6, 8, 26-28 NKJV)

#65 - HYPOCRISY

Anti | DD | Earth | Gov | Israel | **Jesus** | **Leader** | Sky | **Society** | Tech | Trib

> "You hypocrites! Well did Isaiah prophesy of you, saying, 'These people draw near to me with their mouth, and honor me with their lips; but their heart is far from me. And they worship me in vain, teaching as doctrine rules made by men.' " (Matthew 15:7-9)

Jesus is the one speaking in the verses above. He's specifically addressing the religious rulers, the scribes and Pharisees, because they were complaining that Jesus's disciples didn't obey tradition with ceremonial hand washing. A hypocrite is an actor, a pretender. In other teachings of Jesus, he said the hypocrites "said" but didn't actually "do" what they said. Jesus called out many kinds of hypocrisy: not discerning the time of his coming, asking God for an answer then not obeying it, creating religious burdens, tithing yet neglecting more important matters of the Law, appearing beautiful outside but being unclean inside, and not being a wise servant at all times.

Fulfillment - Hypocrisy has always existed. Most recent good examples of this were during the Covid lockdown. Do you remember the US Governors and lawmakers who got busted violating their own rules? They had hair salons open especially for them so they could get their hair done. They didn't wear masks in public. They traveled, attended events, and dined out at restaurants. They had jewelry stores open just for them so they could shop.[1] They did all the things they told their citizens not to do.

Another example is that the Arab nations surrounding Israel state that they support the Palestinians, yet they refuse to accept any of them as refugees when war breaks out. They also refuse to carve out any of their own land for them.²

Police officers and lawmakers who break the law are another way we see this being fulfilled today. I frequently see news about lawmakers or officers getting arrested for Driving While Intoxicated (DWI). There's a current FBI investigation regarding the police department's DWI unit in my hometown, Albuquerque, NM. It's revealing that officers have been colluding with lawyers and accepting bribes to not show up to court for DWI arrests.³

Today Is Different - Sexual and financial scandals involving church leaders make today different. It seems like every month there's another big story breaking about a pastor, priest, church, or religious organization that's caught up in some sex scandal or financial scam. The sins run the gamut whether it's child sexual abuse, adultery, pornography, a secret LGBT relationship, embezzlement, tax evasion, misuse of funds, or living in luxury while members are financially struggling. If you do an internet search on this, the volume of results and examples is overwhelming.

Today, our most trusted leaders don't behave any differently than the rest of society. They are the ones who are making and enforcing the rules and are supposed to be encouraging us to follow those rules by being role models. But they aren't. They're the antithesis of role models.

Additional Scriptures: 1 Timothy 4:1-3. 2 Timothy 3:1-5. Jeremiah 42:19-22. Luke 6:41-42; 12:1, 54-56. Matthew 23:1-36; 24:45-51.

#66 - ENCOURAGING SIN

Anti | DD | Earth | **Gov** | Israel | **Jesus** | **Leader** | Sky | **Society** | **Tech** | **Trib**

> For the wrath of God is revealed from heaven against all ungodliness and unrighteousness of men ... who, knowing the ordinance of God, that those who practice such things are worthy of death, not only do the same, but also approve of those who practice them. (Romans 1:18, 32)

The apostle Paul tells us that God's wrath comes against people "who practice such things." We've looked at this section of Romans 1 many times in this book. It includes a long list of sins. Essentially, it's speaking of people who commit sin and also approve of those who do likewise. By doing so, they're actually encouraging sinful behavior.

In the Old Testament, several kings encouraged their people to commit great sins. King Solomon's many foreign wives encouraged him to worship foreign gods. He built altars for them all over the country that his people worshiped at. King Jeroboam built the golden calves and led his people into worshiping those idols of God. King Manasseh did those same sorts of deeds, but also sacrificed his child to a false god, thereby encouraging others to do the same.

In the book of Revelation, Jesus's letters to two churches reveal that they were both encouraging sinful sexual behavior. During the tribulation period, the Antichrist and False Prophet will commit great sins and encourage the world to do likewise.

Fulfillment - In the prior sign, we discussed several examples of hypocrisy. Hypocrisy fits as an example for this particular sign too. Leaders who break the law or engage in sexual sins are demonstrating to the world that it's okay to do those things. Especially if there's minimal consequence for their behavior.

It doesn't have to be the hypocrisy of a leader though. Anyone in a position of authority or influence can encourage sinful behavior. It's called peer pressure. I'm sure you know someone who wants you to watch the latest movie in theaters with them. Even though it's rated R or has inappropriate content.

Sin is glorified today through entertainment like movies, songs, games, and books. When unholy behavior is constantly fed to a society in entertaining ways, it's no surprise when people get addicted and start doing all the things they've been taught. We believers must strive to separate ourselves from this. We need to stop supporting the junk that's being produced today. All we're doing is encouraging it when we do.

Another way we're encouraging sin today is by refusing to confront sin in others. People use all sorts of excuses. They don't want to hurt the other person's feelings. They don't want to be judgmental. Or they prefer to just love the person. Sin separates us from God. So, none of those excuses are loving. I'm not saying we should go around pointing the finger at others. We should lovingly talk with those closest to us about the gospel and our constant need to repent of our sins. It's the only way that we can have a right relationship with God.

Today Is Different - Social media personalities are a huge influence in the lives of so many people on the planet today. If a popular influencer posts about their cannabis use, praying to mother nature, or their many sexual partners, they're condoning and promoting that behavior. They're encouraging sin. Today, sin can go viral.

We've discussed churches that fail to teach sound biblical doctrine in prior signs throughout this book. Churches and Christian organizations openly supporting unholy lifestyles makes today different in regard to encouraging sin. They used to be the conservative voice and influence in the world. Today, they just blend in with everything else. Our generation encourages people to behave any way they want. We've changed God instead of conforming ourselves to be like God.

Another example that makes today different is the government's disregard for upholding the law. In the US, consider that some states are refusing to arrest and charge people who shoplift when they've stolen below a certain threshold. In California, if you steal below $950 it's only considered a misdemeanor. Officers aren't likely to investigate, and prosecutors will likely let it go. So, it's no wonder that thieves no longer hide their thefts in California. They just walk right in, steal, and casually walk back out. All that law has done is encourage committing a crime.[4] And now it's causing retail stores to close and cease doing business in crime rampant areas.

Additional Scriptures: 1 Kings 11:1-13; 12:25-33; 21:25. 2 Kings 17:21-22; 21:1-9. Ezekiel 13:17-23. Jeremiah 23:13-14; 28. Matthew 23:13-15. Revelation 2:12-14, 18-20; 13; 18.

#67 - PROFANE WORSHIP

Anti | **DD** | Earth | Gov | **Israel** | **Jesus** | **Leader** | Sky | **Society** | Tech | **Trib**

> "I will crush Judah and Jerusalem with my fist and destroy every last trace of their Baal worship. I will put an end to all the idolatrous priests, so that even the memory of them will disappear. For they go up to their roofs and bow down to the sun, moon, and stars. They claim to follow the LORD, but then they worship Molech, too. And I will destroy those who used to worship me but now no longer do. They no longer ask for the LORD's guidance or seek my blessings." Stand in silence in the presence of the Sovereign LORD, for the awesome day of the LORD's judgment is near. (Zephaniah 1:4-7 NLT)

God is speaking to the prophet Zephaniah in this Scripture. We learn that the people claimed to follow the Lord and worship him, but that they also worshiped foreign gods too. I chose the word *profane* to describe this kind of worship because it means unholy and to defile that which is holy. This particular Scripture is also given in the context of the day of the Lord, so it's a reference to behavior that will be prominent in the tribulation period.

There are many instances of this profane worship in the Bible. King Jeroboam's golden calves that were used to worship God. King Manasseh's high places where people worshiped the Lord. Priests of the Lord who took offerings meant for God. The Israelites using the ark of the covenant as a good luck charm in battle. King Uzziah entering the temple and burning incense. Offering unworthy sacrifices to the Lord. Even Judas Iscariot's unholy kiss that betrayed Jesus.

Jesus spoke about this when he told us we should be reconciled to others before we bring offerings to him. Profane worship is also a violation of the fourth commandment, which is to keep the Sabbath day holy.

Of course, the Antichrist is going to commit the biggest profanity in the tribulation period when he declares himself God in God's Temple and demands to be worshiped as such.

Fulfillment - Sunday Christians are a good example of this sign. These are people who attend church service on Sunday, but pretty much just occupy the seat while they're there. Because the rest of the week they don't have anything to do with God. They don't read the Bible or pray outside of Sunday service. They worship the way of the world and behave just like everyone else every day except Sunday.

We should also consider Christian denominations who don't worship or pray to God directly but use an intermediary like what King Jeroboam did with the gold calves. These are denominations who pray to Mary instead of to Jesus, who confess their sins to a priest instead of to Jesus, or who pray to saints instead of to Jesus.

Today Is Different - The rise of churches with LGBT or female pastors makes today unique. In September 2023, the Cathedral of Hope, which is the world's largest LGBT friendly church, held a Sunday service honoring the Sisters of Perpetual Indulgence. That's the group who dresses in drag nun outfits and mocks Catholicism.[5] Today, it's acceptable to blaspheme God and his laws during a profane worship service.

The rise of charismatic Christianity also makes today unique. Back in 2011, the Pew Research Center estimated there were 305 million people practicing this around the world, accounting for 14% of the Christian population.[6] Have you been to a charismatic service or watched any of them online?[7] The preachers and members are known for their crazy behavior. They faint, they jump around, they wriggle on the floor. They say it's because they are overcome by the power of the Holy Spirit. I think most of it is just learned behavior and acting. There isn't a single instance in the Bible of anyone acting like this who was filled with the Holy Spirit. Even on the day of Pentecost when the early church was born, there wasn't any chaos. The only people in the Bible who acted this oddly were those who were demon possessed. The popularity of mimicking demonic activity when worshiping the Lord reveals the prominence of profane worship today.

<u>Additional Scriptures:</u> 1 Kings 12:25-33. 1 Samuel 2:12-17; 4:3-11. 2 Chronicles 26:1, 16-20; 33:10-17. 2 Kings 10:31; 17:21-41. Acts 2. Amos 5:25-27. Daniel 11:21-45. Exodus 20:8-11. Ezekiel 22:8; 23:36-39. Luke 22:47-48. Malachi 1:10-14. Mark 5:1-20; 9:14-29. Matthew 5:23-24. Romans 14:5-6.

#68 - POLLUTED SANCTUARY

<u>Anti</u> | DD | Earth | Gov | <u>Israel</u> | <u>Jesus</u> | <u>Leader</u> | Sky | Society | <u>Tech</u> | <u>Trib</u>

> "When, therefore, you see the abomination of desolation, which was spoken of through Daniel the prophet, standing in the holy place (let the reader understand), then let those who are in Judea flee to the mountains. ... for then there will be great suffering, such as has not been from the beginning of the world until now, no, nor ever will be." (Matthew 24:15-16, 21)

These Scriptures come directly from Jesus, when he was speaking to his disciples on the Mount of Olives and describing the signs of his second coming. He refers to the abomination of desolation that the prophet Daniel wrote about. This is the event in the tribulation period in which the Antichrist will enter God's Temple in Jerusalem, erect an abomination, declare himself God, and demand to be worshiped as God. The word *abomination* means a detestable idol. So, it'll likely be an image of the Antichrist. His actions will pollute God's sanctuary.

In order for the temple to be polluted, it first has to exist, which it currently doesn't. We'll discuss this more in Sign #128 - The Third Temple.

The Bible teaches us about someone else who defiles sanctuaries. Yes, it's Satan. There's an interesting description about how he defiled them too. We're told it was by the sins of his trading. The Greek word for *trading* means merchandise or trade. It's no coincidence that the Babylon of the tribulation period, where we're told the kings will dwell, will be engaged in all sorts of trade with merchants across the earth. You may recall that Jesus drove out all the people who were buying and selling in his temple because they'd turned it into a den of thieves.

Fulfillment - King David was instructed by the prophet Gad to build an altar to God on the threshing floor of Araunah the Jebusite in Jerusalem. So, he purchased the land, built the altar, sacrificed on it, and God sent fire from heaven to burn up his offering. King David recognized that God had chosen that place. It became the location of the temple that his son King Solomon built. After the destruction of Solomon's Temple in 586 BC, it later became the site of the Second Temple. The Second Temple was destroyed in AD 70 by the Roman invasion.

Today, the Dome of the Rock (Al-Aqsa mosque) is located on top of the Temple Mount in Jerusalem. The place that God chose for his altar is currently polluted by an altar to a false god.

Today Is Different - There are many churches today who allow and encourage unholy acts and events in the church building. This could include performing gay weddings, hosting secular concerts with songs laced with profanity, or screening popular movies that draw a crowd but don't honor God. There are also churches that consider it acceptable to hang Pride flags in or outside the church building.

Let's consider churches that permit commerce in the church building. Today, churches rent their space out to third party groups as a way to earn income. They've become places for craft fairs, exercise classes, private grade school, dances, plays, concerts, playing movies, sports leagues, filming a movie, and such. My church does some of this too. Would Jesus think it's okay that today we treat church buildings like government owned convention centers? I get that it's important to be a welcoming place for the community, but where's the line? In many ways it feels like we're no different than the merchants Jesus drove from the temple.

Technology also makes today different. Our society regularly "defiles" buildings by lighting them up in different colors or projecting images and video on them. You may recall that the White House has been frequently lit up in Pride flag colors. Tall skyscrapers have been turned into ancient gods and goddesses, artwork, dinosaurs, and whatever you can think of. Perhaps the relatively new Las Vegas Sphere is the best example of this since the building's exterior is covered in LED displays. I think it's quite reasonable to assume the Antichrist is going to employ this type of innovation when he defiles the Third Temple in Jerusalem. Perhaps he'll project his face or name onto God's Temple.

Additional Scriptures: 1 Chronicles 21-22. 2 Kings 16:10-18; 21:4-5, 7. Daniel 8:9-14, 23-25; 9:26-27; 11:21-45. Ezekiel 8:5-12; 23:38-39; 28:12-18. Jeremiah 7:30. Matthew 21:12-13. Revelation 18. Zephaniah 3:4.

#69 – ONE WORLD RELIGION

Anti | DD | Earth | **Gov** | Israel | Jesus | **Leader** | Sky | Society | **Tech** | **Trib**

> Then one of the seven angels who had the seven bowls came and talked with me, saying to me, "Come, I will show you the judgment of the great harlot who sits on many waters, with whom the kings of the earth committed fornication, and the inhabitants of the earth were made drunk with the wine of her fornication." So he carried me away in the Spirit into the wilderness. And I saw a woman sitting on a scarlet beast [which was] full of names of blasphemy, having seven heads and ten horns. The woman was arrayed in purple and scarlet, and adorned with gold and precious stones and pearls, having in her hand a golden cup full of abominations and the filthiness of her fornication. And on her forehead a name [was] written: MYSTERY, BABYLON THE GREAT, THE MOTHER OF HARLOTS AND OF THE ABOMINATIONS OF THE EARTH. I saw the woman, drunk with the blood of the saints and with the blood of the martyrs of Jesus. And when I saw her, I marveled with great amazement. ... Then he said to me, "The waters which you saw, where the harlot sits, are peoples, multitudes, nations, and tongues. And the ten horns which you saw on the beast, these will hate the harlot, make her desolate and naked, eat her flesh and burn her with fire." (Revelation 17:1-6, 15-16 NKJV)

The apostle John is speaking with an angel who is explaining this vision he's seeing of Mystery Babylon. We looked at the city of Babylon in Sign #49. In this sign, we'll explore the religious aspect of Babylon.

Now, there are two phases to the one world religion.

Phase one of the one world religion is idolatry. Notice that Babylon is called a great harlot, the mother of harlots, and commits fornication with the kings and inhabitants of the earth. The Greek words used for *harlot* and *fornication* are a reference to idolatry. You may recall in the Old Testament that the people of Israel were often called a prostitute, a harlot, or an adulterer for abandoning the Lord and worshiping false gods. That's what this is about. The mother of harlots will worship everything except God. It'll be demonic, full of every evil spirit. That's also why it's drunk with the blood of the saints and martyrs of Jesus. This religion will persecute God's people. After the rapture, this will be the one world religion that someone will be at the helm of.

The harlot is depicted as riding the scarlet Beast (the Antichrist) with the seven heads and ten horns (the kings who pledge allegiance to the Antichrist). Those earthly rulers are going to use phase one of the Babylon religion to aid them in their world dominance.

Phase two of the one world religion is worship of the Antichrist. Notice in the Scripture above that it says the ten horns and the Beast hate the harlot and eventually destroy her. This is a reference to the Antichrist declaring himself God halfway through the tribulation period and then demanding the earth worship him as God. This will destroy the idolatry of phase one. The False Prophet will be at the helm of phase two, and we discussed him in Sign #58.

You know what does a good job illustrating this? It's the *Left Behind* novels by Tim LaHaye and Jerry B. Jenkins. In those books, phase one is Enigma Babylon One World Faith, and phase two is Carpathianism.

The people leading this one world religion, including the Antichrist, are going to appeal to the masses and be excellent communicators. They aren't going to say things that are offensive (except to Christians and Jews). They aren't going to talk about sin, repentance, or hell. It will be easy to follow them. They'll be promoting the broad road that Jesus talked about.

Fulfillment - I'm sure you've seen the bumper stickers that spell out coexist using symbols from different religions. That's a perfect name for phase one of the one world religion. There's an interesting trend that reveals why we're seeing more of this call for unity among religions. Back in 1960, Pew Research Center reported that only 19% of US marriages were interfaith, meaning the couple had differing faiths. In 2010, that number had risen to 39%.[8]

Remember what we discussed about Pope Francis in Sign #58 - The False Prophet, and his efforts to unify the world religions? In June 2024 he stated that Christians, Jews, and Muslims "worship the One God." I agree with Franklin Graham on this one; "Islam denies that God has a Son. They deny that Jesus is God. They do not believe in a Triune God – the Father, the Son, and the Holy Spirit. I can tell you – Islam and Christianity clearly do not worship the same God."[9] This behavior from Pope Francis is exactly what we'd expect from the future leader of phase one of the one world religion.

Today Is Different - X, the platform formerly known as Twitter, makes today different. It's a place for people to follow others, see what they post, read what they comment on, understand their world view and what they have to say about current events. Bucking the trend of prior years, in 2024 some of the most followed people on X are not celebrities like athletes or musicians. They are politicians and businessmen. #1 is Elon Musk with 189.7 million followers (businessman), #2 is Barack Obama with 131.7 million (former US president), #7 is Narendra Modi with 100 million (India's prime minister), #9 is Donald Trump with 87.5 million (former US president).[10]

It's interesting that the world is paying attention to what leaders have to say. Consider how much influence Musk has when he states he's backing Trump in the 2024 US Presidential Election. It's not hard to imagine the future False Prophet being such a person, one who has an enormous following and influence in the world.

Additional Scriptures: Hosea 4:10-19. Jeremiah 3; 50-51. Matthew 7:13-14. Revelation 13:4, 11-12; 17-18; 19:1-2, 20.

#70 - ONE WORLD CURRENCY

Anti | DD | Earth | Gov | Israel | Jesus | Leader | Sky | Society | Tech | Trib

> He causes all, the small and the great, the rich and the poor, and the free and the slave, to be given marks on their right hands or on their foreheads; and that no one would be able to buy or to sell unless he has that mark, which is the name of the beast or the number of his name. (Revelation 13:16-17)

The "he" in the verses above is the False Prophet. During the tribulation period, he will force everyone to get a mark so that they can buy and sell. The mark becomes the foundation of the future one world currency. Now, the problem with getting the mark is that it will condemn anyone who receives it to hell. We're going to discuss the specifics of the mark in Sign #72. In this sign, we'll discuss the economic aspect of it.

The ability to buy and sell is what drives any economy. Consider that this mark will also impact employment. Employees are part of what enables a business to sell products or services. I think it's safe to infer that all employees will be required to have the mark in order for a business to be able to sell. Every business will then have to make sure every customer also has the mark. Otherwise, they won't be able to sell to them.

I'm sure payment controls won't even allow someone to buy from an unmarked establishment or person. You won't be able to use your debit card, credit card, cash, cash app, gold, silver, jewelry, or anything else in this economy. The mark is effectively the currency.

There are numerous financial reasons for why the world leaders are going to push this. When the rapture happens, millions of people across the globe will disappear. Just think of the sheer economic chaos that will ensue. There will be looting, break-ins, identity theft of those who've disappeared, stolen cars, house squatting, and people using stolen credit cards. Auto deposits and withdrawals will continue to happen in raptured people's accounts for a time as well. It's going to take a while for the world to figure out who all vanished and be able to sort through the mess.

Businesses aren't going to trust any source of payment. Banks and credit card companies are going to have to correct a lot of transactions. The entire financial system could quite possibly collapse. The easiest solution to stop the financial crisis will be to stop using all the existing global currencies and payment methods. They'll roll out a completely new, all-in-one solution. People are going to be on board with this too because they'll want life to return to a degree of normalcy.

This isn't unprecedented in history. Recall what happened in Egypt when Joseph was second in command under Pharaoh. There was a terrible famine throughout the region. Joseph knew the famine was coming years in advance because God revealed it to him through Pharaoh's dreams. So, Joseph stored up grain for years. The problem is that the people eventually ran out of money and things to sell in order to buy grain from the government. So, Joseph bought all the land of the people, and the people all worked for Pharaoh in exchange for food. I believe this is a template for what's coming during the tribulation period.

Fulfillment - I'm sure you've noticed the silent war on cash that's been happening in modern times. Most countries are pushing their citizens to adopt cashless systems. I hardly ever need to use cash anymore. Although digital is super convenient, it's an ominous sign revealing how near we are to the Antichrist's economy. If you think about it, we essentially already have a global currency today. Using your credit card, debit card, PayPal, or some other digital form of payment, you can purchase anything you want from anywhere in the world.

So, the next aspect that's needed is for a government or bank to control how our digital money is used. Well, we're starting to see people getting banned from using one of the most popular global online payment systems, PayPal. It's because of government pressure or simply because PayPal doesn't agree with the content the business or user is producing or selling. They banned a popular independent journalist, Alex Jones with Infowars, in September 2018.[11] There have been many others since then.

Another good example of this is China's social credit system. The social credit score is based on how well a person conforms to their ideal citizen. People who don't have a high enough score are unable to buy things, like fuel or train tickets. They also aren't able to attend certain schools or get the best jobs. I like how a person on X described it, "authoritarianism, gamified."[12]

Today Is Different - The government mandated Covid vaccines conditioned society to comply in a way that's similar to what'll happen with the future one world currency. People had to get the vaccine in order to work, travel, attend school, and even enter some places of business.

The global computer outage that happened in June 2024 as a result of an update to a CrowdStrike product exposes the vulnerability of our digitally connected world.[13] It doesn't take much to cripple the whole system. Can you imagine if the financial sector got impacted? We've seen the demise of cryptocurrencies that were hacked, were invested in risky endeavors, had large loan losses, or couldn't meet demand for withdrawals. Outages like this are going to happen after the rapture. These events will drive the need for an entirely new currency and banking system.

That new system is being developed today by the United Nations and 130 countries, including the US. It's called a Central Bank Digital Currency (CBDC). [14] It differs from regular digital currency or cryptocurrency in that those account balances are held at commercial banks or with private cryptocurrency companies. Those private companies are liable for the accuracy of transactions and your balance. With a CBDC, a government's central bank would be the one in control of transactions and liable for balances.[15]

In January 2024, US President Trump promised to never allow CBDC in America because it would "give the government absolute control over your money."[16] He's right. The government would be able to deposit money directly into any citizen's bank account. That also means they could take it out, monitor what you're spending, put expiration dates on deposited money, and implement a whole host of other controls you could think of. Being government backed, it's meant to provide a level of trust and security that privately managed money cannot. This will be the go-to currency for the Antichrist and the False Prophet.

There is a looming threat to our digital world and CBDCs. Quantum computing. Quantum computers can perform complex calculations in record speed because they operate in multiple computational dimensions. In 2019, Google's quantum computer completed a computation in 3 minutes that would have taken the world's fastest supercomputer 10,000 years to finish.[17] That's fast! So, it's not hard to imagine that hacking will become easy with this technology. Passwords and encryption will be no match for this. I believe the events in the tribulation period occur before quantum computing invades the world because this technology will drive people back to physical and cash-based systems and out of digital ones. And that's the opposite of where we're headed. We don't have much time before our technology eclipses what's required for the fulfillment of Bible prophecy.

Additional Scriptures: Genesis 47:13-26. Luke 16:13-14. Revelation 14:9-11; 20:4.

#71 - IMAGE OF THE BEAST

Anti | DD | Earth | Gov | Israel | Jesus | Leader | Sky | Society | Tech | Trib

> He deceives my own people who dwell on the earth because of the signs he was granted to do in front of the beast, saying to those who dwell on the earth that they should make an image to the beast who had the sword wound and lived. It was given to him to give breath to the image of the beast, that the image of the beast should both speak, and cause as many as wouldn't worship the image of the beast to be killed. (Revelation 13:14-15)

In the Scriptures above, "he deceives" is the False Prophet. The "beast" is the Antichrist. So, the image of the Beast that the False Prophet makes the world build during the tribulation period is thus the image of the Antichrist. The word *breath* means a movement of air, life, or a spirit (good or evil). The word *speak* means to utter a voice or emit a sound.

Keep in mind what we learned about the False Prophet in Sign #58, that he will be able to perform signs and wonders through the power of Satan. It could be that the image is able to breathe and speak like a living being because it's inhabited by an evil spirit that's been commanded to take up residence in it. Or it could be one of those lying signs we were warned about, in which case there wouldn't be any real power behind it, but instead just technology.

You may recall that we talked about the abomination of desolation in Sign #68. Jesus even warned about it in his Olivet Discourse. That's when the Antichrist will setup an idol of himself in the Jewish temple in Jerusalem. It's certainly feasible that this image is what gets erected in the temple.

This isn't the first time in the Bible that people were forced to worship an image. King Nebuchadnezzar of Babylon forced his people to bow down in worship to a giant golden statue of himself. Those who refused were thrown into a fiery furnace. Remember Shadrach, Meshach, and Abed-Nego? We'll explore the consequence of not worshiping this image in Sign #115 - War Against God's People.

Fulfillment - The world has been getting prepped for worshiping an image for quite some time. Consider the volume of relics that religions around the world venerate. Every religion even has symbols that are held in high esteem. There are even many Christians who worship or pray to statues of the disciples, Mary, and even the cross.

Some of these images even draw large amounts of tourists, represent national pride, and bring out strong emotions, like the Statue of Liberty. The world is full of such icons.

I've mentioned in prior signs that we also have a propensity to worship celebrities today. Just consider that there are some people who have hundreds of millions of followers on social media today.

Today Is Different - There's an interesting new statue in development that's supposed to debut at the America Dream Mall in New Jersey in January 2025.[18] It's called The Giant.[19] It'll be the tallest moving statue on the planet at 54 feet (16.5 meters) high. It's basically a giant robot that has a head and arms that can move. It can also speak. It's covered in LEDs. So, picture the Las Vegas Sphere as a giant human-like statue. Another fascinating aspect is that the statue will house volumetric scanning pods so visitors can scan themselves and then get projected onto the giant statue. It certainly seems to me that this is exactly the type of technology that the False Prophet could use for the image of the Beast.

One thing that makes today different is that almost everyone has a mobile phone. The number of smartphone mobile network subscriptions worldwide was almost 7 billion in 2023.[20] There are only 8.2 billion people on the planet.[21] So, how might the False Prophet make the image of the Beast visible to everyone on the planet? He could push a video of it to everyone's mobile phone in a similar fashion to emergency alerts. He could simultaneously push the live video to TVs across the globe.

Additional Scriptures: Daniel 3:1-7; 8:9-14; 9:26-27; 11:31. Matthew 24:15. Revelation 14:9-11; 15:2; 16:2; 19:20; 20:4.

#72 - MARK OF THE BEAST

Anti | DD | Earth | Gov | Israel | Jesus | Leader | Sky | Society | Tech | Trib

> He causes all, the small and the great, the rich and the poor, and the free and the slave, to be given marks on their right hands or on their foreheads; and that no one would be able to buy or to sell unless he has that mark, which is the name of the beast or the number of his name. Here is wisdom. He who has understanding, let him calculate the number of the beast, for it is the number of a man. His number is six hundred sixty-six. (Revelation 13:16-18)

"He causes" is the False Prophet. We learn above that everyone, regardless of social status, is given the mark. It's given on the right hand or forehead. The word *mark* means imprinted, stamped, or branded. So, what all do we know about this mark? It will be a literal, physical mark that can be seen on the skin. The mark is the name of the Beast or number of his name. As for the reference to 666, there's a whole lot of speculation about that today. All I can say is that it'll be obvious to those in the tribulation period. The mark enables commerce, buying and selling, and likely employment. It's also associated with worshiping the Antichrist.

We also know that people will not get this mark by accident. Everyone will have a choice. God even sends an angel to fly around the world during the tribulation period, warning people not to get the mark. Because if they do, they'll get a 'you go straight to hell card' at Jesus's second coming. And that's what makes this mark a mystery. It makes a person ineligible for salvation once they get it. There's no repentance allowed for this sin. It seems to me that there's more to it than just worshiping a false god. And why will so many people ignore the angel's warning?

You know there's a curious Scripture in the Bible. It's Hebrews 2:14-17. It basically says that Jesus became flesh and blood to save humanity, that he didn't come to help angels. Why would it be necessary to tell us that bit about angels? Well, recall that Jesus told us it would be like the days of Noah before his second coming. We know there were human-angel hybrids in Noah's day, the Nephilim, or as most translations render it, the giants. They were the offspring of the sons of God, a reference to angels, and human women. Could it be that the mark has something to do with altering human DNA?

I'm glad you asked, because I believe the prophet Daniel revealed that it would. Recall his vision of the giant statue that represented all the world kingdoms to come. The last kingdom which appears in the tribulation period is represented by the ten toes. The toes of the statue were made of iron and clay, partly strong and partly weak. Then it says something quite curious. "They" will mingle themselves with the seed of men, but not adhere, just like iron doesn't mix with clay. The Bible doesn't tell us who the "they" refers to. However, when you put all the tribulation events together, I think the "they" is fallen angels. So, fallen angels will once again be mixing with humanity.

The name and power behind the Beast, the Antichrist, is Satan. The mark of the Beast is the mark of Satan. It'll be his way of marking and sealing people in a similar fashion to what God does with the Holy Spirit. I'm convinced it will transform anyone who gets it. Perhaps not in a way that's visible to us, but certainly visible to God. Due to this spiritual component, we should consider that the fallen angels may have a hand in the technology that'll be used for the mark of the Beast.

If this fascinates you like it does me, I talk a lot more about this in my book *Assault On The Afterlife*.

Fulfillment - We're already seeing payment systems being embedded into people's hands today. It's usually an RFID or NFC chip that's the size of a grain of rice. It works like your phone or credit card.[22] Three of the largest payment card companies are investing in biometric payment systems like this: Mastercard, Visa, and JP Morgan Chase.[23] Since you can now unlock your phone with your face, you might soon be able to pay with your face because these companies are exploring using facial and iris scans for payments too.

Today Is Different - I haven't read about any of these payment chips being implanted in heads though. But guess what has? It's Neuralink. In January 2024, the first human received that brain-chip implant.[24] That person is now able to control a video game on their computer with only their thoughts.[25] Seems unbelievable, doesn't it? Since they can operate anything on the computer, they can make a payment with their thoughts too.

Today they're even developing nanotechnology for use in our bodies, like nanosensors.[26] They'll be able to do similar things to Neuralink, like pay with your thoughts, and then some. This technology is more mark of the Beast oriented because it's minimally invasive. It's injected into the bloodstream.

The technology certainly exists today to enable people to buy and sell through a mark on their hand or forehead.

Now, there's this business about people ignoring the angel who warns everyone about getting this mark. How might that angel be explained away? Well, obviously the Antichrist and False Prophet will lie. Perhaps it'll be simple, and they'll say the angel is a rogue who's jealous of the Antichrist's worship and people will believe them. I think they might explain the angel by saying it's a technological phenomenon. Like a volumetric image (a hologram) that's being projected into the sky. Perhaps by drones equipped with speakers. Of course they'll blame it on the anti-world-government extremists.

Additional Scriptures: 2 Corinthians 1:21-22. Daniel 2:42-43; 3:1-7. Ephesians 1:13-14. Genesis 6:1-8. Hebrews 2:14-17. John 14:16-17. Leviticus 19:19. Matthew 24:37-44; 25:31-34, 41. Revelation 7:1-8; 14:9-11; 15:2; 16:2; 19:20; 20:4.

#73 - FORCED WORSHIP

<u>Anti</u> | DD | Earth | <u>Gov</u> | Israel | Jesus | <u>Leader</u> | Sky | <u>Society</u> | <u>Tech</u> | <u>Trib</u>

> He exercises all the authority of the first beast in his presence. He makes the earth and those who dwell in it to worship the first beast, whose fatal wound was healed. ... He deceives my own people who dwell on the earth because of the signs he was granted to do in front of the beast, saying to those who dwell on the earth that they should make an image to the beast who had the sword wound and lived. It was given to him to give breath to the image of the beast, that the image of the beast should both speak, and cause as many as wouldn't worship the image of the beast to be killed. (Revelation 13:12, 14-15)

We've looked at parts of this Scripture in several signs in this chapter. The "he exercises" is the False Prophet. After the rapture and during the tribulation period, he's going to make everyone worship the "first beast." That's the Antichrist. People will be required to worship both the actual Antichrist and his image. Anyone caught not doing so will be killed.

In prior signs we've discussed the nature of the image (Sign #71) and the one world religion that this worship implies (Sign #69). Here, we're going to explore how this worship could possibly be enforced on a global scale.

Fulfillment - We're used to being forced to do things. Whether that's mask mandates, vaccines, going to school, paying taxes, going to work, using shopper rewards cards, ordering fast food via an app in order to get discounts, or even going through the x-ray machine at the airport. Society is used to complying.

We're also used to being surveilled. There are cameras everywhere today: mobile phones, doorbells, traffic cams, speed cams, red light cams, and cameras in stores to detect shoplifters. Let's not forget about the thousands of satellites in orbit that are taking pictures and keeping track of and providing GPS locations of connected devices like phones and vehicles.

Today Is Different - In September 2023, Iran's parliament passed the "hijab and chastity" bill that introduces more punishments against women who wear hijabs inappropriately. The law requires businesses to have video cameras and upload the footage to police so they can identify violators using AI facial recognition technology. They've even deployed drones with cameras to monitor dress code compliance at events.[27] It's not hard to picture this type of surveillance being used to ensure people worship the Antichrist and his image.

Here's a rather low-tech way the future Antichrist regime might enforce worship. As I mentioned in Sign #71 - Image Of The Beast, the False Prophet could push a video of the image of the Beast to all mobile phones. It wouldn't be hard to make sure everyone gets a phone after the rapture. Governments give them away today already. The image of the Beast might instruct people to go get the mark of the Beast to show their devotion to the Antichrist. And, of course, to be able to buy and sell. I have a feeling an incentive will also be a guaranteed income. It'll be easy to tell who watched the video, who didn't, who muted it, etc. because of existing data-tracking technology. Then anyone who fails to watch the video or get the mark is considered non-compliant and subject to be martyred.

We should also consider that there are going to be fallen angels on earth during the tribulation period. I touched on this in Sign #61 - The Lie, and I explain it in more detail in Sign #146 - The Heavens Shake. The Bible tells us there are a countless number of angels in existence. One third of them aligned with Satan. There could be billions of angels on the planet after the rapture. They are experts in human surveillance. They've been watching us for millennia. They are also experts at accusing us before God. So, they aren't going to have any problems ratting people out to authorities. In fact, they might be the authority and happily martyr anyone who doesn't immediately comply with the forced worship.

Additional Scriptures: 2 Thessalonians 2:3-4. Daniel 3:1-7; 11:36-39. Deuteronomy 28:36, 64. Revelation 5:11; 12:3-4; 13:1-4; 14:9-11; 15:2; 16:2; 19:20; 20:4.

#74 - POLAR OPPOSITE - A STEADFAST HEART

Anti | DD | <u>Earth</u> | Gov | <u>Israel</u> | Jesus | <u>Leader</u> | Sky | <u>Society</u> | Tech | Trib

> "And God will wipe away every tear from their eyes; there shall be no more death, nor sorrow, nor crying. There shall be no more pain, for the former things have passed away." (Revelation 21:4 NKJV)

Throughout this chapter we've looked at signs related to a discouraging heart. This sign is what I call a polar opposite. It's meant to illustrate how far away we currently are from the life we believers are going to live during Jesus's reign on earth in the millennial kingdom. Recall from Sign #6 - The Point Of No Return, that God only lets evil progress so far before he intervenes.

In the Scripture above, we see that God removes sorrow, death, pain, and crying. In the additional verses below, we also learn that we'll rest from our labors, be joyful, go to the house of the Lord in Jerusalem to be taught by God, and that we'll have God's name and Jesus's name written on us.

Everyone will have a steadfast heart, one that not only perseveres with faith and trusts God in all circumstances, but also encourages others to grow in their knowledge of the Lord.

> He will not be afraid of evil news. His **heart is steadfast**, trusting in the LORD. (Psalm 112:7)

Fulfillment - So, how far away are we? Well, as a society we sure aren't encouraging Godly living. It's quite the opposite today because our society encourages and celebrates sin.

A fun way to consider just how opposite we are is to contemplate what the worst-case scenarios might look like and see just how close we are to them.

Worst case, everything we do is monitored and tracked. We can't go anywhere or do anything without a biometric scan. We're not here yet, but I think you'd be hard-pressed to leave your house and go somewhere and never encounter a surveillance camera. If you've got your cell phone with you, it knows where you are. It's probably even listening to you too. We're close to this worst case.

Worst case, everyone idolizes the most popular person in the world and is quick to align with their viewpoint. Oh. I think we might be at the worst case here. Consider how many followers the popular people on the planet have on social media networks, not to mention their broadcast and streaming platforms. It's hundreds of millions, if not even billions. You know there are people who align with what Taylor Swift says only because she said it.

Worst case, churches are no longer exclusive to any particular religion or doctrine. The government takes control of them and makes them open houses for any faith. We're not close to this one. But the government in the US did take control of churches, in a way, during Covid when they forced them all to shut down. In my state, they were closed for quite some time.

Today Is Different - So, what do you think? Is today different? Do we as a society have a discouraging heart that loves to hear lies and that encourages others in sinful endeavors? Do you think we've reached the point of no return? How many people really have a steadfast heart and are encouraging others to live holy lives that honor God?

Additional Scriptures: Ezekiel 43:1-9; 44:15-23. Isaiah 2:2-4; 56:1-7. Revelation 3:10-12; 13:10; 14:12-13; 21:23-27.

CHAPTER 11 - A PERVERSE HEART

A worthless person, a man of iniquity, is he who walks with a perverse mouth, who winks with his eyes, who signals with his feet, who motions with his fingers, in whose **heart is perverseness**, who devises evil continually, who always sows discord. (Proverbs 6:12-14)

#75 - DRUGS AND ALCOHOL

Anti | **DD** | Earth | **Gov** | Israel | **Jesus** | Leader | Sky | **Society** | Tech | **Trib**

They didn't repent of their ... sorceries. (Revelation 9:21)

We're told this regarding the behavior of people during the tribulation period. In this Scripture, the Greek word that's used for sorceries is *pharmakeia*. One of its meanings is the use or administering of drugs. If you're interested in the witchcraft aspect of this, refer to Sign #11 - The Occult.

In fact, Jesus even pointed out drunkenness as a reason people won't be paying attention to the signs of his coming. In the Old Testament, God judged the city of Samaria because it had become a crown of the drunks of Israel.

Also, in the book of Revelation, you'll notice there are many references to the drunkenness of Babylon. In addition, it says that all the nations will be deceived by Babylon's sorcery or drug use. It seems that Babylon will be involved in manufacturing and distributing drugs during the tribulation period.

I believe the apostle Paul also alluded to this substance abuse when he said God gave the people over to a debased mind. And when he told Timothy that in the last days people would have corrupt minds.

Fulfillment - It's not hard to see that drug and alcohol use is prevalent in society today. There are even movies and shows on TV that glorify it, like *Breaking Bad*. You probably know someone who has an alcohol or drug addiction. You can also see it in the homeless population. It's a growing problem in my city, how about yours?

I live in Albuquerque, NM where the city spent $5 million to build a tiny home village with a meager 30 120-square-foot homes and supporting community spaces. It opened in early 2021 and at that time there were an estimated 1,567 homeless in the city. So, you'd think it'd be easy to fill the village. Nope. Six months after it opened, only eight people lived there. People who applied were getting rejected because they hadn't been sober for 30 days, had tested positive for illegal drugs, had a mental health issue requiring intensive care (likely caused by substance abuse), or didn't want to participate in the personal growth program.[1] The city ultimately had to drop the drug and alcohol use restriction in order to fill the village. It just reached full capacity three and a half years after opening.[2]

In the US, 17% of the population aged 12 and over has a substance abuse disorder.[3] It's also reported that 50% of people aged 12 and over have used illicit drugs at least once.

Cannabis (marijuana) is the most used illegal drug worldwide[4]. In late 2022, Pew Research Center indicated 88% of surveyed adults in the US think marijuana should be legal.[5] Thus the reason it's legal in most of the US. It's legal for recreational use in 24 US states and medical use in 38.[6] Legalizing it hasn't shut down the drug cartels though. All it's done is increase the supply. NBC reported in May 2024 that daily marijuana usage outpaced daily drinking in America. From 1992 to 2022, daily marijuana use increased 15-fold.[7] I live in a state where it's legal, and there are a ridiculous number of dispensaries across town. They seem more prevalent than McDonald's.

The Jerusalem Post reported in February 2024 that 1 in 4 Israelis has used an addictive substance to treat anxiety, depression, and PTSD since the Hamas attack in October 2023.[8] It's not hard to see why substance abuse is going to continue to be an issue throughout the tribulation period.

Today Is Different - Opioid abuse makes today different. It's the latest epidemic in this space. Fentanyl is the deadliest drug in America. My city used to have billboards about not drinking and driving. Now, it's billboards warning about fentanyl. If you think it's bad here, Israel is the #1 opioid consumer per capita in the world.[9] Both the US and Israel attribute the dramatic rise in opioid use to marketing by pharmaceutical companies and in turn physicians prescribing them as a quick fix for pain.

I read an interesting article on *Zero Hedge* in July 2024 that explained how Chinese money-laundering is fueling America's fentanyl epidemic. Essentially, Chinese chemical companies give Mexican drug cartels the ingredients needed to make fentanyl. Some of the cash the cartel receives when they sell the drug to people in America is used by the cartel to pay for Chinese students to live and attend school in the US. You see, the cartel pays for the fentanyl ingredients and launders their cash at the same time. The Chinese parents of those students then pay the Chinese chemical company an equal amount of money. It's estimated this amounts to $700 billion annually.[10]

Drug use in the name of religion also makes today unique. Psychedelic churches offer psilocybin mushrooms as part of their worship service. Although the drugs are illegal, these churches are allowed to operate because of a US Supreme Court ruling. One such church in San Francisco with over 100,000 members brings in $5 million annually.[11]

Perhaps the most powerful example of why today is different is that God has allowed America to be governed by President Biden, who clearly has a reprobate mind and is surrounded by drug scandals.

Additional Scriptures: 2 Chronicles 33:1, 6. 2 Timothy 3:1, 8-9. Deuteronomy 18:9-14. Ephesians 2:1-3. Galatians 5:19-21. Isaiah 28:3-7; 47:9. Luke 21:34. Malachi 3:5. Revelation 17:1-6; 18:1-3, 13, 23; 22:15. Romans 1:18, 28; 13:11-13.

#76 – PERVERTED BODIES

Anti | DD | Earth | Gov | Israel | Jesus | Leader | Sky | **Society** | **Tech** | Trib

> For the wrath of God is revealed from heaven against all ungodliness and unrighteousness of men who … traded the glory of the incorruptible God for the likeness of an image of corruptible man, and of birds, four-footed animals, and creeping things. Therefore God also gave them up in the lusts of their hearts to uncleanness, that their bodies should be dishonored among themselves. (Romans 1:18, 22-24)

Here, we learn that when God's wrath comes upon mankind, that God lets people dishonor their bodies. The word *dishonor* means to treat it with contempt. In the very beginning, you may recall that God created mankind in his image, and he created us male and female. The Bible also informs us that our bodies belong to God. We even become part of his temple when we accept Jesus as our savior and receive the Holy Spirit in return. This business about hating our bodies to the point of changing and destroying them comes from Satan. Remember that he is known for defiling temples.

Fulfillment - All you need to do is look around to see fulfillment of this sign. An August 2023 report indicates 32% of Americans have a tattoo. If you just consider adults aged 30-49, that percentage rises to 46%. It's interesting that 47% of those tattooed said they did it to make a statement about what they believe.[12] In Israel, 25% of the population has a tattoo, and it's being reported that since October 7, 2023, there's been a surge in the number of people getting one. They're doing it to show nationalistic pride.[13]

Today, this body modification has progressed beyond the simple tattoo and now includes complete facial tattooing, piercings, studs, eye tattoos, ear gauging, breast implants, tongue splitting, Botox, plastic surgery, and liposuction to name a few. Some people look straight up demonic. Others have had so much work done that they don't even look real anymore.

In the Scripture above, it says people trade the glory of God for animals. Remember that we're made in God's image. So, do we see people trading their bodies for those of animals? Yes! I've started reading articles about a new trend of becoming a "furry." Apparently, kids are dressing up as animals and pretending to be one all day, including during school.[14] I'm sure the new Barbie doll line that came out in 2022 that has Barbie in a fuzzy animal costume has nothing to do with this.[15] Or the popularity of the *Sweet Tooth* TV show about hybrid children being born with animal characteristics, like antlers. There's even a man in Japan who paid $14,000 on a realistic looking collie costume so he could live as a dog.[16]

In a completely different aspect of this perversity toward our bodies, we should also consider the growing trend to glorify obesity.

Today Is Different - The obvious reason today is different is because of transgenderism. The latest survey indicates there are 1.6 million people in the US, or 0.6% of the population, who identify as trans. What's shocking is that 43% of that trans population is under 25 years old. It's estimated the number of people under 25 who identify as trans has doubled since 2017.[17] The survey stated that social media was a significant catalyst for teens questioning their gender identify today.

Modern advancements in medicine and surgery now enable people to change their gender, at least physically. Planned Parenthood is a dominant player in this industry because they're the second largest provider of hormone therapy, like puberty blockers.[18] According to a recent article in *JAMA Network Open*, the number of gender-affirming surgeries performed in the US tripled between 2016 and 2019. There were 4,550 procedures in 2016 and 13,000 in 2019.[19]

Another topic I'd like you to consider is transhumanism. It's the merging of humans and technology. Pacemakers and smart prosthetics fit here. As does Neuralink, the brain chip implant that lets a person control a computer with just their thoughts. The trouble is where's the line? When do these advancements become a perversity of God's creation?

Additional Scriptures: 1 Corinthians 3:16-17; 6:18-20. Deuteronomy 22:5. Ezekiel 28:12-18. Genesis 1:26-27. Leviticus 19:28. Romans 1:26-27.

#77 - ABSTAIN FROM CERTAIN FOODS

Anti | DD | **Earth** | Gov | Israel | Jesus | Leader | Sky | **Society** | **Tech** | Trib

> But the Spirit says expressly that in later times some will fall away from the faith, paying attention to seducing spirits and doctrines of demons, ... and commanding to abstain from foods which God created to be received with thanksgiving by those who believe and know the truth. (1 Timothy 4:1, 3)

In the later times, the days prior to Jesus's return, we're going to see people abstaining from foods that God created for us. God created the plants and animals for food. Initially, Adam and Eve only ate plants, primarily fruit from trees. After they sinned and got banished from the garden of Eden, they also started eating grains and meat. It's evidenced by Cain, their firstborn son, being a farmer and bringing offerings of what the ground produced to the Lord. Also, Abel their second son, was a shepherd and offered the best of the first-born lambs to God.

Jesus said it's not things that enter our body from the outside that defile us. It's what's already inside of us that does the defiling.

Fulfillment - Have you noticed the war against meat? The UN states that one-third of human-caused greenhouse gas emissions is linked to food. Whether that's methane from cows, nitrous oxide from fertilizers, carbon dioxide from cutting down forests for farms or ranches, emissions from manure, or cutting down mangrove forests for shrimp farms. They say beef has the highest carbon footprint followed by lamb, shellfish, cheese, and fish to round out the top five.[20]

So, there's this global push to eat plant-based foods now. I'm sure you've noticed all the plant-based milks at the grocery store. The vegan and vegetarian diets have been around awhile. But now they want to replace animal protein with insect-based protein. That's right. They want us to eat bugs. Just do an internet search on insect diet and you'll get all sorts of results touting the benefits of this. Since most of us clearly find this gross, companies are looking at ways to add powder made from insects into our processed foods. And they're making this difficult for us to know it's in there. If you saw a*cheta domesticus* on a food label, would you know what it is? Would you even look it up? Well, it's cricket powder.

In late 2023, Tyson Foods announced they've invested in Protix, an insect ingredients maker that's going to feed soldier flies animal waste and turn those flies into pet food.[21] How long do we have before this shows up in the breading of chicken nuggets?

Today Is Different - Lab-grown meat created by scientists. This is different than plant-based burgers that you can find in any grocery store today. This is cultivated meat and seafood that's grown using cells from an animal. Obviously, the intent is to get rid of our need to raise animals for food and instead build giant factories to make fake animals for us to eat instead. Apparently, this makes sense to some of the elites fighting climate change.

The US approved the sale of lab-grown chicken in June 2023.[22] Guess who was the first country to approve lab-cultured beef? It's Israel.[23] They just got approval in January 2024. In June 2024, Jeff Bezos's charity just contributed $100 million to companies working on developing fake meat products.[24]

We're going to start seeing this in grocery stores and fast food chains soon.

Additional Scriptures: 1 Corinthians 8. Acts 10:9-15. Genesis 1:26-30; 2:4-17; 3:21-23; 4:1-4. Hebrews 13:9. Mark 7:14-23. Romans 14:1-6.

#78 - CUSSING

Anti | DD | Earth | Gov | Israel | **Jesus** | Leader | Sky | **Society** | **Tech** | **Trib**

> Because of these things the wrath of God is coming upon the sons of disobedience, in which you yourselves once walked when you lived in them. But now you yourselves are to put off all these: ... filthy language out of your mouth. (Colossians 3:6-8 NKJV)

The wrath of God, that's a reference to the tribulation period, is coming because we're committing a whole host of sins. One of those sins is "filthy language." Otherwise known as swearing, cursing, profanity, cussing, vulgar hand gestures, and even telling dirty jokes. It also includes the third commandment, don't use the Lord's name in vain.

Jesus spoke about this when he said we speak out of the abundance of our heart. If you're living in sin and thinking about it, then that's what's going to come out of your mouth. This behavior will continue to be prominent in the tribulation period when people curse the name of God.

Fulfillment - How many of us can say that we never cuss? You've never said fudge, snot, or biscuits instead of their infamous foul word cousins? How about an inappropriate hand gesture to someone who cut you off in traffic?

Giving someone the middle finger is probably the most recognized vulgar hand gesture on the planet. The first documented use of it was in 1866 when a baseball pitcher with the Boston Beaneaters was photographed giving it to a rival on the New York Giants.[25]

If you haven't noticed, most curse words aren't considered taboo anymore. It's just how most people talk today, Christians included. There's no longer a difference between private language among friends and office language among coworkers. Today, even world dignitaries cuss.

Before social media platforms existed, editors filtered everything that was published in the media. Not the case anymore. We're exposed to people's raw informal language and that's normalizing profanity.

Another reason for this is because language changes over time. For younger Americans, the f-word isn't even in the top 20 of what they consider the most offensive words. What's become most offensive today is slurs, like the n-word.[26]

Today Is Different - In the US, profane speech is not protected by the First Amendment. In 1964, the US Supreme Court gave the FCC the authority to police language in broadcasting.[27] You know that radio broadcasts must have started using inappropriate language sometime before that. Otherwise, they wouldn't have needed to control it.

This is also the time tech started to get invented to mask on-air profanity. The bleep sound seems to have first originated in the 1920s and was widely used in the 1960s.[28] TVGuardian, the foul language filter, debuted at the Las Vegas Consumer Electronics Show in 1999.[29]

Do you know when the first movie was released that contained the f-word? 1970. It was *M*A*S*H*. The current Guinness record holder for the most in a movie is *Swearnet: The Movie* from 2014. It has 935 f-words! That's 8.35 of them uttered every minute.[30]

The Wall Street Journal published an interesting article about profanity in movies in December 2023. They interviewed Chad Michael, the CEO of a content filtering service. He said, "we're seeing a big spike in the use of crude and profane language in movies and TV shows." They asked Michael to scan 60,000 popular movies and shows released since 1985 and graph the number of curse words over time. The usage of the f-word was 511 in 1985 compared to 22,177 in November 2023! He did put a caveat on the data and say there's more programming available today than in prior decades.[31]

Are writers just being lazy in creating dialogue? I think Hollywood is just mirroring society because this is how most of the world communicates today.

Additional Scriptures: Ephesians 5:3-7. Exodus 20:7. Hosea 4:1-2. Leviticus 19:12. Matthew 12:33-37. Revelation 13:6; 16:9, 11, 21. Romans 3:10-14.

#79 - SEXUAL PERVERSION

Anti | **DD** | Earth | Gov | Israel | **Jesus** | Leader | Sky | **Society** | **Tech** | **Trib**

> For the wrath of God is revealed from heaven against all ungodliness and unrighteousness of men .... For this reason, God gave them up to vile passions. For their women changed the natural function into that which is against nature. Likewise also the men, leaving the natural function of the woman, burned in their lust toward one another, men doing what is inappropriate with men, and receiving in themselves the due penalty of their error. ... God gave them up to a reprobate mind, to do those things which are not fitting; ... sexual immorality. (Romans 1:18, 26-29)

A sign of God's coming judgment during the tribulation period is sexual immorality. Jesus confirmed that God made people male and female, and that marriage is between a man and a woman. So, this includes every kind of sexual perversion you can think of that goes against God's original design: fornication, adultery (the seventh commandment), gay and lesbian relationships, bestiality, pedophilia, sex changes, gender therapy, and even nudist colonies.

Sexual sin got many of the fallen angels bound because they left heaven to have sexual relations with human women. The people of Sodom and Gomorrah were consumed by this lust of the flesh as well and it resulted in their destruction. During the tribulation period, this will continue to be a dominant behavior. People will refuse to repent of it.

Fulfillment - This is so in your face today that it's difficult to avoid it. Everything has become sexualized: commercials, Hallmark movies, most secular songs, TV game shows, Super Bowl halftime shows, concerts, kids' TV programming, cartoons, and children's books. You can even see it in the clothing choices we have today. They're getting tighter, tinier, and more sheer.

We learned in Sign #44 - Lovers Of Pleasure that of the top 20 websites visited across the world, 4 of them are pornographic. And 2 of those are in the top 5 sites.[32]

In June 2023, Planned Parenthood posted on social media that virginity is a made-up social construct that comes from outdated, patriarchal ways of thinking.[33] In America almost 90% of people have sex before getting married.[34] That means Christians aren't behaving any different than anyone else. In fact, in a Pew Research Center survey in 2020, they reported that 57% of Christians said sex between unmarried adults was acceptable. And 19% consider it okay on a first date![35]

Back in 2012, 3.5% of survey respondents identified as LGBT in the US. In 2023, it had risen to 7.6%.[36] That's a 117% increase! When we look at this by generation there's quite a troubling trend in the younger age groups. For Millennials (born 1980-1996), 5.8% identified as LGBT in 2012 compared to 9.8% in 2023. It almost doubled. In 2020, 15.9% of Gen Z (born 1997-2004) identified as LGBT in the US. Just three years later in 2023 that percentage was up to 22.3%.[37] That's a 40% increase in three short years!

Consider all the new words getting developed and even added to the dictionary to support this sexual immorality: amalgagender, polysexual, gay marry, abrosexual, demisexual, neopronoun, intersex, pansexual, and queer.

Today Is Different - Pride month and Transgender Day of Visibility (inaugurated on Easter 2024) are celebrated in the US. This behavior is no longer considered taboo and sinful. In fact, it's openly celebrated, and that's what makes today unique. The 2024 Olympics even chose to praise this lifestyle by featuring three drag queens as torchbearers, and an opening ceremony with drag queens and nudity in a blatant mockery of Christianity.[38]

If you didn't see it, I'm not sure where you've been hiding. They recreated Leonardo da Vinci's *The Last Supper* painting as a drag queen, LGBT parody, with an obese lesbian woman wearing a halo depicted as Jesus. A depiction of the night that Jesus chose to forfeit his life for our sins. That's what they decided to pervert at an event meant to celebrate elite athletes.

The Olympics aren't the only ones willing to face public backlash to promote this immorality. Consider the companies today that are willing to lose billions of dollars to promote the LGBT community: Anheuser-Busch, Target, and the LA Dodgers for example.

Speaking of the Olympics again, the rise in transgenderism is attacking women's sports. This is no longer about accepting and celebrating the LGBT community. It's now become a war against God's original design for men and women. The Olympics display made that crystal clear. Today, women have to compete against biological males that have a clear advantage, especially if they transitioned after puberty.

It's not even restricted to sports anymore. Biological males are winning women's beauty pageants and woman of the year awards.

And now it's become a war against children. In March 2023, A UN organization published a report titled, "The 8 March Principles for a Human Rights-Based Approach to Criminal Law Proscribing Conduct Associated with Sex, Reproduction, Drug Use, HIV, Homelessness and Poverty." Here's an excerpt from within the report regarding sexual conduct: "Moreover, sexual conduct involving persons below the domestically prescribed minimum age of consent to sex may be consensual in fact, if not in law. In this context, the enforcement of criminal law should reflect the rights and capacity of persons under 18 years of age to make decisions about engaging in consensual sexual conduct and their right to be heard in matters concerning them."[39] So the UN is promoting that children under the age of 18 can consent to sex. It doesn't state what age they believe that is. Nothing good will come of this.

Also consider the drag queen story hour that's invading public libraries and schools. Or the law California passed in July 2024 that prevents schools from informing parents of their children's gender dysphoria.[40] Now, teachers can essentially help a child secretly transition.

Additional Scriptures: 1 John 2:16. Colossians 3:5-6. Ephesians 2:1-3; 5:3-7. Exodus 20:14. Genesis 2:24; 19:1-11. Hosea 4:1-2. Jude 1:6-7. Leviticus 18:22-23. Matthew 5:27-28; 19:1-10. Numbers 25:1-3; 31:15-16. Revelation 2:14; 2:20-21; 9:21; 17; 21:8; 22:15. Romans 1:24.

#80 - ATTACK ON MARRIAGE

Anti | DD | Earth | Gov | Israel | Jesus | Leader | Sky | Society | Tech | Trib

> But the Spirit says expressly that in later times some will fall away from the faith, paying attention to seducing spirits and doctrines of demons, ... forbidding marriage. (1 Timothy 4:1, 3)

Here, we're told that in the last days some people will forbid marriage. Jesus touched on this when he spoke about eunuchs who choose this way of life for God. However, in the Scripture above the teaching originates from the demons, so devoting one's life to God is not why these people aren't marrying.

There is a curious verse in the Bible that might be related to this. It's regarding the Antichrist. It says that he will not regard the desire of women. In the context, it seems like it means the women worship a false god or an idol and he won't desire to do that. Obviously because he'll worship himself instead. But I wonder if it could have a double meaning and refer to the Antichrist not wanting what women want, to be married.

Fulfillment - There are several religions that forbid marriage and demand celibacy of its clergy: Catholicism, Buddhism, and Jainism are examples.[41]

I think we should consider the rise of same-sex marriage as fulfilling this too. After all, God doesn't recognize that as a marriage, and it's definitely an attack on biblical marriage. According to the US Census Bureau, in 2005 couples reporting a same-sex marriage accounted for 0.71% of marriages in the US.[42] In 2022, that percentage had increased to 1.2% of marriages.[43] In Israel, same-sex marriages aren't legal. However, they do recognize foreign same-sex unions and their Supreme

Court in 2022 ruled that these can now occur via Zoom.[44]

Adultery is another type of attack on marriage. In 1960, only 5% of partners admitted to cheating on their spouse. In 2021, that percentage is all the way up to 21%.[45]

I think the best example of fulfillment for this sign is society's disregard for getting married these days. Back in 1920, there were 12 marriages per 1,000 people in the US. The marriage rate has displayed a downward trend since and in 2018 the rate was only 6.5. Almost half of what it was decades prior. Israel has seen a similar trend. Their marriage rate has declined from 10.6 in 1970 to 6.2 in 2016.[46]

Today Is Different - Instead of getting married, today people are choosing to just live together instead. Among adults aged 18-44 in the US, the percentage who have ever cohabited, 59%, is now larger than those who have been married, 50%. This is primarily because society today sees living together as a prerequisite for marriage, not a result of it.[47]

Quoting from an article published on *Forbes* in early 2024, the journalist says, "As society embraces modernity, traditional marriage loses its significance as a cornerstone of societal norms." They hit the nail on the head. The article goes on to describe seven types of contemporary marriages. Three that stick out are starter marriages that are meant to be short lived learning experiences, living-apart-together marriages in which each partner maintains a separate household, and open marriages where couples engage in sex with people outside the marriage.[48]

Additional Scriptures: 1 Corinthians 7. Daniel 11:37. Matthew 19:1-12; 22:23-30.

#81 - WITHOUT NATURAL AFFECTION

Anti | DD | Earth | Gov | Israel | **Jesus** | Leader | Sky | **Society** | **Tech** | Trib

> But know this: that in the last days, grievous times will come. For men will be ... without natural affection. (2 Timothy 3:1-3)

One of the signs that we'll see before Jesus's second coming is that people won't have natural affection. It means people will be unsociable, inhuman, and unloving. In fact, in the Olivet Discourse, Jesus said the love of many growing cold is a sign of his second coming. The Bible tells us that if we don't love it's because we don't know God. Because God is the very definition of love. He demonstrated that love by sacrificing his only begotten son, Jesus, so that we could have eternal life with him.

Fulfillment - One indicator of love in a society is marriage. We looked at the decline in marriage in the prior sign.

Another indicator is the love a parent has for a child. So, let's look at single-parent households. Not surprisingly, the US has the world's highest rate of children living in single-parent households. 23% of children under age 18 live with only one parent and no other adults. For the rest of the world, it's only 7% of children.[49] The US Census Bureau reports that 20% of men in the US who are biological fathers of a child under the age of 18 are considered absent. Meaning they have little or nothing to do with parenting.[50]

Perhaps the best example of fulfillment in this space is to look at population growth over time. Do people even want to have children today? Global population growth peaked in 1963 at 2.3% per year. In 2023, it's down to 0.9%. That's less than half of what it was sixty years ago. Our population is no longer exponentially increasing.[51] When looking at the growth rate for the US and Israel, the data tells the same story.

Today Is Different - It's ironic, but with the popularity of social media today, our society has actually become less sociable. We don't spend as much time around other people as we used to. Covid for sure had a huge impact on that. But so has technology. We don't talk as much anymore because now we just text. We no longer hang out in the same room with friends to play a game, because now it's easier to play with them online.

It's even infected our work lives. We used to go into the office and work side by side with coworkers and engage in conversation with them throughout the day. Not anymore. Many people are still working from home and just engage with coworkers virtually. We've become a society of homebodies.

Abortion is a clear example of having no affection for a child, and the widespread practice of it makes today different. We're going to discuss this in Sign #99 - Child Sacrifice.

Today is also unique because you no longer need an actual human partner if you want to engage in love making. You just need a sex toy or sex doll. Inflatable dolls came on the scene in the 1960s. Today, companies are working on making robots that are lifelike, posable, and incorporate AI so they can have a conversation, and change their look, clothes, or voice.[52] People used to have to call a 1-800 number if they wanted to have a sexual conversation with someone. Not anymore. Like anything else, there's an app for that.

Additional Scriptures: 1 John 4:7-11. Matthew 24:12. Romans 1:18, 28, 31.

#82 - GENETIC ENGINEERING

Anti | DD | Earth | Gov | Israel | Jesus | Leader | Sky | Society | Tech | Trib

> The earth was corrupt before God, and the earth was filled with violence. God saw the earth, and saw that it was corrupt, for all flesh had corrupted their way on the earth. (Genesis 6:11-12)

In the Olivet Discourse, Jesus said it would be like the days of Noah before his second coming. The Scripture above depicts those days of Noah. We learn the earth was corrupt and all flesh had corrupted their way. The word *corrupt* means to be marred, spoiled, ruined, or perverted.

While not a biblical account, there's an interesting description of this period of time in the *Ancient Book of Jasher*. It tells us that men taught the mixture of animals of one species with another and that provoked the anger of God. Which makes sense because one of the laws in the Old Testament speaks of not breeding different animal species and not sowing fields with mixed seed.

Fulfillment - Genetic engineering is modifying the DNA of an organism. The first genetically modified organisms (GMO) were made in the 1970s. Genetically engineered human insulin was first produced in 1978.[53] Now, this scientific advancement is used for all sorts of things: drugs, vaccines, gene therapy in humans, and food.

Genetically modified foods or bioengineered foods are prevalent today. The US FDA approved its use in 1988, and commercial sales of GMO foods began in 1994. The process involves identifying a useful gene from an organism that you'd like to add to the plant or animal. This genetic engineering is usually done to make the food more tolerant of extreme weather, resistant to insects or herbicides, grow faster, and be more nutritious.[54]

Some of this science is actually done in Israel. They're known as a very significant player in the food tech sector with gene-editing of seeds and developing biopesticides.[55]

Today, some mammals are even being modified to produce non-food products. It's called pharming. For example, some genetically modified goats produce a drug through their milk. That product in turn is called a biopharmaceutical.[56] There are even spider-goats that produce spider silk protein in their milk.[57] For real, not making it up. The US Navy is even funding one of these labs so they can research an underwater spider silk web to ensnare hostile ship propellers.

Of the crops grown in the US (like soybeans, cotton, corn, canola, sugar beets), most of them, over 90%, are GMO. Thus, most of the animals we consume eat GMO crops.[58]

We have indeed corrupted God's creation.

Today Is Different - Today is unique because now there's a truly bizarre application of genetic engineering that's reminiscent of the movie *The Matrix*. It was reported in May 2024 that the world's first bioprocessing platform using human brain organoids (lab grown mini brains) performed computational tasks instead of computer chips. It runs on 16 brain organoids, which they state uses one million times less power than a computer.[59] That was in Switzerland. The US is playing in this arena too. Harvard University's Stem Cell Institute created a brain organoid that was able to recognize speech and do simple math.[60]

To me, this development has crossed a whole new line in terms of corrupting and perverting God's creation.

Additional Scriptures: Genesis 1:24-28. Isaiah 24:5. Leviticus 19:19. Luke 17:26-30. Matthew 24:37-39.

Non-biblical accounts:[61] *Ancient Book of Jasher* 4:18.

#83 - NEPHILIM

Anti | DD | Earth | Gov | Israel | **Jesus** | Leader | Sky | **Society** | **Tech** | **Trib**

> The Nephilim were in the earth in those days, and also after that, when God's sons came in to men's daughters and had children with them. Those were the mighty men who were of old, men of renown. (Genesis 6:4)

Just like in the prior sign, we're going to consider the days of Noah because Jesus told us that the time of his second coming would be similar. Here, we're told the Nephilim, the giants, were in the earth. They were the offspring of God's sons, that's the angels, and men's daughters, that's human women.

Several non-biblical accounts confirm the Bible. The *Ancient Book of Enoch* states 200 angels descended from heaven and married human women who then gave birth to giants. The *Ancient Book of Jubilees* tells us the angels who married the human women are now bound in the depths of the earth. Josephus, in *The Antiquities of the Jews*, also wrote about this and said their offspring did what resembled the acts of the Grecian giants.

I mentioned this in Sign #72 - Mark Of The Beast. The prophet Daniel revealed the last kingdom that would rule on earth. It's represented by the ten toes of iron mixed with clay on the statue in his vision. Daniel says "they" will mingle themselves with the seed of men, but not adhere. The Bible doesn't say who the "they" are. Based on all the evidence, I think we can infer it's going to be fallen angels. Will we see the Nephilim return in the tribulation period? It's certainly possible.

Fulfillment - I don't recall the Nephilim coming up in pop culture until relatively recently. Do you? There's a Wikipedia page that's got a list and it looks like an episode of the *X-Files* that aired in 1998 may have been one of the first appearances of them on popular TV.[62]

Now, angel-human hybrids in stories seem commonplace. Just consider all the movies and shows about fallen angels: *Good Omens*, *Lucifer*, *Supernatural*, *Charmed*, and *Angel* as examples. Seems like we're getting prepped and conditioned for their arrival.

Today Is Different - Chimeras are made by placing cells from one animal inside another. A mouse-rat chimera was created in 1973. In 2013, scientists put human brain cells inside mice. The mice actually survived and, perhaps not surprisingly, performed better on cognitive tests.[63] In 2021, a team of scientists created embryos that were part monkey and part human, and they lived for 20 days.[64]

Pigs are being genetically modified with human genes. It's so their organs are more compatible with humans and can thus be used for transplants into humans. In March 2024, it was reported that Harvard Medical School transplanted one of these modified pig kidneys into a human.[65]

This is just a sampling of what's going on. You can read about all sorts of these kinds of experiments being performed today. We live in a unique time because if an angel happened to show up on earth, we have the ability to merge their DNA with human DNA and create something like the Nephilim of old.

Additional Scriptures: 2 Peter 2:4. Daniel 2:32-33, 40-43. Deuteronomy 1:28, 2:10-11, 20-21, 3:11. Genesis 6:11-12; 10:8-9; 19:1-11. Hebrews 2:14-16. Jude 1:6-7. Luke 17:26-30. Matthew 24:37-39. Numbers 13:2, 21-22, 28-29, 32-33. Revelation 14:9-11.

Non-biblical accounts:[66] *Ancient Book of Enoch* 6:1-2, 5; 7:1-2. *Ancient Book of Jubilees* 5:1, 6; 7:21. *The Antiquities of the Jews*, Book 1 Chapter 3.1.

#84 - FADING OF NORMALITY

Anti | DD | **Earth** | **Gov** | Israel | **Jesus** | Leader | Sky | **Society** | **Tech** | **Trib**

> "As the days of Noah were, so will the coming of the Son of Man be. For as in those days which were before the flood they were eating and drinking, marrying and giving in marriage, until the day that Noah entered into the ship, and they didn't know until the flood came and took them all away, so will the coming of the Son of Man be." (Matthew 24:37-39)

Jesus is the one speaking in the verses above. His disciples had asked what the signs of his second coming and the end of the age were. We learn here that one of those signs is that it will be like the days of Noah. Then he lists all the normal things people were doing before the flood came. In a different Scripture, Jesus also said it would be like the days of Lot. In both instances he gave a list of activities that people were engaged in, which includes eating, drinking, marrying, giving in marriage, buying, selling, planting, and building. Essentially, life was normal, and the people were oblivious before judgment came against them.

You might think of this as an anti-sign. When it starts to become difficult to do those activities that Jesus listed, then we know his coming must be near. This is also why we know that he's coming in the rapture before the tribulation judgments begin. Life will be anything but normal during the tribulation period. It will be a struggle to survive.

The book of Revelation points out something interesting too. We're told that the merchants of the earth become rich because of Babylon.

They all weep. Every shipmaster, every sailor, and all who trade when Babylon is destroyed. So, this tells us that some level of normalcy is even still in place up until this judgment against Babylon during the tribulation period.

We shouldn't be expecting Jesus to come when it looks like the Apocalypse has already happened. We should be expecting him when we start to see normal fading away.

Fulfillment - Let's examine how difficult the activities Jesus mentioned have become.

Abnormal eating and drinking: bioengineered food, the push to eat bugs, bird flu, mad cow, war against farmers and ranchers, reduced supply of food, salmonella, listeria, E. Coli, pesticides, healthy food is the most expensive, water contamination, drought, floods, food production plants catching fire.

Abnormal buying: inflation is making goods and services unaffordable, fewer stores, online shopping, delivery, less options for goods and services, counterfeits, fake reviews, self-checkout, ordering through an app, product shrinkage, declining quality, climate regulations mean less choice, increased use of credit cards and loans to pay for stuff.

Abnormal selling: inflation makes the cost of producing goods and services unaffordable, thefts, climate regulations, fewer people working, minimum wage hikes, remote working, online retail, illegal immigration, higher taxes, robot workers, AI.

Abnormal marrying: decline in marriage, open marriages, LGBT marriages, inflation making weddings unaffordable, fear of the future.

Abnormal planting: inflation makes farm equipment unaffordable, war on farmers, climate change regulations, water rights, energy restrictions, bioengineered food, droughts, floods.

Abnormal building: inflation makes lumber and other materials unaffordable, fewer workers, increased regulations, shrinking supply chain, increased demand for housing but high loan rates.

Today Is Different - The new normal. That slogan was spoken everywhere when Covid hit. Remember when we couldn't do most of those activities that Jesus described? We couldn't go anywhere or do anything for a time. We were all stuck at home. The supply chain was a disaster because the cargo ships couldn't offload at US ports. Stores ran out of basic necessities like toilet paper. Anything that could go online did. So, many businesses closed, and people lost their jobs. A lot of people still work from home. We didn't return to the normal we had before Covid.

We almost ran out of normal. How much time do we have before we do run out? Technology and scientific advancements can only progress so far before we eclipse the biblical narrative. AI isn't going to take over everyone's jobs before Jesus comes because that would make buying and selling no longer normal. Inflation isn't going to make it impossible to buy food or have parties because that would make marrying and buying abnormal.

I think the more pressing question is how much time does Israel have before they run out of normal? The war with Hamas seems to escalate every day. Life certainly isn't all that normal for them right now with rockets raining down on them. It's only a matter of time before we start to see the end times wars spoken of in the Bible start to come to pass.

It's almost like we've reached the edge of a cliff. The world is teetering on the edge regarding WWIII. The US is teetering on the edge regarding civil war, insurmountable government debt, the Southern border crisis, the upcoming presidential election, drugs, crime, and inflation. Israel is teetering on the edge regarding a regional war in the Middle East, constant elections, and a strained relationship with the US and the world. It doesn't seem like we can teeter much more before something falls.

All of the signs in this book show that we're losing normal every day.

Additional Scriptures: 2 Timothy 3:1-9. Deuteronomy 28:15-68. Genesis 6. Luke 17:26-30. Revelation 18:3, 11-19.

#85 – DOWNFALL OF THE UNITED STATES

Anti | DD | Earth | **Gov** | **Israel** | Jesus | **Leader** | Sky | Society | Tech | **Trib**

> "Come down, virgin daughter of Babylon, and sit in the dust. For your days of sitting on a throne have ended. O daughter of Babylonia, never again will you be the lovely princess, tender and delicate. ... Never again will you be known as the queen of kingdoms. For I was angry with my chosen people and punished them by letting them fall into your hands. But you, Babylon, showed them no mercy. You oppressed even the elderly. You said, 'I will reign forever as queen of the world!' You did not reflect on your actions or think about their consequences. Listen to this,

> you pleasure-loving kingdom, living at ease and feeling secure. You say, 'I am the only one, and there is no other. I will never be a widow or lose my children.' Well, both these things will come upon you in a moment: widowhood and the loss of your children. Yes, these calamities will come upon you, despite all your witchcraft and magic. ... So disaster will overtake you, and you won't be able to charm it away. Calamity will fall upon you, and you won't be able to buy your way out. A catastrophe will strike you suddenly, one for which you are not prepared." (Isaiah 47:1, 5-9, 11 NLT)

In this set of Scriptures, God is speaking with the prophet Isaiah about the destruction that will come against the "daughter of Babylon." Now, when examining all the Scriptures in the Bible regarding Babylon, a case can certainly be made that the United States fits as a daughter of Babylon. Just look at the adjectives in these verses: lovely princess, queen of kingdoms, queen of the world, pleasure-loving kingdom, living at ease, feeling secure, I will never be a widow or lose my children. In the additional Scriptures below, other descriptions include hindermost of nations (last in terms of founding), mightiest hammer in all the earth, and most haughty one.

If you've read Jonathan Cahn's book, *The Harbinger*, he makes a compelling case that the United States, founded as a Christian nation, is now following the biblical templates of judgment because we've forsaken God. He expounds upon Isaiah 9:8-10:4. In both the Scripture included here and the Scripture Cahn uses, disaster comes upon the nation in one moment.

We know that God often uses a nation's enemies to carry out his judgment. I'm sure Satan is happy to comply, after all the Bible refers to him as the destroyer of cities.

Above, we learn one reason for the judgment is because Babylon didn't show God's chosen people, that's Israel, mercy. There are some wars on the horizon between Israel and her enemies. The biblical accounts make it clear that no nation goes to Israel's aid. Not even the US. God is the one who shows up and defends her supernaturally. For more on this refer to Sign #108 - Gog Of The Land Of Magog and Sign #112 - All Nations Against Israel. Those wars likely happen after the rapture, so it could be that if the US is indeed the daughter of Babylon, that this judgment occurs during the rapture or shortly thereafter. That would render the US incapable of aiding Israel in these future wars.

Fulfillment - Consider all of the things that are currently destabilizing the US: illegal immigration, climate laws and regulations, inflation, government debt, crime, the US presidential election tension, and funding the war in Ukraine to name a few. Health care systems, schools, shelters, and aid organizations can't support the volume of immigrants entering the country. The immigrants are taking all the job growth. And, not surprisingly, it's now being reported that terrorists are taking advantage of our open Southern border.

It's gotten so divisive in California and Oregon that multiple counties within those states are actively trying to secede and either form a new state or join a neighboring state.[67]

Many are having difficulty paying bills and affording groceries because of rising costs. Businesses are struggling to survive, and many are going bankrupt. Fuel prices keep rising. The government has expended our oil reserves in order to artificially lower the price of gas for a time. All on top of increased government regulation that prevents the US from being the largest producer of oil on the planet. We're shackling ourselves.

Since Covid, interest rates have risen from 0.25% to a 23-year high of 5.25-5.50%. It's been at the record high for eight consecutive Federal Reserve meetings, the last one held in July 2024.[68] The Fed doesn't want to lower rates because inflation is so high. This makes loans a lot more expensive for consumers. Another problem is that banks teeter on survival in this type of economy. Banks typically invest in fixed income securities. When interest rates rise, those securities aren't worth as much when the bank needs to sell them to meet deposit requirements. This is why two of the largest bankruptcies in the US happened in early 2023, Silicon Valley Bank and Signature Bank.[69]

America's cities are rotting and turning into ghost towns with empty business and retail space, infrastructure in disrepair, more homeless on the streets, and cities literally covered in human feces. It seems like we're in a death spiral with no way of escape.

Today Is Different - The US used to be the most respected country in the world. Our president had an enormous amount of influence with other world leaders. This is no longer the case, and the reason today is unique.

This is evidenced by the recent emboldened behavior of leaders like Russia's Putin, China's Xi, Iran's Khamenei, and North Korea's Kim. It's also seen in our nation's inability to bring peace and stabilization in a time of need.

Also consider how the US has lost its power over the UN. The US provides one-third of the funding for the UN.[70] In the past, the UN wouldn't have directly opposed the US. The fact that the International Criminal Court of the UN issued arrest warrants in May 2024 for Israel's prime minister and minster for defense, an ally of the US, reveals the changing power dynamics on the international stage.[71]

Instead, what are we doing? God has let America be governed by a debased leader, President Biden, that has no respect on the world stage. Our military withdrawal from Afghanistan in 2021 was an epic failure, seen as weak by world leaders and supplied terrorists with $7 billion worth of sophisticated military equipment.[72] We're exporting the radical agenda that's undermined the morality of our own country by aiding the UN in promoting abortion and the LGBT agenda. Instead of investing in our own military and in replenishing our stockpiles, we continue to pump a seemingly endless amount of money, $175 billion, into the war between Russia and Ukraine.[73]

On top of all of that, our nation's support for Israel is weakening. In March 2024, the UN Security Council passed the Gaza ceasefire resolution for the month of Ramadan and the US didn't veto it. Israel spoke out against US support for this resolution because it doesn't include the immediate release of hostages.[74]

In June 2024, Israel's Prime Minister Netanyahu addressed the US congress and said the US was withholding weapons shipments to Israel. This was thus causing delays in their offensive. Turns out the US government removed procedures they'd put in place to fast-track weapons to Israel when the war with Hamas broke out.[75] Why would they do that when the war isn't over yet, and clearly seems to be escalating instead? We can send endless weapons to Ukraine, but not to Israel? Did you know that over 100 lawmakers boycotted Netanyahu's address?[76] Vice President Kamala Harris was absent as well.[77]

In Israel's time of need the US seems to have less and less mercy every day. This is not going to bode well with God.

<u>Additional Scriptures:</u> Deuteronomy 28:15-68. Ezekiel 38-39. Isaiah 9:8-10:4; 13:19-22; 14:3-17, 22-23; 17:3-9; 21:6-10; 47. Jeremiah 25:11-12; 50-51. Revelation 14:8; 16:17-19; 17-19:3.

#86 - ONE WORLD GOVERNMENT

<u>Anti</u> | DD | Earth | <u>Gov</u> | Israel | Jesus | <u>Leader</u> | Sky | Society | Tech | <u>Trib</u>

> So he said, "The fourth animal will be a fourth kingdom on earth, which will be different from all the kingdoms, and will devour the whole earth, and will tread it down and break it in pieces. As for the ten horns, ten kings will arise out of this kingdom. Another will arise after them; and he will be different from the former, and he will put down three kings." (Daniel 7:23-24)

An angel is speaking to the prophet Daniel in the verses above. Daniel's just had a vision of four beasts who represent the kingdoms who will rule the world. The fourth and last beast is depicted here. We learn that this kingdom starts with ten kings. We're going to talk about them in Sign #105 - Kingdom Vs Kingdom.

In the book of Revelation, it tells us they received no kingdom yet. It seems the world will be in the process of building this one world government of ten kings when the Antichrist comes on the scene and disrupts their plans. They get their authority with the Antichrist for one hour. Then these ten kings all give their authority to the Antichrist.

Now, we know that this one world government cannot come to be until after the rapture, because the Antichrist won't be revealed until then. This is the government that will be in place during the tribulation period.

Fulfillment - All of the nations on earth coming together into one intergovernmental body is clear fulfillment of this. It's the United Nations. Today, there are 195 countries in the world, of which 193 are members of the UN.[78] It officially formed in October 1945.

The UN actually has binding legal authority. The UN Security Council can create resolutions that are binding on all UN member states, like sanctions and military action. There are 15 states on the Security Council, only five are permanent members with veto power (US, UK, France, Russia, China). There's an International Court of Justice with judges chosen by the General Assembly and the Security Council. They resolve disputes between member states and resolutions are binding.[79]

If the UN isn't convincing enough as fulfillment, consider how economically and politically connected the entire world is today. Think of all the treaties between nations, the trade agreements, countries that produce goods and services that are sold across the globe, government debt that's owned by other nations, and massive multinational companies. Today every nation affects another in some way.

Today Is Different - Recently the UN has been trying to expand its power and authority over member states. The World Health Organization (WHO), a UN agency, is negotiating a global pandemic treaty. Critics say it would require member states to share their public health data with the WHO and follow WHO rules on preparing and reacting to the next pandemic. As you can see, this could easily give away US sovereignty or encroach upon the rights of Americans.[80]

There's also the Pact for the Future, and its adoption is on the agenda at the "Summit of the Future" in September 2024.[81] A controversial policy includes giving the UN Secretary General the authority to operate an Emergency Platform in the event of a global crisis with minimal input from member states. So, the UN could make important decisions that are legally binding without US input or approval. Another contentious policy is one regarding information integrity on digital platforms. It's easy to see that something like that would enable censorship and trample rights granted by America's First Amendment.[82]

What would make the world truly unite under a global government? A common enemy. Like climate change. Like another global pandemic. Which you read above is exactly what they're trying to prepare for. Covid had a significant impact regarding advancement of this sign. What if the world thought that an advanced race of aliens made millions of people disappear? Yes, that would unite people too.

Additional Scriptures: Daniel 7. Revelation 13:1-7; 17.

#87 - POLAR OPPOSITE - AN UPRIGHT HEART

Anti | DD | **Earth** | Gov | Israel | Jesus | **Leader** | Sky | **Society** | Tech | Trib

> For our citizenship is in heaven, from where we also wait for a Savior, the Lord Jesus Christ, who will change the body of our humiliation to be conformed to the body of his glory, according to the working by which he is able even to subject all things to himself. (Philippians 3:20-21)

Throughout this chapter we've looked at signs related to a perverse heart. This sign is what I call a polar opposite. It's meant to illustrate how far away we currently are from the life we believers are going to live during Jesus's reign on earth in the millennial kingdom. Recall from Sign #6 - The Point Of No Return, that God only lets evil progress so far before he intervenes.

In the verses above, we're told about the new bodies we're going to have when Jesus returns at the rapture. We believers will exchange our bodies of humiliation for bodies of glory. We won't be subjected to the curse anymore so our bodies will no longer decay, get disease, or die. We'll be completely healed of anything that's perverted what God intended our bodies to be. God will also purify everyone's speech during Jesus's reign on earth.

As for the people who aren't raptured but live through the tribulation period as believers, they'll experience prolonged and abundant life in the millennial kingdom. Like that of a great tree.

Everyone will have an upright heart, one that's pure and resembles its father, God.

> Solomon said, "You have shown to your servant David my father great loving kindness, because he walked before you in truth, in righteousness, and in **uprightness of heart** with you." (1 Kings 3:6)

Fulfillment - So, how far away are we? Looking around, it's hard to see bodies of glory today. Whether that's a person or a nation. Neither are working to glorify God but are instead actively working to pervert God's original design.

A fun way to consider just how opposite we are is to contemplate what the worst-case scenarios might look like and see just how close we are to them.

Worst case, all the food we eat is a perversion of God's original because it's genetically engineered. We discussed that over 90% of the main crops in the US are GMO. We should also factor in that the animals we consume are eating those GMO crops too. It's certainly getting more difficult to avoid this today. We're close to this worst case.

Worst case, there are no more traditional marriages between a man and a woman that are meant to last until death. While we're not at worst case, it's easy to see that traditional marriage is under assault today. Especially since many Christian churches are performing same-sex unions.

Worst case, life has become similar to that portrayed in the movie

WALL-E. No one works, buys, sells, plants, or builds because tech has taken over and provides everything. So, everyone's obese and only cares about being served and entertained all day. I do believe parts of this are true for many people when they get home from work and especially on the weekend. Binging on food and entertainment is common today. We're not at this worst case, but close in some respects.

Today Is Different - So, what do you think? Is today different? Do we as a society have a perverse heart that corrupts God's creation and ruins God's institutions? Do you think we've reached the point of no return? How many people really have an upright heart that's righteous in God's sight?

Additional Scriptures: 1 Corinthians 15:35-57. 2 Corinthians 5:1-3. Isaiah 25:8; 35:6; 65:20-22. Jeremiah 30:17. Revelation 21:4. Romans 8:20-22. Zephaniah 3:9.

CHAPTER 12 - A HATEFUL HEART

> As the ark of the LORD's covenant came to David's city, Michal the daughter of Saul looked out at the window, and saw king David dancing and playing; and she **despised him in her heart**. (1 Chronicles 15:29)

#88 - HATRED

<u>Anti</u> | DD | Earth | Gov | Israel | <u>Jesus</u> | Leader | Sky | <u>Society</u> | <u>Tech</u> | <u>Trib</u>

> As he sat on the Mount of Olives, the disciples came to him privately, saying, "Tell us, when will these things be? What is the sign of your coming, and of the end of the age?" Jesus answered them, ... "Then many will stumble, and will deliver up one another, and will hate one another. ... Because iniquity will be multiplied, the love of many will grow cold." (Matthew 24:3-4, 10, 12)

Jesus is speaking to his disciples and sharing the signs that will point to his second coming. Here, we learn that people will "hate one another" and that love "will grow cold." The word *hate* means to detest or loathe. It's an emotional aversion and intolerance. The religious leaders of Jesus's day were offended at and intolerant of his teachings. Jesus told us believers that the world would hate us because it hated him.

This is related to the fifth commandment which states we should honor our mother and father.

The one who hates us most will be banished to the earth during the tribulation period. Yes, it's Satan. At that time, it says he will have great wrath because he'll know his time is short.

Fulfillment - There's a lot of tension and division today. Consider all the hatred that's building up in the US: teaching critical race theory, affirmative action and DEI for college admissions or workplace hiring, reparations, reverse racism and refusal to hire white men, black lives matter, white privilege, and anti-Semitism.

Israel is experiencing tension in this space as well. Consider the cultural and religious divide just between Jews and Arabs, and Orthodox Jews and Muslims. Up until June 2024, ultra-Orthodox men were exempt from the Israeli military draft which is mandatory for most Jewish men. As you can imagine this exemption created resentment and has been further exasperated by the current war with Hamas. The religious men believe the military is incompatible with their lifestyle and that they'll be secularized.[1] Draft orders just started being delivered in the summer of 2024. Will they comply? We'll see.

Kids today are having to deal with cyberbullying. Social media makes it easier for bullies to target someone and for content to be seen by a large audience. In fact, 53% of teens aged 13-17 say online harassment and online bullying are a major problem for their age group today. Another 40% agree that it's a minor problem. The key takeaway, it's a problem today. Almost half of teens, 46%, say they've experienced some type of cyberbullying like name-calling, being a victim of false rumors, receiving explicit images, stalking, threats, or having explicit images of them shared.[2] On top of all that, with today's technology anyone can become a victim of an AI generated deepfake.

I read an article on Fox News in May 2024 about the latest internet trend of rage rituals. Apparently, women are paying thousands of dollars to go into the woods, scream, and beat the ground with sticks.[3]

Today Is Different - Today is different because the US is on the brink of a civil war because of the increased political divide between the Democrat and Republican parties. Pew Research Center published survey results in June 2024 regarding the key 2024 US Presidential Election issues. Only 27% of people who support President Trump believe slavery affects the standing of Black people in the US today. For supporters of President Biden, it's the opposite at 79%. Here's another one. 90% of Trump supporters say gender is determined at birth as opposed to only 39% of Biden supporters. Illegal immigration is another hot button topic. Supporters in favor of deporting illegal immigrants: 63% of Trump supporters vs 11% of Biden supporters.[4]

Why the big divide? It's primarily a difference between Christianity and the rest of the world, which is a key indicator of end times signs fulfillment. The majority of Protestants (59%), Catholics (52%), and Mormons (75%) align with the Republican party. While the majority of Jewish (69%), Muslim (66%), and Unaffiliated (70%) align with Democrats. The largest religious majority for the Republicans is white evangelical Protestants (85%) and for the Democrats it's Atheists (84%).[5]

If the Republican party, who continues to uphold at least some biblical standards, wins then I don't believe the election results are going to be tolerated by many Americans. Remember what happened after Trump won the 2016 US Presidential Election? There were riots all over the largest cities in America.

Additional Scriptures: 2 Timothy 3:1-3. Colossians 3:5-8. Deuteronomy 28:37. Exodus 20:12. Galatians 5:11. Hosea 4:1. John 15:18-25. Luke 12:51-53. Matthew 10:16-25; 13:54-58. Micah 7:6. Proverbs 6:16-19. Revelation 12:12. Romans 1:30-31.

#89 - VICTIMHOOD

Anti | DD | Earth | Gov | Israel | **Jesus** | Leader | Sky | **Society** | Tech | **Trib**

> "Don't be afraid of the things which you are about to suffer. Behold, the devil is about to throw some of you into prison, that you may be tested; and you will have oppression for ten days. Be faithful to death, and I will give you the crown of life." (Revelation 2:10)

Jesus is the one speaking in the verse above. He's telling his disciple John what to write in the letter to the church in Smyrna. It's a warning about suffering persecution in prison and that being steadfast in the face of it can earn a heavenly crown.

Unfortunately, there are people today who've twisted the meaning of this. They desire to be persecuted, to live through the tribulation period, and to fight against the Antichrist and Satan because they want to earn this crown. They want to be a victim.

Please remember that we cannot earn our salvation. The battle is the Lord's. We get our victory through Jesus.

In the Old Testament book of Amos, we learn that there were people who desired the day of the Lord. Now, many prophets had been prophesying about that time period, so they knew it was a time of God's wrath. Yet, they wanted it. God rebuked them for that and said it would be a day of darkness for them.

Also consider what happened when the Israelites were rescued from Egyptian captivity by Moses and Aaron. Shortly after they left Egypt, they started complaining that God had only brought them into the wilderness to kill them. They did this multiple times before entering the promised land. They constantly acted like victims.

Many Bible scholars believe that Moses may be one of the two witnesses during the tribulation period. If so, he'll be preaching a message of repentance and placing one's faith in Jesus for salvation. He'll be directing people to the promised land, the millennial kingdom, once again. Do you think people in the tribulation period will complain to Moses about being victims of God's wrath instead of realizing how radically God is trying to reach and save them? In the Olivet Discourse, Jesus did say that many people would be offended.

Fulfillment - Do you know people who act like victims, similar to how the Israelites did when they left Egyptian captivity? They compete with others on who has been hurt the most, has the most physical ailments, has the worst boss, has the most problems, and has the most ill-behaved kids. They want attention even if it's negative, so they boast about their victimhood.

We've talked about Christian deconstructionism in prior signs. It's a reason we're seeing fulfillment in this sign today too. I've read that many people start to deconstruct because they've been hurt by a Christian or a church. When they go to social media and start posting about their bad experience, they get attention. I imagine many feel like a hero.

Today Is Different - Consider some of the impacts this victim mentality is having on society today. There are people who go completely berserk if you address them with the wrong pronoun or refer to them as the wrong gender. Instead of just letting it go, they have to make you realize they believe they're a victim and you must pay for hurting them.

It's also evidenced in our sue happy culture. If someone doesn't like what another does or says to them, they sue them in court and hope to get some sort of monetary settlement at a minimum. Or how about the progression we're seeing on reparations for Black Americans due to the wrongs committed by generations past.

Can't we all say that we're a victim of a past wrong? Where does the line on this end?

Additional Scriptures: 1 Corinthians 15:57. 1 Samuel 17:47. Amos 5:18. Exodus 14:11-12; 16:2-3. Jeremiah 17:16. Matthew 24:10. Numbers 14:1-10. Revelation 11:1-14.

#90 - MOCKING

Anti | DD | Earth | Gov | Israel | Jesus | Leader | Sky | **Society** | Tech | **Trib**

> But you, beloved, remember the words which have been spoken before by the apostles of our Lord Jesus Christ. They said to you, "In the last time

there will be mockers, walking after their own ungodly lusts." These are those who cause divisions and are sensual, not having the Spirit. (Jude 1:17-19)

In this Scripture, we're told that one of the signs of the last days is mockers. It means to jeer, deride, ridicule, or make fun of. In the Old Testament, the people mocked the messengers of God. When Nehemiah and the Jewish people were rebuilding the walls around Jerusalem, their enemies constantly mocked what they were doing. You may recall that even Jesus was mocked during his crucifixion. The soldiers gave him a crown of thorns to ridicule him.

During the tribulation period, the two witnesses will be mocked, and their deaths celebrated over.

Fulfillment - Today there are popular TV shows that glorify mocking. Consider *America's Funniest Home Videos*, *Candid Camera*, *Punk'd*, *Jackass*, and *Comedy Central Roast*. The goal of these sorts of shows is to get us to laugh at someone else's misfortune.

There's also a lot of content that mocks Christianity. I've seen several movies made by non-Christians that do such a terrible job at portraying a biblical event. It seems they can't help but mock it. I think the worst one was the movie *Noah* with Russell Crowe. If you didn't see it, the director depicted fallen angels as giant stone creatures, added a stowaway on the ark that started eating the animals, and made Noah a psycho who wanted to murder his own grandchildren.[6] Seriously! It was terrible.

Unfortunately, we Christians give the world plenty of fodder for their mockery. Rapture date setters make it easy to mock the rapture when their predictions fail. Church leaders who are involved in financial and sexual scandals make it easy to mock the Bible's teachings on holy living. There are even Christians who ridicule fellow believers about their views on the end times.

Another clear example of mocking today comes from Iran. Anytime a calamity befalls the US or Israel, we see reports of people in Iran who are celebrating.

Today Is Different - The 2024 Summer Olympics opening ceremony makes today unique. At an event meant to celebrate world class athletes, they instead chose to openly mock a depiction of Jesus at the Last Supper. They presented Jesus's disciples as drag queens and LGBT in a parody of Leonardo da Vinci's famous painting. It also included an obese lesbian woman wearing a halo taking the place of Jesus, and a practically nude, blue-painted man posing as the Greek god Dionysus.[7] The event organizers proved exactly what the Scripture above says. It caused division. It was sensual. They obviously didn't have God's Holy Spirit.

Do you know whose spirit was really behind it all? Well, I discovered that some ancient philosophers regarded Dionysus and Hades as one and the same god. Hades is the god of the underworld.[8] It is no coincidence that Satan chose now as the time to openly mock Jesus at one of the most watched events around the globe.

Additional Scriptures: 2 Chronicles 36:15-16. Deuteronomy 28:37. Isaiah 36. Lamentations 1:7. Luke 22:63-65. Matthew 27:27-31, 38-44. Micah 2:6. Nehemiah 2:17-19; 4:1-3. Revelation 11:7-10.

#91 - BETRAYAL

Anti | DD | Earth | Gov | Israel | **Jesus** | **Leader** | Sky | **Society** | Tech | **Trib**

> So they asked Him, saying, "Teacher, but when will these things be? And what sign [will there be] when these things are about to take place?" And He said: ... "You will be betrayed even by parents and brothers, relatives and friends; and they will put [some] of you to death." (Luke 21:7-8, 16 NKJV)

Jesus is speaking to his disciples on the Mount of Olives and telling them that prior to his second coming that people will betray one another. He specifically mentioned those closest to a person, family and friends.

You may recall that Jesus was betrayed by Judas Iscariot, who was one of his twelve main disciples. Judas accepted 30 pieces of silver to betray Jesus to the religious authorities. In today's money, that would convert to a few hundred dollars at most.[9]

During the tribulation period when the Antichrist and False Prophet are persecuting God's people, betrayal will be commonplace. We're also told that the Antichrist and the kings of the earth who surround him will use the one world religion for a time but end up betraying and destroying it. For more on that refer to Sign #69.

Fulfillment - We see acts of betrayal portrayed in the news daily. Whether it's an act of violence against a friend or family member or the breakup of a celebrity relationship due to infidelity.

One of the best examples of this today is US President Biden's abrupt military withdrawal from Afghanistan in 2021. If you recall, the US war in Afghanistan began on September 11, 2001, when terrorists attacked Americans on US soil. They flew planes into the World Trade Center in New York City. After 20 years of influence in Afghanistan, Biden chose to abandon it and leave it in the hands of terrorists, the Taliban. It created a humanitarian nightmare for residents. Do you remember all the organizations that were trying to help rescue people? *The Atlantic* magazine published a spread on this in their March 2022 issue, aptly titled "The Betrayal."[10]

Today Is Different - Well, up until July 21, 2024, I would have told you that today was special because a clear example of betrayal happened in December 2020 when Vice President Pence signed off on the 2020 US Presidential Election results. There was plenty of evidence of interference, so he could have contested the results and helped get to the truth. Instead, he chose to be complacent in a shocking betrayal of President Trump and the Republican voters.

Today is also unique because as I mentioned in Sign #85 - Downfall Of The United States, the US is now starting to betray one of our closest allies, Israel.

But now, I have to say something even more shocking has happened. It's the betrayal of another US president, this time it was President Biden who was betrayed in a similar manner as President Trump. By his own political party leaders. Biden and the White House were adamant that he wasn't dropping out of the 2024 US Presidential Election, even up until July 20, 2024. Then suddenly the next day he posts a suspicious letter dropping out of the race.[11] It certainly doesn't seem like he chose to quit. Does it to you?

Additional Scriptures: 2 Timothy 3:1-4. Jeremiah 38:1-6. Luke 12:51-53; 22:3-6. Mark 13:12; 14:41-45. Matthew 24:10; 26:47-49; 27:3-10. Micah 7:5-6. Proverbs 6:16-19.

#92 - ANTI-SEMITISM

Anti | DD | Earth | Gov | Israel | Jesus | Leader | Sky | Society | Tech | Trib

"You will be hated by all men for my name's sake." (Luke 21:17)

Jesus is the one speaking in the verse above. He's telling his disciples what the signs of his second coming will be. One of those signs is that they, his disciples, who were all Jewish, would be hated by all men. This anti-Semitism began in the garden of Eden. When God cursed Satan, he said there would be enmity between Satan's seed and Eve's seed.

God created the nation and people group of Israel when he asked Abraham to follow him. God created an unconditional, everlasting covenant with Abraham. That covenant was passed on through Abraham's son Isaac and then his son Jacob, who was later renamed by God to Israel.

During the tribulation period, Satan will severely persecute and try to eradicate God's chosen people. We'll look at that more in Sign #115 - War Against God's People.

Fulfillment - Jew hatred has always existed. Cancel culture provides evidence of this today. There are people who continue to deny the Holocaust happened. It's actually illegal in 18 countries.[12] In 2022, the UN approved a resolution that defines Holocaust denial and encourages member states to preserve sites that were once death or concentration camps and to educate people on the tragedy. No surprise, but Iran disassociated itself from the resolution.[13]

Today, there's also temple denial. It's a form of anti-Semitism which states the Jewish temples in Jerusalem either didn't exist or were not constructed on the site of the current Temple Mount. After Israel became a nation in 1948, the Waqf removed references to Solomon's Temple from its guidebooks.[14] In 2023, the leader of the Palestinian Authority, Mahmoud Abbas, stated in a speech to the UN that there wasn't any proof of Jewish ties to the Temple Mount area. I'm actually writing this on Tisha B'Av, the Jewish day of mourning for the destruction of the two temples. *The Jerusalem Post* has an article titled: " *'Jewish Myth:' In Arab World, Many Still Refuse To Accept The Two Temples' Existence - Analysis.*"[15]

Even within Christianity we see fulfillment in this sign today. It's through replacement theology. It's the belief that the church, the body of people who've put their faith in Jesus, has replaced Israel. They think that because the Jews rejected Jesus as Messiah that Jesus has now rejected them. It's preposterous.

People in this camp don't believe God will fulfill any of his promises to Israel in the future and that the church will get all those benefits instead. The problem with this is that it's not biblical; it's anti-Semitic. I believe Jesus warned us about this in the letter to the church in Smyrna when he said people would claim to be Jews but weren't. That they're really of the synagogue of Satan.

Today Is Different - The BDS movement is another act of anti-Semitism we see that makes today unique. It means boycott, divestment, and sanctions, and its purpose is to pressure Israel into accepting Palestinian demands. Namely that Israel is occupying their land. The movement started in the early 2000s. They boycott goods and services produced by Israeli companies. They want people, governments, schools, and banks to divest from investments in Israel. They want governments to sanction Israel.[16] Most people in America, 84%, hadn't even heard of this movement until war broke out between Israel and Hamas in October 2023.[17]

Since then, this movement has infected college campuses across the US. You've seen the protests on the news and the claims that Israel is apartheid, an occupier, racist, and a terrorist. The January 2024 issue of the *Lamplighter* magazine by Lamb & Lion Ministries (which you can download free on their website) has an article titled, "Deceptive Slogans In The Propaganda War Against Israel."

https://christinprophecy.org/wp-content/uploads/Lamplighter_JanFeb24_War-Raging-Rulers-of-Darkness.pdf

The article explains that slogans like "set Palestine free from the river to sea" are rooted in anti-Semitism. That chant refers to the area from the Jordan River to the Mediterranean Sea. That's the entire nation of Israel! They're calling for the eradication of a people group.[18] It's no surprise that 65% of Jewish students say the BDS movement is now a threat to their safety on campus, according to a 2024 survey.[19]

These protests have escalated to such a degree that the US Congress is now investigating anti-Semitism on college campuses. So far as a result, multiple US university presidents have resigned.[20] What's even more ridiculous is that a Federal judge had to order the University of California, Los Angeles to stop letting anti-Israel protesters ban Jewish people from parts of the campus. The judge was quoted as saying, "In the year 2024, in the United States of America, in the State of California, in the City of Los Angeles, Jewish students were excluded from portions of the UCLA campus because they refused to denounce their faith. This fact is so unimaginable and so abhorrent to our constitutional guarantee of religious freedom that it bears repeating, Jewish students were excluded from portions of the UCLA campus because they refused to denounce their faith."[21]

And in July 2024, we're learning that Iran has a part to play in all this. They're using social media to encourage these US protests, promote their narrative, issue threats, and are even providing financial support to protesters.[22]

Additional Scriptures: Deuteronomy 28:37. Ezekiel 35. Ezra 4:1-5. Genesis 3:15; 12:1-7; 15; 17:1-21; 28:10-22. Luke 21:24. Matthew 10:16-25; 24:9. Nehemiah 2:10. Revelation 3:9; 12.

#93 - UNHOLY PEOPLE CELEBRATED

Anti | DD | Earth | **Gov** | Israel | Jesus | Leader | Sky | **Society** | Tech | **Trib**

> "But he will vent his anger against the people of the holy covenant and reward those who forsake the covenant. ... He will flatter and win over those who have violated the covenant." (Daniel 11:30, 32 NLT)

An angel is speaking to the prophet Daniel in the Scriptures above. The angel is revealing the deeds of the Antichrist during the tribulation period. The Antichrist is "he." He's going to reward, flatter, and win over people who forsake and violate the holy covenant. This sign means unholy people are going to be celebrated and rewarded.

The day Jesus was crucified, the people had a chance to let him go free. But they forsook the one who was holy and chose to reward the one who was unholy. They gave Barabbas the murderer freedom instead.

The Old Testament spoke of this as a time in which people would call evil good and good evil. It makes sense when you realize the world is going to worship the unholy trinity of Satan, the Antichrist, and the False Prophet during the tribulation period.

Fulfillment - One way to gauge who our society celebrates is to look at who's popular on social media. While some church leaders and pastors have a large following, they're not even in the same league as Cristiano Ronaldo, Selena Gomez, Justin Bieber, Dwayne Johnson, and Taylor Swift for example. It's athletes, musicians, and actors who garner hundreds of millions of followers on social media,[23] many of whom are outspoken in their support of abortion and the LGBT community.

Another way we celebrate is through entertainment, like movies. Superhero movies are by far the most popular. The Marvel Comics brand reigns the worldwide box office at $17.2 billion in revenue.[24] No other brand is even close. These movies are starting to reflect our immoral society. Marvel superheroes are now portrayed as being in the LGBT community: Valkyrie, Loki, Phastos, and Deadpool.[25]

The Comics Code Authority started in 1954 and set standards for content in comics. The code prohibited content like sexual perversion, extreme violence, nudity, and profanity. All the major publishers submitted their work and earned their seal of approval on comics up until 2001 when Marvel abandoned it. Then all the publishers followed suit that next decade. The code went defunct in 2011.[26] And now, as a clear sign of the times, the new Superman Jonathan Kent, the son of the original Superman Clark Kent and Lois Lane, was depicted as gay in November 2021.[27]

Today Is Different - There's a lot that can be said for what makes today unique. In May 2024, the UN Security Council had a moment of silence for the death of Iran's President Ebrahim Raisi.[28] This man was nicknamed the Butcher of Tehran. He murdered his own people, attempted to assassinate American officials, and spread terrorism. On top of the UN actions, the US State Department even issued a letter of condolence.[29] It's like giving Hitler a moment of silence. Who would do that? Yet, on that same day the UN International Criminal Court issued an arrest warrant for Israel's Prime Minister Netanyahu.[30]

Do you remember the BLM riots that started in 2020? The protesters caused mayhem in cities across the US but were idolized on the news. Cities even painted BLM murals on city streets to show support for the movement.[31] Wikipedia has a whole list of cities involved. There's probably over a hundred listed with murals. *The New York Times* claims it may be the largest movement in US history with estimates of 26 million people participating in protests.[32]

You know we basically have two days on the US calendar in which we celebrate Jesus. Christmas and Easter. Israel doesn't really celebrate these because their population of Christians is so small. Yet, in the US we have the entire month of June to observe and celebrate the LGBT culture. In Israel it's a week-long observance.

In the US, Pride Month began in 1970.[33] In Israel, Tel Aviv Pride began in 1993.[34] And now there's even an International Transgender Day of Visibility on March 31 each year. It was started in 2009.[35] You may recall that US President Biden officially acknowledged this holiday on March 31, 2024.[36] That day just so happened to be Easter. You won't convince me Biden didn't do that on purpose.

It's also not a coincidence that the symbol Pride has adopted is the rainbow. Did you know that there's a rainbow which surrounds God's throne? That's God's sign! Satan hijacked it. Today, even city streets are painted as rainbows to show support for the LGBT community.

I've mentioned the 2024 Summer Olympics opening ceremony and its drag queen, LGBT mockery of the Last Supper in prior signs. It's obviously another reason that makes today different in regard to fulfillment for this sign. As is the celebration of transgenders competing in the Olympics, winning women's beauty pageants, and being recognized as women-of-the-year by various publications.

<u>Additional Scriptures:</u> Ezekiel 1:28. Genesis 9:12-17. Isaiah 5:20. Luke 21:12-17. Matthew 27:15-26. Revelation 4:3; 6:2; 13:3-4. Romans 1:26-32.

#94 - GOD'S PROPHETS ARE PERSECUTED

Anti | DD | Earth | Gov | **Israel** | **Jesus** | **Leader** | Sky | **Society** | **Tech** | **Trib**

> "I will give power to my two witnesses, and they will prophesy one thousand two hundred sixty days, clothed in sackcloth. ... When they have finished their testimony, the beast that comes up out of the abyss will make war with them, and overcome them, and kill them." (Revelation 13:3, 7)

An angel is speaking to the prophet John in the verses above. This is an event which happens in the tribulation period. God will send two witnesses to prophesy and share their testimony for three and a half years. At the end of that time "the beast," the Antichrist, will kill them. This is just one of the many instances in the Bible regarding the persecution of God's prophets.

For example, before Babylon came against Israel the prophet Jeremiah warned the people and leaders. They refused to listen to him and sought to kill him instead. Jesus warned his disciples that they would suffer persecution too. During Jesus's first coming, he preached a message of repentance and that his kingdom was coming. The religious leaders sought to kill him as soon as he started healing people on the Sabbath. As you know, Jesus was crucified as a result of the persecution against him.

Fulfillment - Today we have prominent church leaders who proclaim the Word of God. It's an element of prophecy. Covid resulted in wide scale persecution against church leaders. In the US, churches were shut down in most states. It was ridiculous. In my state, New Mexico, the bars weren't shut down, but the churches were. If a church wasn't set up with an online presence, they had no way of reaching their congregation during that time. It was the enemy's effort to silence God's voice.

The Johnson Amendment was added to the US tax code in 1954 and prohibits non-profit organizations from endorsing or opposing political candidates in order to maintain their tax-exempt status.[37] It's directly opposed to the First Amendment. It essentially muzzles pastors in America. Church leaders could share a biblical perspective on political party platforms, speeches of political leaders, and contentious issues of today. However, many don't because of this law. They're afraid of losing income that people can write off on their taxes as a charitable contribution because of their exempt status.

Consider all the church leaders who've been silenced over the years on social media. Whether it's a single post that's been taken down, a temporary lockout, or an outright deplatforming. Pastor Jack Hibbs is one such example. He got his entire channel nuked off YouTube in February 2023.[38]

There are also physical attacks against churches in the US today. It's been reported there were 436 incidents in 2023. Double what was reported in 2022 and eight times higher than 2018.[39]

Today Is Different - We've considered Christian deconstructionism in prior signs. It applies to this one too. That movement seeks to invalidate the teachings of the New Testament prophets in particular. Our culture is rejecting biblical doctrine taught by Jesus's disciples.

How about the persecution Pastor Jack Hibbs has received from his opening prayer to the US House of Representatives on January 30, 2024?[40] A group of Democrat lawmakers sent a letter to the House Speaker sharing their disgust. They didn't like that he spoke of national sins and the need for repentance.[41]

Are you familiar with *Rolling Stone* magazine? In October 2023, they published a hit piece on Messianic Rabbi Jonathan Cahn. They state that Cahn blames the Hamas attack on October 7, 2023 squarely on Israel for not accepting Jesus as their savior. Yikes! This is a magazine devoted to music fans. Why did they choose to persecute and speak falsely about a Christian pastor, a Messianic Jew? They can't help it. When you aren't for Jesus, you're against him. They're unknowingly fulfilling Bible prophecy by trying to cancel one of God's chosen spiritual leaders.[42] Cahn posted a video in response and reveals how they pulled things he said completely out of context to make up their story. It has 878,000 views as of August 2024.[43]

Additional Scriptures: 1 Kings 19:1-3. Jeremiah 26:8-24. John 5:1-16. Luke 21:12, 16-17. Matthew 13:9, 53-58; 23:29-39; 27. Revelation 17:7-13.

#95 - OPPRESSION OF GOD'S PEOPLE

Anti | DD | Earth | Gov | Israel | Jesus | Leader | Sky | Society | Tech | Trib

> "But watch yourselves, for they will deliver you up to councils. You will be beaten in synagogues. You will stand before rulers and kings for my sake, for a testimony to them. ... When they lead you away and deliver you up, don't be anxious beforehand or premeditate what you will say, but say whatever will be given you in that hour. For it is not you who speak, but the Holy Spirit. Brother will deliver up brother to death, and the father his child. Children will rise up against parents and cause them to be put to death." (Mark 13:9, 11-12)

Jesus is the one speaking in the Scripture here. His disciples have asked for signs regarding his second coming and the end of the age. He tells them that there will be oppression and persecution against God's people.

Jesus warned about this in a different context prior to this speech. It's in his parable of the sower. He said the seed that was scattered on stony ground sprung up quickly but was scorched by the sun just as quickly because it had no root. That seed is like a believer who immediately receives God's word with happiness, but only endures for a time because tribulation and persecution cause them to stumble.

Another form of oppression against God's people that's mentioned in the Bible is frustrating their purpose. Nehemiah and Ezra both encountered this from their enemies when they were rebuilding

Jerusalem's wall and temple. The enemy doesn't want believers to accomplish anything for God's kingdom.

Fulfillment - Open Doors ranks the top 50 countries where Christians face extreme persecution. In the 2024 list, 68% of the countries have Islam as their main religion.[44] Notable exceptions are North Korea (ranks #1), India (#11), China (#19), and Mexico (#37). Those top 50 encompass 317 million Christians. That's 1 in 7 Christians worldwide who are currently facing high levels of oppression. Almost 5,000 Christians were martyred in 2023 and nearly 15,000 churches or Christian establishments were attacked.

Lawmakers in Israel introduced legislation in March 2023 that would have outlawed evangelism and jailed Christian missionaries preaching the gospel. Thankfully, Prime Minister Netanyahu stepped in and said Israel would not pass laws against the Christian community.[45] This is an ominous progression, nonetheless.

Christian couples are being forced by some US states to attend LGBT training in order to be qualified to foster or adopt children. If they refuse to support gender conversion therapy, they aren't approved. This is the case for a couple I recently read about in Vermont.[46] In November 2023, the US Biden administration proposed a new rule titled "Safe and Appropriate Foster Care Placement Requirements." It would mandate foster families utilize the child's preferred pronouns, chosen name, and dress them according to their preferred gender.[47] Since Christian organizations are a main supporter of the foster program this would have a devastating impact to children in need.

Also consider the persecution that comes against Christian businesses today. I'm frequently seeing in the news small business owners that are being sued for refusing to provide a service to an LGBT customer. Like bake a cake or do wedding photography for a same-sex wedding.

While technology helped Christians continue participating in church during Covid, today it's also being used against us. AI is used to monitor social media, block posts, shadow ban, and deplatform people. It's also used by people to help a boycott against a Christian business go viral.

Today Is Different - The increase in laws that oppress Christians is evidence that today is different. Conversion therapy bans are one such law. A majority of US citizens now live in a state or municipality that's banned gender conversion therapy. That means it's illegal to have a conversation with a child about why they shouldn't change their gender.[48]

In July 2024, California passed a law that prevents schools from informing parents of their child's gender dysphoria.[49] There are currently seven US states which mandate LGBT curriculum in public schools.[50] And unfortunately, a Federal Court just ruled that a school system in Maryland doesn't have to let parents opt their children out of LGBT lessons.[51]

The Equality Act is another law that's on the horizon that would persecute Christians. It keeps getting introduced to congress but hasn't mustered enough support to pass. But the way the country is progressing, it's going to pass one day. This bill would add sexual orientation and gender identity as protected classes to US federal civil rights law.[52] That means those classes of people would trump religious liberty in America. It would force that Christian cake baker we discussed earlier to make a cake for the same-sex wedding he has a religious objection to.

In the face of all this oppression, know that the more unpleasant it is for us believers to be here, the closer the rapture must be.

Additional Scriptures: Acts 7:54-60, 8:1. Deuteronomy 28:15-68. Ezra 4:1, 4-5. Job 2:3. John 12:9-11; 15:20; 16:1-3. Luke 11:52; 21:12, 16-17. Mark 4:1-20. Matthew 24:9. Nehemiah 4:7-8. Revelation 2:10.

#96 - SLAVERY

Anti | DD | Earth | **Gov** | Israel | **Jesus** | **Leader** | Sky | **Society** | **Tech** | **Trib**

> "The merchants of the earth weep and mourn over her, for no one buys their merchandise any more: ... people's bodies and souls." (Revelation 18:11, 13)

John, the prophet and disciple of Jesus, is speaking with an angel who is showing him events in the tribulation period. Here, we see that merchants are weeping over the destruction of Babylon. It's because no one buys their goods anymore, which included people. They were slave traders and human traffickers.

The prophet Joel spoke of this time period too and said God enters into judgment with his people because they sold boys and girls to pay for harlots and wine. We also know that during the tribulation period the Antichrist and False Prophet will enslave people with the mark of the Beast and force the worship of the Antichrist.

Jesus revealed this as a sign prior to his second coming as well. He said that during the tribulation period that people in Jerusalem would be led away captive into all nations when the Antichrist invades it.

Fulfillment - We often think of slavery solely as forced servitude to another person. I think we fail to realize that we can certainly enslave ourselves. Consider how easy it is to get into large amounts of debt today. Banks will give a credit card to almost anyone, the interest rate will just be higher and perhaps the credit limit lower. The same goes for a car loan and, in many cases, a mortgage for a home as well.

Perhaps the easiest and costliest debt to accumulate is for a student loan. It can absolutely cripple young adults. I know adult friends who are still paying off student loan debt 20 years after graduating. The problem with any kind of debt is that it makes the person in debt a slave to that debt. They have to maintain a certain income to pay for it. Sometimes that means sticking with a job that's disliked.

Then there's also government assistance programs like food stamps, welfare, social security, and free public school. You know they're a form of slavery too. They get people trained to depend on the government. In April 2023, 12% of the US population received food benefits from the US government. In 1974, only 6% of the population received this benefit. But we're not currently near the peak of 19% which happened during the Great Recession in 2013.[53]

Today Is Different - Since 2008, the number of human trafficking victims identified worldwide has almost quadrupled! We've gone from 30,961 victims in 2008 to 115,324 in 2022.[54] The UN's Global Report on Trafficking in Persons for 2022 indicates it's primarily forced labor and sexual exploitation, each accounting for 39% of cases.[55] They also state that 84% of sexual exploitation is internet based. In fact, traffickers use the internet to both recruit and exploit victims. With the popularity of online porn sites, it's no wonder this technology is used in trafficking.

On August 9, 2024, the Massachusetts governor signed the Parentage Act into law.[56] The bill allows for the commercial surrogacy of a woman's own biological child. That means a women can now legally sell her own baby in Massachusetts. Our immoral society is going to take advantage of this by turning trafficked women into baby factories. It's only a matter of time before more states follow suit.

Additional Scriptures: Amos 2:6. Deuteronomy 28:15-68. Ezekiel 27:13. Jeremiah 34:8-17. Joel 3:2-3, 6. Luke 21:24. Nehemiah 5:1-13. Revelation 13:14-17.

#97 - POLAR OPPOSITE - A PURE HEART

Anti | DD | Earth | **Gov** | **Israel** | Jesus | **Leader** | Sky | **Society** | Tech | Trib

> The work of righteousness will be peace, and the effect of righteousness, quietness and confidence forever. My people will live in a peaceful habitation, in safe dwellings, and in quiet resting places. (Isaiah 32:17-18)

Throughout this chapter we've looked at signs related to a hateful heart. This sign is what I call a polar opposite. It's meant to illustrate how far away we currently are from the life we believers are going to live during Jesus's reign on earth in the millennial kingdom. Recall from Sign #6 - The Point Of No Return, that God only lets evil progress so far before he intervenes.

When Jesus comes to reign, it'll be a time of peace, quietness, safety, and rest. After all, Jesus is called the Prince of Peace and he'll be the one reigning. In the Scripture above, "my people" is all of God's people. That'll be anyone who survives through the tribulation period as a believer and all the immortal believers who return with Jesus at his second coming. In the additional Scriptures below, we also learn that the Israelites will be brought back to their own land and firmly planted. And then they'll be given fame, praise, and wealth.

Everyone will have a pure heart, one that's full of love.

> Since you have purified your souls in obeying the truth through the Spirit in sincere love of the brethren, **love** one another fervently **with a pure heart** (1 Peter 1:22 NKJV)

Fulfillment - So, how far away are we? It's certainly hard to see love and peaceful coexistence these days. The Jewish people aren't receiving praise either. It's quite the opposite since anti-Semitism is on the rise.

A fun way to consider just how opposite we are is to contemplate what the worst-case scenarios might look like and see just how close we are to them.

Worst case, everyone in society is enslaved by the government in some sort of capacity. If you really think about it, this is truer than you realize. In America, even if you own your home outright, so no mortgage, every single state still requires you to pay tax on real estate. If you don't, the state can seize your property. That means we're really just tenants renting our land from the government. We're already at this worst case.

Worst case, everyone is able to claim some sort of reparation from the government for wrongs committed in generations past. Lawsuits happen because some people get more than others and that's racist, discriminatory, etc. The courts settle the matter by directing the government to give everyone the same payment. In a roundabout way, we arrive at a government basic income. While we're not at this worst case yet, we're certainly seeing forward progress on this.

Worst case, America's most popular pastors and church leaders are deemed terrorists by the UN for promoting hate speech (the gospel) and warrants are issued for their arrests. So, we're not at this worst case yet, but this is certainly happening in pockets around the globe already.

Today Is Different - So, what do you think? Is today different? Do we as a society have a hateful heart that oppresses God's message and his chosen people, yet celebrates unholiness? Do you think we've reached the point of no return? How many people really have a pure heart that demonstrates love for one another?

Additional Scriptures: Amos 9:14-15. Ezekiel 37:21, 25. Isaiah 9:6-7; 60:11-12, 14-15, 22. Zephaniah 3:17-20.

CHAPTER 13 - AN EVIL HEART

> The LORD said to me, "Proclaim all these words in the cities of Judah, and in the streets of Jerusalem, saying, 'Hear the words of this covenant, and do them. For I earnestly protested to your fathers in the day that I brought them up out of the land of Egypt, even to this day, rising early and protesting, saying, "Obey my voice." Yet they didn't obey, nor turn their ear, but everyone walked in the **stubbornness of their evil heart**. Therefore I brought on them all the words of this covenant, which I commanded them to do, but they didn't do them.' " (Jeremiah 11:6-8)

#98 - CONTINUALLY ONLY EVIL

Anti | **DD** | Earth | Gov | Israel | **Jesus** | Leader | Sky | **Society** | Tech | **Trib**

> The LORD saw that the wickedness of man was great in the earth, and that every imagination of the thoughts of man's heart was continually only evil. ... The earth was corrupt before God, and the earth was filled with violence. (Genesis 6:5, 11)

In the Olivet Discourse, Jesus told the disciples that the time of his second coming would be like the days of Noah. This Scripture above reveals what those days were like. Great wickedness, continually only evil, corrupt, and violence are the words used to describe it. In a separate teaching, Jesus said it would also be like the days of Lot. The people of Sodom and Gomorrah were also exceedingly wicked. Sin was at its height.

When examining the additional Scriptures below we can learn that this evil includes murder, having a seared conscience, calling evil good, maliciousness, lawlessness, and violence. In fact, violence is one of the sins that Satan got called out for. During the tribulation period, people won't repent of these deeds, and they'll even double down on murders, a violation of the sixth commandment. In this same vein, we're also told that the Antichrist will be a fierce looking king that's known for murder and destruction.

Fulfillment - Reporting on crime rates seems like it would be an easy task. Not so much given the deceptive tactics used these days to advance an agenda. From 2017 to 2019 the US had an average of 16,641 homicides per year. From 2021 to 2022 the average spiked to 22,000 a year. That's a 32% increase! So, when the news tells you that 2024 homicides are down from the prior year, they might be, but they're still way up from prior years.[1]

During the Covid pandemic, do you recall all the demands to defund the police in major cities? Well, that had an impact. Let's consider Portland, Oregon. In 2023, their homicide rate was 13.2 per 100,000 residents. It was only 5.5 in 2019. It increased 140%. During that same period, they cut 183 officers from their police force and reduced funding by $15 million. Guess what happened as a result? The city had to reverse course and refund their police.[2] This is the behavior pattern in large cities across the US. So, no surprise that the homicide rate appears to be decreasing from its peak.

The US CDC published a report in June 2023 that reveals the homicide rate for people aged 10-24 increased 60% between 2014 and 2021.[3]

Today Is Different - The Hamas attack against Israel in October 2023 crossed a line. It wasn't an attack against the Israeli military with soldiers taken prisoner. They deliberately targeted civilians and murdered children. It was an act of pure terrorism and evil. You saw the news. Hamas hunted down and shot civilians, set homes on fire, desecrated bodies, committed sexual violence, launched rockets into neighborhoods, and took hostages.

When Israel invaded Gaza, they discovered Hamas's headquarters was located under the hospital, a clear violation of the law of war.[4] Terrorists don't care about any laws. Since then, they've also found that Hamas was operating with the cooperation of civilians in Gaza. Tunnels, weapons, and hideouts are in homes, schools, mosques, and hospitals throughout Gaza.[5]

Did Hamas treat the hostages with respect and dignity? Of course not. Victims who were released are reporting the inhumane conditions in which they were kept and the assaults against them.[6] Many hostages have been recovered dead by the Israeli military. Hamas is still refusing to free the remaining hostages. I don't think we could see a clearer display of being continually only evil.

Additional Scriptures: 1 Timothy 4:2. 2 Kings 17:17; 21:1-18. 2 Timothy 3:1-3. Colossians 3:5-8. Daniel 8:23; 11:21; 12:10. Exodus 20:13. Ezekiel 28:16. Genesis 13:13; 18:20-21. Isaiah 5:18-20; 59:2-8. Jeremiah 6:15. Luke 17:26-37. Matthew 24:12, 37-44; 25:14-46. Micah 7:2-4. Proverbs 6:16-18. Revelation 3:1-5; 6:4; 9:21; 21:8. Romans 1:18, 29-30; 3:9-18.

#99 - CHILD SACRIFICE

Anti | DD | Earth | <u>Gov</u> | Israel | Jesus | Leader | Sky | <u>Society</u> | <u>Tech</u> | Trib

> They served their idols, Which became a snare to them. They even sacrificed their sons And their daughters to demons, And shed innocent blood, The blood of their sons and daughters, Whom they sacrificed to the idols of Canaan; And the land was polluted with blood. ... Therefore the wrath of the LORD was kindled against His people. (Psalm 106:36-38, 40 NKJV)

Here, we learn that God's wrath came upon the ancient Israelites because they sacrificed their children to false gods, demons. The Old Testament reveals they learned this from the pagan nations. So, it was a common practice among all peoples. Since this is a form of murder, it's also a violation of the sixth commandment.

In the book of Revelation, one of the sins Jesus told the church in Pergamos to repent of is that they held to the doctrine of Balaam. If you recall, Balaam convinced Moabite women to commit sexual sins with the Israelites. Then they sacrificed to and worshiped the false gods of the Moabites. The Moabites were Canaanites, which we see in the verses above sacrificed children to their idols. Today, we still practice child sacrifice. We just call it abortion.

King David said God formed him in his mother's womb. According to the Bible, life begins even before conception. God told the prophet Jeremiah that he knew him before he created him in his mother's womb.

Fulfillment - This is a shocking statistic that I mentioned in Sign #6 - The Point Of No Return. According to the World Health Organization, 73 million abortions take place worldwide every single year![7] That's the entire population of the 20th largest nation, Thailand. Over the span of 10 years that's 730 million babies, or about double the population of America. Over twenty years, we'd be up to 1.5 billion babies. That's the current population of India.[8] This heinous practice has been going on for far longer than twenty years though.

Let's just consider the US. The number of abortions performed yearly reached its peak in 1990 at 1.6 million. It declined until 2017 and then started increasing again. For 2023, a year after the US Supreme Court overturned Roe v. Wade, we're back over 1 million a year. The highest it's been in a decade. Why has it gone up? Almost every state without a total abortion ban saw an increase. People are traveling to get an abortion. People are now using telehealth services and performing at home medication abortions. I agree with a comment the Guttmacher Institute had in their report: "people will continue to seek abortion care in spite of the policy barriers that anti-abortion policymakers impose."[9]

Pew Research Center conducted a poll in April 2024 and reported that 63% of US respondents said abortion should be legal. For those aged 18-29, it's 76%. Not surprisingly, for the religiously unaffiliated it's all the way up to 86% saying it should be legal. In fact, the only groups that didn't have a majority favoring legal abortion were conservative Republicans (only 27%) and white evangelical Protestants (only 25%).[10]

They conducted that poll in foreign countries too. For Israel, a slight majority, 51% of the respondents, say abortion should be legal. Once again, looking at religious affiliation makes a difference. Support for legal abortion includes Jewish (56%), Hiloni or secular Jewish (89%), Masorti or traditional Jewish (58%). Those who are opposed are the Haredi and Dati or ultra-Orthodox and religious Jews (only 12% support legal abortion) and the Muslims (23%).[11]

Today Is Different - Abortion has been practiced for decades, so what makes today unique is the increasing support for infanticide. We're starting to see states make abortion legal all the way up until the baby is delivered. As of August 2024, we're up to 9 US states that no longer have restrictions on abortions based on gestational period.[12] Planned Parenthood's website even promotes this by stating that, " 'late-term abortion' isn't a thing, except in the imaginations of anti-abortion rights activists."[13]

This also means that doctors in those 10 states aren't forced to provide medical treatment to the baby if it's born alive in a botched abortion attempt. It's mind-blowing considering the advanced medical procedures we have available today to save even micropreemies. In November 2023, a baby who only weighed one pound when she was born at 22 weeks survived and was kept alive by doctors until she was able to go home six months later. The American Medical Association says 30% of babies born at 22 weeks live until they can be sent home. At 24 weeks, 71% of them survive in the hospital until going home.[14]

The reason they don't want to save the babies is because baby parts are big business even though it's a US federal felony to transfer aborted human fetal tissue. You may recall that the Center for Medical Progress

(CMP) released undercover videos in 2015 exposing sales of fetal body parts by Planned Parenthood (PP). PP denied such practices to US congress. Well, in March 2024, it was reported that PP lied to congress about profiting from baby body parts. CMP revealed PP has a contract with the University of California San Diego to provide those fetal tissues in exchange for ownership in the university's intellectual property created through experiments using those baby parts.[15]

Scientists are concerned that abortion restrictions will reduce the availability of fetal tissue and embryonic stem cells. The tissue is used to test drugs, create vaccines, study and treat diseases, and is used in regenerative medicine.[16]

The US Congress has attempted to pass the Born-Alive Abortion Survivors Protection Act since 2015, yet it continues to fail. It either doesn't make it out of a committee or it only passes in one congressional body. For the current 118th congress, so far, it's only passed the House.[17]

In a truly demonic fulfillment of why today is different, *Cosmopolitan* magazine profiled 'Samuel Alito's Mom's Satanic Abortion Clinic.' Yes, it's sadly a real abortion clinic in my home state that's directly mocking the beliefs of a US Supreme Court Justice through its business name. It's run by members of The Satanic Temple. The article claims they don't actually worship Satan. Yeah, I'm not buying that, and here's why. There's an optional ceremonial Satanic abortion ritual they tell patients they can perform before taking the abortion medication. It involves reciting personal affirmations like, "by my body, my blood; by my will, it is done." They even have "ministers" who can help people through the process.[18]

Additional Scriptures: 2 Chronicles 28:1-3. 2 Kings 3:26-27; 17:17; 21:6. Exodus 20:13. Ezekiel 16:20-21; 23:39. Jeremiah 1:4-5. Numbers 25:1-3; 31:16. Proverbs 6:16-17; 139:13-16. Revelation 2:14.

#100 - CANNIBALISM

Anti | DD | Earth | Gov | Israel | **Jesus** | **Leader** | Sky | **Society** | Tech | **Trib**

> He carried me away in the Spirit into a wilderness. I saw a woman sitting on a scarlet-colored beast, full of blasphemous names, having seven heads and ten horns. ... And on her forehead a name was written, "MYSTERY, BABYLON THE GREAT, THE MOTHER OF THE PROSTITUTES AND

OF THE ABOMINATIONS OF THE EARTH." ... "The ten horns which you saw, they and the beast will hate the prostitute, will make her desolate, will strip her naked, will eat her flesh, and will burn her utterly with fire. ... The woman whom you saw is the great city which reigns over the kings of the earth." (Revelation 17: 3, 5, 16, 18)

In this passage, an angel is speaking with Jesus's disciple John. He's seeing a vision of Mystery Babylon. We talked about Babylon in Sign #49 - The Rise Of Babylon and Sign #69 - One World Religion. It represents both a real city and a religious system. The beast the woman sits on is the Antichrist. His ten horns are the ten kings that align themselves with him. These rulers will hate the religious aspect of Babylon. So, at some point in the tribulation period they're going to destroy it. They'll replace it with a different one world religion, worship of the Antichrist.

What we're going to discuss in this sign is the reference to these rulers eating her flesh. Now, we know it's a metaphor for the complete and utter destruction of this religious system. But what if it's literal too? Consider that Jesus told us there would be severe famine and desolate land as a result of the judgments in the tribulation period. Chapter 15 has all the details on those signs. Food is going to be scarce. In the Old Testament, when the Israelites struggled to survive in similar conditions, they resorted to eating their babies, children, and each other. It's worth examining and seeing if there's any modern-day fulfillment of this that would foreshadow the nearness of the tribulation period.

Fulfillment - Cannibalism has been a part of human history for a long time. There's plenty of archaeological evidence that many cultures participated in this practice. Today, we mostly see evidence of it in movies, TV shows, books, and video games. The horror genre is quite popular, and the vampire and apocalyptic zombie type stories often have characters who must resort to cannibalism to survive.

New Scientist, the world's most popular weekly science and technology publication, ran a story in February 2024 titled, "Is it time for a more subtle view on the ultimate taboo: cannibalism?"[19] They said ancient humans ate each other often and perhaps we should reassess our views on the practice. They think dead bodies should be used to feed the hungry, and to honor the dead through funerary rituals that involve eating the deceased.

Today Is Different - Did you know that eating the ashes of a dead loved one is a thing today? Yep. A publication for funeral professionals published an article about this trend in July 2024. Apparently, some people are putting ashes in baked goods and sauces as a way to mourn or honor their loved one. The legality of this is a gray area and ingesting remains could create health issues. They were hoping they didn't need to start putting a "not for human consumption" label on temporary cremains containers.[20]

I didn't know this was a thing either. I guess some celebrities like Kim Kardashian popularized this recently. It's called placentophagy. It's consuming the placenta, otherwise known as the afterbirth. If you do an internet search on this, you'll get conflicting medical opinions. Some tout the benefits of it and recommend new moms do it. Others speak of the risks and infections that could result. Let's just say that enough people are doing it that the US CDC issued a report in 2017 warning about the health risks.[21]

Perhaps the creepiest example of this which makes today different is real life human vampire communities. You can search this one on the internet too and see all sorts of major news publications who've interviewed these people. Or just check out the End Notes in the Appendix for a few I've referenced. Yes, some of them do indeed drink human blood.[22]

<u>Additional Scriptures:</u> Deuteronomy 28:53-57. Ezekiel 5:7-10. Isaiah 9:19-20. Jeremiah 19:9. Lamentations 4:9-10. Matthew 24:7.

#101 – PERILOUS TIMES

<u>**Anti**</u> | DD | Earth | <u>**Gov**</u> | Israel | <u>**Jesus**</u> | Leader | Sky | <u>**Society**</u> | Tech | <u>**Trib**</u>

> But know this, that in the last days perilous times will come: (2 Timothy 3:1 NKJV)

The apostle Paul tells his disciple Timothy that perilous times will be a hallmark of the last days. The Greek word for perilous means fierce, dangerous, and savage. There's one other use of it in the New Testament. It's when Jesus was approached by two demon-possessed men who were described as exceedingly fierce. We might call it insane behavior.

Jesus spoke of this as a sign in the Olivet Discourse when he mentioned lawlessness, that it would be like Noah's day, and the sea and waves would be roaring. We went over that last one in Sign #23 - Anxiety Of Nations With Perplexity.

The Antichrist is referred to as the lawless one. It's a person who doesn't believe or behave like they're accountable to anyone. With a leader who's lawless, it's no surprise that people don't repent of this behavior during the tribulation period.

Fulfillment - Insane people are now randomly punching other people as they casually go about their day. According to one article, there have been 95 unprovoked assaults in Manhattan as of the end of April 2024, 50 of them against women.[23] In May 2024, an elderly woman was hit. Actor Steve Buscemi was attacked in May as well.[24]

New York City is also plagued by what seem to be mentally ill people randomly shoving others onto subway tracks. *The New York Post* has a slew of articles about this.[25] In an August 2024 article, one of the female assailants was arrested and they reported she had prior arrests including for randomly punching someone.[26]

This insanity isn't confined to New York City. Consider the news stories about customers going berserk on cashiers at fast food restaurants. You remember the Georgia woman who drove her car into a Popeyes restaurant in 2023 because she didn't get her biscuits.[27] That's not normal. It's insane!

A report published in 2021 analyzed 911 call data and revealed that between 2017 and 2020 at least 77,000 violent incidents happened at four fast food chains across nine cities in California. They labeled it a "crisis of violence" in which employees have been choked, pushed, grabbed, and hit with food.[28]

The Epoch Times ran an article in July 2024 on crime trends in America's top ten large cities. Car theft has exploded. They compared the first half of 2024 to the same period in 2019. New York City incidents tripled, and Chicago and Philadelphia are each about 2.5 times higher.[29]

Israel is dealing with this insanity too. Lawlessness is preventing much needed aid from being delivered to Gaza. Drivers are being held at gunpoint and cargo is being looted.[30]

We must also consider the mass shootings, drive by shootings, rapes in public during broad daylight, car jackings, street racing, BLM riots, random street stabbings, anti-Israel protesters, and flash mobs looting stores. Violence and lawlessness are an epidemic today which certainly makes it a perilous time.

Today Is Different - The attempted assassination of US President Trump is a clear display of how perilous today is. The shooting happened at an outdoor rally with thousands in attendance. A bullet narrowly missed Trump's head, grazing his ear instead. But three other people were also shot, one fatally.[31] The shooter had reckless abandon in his pursuit to kill Trump.

Criminals have become emboldened today. Do you remember the CHAZ zone in Seattle, WA in the summer of 2020? People protesting the death of George Floyd got unruly, set fires, damaged property, and clashed with police. Protesters across the country started to demand defunding the police. So, in a decision which makes truly no sense, the mayor ordered the police department to surrender. CHAZ became a police-free zone. The protesters blocked off six city blocks, including the abandoned police station.

As you might expect when you let an area become lawless, residents started getting harassed to pay extortion fees to the protesters in order to be inside the zone. The area became overrun with trash, drugs, crime, and a teenager was even murdered. It played out like a mobster movie. Officials let the insanity continue for almost a month. In the aftermath, Seattle was sued by residents within the CHAZ zone. The city ended up settling that lawsuit for $3.6 million.[32]

Additional Scriptures: 2 Peter 2:4-11. 2 Thessalonians 2:1-12. Acts 19:23-32. Isaiah 17:12. Luke 17:26-30; 21:25. Matthew 8:28; 24:12, 37-39. Psalm 10:13. Revelation 9:20-21.

#102 - EVIL INVENTIONS

<u>Anti</u> | DD | Earth | <u>Gov</u> | Israel | <u>Jesus</u> | <u>Leader</u> | Sky | <u>Society</u> | <u>Tech</u> | <u>Trib</u>

> For the wrath of God is revealed from heaven against all ungodliness and unrighteousness of men. ... Even as they refused to have God in their knowledge, God gave them up to a reprobate mind, to do those things which are not fitting; ... inventors of evil things. (Romans 1:18, 28, 30)

In these verses, the apostle Paul tells us that God's wrath comes upon unrighteous men because they are inventing evil things. Throughout the Bible we see the Israelites create and worship idols that they made from metals, stone, and wood. People will continue to do this in the tribulation period as well. Jesus told us that evil men produce evil things from their evil heart.

While not a biblical account, the *Ancient Book of Enoch* states that prior to the flood, one of the fallen angels taught men to make swords, knives, shields, and armor. And he taught the women how to make mirrors, jewelry, and makeup. These things led the people into ungodliness, violence, and fornication.

You know, the Antichrist and False Prophet will be inventors of evil too. Consider that they develop the image of the Beast, the mark of the Beast, and force people to worship the Antichrist.

Fulfillment - Most inventions don't have an inherent value of good or evil. Like a shovel. It's up to the user of the item to determine if they'll use it for good or evil. However, some inventions are only created for evil or sinful purposes.

Weapons used in war—guns come to mind. While I know they can be used for hunting, consider a machine gun attached to a tank. Some were certainly created solely for war. There are also bombs, missiles, suicide drones, chemical weapons (tear gas, nerve gas, mustard gas), and biological weapons (Covid, anthrax, the plague) that exist today.

Sexual inventions. Consider sex robots, sex toys, the abortion pill (a drug), and the abortion procedure itself. I could even argue that a condom is an evil invention because it promotes fornication even though it does prevent disease. How about porn that's generated using AI? AI isn't inherently evil, but it can definitely be used to create something that is. So, now we're getting into the space of using a benign tool to commit evil. But isn't that still inventing evil?

Israel's enemies have used simple things like balloons and kites as weapons of war. They just light them on fire then let them land in Israel's territory to wreak havoc. I've also read that North Korea likes to send trash and poo balloons over into South Korea.

Technology fits here too. There are computer viruses, malware, spyware, ransom ware, and credit card skimming devices. There's technology to deceive, like AI algorithms that suppress or censor content.

Scientific advancements like genetic engineering can be used for evil as well. God says don't mix species, yet we're creating goats that have spider silk in their milk (Sign #82). We now have the ability to create designer babies. Isn't that a perversion of God knitting us together in our mother's womb?

Even a camera is used to commit all sorts of evil today. Consider that it's used to produce porn and X rated movies. Satellites and surveillance systems use cameras to spy on people and nations.

Consider all the ways we've seen science and technology play a part in fulfilling signs throughout this book. Have a look at Appendix A to see all the signs involving technology.

Today Is Different - Weapons of mass destruction make today different. Nuclear weapons have only been used in war twice. When the US dropped two atomic bombs on Japan during WWII on August 6, 1945.[33] That's because the two bombs used killed up to 250,000 people. They caused widespread destruction. Almost 5 square miles of Hiroshima and 1 square mile of Nagasaki were obliterated. That's not to mention the firestorm that burned anything that survived the blast and then some.[34]

The effects of the bombs didn't end that day, they had only just begun. People continued to die from radiation poisoning in the months afterward. Survivors developed cancer. Birth defects increased.

Seeing the US with a weapon like this emboldened other nations to develop them too. For protection against the US or any other nation who pursued this path. In 2024, there are over 12,100 nuclear warheads on the planet. Almost 90% of those belong to the US and Russia. Other nations with them include China, France, the UK, India, Pakistan, Israel, and North Korea.[35]

Additional Scriptures: Matthew 12:35. Revelation 9:20.

Non-biblical accounts:[36] *Ancient Book of Enoch* 8:1-2.

#103 - EVIL LEADERSHIP

Anti | DD | Earth | Gov | Israel | Jesus | Leader | Sky | Society | Tech | Trib

> "And in his place shall arise a vile person, to whom they will not give the honor of royalty; but he shall come in peaceably, and seize the kingdom by intrigue. ... And after the league [is made] with him he shall act deceitfully. ... He shall stir up his power and his courage against the king of the South with a great army. ... Both these kings' hearts [shall be] bent on evil, and they shall speak lies at the same table." (Daniel 11:21, 23, 25, 27 NKJV)

The prophet Daniel is talking with an angel who's explaining events which occur during the tribulation period. The "vile person" is the Antichrist. He reigns during the tribulation period. Notice the descriptions of him and the king of the South: vile, seize the kingdom, deceitful, stir up power, against, bent on evil, speak lies.

In Jesus's Olivet Discourse he reveals many signs of his second coming. He gave several references to evil leadership: false christs, false prophets, lawlessness (implies bad leaders, law enforcement, and judges), nation vs nation (implies evil leaders), kingdom vs kingdom (implies bad leaders), persecution (implies evil leadership in government, churches, and elsewhere).

When reading through the additional Scriptures below, we learn more details about evil leaders. Keep in mind this is anyone in a position of authority: kings, princes, judges, and church leaders for example. They demand bribes and twist justice. They don't defend the poor, fatherless, or widows. They make unrighteous decrees. They hate justice and pervert equity. They commit violence on the law. They seek the praise of mankind. They lead the people in committing sin. They worship false gods. Priests teach for pay and prophets divine for money. The shepherds destroy, scatter, and don't feed God's flock. There are many more sins they commit. Just refer to all the signs in this book that are categorized as Gov or Leader in Appendix A.

Fulfillment - We've had a history of evil leaders. Let's consider the top three most lethal leaders of the 20th century.[37] #3 Adolf Hitler (35 million), #2 Joseph Stalin (40 million), #1 Mao Zedong (65 million). I bet you thought Hitler was the worst.

Today, we have our share of evil leaders around the globe too. People jockeying for political power. Consider Russia's Putin, China's Xi, Iran's Khamenei, Ukraine's Zelenskyy, Syria's al-Assad, and North Korea's Kim to name a few.

The Bible tells us that the love of money is a root of all kinds of evil. It's money and power which are controlling the actions of people in leadership today. In America, it seems like everyone in power is beholden to someone more powerful behind the spotlight who has money.

Lobbyists are one such group behind the scenes. It's illegal for a business to make a direct donation to a US political candidate. Businesses get around this by contributing via candidate fundraisers organized by lobbying firms.[38] The end result is the candidate clearly knowing where the money came from and how their supporter feels about key issues. If the candidate wants the money to keep flowing, they'll align their actions and votes with those supporters.

Since the US Supreme Court overturned Roe v. Wade in 2022, abortion is getting banned in many states. Lobbyists on both sides of the abortion debate spent $3.7 million at the federal level in 2023. Ohio had an abortion measure on their ballot in 2023 and a crazy $106 million was spent lobbying for and against that state level measure.[39]

Donors and lobbyists can easily buy any elected official. Politicians at the federal, state, and local levels. Judges, police chiefs, attorney generals, treasurers, commissioners, and even school board leaders. Just think of all the types of positions that are elected today.

It doesn't stop with elected officials though. Even doctors can be bought today. Enter the pharmaceutical giants. They pay doctors for consulting, for speaking at events, and give them all sorts of gifts. Researchers have found that doctors who receive money and gifts from a pharmaceutical company are indeed more likely to prescribe a drug tied to that company.[40]

Today Is Different - There are evil changes occurring to the status quo of leadership today, and that makes today unique.

The status quo of parents is changing. In America, there's a war against parents as the leaders of their family. Consider the local level school boards that we see on the news because they're allowing teachers to secretly gender transition students. Or they're passing policies that strip parental rights, like the right to not have your child taught LGBT content.

The status quo of the US Supreme Court is changing. It's been in existence since 1789. The number of justices who serve is determined by congress. As the US grew, so did the court. It's had nine justices since 1869.[41] Here we are 155 years later and suddenly that's not working anymore because our nation's leaders don't agree with the recent decisions the justices have made. There's talk of expanding the court and putting term limits on the justices.

The status quo of judges at all levels is changing. Judges are supposed to be impartial and strictly rely on the law to decide cases. Today, judges are brazen about their bias. Think of the legal cases against US President Trump and the conflicts of interest that have arisen. Yet the judges refuse to recuse themselves.[42] Judges are also supposed to imprison criminals, but today they grant them bail and let them roam free.

The status quo of church leaders and pastors is changing. Many now support LGBT, same sex marriage, and are involved in financial and sexual scandals. Today, they resemble our morally degraded society more than Jesus.

The status quo of leaders of terrorists is the most ominous of changes. They used to be public enemy #1. But today young adults are rooting for them on college campuses.

<u>Additional Scriptures:</u> 1 Kings 12:26-33; 14:16. 1 Timothy 6:10. 2 Kings 21:1-18. Amos 5:7-12. Daniel 8:23-25. Deuteronomy 28:15-68. Ezekiel 34:1-10. Isaiah 1:23; 10:1-3. Jeremiah 5:1-5; 23:1-2. Luke 21. Mark 13; 15:6-15. Matthew 24. Micah 3:9-12; 7:3. Psalm 82. Revelation 13:2-7. Zephaniah 3:3-4.

#104 – THE ELECTION OMEN

Anti | DD | Earth | **Gov** | Israel | Jesus | **Leader** | Sky | **Society** | Tech | **Trib**

> "Behold, I have set before you today life and prosperity, and death and evil. For I command you today to love the LORD your God, to walk in his ways and to keep his commandments, his statutes, and his ordinances, that you may live and multiply, and that the LORD your God may bless you in the land where you go in to possess it. But if your heart turns away, and you will not hear, but are drawn away and worship other gods, and serve them, I declare to you today that you will surely perish. ... I call heaven and earth to witness against you today that I have set before you life and death, the blessing and the curse. Therefore choose life, that you may live, you and your descendants, to love the LORD your God, to obey his voice, and to cling to him; for he is your life, and the length of your days." (Deuteronomy 30:15-20)

Moses is conveying a message from God to the Israelites in the verses above. They're about to enter the promised land. God is giving them a choice between life and death, the blessing and the curse. The people can choose whichever path they desire. In order to get life and the blessing, they have to love and obey God and not turn away to other gods.

I've named this sign *The Election Omen* after my book with the same title. In my book, I explain that God gives a nation the ruler they desire. You see, there's a pattern in the Old Testament that we can apply to today. The Israelites started out with a godly leader and by worshiping God. But they started to turn away from God. So, then they got a ruler who drew them further away from God and into worshiping false gods. Then the evil ungodly ruler oppressed them until they finally sought God for help. God then delivered the Israelites by giving them another godly leader.

Then the cycle repeated. It kept repeating until their wickedness had progressed to the point that the evil leader was the polar opposite of the original godly king they started out with. The people had the most wicked rulers (compared to King Ahab) and then a good ruler (compared to King David). The polar opposite king was the clue that they'd hit the point of no return. They reached a point where God didn't give them another godly king because the people didn't want one. They didn't want to repent and turn back to God. Israel advanced in wickedness until it reached the polar opposite of God. At that point judgment was coming. It was the only cure.

It's because a nation that's under an enemy oppressive ruler will remember God and seek him once again. That's why God sent an evil foreign ruler, King Nebuchadnezzar, to take the Israelites into captivity. Since the people didn't want anything to do with God, he gave them exactly what they wanted. He gave them a foreign ruler who didn't know God. Now, the people obviously didn't elect King Nebuchadnezzar, but that doesn't mean they didn't ultimately choose him because of their behavior toward God.

When the world continues to reject God, what they're really asking for is his antithesis. That's Satan and the Antichrist. A time is coming in which God is going to give the world the ruler they've been asking for. It's not going to be through an election, just like it wasn't with King Nebuchadnezzar. In the book of Revelation, we're told that when the Antichrist comes to power in the tribulation period that the world marvels at him, then follows him, then worships Satan, and then worships the Antichrist. Many people choose to do all of those things before the False Prophet ever gets involved in forcing anyone to worship the Antichrist.

Fulfillment - Let's see if our world is reaching the polar opposite of God. Good kings provide freedom while bad kings take it away and oppress people. Failure to turn to God during those bad kings ultimately leads to God taking away the ability for society to choose a king and him giving society the evil leader they crave instead of him.

Freedom House, a non-profit organization, prepares annual reports on freedom across the world. I will warn you it's rather left leaning in some of its views, but it does have helpful insights on democracy. Let's look at the freedom score they give the top 10 most populous nations.[43] Refer to figure 104.1 below. These countries account for 57% of the world population.[44] The scale is 0 to 100. With 100 being totally free and 0 being not free at all, meaning the country has a dictator that's oppressive.

Table 104.1. Freedom Score By Country			
Country	2024 Score	Designation	Change from 2020
India	66	Partly Free	Declined. Free to Partly Free.
China	9	Not Free	Declined
USA	83	Free	Declined
Indonesia	57	Partly Free	Declined
Pakistan	35	Partly Free	Declined
Nigeria	44	Partly Free	Declined
Brazil	72	Free	Improved
Bangladesh	40	Partly Free	Improved
Russia	13	Not Free	Declined
Ethiopia	20	Not Free	Declined

Figure 104.1. Freedom Score By Country[45]
Source: https://freedomhouse.org/explore-the-map?type=fiw&year=2024

As you can see, only two of the most populated countries are considered free, the US and Brazil. And all but two of the countries have less freedom today than just four years ago. Freedom House says global freedom declined for the 18th consecutive year in 2023. They state flawed elections and armed conflict contributed to the decline.

In fact, the manipulation of elections drove down the scores in 26 countries in 2023. This behavior included overturning elections after the fact, controlling who appears on the ballot, changing election rules, using government resources to favor the governing party, violence at polling stations, and military coups.

Today Is Different - Figure 104.2 nicely illustrates that we're becoming less free and less democratic across the globe. And this is a rather recent trend as you can see below. An autocratizing regime is one which is becoming less electorally democratic. While a democratizing regime is one which is becoming more electorally democratic.

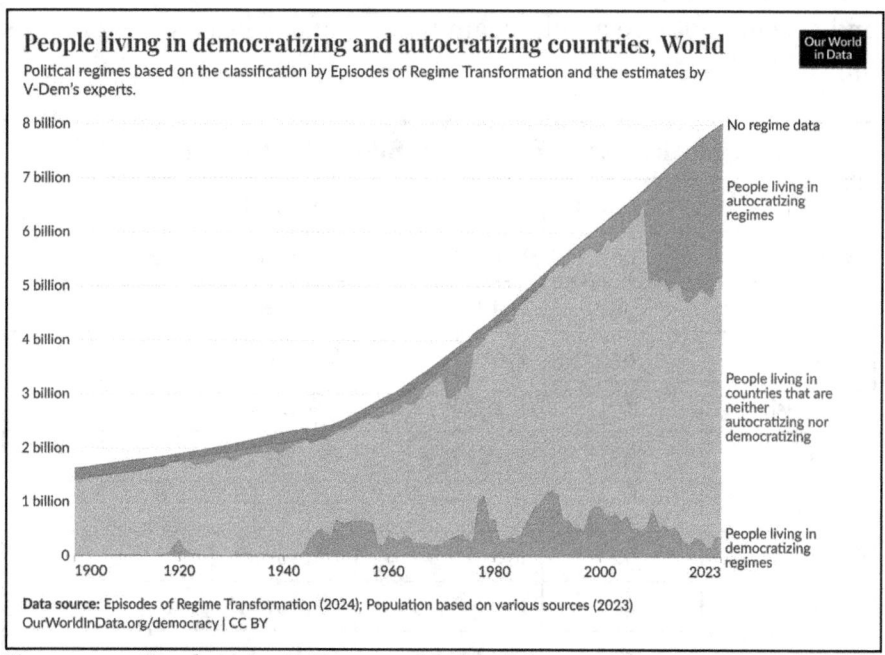

Figure 104.2. People Living In Democratizing And Autocratizing Countries[46]
Source: https://ourworldindata.org/grapher/people-living-in-democratizing-autocratizing-countries-ert

The number of people living in countries that are becoming less and less democratic is at its peak. It started trending upward in the 1970s and then spiked quite a bit in 2008.

While figure 104.2 shows how the world is changing, figure 104.3 below reveals how many people currently live in either an autocracy or a democracy.

Oblivious To The Signs When It's Obvious The King Is Coming 241

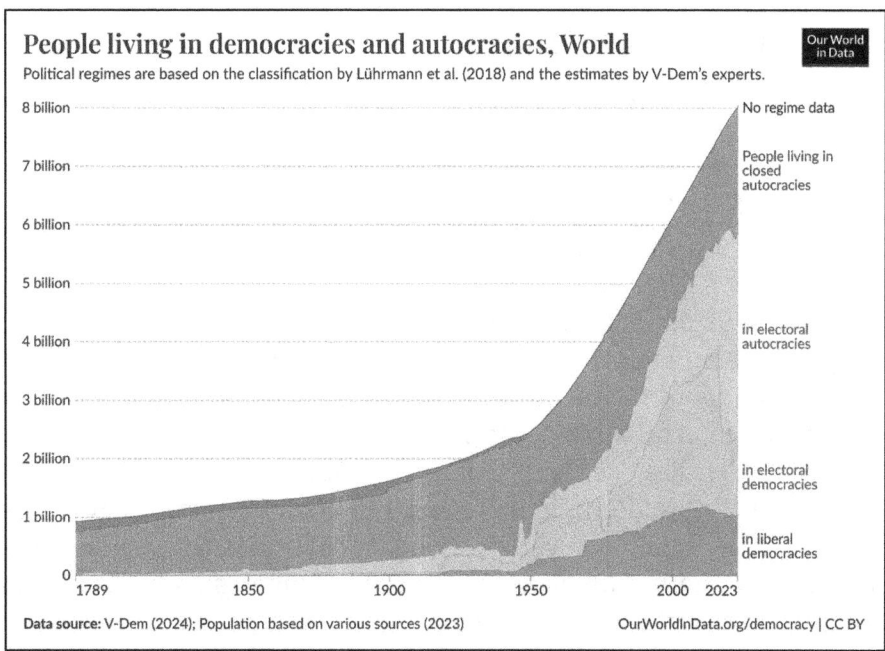

Figure 104.3. People Living In Democracies And Autocracies[47]
Source: https://ourworldindata.org/grapher/people-living-in-democracies-autocracies

A closed autocracy means you can't choose your nation's leader or government. In an electoral autocracy, the people can choose but elections aren't considered meaningful, free, and fair. Electoral democracies mean that people can choose the country's leaders in free and fair elections. Liberal democracies are electoral democracies that include restraint on the executive branch through the legislative and judicial branches.

The US is a liberal democracy, Israel is an electoral democracy, India is an electoral autocracy, and China is a closed autocracy.[48] Figure 104.3 illustrates an upward trend for democracies from 1950 through about 2020. Then there was a big dip in people living in a democratic country and a shift to people living under an electoral autocracy.

In 2023, 5.68 billion people lived under a type of autocracy. That's 71% of the planet!

<u>Additional Scriptures:</u> Deuteronomy 26:6-8. Ezekiel 22:30-31. Jeremiah 11:6-8. Judges 2:12-19. Revelation 13:3-8. Romans 1:21-28.

#105 - KINGDOM VS KINGDOM

Anti | DD | Earth | Gov | Israel | Jesus | Leader | Sky | Society | Tech | Trib

> As he sat on the Mount of Olives, the disciples came to him privately, saying, "Tell us, when will these things be? What is the sign of your coming, and of the end of the age?" Jesus answered them, ... "For nation will rise against nation, and kingdom against kingdom." (Matthew 24:3-4, 7)

Jesus tells us that one of the signs of his second coming will be kingdom rising against kingdom. We'll look at nation vs nation in Sign #111. A kingdom differs from a nation. A nation refers to a people group, which can be a race of people or a group of people who live together. Gentiles, Jewish, China, America can all be considered nations. A kingdom on the other hand refers to a ruler or a territory that ruler has dominion over. The kingdom of God is an example. As is the Roman Empire, which was comprised of many nations. I think in a modern sense it could also refer to a large corporation.

In the tribulation period, ten kings will rise. They are represented by the ten horns that appear on the fourth beast in Daniel's vision. There's an interesting Scripture in the book of Revelation regarding them. It says they receive no kingdom but receive authority for one hour with the Antichrist. I think these ten kings will be in the process of building the one world government when the Antichrist interrupts their plans. When he shows up, they all transfer their authority to him. We also know that three of them will be deposed by the Antichrist. This is illustrated by three of the horns being plucked up by one horn, the Antichrist, who comes up after the ten.

We're also told that these kings live luxuriously in Babylon, taking advantage of phase one of the one world religion (refer to Sign #69), but they'll eventually destroy that religion. Right before Jesus's second coming, they'll be with the Antichrist, False Prophet, and all the people who've gathered to war against Jesus.

Fulfillment - We've progressed from nation vs nation. Today, nations ally themselves with bigger mightier nations and create intergovernmental treaties and military alliances. We have empires battling one another. There is a whole slew of these, so let's just look at a few of them.

NATO started after WWII in 1949 and currently has 32 member

states: the US, Canada, and 30 European nations.⁴⁹ The SCO was established in 2001 and now includes China, Russia, India, Pakistan, and some Central Asia countries. It's the world's largest political, economic, and defense organization, covering 40% of the world population and 80% of Eurasia.⁵⁰ The IMCTC began in 2015 and is a military alliance among 42 Muslim nations and includes Saudi Arabia, Egypt, and Turkey.⁵¹ Notably absent from that group are Iran and Syria. However, they both belong to a different empire created in 2015, the RSII coalition which includes Russia, Syria, Iran, and Iraq.⁵²

The Russia-Ukraine War which began in early 2022 isn't a battle between those two nations. No, it's really a war between NATO and the empires that Russia belongs to.

Today Is Different - Today is unique because our kingdoms are no longer confined to earth. They're battling it out over dominion of the heavens. Space. The space race started in the 1950s. In 1957, the Soviets launched the first satellite into space, Sputnik. Shortly afterward, the US created NASA. In 1961, the USSR launched the first person into space, Yuri Gagarin. Like a month later, the Americans put Alan Shephard into space. The US became the first nation to land on the moon in 1969.⁵³

I'd like to point out that the modern-day space race is no longer between government-led kingdoms. Today, it's between corporate kingdoms and billionaires. Elon Musk's SpaceX versus Jeff Bezos's Blue Origin vs Boeing. I find it quite interesting that nations have relinquished control of such an important part of our planet to the private sector.

This demonstrates the rise of a completely different kind of kingdom that I believe will be prominent in the tribulation period. The rise of the technocrats and oligarchs.

If you were the Antichrist, what industries would you want to have control over right from the get-go? #1 will be defense and military because he's going to conquer and destroy. #2 will be banking because he's going to need funding for his military, and he's going to implement the mark of the Beast economic system. #3 will be media because he'll want to be worshiped, and our society does that through social media these days.

Consider the industries that just a few billionaires control today. Elon Musk owns SpaceX (aerospace, defense, military, communications), Tesla (transportation), the Boring Co. (tunnel construction), Neuralink (brain chip interface), and X Corp (social media).[54] We should keep in mind that he started out in banking. Jeff Bezos has Amazon (marketplace), Blue Origin (aerospace), *The Washington Post* (media), and Altos Labs (biotech).[55] Bill Gates founded Microsoft (software) and runs the Bill and Melinda Gates Foundation (2nd largest charitable foundation on the planet).[56] The Antichrist won't need to control a nation or government to wield significant power. He'll just need a few of these people.

It's no coincidence that billionaires across the planet get together once a year with Klaus Schwab and the World Economic Forum. It's how the new modern kingdom influences the traditional government kingdoms.[57] They also seem more invested in politics these days and are throwing their weight around in the 2024 US Presidential Election. Plenty of the uber rich are coming out in support of both of the key candidates. Seems like a prelude to the ten kings in the book of Revelation who give their authority to the Antichrist.

<u>Additional Scriptures:</u> Daniel 2:40-42; 7:7-8, 23-24. Matthew 24:3-7. Revelation 17; 18:3, 9-10; 19:19.

#106 - THE PRINCE OF PERSIA

Anti | DD | Earth | **Gov** | **Israel** | Jesus | **Leader** | Sky | Society | **Tech** | **Trib**

> Then he said to me, "Don't be afraid, Daniel; for from the first day that you set your heart to understand, and to humble yourself before your God, your words were heard. I have come for your words' sake. But the prince of the kingdom of Persia withstood me twenty-one days; but, behold, Michael, one of the chief princes, came to help me because I remained there with the kings of Persia. Now I have come to make you understand what will happen to your people in the latter days, for the vision is yet for many days." (Daniel 10:12-14)

In these verses, a holy angel is speaking with the prophet Daniel. The angel mentions that the "prince of the kingdom of Persia" had prevented him from arriving sooner and that Michael, a chief prince, had helped him. And that there were also other "kings of Persia" that were there. So, who are these princes and kings? The princes are angelic rulers, and the kings are human rulers. Yes, this means there are angelic rulers (holy ones and fallen ones) behind the scenes, influencing what happens in our human realm.

We should note that this holy angel was sent to tell Daniel about the last days. It's this mission that the prince of Persia, a fallen angel, was trying to stop. Keep in mind that Daniel was one of the first people taken captive to Babylon when King Nebuchadnezzar invaded. He lived in Babylon through the reign of several Persian kings.

In the additional Scriptures below, we learn about other missions the human kings of Persia were involved in. King Cyrus gave the command to rebuild the Jewish temple in Jerusalem and let people return to live there. Work was stopped for a time during King Darius's reign so he could verify its legitimacy in historical records. Two years later, he let the work continue and also commanded the Persians in Jerusalem to stay away and let the work of the temple alone.

Later, in the book of Esther we see the king of Persia put his approval on his trusted adviser Haman's conspiracy to murder all the Jews who remained in their kingdom. Queen Esther helped save the day and prevented the eradication of her people.

Sometime afterwards, King Artaxerxes blessed Nehemiah's and Ezra's missions to return to Jerusalem to rebuild the wall and repopulate the city.

As you can see, there was some back and forth between good and evil in regard to how the kings of Persia treated the Jewish people. I think it reflects the angelic war going on behind the scenes.

Since the unholy prince of Persia withstood a holy angel's mission to just deliver a message about the biblical end times, what do you think he's going to do when that time is actually upon us? Like what happened in Queen Esther's day, he's going to seek to eradicate the Jewish people. He's going to be a key player in the Psalm 83 War (Sign #107) and the Gog of Magog War (Sign #108, #109). So, the question is, can we see any signs of the prince of Persia moving into position?

Fulfillment - I read an interesting news article a few months ago. It said the dominant force in the Middle East is no longer the United States with Egypt, Saudi Arabia, and Israel aligning with them. Now, it's Iran.[58]

Have you heard of the Houthi terrorists in Yemen? They've completely disrupted the Middle East and the Red Sea commercial trade routes. In October 2023, they started launching drone and missile attacks against Israel. Then they started seizing vessels and attacking merchant ships in the Red Sea. Almost every container line has diverted away from using the Suez Canal. It's had a huge impact on revenue for the Suez Canal and all the ports in the Red Sea. Now, those ships have to take the long way around Africa. Iran sponsors the Houthis.⁵⁹

The US has naval ships in the Red Sea. It seems they're only able to destroy some of the missiles and drones that are being launched. The merchant sailors don't trust the US to defend them, because they haven't been able to. We're supposed to have the best military on the planet. Why hasn't the US completely eliminated this threat?

I think it's because Iran has recently allied itself with Russia and China. Iran and the Houthi's know that gives the current US leadership pause in escalating anything in the region. So, Iran's become the bully of the Middle East with their network of terrorist groups operating in the region.

Today Is Different - Iran's nuclear ambitions make today unique. Iran announced that they had enriched uranium for the first time in April 2006. Lots of diplomatic pressure against Iran ensued. It's come from a variety of nations, including the US, and also from the UN. It continues to this day. It seems that no number of economic sanctions against Iran makes a dent against their desire and their continued work to progress their nuclear program.⁶⁰

That's because Iran is mostly comprised of Shia Muslims. They believe that they must destroy Israel and the United States in order to hasten the arrival of the Islamic messiah, their Twelfth Imam or Mahdi. To them this is a holy war.

Iran has also been developing missile technology at the same time. It's one thing to have a nuclear weapon, it's quite another to have a precision guided long range missile or drone to carry that weapon to Israel, for example. They currently have missiles which can travel over 2,000 km (1,200 miles).⁶¹ Israel's only 1,300 km away from them.

Iran proved their ability to reach Israel in an unprecedented direct drone and missile strike against them in April 2024. The strike included 170 drones, 30 cruise missiles, and 120 ballistic missiles. Most were intercepted outside Israel's borders, but several of the ballistic missiles actually reached Israel and caused damage.⁶²

Today is different because the prince of Persia is not only in position but already actively engaged in battle. How long before it's a full-blown war?

<u>Additional Scriptures:</u> 2 Chronicles 36:20-23. Daniel 10:20-21; 11:21-45; 12:1. Esther. Ezekiel 38:1-8. Ezra 1:1-3; 4:3-7, 24; 6:6-15; 7. Nehemiah 1-2:9.

#107 - PSALM 83 ALLIES

Anti | DD | Earth | **Gov** | **Israel** | **Jesus** | Leader | Sky | Society | Tech | Trib

> "Come," they say, "let's destroy them as a nation, that the name of Israel may be remembered no more." For they have conspired together with one mind. They form an alliance against you. The tents of Edom and the Ishmaelites; Moab, and the Hagrites; Gebal, Ammon, and Amalek; Philistia with the inhabitants of Tyre; Assyria also is joined with them. (Psalm 83:4-8)

In this psalm, we see that several nations and people groups conspire together to destroy Israel as a nation. Later in the psalm we're told that they want to take the pastures of God for a possession. If you recall in the Olivet Discourse, Jesus told his disciples that they would be hated by all nations.

Now, there's debate among Bible scholars on whether or not this is a prophecy. Some think it's already been fulfilled. I think there's a good possibility it's a prophecy because later in the psalm it speaks of these people groups being dismayed forever and perishing. Well, these places still exist. Another point mentioned at the very end of the psalm is that once they're defeated that they all come to know the Lord. That hasn't yet happened either.

Some scholars also think this war may actually be a part of the larger Gog of Magog War. We'll look at that war in Sign #108. I'm not convinced of that either though, because none of these groups are named in Ezekiel 38-39 while many others are. Seems odd they'd be left off the list. The Gog of Magog War also has a different motive, to take plunder, and the Scripture makes it seem like Gog enters the war by force and not by choice. These Psalm 83 allies come together willingly. In the Gog of Magog War, it also says Israel will have been brought back from the sword, meaning they'll be recovering from war. Instead, I think it's quite likely this Psalm 83 War is the war that Israel will be recovering from when Gog invades.

As for the timing of this war, I believe it occurs before the rapture and before the Gog of Magog War.

I would also like to mention that at some point between now and Jesus's second coming, that the city of Damascus ceases to exist. We'll look at that in Sign #113. There's certainly a possibility that happens in this Psalm 83 War since Syria is involved.

Figure 107.1 below lists the groups mentioned in Psalm 83 along with their current modern-day location. As you can see, they primarily account for Israel's neighboring countries.

Table 107.1. Psalm 83 People Groups	
Psalm 83	Current Location
Amalek	Jordan, Sinai Peninsula (Egypt)
Ammon	Jordan
Assyria	Iraq, Syria
Edom	Jordan
Gebal	Lebanon
Hagrites	Egypt, Jordan
Ishmaelites	Egypt, Saudia Arabia
Moab	Jordan
Philistia	Gaza
Tyre	Lebanon

Figure 107.1. Psalm 83 Current Locations[63]
Source: 9 Wars Of The End Times by David R. Reagan and The Non-Prophets Guide To The End Times by Todd Hampson.

Fulfillment - Do these current nations have a reason they'd want to destroy Israel from being a nation, as indicated in the psalm? These countries surround Israel geographically. Most of them share a border with Israel. These countries are also Muslim majority nations: Egypt (95%), Gaza (100%), Iraq (99%), Jordan (97%), Lebanon (61%), Saudi Arabia (93%), Syria (93%).[64] The Muslim religion is directly opposed to the Bible and God's promises to the Israelites.

God made an everlasting unconditional covenant with Abraham. It included land and many descendants. God told Abraham that all of his promises would pass through to his son Isaac and then Isaac's son Jacob, otherwise known as Israel. The problem is that Abraham had another son, Ishmael. The Muslims believe that Abraham's first son, Ishmael, is his rightful heir.[65] Thus meaning Ishmael's descendants have the right to the land of Israel. As you know, the Bible says that God didn't recognize Ishmael as the heir because he wasn't the child

God promised through Abraham and Sarah. Ishmael was the product of Abraham trying to fulfill God's promise himself through Sarah's maid Hagar.

You can see this conflict manifest today when these nations tell Israel that they're occupying Palestinian land. When they refuse to even recognize Israel as a nation today. When they want Israel to give up their land in exchange for peace. When they want Israel to revert to 1967 or 1948 borders. Their true intent is to get all the land and eradicate Israel from being a nation.

Today Is Different - The Hamas attack against Israel on October 7, 2023 makes today significantly different. The US considers Hamas a terrorist organization. It has many allies in the Middle East including Iran, Turkey, Syria, Qatar, Egypt, Lebanon's Hezbollah, Sudan, and Algeria. It's had a governing presence over the Palestinians in the Gaza Strip of Israel for quite some time.[66] Many of its allies are listed as participants in the Psalm 83 War or the Gog of Magog War in Ezekiel 38-39.

You've heard the chants of the protesters in America who support Hamas. "From the river to sea, Palestine will be free." The goal of Hamas is to take Israel's land from the Jordan River to the Mediterranean Sea. That's all of their land! You need to know that it's not just the Hamas terrorists that have this view.

In June 2024, Palestinian Media Watch reported results of a poll conducted among Palestinians from the West Bank and Gaza. It reveals that only 9% of Palestinians believe Hamas committed war crimes on October 7, 2023. However, 97% of them believe Israel did. In fact, 67% of them actually support the initial attack by Hamas and 71% think Hamas should govern Gaza after the war.[67]

I want to share part of an interview that *The Media Line* conducted with Lt. Col. Conricus of the Israel Defense Forces in February 2024. The reporter asked him about the weapons they'd found in Gaza. Here is part of his response: "There's hardly a house that our troops go to that doesn't have either an entrance to a tunnel, a shaft, or weapons that are stocked inside, or explosives, or where they are manufacturing weapons, or it's a hideout for terrorist activity, or any of the above combined. And it's pervasive all across the Gaza Strip. We see the same thing in schools, in hospitals, in mosques, in other sensitive humanitarian locations, and I think it's really amazing and unprecedented in the history of warfare to have such a closely enmeshed enemy that is totally embedded within the civilian infrastructure. Nothing in Gaza is detached from Hamas. Almost every building in Gaza is connected or used in some way or another by Hamas for its elicit military activities."[68]

Hamas and those living in Gaza are one and the same. They are allied in their war against Israel. With other allies of Hamas getting involved in the war more each day, it's quite possible this could escalate into the Psalm 83 War.

Additional Scriptures: 1 Chronicles 5:10. Ezekiel 35; 38-39. Genesis 10:6-14, 22; 12:5; 17:1-21; 19:36-28; 25:12-34; 36. Isaiah 17:1. Luke 21:24. Matthew 24:6-9. Psalm 83.

#108 - GOG OF THE LAND OF MAGOG

Anti | DD | **Earth** | **Gov** | **Israel** | **Jesus** | **Leader** | Sky | Society | Tech | **Trib**

> The LORD's word came to me, saying, "Son of man, set your face toward Gog, of the land of Magog, the prince of Rosh, Meshech, and Tubal, and prophesy against him, ... I will turn you around, and put hooks into your jaws, and I will bring you out, with all your army; ... You will come up against my people Israel as a cloud to cover the land. It will happen in the latter days that I will bring you against my land." (Ezekiel 38:1-2, 4, 16)

God is speaking with the prophet Ezekiel here and telling him about the Gog of Magog War. Gog is the ruler of the land of Magog, which includes Rosh, Meshech and Tubal. Gog is a title, not a person's actual name. Later in Ezekiel 38 we're told Magog is a place in the far north.

As you can see God has to put hooks in Gog's mouth to turn him around and drag him into the war. It seems this war is forced upon him and not something he necessarily starts or wants to be involved in by choice. He will come upon Israel in the end times. Upon reading the additional Scriptures below, we also learn that the motive of this war is to take plunder. It occurs after Israel has been brought back from the sword, meaning they'll be recovering from war. I mentioned in the prior sign that it's likely Israel will be recovering from the Psalm 83 War. We're also told Israel is dwelling securely.

Gog will come upon Israel like a cloud. When this happens, Scripture says that at the same time it triggers God's wrath. Now, that's interesting because the time of God's wrath is the tribulation period. This seems to indicate the Gog of Magog war happens shortly after the rapture, at the beginning of the tribulation period. It makes sense when you realize that the second seal judgment is the rider on the red horse who brings war. This also parallels Joel 2 and the army from the north which comes upon Israel during the day of the Lord.

In the Ezekiel passage, when God's wrath is triggered, he causes an earthquake in Israel that makes all people on earth shake at his presence. All the mountains and walls fall. That's a tribulation period type of earthquake that makes me think of the seventh bowl judgment. It's also interesting to consider that the Dome of the Rock that's currently on the Temple Mount will be impacted by that earthquake. You know it's going to fall down. Perhaps enabling the Jews to build the Third Temple?

And then in an awesome display of power, God vanquishes the invading army through infighting, pestilence, and flooding rain of hail, brimstone, and fire. This is also another tribulation type judgment. It makes Israel and many other nations reestablish their relationship with God.

Notice that God supernaturally intervenes and rescues Israel. It implies Israel has no military allies, like the US, that can or are willing to go help them. The Scripture only says that Sheba, Dedan, the merchants of Tarshish, and their young lions basically ask Gog what he's up to. Those are the modern equivalents of the Arabian Peninsula, and the nations West of Israel and those who trade with them. Refer to figure 108.1. Those nations ask Gog if he's invading to take great plunder. But they don't intervene. If this war occurs after the rapture, it would explain why the US isn't involved. America will be severely crippled as a result.

Jesus told his disciples that they would be hated by all nations. It seems to me Israel's enemies take advantage of the chaos that will envelop the planet after the rapture.

Figure 108.1 below lists the groups mentioned in Ezekiel 38 along with their current modern-day location. None of them are neighboring nations of Israel today. The big players are Russia, Turkey, and Iran.

Table 108.1. Ezekiel 38 People Groups	
Ezekiel 38	Current Location
Cush	Ethiopia, Sudan
Dedan	Arabian Peninsula
Gomer	Turkey
Magog	Central Asia republics of Russia, Russia
Meshech	Russia, Turkey
Persia	Iran
Put	Algeria, Libya
Rosh	Russia
Sheba	Arabian Peninsula
Tarshish	Western nations (from Israel)
Togarmah	Armenia, Central Asia, Turkey
Tubal	Russia, Turkey
Young Lions	All trading partners of Western nations

Figure 108.1. Ezekiel 38 Current Locations[69]
Source: 9 Wars Of The End Times by David R. Reagan, The Non-Prophets Guide To The End Times by Todd Hampson, and The Prophecy Watcher 04.2023.

For this sign we're going to focus on Gog. So, that's Rosh, Meshech and Tubal. The modern equivalents of Russia and Turkey. Let's find out if those two nations are behaving like Gog today.

Fulfillment - Well, the world has seen a rise of Russian aggression in the past decade. They annexed the Crimean Peninsula when it was part of Ukraine, in 2014.[70] Tensions between those two countries escalated into the current Russian-Ukrainian War which began in early 2022 when Russia again invaded Ukraine.[71] Both Russia and Turkey are currently involved in the Syrian Civil War, interestingly as opponents.[72]

Global Firepower ranks the nations in the world based on current available firepower. Both Russia and Turkey are in the top 10. For 2024, Russia is #2 and Turkey is #8.[73]

As for religion, 73% of Russians are Christians, 15% are unaffiliated, and 11% are Muslim.[74] You'd think they'd be significantly impacted by the rapture and unable to fulfill the role of Gog in the tribulation period. Well, the primary Christian religion in Russia is Orthodox Christianity. They do not believe that the faith of an individual has any bearing on salvation. They place it entirely in receiving sacraments.[75] It's a works-based faith, not one based on a real saving relationship with Jesus. So, I don't believe they'll be impacted much at all by the rapture.

On the other hand, 98% of people in Turkey are Muslims.[76] You need to know that Islam is intolerant toward other religions and in particular Christianity and Judaism. That's because the Bible directly contradicts the teachings in the Qur'an. Islam is committed to *jihad*, meaning holy war. The Qur'an commands them to war against non-Muslims until they are exterminated.[77]

It's not hard to envision either of these nations as an aggressor in the Gog of Magog War.

Today Is Different - The next question is what does Israel have that Russia or Turkey would want to plunder? I explore Israel's wealth in Sign #125 in more detail. For the purposes of this particular sign, I believe they'll be after natural gas. You know, Israel discovered natural gas in their nation very recently, 1999. They've since discovered several large gas fields. Now, they're even exporting it to Egypt and Jordan. And guess where they're looking at exporting it to next? Europe.[78]

Russia is the second largest exporter of natural gas in the world.[79] They supply Germany and other European countries, and their #2 consumer is Turkey.[80] They deliver it to Turkey via pipelines under the Black Sea. Imagine if Russia could tap into a gas field in the Mediterranean Sea off the coast of Israel instead. Imagine if Russia felt like Israel was starting to encroach on their natural gas territory by expanding into Europe. Imagine if someone, perhaps Ukraine, blew up Russian gas pipelines to Turkey.

The current relationship between Russia and Israel isn't great. Consider that the US is Israel's greatest ally. That puts Israel in a bind because the US is also backing Ukraine in their war with Russia. Iran is Israel's enemy and responsible for the October 7, 2023 invasion by Hamas terrorists. Well, Russia and Iran are allies. Iran even provides suicide drones to Russia for their use in the war with Ukraine. That puts Russia in a bind regarding Israel's war in Gaza.

What will Russia do if the war between Israel and Iran escalates?

Will Iran be the hook in Russia's jaw? We should also keep in mind that Russia has a military presence in Syria. What would happen if Israel killed Russian troops in an air strike in Syria? Might Israel be the hook in Russia's jaw?

Israel's relationship with Turkey is even worse. Turkey banned all import and export activity with Israel in May 2024 because they support the Palestinians and Hamas. Do you recall that Israel assassinated Hamas leader Ismail Haniyeh in Tehran at the end of July 2024? Apparently, he was good friends with Recep Tayyip Erdoğan, the leader of Turkey.[81] Uh oh!

Additional Scriptures: Ezekiel 38-39. Genesis 10:1-7. Joel 2. Luke 21:24. Matthew 24:6-9. Revelation 6:3-4; 8:7.

#109 - GOG'S ALLIES

Anti | DD | Earth | **Gov** | **Israel** | **Jesus** | **Leader** | Sky | Society | Tech | **Trib**

> "Son of man, set your face toward Gog, of the land of Magog. ... Persia, Cush, and Put with them, all of them with shield and helmet; Gomer, and all his hordes; the house of Togarmah in the uttermost parts of the north, and all his hordes—even many peoples with you." (Ezekiel 38:2, 5-6)

Let's continue our discussion of the Gog of Magog War which we started in the prior sign. God is the one speaking in the verses above. We're given a list of nations that join Gog in the war against Israel. Recall that Gog rules over Rosh, Meshech, and Tubal, the modern-day equivalents of Russia and Turkey. As I mentioned in the prior sign, I believe this war takes place after the rapture, at the beginning of the tribulation period.

Jesus said wars like this against Israel would occur before his second coming because he told his disciples that they would be hated by all nations.

Figure 109.1 below lists the nations who join Gog and displays their current modern-day location. The allies of Gog include Iran, Libya, Ethiopia, Sudan, and Central Asia. Let's see if any of these nations are already aligning themselves with Russia and Turkey.

Table 109.1. Gog's Allies	
Gog's Allies	Current Location
Cush	Ethiopia, Sudan
Gomer	Turkey
Persia	Iran
Put	Algeria, Libya
Togarmah	Armenia, Central Asia, Turkey

Figure 109.1. Gog's Allies Current Locations[82]
Source: 9 Wars Of The End Times by David R. Reagan, The Non-Prophets Guide To The End Times by Todd Hampson, and The Prophecy Watcher 04.2023.

Fulfillment - Almost all of these nations are Muslim majority: Algeria (98%), Libya (97%), Iran (99%), Sudan (91%), and Turkey (98%). Even the countries in Central Asia are: Kazakhstan (73%), Kyrgyzstan (89%), Tajikistan (96%), Turkmenistan (93%), and Uzbekistan (97%). The notable exceptions are Armenia (<1%) and Ethiopia (36%). Since I believe this war happens after the rapture, those non-Muslim majority countries might very well become Muslim after the rapture. Perhaps by getting invaded by terrorist groups in the region.

As we've discussed in prior signs, the Muslim religion is directly opposed to the Bible, Christianity, and Judaism. They also believe that the land that Israel possesses is rightfully theirs through Abraham's first son Ishmael. Religion alone gives them a desire to invade Israel and take what they believe is theirs.

Treaties, trade agreements, and diplomatic relations already exist between many of these countries today. Russia is an ally of Iran. Iran provides suicide drones to Russia for use in the Ukraine war. Turkey gets their natural gas from Russia. Russia, Iran, Libya, and Hezbollah are allies in the Syrian Civil War. Russia, Iran, and Ethiopia are members of the BRICS alliance of nations, regarded as a competitor to NATO. In September 2024, Turkey formally requested to join BRICS as well.[83] Russia, Iran, and Turkey even recently formed an alliance to develop new oil and gas pipelines.[84]

Several of these countries also compose what's regarded as the new axis of evil: Russia, China, Iran, and North Korea.[85] Israel's foreign minister recently said Turkey should be considered part of that axis too.[86]

Today Is Different - Tension between Israel and Iran is at an all-time high. Iran supports Hamas, the terrorist group that invaded Israel in October 2023. They also support Hezbollah, the terrorist group that's bombarding Israel with rocket fire from Lebanon.[87] It's estimated they have 150,000 rockets.

In April 2024, Iran launched an unprecedented direct assault against Israel with drones and missiles.[88] It was done in retaliation for an Israeli airstrike in Damascus that killed top Iranian military officials. The most recent escalation occurred when Israel killed the leader of Hamas in Tehran in July 2024.[89] As of writing this, Iran has vowed to respond but has yet to take action.

I mentioned in the prior sign that Turkey was particularly enraged by Israel's action against the Hamas leader because they've also had strong ties with the group. And the president of Turkey was good friends with him. Now, Turkey has threatened to invade Israel.

Today, two of the biggest players in the Gog of Magog War, Iran and Turkey, are at odds with Israel. It's not going to take much for this to escalate into a broader war. Recall that the start of WWI is attributed to the assassination of Archduke Franz Ferdinand of Austria. Might the Gog of Magog War later be attributed as being started by Israel's assassination of Hamas leader Ismail Haniyeh?

Additional Scriptures: Ezekiel 27:13; 38-39. Genesis 10:1-7. Luke 21:24. Matthew 24:6-9.

#110 - THE ANTICHRIST RULES THE WORLD

Anti | DD | Earth | Gov | Israel | Jesus | Leader | Sky | Society | Tech | Trib

> I saw a woman sitting on a scarlet-colored beast, full of blasphemous names, having seven heads and ten horns. ... "The seven heads are seven mountains on which the woman sits. They are seven kings. ... The ten horns that you saw are ten kings who have received no kingdom as yet, but they receive authority as kings with the beast for one hour. These have one mind, and they give their power and authority to the beast."
> (Revelation 17:3, 9-10, 12-13)

The apostle John is speaking with an angel who is explaining the vision he saw of the beast with seven heads and ten horns. Remember that John saw this beast before in Revelation 13. It's the Antichrist.

Here, we see that its seven heads are seven kings. But we see that it has ten horns which represent ten kings. So, why doesn't it have ten heads? Ah, the prophet Daniel sheds light on this. It's the fourth beast in his vision from Daniel 7. The angel who visited Daniel explains that the Antichrist deposes three of the kings. From the verses above, apparently not before all ten kings transfer their authority to the Antichrist. That's right, the Antichrist becomes the ruler of the one world government.

Why would those ten kings do that? We've talked about the Antichrist before in prior signs. Jesus said that he came in God's name and was rejected, but that someone would come in his own name and be accepted. He was referring to the Antichrist, who comes to power during the tribulation period. Something happens to him which causes a seemingly fatal wound that he's seemingly miraculously healed from. It causes the world to marvel, follow, and eventually worship him. Perhaps that's one reason why some of these ten kings transfer their authority to him. They think he's a deity.

I think it's a good explanation for why the Antichrist initially rises to power, at least in his part of the world. After he gets his crown, and this is likely his initial kingship over a specific country, his true nature shines through. He's depicted as the first horseman of the book of Revelation. He has a crown and goes out to conquer. Remember that he'll be possessed by Satan. The rest of the world starts to worship him because they question who can make war with him. He'll have military power and angelic might which will make him formidable. People and nations will be afraid of him. So, many of them will do whatever he says.

As the world is coming together with ten kings and is building their one world government, the Antichrist will force his way in and coerce those ten kings to pledge allegiance to him. The fact that he murders three of them sometime after they transfer their authority reveals that he doesn't like them or doesn't think they'll be loyal. He'll deceive them. From Daniel we learn that his kingdom devours the whole world.

Fulfillment - There are people today who have an enormous amount of power, money, and influence in the world. They could be a world leader, a billionaire in the spotlight, an uber rich person behind the scenes, or a social media influencer with hundreds of millions of followers. Several media outlets publish their lists each year. *Time* magazine's The Most Influential People, *Forbes* The World's Most

Powerful People, *Time* magazine's Person of the Year, and *Forbes* Richest World's Billionaires are all examples.

While Satan could certainly pick a no name from the middle of nowhere to be his chosen vessel, the Antichrist, I doubt it. It'd be far easier to pick someone who's already well known on the world scene and give him the boost needed to rise above everyone else. It's the kinds of people who are on all of these lists who are prime candidates.

Of the top 10 billionaires in 2024, 8 of them are leaders in high tech: Musk (SpaceX, Tesla), Bezos (Amazon, Blue Origin), Zuckerberg (Meta), Ellison (Oracle), Page and Brin (Alphabet), and Gates and Ballmer (Microsoft).[90]

The world's most powerful people in 2024 according to Forbes are: Xi Jinping (China), Vladimir Putin (Russia), Donald Trump, Angela Markel (Germany), Jeff Bezos, Pope Francis, Bill Gates, Mohammed bin Salman Al Saud (Saudi Arabia), Narendra Modi (India), and Larry Page (Alphabet).[91] Four of these people are not current or former government leaders. Three of them are in high tech and one is a church leader.

Our culture is obsessed with these kinds of lists. We want someone to admire, to follow, to rally behind. Putting aside all the requirements that the Antichrist must actually meet, like being from the Roman Empire of old, it's not hard to envision most of these people becoming one of the ten kings of the one world government or rising above them all to become the Antichrist.

Today Is Different - The United Nations makes today different because the structure for the Antichrist and his kingdom is already in place. The UN began right after WWII, at the end of 1945.

The UN Security Council is where the power resides. It can recommend new member states, approve changes to the charter, establish peacekeeping operations, enact sanctions on a state, and even authorize military action. It's the only UN body that has authority to issue resolutions which are legally binding on member states. There are 5 permanent member states who all have veto power: China, France, Russia, the UK, and the US. The other 10 members of the Security Council are elected regionally for two-year terms.[92] It's certainly easy to see how this could be the very foundation for the one world government that the 10 kings are creating when the Antichrist intervenes.

The chief administrative officer of the UN is the secretary-general. It's like the CEO or president of the UN. He's appointed by the General Assembly. But get this, the Security Council must first recommend him.[93]

Could it be that the 10 kings in the tribulation period are a reconfigured UN Security Council? Could it be that they choose the Antichrist as the secretary-general? Could it be that the Security Council then transfers their power to the office of the secretary-general? We'll see, but it certainly seems likely to me that this is how the Antichrist will come to rule the world.

Additional Scriptures: 2 Thessalonians 2:8-12. Daniel 7:7-8, 19-27; 8:9-14, 17, 23-25; 11:21-45. John 5:43. Revelation 6:1-2; 13:1-8; 17; 18:2-3, 9-10.

#111 – NATION VS NATION

Anti | DD | Earth | **Gov** | Israel | **Jesus** | Leader | Sky | Society | **Tech** | **Trib**

> As he sat on the Mount of Olives, the disciples came to him privately, saying, "Tell us, when will these things be? What is the sign of your coming, and of the end of the age?" Jesus answered them, ... "You will hear of wars and rumors of wars. See that you aren't troubled, for all this must happen, but the end is not yet. For nation will rise against nation." (Matthew 24:3-4, 6-7)

Jesus tells us that one of the signs of his second coming is rumors of wars and nation rising against nation. The tribulation period will be a time of war. The first, second, and fourth seal judgments in Revelation all mention war. Evil rulers will take advantage of the chaos following the rapture, the Antichrist included. He will be conquering. That means nations will be against him. Nations will also be against each other. One half of the population remaining on earth after the rapture will not survive the initial years of the tribulation.

Here are some of the wars which take place during the tribulation period that are discussed in more detail throughout this book. The Gog of Magog War in which several nations rise against Israel (Sign #108). The war against God's people in which the Antichrist murders anyone who doesn't get his mark (Sign #115). The war between Israel and Syria (Sign #113). The war between the Antichrist and Israel (Sign #62, #112, #115). The gathering of all the earth's kings at Armageddon to war against Jesus (Sign #116).

There are many other wars that occur during the seven-year tribulation period. The directions north, south, east, and west are from Israel. The Antichrist will rise against a king of the South (maybe Egypt, Saudi Arabia?). Ships from the West (maybe Europe?) will advance against the Antichrist. The king of the South will rise back up against the Antichrist. Then a king of the North (perhaps Russia, Turkey, Syria, Central Asia?) will surge against the king of the South. The Antichrist will conquer Egypt. Kings from the East (maybe India, China?) and the North will mount against the Antichrist.

So, let's consider how close we are today to nations rising against other nations.

Fulfillment - I think this one is pretty obvious. Nations still war against other nations today. Let's look at some data that illustrates this. Figure 111.1 reveals the number of state-based conflicts across the world since 1946.

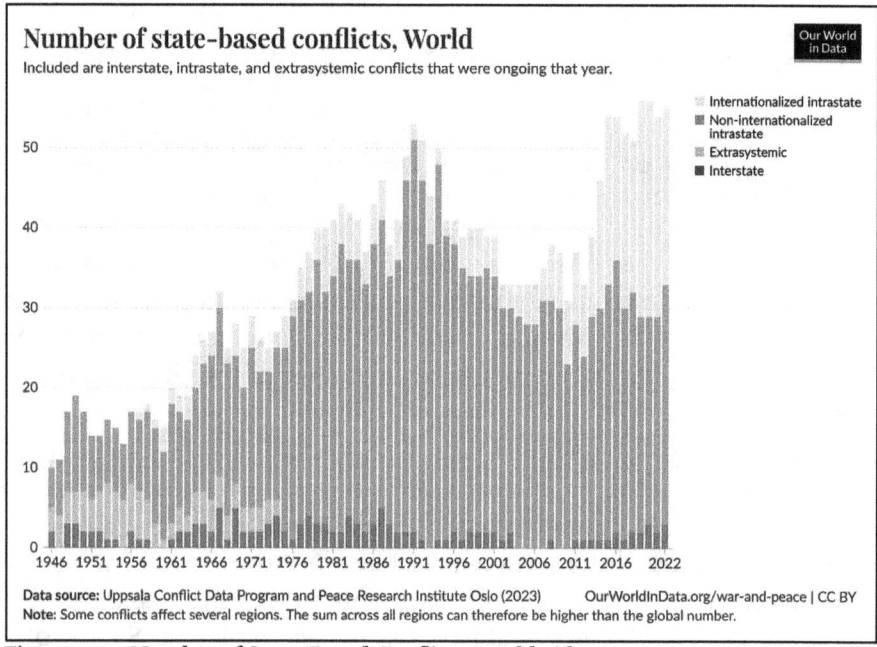

Figure 111.1. Number of State-Based Conflicts Worldwide[94]
Source: https://ourworldindata.org/grapher/number-of-state-based-conflicts

As you can see, there's been an upward trend over the years and even a spike in the last decade. The top-level bar indicates internationalized intrastate conflicts. Those weren't prominent until the 1960s. Starting around 2010, they've become a substantial percentage of the conflicts. Our nation vs nation conflicts are turning into kingdom vs kingdom conflicts.

Today Is Different - Rumors of WWIII makes today different. Even though Russia is warring with Ukraine, it's really between the US and NATO and Russia and its allies, like Iran. But it seems to boil down to Russia versus the US. WWII ended in 1945. That was 79 years ago.

The difference between then and now is that today all of the world's superpowers have nuclear weapons. The US has 5,748 and Russia has 5,580.[95] Both considerably more than China has at 500. You know, all it's going to take is for either nation to just launch one nuke in the other nation's direction. It might get blown out of the sky by anti-missile tech and not reach its intended target. Landing anywhere and destroying anything is irrelevant. In that moment, WWIII would begin.

That's also the reason WWIII hasn't started yet and is just a rumor. The superpowers threaten nuclear war, but none of them really want it to escalate to that. It would be devastating for all involved if it did.

I do not believe we'll see WWIII before the rapture because our normal lives would no longer be normal. Life wasn't normal during WWI or WWII. It was hard to buy and sell. People weren't celebrating and getting married. As we learned in Sign #84 - Fading Of Normality, normal exists before the rapture.

Additional Scriptures: Daniel 8:23-25; 9:26-27; 11:21-45. Deuteronomy 28:15-68. Isaiah 14:12, 16-17. Luke 21:9. Revelation 6:1-4, 7-8; 13:1-7; 16:12.

#112 - ALL NATIONS AGAINST ISRAEL

Anti | DD | Earth | Gov | Israel | Jesus | Leader | Sky | Society | Tech | Trib

> "I will make Jerusalem like an intoxicating drink that makes the nearby nations stagger when they send their armies to besiege Jerusalem and Judah. On that day I will make Jerusalem an immovable rock. All the nations will gather against it to try to move it, but they will only hurt themselves." (Zechariah 12:2-3 NLT)

God is the one speaking in the Scripture above. We're told that all nations will be against Israel. But though they try to influence Israel or war against it, they will only hurt themselves. In later verses in Zechariah 12 we learn it's at this time that God will defend Israel, give them the victory, and begin destroying the nations that rose against them. This aligns with what Jesus said in the Olivet Discourse about Israel. That they would be hated by all nations before his second coming.

Consider these wars that we know Israel will be involved in between now and Jesus's second coming. Psalm 83 War (Sign #107), Gog of Magog War (Sign #108, #109), Syria (Sign #113), and the Antichrist (Sign #62, #115). On top of this, we're told that many nations will rush against Israel in the wake of their war with Syria. But God rebukes them, and they flee.

During the tribulation period, the Antichrist is going to break his peace treaty with Israel (Sign #62). He's going to commit an abomination in their rebuilt temple and declare himself God (Sign #67, #68). This will of course offend all the Jews. Jesus warned about this in the Olivet Discourse too. For those alive during that time period, he said when Jerusalem is surrounded by armies to know the abomination is coming. He further instructed that the people living there should flee the city immediately.

Israel's enemies will want to eradicate them as a nation, take over their land, and plunder their wealth. The closer we are to all nations being against Jerusalem, the closer we are to Jesus's return.

Fulfillment - Israel's military is a top 20 power. It ranks 17th out of the 145 countries included in the yearly Global Firepower report.[96] That puts them ahead of Germany and Ukraine. It's estimated Israel has 90 nuclear weapons.[97] No one else in the Middle East has any, that we know of. There's speculation that Iran might. Israel has four different air defense systems in use: the Arrow anti-ballistic missile system, the Iron Dome system for short range rockets, David's sling for medium range rockets, and Iron Beam, a short-range laser system.[98]

There's another weapon that Israel has which is unique to them and makes all the difference. It's God. Over the years, I've read so many accounts of miraculous events that led to Israel obtaining victories in prior wars.[99] Jonathan Cahn's book *The Oracle* reveals some of them too.

During Israel's Independence War, a small platoon was almost out of ammunition when suddenly the Jordanian soldiers they were fighting all dropped their weapons and ran away screaming "Abraham!" The soldiers who ran claimed to have seen a vision of Abraham defending the Jews in the sky above.

During the Six-Day War, when Israel went against Egypt's Kusseima outpost they discovered the Egyptians had destroyed their equipment and abandoned their base. The Egyptian soldiers said they saw a gigantic hand come out of the sky which terrified them. In a separate battle during this war, an Arab tank commander was asked why he surrendered to a small number of Jewish tanks. He said he saw a vision of hundreds of Israeli tanks.

During the Gulf War, Iraq threatened to attack Israel with chemical weapons. While they did attack Israel with rockets, a chemical attack never occurred. It's because the normal wind patterns over Israel shifted to blow east toward Iraq. Any chemical attack would have blown into Iraq and harmed their own people, so they didn't make good on the threat.

Today Is Different - Even before the Hamas attack against Israel in October 2023, the world was gathered against Israel regarding the Palestinians. Countries, including the US, were pressuring Israel to agree to a two-state solution.

In fact, UN Watch reports that between 2015 and 2022, the UN General Assembly adopted 140 resolutions on Israel vs 68 for the rest of the world. Between 2006 and 2022, the UN Human Rights Council issued 99 resolutions against Israel and only 13 against Iran.[100] It hasn't eased up either. In 2023, the UN General Assembly rebuked Israel 14 times compared to 7 for the rest of the world combined.[101]

Now, all the nations are speaking out against Israel regarding their actions in Gaza against the Hamas terrorists. They want Israel to cease fire. But Israel's not budging. They are determined to finish this war and eliminate the enemy.

In March 2024, the UN Security Council passed a Gaza ceasefire resolution for the month of Ramadan. The US didn't veto it. Israel spoke out against US support for this because it didn't demand Hamas release any hostages.[102]

In April 2024, in speaking with a US Republican Congressional delegation, Israel Prime Minister Netanyahu was quoted as saying, "there is a contrary move, an attempt to force, ram down our throats a Palestinian state, which will be another terror haven, another launching ground for an attempt, as was the Hamas state in Gaza. That is opposed by Israelis, overwhelmingly. We just had a vote in the Knesset: 99 to 9."[103]

Also in April 2024, the UN Human Rights Council adopted a resolution condemning Israel and calling for an arms embargo against them.[104]

In May 2024, the United Nations International Criminal Court issued an arrest warrant for Israel's Prime Minister Netanyahu and Minister of Defense Gallant. They're being accused of war crimes in Gaza.[105] Netanyahu responded by stating this is "what the new anti-Semitism looks like." Then he vowed to achieve victory over Hamas.[106]

In June 2024, the UN placed Israel on its "List of Shame" for wartime children's rights violations.[107] In July 2024, the UN International Court of Justice stated Israel's presence in Palestinian territories is unlawful.[108]

In August 2024, the UN fired nine employees working in its Palestine refugee agency, UNRWA, because they were found to be involved in the Hamas attack against Israel.[109]

In September 2024, the UK announced that it's suspending some arms and defense sales to Israel. They are concerned the weapons will be used to violate international humanitarian law. While British exports only make up 1% of external arms sales to Israel, this is indicative of the beginning of an ominous trend.[110]

This looks like it'll be a record-breaking year for the United Nations against Israel.

Additional Scriptures: 2 Kings 21:11-15; 24. 2 Thessalonians 2:3-4. Daniel 9:24-27; 11:21-39. Deuteronomy 28:15-68. Ezekiel 38-39. Isaiah 17. Joel 2. Luke 21:20-24. Matthew 24:9, 15-21. Psalm 83. Revelation 11:1-2; 12. Zechariah 12; 14:1-15.

#113 - DESTRUCTION OF DAMASCUS

Anti | DD | Earth | **Gov** | **Israel** | **Jesus** | Leader | Sky | Society | **Tech** | Trib

> The burden of Damascus. "Behold, Damascus is taken away from being a city, and it will be a ruinous heap." (Isaiah 17:1)

God is giving a prophetic message to the prophet Isaiah in the verse above. We learn that Damascus will no longer be a city, but instead a ruinous heap. Damascus is the capital of Syria. In the Bible, it was the ancient nation of Assyria. You may recall that Assyria was one of the nations that God sent against the Israelites to take them into captivity. God promised to hold them accountable for that and this will be the fulfillment of that promise.

As I mentioned in Sign #107 - Psalm 83 Allies, I think it's feasible that this destruction of Damascus happens during the Psalm 83 War against Israel because Assyria is listed as one of the participants. But it could be a completely separate war between Israel and Assyria that results in this.

Israel will also sustain heavy losses in this war. Later in Isaiah 17 we're told that Israel will look like a grain field after the harvest. They'll be like an olive tree that's shaken and only has two or three olives left on the top branches and a handful scattered among the rest of the limbs.

The very last verse in Isaiah 17 infers that Syria will attack Israel first and cause their devastation, and then Israel will respond by completely destroying Damascus. This war against Israel is because they'll be hated by all nations, as Jesus mentioned in the Olivet Discourse as being a sign of his second coming.

Fulfillment - Damascus is the capital of Syria. It's one of the oldest continually inhabited cities on the planet, originating around 3000 BC.[111] As we learned in Sign #107, Syria is 93% Muslim.

The Syrian Civil War has been ongoing since 2011. It's a battle between the rule of Bashar al-Assad and those against him. There are many foreign nations involved in this. Those backing Assad's regime include Iran, Russia, and Hezbollah. Those opposed to him include the United States and Turkey.[112]

Israel considers itself neutral in the civil war. However, Israel intervenes to prevent Iran from gaining influence in Syria. Israel doesn't want Iran smuggling weapons to Hezbollah. Israel doesn't want Iran building up a military presence in Syria on its border with Israel. Thus, they frequently conduct airstrikes in Syria against targets they see as a threat.[113]

Today Is Different - In April 2024, Israel destroyed the Iranian consulate in Damascus, killing two Iranian generals and five other officers.[114] That action seems to have escalated tension between Israel and Iran because Iran responded with a direct drone and missile strike against Israel in April 2024. Then Israel killed the leader of Hamas in

Tehran at the end of July 2024. Now, Iran has threatened to retaliate.

What does that have to do with Syria and Damascus you ask? Well, the Iranian military and the terrorist regimes they sponsor operate out of Syria. It's certainly feasible for Iran to launch an assault against Israel from Syria.

Based on the biblical text, it appears this war will be nuclear given the amount of destruction which takes place on both sides. So, does anyone in this group of nations have nuclear weapons? While they haven't admitted it, it's estimated Israel has at least 90.[115] It's uncertain if Iran already has some. We know Iran has a nuclear program and that it's enriching uranium. Several leaders have recently raised the alarm that it could be just a matter of weeks before Iran has a nuke. Some have even speculated that this is why Iran recently decided to brazenly attack Israel directly instead of through a terrorist proxy.[116] Because they already have a nuke or two.

I honestly don't think Iran having a nuke that they manufactured themselves is a constraint. If Iran wanted to nuke Israel, I think they could buy one from North Korea or Pakistan. Sure, it would put the nation they purchased it from at risk of retaliation from Israel. But if that nation had an ally like Russia, then that would certainly change the game.

<u>Additional Scriptures:</u> 1 Chronicles 5:26. 2 Kings 15:29; 17. Isaiah 10:5-19; 17. Jeremiah 49:23-27. Luke 21:24. Matthew 24:6-9. Psalm 83.

#114 – SHOCKING AMOUNT OF DESTRUCTION

<u>Anti</u> | DD | Earth | <u>Gov</u> | Israel | <u>Jesus</u> | <u>Leader</u> | Sky | Society | <u>Tech</u> | <u>Trib</u>

> "He will become very strong, but not by his own power. He will cause a shocking amount of destruction and succeed in everything he does. He will destroy powerful leaders and devastate the holy people. He will be a master of deception and will become arrogant; he will destroy many without warning." (Daniel 8:24-25 NLT)

The prophet Daniel is speaking with the angel Gabriel in these verses. The "he" is the Antichrist. We're told he's going to cause "a shocking amount of destruction," including destroying powerful leaders, the holy people, and many who don't see him coming. We're told he worships a god of fortresses with silver and gold. A fortress is a place of safety and protection. Since he will have so much military might, perhaps that's what he worships. Examining the additional Scriptures below we also know this destruction includes his looting of the nations he conquers.

There's an interesting definition for the Hebrew word that's used for *shocking*. It means beyond one's power. Makes sense. We know that he'll be possessed by Satan. So, that's one reason why he's going to succeed at everything he does. Satan is known for being a destroyer of cities.

There's another angel who's named as a prominent character in the tribulation period. His name is Apollyon. This fallen angel gets let out of the bottomless pit and is the king of the demonic locust creatures that'll be torturing unbelievers. Do you know what his name means? Destruction.

Jesus warned that this would be a time of great tribulation. Worse than any other time in history.

So, how close are we to being able to cause a shocking amount of destruction without the help of fallen angels?

Fulfillment - When we think of a destructive weapon, we usually think of nuclear weapons. We're going to talk about that below, but there's another type of weapon that can certainly be destructive in a different way. It's an electromagnetic pulse weapon or EMP. You see, this weapon wouldn't cause any damage to structures. The blast wouldn't even kill anyone. But this type of weapon would fry an electric grid.

Electricity is used to pretty much power everything. Without power, that means defense systems, communication systems, and navigation systems wouldn't work anymore. A military wouldn't be able to easily respond to such an attack. They'd be crippled. If one was detonated in space, it would destroy satellites. Mounted to an autonomous drone, it could fly over a city and disable targets at will.[117]

All the global superpowers are developing weapons like this. It's not hard to envision the Antichrist using such a weapon to conquer nations. Since the Bible tells us that he plunders, this seems like the weapon that could cause a shocking amount of destruction while still keeping valuable items safe and available for the taking.

Today Is Different - We talked about weapons of mass destruction in an earlier sign. That the US dropped two atomic bombs on Japan during WWII which caused massive devastation and death. Well, those pale in comparison to the upgraded nuclear weapons of today. Now, we have hydrogen bombs, otherwise known as thermonuclear bombs.

The explosive yield of the two atomic bombs were 15 and 21 kilotons. The Soviet Union tested a hydrogen bomb in 1961 named Tsar Bomba. Its explosive yield was 50,000 kilotons (or 50 megatons)! The heat this bomb generated was 10.6 billion °F. That's 392 times hotter than the sun. It's the most powerful weapon ever detonated on earth. The island they dropped it on during their test was leveled and looked like a skating rink afterward.[118]

The most powerful bomb in the US arsenal is the Mark 41 thermonuclear bomb at 25 megatons. The B-52 bomber can carry two of them.[119]

There are enough nuclear weapons on the planet today that the Antichrist would have no problem committing a shocking amount of destruction if he got his hands on them.

Additional Scriptures: 2 Thessalonians 2:3-4. Daniel 7:7, 23; 11:21-45. Isaiah 14:12-17. Matthew 24:6-9, 21-22. Revelation 6:1-4, 7-8; 9:1-11; 12:7-12; 13:1-4.

#115 - WAR AGAINST GOD'S PEOPLE

Anti | DD | Earth | Gov | Israel | Jesus | Leader | Sky | Society | Tech | Trib

> I saw thrones, and they sat on them, and judgment was given to them. I saw the souls of those who had been beheaded for the testimony of Jesus and for the word of God, and such as didn't worship the beast nor his image, and didn't receive the mark on their forehead and on their hand. They lived and reigned with Christ for a thousand years. (Revelation 20:4)

In this Scripture, the apostle John is seeing a vision of events during the second coming of Jesus. We see souls of the people who were beheaded for their testimony. They had put their faith in Jesus and the Word of God. They didn't worship the Antichrist, his image, or get his mark. These are the tribulation saints, the people who come to faith in Jesus after the rapture and during the tribulation period.

In the additional Scriptures below, you'll discover the Antichrist wages a war against God's people during the tribulation period.

Refusing to worship him, his image, and receive his mark is punishable by death. This will of course include people who've put their faith in Jesus.

We get further clarification that this is indeed a holy war when we see references to the Antichrist warring with the saints, devastating the holy people, and being against the holy covenant. That means the Antichrist will murder Christians and Jews. The Antichrist also executes God's two witnesses preaching the gospel, and the entire world will see their dead bodies for three and a half days.

Babylon also gets drunk off the blood of the saints, meaning the one world religion is going to have a hand in killing God's people too.

Jesus spoke of this time of great tribulation and said his followers would suffer persecution, betrayal, hatred, and some would be martyred. Do we see a war against God's people today? It would be an indicator that Jesus is at the door.

Fulfillment - Well, the Holocaust certainly comes mind as a contemporary fulfillment of this. Hitler murdered six million Jews during the Holocaust of WWII.[120] Since then, we haven't witnessed a war against God's people to such a degree. We discussed anti-Semitism toward the Jews in Sign #92, oppression against God's people in Sign #95, and the current situation against the Jews regarding Hamas terrorists in Sign #107.

Open Doors publishes a world watch list of 50 countries where Christians face the highest levels of persecution. It's difficult to get actual counts of people who are martyred. As you can imagine, a country isn't going to blast that on TV, in newspapers, or on social media. It's kept secret. They don't want the world to know what they're doing.

Given all that, they estimate 1 in 7 Christians are persecuted worldwide. Refer to figure 115.1 for the top 10 countries where the overall highest levels of persecution are occurring. North Korea tops the list.

Table 115.1. Open Doors World Watch List 2024, Top 10 Overall	
Rank	Country
1	North Korea
2	Somalia
3	Libya
4	Eritrea
5	Yemen
6	Nigeria
7	Pakistan
8	Sudan
9	Iran
10	Afghanistan

Figure 115.1. Open Doors World Watch List 2024, Top 10 Overall[121]
Source: https://www.opendoors.org/persecution/reports/North_Korea-Full_Country_Dossier-ODI-2024.pdf

While North Korea has no religious affiliation, almost all the other countries have a Muslim supermajority population. The exceptions are Eritrea (63% Christian, 37% Muslim) and Nigeria (51% Muslim, 47% Christian).[122]

Nearly 5,000 Christians were murdered in 2023. Figure 115.2 displays the top 10 countries where the highest levels of violent persecution are happening, Nigeria being the deadliest place to live as a follower of Jesus. 82% of the deaths happened there.

Table 115.2. Open Doors World Watch List 2024, Top 10 Violence	
Rank	Country
1	Nigeria
2	Pakistan
3	India
4	Myanmar
5	Niger
6	DRC
7	Cameroon
8	Uganda
9	Mali
10	Burkina Faso

Figure 115.2. Open Doors World Watch List 2024, Top 10 Violence[123]
Source: https://www.opendoors.org/persecution/reports/North_Korea-Full_Country_Dossier-ODI-2024.pdf

In figure 115.2, these countries have a Muslim majority population: Nigeria (only slightly though), Pakistan, Niger, Mali, and Burkina Faso. India is mostly Hindu. Myanmar is mostly Buddhist. That leaves the DRC, Cameroon, and Uganda who have majority Christian populations.[124] Christians in those three nations are suffering from violence in specific regions of the country.

In 2023, almost 15,000 churches or Christian properties were attacked.[125] While not in the top 10 for violence, China saw at least 10,000 churches close. The majority of people in China have no religious affiliation while the rest are mostly folk religions or Buddhist.

Today Is Different - Something that makes today different is the sophisticated surveillance technology that exists. It's used to persecute people today, not just Christians. Technology like this is going to get used in the tribulation period to help track down God's people.

One example is Iran's draconian surveillance of women to ensure they're wearing head coverings in public. There are random road checks to stop women drivers, traffic cameras that snap photos of women in their cars, cameras in public places, and citizens are encouraged to report dress code offenders. Businesses must upload camera footage or face fines. On top of that, the government is using AI to link facial recognition with cell phone and GPS data to help them track down female offenders.[126] Offenders are often sent text messages demanding they report to the morality police.

Then there's China, who uses AI and big data to create a social credit score for each person and business. They've got cameras everywhere in society that monitor people's behavior, like jaywalking, so it can be analyzed and fed into the score. As you might expect, a lot of the data that determines a score comes from financial information. People now have to do a facial scan and have a good score in order to purchase fuel for cars. It's estimated 23 million people have been banned from traveling by plane or train because their score is too low.[127]

We're also seeing advances in biometric surveillance today. I already mentioned facial recognition. Did you know they've put that in AR glasses for police officers? There are also cameras doing iris scans instead of full facial recognition. Now, there's even gait recognition that can identify an individual by how they walk.[128] Partner all this technology with a miniature drone that's flying around recording video, and you've got something out of a sci-fi movie.

Also consider that without modern technology like cameras, the internet, and TV broadcasting, the world that's left behind after the rapture wouldn't be able to watch the two witnesses in Jerusalem.

Additional Scriptures: 1 Peter 5:8. Daniel 7:19-25; 8:24; 9:26-27; 11:21-45. Luke 21:12-24. Mark 13:9-20. Matthew 24:9-22. Revelation 6:9-11; 11:1-7; 12; 13:7; 17:6; 18:24.

#116 – GATHERED TO ARMAGEDDON

Anti | DD | **Earth** | **Gov** | **Israel** | **Jesus** | **Leader** | Sky | **Society** | Tech | **Trib**

> Then the sixth angel poured out his bowl on the great river Euphrates, and its water was dried up, so that the way of the kings from the east might be prepared. And I saw three unclean spirits like frogs [coming] out of the mouth of the dragon, out of the mouth of the beast, and out of the mouth of the false prophet. For they are spirits of demons, performing signs, [which] go out to the kings of the earth and of the whole world, to gather them to the battle of that great day of God Almighty. ... And they gathered them together to the place called in Hebrew, Armageddon. ...

> And I saw the beast, the kings of the earth, and their armies, gathered together to make war against Him who sat on the horse and against His army. (Revelation 16:12-14, 16; 19:19 NKJV)

In these verses, the apostle John is describing his vision of events in the tribulation period. We're told the Euphrates River will dry up, and the kings from the East will cross that dried-up river on their way to the place called Armageddon. In Hebrew it's the word *Har-Magedon*, which means the city of Megiddo. It's an actual place that exists in the Jezreel Valley, also known as the Valley of Megiddo, in Israel today. It's a large fertile plain with some surrounding mountains.

The kings from the East aren't alone. In Revelation 9, we come to find out that four angels who've been bound at the Euphrates River are released. They have a demonic army of horsemen that numbers 200 million. We also see in the above Scripture that the spirits of demons gather all the kings of the world along with their armies to this battle against God Almighty. As you would expect, the Beast who is the Antichrist is there too. Though not mentioned above, the False Prophet is as well. In fact, I'm sure every fallen angel and every demon will be front and center with Satan. They think they're going to win.

It's interesting to contemplate how long it's going to take for all these people to mobilize and get to Israel. Satan knows the Bible better than we do. Of course, he's going to know the exact date that Jesus will return because God's Word tells us how many days to count from when the Antichrist declares himself God. It's 1,260 days.

When Jesus gave us all the signs to watch for regarding the end of the age, he culminated his teaching with details about his actual second coming. He said everyone would see him coming. He also shared the sheep and goats parable so we would know that he will separate whoever survives through the tribulation period. Only people who've put their faith in him will get to live in his kingdom. That means all those people who gather to war against Jesus get destroyed when he returns.

Fulfillment - Let's talk about the Euphrates River first. Guess what? It's drying up. This river begins in Southern Turkey, flows through Syria and Iraq, merges with the Tigris River, and then flows into the Persian Gulf. Today, there are 22 dams along the river for irrigation and hydroelectric power. So, less water in the river flows downstream. It's also been impacted by severe drought. The water level is historically low, and it's estimated the river could run dry by 2040.[129]

The Valley of Megiddo is southwest of the Sea of Galilee in a large plain. In 1799, Napoleon Bonaparte battled the Ottomans in the valley. It's reported that he said, "All the armies of the world could maneuver their forces on this vast plain. ... There is no place in the whole world more suited for war than this. ... [It is] the most natural battleground of the whole earth."[130]

I also want to touch on the army of 200 million. I'm convinced it's a demonic army, but if it actually is comprised of humans led by kings from the East, let's see if any nation in the East could field an army that size today. Today, India could field an all-male army, ages 15-64, that is 495 million strong.[131] China's would be slightly higher at 496 million.[132] However, we must consider that half of the world that's left behind after the rapture is going to perish in just two of the tribulation period judgments. Even if we cut those armies in half, each of those nations could still have an army of over 200 million.

Today Is Different - I can sort of understand why Satan and the fallen angels think they have a chance at defeating Jesus. I think it's because they were able to get him crucified two thousand years ago. Perhaps they think they can do it again and make it permanent this time.

Now, I don't think they were expecting Jesus to conquer death the first time. I sure don't think they were expecting his death and resurrection to end up paving the way for us to have eternal life. They would have done everything possible to prevent Jesus's crucifixion if that was the case. However, since the fallen angels have some superpowers and people are going to worship them during the tribulation period, I can see how that could go to their head so to speak. Like Satan's beauty did with him. Perhaps it all just boils down to sheer pride.

So, why are humans going to join the demonic army in the Valley of Megiddo to war against Jesus? Why would they think they could defeat God? Because they are not going to believe that Jesus is God. They are going to believe that Satan and the fallen angels who invade earth are the true gods. The Bible tells us that God will send strong delusion in the tribulation period and that people will believe the lie. We looked at that lie in Sign #61. This is just another facet and consequence of it.

They'll all choose to get Satan's mark of the Beast which reveals their allegiance to him.

Additional Scriptures: Daniel 8:25; 12:6-13. Joel 3:1-2, 9-16. Matthew 24:28-31; 25:31-46. Revelation 9:13-17; 17:11-14; 19:17-21.

#117 - POLAR OPPOSITE - A GOOD HEART

Anti | DD | Earth | **Gov** | **Israel** | Jesus | **Leader** | Sky | **Society** | Tech | Trib

> For a child is born to us. A son is given to us; and the government will be on his shoulders. His name will be called Wonderful, Counselor, Mighty God, Everlasting Father, Prince of Peace. Of the increase of his government and of peace there shall be no end, on David's throne, and on his kingdom, to establish it, and to uphold it with justice and with righteousness from that time on, even forever. The zeal of the LORD of Armies will perform this. (Isaiah 9:6-7)

Throughout this chapter we've looked at signs related to an evil heart. This sign is what I call a polar opposite. It's meant to illustrate how far away we currently are from the life we believers are going to live during Jesus's reign on earth in the millennial kingdom. Recall from Sign #6 - The Point Of No Return, that God only lets evil progress so far before he intervenes.

In the Scripture above, the prophet Isaiah tells us about Jesus, the child born to us, reigning during the millennial kingdom. The names of Jesus reveal many character traits that are important. After seven years of intense tribulation, wars, and unbridled evil, the Prince of Peace will be a celebrated leader. We're told his kingdom will not end. Neither will justice, righteousness, and peace. In the additional Scriptures below, we also discover that Jesus bestows rulership on believers in the church age during the millennial kingdom. Gone will be the days of evil leaders and bad judges. War will be a thing of the past because nation will never rise against nation ever again.

Everyone will have a good heart, one that bears fruit and keeps away from evil.

> "The **good man** out of the **good treasure of his heart** brings out that which is **good**, and the evil man out of the evil treasure of his heart brings out that which is evil, for out of the abundance of the heart, his mouth speaks." (Luke 6:45)

Fulfillment - So, how far away are we? Well, we just looked at nineteen different signs that indicate how evil the world has become. It's obvious we're not in a state of peace. It seems like nations are at a tipping point where conflicts and tension could easily escalate into devastating wars.

A fun way to consider just how opposite we are is to contemplate what the worst-case scenarios might look like and see just how close we are to them.

Worst case, every nation on earth is involved in a conflict or war with another nation. This is truer than you realize. It's because of all the treaties nations have with others today. Even if a nation isn't physically participating in a conflict, they might be providing funds or military equipment for use in the conflict. From what I can tell, there's maybe a handful of nations that aren't involved in a current conflict and haven't been in decades. We're essentially at the worst case here.

Worst case, the criminals are in control because there's no lawman and no justice. It's like the Wild West. While we haven't degraded to this state on a wide scale, it certainly happens in pockets today. We're not at this worst case yet.

Worst case, Israel no longer has any allies. Every nation on the planet is critical of them. All the nations which will war against them in the last days are already making threats and attacking them. Israel doesn't have many allies today. Support from the US is on shaky ground, as are the peace agreements Israel has with its neighboring countries. The UN, which represents all the nations on the planet, has issued more resolutions against Israel than all the other nations combined. There are indeed several nations already attacking Israel who will war against them soon. We're really close to the worst case here.

Today Is Different - So, what do you think? Is today different? Do we as a society have an evil heart that wars against God's people, opposes the law, and murders the most innocent? Do you think we've reached the point of no return? How many people really have a good heart that's longing for the return of King Jesus?

Additional Scriptures: 1 Corinthians 6:2-3. Acts 3:20-21. Daniel 7:13-14. Ezekiel 37:24-25. Isaiah 2:4; 32:1; 60:17-18. Revelation 4:4; 19:1-16; 22:1-2.

PART 3

SUPERNATURAL SIGNS

CHAPTER 14 - POSITIVE SIGNS

#118 - GOD'S PRESENCE IS OBVIOUS

Anti | DD | **Earth** | Gov | Israel | Jesus | Leader | **Sky** | Society | Tech | **Trib**

> For the wrath of God is revealed from heaven against all ungodliness and unrighteousness of men ... because that which is known of God is revealed in them, for God revealed it to them. For the invisible things of him since the creation of the world are clearly seen, being perceived through the things that are made, even his everlasting power and divinity, that they may be without excuse. (Romans 1:18-20)

Here, we're told that God has revealed himself to each person. That we can also clearly see God through all the things he's created. He's made his power and divinity obvious. So, no one will be able to use the excuse that they didn't know God existed on judgment day. In fact, in Psalm 19 we learn that the heavens themselves declare God's glory and speak of his existence to us.

Other ways that God makes his presence obvious is through signs, fulfilled Bible prophecy, and eyewitness accounts. Observing all the signs of Jesus's second coming should be enough to convince someone that God is real. God gave Moses signs to perform for the Israelites and the Egyptian Pharaoh to prove that God had sent him. Jesus even stepped out of heaven and came to earth to demonstrate God's existence. We have many eyewitness accounts of Jesus's life, death, and resurrection.

Yet, in the tribulation period we're told that people still refuse to believe and repent, even when the sky rolls up like a scroll and everyone can see Jesus on his throne. The more that God makes his presence obvious, the closer Jesus is to returning.

Fulfillment - God is Reliable. God will do everything he's promised to do because he's always done what he said he would do. God's past actions prove that he is reliable and worthy of our trust. A concrete way we can examine this is by looking at Bible prophecies. A Bible prophecy is a Scripture that speaks about something in the future. By comparing history against Bible prophecy, we can see if what God said would happen actually did.

One clear example that we've been given is that Israel is a nation again. It's that important that I put it as Sign #1. In my book *Rapture*

911, I have an entire section of the book (Part 6 - Trusting The Bible) that's dedicated to fulfilled Bible prophecies.[1] There's one particular example that I'd like to mention here.

A college professor of mathematics and astronomy, Peter W. Stoner, wrote a book titled *Science Speaks* in which he analyzed the likelihood of one man fulfilling the first coming prophecies that Jesus fulfilled. His analysis was peer reviewed by members of the American Scientific Affiliation, and they determined the mathematical probabilities he presented were "thoroughly sound" and applied in a proper way.[2]

Now, consider there are over 300 prophecies in the Bible about the first coming of Jesus. Jesus fulfilled every single one of them. Even if you had a ridiculously conservative probability for each prophecy that 1 man in 10 could fulfill it, the likelihood of that 1 man fulfilling all 300 would be 1×10^{300}. To picture this, you need to envision an electron. You mark one of these electrons, blindfold yourself, and then try to pick the right one throughout the whole universe. Physicists tell us there are only 10^{80} electrons in the entire universe. You'd have to search through a universe almost 4 times the size of ours before you'd have a chance of finding the one electron you marked!

As Stoner put it, "It is proof of the Bible's inspiration by God—proof so definite that the universe is not large enough to hold the evidence."[3] It's utterly inconceivable that these prophecies were fulfilled by Jesus as a mere coincidence or matter of chance. The only one who could orchestrate such a feat is God. The Bible is the Word of God. God really did come to earth in the flesh as Jesus Christ and die for your sins.

If you're someone who favors logic, science, and facts that can be tangibly proven, this evidence should give you enormous confidence.

Today Is Different - Recent scientific discoveries which validate the Bible make today unique. One is the potential discovery of the ancient Old Testament city of Sodom. You may recall that God destroyed Sodom and Gomorrah by making it rain fire and brimstone.

A research article was published in *Scientific Reports* in September 2021 regarding this. Archaeologists have been excavating Tall el-Hammam. It's in the Jordan Valley near the north end of the Dead Sea. They discovered an odd 3600-year-old charcoal-rich destruction layer that marks the sudden abandonment of the urban center. The remains of the city are unique and point to the occurrence of a catastrophic event.

After performing lots of tests, they concluded the only plausible way that destruction layer could have formed was by a crater-forming impact or cosmic airburst. If it was an airburst, it would have been larger than the 22-megaton airburst at Tunguska, Siberia in 1908. It would have caused a high-temperature thermal pulse from a fireball that melted materials like clay, mudbricks, and pottery. The subsequent blast wave would then have pulverized the walls across the city, leveling it.

The conclusion of their paper states: "Regarding this proposed airburst, an eyewitness description of this 3600-year-old catastrophic event may have been passed down as an oral tradition that eventually became the written biblical account about the destruction of Sodom."4

Additional Scriptures: 1 Corinthians 15:1-8. Exodus 4:1-9. Genesis 19:24-25. Psalm 19:1-6. Revelation 6:12-16. Romans 1:32.

#119 - PROPHETS WARN ABOUT THE FUTURE

Anti | DD | Earth | Gov | Israel | **Jesus** | **Leader** | Sky | Society | **Tech** | **Trib**

> Yet the LORD testified to Israel and to Judah, by every prophet and every seer, saying, "Turn from your evil ways, and keep my commandments and my statutes, according to all the law which I commanded your fathers, and which I sent to you by my servants the prophets." (2 Kings 17:13)

In this Scripture, we learn that God sent every prophet and seer to warn the people. Upon reading the additional Scriptures below, you'll also discover that God doesn't do anything until he reveals it to his prophets. That's because he wants to get the credit for it when it comes to pass. In this way we'll learn to trust him because we know he's going to do what he says.

God told Noah about the flood years in advance. Then God gave him a seven-day advanced warning to pack up before it started raining. God told Abraham about Sodom and Gomorrah before he destroyed the cities. God sent two angels to warn Lot, give him one last time to warn others, and then rescue him before those cities were destroyed. God sent prophets like Jeremiah, Ezekiel, and Isaiah to warn about the coming captivity of the Israelites. God had Isaiah and Ezekiel be signs themselves by acting out coming events.

God even came to earth, that's Jesus, to warn all of us about the future. All of the Gospel accounts are full of warnings. In particular Jesus's Olivet Discourse. His message was one of repentance because his kingdom was coming soon.

During the tribulation period, God will even send two witnesses to prophesy for three and a half years.

Fulfillment - For purposes of this sign, when I speak of a modern-day prophet, it's not someone like the prophet Ezekiel who spoke prophetic words from God regarding the future. It's more like a watchman. Someone who expounds upon God's already spoken word and warns about what's coming.

I think a great example of this is the *Left Behind* book series by Jerry B. Jenkins and Tim LaHaye. It's a set of sixteen thriller novels about people left behind after the rapture who are living through the tribulation period. Even though it's fiction, it's rooted in the Bible. Much like *The Chosen* TV series is a biblical historical fiction about the ministry of Jesus during his first coming and the disciples who followed him. The first *Left Behind* book was published at the end of 1995. By 2017, the series had sold more than 65 million copies! It's one of the most popular Christian fiction series of all time.[5]

Another example is Jonathan Cahn and the books he writes which expound on modern-day events happening in America and how they follow the biblical patterns of judgment. *The Harbinger* was published in 2011. It was on *The New York Times* bestseller list for over 100 weeks (that's like 2 years) and has sold over two million copies.[6]

You know, God called me into this mission field as well. You can read the details about it in my testimony in the Appendix. God asked me to leave the career I had at Intel Corporation and write a book about the rapture, but not just any book. He asked me to write a book for those who would be left behind afterwards, *Rapture 911: What To Do If You're Left Behind*. I'm convinced this illustrates how very near the rapture must be.

God is using me and these other authors to spread the gospel and Bible prophecy in easily understandable and sometimes entertaining ways. We're all modern-day prophets warning about the future.

Today Is Different - The rise of biblical end times focused ministries makes today unique. Consider these popular ones: Lamb & Lion Ministries, Prophecy Watchers, Olive Tree Ministries, Behold Israel, and SkyWatch TV.[7] These ministries and many more like them are reaching millions of people through cable television, the internet, radio, and Bible prophecy conferences throughout America. They're all helping to educate people on the nearness of Jesus's return.

Additional Scriptures: Acts 2:16-21. Ezekiel 2:4-7; 12:1-6; 33:33. Genesis 6:3, 13-22; 7:1-5; 18:16-33; 19:12-14. Isaiah 20. Jeremiah 7:25; 25:1-4; 29:19. Luke 7:11-17; 21. Mark 13. Matthew 4:17; 24-25. Revelation 11:1-14.

#120 - MANY RUN TO AND FRO

Anti | DD | **Earth** | Gov | Israel | Jesus | Leader | **Sky** | **Society** | **Tech** | Trib

> "But you, Daniel, shut up the words, and seal the book until the time of the end; many shall run to and fro." (Daniel 12:4 NKJV)

An angel is speaking to the prophet Daniel here. He tells Daniel that in the end times people will run to and fro. It means to travel, go about. In other Scriptures, we're told that God's eyes run to and fro and that Satan goes to and fro on the earth.

As we discussed in Sign #37 - Censorship, God will send a famine on the words of the Lord during the tribulation period. The people will run to and fro to seek the Word of the Lord, but not find it. Speaking of seeking God's Word, we'll explore that in Sign #122 - Prophecy Sealed Until End Times.

Fulfillment - I think this one's pretty obvious to us today. People used to travel primarily by foot, horse, carriage, and boat. No one was going anywhere fast, and most people didn't travel far. Then the industrial revolution happened in the 1800s. Passenger trains and ships became popular in the mid-1800s.[8] Cars came into being around the turn of the 20th century with Ford's Model T being produced in 1908[9]. In the 1950s came the big jetliners.[10]

Now, the majority of people in many nations owns a vehicle: the US, Canada, Italy, France, the UK, New Zealand, and Australia for example. About 290 million vehicles are in use in the US. The number of cars on the road in America has doubled since the 1960s.[11]

In 1945, there were 9 million global airline passengers per year. In 2019, before Covid, it had skyrocketed to 4.5 billion passengers a year.[12]

We are certainly a people who are running to and fro.

Today Is Different - Now, we're no longer confined to running to and fro on the earth. We talked about the space race in Sign #105 - Kingdom Vs Kingdom. Today is different because we even have space tourism now. This industry started in the 2000s. A widely broadcast event occurred in 2021 when actor William Shatner traveled to space aboard Jeff Bezos's Blue Origin space shuttle.[13] Elon Musk's SpaceX routinely takes astronauts to the International Space Station.[14] And his company is doing test flights of the Starship, which is intended to take passengers to Mars.[15]

Additional Scriptures: 2 Chronicles 16:9. Amos 8:12. Job 1:7.

#121 - KNOWLEDGE SHALL INCREASE

Anti | DD | Earth | Gov | Israel | Jesus | Leader | Sky | **Society** | **Tech** | Trib

> "But you, Daniel, shut up the words and seal the book, even to the time of the end. ... Knowledge will be increased." (Daniel 12:4)

In this verse, an angel is speaking to the prophet Daniel. He tells Daniel that in the end times knowledge will increase. In this sign, we'll explore knowledge in general. In the next sign, Sign #122 - Prophecy Sealed Until End Times, we'll apply this to Bible prophecy being understood with greater clarity today.

Fulfillment - A futurist published a book in 1981 and revealed that all the knowledge mankind had accumulated in the year AD 0 was equivalent to 1 unit of information. In AD 1500 the accumulated knowledge of mankind had doubled to 2 units. Then knowledge doubled again in 1750. By 1900 it had doubled again and was up to 8 units. By 1945 it was doubling every 25 years. By 1982 every 12 months. IBM added to his prediction and stated that in 2020 knowledge was now doubling every 12 hours.[16] The rate at which information doubles is getting faster and faster. It's growing exponentially.

This is evidenced in all sorts of ways. Consider how much information we can store today on portable USB drives versus how much we could store on the first floppy disks. Think of how much new content is added to the internet everyday through social media posts, blogs, videos, and news.

Another way we can see this is by looking at how many people on the globe have a formal basic education today. Back in 1820, a whopping 83% of the global population didn't have any formal education. In

2020, it was completely the opposite. Only 14% were uneducated.[17] When we look at the percentage of people who can read, it tells the same story. In 1820, only 12% of the global population could read. In 2022, 87% of the world was literate.[18]

Today Is Different - Today is unique because technology has enabled us to have gobs of information available at our fingertips. When I was growing up, I had to check out the massive and heavy encyclopedia volume I needed for research papers from the local library. Today, encyclopedias are online and can be searched easily. Can you imagine how many books it would generate if Britannica or Wikipedia printed out all their content?

Today, information, otherwise known as data, is gold. There are entire industries dedicated to collecting it, storing it, and analyzing it. We've even reached the point that AI and quantum computers are needed to help us make sense of all the information we have.

Today, we have information overload. Even though we have all sorts of search engines and AIs to help us find the knowledge we need, sometimes it proves impossible. With so much content available, the best stuff doesn't always make it to the top of the search results.

There's a Scripture in the book of Romans that says God's knowledge is unsearchable. I find it interesting that our society's volume of knowledge is able to mimic in a small way the vastness of God's knowledge.

When God saw that nothing was going to be impossible to achieve for the people building the Tower of Babel, he directly intervened. Does anything seem impossible for us to achieve with our knowledge and technology today? Our increase in knowledge is a sign of the nearness of Jesus's return.

Additional Scriptures: Genesis 11:1-9. Romans 11:33.

#122 - PROPHECY SEALED UNTIL END TIMES

Anti | DD | **Earth** | Gov | **Israel** | **Jesus** | Leader | Sky | **Society** | **Tech** | **Trib**

> "But you, Daniel, keep this prophecy a secret; seal up the book until the time of the end...." ... I heard what he said, but I did not understand what he meant. So I asked, "How will all this finally end, my lord?" But he said, "Go now, Daniel, for what I have said is kept secret and sealed until the time of the end. ... Only those who are wise will know what it means." (Daniel 12:4, 8-10 NLT)

An angel is speaking to Daniel the prophet. He's just explained Daniel's visions about the end times. The angel tells him that the prophecy is a secret. That means it's not going to be understood in Daniel's time. He's instructed to seal up the book until the end times and that only those who are wise will know what it means. The book was sealed up to preserve it until the end times. In fact, in the Olivet Discourse Jesus said that his words wouldn't pass away. The preservation of his Word is a sign of the second coming. This also means that in the end times we should see a greater understanding of Bible prophecy.

The Bible reveals that the fear of the Lord is the beginning of wisdom. That if we lack wisdom all we have to do is to ask God, and he'll give it to us. One of the purposes of the Holy Spirit is to teach us all things.

You know Jesus taught in parables and his disciples asked him why. He revealed it was because his followers were given the ability to understand the mysteries of the kingdom of heaven, but to everyone else it was hidden. Throughout the New Testament we learn about mysteries that were revealed to the disciples. That the gentiles, non-Jewish, who come to faith in Jesus are heirs of God's promises too. That Jesus's second coming happens in two events, the rapture and the second coming. That God would pour out his spirit on people in the last days.

The Bible ends by telling us that prophecy is no longer sealed because the time is at hand. During the tribulation period, the people will have an even greater understanding than we do. That's because God will seal 144,000 Jewish believers who will share God's Word with the world. And there's also the two witnesses God sends to prophesy for three and a half years.

Fulfillment - *The Dead Sea Scrolls* were discovered from 1947 to 1956 in caves near the Dead Sea. The scrolls were almost 2,000 years old. They dated from the first to the third centuries AD. Fragments from every book of the Hebrew Bible (except Nehemiah and Esther) were discovered there.

The Isaiah Scroll is probably the most famous of the discoveries. It contains many prophecies regarding the last days, including the fall of Babylon, the destruction of Damascus, the day of the Lord, and the millennial kingdom.

Some non-biblical works were also found in the caves, including the *Ancient Book of Jubilees* and the *Ancient Book of Enoch*. Both contain end times prophecies. They also found the *Temple Scroll*, which interestingly has details for constructing the Third Temple, meant to replace the one destroyed in AD 70 by the Romans.[19]

Eight scrolls representing the book of Daniel were found in the caves too. This was significant because many Hebrew scholars questioned the value and authenticity of the book of Daniel. The ancient scrolls revealed overwhelming conformity to the current Masoretic Text of the Hebrew Bible.[20]

The Dead Sea Scrolls were discovered around the same time that Israel became a nation. In fact, it's far more exciting than that. You should read Jonathan Cahn's book, *The Oracle*, and see how God orchestrated some cool details. For example, the day that Israel was voted into existence at the United Nations is the same day *The Isaiah Scroll* was first being read by a professor of Bible archaeology in Jerusalem.[21]

These discoveries illustrate that prophecy was no longer sealed, and the end time was upon us. If you think about it, since the temple was destroyed in AD 70, there was essentially a void in Bible prophecy being fulfilled from that time until the 1940s. Nothing much happened during those 1,900 years.

Then the Holocaust happened between 1941 and 1945, when Ezekiel's vision of dry bones became a reality. Then Israel became a nation in 1948, and those dry bones had new life just as Ezekiel's vision foretold. It seems that God breathed life into Bible prophecies at the same time.

Today Is Different - Bible prophecy regarding the last days is certainly understood better today than in times past. There are many good authors publishing content in biblical eschatology. Today, you can even learn about Bible prophecy from several end times ministries that make their teachings and programs available online and through television and radio broadcasts.

Some reasons it's understood better is because of the Bible study tools that are available today. It's easy to use a modern-day Bible app to do a word study of the ancient text. They enable us to quickly see all the verses the same word was used in and get an even bigger understanding of a word's meaning and context. These apps also put Bible commentaries at our fingertips. We can see what many Bible scholars have to say about a difficult passage.

Something else that's really unique about today is that we have tech that enables us to read text on ancient scrolls that are now invisible to the naked eye because of deterioration. Multispectral imaging developed by NASA is being used to help read *The Dead Sea Scrolls*. Today, AI algorithms can even virtually unroll scrolls that are stuck together and reveal what's written on them.[22]

Additional Scriptures: 1 Corinthians 15:50-58. Acts 2:16-21. Colossians 1:24-29. Daniel 12:10. Ephesians 1:7-10; 3:1-7. Ezekiel 37. James 1:5. John 14:26. Luke 8:16-18. Matthew 13:10-17; 24:35. Proverbs 1:7. Revelation 1:3; 7; 11:1-14; 22:10. Romans 16:25-27.

#123 - POPULATION EXPLOSION

Anti | DD | **Earth** | Gov | Israel | Jesus | Leader | Sky | **Society** | **Tech** | **Trib**

> After these things I looked, and behold, a great multitude which no man could count, out of every nation and of all tribes, peoples, and languages, standing before the throne and before the Lamb, dressed in white robes, with palm branches in their hands. (Revelation 7:9)

Jesus's disciple John is seeing a vision of events taking place in heaven after the rapture and during the tribulation period. Later in this chapter, John asks an angel who these people are. We find out they're the tribulation saints who've died and are in heaven. These are people who will be left behind at the rapture but put their faith in Jesus for salvation during the tribulation period. The number of them is a great multitude that no man could count.

Keep in mind this is after the rapture, in which millions of people are going to disappear. There will still be millions more who come to faith. In order for this to be possible there has to be a large population on the planet during the end times and prior to Jesus's second coming.

Fulfillment - The world population has increased rapidly over the past few centuries. In 1700, there were 600 million people. It took 140 years to double that. In 1840, there were 1.2 billion people. By 1950, 110 years later, it had doubled again to 2.5 billion. A short 37 years later, in 1987, it had doubled again to 5 billion.[23] Now, in 2023, we're over 8.2 billion people.[24] That's a 64% increase in 36 years.

This exceptional growth was due to a number of reasons. In the past, years of very high death rates due to disease or famine were common. Advancements in medicine, hygiene, and clean water all led to increased childhood mortality, the eradication of some diseases, and a higher life expectancy. The death rate decreased, and the birth rate increased, causing the population growth.

Today Is Different - You might think that the global population is exponentially increasing, but it's not. The number of people on the planet is increasing in absolute numbers, but the rate of growth (the difference between births and deaths) peaked decades ago in 1963 at 2.3%. In 2023, the growth rate is down to 0.9%. The growth rates for the US and Israel tell the same story. In 2023, the US had a dismal 0.2% growth rate while Israel was higher than the world rate at 1.3%.[25]

Today, there's an interesting dynamic at play. China instituted its one child per family policy in the late 1970s to reduce its population growth. In 2016, they increased it to two children per family. Then in 2021, they upped it to three children per family. This is all because China is seeing the fallout of its prior policy. They have an aging population, a shrinking workforce, less children to take care of their aging parents, and more men than women.[26]

But now we also have climate alarmists telling us the planet is overpopulated and unable to sustain humanity. They're in favor of population reduction measures.

I would like to conclude by saying the massive population that's required to fulfill end times prophecies like the one we just read means population reduction won't happen on a global scale. It also means nothing cataclysmic or apocalyptic is going to happen to the world prior to the tribulation period.

Additional Scriptures: Genesis 22:15-17. Jude 1:14. Revelation 5:11; 7:9-17; 9:13-17; 14:18-20.

#124 - SECRETS REVEALED

Anti | DD | Earth | Gov | Israel | **Jesus** | Leader | Sky | **Society** | **Tech** | Trib

> "But there is nothing covered up that will not be revealed, nor hidden that will not be known. Therefore whatever you have said in the darkness will be heard in the light. What you have spoken in the ear in the inner rooms will be proclaimed on the housetops." (Luke 12:2-3)

Jesus is the one speaking in these verses. He indicates that secrets will become known. In the additional Scriptures below, we learn that when Jesus comes that he'll bring to light these hidden things.

As we get closer to his second coming, might we see this already coming to fruition as a sign for us?

Fulfillment - Let's consider if there are any big lies and secrets that are now being exposed. The UFO cover-up comes to mind. You may recall that a former US Air Force intelligence officer testified to congress in July 2023 that the US had been conducting a multi-decade UAP crash retrieval and reverse engineering program. He also said the US has been aware of non-human activity since the 1930s. And that the US is in possession of recovered craft and non-human pilots.[27]

You remember Covid, right? The Heritage Foundation published an article in May 2024 titled, "The Lie of the Century: The Origin of COVID-19." It seems like the truth is finally coming into the open. That it was a manmade virus that escaped from a lab in China. That lab was receiving funding for gain-of-function research from the US government. A practice which the US banned back in 2014. Instead of the Chinese government helping expose this, they just aided in the cover-up and mysteriously got a vaccine developed before anyone else. Prominent scientists perpetuated the lie for financial reasons. They didn't want their research projects or funding jeopardized.[28]

In fact, Mark Zuckerberg, the CEO of Facebook, revealed a secret regarding Covid content too. He published a letter in August 2024 revealing his company was pressured by the US government to censor that information on his social media platforms.[29]

Now, the hype and bubble are bursting on electric vehicles (EVs). A study quoted in *The Wall Street Journal* in May 2024 revealed that EVs release more toxic particles into the air and are worse for the environment than gas-powered vehicles. It said today's gas vehicles have efficient tailpipe exhaust filters, so most pollution comes from tire wear. EVs are quite a bit heavier than standard vehicles, so their tires wear out quicker.[30] That's not to mention the issues with battery fires, the cost of replacing the battery, and infrastructure issues with charging the vehicle.

Today Is Different - The rise of the whistleblower certainly makes today different. Some noteworthy examples include Julian Assange, Edward Snowden, Karen Silkwood, Daniel Ellsberg, and W. Mark Felt.

Julian Assange founded WikiLeaks in 2006. He and his site gained popularity in 2010 when he published leaks provided by Chelsea Manning, a US Army intelligence analyst at the time. That year, he also leaked a quarter million US diplomatic cables.[31] In this same vein, there's also Edward Snowden. He gained notoriety in 2013 when he leaked classified information from the US NSA.[32]

In 1974, Karen Silkwood blew the whistle on safety issues at a nuclear power plant in Oklahoma where she was employed as a chemical technician. You've heard of the *Pentagon Papers*. They revealed the truth about US involvement in Vietnam. They were leaked by Daniel Ellsberg in 1971. And of course there's the Watergate scandal of 1972. W. Mark Felt was the secret informant to reporters with *The Washington Post*.[33]

Whether or not you agree with what any of these people did, they all fulfilled Jesus's prophecy about secrets being revealed, didn't they?

Perhaps the biggest lie that was recently exposed and makes today unique is the one regarding US President Biden's mental acuity. It seems like the bubble on this one burst with George Clooney's op-ed in *The New York Times* calling for Biden to drop out of the 2024 US Presidential Election.[34] Suddenly many other celebrities and politicians jumped on that train. A couple weeks later, near the end of July 2024, Biden announced he was dropping out of the 2024 US Presidential Election.[35]

Additional Scriptures: 1 Corinthians 4:5. Ecclesiastes 12:14. Jeremiah 23:24. Luke 8:17. Romans 2:11-16.

#125 - ISRAEL'S WEALTH

Anti | DD | **Earth** | **Gov** | **Israel** | Jesus | Leader | Sky | Society | **Tech** | **Trib**

> "Sheba, Dedan, the merchants of Tarshish, and all their young lions will say to you, 'Have you come to take plunder? Have you gathered your army to take booty, to carry away silver and gold, to take away livestock and goods, to take great plunder?' " (Ezekiel 38:13 NKJV)

God is speaking to the prophet Ezekiel in this verse. He's telling him about the Gog of Magog War which we discussed in Signs #108 and #109. You may recall that it's a future war that I believe takes place in the tribulation period. Many nations invade Israel under the leadership of Gog. Here, we're told that some nations witnessing this will question

Gog's intent by asking if they're doing it to take plunder.

God promised blessings upon the Israelites if they loved and obeyed him. In the Bible, the promised land is described as a good land, without scarcity, lacking nothing, and as having natural resources. God promised that everything his chosen people had would be multiplied. It's evidenced through people like Abraham, who was very wealthy, and King Solomon, whose wealth was unsurpassed.

In order for this sign to see fulfillment, Israel must have something worth taking and a lot of it. That's what we'll explore here.

Fulfillment - Israel is considered the world's leader in desalination and wastewater treatment technology. Sewage is almost 100% reused in Israel with 90% of the treated water going to agriculture. They also desalinate seawater which now produces 60-80% of Israel's drinking water.[36] Even more recently, in 2018, scientists in Israel figured out how to grow crops in salt water by applying a solution that makes them immune to salt. They've been using it on a variety of crops and are experimenting with it on cotton crops in India.[37]

All sorts of discoveries are happening today in Israel. In 2020, the Israeli government issued a certificate of discovery to an Israeli company who discovered precious gems in a valley near Haifa. It's the first mine of precious gems in Israel.[38] Their gems include sapphires, rubies, garnets, and even some diamonds. The Carmel Sapphire is their most iconic with its sky-like appearance. It contains a mineral only previously known to exist in space. It was chosen as the 2018 mineral of the year.[39]

Today Is Different - Speaking of diamonds, Israel is one of the world's three major centers for polished diamonds. They produce 12% of the world's cut diamonds for wholesale.[40] Diamonds are Israel's largest export product. In fact, they're the 5th largest exporter of diamonds in the world. They exported $10.5 billion worth of them in 2022.[41]

Israel was considered devoid of energy resources until quite recently. In 1999, Israel discovered natural gas off the coast of the Mediterranean Sea. They began producing it for themselves in 2004. They've since discovered several large gas fields. Now, they even export it to Jordan and Egypt.[42]

Perhaps the most shocking of recent wealthy discoveries in Israel is shale oil. In 2011, scientists reported that Israel has the third largest shale oil deposit in the world. That would put it behind the US and China. They believe there's the equivalent of 250 million barrels of oil in Israel. So that you understand the magnitude of this, Saudi Arabia has 260 million barrels.[43] So far, shale oil is a largely undeveloped industry in Israel due to technological limitations.

These technologies and areas of wealth could certainly be the reasons Gog of the land of Magog and its allies decide to invade Israel.

Additional Scriptures: 1 Kings 10:14-29. Deuteronomy 8:7-13; 28:1-14. Ezekiel 38. Genesis 13:2. Numbers 13:27.

#126 - ISRAEL'S BIRDS OF PREY

Anti | DD | **Earth** | Gov | **Israel** | **Jesus** | Leader | **Sky** | Society | Tech | **Trib**

> I saw an angel standing in the sun. He cried with a loud voice, saying to all the birds that fly in the sky, "Come! Be gathered together to the great supper of God, that you may eat the flesh of kings, the flesh of captains, the flesh of mighty men, and the flesh of horses and of those who sit on them, and the flesh of all men, both free and slave, small and great." (Revelation 19:17-18)

The apostle John is seeing a vision of Jesus's second coming. We see an angel tell all the birds to gather so they can eat the carcasses of the men and horses. This is the end result of the war against Jesus where everyone's gathered in the Valley of Megiddo. We discussed that in Sign #116 - Gathered To Armageddon.

God gathers these birds at the end of the war of Gog of Magog as well (Sign #108). You may recall that battle likely occurs during the tribulation period. It's when many nations, led by Gog, attack Israel.

Jesus mentioned these birds of prey in the Olivet Discourse too. He compared their appearance as a sign of a carcass nearby to the appearance of all the signs Jesus mentioned as the indicator that his coming is near.

Fulfillment - Did you know that Israel is known as the bird migration capital of the world? Apparently, it's at the crossroads of migration flyways. 500 million birds converge on Israel twice each year, in the spring and fall. Most of the birds are traveling from nesting grounds in Europe and Asia to where they winter in Africa.[44] Then they fly back home again in the spring. They even have a network of HD cameras in several locations throughout Israel so you can watch this migration live from your own home.[45]

Today Is Different - I learned that birds of prey are included in this mass migration. Experts say 150,000 of the half a billion birds are in fact birds of prey from 27 different species.[46] This includes half of the world's population of lesser spotted eagles (50,000 of them).[47]

I read an interesting article regarding Israel's birds of prey and its war with Hamas. During the initial attack in October 2023, many victims were scattered throughout a large area of dense foliage. It made it difficult for Israel Defense Forces to locate bodies. They came up with a clever idea to use the fall migration of birds to help them. Many of the migratory raptor birds are equipped with a GPS transmitter. They simply looked for where the birds of prey were gathering and were able to locate many bodies that way.[48]

Vultures are probably the best known of the carrion birds who eat decaying flesh. It's estimated that in the 1950s when Israel first became a nation there were 1,000 pairs of griffin vultures in Israel. Today, there are less than 200. Since farmers often use poisons to kill unwanted predators, their dwindling numbers are due in part to eating animals that have died from being poisoned.[49]

The Bible says the vultures and birds of prey will gather to clean up the mess left behind from wars in Israel. Since those vultures are near extinction in Israel, it must mean those wars are on the horizon. It all points to the nearness of Jesus's return.

Additional Scriptures: Ezekiel 39:4, 17-20. Jeremiah 7:32-34. Luke 17:37. Matthew 24:27-28.

#127 - ISRAEL'S BEASTS

Anti | DD | **Earth** | Gov | **Israel** | Jesus | Leader | Sky | Society | Tech | **Trib**

> "And you, son of man, prophesy against Gog, and say, 'Thus says the Lord GOD: "Behold, I [am] against you, O Gog, ... I will ... bring you against the mountains of Israel. ... You shall fall upon the mountains of Israel, you and all your troops and the peoples who [are] with you; I will give you to birds of prey of every sort and [to] the beasts of the field to be devoured." ' " (Ezekiel 39:1-2, 4 NKJV)

God is speaking with the prophet Ezekiel here. It's regarding the war of Gog of Magog against the nation of Israel. We talked about that war in Sign #108. I think it's most likely that this war takes place after the rapture and during the tribulation period. I'd like to point out that there are "beasts of the field" to devour the army on the mountains of Israel. In order for it to see fulfillment there must be beasts of prey in the mountains of Israel.

This is also going to be one of the judgments during the tribulation period. When the fourth seal is opened, the rider on the pale horse, death, kills with the sword, famine, and beasts.

Fulfillment - Lions have long been extinct in Israel. The largest beast of prey currently in the area is the Arabian Leopard. There aren't many of them either. It's a critically endangered species. As of 2023, scientists estimate there's only 120 of them on the entire Arabian Peninsula, mostly in the mountains along the Red Sea.[50]

There are other carnivorous predators in the Arabian Peninsula though, including the grey wolf, Arabian wolf, golden jackal, caracal, and striped hyena. While the wolves are not abundant in Israel, the other animals are. The golden jackal looks like a small wolf. Striped hyenas are known to scavenge human corpses. The caracal is a medium-sized wild cat with long canine teeth.[51]

Today Is Different - There's a biblical beast of the field that is currently extinct in Israel. It's the Syrian brown bear. This is the species of bear that attacked the group of boys mocking the prophet, Elisha. Today they mostly live in Turkey and Central Asia. They were thought to have been extinct in its namesake Syria as well, but guess what? In 2004, their bear tracks were recorded in the snow in the Anti-Lebanon Mountains of Southwestern Syria. It's the first time they've seen evidence of them in Syria in the past 50 years! Then in 2011, three more sets of bear tracks were found in the same area.[52]

Why is this a big deal? Those mountains form the border between Syria and Lebanon. Both of those nations are north of Israel. The biblical beasts of the field are returning to the mountains near Israel where this battle of Gog of the land of Magog will take place.

Additional Scriptures: 2 Kings 2:23-24. Ezekiel 5:17; 14:21; 39:17-20. Jeremiah 7:32-34; 15:3. Revelation 6:7-8.

#128 - THE THIRD TEMPLE

Anti | DD | **Earth** | **Gov** | **Israel** | **Jesus** | **Leader** | Sky | Society | Tech | **Trib**

"When, therefore, you see the abomination of desolation, which was spoken of through Daniel the prophet, standing in the holy place" (Matthew 24:15)

Jesus is the one speaking in this Scripture. His disciples have asked him what the signs of his second coming are. Here, we see that one sign is the abomination of desolation in the holy place. We talked about the abomination in Sign #68 - Polluted Sanctuary. In order for the Antichrist to stop the daily sacrifices in the temple, erect an image of himself inside, and declare himself God, the temple needs to exist. The Antichrist does this halfway through the tribulation period.

King Solomon built the First Temple which was destroyed by the Babylonians in 586 BC. The Second Temple was constructed after the Israelites returned to their land. It was finished in 515 BC. It was later destroyed by the Roman Empire when they invaded Jerusalem in AD 70. The Muslim's Dome of the Rock (Al-Aqsa mosque) now stands in its place on top of the Temple Mount in Jerusalem.

Obviously, something happens between now and halfway through the tribulation period that enables the construction and completion of the Third Temple. In the additional Scriptures below, you can learn about the temple furnishings and other items which are needed for temple services. In this sign, we'll discuss the current status of the Third Temple, temple furnishings, Levitical priests for the temple, and red heifers which are needed for the water of purification.

Fulfillment - I had the privilege of traveling to Israel on a tour with my pastor. One of the places we toured in Jerusalem was the Temple Institute. It's quite fascinating. They're a non-profit dedicated to building the Third Temple. As such, they've started restoring and reconstructing all the articles required for use in the temple. They have many of them on display in their museum.

They have everything that's needed, including musical instruments, the Menorah, the Incense Altar, the Table of the Showbread, and the clothes the priests wear. They also conduct re-enactments of temple services right next to the Temple Mount. The Levitical Choir is already performing. The men who will be priests are receiving regular instruction. As soon as the Third Temple is reconstructed, they are literally ready to go on day 1.[53]

Today Is Different - The red heifers make today unique. In order for the Jews to have services in the Third Temple they first need to sacrifice a red heifer, that's a cow, whose hair is completely red. The animal must also be free of defects and never have performed work. In the Old Testament, the blood of the animal was sprinkled in front of the tent of meeting and the ashes were used in the water of purification. Before they can sacrifice the red heifer, they have to wait for it to reach maturity, three years old. It's ideal they use it soon after that because they risk it growing hairs of other colors, which would make it unusable.54

In September 2022, five red heifers arrived in Israel. They came from a farmer in Texas.55 As of May 2024, three of them have been disqualified and will be bred to produce more red heifer offspring.56

There's something else unique about these red heifers. A military spokesman for Hamas gave a televised speech in January 2024. Here's part of what he said, "an aggression that reached its peak against our path (Al-Quds) and Al-Aqsa, with the start of its actual temporal and spatial division, and the bringing of red cows as an application of a detestable religious myth designed for aggression against the feelings of an entire nation in the heart of its Arab identity." Wow! They considered the red heifers arriving in Israel as an act of aggression.

These cows have certainly set some end times events in motion.

Additional Scriptures: 1 Kings 5-8. 2 Chronicles 2-7. 2 Thessalonians 2:1-4. Daniel 8:9-25; 9:24-27; 11:21-45. Exodus 29:9. Numbers 19. Revelation 11:1-2.

#129 - THE BLESSED

Anti | DD | Earth | **Gov** | **Israel** | **Jesus** | **Leader** | Sky | **Society** | **Tech** | Trib

> "Behold, I am coming soon! Blessed is he who keeps the words of the prophecy of this book. ... Behold, I am coming soon! My reward is with me, to repay to each man according to his work. I am the Alpha and the Omega, the First and the Last, the Beginning and the End. Blessed are those who do his commandments, that they may have the right to the tree of life, and may enter in by the gates into the city." (Revelation 22:7, 12, 14)

Jesus is speaking with the apostle John in these Scriptures. The conversation happens during John's vision of events that are taking place during the tribulation period. This is well after Jesus's death and resurrection, so Jesus is in heaven. He speaks to John of people who are blessed. It's those who keep the words in the book of Revelation and those who keep his commandments. Jesus is going to bring a reward with him at his second coming to pay everyone back according to what they have done.

In the Olivet Discourse, when Jesus was speaking about signs of his second coming, he talked about judging everyone when he returns. He said people who are blessed get to inherit his kingdom. It's those who feed and clothe the needy, are hospitable to strangers, and visit the sick and imprisoned.

Very early on in the Bible God tells us that he will bless people who bless his chosen people, the Israelites. What's more is that even if we as individuals don't bless them, the world will still be blessed through Israel. God even reiterated this promise to Abraham by telling him that all the nations of the world would be blessed through his seed. Both of these statements saw their ultimate fulfillment in Jesus.

What we're going to consider in this sign is the blessed people that Jesus speaks of. Is there evidence of blessings upon the world through the nation of Israel? How about blessings for people who support Israel? Jesus is bringing rewards for this with him. If we're already starting to see rewards manifest, then Jesus must not be far behind.

Fulfillment - Let's start with blessings upon the world that originate in Israel or through the Jewish people. Some of Israel's world-changing inventions include the pressure bandage, USB drive, cherry tomatoes, drip irrigation, Voice over Internet Protocol, Iron Dome air defense system, pillcam, spectral CT, 8088 Intel processor, flexible stent, and Waze.[57]

Thirteen Israelis have received the Nobel Prize. They have more awards per capita than Germany, the US, and France.[58] Those efforts include the peace treaty between Israel and Egypt, enhancing our understanding of game-theory in economics, and the discovery of quasicrystals.

Jews across the world are also credited with inventing the teddy bear, ballpoint pen, Polaroid camera, flashlight, shopping cart, TV remote, Barbie dolls, PEEPS marshmallows, Levi's jeans, Duracell batteries, lasers, gas powered vehicles, stainless steel, sewing machine, digital camera, mobile cell phone, antibiotics, cardiac defibrillator, aspirin, polio vaccine, and nuclear weapons.[59]

Perhaps you also know that one of the world's largest companies and a technology you likely use every day was created by two Jewish men. Larry Page and Sergey Brin created Google.[60]

Israel and the Jewish people have certainly impacted and blessed the world.

Today Is Different - Evidence of blessings for supporting Israel and the Jewish people makes today different. The British Empire helped Israel become a nation. They issued the Balfour Declaration way back in 1917 and declared their support for a national home for the Jewish people. In 1922 the League of Nations (precursor to the UN) granted Britain the Mandate for Palestine. That paved the way for the creation of the nation of Israel.

Britain had a major role in WWII and the victory against Nazi Germany. The British Empire was the global superpower through WWII. You know the saying, "the empire on which the sun never sets." Although the empire dissolved after WWII, the UK still has a powerful standing in the world. Despite not being one of the more populous countries on the planet, they're one of the five permanent members of the UN Security Council.[61] God blessed Britain because they supported his chosen people.

When Israel became a nation on May 14, 1948, US President Harry Truman recognized Israel as a nation eleven minutes later.[62] Israel is the largest cumulative recipient of US foreign aid, over $150 billion in assistance. America's first trade agreement was with Israel. The US is now Israel's largest trading partner.[63] Until recently, the US had consistently supported Israel at the UN and vetoed resolutions condemning them.

One could easily argue that the United States is the most prosperous nation that's ever existed. Our currency, the US dollar, is the world's reserve currency. In 2023, the US still had the highest GDP of all other nations, accounting for 25% of the global economy. We also have the highest disposable income per capita.[64]

It is no coincidence that the United States became the global superpower when the British Empire fell. God blessed America because we blessed Israel. But, as we discussed in Sign #85 - Downfall Of The United States, that's all changing, and it's partly because we're not the rock-solid ally of Israel as we once were.

<u>Additional Scriptures:</u> Daniel 12:12. Genesis 12:3; 22:15-18; 27:26-29. John 3:16. Matthew 24:31; 25:31-46. Numbers 24:9. Revelation 1:3; 16:15; 19:9; 20:6. Romans 15:25-27.

#130 - THE ACCURSED

Anti | DD | Earth | Gov | Israel | Jesus | Leader | Sky | Society | Tech | Trib

> For the LORD of Armies says: "For honor he has sent me to the nations which plundered you; for he who touches you touches the apple of his eye. For, behold, I will shake my hand over them, and they will be a plunder to those who served them; and you will know that the LORD of Armies has sent me. ... Many nations shall join themselves to the LORD in that day, and shall be my people; and I will dwell among you, and you shall know that the LORD of Armies has sent me to you. ... Be silent, all flesh, before the LORD; for he has roused himself from his holy habitation!" (Zechariah 2:8-9, 11, 13)

God is speaking to the prophet Zechariah in these verses. We learn that anyone who harms Israel is touching the "apple" of God's eye. When this happens, God will shake his hand over the enemy and let them be plundered by Israel. We're given the timeframe of this prophecy. It's when God is roused "from his holy habitation" and ready to "dwell among" us. That means this is a sign of Jesus's second coming. It happens in the last days.

In the Old Testament, there are several Scriptures that teach us that God curses those who curse Israel and his chosen people. Satan was cursed for deceiving Eve and causing her to sin. During the tribulation period, the nations who war against God's people and Israel see destruction. Babylon and Gog of Magog and its allies for example.

At Jesus second coming, he's going to throw the Antichrist and False Prophet into the lake of fire and imprison Satan in the bottomless pit for a thousand years. Jesus also mentioned in a parable in the Olivet Discourse that those who refuse to feed and clothe the needy, aren't hospitable to strangers, and don't visit the sick and imprisoned are cursed and destined for hell.

Let's see if there's any evidence of the accursed. It would reveal that Jesus has been roused from his heavenly habitation and on his way.

Fulfillment - We can see clear evidence of this being fulfilled by examining what's happening to the United States. We talked about some reasons for America's downfall in Sign #85. It's also due to the US pressuring Israel for a two-state solution. God promised Israel a plot of land and gets mighty unhappy when nations try to take it away.

Israel warred against its surrounding enemy nations in 1967 and gained expanded territory including the entire city of Jerusalem and the Temple Mount. It's the aftermath of that war where we can clearly see the US taking an active role in brokering a two-state solution between Israel and the Palestinians. The UN Security Council unanimously adopted resolution 242 after the Six-Day War. It called for Israel's withdrawal from all gained territory. It's also the document that established the whole land for peace business.[65]

Then I believe America hit a point of no return with the 2000 Camp David Summit. You may remember that US President Bill Clinton met with leaders from Israel and the Palestinian Authority in an effort to bring about peace. The parties failed to reach an agreement which then led Clinton to write the Clinton Parameters. It proposed a Palestinian state in the West Bank and Gaza Strip, including Palestinian sovereignty over the Temple Mount and the Arab neighborhoods in East Jerusalem. Both Israel and the Palestinian Authority seemed close to agreeing to it.[66]

Although US President George W. Bush formally repudiated the Clinton Parameters when he took office in early 2021, he approved UN Security Council resolution 1397 in early 2002. It was the first UN Security Council resolution to call for a two-state solution in Israel.[67] The American government hasn't stopped pressuring Israel to divide its land, and in particular Jerusalem, since.

Today Is Different - The Bible reveals that God will supernaturally intervene to protect Israel in the tribulation period. Today is unique because we're starting to clearly see evidence of his divine protection.

In December 2023, Turkish lawmaker Hasan Bitmez was delivering a speech in his nation's parliament. He held up a poster that read "Murderer Israel; collaborator AKP." The AK Party is the political party of the president of Turkey, Erdogan. Bitmez's speech was very critical of Israel. He was quoted as saying of Israel, "Even if you escape the torment of history, you will not be able to escape the wrath of God (Allah)." Literally, the moment he finished that sentence he had a massive heart attack and collapsed to the floor. He died two days later.[68] That was not a coincidence!

In April 2024, the president of Iran, Ebrahim Raisi, threated Israel with annihilation. He was quoted as saying, "an attack on Iranian territory will bring about a complete change of circumstances ... could result in nothing being left of the Zionist regime." This threat came on the heels of an Israeli military airstrike on Damascus that resulted in the death of Iranian military leaders.[69] Do you think it's a coincidence that Raisi died in a helicopter crash caused by adverse weather conditions in May 2024?[70]

Jonathan Cahn posted a YouTube video revealing divine curses such as these and expounding upon their biblical meaning. I recommend you check it out because it's fascinating. It's titled *The Iranian Mystery: 12 End-Time Signs!*[71]

Additional Scriptures: Ezekiel 38-39. Genesis 3:1-5; 12:3; 15:18-21; 17:19-21; 27:26-29. Joel 3:1-2. Matthew 25:31-46. Numbers 24:9. Psalm 83. Revelation 18; 19:17-21; 20:1-3.

#131 - BROKEN PAGAN ALTARS

Anti | DD | **Earth** | Gov | Israel | **Jesus** | Leader | Sky | **Society** | Tech | **Trib**

> Jesus went out from the temple, and was going on his way. His disciples came to him to show him the buildings of the temple. But he answered them, "You see all of these things, don't you? Most certainly I tell you, there will not be left here one stone on another, that will not be thrown down." (Matthew 24:1-2)

Jesus is speaking to his disciples here. They've all just left the temple, and his disciples are admiring it. Jesus tells them a day is coming in which its stones will be thrown down. Now, this was already fulfilled in AD 70 when the Roman Empire invaded Jerusalem, burned the temple, and disassembled it to collect all the gold that had melted. What we're going to look at in this sign is a broader view of this torn down altar. You see, in the verse right after this, his disciples ask when this will happen and what's the sign of his second coming. Then Jesus began his Olivet Discourse. Broken altars and temples are a sign of the second coming.

In the Old Testament, when Israel had a king who did good in the eyes of the Lord, they were known for tearing down the pagan altars where people worshiped the false gods. They also cleansed the temple which had become polluted with altars and images. King Josiah and King Hezekiah are two examples. God ultimately cleansed the First Temple when he allowed it to be destroyed during the Babylonian invasion.

In the tribulation period, we see fulfillment of this through all the earthquakes that bring walls down and when Babylon, the false one world religion, is destroyed.

Fulfillment - The US Affordable Care Act prohibits health insurance plans from discriminating on the basis of gender. The US government used this to try and force employer health insurance plans into covering gender transition procedures. Well, the US government got sued by the Christian Employers Alliance stating the law violates religious rights under the First Amendment. In March 2024, a US District Judge agreed and ruled that the US government cannot force Christian employers to comply and require that coverage.[72] An altar which had been erected against Christians came down.

In November 2020, Oregon became the first state to decriminalize possession of small amounts of cocaine, heroin, meth, and other drugs. Instead of being criminally charged with drug possession, people would merely be issued a violation, just like a traffic ticket. Keep in mind that the citizens actually voted for this first.[73] As you might imagine, this didn't work out. The city of Portland was overrun with lawlessness. It saw a surge in homelessness, a rapid spread of fentanyl, soaring overdose deaths, street protests, record homicides, and people passed out on sidewalks during the day. The Oregon governor signed a law recriminalizing drug possession in April 2024.[74] An altar for lawlessness was just torn down.

Today Is Different - Have you heard of Burning Man? It takes place in Black Rock City, Nevada every year around Labor Day. Tens of thousands of people gather on the dried-up, dusty lakebed. They erect all sorts of altars to false gods and then burn them, including a giant effigy of a man. It's an anything goes, completely demonic event full of alcohol, drugs, and sexual perversion.[75]

It's in the desert so it's normally very dry and dusty. Well, in 2023, more than 70,000 people were in attendance when God opened up the sky and flooded the whole place. It received three months' worth of rain in a matter of hours! No one could leave because the mud was so intense that it prevented vehicles from moving. It took days for the place to dry out.[76] God tore this altar down himself in what I consider a teaser trailer of what's to come in the tribulation period. That certainly makes today unique.

In June 2022, the US Supreme Court overturned Roe v. Wade. This removed the federal law granting a woman the right to have an abortion.[77] One of the most egregious altars against God's sacred creation, human life, was torn down. That makes today different as well. This left it up to each individual state to decide if they would erect an altar for child sacrifice by making abortion legal in their territory. Currently, 14 states have a total ban on abortion, 27 states have bans based on gestational period. Only 9 states and D.C. have chosen to build that altar again by making abortion completely legal.[78]

Additional Scriptures: 2 Chronicles 31:1-2; 34:1-7; 36:15-21. 2 Kings 18:1-4; 22:1-2; 23:1-25; 25:1-21. Jeremiah 52:1-30. Matthew 24:7. Revelation 18.

#132 – CHRISTIAN REVIVAL

Anti | DD | Earth | Gov | Israel | **Jesus** | Leader | Sky | **Society** | **Tech** | **Trib**

> But Peter, standing up with the eleven, lifted up his voice and spoke out to them, "You men of Judea and all you who dwell at Jerusalem, let this be known to you, and listen to my words. ... This is what has been spoken through the prophet Joel: 'It will be in the last days, says God, that I will pour out my Spirit on all flesh. ... It will be that whoever will call on the name of the Lord will be saved.'" (Acts 2:14, 16-17, 21)

As you can see, the apostle Peter is standing with the other original disciples of Jesus and is speaking to a crowd. This is the day of Pentecost when all the believers received the Holy Spirit. Peter tells us this is also a sign of the last days. That God will pour out his spirit and people will call on his name and be saved. It's the sign of Christian revival.

An angel revealed this sign to the prophet Daniel too. The angel said many people would be purified, made white, and refined in the time of the end. We see evidence of this even in the tribulation period because the number of tribulation saints is a multitude which can't be counted. In fact, many people come to faith in Jesus during that period because of God's supernatural intervention to protect Israel from its enemy invaders.

Of course, this is also because Jesus said the gospel would be preached throughout the world before his second coming. We're going to look at that in the next sign.

Fulfillment - The Jesus revolution is a clear example of a modern

Christian revival. It took place in America in the 1970s. Thousands of young people were suddenly drawn to church and Christian worship music. They were getting baptized, studying the Bible, and spreading their faith.[79] *Time* magazine published a cover story about it in 1971.[80] This time period of spiritual transformation and turning to Jesus was also depicted in a movie released in 2023 titled *Jesus Revolution*.

Perhaps another such revolution is beginning today. Pastors in California have been doing mass baptism events the past two summers. Thousands of people are attending and getting baptized. In May 2024, the Baptize California event saw a record number of people get baptized across the state. Hundreds of churches are participating. The event's founders were inspired by reading about the large baptism events that have been taking place in Pirate's Cove, California ever since pastor Chuck Smith held one during the Jesus revolution.[81]

Today Is Different - The Asbury outpouring makes today different. In February 2023, Asbury University in Kentucky witnessed a regular campus church service turn into a 16-day event that garnered nationwide and even worldwide attention. It's estimated 50,000 visitors ended up participating in the Christian worship, prayer, and outpouring that took place.[82] It soon spread to other college campuses across the nation, like Auburn University where 5,000 students attended an evening worship event and hundreds of them were baptized in a nearby lake.[83]

Modern technology is helping share these revivals and spread their reach. Consider how many people witnessed the outpouring of God's spirit in Asbury on social media or television and then decided to go there themselves.

We're starting to witness a revival in Israel too. In 1999, there were 5,000 believers worshiping in Messianic congregations in Israel. In 2022, there were over 15,000.[84] While the numbers are still small, they are encouraging, nonetheless.

A Christian revival is growing in of all places, Iran. It's estimated there could be 1-3 million Christians there. It's illegal to be a Christian in Iran, so they face extreme persecution. An Iranian woman who immigrated to the US after being sentenced to death for converting to Christianity confirmed the revival there. She shared her faith in Iran for five years before being arrested. She connected with thousands of Iranians who were all receptive of the gospel. She said there are many

Christian churches in Iran.[85]

In fact, God is doing something amazing in Muslim nations today. Growing numbers of Muslims are receiving visions of Jesus in their dreams. It's being reported that 200 Muslim men in Gaza saw Jesus appear to them in dreams in December 2023.[86] The internet is full of these accounts. Check out the *I Found The Truth* channel on YouTube. They're posting testimonies of this.[87] So far, they've got 1.2 million subscribers.

Additional Scriptures: Acts 2. Daniel 12:9-10. Ezekiel 36:22-23, 36; 38:23; 39:6-7, 22-29. Malachi 4:4-5. Matthew 24:14, 30. Revelation 6:9-11; 7:9-14. Zechariah 12:10-14.

#133 – THE GOSPEL PREACHED EVERYWHERE

Anti | DD | Earth | Gov | Israel | **Jesus** | Leader | Sky | **Society** | **Tech** | **Trib**

> As he sat on the Mount of Olives, the disciples came to him privately, saying, "Tell us, when will these things be? What is the sign of your coming, and of the end of the age?" Jesus answered them, … "This Good News of the Kingdom will be preached in the whole world for a testimony to all the nations, and then the end will come." (Matthew 24:3-4, 14)

Jesus is speaking with his disciples and sharing the signs they should be looking for regarding his second coming. He tells us the "Good News," which is the gospel, will be preached across the entire world. And then here's the best part, "then the end will come." When we see this particular sign getting fulfilled then we know Jesus is on his way!

Now, you need to know that we humans aren't going to be the ones to fulfill this 100 percent. During the tribulation period, God spreads the gospel across the whole world in three different ways to ensure no one will have an excuse. There's the 144,000 Israelites who will be sealed by God and go forth to preach. Just imagine if they're all like the apostle Paul. Then there's the two witnesses who preach from Jerusalem for three and a half years. The Bible tells us the whole world watches them. Lastly, God sends an angel to fly around the world sharing the gospel.

If we're already getting close to fulfilling this one ourselves, then that right there shows how near the rapture is.

Fulfillment - Billy Graham is a very clear example of this. His preaching in 1949 at a citywide crusade in Los Angeles caught the eye of major newspapers. He became a household name after that. He was known for filling stadiums in which he shared the gospel and called people in attendance to repentance. His events were broadcast on the radio and TV. It's estimated he spoke to 210 million people in live audiences across 185 countries and territories. Over 3 million people responded to his invitations to accept Jesus at those events. It's truly mind boggling to think about.[88]

Consider the number of Christian megachurches today. They have a weekly attendance of over 10,000. A list from 2010 estimated there were 50 of them in the US. Some of the largest have 50,000 plus attendees.[89] You know that all of these have an online presence and are probably being broadcast on TV too. My church in Albuquerque, NM is considered one of these, and it even has satellite campuses in other countries.[90] Just these churches alone are reaching millions of people across the world.

Today Is Different - One thing that makes today special is the popularity of *The Chosen* TV series. I have to admit, I'm a fan. It's a historical fiction based on the Bible. It focuses on the life and ministry of Jesus and his disciples. It's controversial because creative liberties are obviously taken. However, you cannot deny that this show is having a huge impact in reaching people with the gospel. It's reached 200 million viewers in the US alone. It's encouraging people to read their Bible, to pray, and to go to church. I witnessed my eleven-year-old niece want to read the Bible all on her own because she loves the show so much. In May 2024, it broke a record for being the most translated TV show. It's now available in 50 languages.[91]

Long before *The Chosen* was released, the Jesus Film Project was breaking into using movies to reach people across the world with the gospel. They premiered the film *JESUS* in 1979. It's based on the Gospel of Luke. Today, it's available in a remarkable 2,000 languages and it's had over 5 billion viewers.[92]

Having the Bible available in local languages is key to spreading the gospel. This used to be quite a tedious task. However, today's technologies, like AI, help make translations available quickly. At the end of 2023, Wycliffe Bible Translators reported that the entire New Testament now becomes available in a new language every week. Today,

4 out of 5 people on the planet, that's 80%, have the Bible available in their own language.[93]

Additional Scriptures: Matthew 24:13, 35. Revelation 7; 11:1-14; 14:6-7.

#134 – A PLACE PREPARED BY GOD

Anti | DD | **Earth** | Gov | **Israel** | **Jesus** | Leader | Sky | Society | Tech | **Trib**

> The woman fled into the wilderness, where she has a place prepared by God, that there they may nourish her one thousand two hundred sixty days. ... When the dragon saw that he was thrown down to the earth, he persecuted the woman who gave birth to the male child. Two wings of the great eagle were given to the woman, that she might fly into the wilderness to her place, so that she might be nourished for a time, times, and half a time, from the face of the serpent. (Revelation 12:6, 13-14)

The apostle John is seeing a vision of events which occur during the tribulation period. The "woman" is Israel. We see that Israel is persecuted by the Dragon, that's Satan, but escapes into the wilderness. It's a place prepared by God. Israel will be protected there for a time (that's a year), times (two years), and half a time (half a year). So, that's three and a half years or the last half of the tribulation period.

Upon reading the additional Scriptures below, you'll discover this takes place when the Antichrist desecrates the temple halfway through the tribulation period. In fact, Jesus warned of this specific event in his Olivet Discourse. He told the people in Jerusalem to flee to the mountains when this happens.

So, where are the mountains and the wilderness? Well, Jerusalem is in the mountains, and the temple will be on Mount Moriah. The Mount of Olives is directly east. The only directions the people will be able to flee and end up in a wilderness are south or east. That'll put them in the wilderness area the Israelites actually came from and lived in for forty years before they entered the promised land.

South is Egypt's Sinai Peninsula and south and east is the nation of Jordan. What's interesting is that both of those locations are mentioned in the Psalm 83 War that Israel wins (Sign #107). It's a good possibility those areas will be Israel's territory when this prophecy comes to pass.

Some Bible scholars think Jordan is the likely location because there are yet to be fulfilled prophecies against Ammon, that's modern-day Jordan, that speak of the remnant of Israel plundering and possessing it. Let's see where this place prepared by God might be.

Fulfillment - Did you see the movie *Indiana Jones and the Last Crusade*? It's the one about the quest for the Holy Grail. The last part of the movie was filmed at Petra, Jordan. The famous rock-cut tomb in Petra, The Treasury, is shown on the map in figure 134.1 below. You can also see Jerusalem in the north just west of the Dead Sea.

Figure 134.1. Google Map of Jerusalem and Petra[94]
Source: https://maps.app.goo.gl/NMH3Uo1yKto7UssS6

This large view of the area also gives you a better sense of where the ancient Israelites traveled in the wilderness on their journey from Egypt. The body of water in the southwest that's labeled Gulf of Suez is the start of the Red Sea. The pointy mountainous end of the Sinai Peninsula (the triangular land between Israel and Egypt) is where Mount Sinai is located.

Petra is currently uninhabited, although there are local Bedouin communities in the area. What's special about Petra is that the terrain provides a natural defense, and it has an ancient water system. Both would certainly be useful if a large number of people fled there from Jerusalem.

Petra is a city carved into the mountains. So, the mountains provide a natural wall to protect the area from enemies. The main entrance is through a narrow gorge. It's only 3 meters wide in some spots and it's almost a mile long.[95] Another interesting tidbit is that the gorge wasn't formed by water. It's a geological fault. So, it was split apart by tectonic forces.

The reason I find that fascinating is because of the Scripture we started with for this sign. A few verses later in Revelation 12 we're told that Satan sends a flood upon the people who are fleeing from Jerusalem. But get this, the earth will help them by opening up and swallowing the flood waters. Now, isn't it convenient that Petra is right on top of a fault line where the earth splits apart?

As for water, there are nine natural springs located in the area which were the primary source of water for the ancient community who dwelt there. Several dams were built along stream beds in the mountains which capture and divert runoff water. I'm sure those will also come in handy regarding the flood that Satan sends. There's a multitude of water reservoirs or cisterns to store water. It also has a network of clay pipelines and water channels that transported water throughout the area.[96]

The ancient city of Petra is definitely a prime candidate for fulfilling this sign.

Today Is Different - The reason today is unique is because Petra was all but forgotten and crumbling away until relatively recently. That significantly changed in the late 1900s. You see, in 1985 Petra was designated a UNESCO World Heritage Site and named one of the New 7 Wonders Of the World. Lots of restoration and archaeological projects since ensued. Many of the structures which had fallen down were restored.[97] God's busy at work preparing this place for a people who will need it in the near future.

Additional Scriptures: Daniel 9:27; 11:21-45; 12:6-11. Exodus 23:20-23. Jeremiah 49:1-6. Matthew 24:13, 15-20. Psalm 83. Revelation 12. Zephaniah 2:8-9.

CHAPTER 15 - SIGNS ON THE EARTH

#135 - THE CURSE

Anti | DD | **Earth** | Gov | Israel | Jesus | Leader | Sky | Society | Tech | **Trib**

> The earth mourns and fades away. The world languishes and fades away. The lofty people of the earth languish. The earth also is polluted under its inhabitants, because they have transgressed the laws, violated the statutes, and broken the everlasting covenant. Therefore the curse has devoured the earth, and those who dwell therein are found guilty. (Isaiah 24:4-6)

The first sign that we'll look at regarding the earth is the curse that God placed upon all creation when Adam and Eve sinned in the garden of Eden. Adam was told that if he ate the forbidden fruit that he would die. And that's exactly what happened. Death and decay entered creation on that day. The ground was cursed to produce thorns and thistles, and it was going to take hard, sweaty work from then on to survive. The verses above will be fulfilled during the tribulation period.

Before the flood, people lived to be hundreds of years old. Methuselah survived the longest at 969 years. After the flood, the lifespan changed dramatically. We're told in Psalm 90:10 that the days of our lives are 70 to 80 years.

Fulfillment - Based on your own observations, do you think nature is getting more and more bountiful over time? It certainly doesn't appear that way to me. Consider how difficult farming still is. It seems like nature is against us with pests, weeds, and diseases. Even with all the herbicides and pesticides that we have today, some weeds and bugs are indestructible. We've resorted to bioengineering our food supply to make it more resilient and to increase its yield.

How about humanity? Do you think we're continually improving by getting healthier, smarter, and stronger over time? Not a chance. Let me call attention to the obesity epidemic that's plaguing the entire planet, not just America. The World Health Organization reports that 2.5 billion adults, or 43% of the adult population, were overweight in 2022. Worldwide obesity has more than doubled since 1990, with 16% of adults living with obesity. It's no different with children. In 2022, 37 million children under the age of 5 and 390 million aged 5-19 were overweight.[1]

Even with all our scientific advancements in medicine and our ability to edit DNA, we still haven't figured out how to cure the most common diseases. If we look at life expectancy, we see something interesting. Back in 1964 worldwide life expectancy was 52 years from birth. Today it's 73 years. That's a big improvement. However, if you look at the rate of growth, it's been decreasing every year since then. In 1964 the growth rate was 1.66% while today it's only 0.23%.[2] When looking at the US and Israel, the data tells a similar story. Life expectancy in the US is currently 79 years, while in Israel it is 83 years.[3] The rates of growth for each have been declining each year for at least the past twenty years. It's clear that we've hit a plateau in regard to how long we're expected to survive. Don't you think it's interesting that it coincides with what we're told about life expectancy in the Bible?

There's a reason life isn't getting better. Instead, it just continues to decay. It's clear evidence of the curse that God placed upon creation. The curse will continue to progress until Jesus returns.

Today Is Different - The living planet index is a metric that illustrates why today is different. The latest report covered 31,821 populations of 5,230 vertebrate (mammal, bird, fish, reptile, and amphibian) species across the world. It's much easier to count bears than ants. It reveals that from 1970 to 2018, the size of animal populations for which data is available have declined by 69% on average.[4] Even though this metric isn't perfect, it paints a compelling picture that the curse is evident in nature too.

Additional Scriptures: 1 John 2:17. Deuteronomy 28:23. Genesis 2:16-17; 3:14-19. Psalm 90:10. Revelation 22:3. Romans 8:20-22.

#136 - THE DAY OF THE LORD

Anti | DD | **Earth** | Gov | Israel | **Jesus** | Leader | **Sky** | Society | Tech | **Trib**

> "Blow the trumpet in Zion, and sound an alarm in my holy mountain! Let all the inhabitants of the land tremble, for the day of the LORD comes, for it is close at hand: ... I will show wonders in the heavens and in the earth: blood, fire, and pillars of smoke. The sun will be turned into darkness, and the moon into blood, before the great and terrible day of the LORD comes." (Joel 2:1, 30-31)

The day of the Lord has many names in the Bible, including Jacob's

Trouble, Daniel's 70th week, the hour of trial, and the great tribulation. It starts after the rapture, and the official countdown begins when the Antichrist signs a peace treaty with Israel. We went over that in Sign #62 - A Covenant With Death. The seven-year period culminates in Jesus's second coming.

In the Scripture above, we're told there will be wonders in the earth that include things like blood, fire, and smoke. Aside from the blood, in the context of the earth that sounds like a volcano. We'll be looking at fire in Sign #140 - Planet On Fire.

In the book of Micah, it's explained that the wonders will be similar to what the Israelites witnessed when they came out of Egypt. They experienced water turned into blood, frogs, lice, flies, livestock diseases, boils on their skin, hail, locusts, darkness, and the death of the firstborn. Most of those plagues devastated the land, and we'll discuss that in Sign #138 - Earth Made Desolate. For the other plagues, refer to Sign #137 - Pestilences, Sign #141 - Severe Storms, and Sign #147 - The Black Sun.

Jesus described the tribulation period as a time of great distress in the land, troubles, and tribulation.

Fulfillment - Perhaps the reference to blood being a wonder in the earth speaks to the mass mortality events (MME) that are occasionally in the news. Like when thousands of birds drop from the sky for no apparent reason, or thousands of dead seals wash ashore.

A group of researchers conducted a broad review of all the reports of large animal die-offs in scientific literature since 1940. They found 727 papers documenting MMEs of 2,407 global populations of mammals, birds, fish, reptiles, amphibians, and marine invertebrates (like starfish). Their analysis revealed that the events are becoming more frequent and increasing in magnitude. That describes what birth pains look like. Between 1940 and 2012, there was one more MME each year. "Going from one event to 70 each year is a substantial increase, especially given the increased magnitudes of MMEs for some of these organisms," said Adam Siepielski, University of San Diego assistant professor of biology and the study's co-lead author.[5]

Today Is Different - Let's talk about volcanoes and see if there's anything that could be considered a wonder happening here. Of the 12 biggest volcanic eruptions that scientists are aware of throughout history, five of them have happened since 1883. I'm sure you've heard of Krakatoa. It famously exploded in 1883 and created the loudest sound ever recorded on earth. Since then, there's been Santa María (1902), Novarupta (1912), Mount Pinatubo (1991), and Hunga Tonga-Hunga Ha'apai (2022).[6]

You may recall that in January 2022 the Hunga Tonga-Hunga Ha'apai volcano exploded in spectacular fashion. It produced the largest underwater explosion ever recorded, and it blasted water and volcanic gases higher than any other eruption since we've been monitoring them via satellite.[7] The blast extended 162 miles and shot 35 miles into the air, the tallest in recorded history.[8] It reached the third layer of the atmosphere, the mesosphere. No other volcano in modern times has ever achieved that. Most eruptions only go 7 miles up, impacting the first layer of the atmosphere. It generated the fastest atmospheric waves ever recorded, reaching 720 miles per hour. It triggered a record 590,000 lightning strikes.[9]

Here's another thing that was cool about it. The eruption had the power of 10 megatons of TNT or 500 times that of the bomb dropped on Hiroshima in WWII. It caused the atmosphere to ring like a bell, apparently a phenomenon that was theorized over 200 years ago but never witnessed before.[10]

I'd say that's quite the wonder we recently witnessed on the earth. You could even say God wanted to get our attention with that one.

Additional Scriptures: Daniel 9:24-27; 12:1. Exodus 7-12. Isaiah 13:9; 51:6. Jeremiah 30:7. Luke 21:23. Mark 13:8, 19-20. Matthew 24:8, 21. Micah 7:15. Revelation 3:10.

#137 - PESTILENCES

Anti | DD | **Earth** | Gov | Israel | **Jesus** | Leader | **Sky** | Society | **Tech** | **Trib**

> As he sat on the Mount of Olives, the disciples came to him privately, saying, "Tell us, when will these things be? What is the sign of your coming, and of the end of the age?" ... "For ... there will be ... plagues." (Matthew 24:3, 7)

Jesus is the one who sat on the Mount of Olives and who answered the disciples. One of the signs of his second coming is plagues, which also means pestilence or disease. During the tribulation period this gets pretty intense. The fifth trumpet judgment is torture by demonic locust-scorpion creatures that are released from the bottomless pit. The first bowl judgment is boils on people who take the mark of the Beast.

There's even a plague during the tribulation period which comes upon people who fight against Jerusalem that dissolves their flesh while they stand on their feet. It's certainly possible that's describing the result of a nuclear bomb, but it could also be some sort of biological weapon.

Fulfillment - Humanity has been dealing with plagues for thousands of years. What we need to consider for this sign is if we've seen an increase in the frequency and severity of illnesses in modern times, like the birth pains Jesus described in the Olivet Discourse. When looking at pandemics there's debate about how many people died from each one. We don't even agree on how many died from Covid, and that just happened to us all. I found a couple interesting infographics though.[11]

https://www.visualcapitalist.com/history-of-pandemics-deadliest/

https://ourworldindata.org/historical-pandemics

Since 1900, there have only been 3 large-scale pandemics on the globe where more than 2 million people died. The Spanish flu in 1918 (50-100 million deaths), HIV/AIDS began in 1981 (33 million deaths since), and Covid in 2019 (27 million deaths since).

There's a gap of 63 years between the first two pandemics and a gap of only 38 years between the most recent two. Keep in mind we haven't cured either of the last two. So, the death tolls will continue to climb. With that limited dataset the frequency increased, but the intensity not so much.

The narrative is different if we look at specific diseases. I mentioned obesity is on the rise in Sign #135 - The Curse. I also researched autism because I hear more about this now than in times past. It's no wonder. In the US in 1970, autism prevalence was 1 in 10,000 people. In 2020, it was all the way up to 1 in 36.[12] It's similar in Israel. Their rate of autism prevalence has doubled in the last five years.[13] I'm sure we'd see comparable data if we looked at other modern-day diseases.

Now, what if we look at pestilence in animals? After all, that was one of the plagues of the Exodus. Have you noticed that Avian flu is in the news a lot today? Bird flu outbreaks have come and gone over the decades. Some media outlets are making this latest flu strain seem like it could turn into the next Covid. Turns out this new strain of H5N1 started in 2020 in Russia and has been spreading around the globe since.[14]

Israel saw the death of 8,000 cranes and 1.6 million chickens and turkeys in 2021.[15] From January 2022 through July 17, 2024, the US reports 99 million birds in America have been affected.[16] It's estimated over half a billion farmed birds have died globally. And now it's spreading to mammals. It's believed 17,000 elephant seals died from the virus in 2023. As of April 2024, it was confirmed in dairy cows across the US. A veterinarian at UC Davis comments: "With this virus, the conservation impact is already unprecedented. It's on a scale we've never seen: in terms of the number of species and regions affected, we've never seen anything like it."[17] It certainly looks like the animal kingdom is getting hit with a unprecedented pandemic today.

Today Is Different - I think one of the most revealing pieces of evidence for this sign is to look at the use of prescription drugs over time. It would be indicative of a population treating diseases. In 1960, Americans spent $2.7 billion on retail prescription drugs. In 2000, we spent $122 billion. In 2022 it's up to $405.9 billion. Wow! Even if we just look at this century, the spending has more than tripled in the last twenty years.[18]

If we look at global spending, it tells the same story. In 2010, $887 billion was spent globally on medicine and in 2022 it was up to $1.48 trillion. That's a 67% increase in just twelve years.[19] We're a nation and a world that's spending more and more on treating the diseases which plague us.

This particular sign also has a scientific and technology component. The Scripture above doesn't say God is the one who creates the plague. We could easily inflict this upon ourselves today. After all, Covid was a man-made virus, a bioweapon.[20]

Additional Scriptures: Deuteronomy 28:15-68. Exodus 7-12; 9:8-12, 11. Habakkuk 3:5. Jeremiah 21:6; 32:23-24. Revelation 9:2-11; 16:2, 10-11. Zechariah 14:12, 15.

#138 - EARTH MADE DESOLATE

Anti | DD | **Earth** | Gov | Israel | **Jesus** | Leader | Sky | Society | **Tech** | **Trib**

> Behold, the day of the LORD comes, cruel, with wrath and fierce anger; to make the land a desolation. (Isaiah 13:9)

This Scripture from the Old Testament is about the tribulation period, the day of the Lord. We learn that the land will be made desolate during this time. The word *desolation* means waste, a horror, and ruin. Jesus said there would be famines. The book of Joel has a detailed account of locusts devouring all the food. So, the harvest perishes, the trees wither, and the wine and oil dry up.

All sorts of judgments against the earth happen during the tribulation period and cause this desolation, including no wind, scorching sun, the rivers and sea turning to blood and destroying all fish and sea life, and fire. We also know that the Euphrates River dries up during the tribulation period.

Fulfillment - Since Jesus said there'd be famines, what's the data look like? As you can see in figure 138.1 below, since 1860 the number of global famine victims saw a big wave of increase in the early 1900s. However, the number of famine victims has been low since the 1960s.

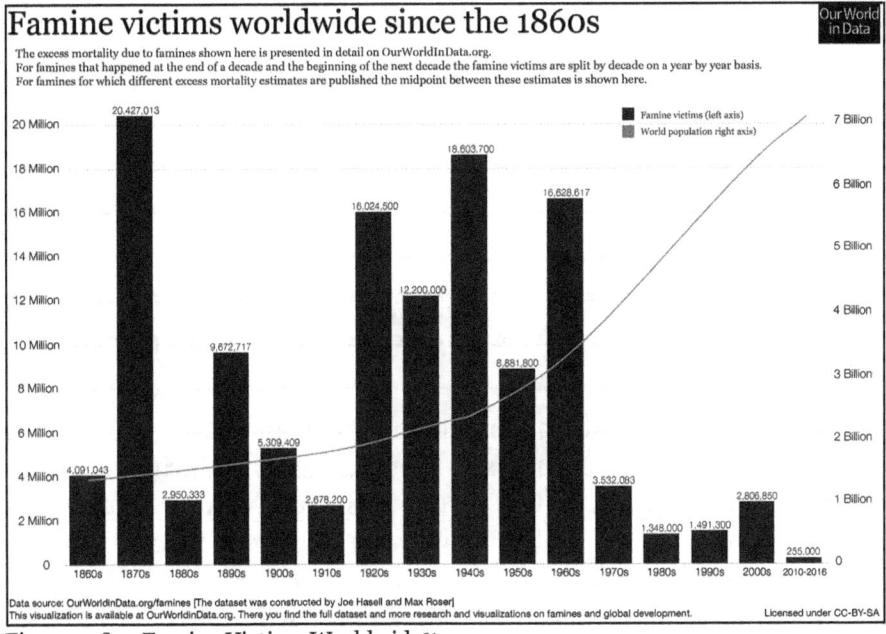

Figure 138.1. Famine Victims Worldwide[21]
Source: https://ourworldindata.org/famines

There are a lot of aid organizations today that help fight hunger. I think that's one reason deaths have decreased. But the root of the problem hasn't really gone away.

Here's another way to look at who isn't getting enough food. Figure 138.2 shows the worldwide number of people who reported they are severely food insecure, meaning they don't have enough to eat to support normal growth and activity. Back in 2015, there were 576 million people who were severely food insecure. It's risen steadily since then. In 2022, it was up to 893 million people.[22]

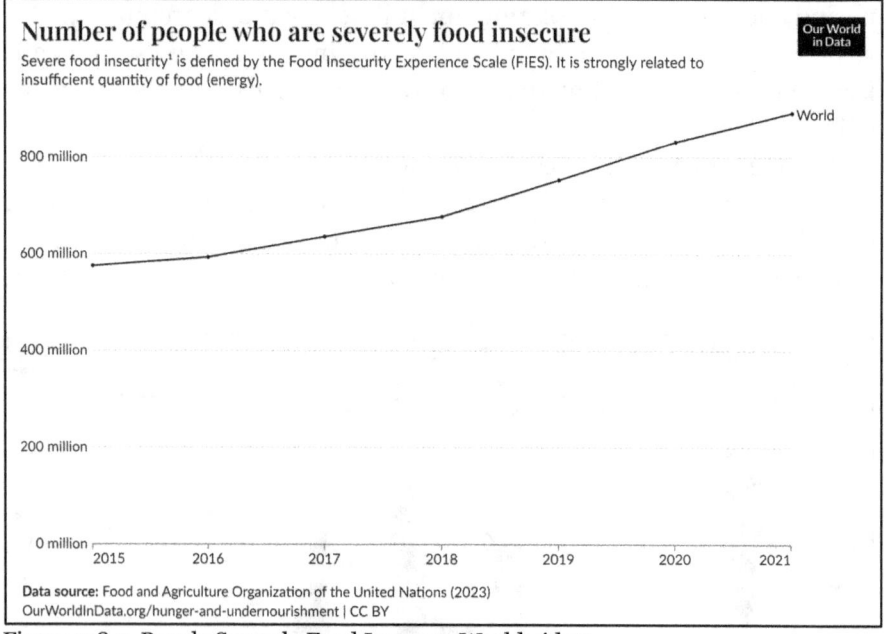

Figure 138.2. People Severely Food Insecure Worldwide[23]
Source: https://ourworldindata.org/grapher/number-of-people-severely-food-insecure?tab=chart

This means 11% of the population on the planet is hungry.[24] In the US, almost 13% of households were food insecure during 2022, up from 10% the prior year.[25] In Israel, 16% of families suffered from food insecurity in 2021.[26] The key drivers for this are war and conflicts, weather extremes, and economic shocks.

Let's see if the planet is drying up and becoming more desert like. It actually is. A team of international researchers reported in May 2023 that half of the world's large lakes and reservoirs have shrunk since the 1990s. The freshwater sources from the Caspian Sea to Lake Titicaca have lost 22 gigatonnes of water per year for the past three decades. That's 17 times the size of Lake Mead, the largest reservoir in the US.[27]

In fact, Lake Mead has dropped 60% in just over a decade.[28]

Even the Euphrates River is drying up today. It starts in Southern Turkey, flows through Syria and Iraq, combines with the Tigris River, and then empties into the Persian Gulf. It's a vital source of freshwater to 23 million people. One reason it's drying up is because of modern-day technology, like the Ataturk Dam in Turkey that was finished in the 1990s. The dam blocks the river for irrigation and hydroelectric power. It's estimated the river could completely dry up as early as 2040.[29]

Today Is Different - I doubt most of us realize how much impact a war, like the Russia-Ukraine War, can have on the entire globe. Today is different because we live in a world that's intertwined economically. Many nations depend on importing basic food staples from other countries in order to feed their people. Turns out Ukraine is the fifth largest exporter of wheat with the majority of it going to Africa, Asia, and the Middle East.

The largest wheat producers like China and India don't export it. When Ukraine wasn't able to export as much wheat, due to the war, prices skyrocketed. There would have been famines if other countries like the US, Canada, and interestingly Russia hadn't stepped in to fill the supply gap and bring prices down.[30]

That war is also having a global impact on fertilizer. Guess which nation has the largest source of mineral fertilizers? It's Russia. Well, their ability to export fertilizer has been severely hampered due to all the economic sanctions placed upon them by various countries, insurers not wanting to cover shipments in a war zone, and export routes being closed. The price of fertilizer rose 200% by the end of 2022.[31] Without fertilizer, crop yields are going to be lower. That in turn will lead to higher food prices and even higher food insecurity.

A war between two countries in the far north of the world is currently contributing to the earth becoming desolate, to increasing food insecurity, and even to famine for millions of people.

Speaking of war, there's a global war on farmers, and it's another reason today is different. This has never happened before. Some scientists say that farming contributes to global warming and accounts for one-third of greenhouse gas emissions globally.[32] In early 2024, we saw farmers across Europe protesting because they're facing rising costs and taxes, environmental regulations, and competition from cheap food imports.33

Even in the US farmers are now being encouraged to leave their land fallow by being paid to not farm. All in the name of science, climate change, carbon reduction, and green energy technology. Some of these climate laws include reducing nitrogen (that means reducing the volume of fertilizer and manure, so less plants and animals), reducing emissions from animals (also means less animals), and reduce fossil fuels (that means stop using diesel fuel which powers farm equipment). Today we're causing desolation by revolting against our own survival.

Additional Scriptures: Deuteronomy 28:15-68. Exodus 7:14-25; 8:1-32; 9:1-7; 10:1-20. Jeremiah 32:23-24. Joel 1. Luke 21:23. Matthew 24:7. Revelation 6:5-8; 7:1, 16; 8:7; 16:3-4, 8-9, 12.

#139 - GREAT EARTHQUAKES

Anti | DD | **Earth** | Gov | Israel | **Jesus** | Leader | Sky | Society | **Tech** | **Trib**

> As he sat on the Mount of Olives, the disciples came to him privately, saying, "Tell us, when will these things be? What is the sign of your coming, and of the end of the age?" ... "For ... there will be ... earthquakes in various places." (Matthew 24:3, 7)

In these verses, Jesus is the one answering the disciples' question about his coming and the end of the age. He tells them that there will be "earthquakes in various places."

When Gog of Magog goes to invade Israel in the last days, God creates a great earthquake in Israel that causes every person on earth to shake at God's presence. To learn more about that war, refer to Sign #108 - Gog Of The Land Of Magog and Sign #109 - Gog's Allies.

That'll just be the beginning of what's to come. When reading the additional Scriptures below, you'll learn that there are many violent earthquakes which occur during the tribulation period. The seventh bowl judgment is described as the worst earthquake since people have inhabited the earth. It levels every mountain, all the islands disappear, and the cities fall.

Fulfillment - Let's have a look at some earthquake data. Figure 139.1 shows the number of deaths from earthquakes across the globe from 1801 to 2023. This graph looks exactly how Jesus described earthquake data would appear in the end times. It resembles labor pains, doesn't it? You can clearly see that the deadliness of earthquakes is increasing over time and happens in waves.

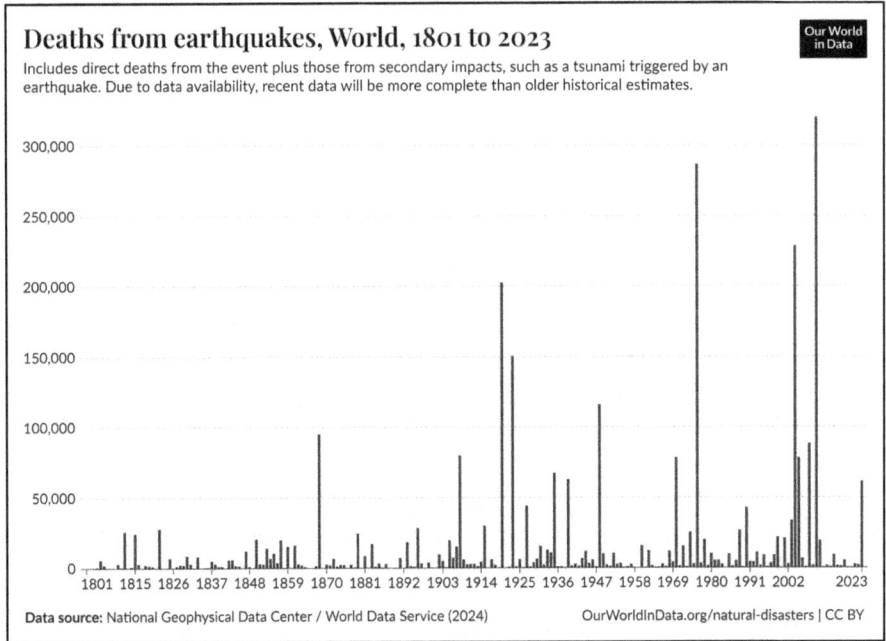

Figure 139.1. Deaths From Earthquakes Worldwide[34]
Source: https://ourworldindata.org/grapher/earthquake-deaths?time=1801..latest

Figure 139.2 shows the number of significant earthquakes from 1800 to 2023. That means they were either magnitude 7.5 or greater, caused deaths, inflicted at least $1 million in damage, or generated a tsunami. There are certainly more of them happening across the globe today than in decades prior. This graph looks a little like labor pains too.

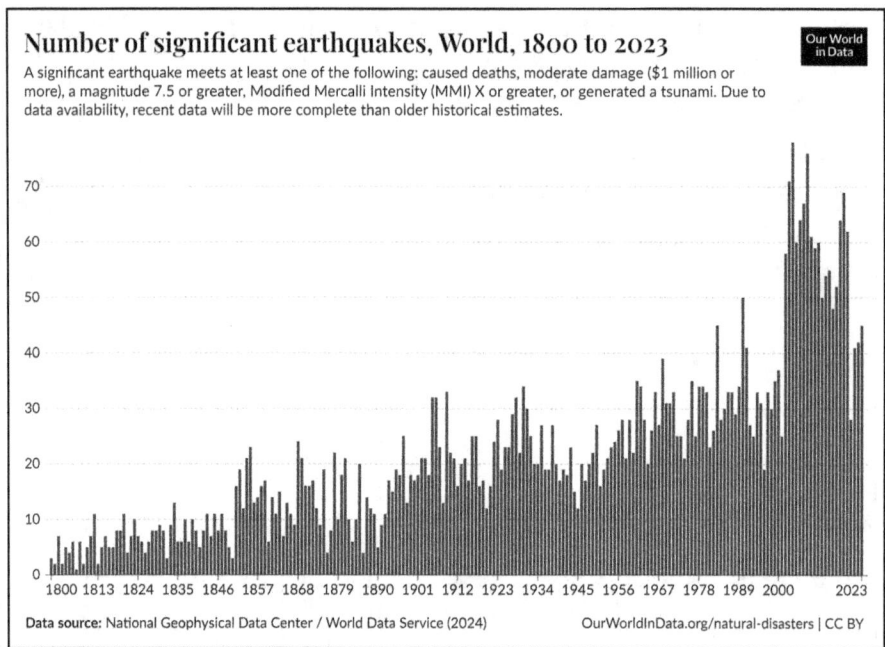

Figure 139.2. Significant Earthquakes 1800-2023 Worldwide[35]
Source: https://ourworldindata.org/grapher/significant-earthquakes?tab=chart&time=1800..latest

Figure 139.2 could be a bit misleading though because earthquake detection technology, the seismograph, was invented in the late 1800s. Because of this, we shouldn't compare the 1800s data with today. So, let's look at the last fifty years, when we know seismographs were all over the globe.

In figure 139.3, since 1970 you can clearly see a labor pains looking upward trend in the number of significant earthquakes. The last big wave started in 2002 and ended in 2019. But the next wave picked up in 2021 and it's still increasing.

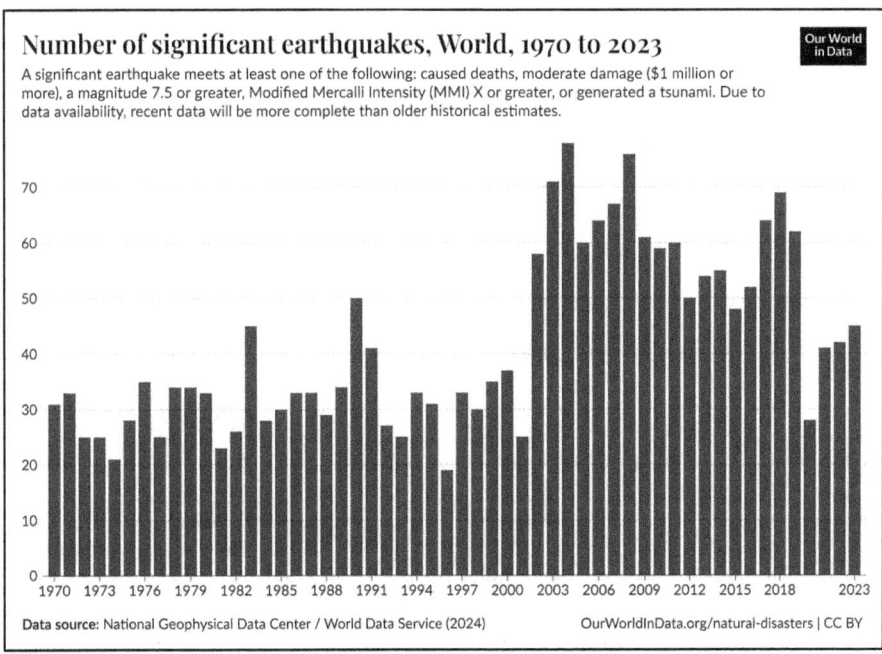

Figure 139.3. Significant Earthquakes 1970-2023 Worldwide[36]
Source: https://ourworldindata.org/grapher/significant-earthquakes?tab=chart&time=1970..latest

What about the severity of earthquakes? Figure 139.4 displays the number of magnitude 7+ earthquakes since 1990 across the world. The average number of quakes magnitude 7-7.9 during this time is 14 per year. There were 5 above that in the 1990s while there have been 8 above that since 2010.

324   Chapter 15 - Signs On The Earth

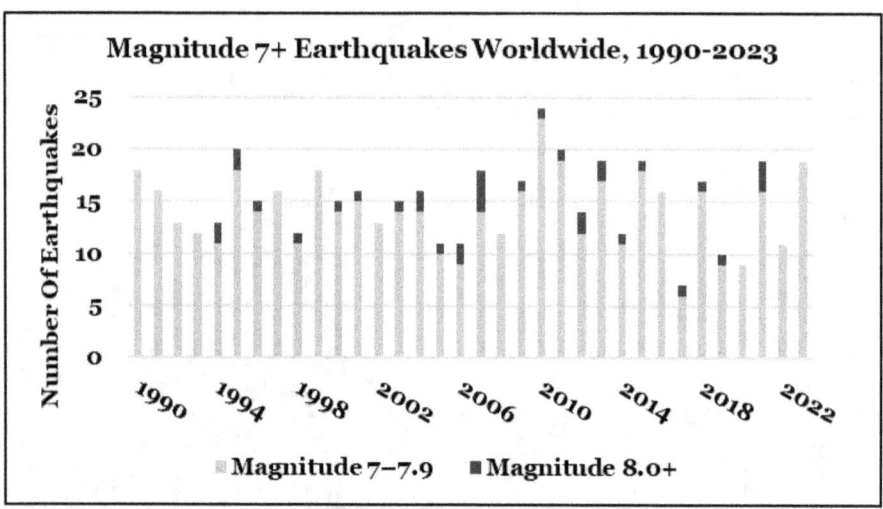

Figure 139.4. Magnitude 7+ Earthquakes Worldwide, 1990-2023[37]
Source: Compiled from USGS earthquake data at https://www.usgs.gov/programs/earthquake-hazards/lists-maps-and-statistics

Of note is the magnitude 8+ earthquakes. In the 1990s, there were 6. In the 2000s there were 13. Then in the 2010s it was 11. In the 2020s so far there's been 3. It appears the intensity of earthquakes may be gradually going up as well.

Today Is Different - Technology plays many roles in this particular sign. We wouldn't know all this earthquake data if it wasn't for modern seismograph technology. And because the earth shakes so much, the building industry has been using earthquake resistant construction techniques to mitigate destruction and deaths.

Let's also consider the role that science and technology has in man-made earthquakes. We normally think earthquakes happen along fault lines when tectonic plates slide or slip across each other. Well, today our technology is to blame for some earthquakes. Here are some examples. Mining removes material from the earth, leading to collapses that can trigger an earthquake. Dam building is another. The 7.9 earthquake in China in 2008 that killed 80,000 people was triggered by the weight of all the water in the reservoir. It sat over a fault line. Fracking for oil and gas along with wastewater disposal can also create an earthquake by cracking rocks and lubricating faults. You can also envision that a nuclear bomb could certainly trigger an earthquake too.[38]

Today, there's also the possibility of tectonic weapons. Good luck doing an internet search on that. It's been deemed a conspiracy theory. Regardless, I have no doubt that governments today are investing in tectonic weaponry. It could very well be that some of the earthquakes which happen during the tribulation period are man-made, and that wasn't possible until recently.

Additional Scriptures: Ezekiel 38:18-20. Isaiah 13:6, 13; 24:19-20. Joel 2:10. Matthew 27:50-54. Revelation 6:12-14; 8:1-5; 11:15, 19; 16:17-20. Zechariah 14:1, 4, 10.

#140 – PLANET ON FIRE

Anti | DD | **Earth** | Gov | Israel | **Jesus** | Leader | **Sky** | Society | **Tech** | **Trib**

> But the day of the Lord will come as a thief in the night, in which the heavens will pass away with a great noise, and the elements will be dissolved with fervent heat; and the earth and the works that are in it will be burned up. Therefore, since all these things will be destroyed like this, what kind of people ought you to be in holy living and godliness, looking for and earnestly desiring the coming of the day of God, which will cause the burning heavens to be dissolved, and the elements will melt with fervent heat? (2 Peter 3:10-12)

For this sign, we learn that during the tribulation period, the day of the Lord, that "the elements will be dissolved with fervent heat" and that the earth will be "burned up." The planet is going to be on fire. Jesus did say in the Olivet Discourse that there would be great distress in the land prior to his second coming. With the first trumpet judgment, one-third of the trees and all the grass on earth is burned when fire rains from heaven. The sun's heat is going to be so intense that it'll start fires. Perhaps the most terrifying is the demonic army that's let out of the bottomless pit. They ride horses that billow fire, smoke, and brimstone from their mouths.

Fulfillment - In order for the trees or grass to burn easily, they need to be dry. That means heat and drought. Unless you've been living in a cave for the last couple decades, you're familiar with global warming. While there's much debate about the legitimacy of climate data these days, it does align with what the Bible says is going to happen in the last days. It's going to get hotter.

Worldwide, 2023 was the warmest year on record. 2016 was the next warmest. And 2014-2023 was the warmest decade. Global average surface temperatures have risen by an average rate of 0.17°F per decade since 1901.[39]

June 2024 was the thirteenth month in a row where it was the warmest for its respective month of the year. This type of streak also happened in 2015-2016. The past twelve months have also all been at least 1.5°C above the temperature average of the pre-industrial era (1850-1900). The global temperature average over the last twelve months was also the highest on record. It was 0.76°C above the 1991-2020 average and 1.64°C above the pre-industrial average.[40]

The US National Weather Service states that the deadliest weather hazard in America is in fact heat. In 2023, there were 207 fatalities attributed to the heat. The 30-year average is 183 deaths, and the 10-year average is 188. Did you notice that it's been trending upward? For weather hazards, it leads fatalities by a large margin too. The next deadliest is a flood, and its 10-year average of fatalities is only 103.[41]

The 2003 European heatwave was the hottest summer recorded since 1540. It's estimated 70,000 people died. Temperatures rose to 40°C (104°F) in France. The death toll was high because air conditioning isn't widely used there.[42] It had additional and sometimes devastating impacts. Crops suffered from drought. The River Danube fell to its lowest point in 100 years. Forest fires broke out. The trains had to run at reduced speeds in case railway lines had buckled. Workers altered their working hours to avoid the heat. Water supply shortages occurred that led to bans on watering.[43]

Have you noticed the extreme heat wave in the US this summer of 2024? Temperatures are easily 10°F above normal. In the first week of July 2024, 10 US cities set all-time record high temperatures including Las Vegas, NV (120°F) and Raleigh, NC (106°F). It even reached 129°F in Death Valley, CA.[44]

It's not just impacting the US either. Tel Aviv, Israel shattered an 85-year-old temperature record in April 2024 with 105.3°F. [45] Temperatures in Saudi Arabia reached 117°F and resulted in 1,300 deaths during the haj pilgrimage.[46]

Figure 140.1 is a look at some interesting data for the US. It shows heat wave characteristics by decade. Notice that the frequency, duration, length in days, and average temperature of heat waves have all increased every decade since the 1960s.

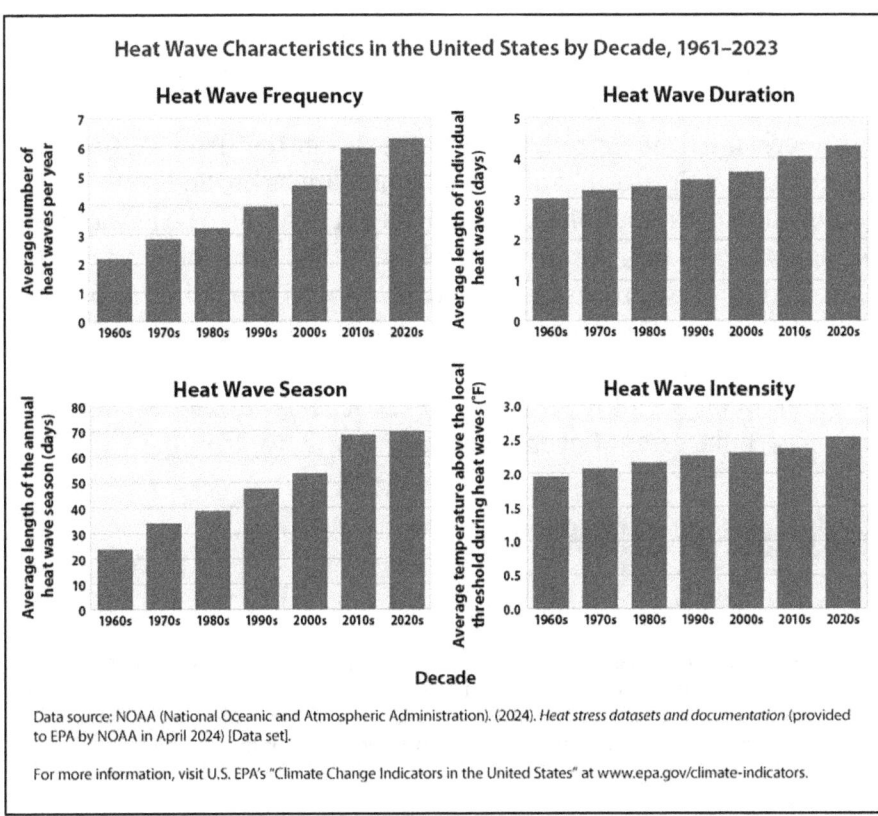

Figure 140.1. Heat Wave Characteristics United States[47]
Source: https://www.epa.gov/climate-indicators/climate-change-indicators-heat-waves

Today Is Different - Hot nuclear fireball and thermal radiation. That's what makes today so very different than prior generations. A nuclear detonation heats the air to extremely high temperatures, causing the air to form a large fireball within a fraction of a second. According to *The Nuclear Matters Handbook 2020*, the immediate fireball is as hot as the interior temperate of the sun! It causes a complete disintegration of atoms.[48] A nuclear weapon detonated in the air with a 10-kiloton blast yield (the Hiroshima bomb was 15 kt) has a fireball blast radius of 65 meters.[49] For you American football fans, that's 71 yards.

That's not the worst of it. Thermal radiation is also generated in a nuclear explosion. It can ignite wood, vegetation, anything combustible, and severely burn skin. Considering that same weapon with a 10-kiloton blast yield, third degree burns would happen to people within

1.7 kilometers (about 1 mile) of the detonation.

In nuclear detonations, the fires created by the fireball and the thermal radiation often merge into a giant fire, a firestorm. The wind can reach hurricane strength and in turn fan the flames. Hiroshima experienced a firestorm, and over 4 square miles burned.[50]

During the tribulation period, the planet is going to be at war. Refer to Sign #111 - Nation Vs Nation and Sign #114 - Shocking Amount Of Destruction. We can assume nuclear weapons are going to be used. Today, we have the power to quickly set the planet on fire all by ourselves, without God's intervention.

Additional Scriptures: Amos 9:5. Genesis 19:24-28. Jeremiah 52:12-13. Luke 21:23. Revelation 8:1-5, 7; 9:14-19; 16:8-9.

#141 - SEVERE STORMS

Anti | DD | **Earth** | Gov | Israel | **Jesus** | Leader | **Sky** | Society | **Tech** | **Trib**

> The seventh poured out his bowl into the air. A loud voice came out of the temple of heaven, from the throne, saying, "It is done!" There were lightnings, sounds, and thunders. ... Great hailstones, about the weight of a talent, came down out of the sky on people. People blasphemed God because of the plague of the hail, for this plague was exceedingly severe. (Revelation 16:17-18, 21)

During the tribulation period there will be some intense storms that include lightning, loud sounds, thunder, and hail. These hail stones mentioned in the Scripture above weigh one talent. A Roman talent was 71 pounds (32 kg).[51] Wow! To put that into perspective, if you filled a gallon jug with ice it would weigh about 8 pounds. So, imagine almost 9 gallons of ice falling from the sky. It would be falling at such a high rate of speed that it would cause mass destruction.

The Scripture doesn't specifically mention wind, but we can make an inference that the "sounds" could be the noise a tornado makes. Tornadoes make sense because hail requires a strong updraft of wind in order to form. When the hail weighs more than the updraft is able to support, that's when it falls.

I would like to call out that there's no mention of snow in the Scripture above. However, we're told in the Old Testament that God has reserved the storehouses of both hail and snow for use during the tribulation period.

Severe storms are certainly a type of great distress in the land. In the Olivet Discourse, Jesus said this would be a hallmark of his second coming.

Fulfillment - The most violent type of storm on land that comes to mind is a tornado. It has all the elements: thunder, lightning, hail, wind, rain, and noise. Here's something really interesting. The United States is pretty much the only country on the planet that's plagued by tornadoes. The US has an average of 1,200 a year. Canada is next and they only average 100 a year.[52] So, what's up with America?

We have a perfect mix of the right kind of air. Tornadoes form when there's warm, moist air near the ground, when there's cool, dry air higher up, and when there are horizontal winds that increase and change direction with elevation. In the US, the warm, moist air comes in from the Gulf of Mexico. The dry air comes from the Southwest states and Mexico. And the cold air comes from the northeast over the Rocky Mountains. It all mixes together and forms severe thunderstorms with tornadoes in the areas and states east of the Rocky Mountains.[53]

Figure 141.1 displays the number of tornadoes in the US each year from 1950 to 2023. As you can see, there's been an upward trend in the number of these severe storms. The number of tornadoes peaked in 2004 at 1,817. Between 1950 and 1989, the US averaged 709 tornadoes each year. Since 1990, the average has jumped to 1,224 per year.

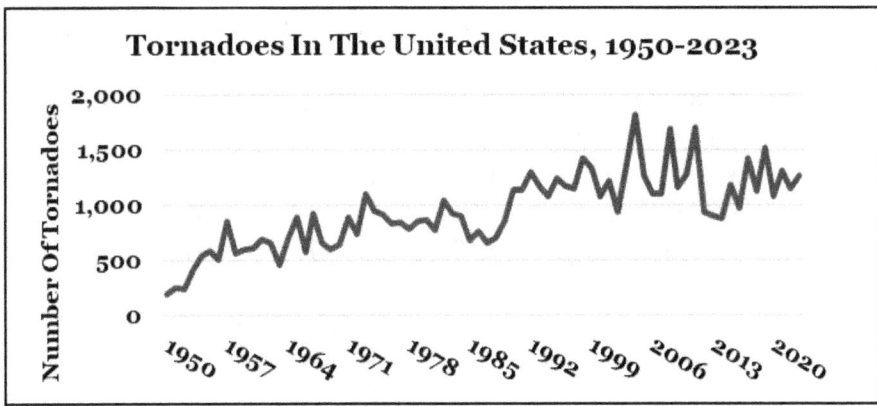

Figure 141.1. Tornadoes In The United States[54]
Source: Compiled from tornado data at https://en.wikipedia.org/wiki/List_of_tornado_events_by_year

Today Is Different - Have you heard of cloud seeding? If you saw the new movie *Twisters*, then you have. This technology was actually invented in the 1940s. Today, there are many ways to accomplish it using a variety of cloud seeding materials. The most common material used is silver iodide. They can shoot it into clouds from the ground, release it from planes into an updraft, or drop a flare into a cloud formation from above. This essentially makes it more likely to rain or snow.

This was used as a weapon of war by the US Air Force during the Vietnam War.[55] It extended the monsoon season and led to floods and landslides. Today, countries use it for all sorts of things: to suppress heat waves, to combat wildfires, to boost agricultural capabilities, for drought mitigation, to minimize hail, and even for more snow at ski resorts. Apparently, it also aids in fog clearance and is used at airports to enhance visibility.[56]

Scientists are also experimenting with modifying extreme weather phenomena, like seeding a thunderstorm in an effort to diminish tornado intensity.[57] In fact, this was illustrated in the movie *Twisters*. What could possibly go wrong there? Maybe we're the ones who create the enormous 71-pound hailstones of the tribulation.

As you might imagine, this doesn't come without risks. Some scientists say it doesn't create rain, that it just moves it from one location to another. Thus, it could be used as a weapon. Not just to flood an enemy, but to divert the rain they would normally get and give them a drought instead. The chemicals used can pollute the air and contaminate the ground and water. It can also cause unexpected extreme weather. Severe flooding and a deadly blizzard have been linked to cloud seeding.[58]

Considering the weather extremes we've been reading about in this chapter, it's almost guaranteed that cloud seeding is going to get used to combat what we read about in Sign #138 - Earth Made Desolate and Sign #140 - Planet On Fire.

Additional Scriptures: Deuteronomy 28:22. Exodus 9:13-35. Genesis 7:11-24. Job 38:22-23. Luke 21:23. Revelation 8:7; 10:1-7; 11:15-19.

#142 - SEA AND WAVES ROARING

Anti | DD | **Earth** | Gov | Israel | **Jesus** | Leader | **Sky** | Society | **Tech** | **Trib**

> "There will be signs in the sun, moon, and stars; and on the earth anxiety of nations, in perplexity for the roaring of the sea and the waves." (Luke 21:25)

Jesus is the one speaking here. He says one of the signs of his second coming will be the "roaring of the sea and the waves." As we discussed in a prior sign, this could have a double meaning. It could be a literal reference to a storm on the water, which we'll consider in this sign. The other is that it's a metaphor for people making a noise like the roar of the sea and a rushing sound like the flow of water. Refer to Sign #23 - Anxiety of Nations With Perplexity for more discussion on that aspect.

When I picture a storm on the sea, a hurricane comes to mind. We're told of another type of storm in the book of Revelation. A burning mountain is thrown into the sea for the second trumpet judgment. Makes me picture an island volcano that's exploded or an asteroid that's landed in the ocean. Either would create a tsunami.

Another event that happens in the tribulation period is the war between Gog of Magog and Israel. We're told that God creates a great earthquake as a result of that invasion. An earthquake of that magnitude near Israel will likely generate a tsunami in the Mediterranean Sea.

Fulfillment - Let's talk about tropical cyclones, otherwise known as hurricanes and typhoons.

Figure 142.1 depicted below shows the hurricane landfalls in the United States between 1851 and 2022 by category. The data doesn't look all that noteworthy until you look at the most destructive of them. 2005 stands out for having 4 category 3 storms, which are considered major. Did you notice that the first category 5 storms didn't occur until 1935? 84 years went by before we had one. Since then, we've had 4 in 83 years, the most recent being in 2018.

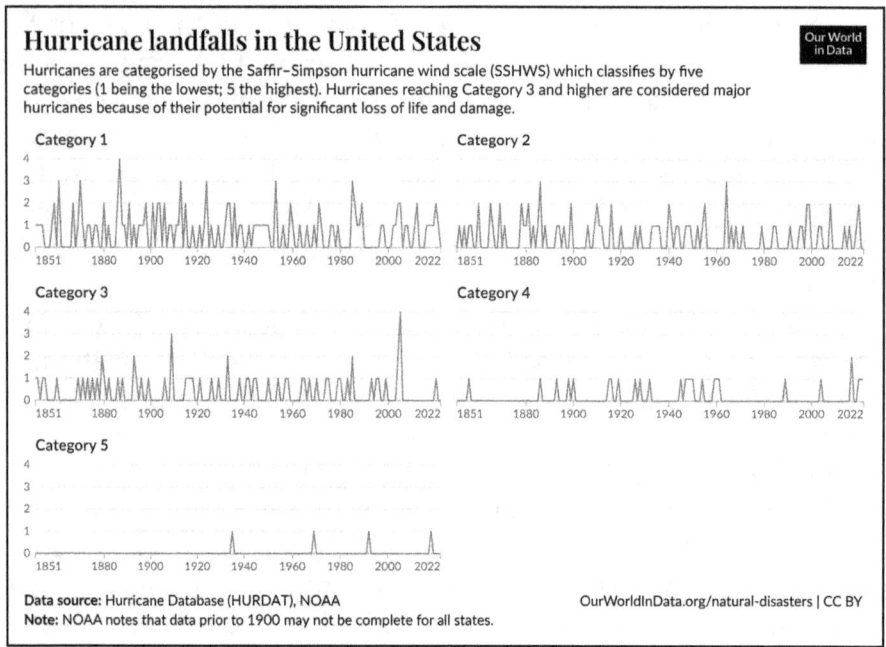

Figure 142.1. Hurricane Landfalls In The United States[59]
Source: https://ourworldindata.org/grapher/hurricane-landfalls-us

Beginning with hurricane Matthew in 2016 and going to hurricane Nicholas in 2021, 19 hurricanes and tropical storms have each caused at least $1 billion in damage to the US. Seven of those billion-dollar storms happened in 2020. The damage estimates for all of them is estimated at $508 billion![60]

Did you know that even Israel can be impacted by a tropical cyclone? They're known as Mediterranean cyclones or medicanes when they occur in the Mediterranean Sea. On rare occasions they can reach the strength of a category 1 hurricane, and at least one was recorded at a category 2.[61] Storm Daniel was the deadliest of these in recorded history. It formed in September 2023. It caused severe flooding in Greece and Libya and killed almost 6,000 people. Even Israel was hit with its remnant and experienced heavy rains.[62]

Today Is Different - There are several things that can generate a tsunami: an earthquake, a landslide (above ground or submarine), a volcanic eruption, and extreme windy weather called a meteotsunamis.[63]

Of the 10 deadliest tsunamis in history, only two were caused by a volcano. The others were triggered by an earthquake. The volcanoes that exploded were Kyushu Island, Japan in 1792 and Krakatoa,

Indonesia in 1883. Of those 10 deadliest tsunamis, two of them happened in the past twenty years. None of them occurred in the 20th century. Seems like God woke up the ocean recently, wouldn't you say?[64]

The deadliest tsunami in history occurred just twenty years ago in December 2004. You may remember it. It was triggered by the 9.1 earthquake off the coast of Sumatra. It also happened to be the third largest earthquake since 1900. The tsunami was as high as 167 feet (51 meters)! It caused inland flooding up to three miles. 230,000 people died and 1.7 million people were displaced as a result.

The most expensive natural disaster in history occurred just thirteen years ago in 2011. It was triggered by another 9.1 earthquake, this time off the coast of Japan. The tsunami reached a height of 127 feet (39 meters) and caused inland flooding up to five miles. 18,000 people died and 500,000 people were displaced as a result. The damage amounted to $243 billion! That's due in part to the destruction of a nuclear power plant. That tsunami traveled all the way over to California and Hawaii too, resulting in over $100 million in damage.

In case you're wondering, I did research on what would happen if you dropped a nuke into an active volcano. Surprisingly, the consensus seems not much. That's because the magma is too far down for a nuke to trigger an eruption. It would just make a dent in the mountain. If you somehow got the nuke into the magma chamber, the bomb would melt before you could detonate it.[65]

Do you know what else can generate a tsunami? It's a nuclear weapon. Russia revealed Poseidon, a nuclear armed torpedo drone, in 2015. It can be equipped to carry a 100-megaton warhead. It's designed to trigger a radioactive tsunami that would destroy a coastal city and render it uninhabitable.[66] Tsunamis reaching 100 meters (330 feet) in height would be possible with this weapon.[67] While it's unclear if Russia has a weapon that size, we do know from Sign #114 - Shocking Amount Of Destruction, that they have a 50-megaton warhead named Tsar Bomba.

Another thing that makes today different is that NASA is continually monitoring for near earth objects (NEO). These are asteroids larger than 1 kilometer (0.62 miles) that have the potential to impact earth. NASA says they already know that none of the large NEOs that have been discovered have any risk of impacting earth over the next 100 years. An asteroid that size would essentially be a planet killer, the equivalent of 6.6 million Hiroshima bombs.[68]

The glaring vulnerability I see with this is that NASA is only looking for the really big asteroids. If it is an asteroid that slams into the ocean in the tribulation period, it's not going to be a planet killer. But it would be devastating to the area it hit. A small 30-meter asteroid (98 feet) exploded over Tunguska, Russia in 1908. It leveled 80 million trees over 2,150 square kilometers (830 square miles).[69] The Bible is full of examples of God coming against human hubris. I think it's quite likely he'll use an asteroid to do just that.

Additional Scriptures: Exodus 7:14-25. Ezekiel 38:18-20. Isaiah 17:12. Revelation 8:8-11; 16:3-4.

#143 – GOD'S WRATH

Anti | DD | Earth | Gov | Israel | Jesus | Leader | Sky | Society | Tech | Trib

> "For there will be great distress in the land and wrath to this people." (Luke 21:23)

Jesus is delivering the signs of his second coming in the Olivet Discourse in the verse above. We're told it'll be a time of "wrath." It means anger, vengeance, and punishment. Since God is perfect and holy, that means he's also the perfect judge. The tribulation period is a time in which he judges sin.

In the fourth seal judgment, we're told one-quarter of the world dies due to war, famine, death, and wild beasts of the earth. Then in the sixth trumpet judgment another third of the world perishes from the demonic army let out of the bottomless pit. Just those two judgments result in the death of half of the world that's left behind after the rapture. In Revelation 6:8, the Greek word used for wild beasts means a beast, venomous, and ferocious.

Throughout this book we've discussed a myriad of ways in which the wrath of God is displayed. Chapter 13 has several signs that involve war. In this chapter, we considered famine and death by all sorts of things that occur on the earth. As for the angelic war that's occurring in heaven, we'll go over how we can see that impacting us today in Sign #148 - War In Heaven.

The tribulation period ends with Jesus's second coming. It's at that time that Satan, the other fallen angels, the Antichrist, the False Prophet, and the unrepentant sinners who survived the tribulation period are defeated and either bound or cast into the lake of fire. I'll cover that in more detail in Chapter 20.

Ok, so that leaves wild animals as the judgment that we need to touch on here.

Fulfillment - Want to take a guess at what the deadliest species to humans is? Maybe it's all the Bible stories with lions, but that's where my brain goes. But it's not them. They only accounted for 250 deaths worldwide in 2022. It's not snakes, either. They're the second deadliest though, causing 100,000 deaths in 2022. It's one of the most annoying insects, the mosquito. Mosquitoes killed 1 million people in 2022. They are the deadliest because they transmit a number of deadly diseases like malaria, West Nile virus, dengue, and Zika. The worst is malaria.[70]

Well, when I think of ferocious and venomous like the Scripture says, mosquitoes just don't fit. So, I don't think that's what God is portraying. Here are the deadliest ones that fit: snakes (#2), dogs (#3), crocodiles (#8), hippos (#10), elephants (#11), and lions (#12). You may recall that God sent poisonous snakes into the camp of the Israelites when they started complaining and speaking against him and Moses. There are several references in the Old Testament about wild dogs eating people who died. And of course there are lions in the Old Testament too.

While nearly 5 million people worldwide are bitten by snakes every year, turns out snakebite mortality has been steadily decreasing.[71] Between 1990 and 2019 the rate of death decreased 36%.[72] This is due in part to scientific advancements in the development of antivenom. As for dog bites, it's not just the initial attack that you have to worry about. Any bite by an animal is likely going to get infected, and dogs can carry diseases like rabies. In the US, dogs bite more than 4.5 million people annually with tens of millions of bites occurring worldwide.[73]

I think it's obvious that the animal kingdom isn't always friendly toward us and can certainly be used by God to deliver his wrath.

I'll wrap up with a bizarre example that's happening today. Killer whales are not only attacking but also sinking boats today. It's not just one crazy orca out there either. It's pods of them doing this in the North Atlantic Ocean. Apparently, they've been at it for several years now.

From 2020 to 2023, 500 interactions with these whales have been documented. At least three boats have been sunk and dozens damaged as the whales rip off the boat rudders. Scientists have no idea why they started behaving this way.[74]

Today Is Different - The World Economic Forum publishes a Global Risks Report each year. The 2024 report states extreme weather is the #1 risk. Survey respondents believed it was most likely to present as a material crisis on a global scale in 2024. It's the only environment-related risk in the top 20. With the bombardment we constantly get about climate change I would have figured environmental risks would have made up a majority of the top 20. Nope. The other risks are classified as economic, geopolitical, societal, or technological. In fact, #2 is AI generated misinformation and disinformation. It seems the respondents believe that we are our own biggest risk.[75]

If you do an internet search on extinction level threats today, most of the articles discuss how unlikely it is to be an environmental crisis. And how much more likely it is for nuclear war to break out. I sometimes wonder why so many people will dig in their heels and refuse to repent during the tribulation period. What will keep them from seeing the obvious, that God is in control and judging sin?

I have a feeling that God is going to be explained away in the name of science and technology. You see, we've reached the point that we can mimic God's wrath. That's what makes today so different. Are people more likely to believe that God sent the famine or that geoengineering and human-caused climate change are the culprits? Are people going to believe that God sent the pestilence or that it was bioengineered in a lab and dispersed as a weapon?

It's the classic tug of war between fate and free will. God lives outside of time and knows all things—past, present, and future. Because he knows what's going to happen in the future, he can reveal it to us in the past. That's prophecy, predestination, or fate. However, you have free will. You know this because you make choices all the time. You can choose to follow God or not. You can choose to sin or not. God's plan and our choices work together in perfect harmony.

King Nebuchadnezzar didn't know that God was working behind the scenes using him as his servant to discipline Israel because they kept sinning and worshiping false gods. He wasn't a leader the people of Israel chose because they certainly didn't elect him. But their choices resulted in him being their leader. So, in a sense, they did pick him. But God also promised to hold King Nebuchadnezzar accountable for his own sins too, and he did. This same principle applies today.

During the tribulation period, God will use the Antichrist and all the kings of the earth to deliver his wrath, just like he did with King Nebuchadnezzar.

Additional Scriptures: 2 Thessalonians 1:6-10. Daniel 4:28-34; 7:11-12, 23-27; 8:25. Deuteronomy 28:15-68. Hebrews 10:28-31. Isaiah 13; 14:12-21; 24:21-22; 33:22. Jeremiah 15:1-9; 21:5-7; 25:2-12. Matthew 25:31-46. Numbers 21:4-6. Psalm 78:31. Revelation 6:7-8; 9:13-21; 14:14-20; 19:17-21; 20:1-3. Romans 2:2-16. Zechariah 14:12-15. Zephaniah 1:14-15.

#144 - POLAR OPPOSITE - RESTORED EARTH

Anti | DD | **Earth** | Gov | **Israel** | **Jesus** | **Leader** | Sky | Society | Tech | Trib

> He showed me a river of water of life, clear as crystal, proceeding out of the throne of God and of the Lamb, in the middle of its street. On this side of the river and on that was the tree of life, bearing twelve kinds of fruits, yielding its fruit every month. The leaves of the tree were for the healing of the nations. There will be no curse any more. The throne of God and of the Lamb will be in it, and his servants will serve him. (Revelation 22:1-3)

Throughout this chapter we've looked at signs on the earth that result in its destruction. This sign is what I call a polar opposite. It's meant to illustrate how far away we currently are from the life we believers are going to live during Jesus's reign on earth in the millennial kingdom. Recall from Sign #6 - The Point Of No Return, that God only lets evil progress so far before he intervenes.

We're told about the millennial kingdom in the verses above. There's a river in Jerusalem which flows from God's throne with trees along the banks that bear all kinds of fruit and whose leaves have the ability to heal. The main feature I want to draw your attention to is that "there will be no curse any more."

It's a time in which God restores the planet and makes all things new. In fact, in the Olivet Discourse Jesus said heaven and earth would pass away. This is the culmination of that sign of the second coming. Animals will no longer exist as prey and predator because they'll all live together peaceably, including peace with us. The dry and barren deserts are going to bloom. There will also be an abundance of food.

Fulfillment - So, how far away are we? Well, we learned that the curse upon creation just keeps progressing even in the midst of all the scientific advancements we're using to fight against it. I certainly haven't seen a river that's as clear as crystal. The closest river to me is the Rio Grande, and it's the color of mud. Today, when I drive around my city, I can't help but notice how many trees are dead or dying. They don't look like the abundantly fruitful trees described above.

A fun way to consider just how opposite we are is to contemplate what the worst-case scenarios might look like and see just how close we are to them.

Worst case, nature seems to have dominion over us instead of us having dominion over it. Oh. We live in a world that worships nature, don't we? In that respect, we've given nature its supreme status. At the same time, we can clearly see in the signs we've considered that the planet is very much at times against us. We're close to this worst case.

Worst case, we see every type of natural disaster impact every nation every year. So, not every nation experiences every type of natural disaster. We learned the US is in a unique situation to experience tornadoes for example. However, if we consider how interconnected the global economy is today, you could make a case for how any natural disaster regardless of where it is has an impact felt across the globe. We might be close to this worst case.

Worst case, we can't tell when God's trying to get our attention through signs on the earth because we chalk up the sign to a natural random occurrence or attribute it to mankind. Yikes! We've reached the worst case on this one and have been here for a while now.

Today Is Different - So, what do you think? Is today different? Could the curse upon the earth get any worse before it's considered the time of God's wrath? If not, that would mean the tribulation period and thus the rapture are close at hand. Is anyone paying attention to all of God's signs on the earth, or is it now going to take something truly extraordinary to get our attention?

Additional Scriptures: 2 Peter 3:13. Acts 3:19-21. Amos 9:13-15. Ezekiel 47:1-12. Isaiah 11:6-9; 35:1-2, 6-7; 65:17, 25. Joel 2:19-27. Matthew 24:35. Revelation 2:7; 21:5-6; 22:14.

CHAPTER 16 - SIGNS IN THE HEAVENS

#145 - WONDERS IN THE SUN, MOON, AND STARS

Anti | DD | Earth | Gov | Israel | **Jesus** | Leader | **Sky** | Society | **Tech** | **Trib**

> "There will be terrifying things and great miraculous signs from heaven. ... And there will be strange signs in the sun, moon, and stars." (Luke 21:11, 25 NLT)

Jesus tells us here that we should be looking at signs in the heavens and in particular the sun, moon, and stars. In the very beginning when God created the universe, we're told that the lights he created in the sky are signs to mark the seasons, days, and years.

God also uses them to mark special occasions. Recall that when Jesus was born a star appeared in the sky that guided the magi. God created the rainbow as a sign of his covenant with us and the earth, to not destroy it by flood again. It's interesting to note that God's throne is surrounded by a rainbow. Perhaps we can think of the rainbow as his seal or stamp. In the US, the presidential seal is recognizable because of the eagle, and Israel's national emblem is evident because it's a menorah.

During the tribulation period, all sorts of strange things are going to happen in the heavens. We're going to look at the particulars of those as we discuss each sign in this chapter.

Fulfillment - Did you know that God also uses the stars to communicate information and tell a story? I read several books about this that are really fascinating. One is *The Gospel In The Stars* by Joseph Seiss. It's in the public domain and available as a free download. Another is *God's Voice In The Stars* by Ken Fleming. And there's also *Story In The Stars* by Joe Amaral.[1] Joe even has a YouTube video you can check out that provides a nice summary.[2]

God literally wrote the entire gospel account in the stars when he created them. He must have taught Adam and Eve the names of the stars and all the constellations. The evidence reveals that every ancient civilization used the same zodiac. And the major stars in the zodiac constellations all have names which mean the same thing when translated. I believe this is yet another reason why God says no one has an excuse for not knowing him.

In the book of Revelation, we're given a description of an event that takes place in the stars.

> A great sign was seen in heaven: a woman clothed with the sun, and the moon under her feet, and on her head a crown of twelve stars. She was with child. She cried out in pain, laboring to give birth. Another sign was seen in heaven. Behold, a great red dragon, having seven heads and ten horns, and on his heads seven crowns. His tail drew one third of the stars of the sky, and threw them to the earth. The dragon stood before the woman who was about to give birth, so that when she gave birth he might devour her child. (Revelation 12:1-4)

It's a story about Jesus. The woman is the nation of Israel, and her crown of twelve stars is the twelve tribes. The Dragon is of course Satan. He's ready to devour the woman's child, Jesus. Well, on September 23, 2017, this sign actually appeared in the night sky over Jerusalem, Israel. It centered around the constellation Virgo. Twelve stars appeared over her head. The sun was in the constellation near her back. The moon was near her feet. The planet Jupiter, which had been in the belly of the constellation for nine months, departed as though the constellation had birthed it.

It was the first time this sign manifested in the sky since that prophecy was written some 2,000 years ago. It's certainly not something that happens frequently. You can see it for yourself in a constellation app like Stellarium, and there are many YouTube videos about it.[3]

So, what do you think it means? I think it's meant to get our attention. To get us to read the book of Revelation and start thinking about the nearness of Jesus's return. It's telling us that we're in the season of Jesus's second coming.

Today Is Different - In Sign #4 - Birth Pains, we discussed that the signs would manifest like birth pains. They appear more frequently and more intensely. In the past year, there has been a whole bunch of unusual activity in the heavens.

I want to start by mentioning the total solar eclipse that traveled across the US on April 8, 2024. A solar eclipse involves both the sun and the moon. The light from the sun gets blocked when the moon crosses in between the sun and the earth at the perfect distance. The April 2024 eclipse crossed over seven cities named Ninevah. You can't tell me that's not foreboding.

It also intersected the paths of two other recent eclipses in the US. The annual solar eclipse of October 14, 2023, and the total solar eclipse of August 21, 2017. The total eclipse paths created a giant X across the US. The X is also known as the paleo-Hebrew letter "tav." While all three eclipse paths formed the paleo-Hebrew letter "aleph."[4] The aleph is the first letter of the Hebrew alphabet and the tav is the last. Recall that Jesus referred to himself as the first and the last.

At the intersections of those eclipse paths, there's a 111-foot-tall cross and a 77-foot-tall cross.[5] Do you think that's a coincidence? Here's another interesting fact. The total eclipse in 2017 crossed over seven cities named Salem, short for Jerusalem.

Here's something else interesting that occurred during the 2024 total eclipse. NASA launched three rockets during the eclipse for scientific tests. Guess what they named this science project? APEP. Straight from NASA: "choosing the acronym because it is also the name of the serpent deity from ancient Egyptian mythology, nemesis of the Sun deity Ra. It was said that Apep pursued Ra and every so often nearly consumed him, resulting in an eclipse."[6] Seriously? This sounds a lot like the Revelation 12 sign of the Dragon ready to consume Jesus, doesn't it?

It keeps getting better. There was a planet parade during the 2024 total solar eclipse that involved seven planets.[7] A parade is when a group of planets appear in the sky on one night. These are pretty rare to begin with and now one happened on the exact date of the eclipse. Another one happened with six planets on August 28, 2024.

Then there's the appearance of comet 12P/Pons-Brooks, also known as the "devil comet" and the "mother of dragons" comet. I'm not making this up. It's a Halley-type comet that orbits the sun every 71 years. It has a horned appearance which is how it got its nickname. It's a cryovolcanic comet because it has volcanoes on its icy, rocky surface that erupt volatile materials. It was visible in the night sky during the 2024 total eclipse.[8]

Ooh and here's my favorite part, cities in totality for the 2024 eclipse were Enoch, Texas and Elijah, Missouri.[9] The Bible tells us that both Enoch and Elijah were raptured! There are plenty more just as interesting facts about these eclipses that are worth looking into. I read a book titled *The Great American Writing On The Wall* by A.C. Katz.[10] Bill

Koenig also has a detailed article about these eclipses on his website.[11]
https://watch.org/node/111110

The "Blaze Star" is expected to explode any day now. It's a rare recurrent nova that explodes about every 80 years. It'll be visible to the naked eye, at the same brightness as the North Star, for the first time since 1946.[12]

There's also something astronomers had never seen a galaxy do. Five years ago, the galaxy SDSS1335+0728 threw the lights on. They believe a supermassive black hole at its center awoke. Seeing an entire galaxy light up and remain lit, as this one has for many years, is unprecedented.[13]

Have you ever seen the Aurora Borealis? If you happened to be at the North Pole on Christmas day in 2022, you got to see an event that's never happened before. Normally, the auroras pulsate and move around. This one on Christmas was smooth and didn't pulsate. They've called it a polar rain aurora. It's only ever been observed from satellites in space, never on earth before.[14]

I don't think it's a coincidence that the flat-earth conspiracy is coming up at a time like this. Satan doesn't want us paying attention to God's signs in the heavens because God's made it obvious something's up. If our enemy can get people to believe that the sky is just a sophisticated projection onto a dome, then suddenly those strange signs aren't anything to care about at all.

This sign requires a lot of modern technology and scientific advancements in order to see its fulfillment. We wouldn't be able to see most of these things in the sky if it wasn't for telescopes and satellites. In particular, the Hubble and James Webb telescopes that are out in deep space and got there on sophisticated rockets.

Additional Scriptures: Acts 2:16-21. Amos 5:8. Ezekiel 1:28. Genesis 1:14; 9:13-17. Jeremiah 10:2. Matthew 2:2; 24:27, 29-30. Revelation 1:17; 4:3; 12:1-4. Romans 1:19-20.

#146 - THE HEAVENS SHAKE

Anti | DD | Earth | Gov | Israel | **Jesus** | Leader | **Sky** | Society | **Tech** | **Trib**

> "But immediately after the suffering of those days, ... the powers of the heavens will be shaken." (Matthew 24:29)

Jesus tells us in his Olivet Discourse that during the tribulation period, "the powers of the heavens will be shaken." The word *powers* can mean the inherent power that things in the heavens possess, like the power of the sun. It can also mean the powers of the angels and the powers resting in an army. The word *shaken* means to shake down, overthrow, or to agitate.

During the tribulation period, some really freaky things are going to happen in the heavens. The sixth seal judgment speaks of the stars of heaven falling to earth like figs falling from a shaken tree. This could literally be stars falling. Perhaps it would look like an intense meter shower to us. In the Bible, stars can also refer to angels. So, it could be a reference to fallen angels losing their authority and power and falling to earth. We'll talk more about the war that happens in heaven in Sign #148 - War In Heaven.

The sixth seal also states the sky will recede like a scroll rolling up. Talk about shaking the heavens. Now, some Bible scholars think that might be describing a nuclear bomb exploding and how that appears in the sky. Perhaps, but what I find interesting is what happens afterward. We're told the people on earth want to hide from Jesus who sits on the throne. Now, to me that implies the sky literally recedes and the barrier that's been keeping us from seeing into heaven is removed. How else would they see Jesus in heaven?

The seventh seal judgment starts off with utter silence in heaven before a censor filled with fire is thrown down to earth and creates a great noise and thunder. Then, after the fifth seal judgment, seven thunders utter something that John wasn't allowed to write down for us. Have you ever experienced thunder that you could feel, shaking the walls of your house?

Fulfillment - How might we see what's depicted in the Bible regarding the heavens shaking? If the stars actually fall, we'd be able to see that with our naked eye. The thunder we're familiar with is powerful enough to shake walls, so we'd feel and hear that for sure.

What if it's angels getting their power revoked and then falling from heaven? Might the people left behind on earth after the rapture be able to witness these events in heaven before the fallen angels arrive on earth? I think so. Let's consider radio astronomy.

Space is a vacuum and as such sound waves don't have anything to travel through, like air. So, we can't hear anything from space from a sound wave. But we can hear space through radio waves. The first radio wave from an astronomical object was detected in 1933. Today, scientists use radio telescopes and arrays of them like the Very Large Array, to observe and listen to space.[15] Using this technology, I have a feeling they'll be able to see and hear what's going on in the heavens before the aftermath arrives on earth. I also think people will be able to use radio telescopes to detect the eerie silence in heaven.

If the sky receding like a scroll is the result of a nuclear weapon that's perhaps detonated in the atmosphere, that's a modern weapon of war that was first used in 1945. It wouldn't have been possible to blow up the sky until recently.

Today Is Different - A technology that makes today different is sonification astronomy. It's enabling us to hear space in a whole new way. NASA just started doing this in the past few years. They are taking images from telescopes like the Hubble and using data sonification to translate the images into sound. They've got a website with a bunch of space objects like galaxies and black holes that you can listen to.[16]

https://science.nasa.gov/mission/hubble/multimedia/sonifications/

Here's something else exciting. NASA recently released a sonification of the Perseus galaxy cluster. While space is essentially a vacuum, it isn't everywhere. A galaxy cluster is enveloped by a lot of gas that provides a medium for sound waves to travel through. Scientists were able to record actual sound waves from Perseus and use sonification to make them audible to the human ear.[17]

While we can't see or hear most events happening in space with our naked eye, today we have the ability to both see and hear the heavens through deep space telescopes, radio astronomy, and sonification astronomy. While we might not be able to see the powers in the heavens shake during the tribulation period, we certainly might be able to hear it.

Additional Scriptures: Hebrews 12:25-26. Isaiah 13:13. Joel 3:16. Luke 21:11, 25; 23:44-45. Revelation 1:20; 6:12-16; 8:1-5; 10:1-7; 11:15-19.

#147 - THE BLACK SUN

Anti | DD | Earth | Gov | Israel | **Jesus** | Leader | **Sky** | Society | **Tech** | **Trib**

> "But immediately after the suffering of those days, the sun will be darkened, the moon will not give its light, the stars will fall from the sky." (Matthew 24:29)

In this verse from the Olivet Discourse, Jesus provides us another glimpse into the future during the tribulation period. Here, we're told the heavens are going to get dark.

During the sixth seal judgment, the sun becomes black, and the moon becomes like blood. The fourth trumpet judgment involves one third of the sun, moon, and stars being stricken and darkened. The Bible tells us that event results in one third of the day and one third of the night being dark. When the bottomless pit is opened, the smoke that rises from it darkens the sun. If that's not enough, the fifth bowl judgment is a plague of darkness.

Fulfillment - Did you know that stars are disappearing today? When massive stars die it's because their fuel runs out and they explode in a violent supernova before forming a neutron star or black hole. What's been discovered recently is that some massive stars are vanishing without a trace. Scientists published their findings in May 2024.[18] They've documented 800 cases over the past 70 years.[19] Scientists believe it's because these stars collapse so completely that nothing is able to escape and be visible in a supernova. They've observed at least one such star that they know used to exist, didn't supernova, and now there's a black hole where it used to be.[20]

I think it's certainly possible that stars falling from the sky or being stricken is a reference to this phenomenon. Perhaps God just speaks a word, and thousands of stars just go dark and become black holes. We now have the technology that astronomers will be able to witness that.

Today Is Different - The Bible tells us that the sun and moon endure all generations, so it doesn't seem to make sense that part of the sun and moon suddenly don't exist or function like they always have. And what would make only one third of the day dark? If one third of the sun was stricken, then the entire day and entire night would be darker.

One thing that stands out today is that we have the technology to block out the sun ourselves. I think it's in the realm of feasibility that God's not the one who supernaturally darkens the sun during the tribulation, at least not each time it's mentioned. It could be humanity that does it.

It's called solar geoengineering, and it's in the news today. Switzerland proposed in early 2024 that the UN form a group to explore using technology to prevent the sun from changing the climate. The technology would block the sun with reflective materials. The solar radiation would bounce off of it back into space and not hit the earth. It would theoretically make the earth's climate cooler.[21] The UN didn't agree to do anything because it was too controversial.

Just because the UN isn't exploring this doesn't mean it's not advancing. There are all sorts of ways this could be achieved today. Reflective objects in space, aerosols in the atmosphere, and reflective materials on the earth's surface. There are startup companies in both the US and Israel working on this.[22] Billionaires George Soros and Bill Gates are pouring money into it.[23]

So, here's a theory. After the rapture, we know the weather is going to get hot during the tribulation period. I think governments will decide to deploy something into space or the atmosphere that they can turn on and off to block the sun's rays. It would also block visibility to the stars. This type of technology would explain how the darkness only affects one third of the day or night and one third of what can be seen in the sky.

Additional Scriptures: Acts 2:16-21. Amos 8:9. Exodus 10:21-29. Isaiah 13:10. Joel 2:10, 31. Luke 21:25; 23:44-45. Psalm 72:5; 89:37. Revelation 6:12-16; 7:16; 8:12; 9:2; 16:10-11.

#148 - WAR IN HEAVEN

Anti | DD | Earth | Gov | Israel | Jesus | Leader | Sky | Society | Tech | Trib

> And war broke out in heaven: Michael and his angels fought with the dragon; and the dragon and his angels fought, but they did not prevail, nor was a place found for them in heaven any longer. So the great dragon was cast out, that serpent of old, called the Devil and Satan, who deceives the whole world; he was cast to the earth, and his angels were cast out with him. (Revelation 12:7-9 NKJV)

In Sign #146 - The Heavens Shake we learned that Jesus told us the heavens would be shaken during the tribulation period. Here, we see one of the reasons why. War breaks out in heaven. Michael and the holy angels war against Satan and his evil fallen angels. The result is Satan's defeat and permanent ousting from heaven.

I have a feeling many of you are wondering how this is feasible because you think angels are just spirit beings that don't consist of physical matter. That is not biblical. Throughout the entire Bible we see that angels are physical beings with powers that are honestly difficult to comprehend. Let's consider some examples.

Two angels appeared with the Lord when he met with Abraham. Abraham described them as looking like men. They all ate a meal together. That requires a body that functions with some similarity to ours. Those two angels then saved Lot and his daughters before God destroyed Sodom and Gomorrah. The men of the city were so enamored with the angels that they wanted to have sex with them. Those angels obviously had a body and were physically attractive. The angels were able to strike the men of the city with blindness.

How about the angel that killed 185,000 Assyrians in one evening because King Hezekiah prayed for help? That angel was clearly wielding more than a sword.

We can't forget about Satan. The apostle Paul tells us that Satan is able to transform himself into an angel of the light. That word *transforms* means to change the figure of or to assume one's appearance. Now, that's just freaky to think about. Is it just Satan who has this shape-shifting ability or do other angels as well?

As you can see, angels are not intangible balls of light or energy. They are as real as you and I.

During the tribulation period, this war in heaven is going to spill over onto earth. In addition to the unholy angels being banished to earth, we're told the bottomless pit is going to be opened and that the angel Apollyon will be let loose along with a horde of demonic creatures. Four angels that have been bound at the Euphrates river are also freed. They are the ones who round up the army of 200 million for the final war against Jesus. And we mustn't forget that Satan is going to be worshiped by almost everyone on earth and gives the Antichrist his power.

Fulfillment - This war in heaven started a very long time ago. Satan sinned sometime before he convinced Eve to disobey God and eat from the Tree of the Knowledge of Good and Evil. During Jesus's first coming, he mentioned that he saw Satan fall like lightning from heaven. With a war that's been raging for thousands of years, is there any tangible evidence of it here on earth?

Consider all the weird stuff that happens on the planet that we can't explain. How about some of the crop circles? Consider events that have a demonic nature. How about cattle mutilations or demonic possessions?

Consider events that involve something high tech that's beyond any capabilities any government has today. How about a UFO sighting by an experienced US Navy pilot? Consider events that are truly frightening. How about a UFO abduction?

The National UFO Reporting Center is celebrating their fiftieth anniversary this year, 2024.[24] During that time, they've processed over 170,000 UFO sightings. In 1990, they received 346 reports, while in 2022, they got 5,035.[25]

The Pentagon has an office for investigating potential UFOs, or UAPs as they're now called, the All-Domain Anomaly Resolution Office. That alone should reveal something. In 2021, they had a list of 144 sightings over a 17-year period. In 2022 they received 366 sighting reports. They're still trying to figure out the origin of 171 of those because they "appear to have demonstrated unusual flight characteristics or performance capabilities, and require further analysis."[26]

Perhaps you recall that US Air Force veteran David Grusch testified to congress in July 2023. He accused the Pentagon of covering up decades of programs to reverse engineer technology that had been retrieved from UFO crash sites as well as the non-human biologics of the pilots.[27] Non-human. Let that sink in.

In April 2024, Tucker Carlson was a guest on Joe Rogan's podcast. They talked about UFOs. Keep in mind Tucker has interviewed many people who were eyewitnesses to sightings. Here's what Tucker said: "They're from here and they've been here for thousands of years." He described them as "spiritual entities" that defy conventional scientific explanations and operate outside the bounds of observable nature.[28] Wow! That certainly sounds like angels or demons, doesn't it?

Don't let the media or Hollywood fool you into thinking "aliens" don't exist or that they come from another planet far, far away. They go by another name to those of us familiar with God's Word. They are angels, fallen angels, demons, or evil beings that the fallen angels have bioengineered and who do their bidding.

Today Is Different - I have to mention another Jonathan Cahn book that exposes what makes today so different than any other time. It's his book *The Return Of The Gods*.[29] He reveals how Jesus's teaching of the unclean spirit who returns has manifested today. The biblical account tells us that when an unclean spirit goes out of a person, he looks for rest and can't find any. So, he returns to his former house, finding it put in order. Then the spirit goes and gets seven other spirits more wicked than himself, and they all dwell in there.

This can be applied to any nation that has known God and turned away. A person or nation who has emptied itself of God will not remain empty. The demons will come and inhabit that space. It was a chilling read about the very real war that's taking place in the realm where the angels and demons currently dwell.

It's also interesting to note that it certainly seems like most of the government whistleblowers regarding UFO encounters are pilots. Why is it they are being targeted? Do these beings want to be seen or chased and know it's going to take a person in a jet to even spot them? Or perhaps we're just seeing some of this war in the heavens cross into our dimension from time to time.

<u>Additional Scriptures:</u> 2 Corinthians 11:14. 2 Kings 19:35. Daniel 10:12-13; 12:1. Ephesians 6:12. Ezekiel 28:11-19. Genesis 3:1-6; 18-19. Luke 10:18; 21:25. Matthew 12:43-45; 24:29. Revelation 9:2-11, 14-19; 13:4; 16:13-14.

#149 – POLAR OPPOSITE – NEW HEAVENS

Anti | DD | **<u>Earth</u>** | Gov | Israel | **<u>Jesus</u>** | **<u>Leader</u>** | **<u>Sky</u>** | Society | Tech | Trib

> I saw a new heaven and a new earth, for the first heaven and the first earth have passed away, and the sea is no more. I saw the holy city, New Jerusalem, coming down out of heaven from God, prepared like a bride adorned for her husband. ... Her light was like a most precious stone, like a jasper stone, clear as crystal; having a great and high wall with twelve gates, and at the gates twelve angels, and names written on them, which are the names of the twelve tribes of the children of Israel. ... The wall of the city had twelve foundations, and on them twelve names of the twelve Apostles of the Lamb. ... The city is square. Its length is as great as its width. He measured the city with the reed: twelve thousand twelve stadia. Its length, width, and height are equal. Its wall is one hundred forty-four cubits, by the measure of a man, that is, of an angel. The construction of its wall was jasper. The city was pure gold, like pure glass. The foundations of the city's wall were adorned with all kinds of precious stones. ... The twelve gates were twelve pearls. Each one of the gates was made of one pearl. The street of the city was pure gold, like transparent glass. ... The city has no need for the sun or moon to shine, for the very glory of God illuminated it and its lamp is the Lamb. ... Its gates will in no way be shut by day (for there will be no night there). (Revelation 21:1-2, 11-12, 14, 16-19, 21, 23, 25)

Throughout this chapter we've looked at signs in the heavens. Frightening things that are going to happen in the heavens and to the heavenly objects during the tribulation. This sign is what I call a polar opposite. It's meant to illustrate how far away we currently are from the life we believers are going to live during Jesus's reign on earth in the millennial kingdom. Recall from Sign #6 - The Point Of No Return, that God only lets evil progress so far before he intervenes.

In the verses above, we learn that God will create a new heaven and a new earth. Jesus said that heaven and earth would pass away in his Olivet Discourse. This is the ultimate fulfillment of that sign of his second coming. There's a vivid depiction of the holy city, New Jerusalem, which is currently in heaven. It has streets of gold, foundations of precious gems, and pearl gates. It's going to come down to the earth. If we translate its measurements into something we can understand, it equals a 1,400-mile cube.[30] There won't be any more separation between heaven and earth in the future. Jesus told us in the Olivet Discourse that even all the holy angels are going to come with him at his second coming.

Fulfillment - So, how far away are we? Well, the current Jerusalem in Israel doesn't look anything like what's pictured here, does it? Even the most opulent cities on earth don't compare with the glory of New Jerusalem.

A fun way to consider just how opposite we are is to contemplate what the worst-case scenarios might look like and see just how close we are to them.

Worst case, God turns off all the lights. The sun, moon, and stars all go dark. There's a darkness you can even feel, just like what the Egyptians experienced during the Israelite exodus. Well, this hasn't happened. The closest we can get to this and be outside is during a total solar eclipse. But even then, the stars are still visible. Those only last a few minutes and then it's bright again. Perhaps a prolonged power outage might help us understand what this would be like. While we haven't gotten close to this worst case, it's going to actually happen in the tribulation period.

Worst case, God separates the veil between heaven and earth so that people can see God, yet people still refuse to turn to God. This totally happened 2,000 years ago. Jesus literally stepped out of heaven and came down here to live with us. We as a society rejected him and crucified him. It's not going to be any different during the tribulation period when people see Jesus on his throne. We're told they hide in caves. Right before Jesus's second coming, they'll all gather to war against him in hopes they'll be able to defeat him. We've hit this worst case.

Worst case, the unholy angels are here among us and wage war against us. This is true for today. This war between us and Satan started in the garden of Eden, and it's still going. We're at the worst case here too.

Worst case, the entire planet is destroyed by things falling from the sky, like asteroids. Ok, this one hasn't happened to us. We're not near this worst case. But it's going to happen during the tribulation period, and we know that's not very far off.

Today Is Different - So, what do you think? Is today different? Are you seeing foreshadows today of events that take place in the heavens during the tribulation period?

Additional Scriptures: 2 Peter 3:13. Exodus 10:21-29. Isaiah 65:17. Matthew 24:35; 25:31. Revelation 6:14-17; 16:10; 19:11-19.

CHAPTER 17 - THE RAPTURE

#150 - THE RAPTURE

Anti | DD | **Earth** | Gov | Israel | **Jesus** | Leader | **Sky** | Society | Tech | Trib

> But we don't want you to be ignorant, brothers, concerning those who have fallen asleep, so that you don't grieve like the rest, who have no hope. For if we believe that Jesus died and rose again, even so God will bring with him those who have fallen asleep in Jesus. For this we tell you by the word of the Lord, that we who are alive, who are left until the coming of the Lord, will in no way precede those who have fallen asleep. For the Lord himself will descend from heaven with a shout, with the voice of the archangel and with God's trumpet. The dead in Christ will rise first, then we who are alive, who are left, will be **caught up** together with them in the clouds to meet the Lord in the air. So we will be with the Lord forever. Therefore comfort one another with these words. (1 Thessalonians 4:13-18)

Notice the phrase "caught up." In Latin it's translated *rapio*. It's where we get the English word *rapture* from. This Scripture tells us about the rapture. The word *rapture* means to be caught up, snatched away, seized, or carried off to another place of existence. It's Jesus's promise to remove all people who've put their faith in him from the planet before the Antichrist's reign and all the horrible judgments of the tribulation period. You can read a lot more about the rapture in my book *Rapture 911: What To Do If You're Left Behind*.

Jesus will come down from heaven and gather believers in the clouds with him. It tells us why Jesus takes them. It's because they believed "Jesus died and rose again." The people who will be taken are described as "alive" and "who are left until the coming of the Lord."

They aren't going to be the only ones Jesus takes. We also learn that "the dead in Christ" will be gathered too. These are people who had put their faith in Jesus but already died. Death is also referenced in the Scripture as "fallen asleep." They died between the resurrection of Jesus and the rapture. Yes, they're already with Jesus in the present heaven. However, this is when they get their new body, which you'll see clearly in a bit.

This Scripture also gives us a glimpse of what everyone gathered will be doing. It says they "will be with the Lord forever." That means from this event forward they'll be with Jesus, the Lord, for all eternity.

Many say that Jesus never taught about the rapture. Well, let's see the truth for ourselves. Jesus is the one speaking in the verses below.

> "Don't let your heart be troubled. Believe in God. Believe also in me. In my Father's house are many homes. If it weren't so, I would have told you. I am going to prepare a place for you. If I go and prepare a place for you, I will come again and will receive you to myself; that where I am, you may be there also." (John 14:1-3)

Jesus told his disciples to believe in God and in "me" which is himself. Then he says there are "many homes" in his "father's house." That's God's house. He was leaving to go "prepare a place" for them there. We know that God's house is in the present heaven. So, Jesus was going to the present heaven, and he would return to get them at a later time. This was the next thing Jesus wanted his disciples to be expecting, his future return to get them.

The phrase "receive you to myself" means to take to one's own self. That's literally what happens in the rapture. Jesus will take the believers to himself. He will do this so that believers can be where he is. Jesus is currently in the present heaven. In the rapture, Jesus will meet the believers in the clouds and take them to himself in heaven.

Let's consider if he's talking about the second coming instead of the rapture. At Jesus's second coming, believers will already be with him in the present heaven and will be going with him to earth. Jesus won't be receiving or taking anyone to himself at his second coming. Also remember that once Jesus returns to earth physically at the second coming that he sets up his millennial kingdom. Then after that creates a new earth. Jesus doesn't ever leave earth again and go back to heaven. That's because heaven will essentially become earth. Jesus is clearly talking about the rapture in this Scripture, not his second coming.

This Scripture applies to anyone who puts their faith in Jesus. If you put your faith in Jesus, you get this promise too. Jesus has a place prepared just for you in the present heaven. There you have it, Jesus most certainly taught about the rapture! Multiple times he told his followers to be watching for his return. He even told us what to be watching for.

Here's another description of the rapture from Paul the apostle.

> Now I say this, brothers, that flesh and blood can't inherit God's Kingdom; neither does the perishable inherit imperishable. Behold, I tell

> you a mystery. We will not all sleep, but we will all be changed, in a moment, in the twinkling of an eye, at the last trumpet. For the trumpet will sound and the dead will be raised incorruptible, and we will be changed. For this perishable body must become imperishable, and this mortal must put on immortality. But when this perishable body will have become imperishable, and this mortal will have put on immortality, then what is written will happen: "Death is swallowed up in victory." (1 Corinthians 15:50-54)

"Flesh and blood" is a reference to our current bodies. They're temporary and not eternal. That's why they can't live in God's kingdom, which is heaven. Paul tells us not everyone will "sleep" which means some people won't die. Instead, those people who won't die will be changed in a moment. This will happen at the sound of a trumpet. That trumpet was mentioned in the first Scripture we looked at too.

We learn some extra details about what happens to the people Jesus gathers. They get new immortal bodies that are suitable for living in heaven for eternity. In a moment, our bodies that decay and eventually die will be transformed into immortal bodies which live forever. This new body applies to believers in heaven as well. The "dead in Christ" from 1 Thessalonians 4:16 are described in these verses as "the dead will be raised incorruptible."

Don't worry, the Old Testament believers who are in the present heaven get a new body too, just not until the second coming (Daniel 12:1-3, 13). Anyone who misses the rapture yet makes it alive through the tribulation period as a believer will also get their new body at the second coming (Revelation 20:4-6). Everyone else, like any unbeliever throughout history, or people who die during the millennial kingdom, will all get their new body after Jesus's 1,000-year reign on earth (Revelation 20:5).

While we're talking about the rapture, I'd also like to address the belief that some people have about a partial rapture. Some think that only truly faithful Christians will be taken by Jesus in the rapture. They get this from the parable of the ten virgins (Matthew 25:1-13). Remember in that parable that only five of the virgins had enough oil in their lamps and were ready for the wedding. The other five ran out of oil, had to go find some, and then got left out of the wedding. These people are assuming the oil is a reference to good works or faith. It's not. Just think about that for a second. Does it jive with the rest of the Bible's teaching on how we're saved? Nope. Our salvation is not about works. We are saved by God's grace through our faith in what Jesus did (Ephesians 2:8-9).

The oil is a reference to the Holy Spirit. We're told that King David was anointed with oil and then received the Holy Spirit (1 Samuel 16:13). We're also told that the Spirit of the Lord was upon Jesus because he was the anointed one (Luke 4:18). Then we also learn that the anointing believers receive abides in them and teaches them all things (1 John 2:27). That's the Holy Spirit (John 14:26). The virgins in the parable that entered the wedding were true believers because they were sealed with the Holy Spirit. The other virgins didn't have a real relationship with Jesus and never received the Holy Spirit. That's why Jesus told them that he didn't know them when they tried to enter the wedding.

That brings me to my next point about the rapture. Only those who have put their faith in Jesus for salvation—believing that he is the Son of God, died for their sins, and rose from the grave—will be included in this most spectacular event. It's not a "bring a plus one" type of wedding invitation. You don't get to bring your family and friends along. Everyone is invited, but only those with the Holy Spirit will get in.

GOD'S PURPOSE FOR THE RAPTURE

There are many purposes for the rapture. Let's consider a few of them.

It's one last sign for unbelievers before the tribulation events start to kick in. It's God proving one more time that he exists and that he's faithful to do what he says he's going to do. Even if none of the rapture events are witnessed by unbelievers left behind, the disappearance of all those people is certainly going to make some of them think it was the rapture. Many of those people will come to believe and be saved.

In fact, the Bible reveals that this may be one of the reasons that all of Israel becomes saved. Israel will be blind until the fullness of the gentiles has come (Luke 21:24, Romans 11:25). That's a reference to the rapture.

The rapture is also protecting believers from God's wrath as noted in the Scriptures below.

> For God didn't appoint us to wrath, but to the obtaining of salvation through our Lord Jesus Christ, who died for us, that, whether we wake or sleep, we should live together with him. (1 Thessalonians 5:9-10)

> "Because you kept my command to endure, I also will keep you from the hour of testing which is to come on the whole world, to test those who dwell on the earth." (Revelation 3:10)

Jesus is the one speaking in Revelation 3:10. One of the meanings of the phrase *will keep* is to guard, to cause one to escape in safety. Believers won't be kept alive on earth and protected through the tribulation, like Noah was through the flood. No, at the rapture believers will be removed from earth. Like Lot was removed from the cities of Sodom and Gomorrah before judgment came against them.

The wrath that's mentioned is clearly portrayed in the Bible as the tribulation period (Revelation 6:16-17, Mark 13:19), otherwise known as the day of the Lord (1 Thessalonians 5:1-4), Jacob's trouble (Jeremiah 30:7), and a time of trouble (Daniel 12:1).

Consider God's behavior in the past when similar judgments happened. You know that Noah was delivered from God's wrath during the flood (Genesis 6-8). We're told in the *Ancient Book of Jasher* (not biblical, but a historical account) that all the other believers died before the flood. Methuselah died right before Noah and his family entered the ark (*Jasher* 5:5, 6:1). We also know that Lot and his daughters were delivered from God's wrath upon Sodom and Gomorrah. Remember that two angels arrived to escort them out of the city (Genesis 19:1-29).

Jesus already took God's wrath for our sin upon himself when he died on the cross. The church is referred to as the body of Christ with Jesus as the head (1 Corinthians 12:12-27, Colossians 1:15-18). The body of Christ isn't going to experience God's wrath a second time. Jesus suffered once for all (1 Peter 3:18). Thus, we believers have nothing to fear regarding the tribulation events and the wrath to come.

This is perhaps the most important reason for the rapture. It's also the time for Jesus to be glorified and to be admired among all of those who believe in him (Revelation 4-5, 1 Thessalonians 1:10). The people who are raptured will be in heaven to witness Jesus receiving all of this glory. While the raptured people are in heaven, one event they partake in is the wedding of the Lamb (2 Corinthians 11:2, Revelation 19:7-8). They are celebrating Jesus being married to the believers who were raptured and resurrected at the rapture, his bride. If we look up synonyms for *husband*, we get words like safeguard, steward, preserve, and hold fast. Jesus will indeed be protecting everyone he gathers to himself at the rapture.

In these verses below, "he had taken the book" and the "Lamb" both refer to Jesus. The "twenty-four elders" and "the saints" are believers who are in heaven after the rapture.

> Now when he had taken the book, the four living creatures and the twenty-four elders fell down before the Lamb, each one having a harp, and golden bowls full of incense, which are the prayers of the saints. They sang a new song, saying, "You are worthy to take the book and to open its seals, for you were killed, and bought us for God with your blood out of every tribe, language, people, and nation, and made us kings and priests to our God; and we will reign on the earth." I looked, and I heard something like a voice of many angels around the throne, the living creatures, and the elders. The number of them was ten thousands of ten thousands, and thousands of thousands, saying with a loud voice, "Worthy is the Lamb who has been killed to receive the power, wealth, wisdom, strength, honor, glory, and blessing!" I heard every created thing which is in heaven, on the earth, under the earth, on the sea, and everything in them, saying, "To him who sits on the throne and to the Lamb be the blessing, the honor, the glory, and the dominion, forever and ever! Amen!" (Revelation 5:8-13)

Did you notice how many holy angels are present to see Jesus in all his glory? If you multiplied the ten thousands together, it'd be a hundred million. But it's thousands times thousands more than that. It's hard to even fathom a choir that size! It's like if you looked up at the night sky and all the stars started singing. But even then, did you know that in a place far away from city lights, on a moonless night, that you can only see a couple thousand stars?[1] So it truly is hard to imagine.

RAPTURE PRECEDENTS

The millions of people who will disappear in the rapture aren't the only people who will have disappeared throughout time. The Bible tells us of a couple men who had the pleasure of being raptured, per se. Let's take a look at their stories and learn why God took them so that we can further understand the rapture.

The first person God removed from the earth was Enoch. He was the great-grandfather of Noah. He preached righteousness and warned about God's coming judgment (Jude 1:14-15). Enoch lived during a time that's very similar to today. He lived right before a period of judgment, the flood.

We know it was a time of unprecedented wickedness on the earth.

Every thought of man was "continually only evil" (Genesis 6:5). Enoch was different than almost everyone else who lived during his time. He walked with God (Genesis 5:22-24). "Walk" in this instance reflects how Enoch behaved. He pursued God. He had a close relationship with God. Because of his special relationship with God, the Scriptures tell us God took him. He was caught up into heaven, raptured. That's right, Enoch didn't die.

The second person God removed from the earth was Elijah. Like Enoch, Elijah was also very special to God. He was a man of God (1 Kings 17:24). To be "a man of" something means you reflect or represent that something. Elijah reflected and represented God. He had such a close relationship with God that he was even able to pray for fire from heaven and God answered and did it (2 Kings 1:10).

Elijah lived during a time of terrible persecution against God's people. He stood against evil King Ahab and perhaps Ahab's even more evil wife Queen Jezebel. Once Elijah completed the work God set out for him, God took him up to heaven in quite a spectacular fashion. A chariot of fire drawn by horses of fire came out of heaven, picked him up, then went back into heaven in a whirlwind (2 Kings 2:11). Elisha, his successor, witnessed the whole event. Can you imagine how cool that must have been?

Noah and Lot are two more examples (Genesis 6-8, Genesis 19:1-29). God protected them from his wrath. And Jesus even referred to them as examples for our time in the Olivet Discourse. Noah and Lot were both taken into salvation while everyone else was left behind for judgment. Noah was supernaturally protected from the flood. God was the one who closed the door of the ark after all. Lot and his daughters were supernaturally protected from God's rain of fire and brimstone on Sodom and Gomorrah. God sent two angels to rescue them before judgment came.

Something interesting to think about regarding all of these men is that they all knew beforehand that they were about to be rescued. We touched on this in Sign #119 - Prophets Warn About The Future.

> Surely the Lord GOD will do nothing, unless he reveals his secret to his servants the prophets. (Amos 3:7)

An angel told Enoch that he was required in heaven (*Ancient Book of Jasher* 3:23-24 a historical account, not biblical). The day that Elijah was raptured, he knew it was coming. As did Elisha and two other groups of prophets (2 Kings 2:1-18). God told Noah 120 years beforehand that the flood was coming. When the ark was completed and the day got closer, God gave Noah seven days advanced notice (Genesis 6:13, 7:1-4). Lot knew beforehand too because the angels came to him the night before and even let him warn his sons-in-law before they rescued him out of the city the next morning (Genesis 19:12-13). Abraham knew about Sodom and Gomorrah prior to its destruction too. God and the two angels shared a meal with Abraham the evening prior. God said he didn't want to withhold what he was about to do from Abraham (Genesis 18:16-33).

So, do you think we're going to get a heads up before the rapture happens too? Let's talk about that.

WILL THE RAPTURE BE WITNESSED?

This is something really fascinating to consider. Will the people who are alive on earth witness any of the rapture events? Will we all somehow know beforehand that it's about to happen?

We know the rapture event is going to be loud since there's the Lord's shout, the voice of an archangel, and the trumpet of God (1 Thessalonians 4:16). When Moses and the Israelites heard the Lord and the trumpet of God at Mount Sinai, they were all terrified because it was so loud (Exodus 19:16-19, 20:18). Who is going to hear all of those things at the rapture? Just the believers included in the rapture? Or do you think the entire world might hear it? The Bible doesn't say. The more I think about this though, the more I think it's going to be heard by everyone. I don't think God wants the rapture to be a secret. His heart is after every person's soul. Seems to me that he'd want everyone to have one last opportunity to be saved before the horrible events of the tribulation period.

Let's explore more reasons I've come to believe this. We're told that people who are alive at the rapture are changed in a moment from their current body into an immortal body (1 Corinthians 15:52). Well, for some reason we've applied that specific change happening in an instant to the entire rapture event happening in an instant. Should we do that?

I read an eye-opening article written by Jeff Van Hatten about this in the July 2023 *The Prophecy Watcher* magazine.[2] Scripture says the "dead in Christ will rise first" (1 Thessalonians 4:16). This implies there's an order of events and illustrates it doesn't all happen instantly at the same time.

Van Hatten does a word study to explain why he believes people are going to see these resurrected believers before they and the believers who are alive are all taken up into the clouds to meet Jesus. The phrase "will rise" comes from the Greek word *anistēmi*. One of its meanings is to arise and enter into conversation with someone. In 1 Corinthians 15:52 we're told the dead "will be raised." That comes from the Greek word *egeirō* and one of its meanings is to cause to appear before the public.

Wow! Just contemplate that for a few moments. Can you imagine if the dead believers rise from the grave, appear in public, and start talking to people?

Do you know there's actually a precedent for it? It happened at Jesus's resurrection. We're told that many of the dead believers were raised and appeared to many people in Jerusalem (Matthew 27:50-53). You know what else? Every resurrection in the Bible was witnessed.[3] None of them were a secret.

Just think of the resurrections that Jesus performed. He raised Jairus's daughter, and Peter, James, John, and the girl's parents all saw it (Luke 8:51-56). He resurrected the son of a widow, who was in a coffin, in the presence of a large crowd (Luke 7:11-17). Then he resurrected Lazarus when his disciples and a crowd were gathered at Lazarus's tomb (John 11:11-46). And, of course, Jesus was resurrected and seen by all the disciples, the apostle Paul, and a crowd of over 500 (1 Corinthians 15:1-8).

We should also consider that the other rapture or rapture-like events in the Bible were witnessed too. The people didn't just vanish. The prophet Elijah was taken into heaven by a fiery horse drawn chariot. He was seen by his successor Elisha and likely a group of 50 other prophets (2 Kings 2:11-15). When Jesus ascended into heaven, he was watched intently by the disciples. Jesus didn't just disappear (Acts 1:9-11). There's also Enoch (Genesis 5:24). The *Ancient Book of Jasher* (not a biblical book, more like a historical account) tells us that Enoch was seen by 800,000 people when he was taken by God into heaven (*Jasher* 3:27-29, 32-36).

In an article on his website, Van Hatten also explains that Moses on Mount Sinai is another example and a pattern of the rapture. [4] Consider that God came down from heaven to Mount Sinai. He met Moses on top of the mountain, in the clouds. All the Israelites watched Moses climb the mountain and vanish into the cloud cover (Exodus 19:16-20).

https://raptureparty.net/2022/11/11/the-rapture-part-seventeen/

Okay, so it seems like this could be legit. Doesn't it to you? I told you it was going to be interesting to think about! How do you think people would react to seeing their dead Christian loved ones alive again and talking to them?

I think some would have even more faith than they already do. Believers who are rapture skeptics might change their mind and earn a crown for looking forward to Jesus coming.

Many unbelievers would definitely come to believe in Jesus after listening to the testimony of a resurrected loved one. There are lots of people today that don't think there's life after death. Wouldn't this be the ultimate proof of God's existence?

But then I think of Abraham in paradise and his response to the rich man begging him to send someone to tell his relatives about hell. Abraham told him that even if someone rose from the dead that they wouldn't believe (Luke 16:19-31). Look at how many people don't believe that Jesus rose from the grave. So, then I have a sinking feeling that many people would scoff at it. They wouldn't believe it's real. And, if the rapture is visible to everyone, Satan certainly isn't going to want people to believe what they're seeing. He's going to be pushing the biggest lie to explain it away. Scoffers are going to think it's something like a highly sophisticated technological feat using advanced AI and volumetric imaging.

And then there are others who would just freak out. They might think it's the zombie apocalypse. That the resurrection wasn't by the power of God, but by science or a virus. I imagine they'd be so full of fear that they wouldn't even listen to any of the resurrected people.

If this is what's going to happen at the rapture, how long do you suppose the resurrected believers would be out milling among the people on earth? Well, Jesus was on earth for 40 days after his resurrection, meeting with the disciples before he went up into heaven (Acts 1:1-3). I wonder if that's when the other people who were resurrected with him ascended too. I can only imagine the volume of evangelism that would be done by these people if that were the case. We know that people from every tribe, nation, language, and people are included in the rapture (Revelation 5:9). Perhaps this is how God accomplishes that?

Now, let's consider all the believers floating up to heaven into the clouds. Do you think that part of the rapture will be witnessed by the unbelievers left behind on earth? There's no biblical evidence that points to the raptured leaving a pile of ashes or their clothes behind. None of the men who were rapture precedents, that we considered in the prior section, left anything behind. Except Elijah who dropped his mantle. But I believe he did that on purpose so Elisha could have it (2 Kings 2:13). All of them had witnesses to their being taken up into heaven.

Even if none of the rapture event is visible to unbelievers who will be left behind, I do believe there will be evidence for them that the rapture occurred. The *Left Behind* novels portray this. The dead bodies of believers will disappear because they got resurrected. So, that means some empty graves, empty urns, and empty morgues. Seems like that'll be tricky for Satan to concoct a lie about.

The Bible tells us about another interesting event that happens after the rapture. Every creature in heaven, on earth, under the earth, and in the sea sings praises (Revelation 5:13). The party and celebration aren't limited to heaven. It's happening on earth and under earth. Which implies hell, as well. It says every creature worships Jesus. That word *creature* means created thing.

Do you think God will cause unbelievers who are left behind, or those who are already dead in the present hell, or even the fallen angels and demons to spontaneously shout out in praise? And what about the animals and birds and such? Is God going to open their mouth like he did for Balaam's donkey (Numbers 22:28)? It's a curious mystery indeed! What will the left behind make of all these signs?

TIMING OF THE RAPTURE

There's much confusion today regarding the timing of the rapture. Some think it happens before the tribulation, some say it happens after, some believe it'll be on a Jewish feast day, etc. So, let's clear all this up.

The rapture is an imminent event. That means it can happen at any time. There aren't any specific things that must occur beforehand. Jesus told us multiple times in the Olivet Discourse that we wouldn't know the day or hour and that it'd be at a time we didn't expect (Mark 13:32, Matthew 24:36, 42, 44). As we've discussed throughout this book, this is why we're supposed to be looking for and watching all the signs (Titus 2:13).

The rapture happens before the tribulation period and thus the second coming of Jesus. It's what's referred to as pre-tribulational. This is because believers are not meant for God's wrath (1 Thessalonians 5:9-10). We started discussing this in an earlier section of this chapter. Here's some additional support for this viewpoint.

As a believer, you're an ambassador of heaven (Ephesians 6:20). You reside on earth, but your true home is heaven. When war breaks out between nations, ambassadors of those nations get recalled back to their home country so that they'll be safe. That's what God is doing in the rapture, calling all ambassadors home.

We also know that in order for the Antichrist to rise to power that Christians can't be around. We'd totally get in the way of that by calling him out and hindering his agenda (Isaiah 59:19). The apostle Paul explains that to us in the Scripture below.

> Now, dear brothers and sisters, let us clarify some things about the coming of our Lord Jesus Christ and how we will be gathered to meet him. Don't be so easily shaken or alarmed by those who say that the **day of the Lord** has already begun. Don't believe them, even if they claim to have had a spiritual vision, a revelation, or a letter supposedly from us. Don't be fooled by what they say. For that **day will not come until there is a great rebellion against God** and the **man of lawlessness is revealed**—the one who brings destruction. He will exalt himself and defy everything that people call god and every object of worship. He will even sit in the temple of God, claiming that he himself is God. Don't you remember that I told you about all this when I was with you? And **you know what is holding him back**, for he can be revealed only when his time comes. For this lawlessness is already at work secretly, and it will remain secret **until the one who is holding it back steps out of the way. Then the man of lawlessness will be revealed**, but the Lord Jesus will kill him with the breath of his mouth and destroy him by the splendor of his coming. This man will come to do the work of Satan with counterfeit power and signs and miracles. (2 Thessalonians 2:1-9 NLT)

Some people thought "the day of the Lord," which is the tribulation period, had already started. Paul told them that wasn't the case and revealed the sequence of events. First, there's a "great rebellion against

God." The word *rebellion* isn't a great translation. It's the Greek word *apostasia*, which means apostasy or falling away.

Second, were told that someone is holding back the "man of lawlessness." That's the Antichrist. So, who is the one holding him back? It's obviously a reference to God. It can't be anyone else. No one other than God has the power to hold back Satan, who we know is the power behind the Antichrist.

Third, "the one who is holding it back steps out of the way." So, God, who's holding back the Antichrist, steps out of the way. This is a reference to the rapture. God's Holy Spirit lives inside all believers. Once all the believers are removed and taken to heaven, the Holy Spirit will be out of the Antichrist's way. The rapture also explains the falling away that was mentioned first. The rapture will indeed cause a great apostasy on earth.

Lastly, "the man of lawlessness will be revealed." With believers out of his way, the Antichrist will be able to deceive the world.

The book of Revelation also reveals the pre-tribulational timing of the rapture. Chapters 2 and 3 are letters to specific churches on earth. Then in chapters 4 and 5 we see the church in heaven with Jesus. Chapter 6 is when Jesus opens the scroll and the tribulation judgments begin. The church isn't mentioned again until chapter 19. That's Jesus's second coming in which the church is depicted as leaving heaven with Jesus and returning to earth with him.

Jesus also told us that the rapture happens before the tribulation in the Olivet Discourse. Consider what he said regarding the days of Noah and Lot. People were eating, drinking, buying, selling, farming, and marrying before judgment came against them. That means the rapture must happen before the mark of the Beast, before famine, and during a time when people have hope since they are marrying. No one is going to be living a normal life after the rapture. It'll be a time of immense fear, hardship, and chaos. The second judgment in Revelation is worldwide war. A worldwide famine is going to result from that and is in fact the very next judgment. Refer to Sign #84 - Fading Of Normality for more on this.

The rapture does not happen at any point during the tribulation period. We already discussed that the rapture occurs prior to God's wrath. Other points to consider here include that if the rapture occurred after the tribulation, then it wouldn't be imminent anymore.

It would require the tribulation to start beforehand. Then we'd be looking for the Antichrist instead of Jesus Christ. That would bring Satan glory, not Jesus.

The rapture doesn't happen at the end of the tribulation period either. This one just requires a bit of logical thinking. Jesus said he would be separating believers from unbelievers when he returns to earth at his second coming (Matthew 25:31-41). If all the believers got raptured right before Jesus returned to earth, so that they could return with him (like a U-turn), then there wouldn't be any believers for him to separate from unbelievers once he got to earth. So, then who on earth would populate Jesus's millennial kingdom? No one. This explanation clearly doesn't work.

The apostle Paul told us that the rapture is meant to encourage us (1 Thessalonians 4:18). There's absolutely nothing encouraging about living through the tribulation events and God's wrath. God's Word does not contradict itself. The only timing that fits all of Scripture is the pre-tribulational view.

Now, I'd like to talk about the season of the Lord's return because the Bible gives us some really good indications of the season in which the rapture might happen. We're told that Jesus's resurrection was a type of firstfruits (1 Corinthians 15:22-24). It's like a harvest. When examining the harvests mentioned in the Bible, we can figure this out.

First, let's consider the fall because that's when I think of harvesting. We're told that the grape harvest happens in the late summer and fall period. Well, the harvest that happens at Jesus's second coming is compared to a grape harvest and it's a harvest of unbelievers (Revelation 14:18, Matthew 13:39-42). So, that's not a good clue for the rapture.

Next up is the winter season, and there's no harvest then. I want to skip spring for a minute and touch on summer. The prophet Micah gave a prophecy about the summer harvest.

> Misery is mine! Indeed, I am like one who gathers the summer fruits, as gleanings of the vineyard. There is no cluster of grapes to eat. My soul desires to eat the early fig. The godly man has perished out of the earth, and there is no one upright among men. They all lie in wait for blood; every man hunts his brother with a net. Their hands are on that which is evil to do it diligently. The ruler and judge ask for a bribe. The powerful man dictates the evil desire of his soul. Thus they conspire together. The best of them is like a brier. The most upright is worse than a thorn hedge. The day of your watchmen, even your visitation, has come; now is the time of their confusion. (Micah 7:1-4)

Notice that he's gathering "summer fruits," but there are none to eat. Then he makes a rather curious statement when he says, "the godly man has perished out of the earth." I like how the NLT version translates that better, "the godly people have all disappeared." Then he goes on about all the evil there is and that their day of visitation and confusion has come. Wow! It sure seems like Micah is talking about the rapture, doesn't it? The clue here is that the rapture happens before the summer harvest. Because it's summer, and all of the fruit, believers, are already gone.

So, then let's look at the spring harvest season. Jesus told a parable of the wheat and the tares (Matthew 13:24-30). He said the wheat, the believers, and the tares, the unbelievers, would grow together until the harvest. Then he'd gather the wheat into his barn and burn the tares. The grain harvest happens in the spring and is celebrated during the Feast of Firstfruits.

Then there's the book of Ruth. The story takes place during the barley and wheat harvest, in the spring. Ruth, a gentile, gets betrothed to Boaz, her redeemer, at the end of the grain harvest. That's definitely a picture of the rapture.

There's also a mention in the Song of Solomon which is about a bride and groom. When the groom asks the bride to rise up and come away, the winter has passed, the flowers have appeared, the figs trees have green figs, and the vines have grapes with a nice smell (Song of Solomon 2:10-13). So, it's the springtime when the bride gets whisked away.

And you're also familiar with Jesus's parable of the fig tree from Sign #2 - The Timing Is Right. To recap, the fig trees are budding, and the branches are putting out leaves. Just like we know that summer is near when we see that, we can also know that God's kingdom is at the doors (Matthew 24:32-35).

The spring season is definitely a time to be watching for the Lord's return!

Since I mentioned a Jewish feast day earlier, let's consider if the rapture could occur on one. The feasts are described in Leviticus 23. There are some Bible scholars who think so. Other biblical events were fulfilled on feast days. We know that Jesus is fulfilling all of them. On Passover he was crucified. Unleavened Bread represents his sinless life. He was resurrected on Firstfruits. Jesus gave the Holy Spirit and began the church on Pentecost. Thus, scholars believe Jesus's second coming and establishment of the millennial kingdom will fulfill the remaining fall feasts of Trumpets, the day of Atonement, and Tabernacles. But could one of them also be fulfilled with the rapture?

The two feasts most people think are in contention are Pentecost and Trumpets. The Feast of Trumpets is in contention because it involves sounding the shofars and there's a trumpet at the rapture.

Pentecost is considered because Jesus is the firstfruits and believers are the fruits afterward (1 Corinthians 15:22-24). Pentecost is the feast right after Firstfruits. It's also a feast in which ancient Israelites didn't know the day or time of it in advance. That's because it's supposed to occur 50 days after the first fruits from the grain harvest are offered in the temple. Today, it's a fixed date, but biblically it's not. So, this could fit with not knowing the day or hour of the rapture.

I'm not convinced the rapture is going to happen on a feast day. It could, but it doesn't have to. God gave the Jewish people those feasts to celebrate, not the church. So, I don't think they should be forced to apply to the church and the rapture. I do think it's more likely that the rapture will occur between those spring and fall feasts.

How about the time of day of the rapture? Jesus said we wouldn't know the hour, but is there a clue that hones that in for us? I think so. Jesus is the one speaking in the verse below. It's one of his quotes from the Olivet Discourse in which he's talking about the signs of his second coming.

> "Watch therefore, for you don't know when the lord of the house is coming—whether at evening, or at midnight, or when the rooster crows, or in the morning." (Mark 13:35)

I think this is telling us the rapture could happen anytime between the evening through the morning. Since he was talking to disciples in Israel, we should use that location to adjust for our local time. Here's what this translates to for the US. I'm writing this in June. At 6pm Jerusalem time it's 10am in Dallas, Texas. At 8am Jerusalem time it's midnight in Dallas, Texas. In summary, if the rapture happened between 6pm and 8am in Jerusalem that would be between 10am and midnight in Dallas, Texas.

There's another tidbit we can glean from Scripture regarding the timing of the rapture. It's the Gog of Magog War in Ezekiel 38-39. The

United States isn't mentioned as an ally of Israel's or even as speaking against the countries that come against Israel. As we discussed in Sign #112 - All Nations Against Israel, it seems like the rapture must have happened before this. I don't see how the volume of Christians in the US would allow the US to just sit by and let this war happen. We can certainly see this war on the horizon, can't we? That points to the nearness of the rapture.

Fulfillment - Well, I'm still here writing this book, so the rapture hasn't happened yet. However, only you will know if it's happened by the time you're actually reading this. Did millions of people disappear? If so, you need to get my book *Rapture 911: What To Do If You're Left Behind*.

Today is Different - People have been predicting the date of the rapture and the second coming of Jesus for centuries. Don't get discouraged because the day or time of year that you were expecting the rapture to occur came and went.

Today is different because we've just examined 149 other signs that indicate it is. We can see the day approaching. It's obvious. The rapture is going to happen, and it's going to be very soon. You are not going to be caught unaware because you're diligently paying attention to all the signs. Take comfort in knowing we don't have much longer to wait and that you still have time to help others be invited into the party.

<u>Additional Scriptures:</u> 1 Corinthians 15:50-54. 1 Thessalonians 1:10; 4:13-18; 5:9-10. 2 Thessalonians 1:6-7; 2. Daniel 8:19. Ephesians 5:25-27. Isaiah 26:20-21. John 14:1-3. Luke 21:28, 36. Mark 13:19. Matthew 24:31-44; 25:1-13, 31-46. Revelation 3:10; 4-5; 6:16-17; 19:7-21. Titus 2:13.

CHAPTER 18 - GOD'S JUDGMENT HAS A PURPOSE

Now that we've explored all the signs that point to Jesus's soon return and better understand what's coming upon the world during the tribulation period, I want to make sure you know that God's judgment isn't just to punish unrighteousness. God's judgments reveal God's character to us and are ultimately for our own benefit.

God's judgments are for God's own glory. Just consider all the credit that false gods get for orchestrating events that God is actually the one behind. Mother nature is one in particular that comes to mind. Or how about all the false gods of Greek and Roman mythology. When God spoke through the prophet Ezekiel about the reason Israel would be taken into captivity, God said one reason was so his name was no longer profaned but sanctified (Ezekiel 36:22-23).

At the same time, it also brings nobility low. Many of the ancient rulers considered themselves gods. God's judgments cut their pride and put them back into their place (Isaiah 23:9, Zephaniah 2:11). One such ruler was King Nebuchadnezzar, a ruler of Babylon during Israel's captivity there. God's judgment against Nebuchadnezzar brought about his recognition of God and thus his worship of God (Daniel 4:37). That's what brings God the most glory, our worship.

God's judgments display God's power. God shows signs and wonders so that we'll believe he exists and know that he is all-powerful. When the Israelites were under Egyptian captivity and slavery, they didn't worship God. They worshiped the same false gods that the Egyptians did. It wasn't until God revealed himself through all the plagues against Egypt, that they knew he was indeed God (Exodus 10:1-2, 14:31).

Judgments also give us something to remember and pass along to our families and friends. Like it did with the Israelites who were rescued from Egypt.

God also knows that he has to get our attention, often with a major event or display of his power, for us to take him seriously. Recall the display of power that God revealed to Israel at Mount Sinai right after he'd already shown a whole bunch of signs and wonders to them in Egypt. God's presence came upon Mount Sinai in a thick cloud with lightning, thunder, fire, smoke, an earthquake, and a loud trumpet (Exodus 19:16-19, 20:20). The people were absolutely terrified. But it was a holy fear that was meant to keep them obedient to him.

God's judgments show God's faithfulness. It's important for us to know that God is trustworthy. He's going to do what he says. And he can indeed do what he says. Jesus himself said all the Law would be fulfilled (Matthew 5:18). When Israel was about to be taken into Babylonian captivity, God said, "They will know that I am the LORD. I have not said in vain that I would do this evil to them" (Ezekiel 6:10). God wants our trust so that when trouble comes upon us, we'll cry out to him for help, which is exactly what the Israelites did after God rescued them from the Egyptians and the Egyptian army had chased them to the Red Sea (Exodus 14:10). Signs and wonders demonstrate that God is able to save us. That the gospel message is legit (Mark 16:20).

God's judgments proclaim God's righteousness. Our world is full of unjust judges and leaders who aren't fair. They don't give people what they deserve. It seems like bad people get away with everything at the expense of good people. Judgments show that God is fair, full of justice, and that he punishes evil.

Right at the beginning, with the first sin and fall of man in the garden of Eden, God made it clear that he judges sin when he punished Adam and Eve and cursed the earth (Genesis 3:14-19). The Bible tells us the reason Israel was taken into captivity is because of their iniquity (Ezekiel 39:23).

Every one of us is accountable to God (Hebrews 4:13, Romans 14:10-12). Since God is perfect and holy, he has to judge our sin. It doesn't matter whether your parents were believers or are incarcerated unbelievers. Their good or bad deeds don't get passed on to you. God judges each person individually (Ezekiel 18:20). God makes a difference between the righteous and the wicked.

Consider the many examples of this in the Bible. Noah was saved while the wicked died in the flood (Genesis 7). Lot was saved while the wicked in Sodom were destroyed (Genesis 18:16-19:29). During the tribulation period, those who choose to get the mark of the Beast will be punished with boils on their body, but worse, an eternity in hell (Revelation 14:9-10, 16:2). Jesus will even separate those who survive the tribulation period, the righteous from the wicked, when he returns at his second coming (Matthew 25:31-46).

It's not just our sin that God deals with during judgments, it's also that of the false gods, fallen angels, and demons. That was one of the reasons for God's mighty works against the Egyptians during the Exodus (Exodus 12:12).

Know that it's not our righteousness that saves us from God's justice; it's the perfect righteousness of Jesus. You must put your faith in Jesus in order to be saved. Refer to Chapter 19 if you aren't sure you're covered with Jesus's holiness.

God's judgments reveal God's compassion. God's warnings are meant to lead us into repentance so that God can be compassionate to us. God sent the prophet Jonah to Nineveh, a very wicked city at the time, to warn them of God's impending judgment against them. The people of Nineveh believed what Jonah said, cried out to God, and turned from their evil way (Jonah 3). Because of that, God relented from destroying them.

God wants to rescue us, and he often gets our attention through adversity (Job 36:15-16). Before the Israelites were taken into Babylonian captivity, the Bible tells us that, "God of their fathers sent [warnings] to them by His messengers, rising up early and sending [them], because He had compassion on His people and on His dwelling place" (2 Chronicles 36:15 NKJV). This is why God has sent us so many warnings, many prophets, and over 150 different signs. God doesn't want to send anyone to hell. He wants everyone to turn away from their sin and be saved.

> Tell them, ' "As I live," says the Lord GOD, "I have no pleasure in the death of the wicked, but that the wicked turn from his way and live. Turn, turn from your evil ways! For why will you die, house of Israel?" ' (Ezekiel 33:11)

Speaking of salvation, **God's judgments lead us to belief and repentance**. When God displayed his power against the Egyptians during the Exodus, the people of Israel were full of awe with all that God did, and they put their faith in him. What's more is that a bunch of non-Israelites believed too and left Egypt with them (Exodus 12:38, 14:31).

God desires for everyone to know him as Lord. When Babylon came against ancient Israel, King Manasseh was taken captive to Babylon. When he arrived and saw that God did what he said he was going to do to them, King Manasseh cried out to God and repented. God heard him

(2 Chronicles 33:10-16). God restored King Manasseh to leadership in Jerusalem, where he then tore down the altars to false gods, repaired the altar to God, and told his people to serve God.

When Jesus was crucified, there was darkness, an earthquake, the veil in the temple was torn, and people even rose from their graves! All those signs led the Roman centurion and his men who were guarding Jesus to believe that Jesus "was the Son of God" (Matthew 27:45-54).

Once we've turned to God, the remembrance of those judgments is meant to keep us obedient to God. King David recognized that before God's judgments came upon him that he went astray, but afterwards he kept God's word (Psalm 119:67).

God's judgments refine our faith. If you've read the book of Job, you know that Job didn't deserve all the horrible things that happened to him. He was a righteous man. Yet, God allowed Satan to afflict him. Job's friends thought God's wrath had come upon him. Judgments, trials, obstacles, and adversity often all look the same.

Since Job already had faith in God, this act which seemed like judgment was actually a trial. You see, God used Satan to test Job's faith. Job did well initially and held onto his integrity (Job 2:3). But as the affliction continued, Job began to question God. When God answered Job's accusations, Job quickly humbled himself before God (Job 42:1-6). Job's faith was refined just as the apostle Peter described when he said our faith is tested by trials like gold is by fire (1 Peter 1:6-7).

Lastly, **God's judgments bless us**. God loves us so much that he sent Jesus to die for us. He wants to shower us with blessings. He gave the Israelites a long list of blessings they would reap if they obeyed him (Deuteronomy 28:1-14). It sounds as close to heaven as we can get on this side of it: the land would be blessed, everything they put their hand to do would be blessed, and they'd be above all nations. Essentially, nothing would be hard, life would be easy and fruitful.

It didn't happen to the nation of Israel, but it will one day. In the meantime, God has demonstrated his desire to bless us through individuals that judgment seemingly came upon. Three people come to mind when I think of overcoming adversity: Job, Joseph, and Daniel. God let Satan afflict Job. Job lost all his wealth, his children, and his health (Job 1-2). Joseph was sold into slavery by his own brothers and then imprisoned in Egypt (Genesis 37-40). In Babylon, Daniel was almost executed when the wise men couldn't interpret King

Nebuchadnezzar's dream. Then later he was thrown into a lion's den by King Darius (Daniel 2, 6).

Because those three men maintained their faith through the judgments against them, God blessed them as a result. Job was blessed more in his later years than the beginning (Job 42:12). Daniel was made ruler over Babylon by King Nebuchadnezzar (Daniel 2:48) and had blessings bestowed on him by King Darius (Daniel 6:25-28). Joseph became the ruler of Egypt under Pharaoh (Genesis 41:39-45).

Jesus promises that those who overcome will inherit all things (Revelation 21:7). If you're a believer, you have more in common with these men than you might think. We're going to go over rewards awaiting us in heaven in Chapter 20, but know that leadership in the millennial kingdom is a blessing promised to us.

It's easy to think that God's judgment is only about punishing wicked behavior. As you've just read, it's far more purposeful than that. In the next chapter, we're going to discuss Satan's tactics in blinding us to the truths that God's judgments are meant to reveal.

PART 4

THE KING IS COMING

CHAPTER 19 - WAS BLIND, NOW I SEE

Throughout this book, we've looked at 10 bad heart conditions that reveal signs that have gotten us to the point of no return regarding God's judgment and reveal that Jesus is about to burst onto the scene. But even with so many signs, most people are oblivious to them. You see, Satan wants us blind to God, the truth, and the signs of Jesus coming. He can inflict blindness upon us by targeting our heart. So, we're going to look at 10 ways that Satan blinds us to the signs. For the sake of our discussion, I've applied each blindness to one bad heart. However, keep in mind these bad heart conditions could easily apply to multiple blindnesses. As we explore each blindness, we'll also look at the good heart strengths that directly oppose the bad heart and cure the blindness, enabling us to see.

Since this blindness is all about a heart problem, the cure begins with a heart of flesh and is fully developed by being a doer of God's Word (James 1:22-25) and by being suited up in the armor of God (Ephesians 6:10-18). The heart of flesh is the most important and will be discussed first because it all starts with getting your heart right with Jesus. You see, that's the foremost cause of blindness to the signs, not being a Christian who has the Holy Spirit.

The nine other blindnesses I cover could certainly be caused by not having God's Holy Spirit, but for the sake of our discussion we're going to focus on how these blindnesses happen specifically to Christians.

There are many ways in which you can be a doer of God's Word. So, with each blindness we'll also discuss how the good heart strength that cures it also enables you to walk in that truth. The key message is to stay occupied and not be idle while we wait for Jesus to return. Idleness gives an opportunity for the devil to tempt us and shift our focus away from and back into blindness. Peter demonstrated this principle while he was waiting for Jesus to arrive in Galilee after his resurrection. Instead of standing around or just hanging out with the disciples, Peter went fishing (John 21:1-3). He did something productive with his time.

Let's look at the first type of spiritual blindness to the signs of Jesus coming.

BLINDED BY YOUR INTELLIGENCE

This type of spiritual blindness is born from a hardened heart. People who have put their faith in their own intelligence usually don't believe in God, Satan, the rapture, the Bible, or anything regarding religion. Some believe they are smarter than the religious folks. Others may think religion is just a crutch for weak minds and unnecessary. Yet, others may not really have an opinion either way, choosing to just see what happens when they die.

These people may not even debate topics as being moral choices or sin. For example, homosexuality becomes genetic, not a choice. So, they're oblivious to the signs of Jesus coming because they don't know Jesus and certainly aren't expecting him to return.

I can understand why Christianity gets a bad reputation. Just consider the prominence of immorality and fraud in the churches today with wealthy preacher scams, the prosperity gospel, the word faith movement, and pedophilia. How about all the Christians who don't act like it and thus give a bad witness to unbelievers. On top of that, think about other religions that are extreme, like Islam. All of these things make atheism and agnosticism attractive.

> Let no one deceive himself. If anyone thinks that he is wise among you in this world, let him become a fool that he may become wise. For the wisdom of this world is foolishness with God. (1 Corinthians 3:18-19)

Since the "wisdom of the world is foolishness," this is exactly what Satan gets us to focus our attention on. A good example from the Bible is the Egyptian Pharaoh that Moses confronted about letting the Israelites go. When Moses told him what "the Lord, the God of Israel" had spoken to him, Pharaoh said he didn't know the Lord. So why should he listen to what he says (Exodus 5:1-2). You see, in Egyptian religion, Pharaoh was a god and an intermediary between the people and the gods.[1] If you're trusting in your own intelligence, you're essentially making yourself a god, just like Pharaoh did.

What's more is that even with all the signs and wonders that God did through Moses, Pharaoh refused to believe. There was an enormous amount of evidence for God's existence and power. That didn't matter. It wasn't about the signs. Pharaoh was completely blind to the source of them. That's because he refused to make a decision about the source of those signs. He didn't want to acknowledge God.

The Bible tells us there's a spiritual veil upon unbelievers which blinds them to the things of God (2 Corinthians 4:3-4). The veil is removed once someone places their faith in Jesus (2 Corinthians 3:14-16). In order to put your faith in Jesus, you must trade your hard heart for a **heart of flesh**.

> I will also give you a new heart, and I will put a new spirit within you. I will take away the stony heart out of your flesh, and I will give you a **heart of flesh**. (Ezekiel 36:26)

Let me tell you how to do that. God loves you and wants to spend eternity with you. But there's a problem, and it's called sin. Sin is doing and even thinking anything that isn't perfect and holy. Every single one of us commits sin. We can't help it. It's our nature. It doesn't matter what your sin is or how big or little you perceive your sin to be. It could be lying, lust, pride, or murder (Galatians 5:16-26). Any sin is sin in God's eyes.

> As it is written, "There is no one righteous; no, not one. There is no one who understands. There is no one who seeks after God. They have all turned away. They have together become unprofitable. There is no one who does good, no, not so much as one." (Romans 3:10-12)

> For all have sinned, and fall short of the glory of God. (Romans 3:23)

God is perfect and sinless and righteous in every way. Thus, so is where he lives, heaven. Sin is the opposite of God. Sin cannot exist in heaven. Since people are inherently sinful, no one can live with God unless the sin problem is taken care of first.

Sin leads to death and keeps us from the heavenly afterlife that God desires for us. Case in point: Adam and Eve. They lived in the garden of Eden with God. They saw God every day. Heaven is wherever God is, so they essentially lived in heaven. After they sinned and ate from the forbidden tree, they got kicked out of the garden. They couldn't live with God anymore. They couldn't live immortally anymore. That's why they were forbidden from eating from the Tree of Life. They were destined to die because of sin (Genesis 3).

Here's the good news. God has a solution for the sin problem. He demands a perfect and spotless sacrifice to atone for sin. When Adam and Eve first sinned, God killed an animal to clothe them and atone for their sin (Genesis 3:21). In the Old Testament times before Jesus came, God's people sacrificed animals to atone for their sin (Leviticus 4:27-29, Hebrews 13:11). It's because the payment required for sin is death.

> For the wages of sin is death, but the free gift of God is eternal life in Christ Jesus our Lord. (Romans 6:23)

Now, don't run off to find an animal that you can sacrifice to atone for your sin. God's already taken care of the sacrifice offering permanently for you. He loves you so much that he sent Jesus, his perfect, sinless, and righteous only begotten son, down to earth to live as a man. Now, don't confuse Jesus being the son of God with people being children of God. It's not the same. Jesus being the only begotten son equates Jesus with God (John 3:16). Jesus is God in a human body (Colossians 1:15, 2:9, John 10:30). He's fully God and fully human. Jesus sacrificed himself for you (John 19). He was crucified to atone for your sin. That's right, Jesus died for you long ago, before you ever came to faith in him. While you were still a sinner.

> But God commends his own love toward us, in that while we were yet sinners, Christ died for us. (Romans 5:8)

We know this worked because Jesus isn't dead! God raised him from the dead.

> Now after the Sabbath, as it began to dawn on the first day of the week, Mary Magdalene and the other Mary came to see the tomb. Behold, there was a great earthquake, for an angel of the Lord descended from the sky and came and rolled away the stone from the door and sat on it. His appearance was like lightning, and his clothing white as snow. For fear of him, the guards shook, and became like dead men. The angel answered the women, "Don't be afraid, for I know that you seek Jesus, who has been crucified. He is not here, for he has risen, just like he said. Come, see the place where the Lord was lying. Go quickly and tell his disciples. ... As they went to tell his disciples, behold, Jesus met them, saying, "Rejoice!" (Matthew 28:1-7, 9)

Then Jesus appeared to hundreds of people in his risen state (1 Corinthians 15:3-8). All you have to do now is believe.

> If you will confess with your mouth that Jesus is Lord and **believe in your heart** that God raised him from the dead, you will be saved. For

> **with the heart one believes** resulting in righteousness; and with the mouth confession is made resulting in salvation. (Romans 10:9-10)

Believe in your heart. It seems too simple, doesn't it? But that's the irony of it. It's not simple at all. In fact, belief is really hard. The Bible says the path to God is narrow and most don't find it. That's because we're accustomed to striving for what we want down here on earth. The harder we work, the more we get.

We love to boast about our accomplishments. We love to be in control. We want to earn our way into heaven, and it's one of Satan's go-to lies. That's not God's way. God is in control, and it's about what God did, not what you've done. His solution is a gift. He gave his son as a gift to you. You just have to accept it.

"You once walked" "dead" in transgressions and through trespasses means we were condemned to death because of our sin.

> You were made alive when you were dead in transgressions and sins, in which you once walked according to the course of this world, according to the prince of the power of the air, the spirit who now works in the children of disobedience. ... But God, being rich in mercy, for his great love with which he loved us, even when we were dead through our trespasses, made us alive together with Christ—by grace you have been saved— ... for by grace you have been saved through faith, and that not of yourselves; it is the gift of God, not of works, that no one would boast. (Ephesians 2:1-2, 4-5, 8-9)

Perhaps you believe Satan's lie that you don't deserve to go to heaven. That you're a bad person and committed sins that can't be forgiven. That's where grace comes in. You see, it's God's grace that saved you.

As sinners, we are doomed to an eternal life far removed from God. That's God's rule. Grace is God demonstrating his love for us. He pardons us when we believe that Jesus died for our sins. You see, God treated Jesus the way we deserve to be treated. Jesus was crucified. We deserve to be crucified for our sins against God. But Jesus took that punishment for us.

It doesn't matter what you've done. No sin is too big for Jesus to absolve! God did that so he can treat you the way that Jesus is treated now. Jesus is now in heaven with God, reigning. God wants you in heaven with him too. He doesn't want you to miss out on being included in the rapture. He doesn't want you to experience his wrath during the tribulation period. Jesus already took God's wrath upon himself for you.

A person who believes in what they can't yet see has faith. They believe God and that Jesus died for their sins. Have faith.

> Now faith is assurance of things hoped for, proof of things not seen. (Hebrews 11:1)

Here's what you must come to believe:
You recognize that you are a sinner.
You don't want to be a sinner anymore. So, you ask God to forgive you.
You want to live with God for eternity in heaven.
You know that you can't save yourself or earn your way into heaven.
You believe that God sent his only begotten son Jesus to atone for your sin by dying on the cross.
You believe that God raised Jesus from the dead and that Jesus reigns with God in heaven.
You surrender your salvation to Jesus and ask him to come into your life.

Now, you can't just go through the motions and say these things. You have to actually mean them, deep down, from your heart. That's what faith is all about.

This is the good news of the Bible. That Jesus, God in the flesh, died for your sins, rose from the grave, and reigns from heaven.

> Now I declare to you, brothers, the Good News which I preached to you, which also you received, in which you also stand, by which also you are saved, if you hold firmly the word which I preached to you—unless you believed in vain. For I delivered to you first of all that which I also received: that Christ died for our sins according to the Scriptures, that he was buried, that he was raised on the third day according to the Scriptures. (1 Corinthians 15:1-4)

If you truly believe all those things, then tell God. That's what praying is, just talking to God. Tell him you believe each of those truths and ask him to come into your life. And he will indeed!

Here's an example prayer you can say to God:

"Lord Jesus, I know that I'm a sinner. I need your forgiveness so that I can live with you for eternity in heaven. Please forgive me. I believe that you are the son of God, God in the flesh, and that you died on the cross for my sins. I believe that you alone have the power of life and death and that you rose from the grave! I want to turn from my sins and trust and follow you as Lord and Savior. Please come into my heart and life. In Jesus's name, amen."

Now, be confident that you are truly saved! You are sealed with God's Holy Spirit as a guarantee of your salvation (Ephesians 1:13-14). Nothing, not even Satan himself, can steal you from Jesus.

> Jesus answered them, "... I give eternal life to them. They will never perish, and no one will snatch them out of my hand. My Father who has given them to me is greater than all. No one is able to snatch them out of my Father's hand. I and the Father are one." (John 10:25, 28-30)

This is your helmet of salvation in the armor of God (Ephesians 6:17). Your salvation protects you from the devil's efforts to steal you away from God.

Now that we've discovered the main blindness affecting unbelievers, we're going to learn how Christians in particular can be blind to the signs.

BLINDED BY MAGIC

This type of spiritual blindness comes from a heart that's turned away. These are Christians who are curious about what's in store for humanity and themselves. They are open to new teachings and might read all sorts of nonfiction books that seem Christian but, in reality, aren't. Or perhaps this person goes to church every week and appears to be a Christian. But in reality, they're just a cultural Christian who doesn't have any real relationship with Jesus.

Since Satan makes magical and mystical things appear attractive, they've gone looking for answers in new age teachings and maybe even in the occult by consulting psychics, mediums, and tarot and palm readers. Maybe you even know a fellow church member who's mentioned they talk with a deceased loved one through a medium. Some of these people may even be involved in a secret society that claims to have hidden or forbidden knowledge, like the free masons.

Christians who aren't very knowledgeable with the Bible aren't going to know the true source behind these things. It's Satan by the way.

That's why God warns us against participating in this (Deuteronomy 18:9-14, 1 Timothy 4:1).

They're oblivious to the signs of Jesus coming because they're seeking truth from the wrong source.

There's an example of this in the Bible which comes to mind. It's regarding the Egyptian Pharaoh that Moses dealt with when rescuing the Israelites from captivity. We talked about him in the prior spiritual blindness regarding intelligence.

Well, Pharaoh had multiple blindnesses because he had a lot of bad heart conditions. Pharaoh had his own magicians who were able to replicate some of the signs that Moses and Aaron performed with God's power. His magicians could turn their staffs into serpents like Aaron could (Exodus 7:10-13), turn water into blood (Exodus 7:19-22), and make frogs appear (Exodus 8:5-7). Of course, Pharaoh's magicians had Satan's power. The Bible warns us that Satan is able to perform signs and lying wonders (2 Thessalonians 2:9). They lie because they deceive. Pharaoh was blinded to the source of Moses's power.

The cure for this spiritual blindness is to trade your heart that's turned away from God for a **seeking heart**.

> Blessed are those whose ways are blameless, who walk according to the LORD's law. Blessed are those who keep his statutes, who **seek him with their whole heart**. (Psalm 119:1-2)

The word *seek* means to consult, investigate, study, follow, and to frequent a place. A heart that seeks God is one who trusts and abides in God. Consider Noah. He lived for hundreds of years before the flood. I can only imagine the crazy wickedness of his day and the things he saw and had to deal with. Yet, he walked with God and did everything God asked him to do (Genesis 6:9, 22).

I also think of the prophet Jeremiah. He lived in Jerusalem during the Babylonian invasion and prophesied about that to the people and the leaders before it happened. No one listened to him. They persecuted him instead. Even though Jeremiah knew the destruction of his city was coming, Jeremiah hoped in God and knew God was good to those who wait on him and seek him (Lamentations 3:21-26).

When their worlds were falling apart, they didn't turn away from God and look for answers elsewhere, they sought God all the more.

You know, Jesus tells us in Revelation 3:1-3 that if we're not being watchful, that his coming will be a surprise, like a thief breaking into a house unexpectedly. That's why it's important to stop walking as unbelievers walk, which is blind (Ephesians 4:17-18). We're called to wear the armor of God and be watchful (Ephesians 6:18).

BLINDED BY BIBLICAL IGNORANCE

This type of spiritual blindness comes from a foolish heart. You might think someone who doesn't know the Bible is someone who isn't a Christian. While that is one example, unfortunately today most Christians are biblically ignorant. We discussed that in Sign #7 - Apostasy. The reason these believers are so oblivious to the signs of Jesus coming is because they don't understand the rapture, the second coming, or Bible prophecy.

They likely just go to church each week and listen to a pastor who doesn't teach through the entire Bible, especially not prophecy. They don't read the Bible much on their own, and they frankly think it doesn't matter if they know the Bible that well. They just focus on being a good person.

Or perhaps they prefer to be in the dark on all this prophecy stuff because they've read some articles about it and it's just too confusing. The danger here is that it's very easy for this type of person to be led astray by false doctrine or start doing things out of fear of what they see happening in the world. Would they believe it and then quit their job if someone on TV told them Jesus was coming back next week? They might. Would they buy a bunch of guns, a cabin in the woods, and start prepping for the end of the world? Yes, they might do that too.

And of course, this could be a cultural Christian. They say they're a Christian and might act like one, but they don't have a real relationship with Jesus.

There are several examples of this in the Bible. Jesus himself said not everyone who professed his name and did good works in his name would enter his kingdom (Matthew 7:21-23). He was referring to cultural Christians who identify with the goodness of the faith, but don't have a relationship with Jesus. His parable of the sower describes this group as receiving the seed of his word by the wayside (Matthew 13:19). They hear, but don't understand.

Also consider Jesus's rebuke of the people because they didn't know the time of their visitation (Luke 19:21-44). That means Jesus expected them to understand the Scriptures and be watching for him, but they didn't know and weren't watching.

Or how about the people who were absolutely terrified at some of the miracles that Jesus performed, like when he healed a demoniac and cast the demons into a herd of pigs (Mark 5:1-20). They begged Jesus to leave because they were so afraid. Their lack of understanding resulted in fear.

And then there's the people the apostle Paul talked about in his letters. Some early Christians thought the day of the Lord had already happened (2 Thessalonians 2), and some thought the resurrection of the dead had already happened (2 Timothy 2:18). Jesus even warned people about false christs appearing (Matthew 24:5, 23-26).

Jesus doesn't want us to be in the dark about what's going on. The cure for this spiritual blindness is to trade your foolish heart for a **wise heart**.

> The **heart of the wise** instructs his mouth, and adds learning to his lips. (Proverbs 16:23)

The word *wise* means learned, intelligent, and prudent. It's not enough to attend church each week and listen to a half hour sermon. You are going to learn very little that way. Know that you are responsible for your own biblical knowledge.

Yes, Jesus is going to hold bad preachers accountable for doing a poor job. But he's also going to hold every single one of us accountable for what he expected us to know. Jesus said you need to receive his word in good soil so you can hear it, understand it, and then be able to produce good fruit (Matthew 13:23). And he also taught a rather interesting principle about learning. Jesus is the one speaking in the Scripture below.

> "Anyone with ears to hear should listen and understand." Then he added, "Pay close attention to what you hear. The closer you listen, the more understanding you will be given—and you will receive even more." (Mark 4:23-24 NLT)

The more we listen, the more we'll understand. It makes sense, doesn't it? We don't expect to get good at any school subject by listening to it once a week for 30 minutes. Why would we expect to become Bible scholars by doing that?

It starts with reading the Bible every day or listening to it being read to you while you follow along in a Bible app. Supplement that with a devotional, study Bible, or commentary to help you learn more about what you're reading. Check out my website for some helpful resources - www.rapture911.com.

If your preacher isn't teaching you the Bible, find another one. Go to a different church that is teaching good doctrine. In today's day you can even find one online and watch with family and friends. There are still good preachers out there. My church puts all of their teachings online for free - www.calvarynm.church.

Now that you're wearing the belt of truth in the armor of God (Ephesians 6:14), you'll be able to walk as someone who is wise (Ephesians 5:15).

BLINDED BY BEING OFFENDED

This type of spiritual blindness comes from a prideful heart. While non-Christians could easily be offended at biblical teaching because it goes against a deeply held belief, we're going to focus on Christians who get easily offended at end times topics, discussions, or teachings.

Do you know people like this? You mention the rapture and they freak out and tell you they've read the Bible and that the word isn't in there. Then they refuse to listen to you explain. Or how about those who are convinced the rapture happens sometime after the tribulation period starts? They can't explain their position with any Scripture, nor can they have a civil conversation with you about it. They even refuse to read articles or books you suggest that explain the different end times viewpoints.

I was doing a book signing in a store once, and I asked a woman who walked by my table if she was interested in Bible prophecy. She shouted "NO!" at me and then left. Yikes. What was that about?

Yeah, I know people like this too. These Christians are oblivious to the signs of Jesus coming because they're offended by even looking since it goes against their world view.

This starts with bad doctrine and bad eschatology coming from a foolish heart. Then it morphs into being offended because people don't want to admit they were wrong, were deceived, or here's the kicker, that you might be correct. They don't want to lose face. And that's all pride.

The Pharisees and Sadducees were prime examples of this. Jesus's teachings and behavior went against their deeply held beliefs and traditions. They considered themselves more righteous than Jesus! Can you imagine? They really didn't like that Jesus broke their rules by healing people on the Sabbath (Mark 3:1-6). So, they sought to kill him because they reasoned he must not be from God but was a sinner instead (John 19:16). The irony of this is that one of the people Jesus healed on the Sabbath was a blind man.

The Pharisees and Sadducees were also blinded by their jealousy of Jesus because he was getting all the attention (Mark 11:18, 15:10). We also learn they loved money and didn't like Jesus's parable of the shrewd manager where Jesus taught that we can't serve both God and money (Luke 16:1-14). Their hatred toward Jesus was coming from pride.

But the Pharisees and Sadducees weren't the only ones offended by Jesus. Jesus's own family and friends didn't believe he was God and were offended (Mark 6:1-6, John 7:5). This shows that it's often going to be harder for us to deliver biblical truths to those closest to us.

And then there's Thomas, one of the twelve disciples. After Jesus's resurrection, when all the other disciples told Thomas that Jesus was alive and that they'd seen him, Thomas refused to believe them. Really, why? Perhaps he was put off that Jesus appeared to them and not him. That's pride again.

The cure for this spiritual blindness is to trade your prideful heart for a **worshiping heart**.

> Let's **lift up our heart** with our hands to God in the heavens. (Lamentations 3:41)

When worshiping God, we're exalting him, revering him, and lifting his name up. It includes talking to God in prayer too. It turns the focus from ourselves back toward God. If you find yourself getting worked up and offended like what I described above, it's time to ground yourself by praying to God, singing to God, or listening to worship music.

The apostle Paul tells us that we need to pray to God in order to receive his peace (Philippians 4:6-7), and that our prayers should include rejoicing and thankfulness. Even the apostle Peter says we need to be especially watchful in our prayers in the last days (1 Peter 4:7). I also find it interesting that when Paul described the spiritual pattern we see today, one of the first reasons he mentions for the apostasy is that people didn't worship God or give God thanks (Romans 1:21).

Another tip that I find helpful for myself is to write about whichever Bible topic I want to learn better. You don't have to show it to anyone if you don't want to. When you decide your position on a topic, have to go hunt for the Bible verses to support it, and then figure out all the arguments against it and which verses could support that, it's quite informative. I learn a lot doing that.

Once we're suited up in the armor of God, we're told to pray always (Ephesians 6:18). It protects us from bad heart conditions and enables us to walk in reverence of God and be comforted by his Holy Spirit (Acts 9:31).

BLINDED BY THE CARES OF THE WORLD

This type of spiritual blindness comes from a coveting heart. This Christian is oblivious to the signs of Jesus's soon return because they're distracted and focused on life, daily activities, work, and you name it.

Many people are in this camp today whether it's Christians or unbelievers. I see how busy the lives of some of my family and friends are, and it's no wonder they aren't paying attention to the signs. Some of these people want to have the best stuff and want themselves and their kids involved in every activity. Thus, they need money and work a lot to earn it. Others are just stuffing too much into their day, maybe because they don't want to say "no" to anyone or anything. They think they can do it all. This comes down to not effectively prioritizing what really matters.

Some examples of this in the Bible that come to mind include the disciples Peter, James, and John when they were at Jesus's transfiguration (Luke 9:27-36). They were so tired that they fell asleep and pretty much missed the entire conversation that Jesus had with Moses and Elijah. What were they talking about? We don't know because they fell asleep! Jesus is fully human, just like us, and he didn't fall asleep. What were those disciples so busy doing all day that they couldn't focus on something so important? Makes you wonder, doesn't it?

Or how about Martha, when she was busy running around her house trying to cook dinner for everyone instead of listening to Jesus teach like her sister Mary was (Luke 10:40). Jesus told Martha that only one thing was needed. She was distracted by the wrong things and needed to focus on the most important thing.

I also think of the many people who went to hear Jesus teach but left once the free lunch was over (John 6, 6:26). They only wanted to satisfy their tummies and couldn't care less about satisfying their spiritual needs.

Then there's Judas Iscariot, the disciple who spent years with Jesus and then betrayed him for silver coins (Matthew 26:14-16). He completely missed Jesus being the Messiah because he was focused on his love of money instead of on Jesus (John 12:4-6, Acts 1:16-19).

In the parable of the sower, Jesus described these people when he said his word is like seed among thorns. The thorns, which are the cares and riches of the world, choke out the truth (Matthew 13:22).

The cure for this spiritual blindness is to trade your coveting heart for a **serving heart**.

> Now, Israel, what does the LORD your God require of you, but to fear the LORD your God, to walk in all his ways, to love him, and to **serve the LORD your God with all your heart** and with all your soul (Deuteronomy 10:12)

The word *serve* means to labor and to work. There's nothing wrong with working. It's when we're working for ourselves and what we desire, instead of for God, that we risk becoming oblivious. Did you know that Jesus told each of the seven churches in the book of Revelation that he knew their works (Revelation 2-3). Jesus is keeping track of how we spend our time.

In the Olivet Discourse, Jesus even told us to pay attention to what we're doing so that the cares of life don't distract us and make his return come upon us unexpectedly (Luke 21:34-36). As such, we're told not to entangle ourselves in the affairs of the world (2 Timothy 2:3-5). The vast majority of things the world cares about are unimportant and a distraction. It's imperative that we figure out how to appropriately spend our time.

It starts with being content (1 Timothy 6:6). If you think about it, does it really make sense to strive for a mansion, a fancy car, designer clothes, and work multiple jobs to look good and send your elementary school kids to the best college if you know Jesus is coming back any minute to take you to heaven? What's the point of all your hard work to get all that? Think of all the important things you're missing out on right now by being so busy focused on worldly things.

Perhaps you're not necessarily overworked because instead you're racking up a ton of debt on credit cards in order to live it up. You think if Jesus comes, yay, you won't have to pay it back. Well, Jesus expects us to be good stewards of the resources he's given us. That's why some of his parables are about good versus bad servants (Luke 16:1-13, Luke 19:12-27).

The people listening to Jesus were worried about providing for themselves too. Jesus tells us to seek God first and if we do, then he'll handle all the other daily things that we worry about (Matthew 6:24-33). Jesus says we're going to inherit all things after his coming (Revelation 21:7). All that cool stuff we desire is already ours. We just have to wait for it and be at peace in the meantime. It's okay to have a modest house, a used car, and clothes from Walmart. And if we happen to still be here in a decade, it's okay for your elementary age kids to attend a cheaper university, a trade school, or just get a job out of high school.

To help us work for God, Jesus has given each of us a spiritual gift (1 Corinthians 12:4-11, Romans 12:3-8). Gifts like wisdom, faith, healing, discerning, teaching, and giving. Jesus wants you to use the special gift he's given you to benefit others and bring him glory. Consider the parable of talents in which the master gave each servant a different amount of money (Luke 19:12-27). The good servants invested it and were fruitful. The wicked servant just buried what the master gave him.

Don't bury the spiritual gift that God gave you because you say you don't have time for God. Make time for God. Figure out what your gift is and use it to serve him in these last days. With your attention turned toward God, you'll stop caring about what the world wants you to desire. You'll be walking in the good works that God prepared for you to accomplish before Jesus comes (Ephesians 2:10).

BLINDED BY PEER PRESSURE

This type of spiritual blindness comes from a discouraged heart. These are Christians who are curious about the signs, end times, and prophecy, but don't pursue it because their friends mock it. Anyone know someone who thinks the rapture is stupid? Or maybe a pastor is the one who discourages this person from studying Bible prophecy because they don't see the value in it.

It could also be that these believers have a close relative they love who's living a sinful lifestyle and the thought of Jesus coming soon makes them sad, so they prefer not to think about it. A similar group of people are Christians who had a close relative or friend die as an unbeliever and they can't bear the thought of them being in hell, so now they pick and choose Scripture to believe that suits their world view.

All of these people are oblivious to the signs of Jesus coming any minute because someone or something has discouraged them from even looking. They've become a victim of peer pressure.

The Bible is full of examples. While Moses was on Mount Sinai getting the Ten Commandments from God, Aaron made a golden calf for the people to worship because they pressured him to (Exodus 32). In a way, Eli the priest was blind to the sins of his sons (1 Sam 2:12-36, 3:11-14). He knew of their wickedness but refused to do anything about it. As a result, he became oblivious to God speaking to him. God had to speak to him through an unnamed prophet and the prophet Samuel who was just a boy at the time. We're told that Eli gave his sons more honor than he gave God. That's what we're doing when we're listening to and then obeying someone other than God.

The Pharisees and Sadducees were the best demonstrators of this. They always wanted to do what pleased the people (Mark 11:27-33, 12:12). But since they were in authority it was mostly about the people doing what pleased those religious leaders. The Pharisees, Sadducees, and the people ultimately pressured Pontius Pilate into crucifying Jesus (John 19:5-16, Matthew 27:20-24). Those who did believe in Jesus wouldn't admit it because they feared the religious leaders and didn't want to be expelled from their synagogue (John 12:42-43, 19:38). Even the apostle Peter denied knowing Jesus three times after Jesus was arrested because he was afraid of the people and religious leaders (John 18:15-27).

Jesus doesn't describe these people who discourage others in a good light. He calls them sons of Satan in the parable of wheat and tares (Matthew 13:24-38).

This tactic of Satan's works so well because most people are afraid of confrontation, of being different, and of being labeled something unpleasant. Nobody wants to be called a racist or right-wing extremist, even if it isn't true. Ridicule and shaming are weapons these discouragers use to control the behavior of others.

One of their marketing tactics is to inundate us with whatever they want us to believe in the least offensive way they can think of. Like adding LGBT content to Disney and Hallmark movies to get us accustomed to that lifestyle, so we'll eventually become calloused to it (Acts 28:26-27).

These strategies can be very difficult to counterattack. That's why the cure for this spiritual blindness is to trade your discouraged heart for a **steadfast heart**.

> He will not be afraid of evil news. His **heart is steadfast**, trusting in the LORD. (Psalm 112:7)

The word *steadfast* means firm, established, fixed, secure, and determined. Once we're wearing the armor of God, there's a reason we're told to stand four different times (Ephesians 6:11, 13-14). You often can't even reason with someone who's a discourager. You have to stand in firm opposition to those who come against God, the Bible, and your faith in Jesus. Don't give in or compromise.

It can certainly be intimidating to stand against someone else, especially someone you care about. But know that if you resist the devil, that he will flee from you (James 4:7). God allows Satan to come against us because it tests and strengthens our character (Romans 5:3-4).

Being steadfast involves more than just yourself. Flip this negative peer pressure on its head with a dose of positive peer pressure. Encourage and motivate others to draw near to God, and to be watching for Jesus's coming (Hebrews 10:22-25). When King David was in the wilderness on the run from the wrath of King Saul, David's friend Jonathan strengthened him in God (1 Samuel 23:16). I wonder what Jonathan said. Perhaps it inspired one of David's psalms.

Sometimes being steadfast does require the use of a weapon. The

Bible tells us that our weapons can pull down spiritual strongholds (2 Corinthians 10:4). The sword of the spirit, the Word of God, is our weapon against discouragers (Ephesians 6:17, Hebrews 4:12). When Jesus was fasting in the wilderness before he started his ministry, Satan came against him, seeking to discourage him from his mission to save us. Jesus countered Satan's attacks with Scripture and Satan eventually left (Matthew 4:1-11).

In order for you to wield God's Word as a weapon, you first have to know it. So, I'd like to encourage you to make reading and studying the Bible a habit so that you're better equipped to deal with people who will try to discourage your biblical pursuits.

BLINDED BY ESCAPISM

This type of spiritual blindness comes from a perverse heart. Today, many people just can't deal with what's going on in the world, so they choose to escape it through using drugs and alcohol, watching porn, playing video games all day, or binge-watching TV shows every night and weekend. Yes, Christians are doing these things too. These believers aren't living in reality.

This person is oblivious to the signs of Jesus coming because they're drugging their conscience, putting themselves into a stupor, thereby silencing the Holy Spirit.

In the Bible, the clear examples of this all come from the book of Revelation and occur during the tribulation period. While the world is being inundated with God's judgments, we're told the people refuse to give up their sorceries (Revelation 9:21). Now, that word *sorceries* has an interesting biblical definition. While it can mean magic or witchcraft, it's the Greek word *pharmakeia*, where we get the word *pharmacy* from. So, it also means drugs. Instead of waking up to reality, they double down on using drugs. Even Babylon gets called out in Revelation 18:23 for deceiving the nations with its sorceries. It must become the drug supplier of the world. If people are tuning out of the world today, I understand why they'd especially want to disengage during the tribulation period.

The cure for this spiritual blindness is to trade your perverse heart for an **upright heart**. King Solomon is speaking to God in the Scripture below.

> Solomon said, "You have shown to your servant David my father great loving kindness, because he walked before you in truth, in righteousness, and in **uprightness of heart** with you." (1 Kings 3:6)

The word *uprightness* means straight, correct, pleasing, and proper. One of the first things to do to conquer this stupor is to avoid whatever is tempting you (Proverbs 4:14-16). If it's drugs or alcohol, get the help you need to overcome that addiction. Stop hanging out with your friends who encourage that behavior. The apostle Paul tells us to turn away from people who engage in wicked behavior (2 Timothy 3:1-5). Throw away all of your paraphernalia. If it's a screen-related addiction, turn it off.

I recently did a 40-day news fast in which I didn't read or listen to any news. For someone like me who likes to stay up to speed on current events, that was really hard. But I needed that reset before I started writing this book. I bought a new devotional and read that every day instead of the news.

The next step is to escape into heavenly things instead of dwelling on and worrying about earthly things (Colossians 3:2) that get you depressed and wanting to escape into a worldly addiction. Consider joining a small group at church to make new friends and to have new activities to do. Replace that unproductive screen time with biblical content. Watch some sermons or Bible prophecy conferences. Better yet, go outside! Go walking every day, sit outside in your yard for a bit and watch the birds, or try just having a meal outside every day.

We need to be focused on Jesus coming, heaven, and what awaits us there. The Bible tells us that those with an eager expectation of Jesus's return stay pure (1 John 3:2-3). Jesus is the one speaking in the verse below.

> "But when these things begin to happen, look up and lift up your heads, because your redemption is near." (Luke 21:28)

When you accepted Jesus as your savior, you received his righteousness in return. That's the breastplate of righteousness in the armor of God (Ephesians 6:14). It will enable you to walk in righteousness and uprightness like King David did.

Now that you're watching for Jesus's return, you'll be able to open the door when he arrives (Luke 12:35-40).

BLINDED BY LOOKING FOR THE WRONG SAVIOR

This type of spiritual blindness comes from a deceived heart. You know there are many people who are looking for a savior these days. The Jewish people are still expecting their Messiah. The Muslims are waiting for their Mahdi. Every religion on the planet, except biblical Christianity, expects you to be your own savior through good works.

For Christians in particular, many of them today are putting their faith into a politician to save humanity. It's especially prominent since this is an election year. Then we also have Christians expecting science to save us, through environmental policies, Mars colonization, or bioengineering us to live forever. There are even some Christians who believe they must live through the tribulation period and are thus looking for the person the world will eventually worship as their savior, the Antichrist.

These believers are oblivious to the signs of Jesus's next visitation because they're not looking for Jesus, they're looking for the wrong savior.

During Jesus's first coming, the Jewish people were looking for a savior who would rescue them from Roman oppression. They were looking for a conqueror. John the Baptist was taken prisoner by King Herod, and while in prison he sent people to ask Jesus if he really was the savior or if they should be looking for another (Matthew 11:2-6). This was John the Baptist! He knew Jesus was the Messiah (John 1), yet he started to doubt when Jesus didn't vanquish King Herod from the throne and rescue him from prison.

After his resurrection, Jesus secretly appeared to two of his disciples who were walking on the road to Emmaus (Luke 24:21-26). He hid himself from being recognized as Jesus. He asked them what they were talking about and why they were sad. They told him Jesus was crucified and they thought he was the one who was going to redeem Israel. They were expecting a different savior.

The cure for this spiritual blindness is to trade your deceived heart for a **discerning heart**. King Solomon is the one speaking in the verse below.

> "Give your servant therefore an **understanding heart** to judge your people, **that I may discern** between good and evil; for who is able to judge this great people of yours?" (1 Kings 3:9)

The words *understanding* and *discern* mean to hear, listen, obey, and perceive. After those two disciples told Jesus why they were sad, Jesus expounded the Scriptures to them so they would understand everything about him (Luke 24:27-35).

If you're looking for a savior other than Jesus, I encourage you to get to know Jesus by reading the Bible and studying it. Cast aside whatever beliefs you already have about who or what could save humanity. Jesus is our only hope and only savior (Acts 4:12). I think an excellent place to start is the book of John.

Perhaps you're more like John the Baptist and you're wavering on if Jesus really is coming before the tribulation begins. Go back and read Chapter 17 about the rapture. Then grab your shield of faith in the armor of God (Ephesians 6:16) and have the same kind of faith in Jesus that Peter did when he was able to walk on water (Matthew 14:22-33).

BLINDED BY HURT

This type of spiritual blindness comes from a hateful heart. There are plenty of Christians today who've been hurt by someone, a fellow believer, a church, a Christian school, a charity, or even an employer. Perhaps they gave a bunch of money to a church who promised something in return that didn't come to pass. Maybe they were treated poorly at the last church they attended. Some were probably hurt when a relationship ended badly. It could even be that they were called out for sinful behavior by another Christian.

There are those who lost their job due to tough economic times. I think some of these people were even hurt when they got sick or when a loved one died. Other believers may have been the ones who hurt someone else, and now they struggle with shame and are unable to forgive themselves.

The hurt these people experienced festered into unforgiveness toward other people, Christians, and themselves. They might even blame God for what's happened. These believers are oblivious to the signs of Jesus's soon return because they've walked away from God and his church due to the pain they experienced.

There are several examples in the Bible of people who were blinded by the hurt, pain, or grief they experienced. The prophet Elijah had just witnessed a grand display of God's power when God burned his water-soaked sacrifice in front of all the prophets of Baal and then enabled him to execute them all (1 Kings 18). But shortly after this, Queen Jezebel threatened his life and so he took off running. Elijah told God that he was the only prophet of God's left alive (1 Kings 19:10). God told him there were over 7,000 who hadn't worshiped Baal (1 Kings 19:18). Before that happened, Obadiah even told Elijah about him saving 100 of God's prophets from Jezebel (1 Kings 18:7-13). The persecution Elijah experienced from a wicked ruler blinded him to what was really going on.

In the parable of the sower, Jesus himself said that people like this are the seed on stony places that don't have a root and stumble when tribulation or persecution comes (Matthew 13:20-21).

Then there are the disciples who were so grieved after the death of Jesus that they couldn't believe Mary when she told them she saw and spoke to Jesus (Mark 16:9-11). After that, they also couldn't believe the two disciples Jesus spoke to on the road to Emmaus after his resurrection (Mark 16:12-13).

I think the best example is Judas Iscariot, the disciple who betrayed Jesus. After Judas realized the religious leaders wanted Jesus crucified and he saw them turn Jesus over to Pontius Pilate, he was sorrowful. He even returned the bribe he received from the religious leaders for betraying Jesus (Matthew 27:1-4). But his sorrow didn't make him turn toward God for forgiveness. It led to his suicide (Acts 1:16-18) and his being doomed to destruction (John 17:12, Matthew 26:24). The Bible tells us that sorrow that doesn't result in repentance leads to spiritual death (2 Corinthians 7:10).

The cure for this spiritual blindness is to trade your hateful heart for a **pure heart**.

> Since you have purified your souls in obeying the truth through the Spirit in sincere love of the brethren, **love** one another fervently **with a pure heart**. (1 Peter 1:22 NKJV)

The word *pure* means clean, purified, blameless, and sincere. It's hard to let go of hurt and hate because it feeds our pride and makes us feel righteous. That's just an illusion. God wants us to be at peace with all people (Hebrews 12:14-15). He even asks us to love our enemies (Matthew 5:44).

It's impossible to do this on our own. We need God's supernatural love in order to accomplish this. So, you must return to God and pour your heart out to him in prayer (Philippians 4:6). If you don't feel like it, turn on a Christian radio station and listen to a few songs first to help get your heart in the right place. If you still don't want to, well, do it anyway. Trust me, this will work, and you'll be amazed at how faithful God is to restore you (1 John 1:9). Repent of your unforgiveness either toward yourself or others. Repent of blaming God and walking away. Ask God to help you forgive all the people you need to forgive.

Now, you'll be able to wear the breastplate of faith and love (1 Thessalonians 5:8) and walk in love toward yourself and others (Ephesians 5:2).

BLINDED BY UNRIGHTEOUSNESS

This type of spiritual blindness comes from an evil heart. Just because a person is saved and has the Holy Spirit living in them doesn't mean they always behave like they're saved. There are some Christians who live an openly sinful lifestyle. They use their salvation as a type of "get out of jail free" card, so to speak. They want to party it up while they're alive and be holy when they're old or after they die and go to heaven.

Some Christians in this camp have become so broken down by the sin and evil in the world that they give in to it themselves. Others might perceive that there isn't a consequence for bad behavior or a reward for good these days, so why bother trying so hard to be good.

I think many of these believers grew up in a righteous Christian family, and now they want to see what they missed out on. And unfortunately, some people with this type of blindness think that as long as something is legal that means it's moral.

These believers are oblivious to the signs of Jesus's return because they are a prodigal.

You guessed it, the parable Jesus told about the prodigal sons fits this one perfectly (Luke 15:11-32). The younger son demanded his portion of his father's inheritance. Then he left town and blew it all on wild living.

Another example is in the book of Revelation where we see that during the tribulation period people are so consumed by their wicked behavior that instead of repenting when they clearly know the judgments are from God, that they double down on their sins instead (Revelation 9:20-21, 16:9, 11, 21). The apostle Paul tells us this is because God's truth is suppressed in unrighteousness (Romans 1:18-19).

Here's another one. Before the Babylonian invasion, the ancient Israelites decided to worship the queen of heaven because they remembered how good life was back when they did that. The prophet Jeremiah told them that all the troubles they were experiencing were because God could no longer put up with all their sin. Some people mistake God's longsuffering and his desire to see everyone saved for inaction.

The cure for this spiritual blindness is to trade your evil heart for a **good heart**.

> "The **good man** out of the **good treasure of his heart** brings out that which is **good**, and the evil man out of the evil treasure of his heart brings out that which is evil, for out of the abundance of the heart, his mouth speaks." (Luke 6:45)

The word *good* means pleasant, happy, and excellent. God's Word tells us that evil deeds are exposed when the light shines on them (Ephesians 5:13). So, what's the light? It's the gospel, the good news about Jesus (2 Corinthians 4:4-6).

The person who comes to mind in the Bible who had a radical change from being evil to being righteous is the apostle Paul (Acts 22). Jesus's light shone on him, and he was never the same.

Now, I know that we're talking about prodigal Christians here, so the assumption is that they're already saved. But the apostle Paul did something after his conversion that's key. He was immediately baptized and then started sharing the gospel everywhere he went.

So that's what you should do if this is your type of blindness. Return to God, just like the prodigal son returned to his father. Recommit your life to Jesus. Get baptized again, or perhaps for the first time, to demonstrate your commitment to God.

Then instead of spending your time partying, spend it helping others come to know Jesus. Be the light of the world that Jesus told us we are (Matthew 5:13-16). It's as simple as inviting someone to go to church or your small group or even a fun church event with you. I think another great way to encourage people to discuss biblical content and spark a desire to learn more is through movies and TV shows. Watch a movie like *Jesus Revolution* or *Risen* with some friends or invite them over and stream *The Chosen* series.[2]

Now that your heart is right, you'll be able to walk as a child of the light (Ephesians 5:8) and share the gospel of peace wherever your feet take you (Ephesians 6:15).

In our quest to overcome spiritual blindness to the signs, we've learned about ten of the good heart strengths mentioned in the Bible that we can use to overcome all the bad heart conditions. For a quick look at all the heart conditions and strengths that we've reviewed and their associated Scriptures, refer to Appendix B.

After all this talk about blindness and how to overcome it, are you able to see clearly now? I certainly hope so. Join me in the final chapter where we'll get ready to reign with Jesus, because it's obvious that he's on his way!

CHAPTER 20 – READY TO REIGN

THE KING IS COMING

Jesus is the King of kings and Lord of lords (Revelation 19:16). I hope it's obvious by now, Jesus is ready to reign by setting up his millennial kingdom on earth!

Jesus's second coming is a sequence of events that begins after the last judgment is poured out against unrepentant mankind. The seventh bowl judgment is the last and is described as the worst earthquake since people have existed (Revelation 16:17). We discussed it as Sign #139 - Great Earthquakes. The angel proclaims that "It is finished!"

Then we're told that immediately afterward the sources of natural light won't shine but that it'll be like a continuous day anyway (Matthew 24:29, Zechariah 14:6-7). That's curious, isn't it? We'll see where that light is coming from in a minute.

The sign of the Son of Man, that's Jesus, appears in the sky first (Matthew 24:30). A sign is a mark or token that distinguishes something and is known. It can also be an unusual occurrence. I think both of those apply to Jesus's second coming. So, what's the sign going to be? The Bible doesn't specifically say. I think we can take some educated guesses though based on Scripture.

We're told that a star, a reference to Jesus, would come out of Jacob (Numbers 24:17). The wise men who journeyed from the East to worship Jesus after his birth followed his star (Matthew 2:1-2). Then there are the shepherds who were informed of Jesus's birth by angels in the sky. Those shepherds were told to look for a baby in a manger as their sign (Luke 2:1-15). The rainbow is another good candidate since it's the sign of God's covenant with us (Genesis 9:13). And a rainbow surrounds God's throne in heaven (Revelation 4:3). The Bible also tells us that Jesus himself is the sign (Isaiah 7:14, Luke 11:30). We can't possibly forget the cross of Christ (1 Corinthians 1:17). Of all the signs of Christianity, that one is the most well-known. Perhaps it'll be a star that looks like a cross.

Next, the Son of Man comes on the clouds (Matthew 24:30). The disciples were told that Jesus would return the same way he left (Acts 1:11-12). They stood on the Mount of Olives, just east of Jerusalem, and watched him float up into the clouds. So, we should expect that he's going to float back down from the clouds and touch down on the Mount of Olives. But this time he's going to be riding a white horse (Revelation 19:11). When Jesus does touch the earth, the mountain will split into two (Zechariah 14:4-5).

Now, about it being like daytime when the sun's not shining. Here's why. Jesus told us that his coming would be like lightning (Matthew 24:27). We also know that he comes in flaming fire (1 Thessalonians 1:7), his countenance is like the sun (Revelation 1:6), his clothes are as white as light (Matthew 17:2), and all of his glory covers the heavens because the brightness is like light (Habakkuk 3:3). There are even rays that shoot out of Jesus's hands! Another cool thing about this is that somehow everyone is going to witness this (Revelation 1:7).

God's Word also reveals what Jesus will look like when he returns again. He's going to be seen in all his glory. Eyes like flames, hair like white wool, and feet like brass (Revelation 1:14-15). His garment will go to his feet. It has a golden band around the chest, is dipped in blood, and has the King of kings and Lord of lords inscribed on it (Revelation 1:13, 19:13, 16). And of course, he'll be wearing many crowns (Revelation 19:12).

Jesus's voice is like the sound of many waters (Revelation 1:15). I imagine that might be like being near a waterfall. It's loud and you can feel the power in the water.

It's hard to fathom what this is going to be like. If you've put your faith in Jesus, you won't need to wait until the second coming to experience this. You're going to see Jesus in all his glory face-to-face at the big party in heaven that happens right after the rapture.

When we see Jesus like this, are we going to fall on our face as though dead, like the apostle John did who witnessed these events and wrote those descriptions? I don't think we'll be able to help it! We'll be awestruck.

Lastly, Jesus doesn't return to earth by himself. His mighty angels will be there (1 Thessalonians 1:7). Along with everyone else in heaven. Everyone who was raptured, anyone resurrected at the rapture, all the Old Testament believers, and people who come to faith after the rapture and die during the tribulation (Revelation 19:14, 20:4-6, Daniel 12:1-3).

All of us will be riding white horses. I can't help but put a smile on my face when I think of how cool this is going to be. Can you imagine riding a horse across the sky with millions upon millions of others? And then we're going to see the reactions of the people on earth who are gathered at Armageddon (Sign #116). The evil angels and unrepentant sinners will be terrified at the sight of us. But the believers on the ground are going to be so completely overwhelmed with joy.

WHAT JESUS DOES WHEN HE RETURNS

When Jesus returns to earth at his second coming there are several things he's going to do.

Jesus is going to deal with all the unrepentant sinners left behind. Let's look at the War of Armageddon that he's going to end. All the nations, their kings, and their armies which are gathered to fight Jesus are going to be destroyed by Jesus simply speaking a word (Matthew 25:32, Revelation 19:19-21). Remember his Word is like a sharp sword. That's it, no battle. And this is no small army either. It's the army that the demonic angels gather of 200 million (Revelation 9:15-16). I imagine this is how every unbeliever left remaining on the planet meets their demise. Then an angel is going to shout for all the vultures to gather so they can feast on these victims of war (Revelation 19:17-18).

Jesus's parable of the sheep and goats speaks of this too (Matthew 25:32-46). The goats are the unbelievers who are destined for the lake of fire.

The Antichrist and the False Prophet will be captured and thrown alive into the lake of burning sulfur.

Next, Satan is going to be bound. Jesus instructs an angel to bind Satan in the bottomless pit for 1,000 years (Revelation 20:1-3). Yes, that's it. No epic superhero type battle of the ages takes place between Jesus and Satan. All it takes is Jesus's command and it's done. Satan will be rendered powerless. That's how mighty God is!

The Bible also tells us that the "host of exalted ones," which appears to reference the fallen angels, will be shut up in prison at this time too (Isaiah 24:21-23). With all those demonic beings imprisoned, there will be no deception until after Jesus's millennial reign, when we're told Satan is released for a time.

Once Jesus has vanquished the enemy, he'll setup his kingdom. Jesus's kingdom will cover the entire earth and never be destroyed (Daniel 2:34-35, 44, Zechariah 14:9). Jesus will reign here on earth forever.

Only people who've put their faith in Jesus for salvation from their sins will be able to live in Jesus's kingdom on earth (Daniel 7:18, 22).

That's not all though! Jesus is going to lift the curse he placed on earth and mankind when Adam and Eve first sinned in the garden of Eden (Genesis 3:14-19).

> For the creation waits with eager expectation for the children of God to be revealed. For the creation was subjected to vanity, not of its own will, but because of him who subjected it, in hope that the creation itself also will be delivered from the bondage of decay into the liberty of the glory of the children of God. For we know that the whole creation groans and travails in pain together until now. Not only so, but ourselves also, who have the first fruits of the Spirit, even we ourselves groan within ourselves, waiting for adoption, the redemption of our body. (Romans 8:19-23)

We've been discussing God's promises that await us in the millennial kingdom throughout this entire book. They are the polar opposite signs in each chapter. I for one am certainly ready for my new body and to see firsthand what God has planned for us. The Bible tells us that our hearts can't even imagine what God has prepared for us (1 Corinthians 2:9). I can think of some pretty fantastic things. So, it's going to be truly amazing!

TIMING OF THE SECOND COMING

Unlike the rapture, the date of the second coming won't be a secret. God gives us the exact number of days to count and when to start counting. We're supposed to start counting when the Antichrist confirms a covenant with Israel (Daniel 9:27). It's going to be a seven-year peace treaty. The Scripture says a "week" which translates to seven years on our calendar. We're told that in the middle of that timeline, the Antichrist will commit an abominable act in the temple when he declares himself God (2 Thessalonians 2:4). He'll likely erect a statue of himself for worship. This of course will end the daily sacrifices.

The prophet Daniel was so distraught by these visions of the end, that he asked the angel when it would all be over. He was told, "a time, times, and half a time" (Daniel 12:6-7). A time is a year on our calendar. So that's 3.5 years or 1,260 days.

The angel further states to Daniel that anyone who waits until day

1,335 gets a blessing (Daniel 12:12). That's 75 days after Jesus's second coming. What's this about? Wouldn't believers alive on earth at Jesus's second coming be getting a blessing on day 1,260? Well, of course they would because they'll finally see Jesus! But keep in mind all of the things we discussed in the prior section that Jesus does when he returns. I believe it means the millennial kingdom and the lifting of the curse officially starts on day 1,335. We'll see.

The next aspect of the timing of Jesus's second coming that I want to explain is when it happens in relation to the tribulation period and millennial kingdom. Now, it should be obvious by now that I hold a pre-millennial viewpoint on this. The *pre* in pre-millennial means Jesus's second coming occurs prior to the millennial kingdom.

I take a literal interpretation of the Bible and believe there's a literal 1,000-year reign by Jesus on earth that starts after the literal tribulation period. We shouldn't pick and choose which Scriptures to interpret literally. That's a very slippery slope. It's how people make the Bible fit their world view. The entire Word of God is literal unless it says otherwise in the Scripture.

The present time in which we live is the church age. I also believe that God will literally fulfill all of his promises to Israel and the Jewish people during the millennial kingdom.

> Long ago the LORD said to Israel: "I have loved you, my people, with an everlasting love. With unfailing love I have drawn you to myself. ... Is not Israel still my son, my darling child?" says the LORD. "I often have to punish him, but I still love him. That's why I long for him and surely will have mercy on him. ... How long will you wander, my wayward daughter? For the LORD will cause something new to happen—Israel will embrace her God. ... I am as likely to reject my people Israel as I am to abolish the laws of nature!" (Jeremiah 31:3, 20, 22, 36 NLT)

Okay, that's crystal clear. God has not forsaken Israel. The church, believers who've put their faith in Jesus, certainly hasn't replaced them because they rejected Jesus as their savior. God's covenant with them isn't dependent on their behavior, it's unconditional and eternal (Genesis 15, 17). As we've discussed throughout this book with the polar opposite signs, there are a lot of promises God has yet to bestow upon his chosen people.

Let's understand the other two viewpoints, post-millennialism and amillennialism, so that we can have an intelligent conversation about it with others. They are actually very similar. So, let's start there.

Neither of them relies upon a literal interpretation of the Bible. They start by spiritualizing the 1,000-year millennial kingdom. They think it's symbolic of the church age and believe it's about Jesus reigning in the hearts of Christians and impacting society. Thus, they believe the present era that we're living in is the millennial kingdom.

As for the tribulation events depicted in the book of Revelation and at least 19 other books of the Bible, both viewpoints also spiritualize those events or think they already happened in the past.[1]

They also both believe that the church has replaced Israel and that there will be no literal fulfillment of God's promises to the Jewish people. They believe God is blessing the church with those promises instead.

The difference between them is simple. Post-millennialists think Christians will evangelize the world and usher in a period of righteousness on earth before Jesus returns at his second coming. Amillennialists think the second coming could happen whenever.

As you might be thinking, it's difficult to counter a Christian who doesn't regard the Word of God as literal. I would simply ask them if they believe that Jesus literally fulfilled every single prophecy in the Bible regarding his first coming. If they believe that, then ask why they don't believe that Jesus will do that again regarding his second coming. I mean those prophets who wrote about his first coming also wrote about his second coming. The source is reliable. After all, God wrote the entire thing (2 Peter 1:20-21, 2 Timothy 3:16-17).

God's going to do what he says. That's how he gets credit for doing it instead of the enemy.

ARE YOU READY TO REIGN?

Are you ready to get promoted from being a watchman and a soldier to being a king or queen? We're going to reign with Jesus!

In order to reign, you're going to need a crown. It's one of the many rewards we can earn while we're here on earth. You're going to want a crown because it's mentioned as the gift we get to bring to Jesus's party after the rapture (Revelation 4:9-11).

There are five specific crowns mentioned in the Bible. The crown of righteousness is for believers who are looking forward to Jesus's return (2 Timothy 4:7-8). The incorruptible crown is for Christians who are self-controlled and persevere, just like an athlete (1 Corinthians 9:25). The crown of life is for believers who were faithful unto death, or Christian martyrs (Revelation 2:10). There's also the crown of glory that's for church leaders who are good shepherds to God's flock of believers (1 Peter 5:1-4). Lastly, there's the crown of rejoicing for Christians who help others come to faith in Jesus (1 Thessalonians 2:19-20).

As you should expect, a crown comes with responsibility and work. It's not just for show. In Jesus's parable of the faithful and evil servant, the faithful servant is rewarded with becoming the ruler over all the master's goods (Matthew 24:45-47). One aspect of this is authority over nations (Revelation 2:26). In the millennial kingdom, all of us believers are going to be government employees. Some of us will be ruling over cities or nations. But that's not the only thing that's going to need leaders.

Just think of how complex our own cities are. I'm sure Jesus is going to want us leading churches, schools, construction projects, events, eateries, and other places of employment for those living in the millennial kingdom. Some of us are going to be judges too. Remember the kingdom is going to be populated with Christians who come to faith in Jesus after the rapture and live through the tribulation period. There will be disputes because they will still be living in sin.

Now, crowns are just some of the rewards we can earn and store in heaven.

> "Don't lay up treasures for yourselves on the earth, where moth and rust consume, and where thieves break through and steal; but lay up for yourselves treasures in heaven, where neither moth nor rust consume, and where thieves don't break through and steal; for where your treasure is, there your heart will be also." (Matthew 6:19-21)

There are a whole slew of rewards or treasures that we can earn for heavenly living. Refer to Appendix B for a list I compiled. They are all based upon things we do here while we wait for Jesus. Here's a quick look at what'll secure you a reward: being ready for Jesus's return, reading the book of Revelation, caring for your enemies, suffering for your faith, praying to God in private, inviting the poor to a party, and living righteously.

It's worth contemplating why the Bible doesn't specifically tell us what all the rewards for doing those things are. I'm sure there's the surprise element that's involved in getting a gift. I also think it would be hard for us to fully comprehend. We don't look at rewards the same way that God does. We typically consider things like money and possessions as treasures here on earth. But I've found that earthly treasure is often a burden. Like how it just takes more time and money to maintain a bigger, fancier house. That's not going to be the case in heaven. I do believe some rewards in heaven will be receiving special skills that we'll be able to use in the millennial kingdom (1 Corinthians 12).

If you're worried that your lifestyle isn't up to par, the good news is that there's also a bunch of rewards we just inherit for being saved by Jesus. These are also listed in Appendix B. They include eternal life, fruit from the Tree of Life, hidden manna, sitting on Jesus's throne, and a new name.

I think one of the most important teachings in the Bible about these heavenly treasures is that Satan is after our rewards (Revelation 3:8-11). Not everyone included in the rapture or resurrected at the rapture is going to be crowned. And some believers are even going to arrive in heaven and find out they didn't earn any treasure (1 Corinthians 3:13-15). We're told that we can lose our rewards by doing good deeds publicly for human praise (Matthew 6:1-5, 16). If we don't love one another or do what God commands, we'll lose rewards too (2 John 1:8).

You don't want to show up in heaven empty handed without a gift for Jesus. That's not cool. The entire point of rewards is that they reflect our faith and God's glory in our lives. Jesus said that when we do something good and helpful for one of the least of our brethren, that we're really doing it to Jesus (Matthew 25:34-40). These treasures ultimately bring glory back to Jesus.

As we wrap up our study about the signs of Jesus's soon return, the bad heart conditions that are so obvious in the world, and the good heart strengths that we need to overcome it all, there are a few things the Bible tells us to do "above all" that apply to us today.

> **The heart is deceitful** above all things and it is exceedingly corrupt. (Jeremiah 17:9)

> **Guard your heart** above all else, for it determines the course of your life. (Proverbs 4:23 NLT)

Seek the Kingdom of God above all else, and live righteously, and he will give you everything you need. (Matthew 6:33 NLT)

Above all these things, **walk in love**, which is the bond of perfection. (Colossians 3:14)

Above all, you must **live as citizens of heaven**, conducting yourselves in a manner worthy of the Good News about Christ. (Philippians 1:27 NLT)

Above all, **taking up the shield of faith**, with which you will be able to quench all the fiery darts of the evil one. (Ephesians 6:16)

These are the five things we should focus on doing above all others. Since our heart is deceitful, we must guard our heart, seek the kingdom of God, walk in love, live as citizens of heaven, and take up the shield of faith. I'd like to throw one more in by reminding you that God himself is "able to do exceedingly abundantly above all." God's given us a short window of time in order to make an impact and help lead others to him. I implore you to use the remaining time we have wisely.

You're no longer oblivious to the signs that are all around us because today is different. It's obvious that we've passed the point of no return. You've learned it's not "seeing is believing," but rather, "believe and then you'll see." You're equipped to help yourself and those you care about overcome spiritual blindness to the signs. You know you'll be included in the rapture and not left behind. You've traded your bad heart condition for a good heart strength. You won't be ashamed at Jesus's return because you're storing your treasure and rewards in heaven. You're not living in fear of what you see in the world. You know it reveals Jesus is coming and you know God's wrath isn't meant for you. You know you're saved and you're ready for Jesus's second coming. You're ready to wield the sword of the spirit and share the gospel with those you love because you know how little time is left. You're bringing a gift to Jesus's party, the crown of righteousness, because you're eager for Jesus's imminent return. You're standing, wearing the full armor of God, watching intently **because it's obvious the King is coming!**

Chapter 20 - Ready To Reign

I hope you enjoyed this journey through the signs. If you'd like to show your support for my work, please leave a review wherever you purchased this book. Your review is very important to independent, self-published authors like me. Internet and online bookstore algorithms favor books with reviews. They display in search results and at the top of search results more often than books without reviews. I even need a minimum number of reviews before I can purchase certain advertising. Ultimately, your review will help more people find this book and come to realize how obvious it is that Jesus is coming! Go to rapture911.com/reviews if you need a link to where you can leave a review.

Thanks for your support!
Marsha

APPENDIX

A. SIGNS BY CATEGORIES

SIGN LEGEND

You'll notice the following elements included for each Sign # in this book.

Category Bar - you'll see the category bar that's shown below. Figure A describes what each category includes. The categories I've placed the sign into will be bold, underlined, and appear in black text as shown here:

Anti | DD | Earth | Gov | Israel | **Jesus** | Leader | Sky | Society | Tech | Trib

Scripture - A Scripture that describes the sign.

> But know this: that in the last days, grievous times will come. (2 Timothy 3:1)

An explanation of the Scripture and the sign.

Fulfillment - Examples that reveal how the sign is being fulfilled.

Today Is Different - A discussion of why today is different when compared to prior generations regarding fulfillment of the sign.

Additional Scriptures: A list of additional Scriptures to read regarding the sign. If I refer to any other biblical content when describing the sign, like a parable of Jesus or an event in the Old Testament, you'll find the Scriptures for those in this list.

Table A. Sign Legend	
Category	Description
Anti	The sign is a characteristic of the Antichrist.
DD	The sign is a double down. When judgment came, instead of repenting, the people were often called out for continuing to do specific sins. Sometimes even worse than before. *1 Kings 13:33-34, 2 Kings 17:13-17, Jeremiah 44:7-10, Revelation 9:21.*
Earth	The sign is in nature or on the earth.
Gov	The sign is about nations, governments, wars, or politics.
Israel	The sign is about the Jewish people or the nation of Israel.
Jesus	The sign is a direct quote of Jesus.
Leader	The sign is about leaders, kings, rulers, teachers, prophets, and judges.
Sky	The sign is in the heavens, sky, space, or is about angels.
Society	The sign is about human behavior and society.
Tech	The sign requires a technology, scientific advancement, or modern invention for fulfillment or substantial progression in fulfillment.
Trib	This sign takes place during the tribulation period.

Figure A. Sign Legend

SIGNS IN JESUS'S OLIVET DISCOURSE

Not One Stone Will Be Left On Top Of Another
Matthew 24:1-2, Mark 13:1-2, Luke 21:5-6

Sign #131 - Broken Pagan Altars

The Sign Of Your Coming And Of The End Of The Age
Matthew 24:3-4, Mark 13:3-4, Luke 21:7-8

Sign #119 - Prophets Warn About The Future

Don't Be Deceived
Matthew 24:4, Mark 13:5, Luke 21:8

Sign #51 - Deception	Sign #61 - The Lie

Many Will Come In Jesus's Name (False Christs) And Deceive
Matthew 24:5, Mark 13:6, Luke 21:8

Sign #54 - Blasphemy	Sign #61 - The Lie
Sign #59 - False Christs	Sign #103 - Evil Leadership
Sign #60 - The Antichrist	

Wars
Matthew 24:6, Mark 13:7, Luke 21:9

Sign #103 - Evil Leadership	Sign #109 - Gog's Allies
Sign #105 - Kingdom Vs Kingdom	Sign #111 - Nation Vs Nation
Sign #107 - Psalm 83 Allies	Sign #113 - Destruction Of Damascus
Sign #108 - Gog Of The Land Of Magog	Sign #114 - Shocking Amount Of Destruction

Rumors Of Wars
Matthew 24:6, Mark 13:7

Sign #103 - Evil Leadership	Sign #111 - Nation Vs Nation

Commotions
Luke 21:9

Sign #103 - Evil Leadership	Sign #111 - Nation Vs Nation

These Things (Wars) Must Come, But End Is Not Yet
Matthew 24:6, Mark 13:7, Luke 21:9

Sign #103 – Evil Leadership	Sign #111 – Nation Vs Nation

Nation Will Rise Against Nation

Matthew 24:7, Mark 13:8, Luke 21:10

Sign #103 – Evil Leadership	Sign #111 – Nation Vs Nation
Sign #107 – Psalm 83 Allies	Sign #113 – Destruction Of Damascus
Sign #108 – Gog Of The Land Of Magog	Sign #114 – Shocking Amount Of Destruction
Sign #109 - Gog's Allies	

Kingdom Will Rise Against Kingdom

Matthew 24:7, Mark 13:8, Luke 21:10

Sign #103 - Evil Leadership	Sign #108 - Gog Of The Land Of Magog
Sign #105 - Kingdom Vs Kingdom	Sign #109 - Gog's Allies
Sign #107 - Psalm 83 Allies	Sign #114 - Shocking Amount Of Destruction

Famines

Matthew 24:7, Mark 13:8, Luke 21:11

Sign #100 - Cannibalism	Sign #138 - Earth Made Desolate

Pestilences

Matthew 24:7, Luke 21:11

Sign #137 - Pestilences

Earthquakes In Various Places

Matthew 24:7, Mark 13:8, Luke 21:11

Sign #131 - Broken Pagan Altars	Sign #139 - Great Earthquakes
Sign #138 - Earth Made Desolate	

Troubles

Mark 13:8

Sign #4 - Birth Pains	Sign #136 - The Day Of The Lord

Beginning Of Sorrows

Matthew 24:8, Mark 13:8

Sign #3 - When You See All These Things	Sign #5 - Tribulation In View
Sign #4 - Birth Pains	Sign #136 - The Day Of The Lord

Fearful Sights And Great Signs From Heaven

Luke 21:11

Sign #13 - Great Fear	Sign #146 - The Heavens Shake
Sign #145 - Wonders In The Sun, Moon, Stars	

A. Signs By Categories

God's People Delivered To Tribulation Or Persecution
Matthew 24:9, Mark 13:9, Luke 21:12

Sign #37 - Censorship	Sign #103 - Evil Leadership
Sign #94 - God's Prophets Are Persecuted	Sign #115 - War Against God's People
Sign #95 - Oppression of God's People	

God's People Killed Or Martyred
Matthew 24:9, Mark 13:12, Luke 21:16

Sign #94 - God's Prophets Are Persecuted	Sign #103 - Evil Leadership
Sign #95 - Oppression of God's People	Sign #115 - War Against God's People

God's People Hated By All Or All Nations
Matthew 24:9, Mark 13:13, Luke 21:17

Sign #92 - Anti-Semitism	Sign #108 - Gog Of The Land Of Magog
Sign #94 - God's Prophets Are Persecuted	Sign #109 - Gog's Allies
Sign #95 - Oppression of God's People	Sign #112 - All Nations Against Israel
Sign #103 - Evil Leadership	Sign #113 - Destruction Of Damascus
Sign #107 - Psalm 83 Allies	Sign #115 - War Against God's People

God's People Delivered To Councils
Mark 13:9

Sign #94 - God's Prophets Are Persecuted	Sign #103 - Evil Leadership
Sign #95 - Oppression of God's People	

God's People Beaten
Mark 13:9, Luke 21:12

Sign #94 - God's Prophets Are Persecuted	Sign #103 - Evil Leadership
Sign #95 - Oppression of God's People	

God's People Brought Before Rulers
Mark 13:9, Luke 21:12

Sign #94 - God's Prophets Are Persecuted	Sign #103 - Evil Leadership
Sign #95 - Oppression of God's People	

God's People Arrested Or Imprisoned
Mark 13:11, Luke 21:12

Sign #94 - God's Prophets Are Persecuted	Sign #103 - Evil Leadership
Sign #95 - Oppression of God's People	

God's People Delivered To Synagogues
Luke 21:12

Sign #94 - God's Prophets Are Persecuted	Sign #103 - Evil Leadership
Sign #95 - Oppression of God's People	

God's People Betrayed By Family And Friends

Mark 13:12, Luke 21:16

Sign #91 - Betrayal

Many Will Be Offended

Matthew 24:10

| Sign #88 - Hatred | Sign #89 - Victimhood |

Many Will Betray One Another

Matthew 24:10, Mark 13:12

| Sign #53 - Conspiracy | Sign #91 - Betrayal |

Many Will Hate One Another

Matthew 24:10

Sign #88 - Hatred

False Prophets Deceive Many

Matthew 24:11

| Sign #57 - False Prophets | Sign #103 - Evil Leadership |
| Sign #58 - The False Prophet | |

Lawlessness Will Abound

Matthew 24:12

| Sign #98 - Continually Only Evil | Sign #103 - Evil Leadership |
| Sign #101 - Perilous Times | |

Love Grows Cold Because Of Lawlessness

Matthew 24:12

| Sign #81 - Without Natural Affection | Sign #101 - Perilous Times |
| Sign #88 - Hatred | |

God's People Who Endure To The End Will Be Saved

Matthew 24:13, Mark 13:13, Luke 21:18-19

| Sign #133 - The Gospel Preached Everywhere | Sign #134 - A Place Prepared By God |

Gospel Preached In All The World, Then The End Comes

Matthew 24:14, Mark 13:10

| Sign #132 - Christian Revival | Sign #133 - The Gospel Preached Everywhere |

A. Signs By Categories

Abomination Of Desolation In The Temple
Matthew 24:15, Mark 13:14, Luke 21:20

Sign #43 - Entitlement	Sign #103 - Evil Leadership
Sign #60 - The Antichrist	Sign #115 - War Against God's People
Sign #68 - Polluted Sanctuary	Sign #128 - The Third Temple
Sign #71 - Image Of The Beast	

Those in Judea Flee To The Mountains
Matthew 24:16-20, Mark 13:15-18, Luke 21:21

Sign #134 - A Place Prepared By God

Jerusalem Surrounded By Armies
Luke 21:20

Sign #60 - The Antichrist	Sign #112 - All Nations Against Israel
Sign #103 - Evil Leadership	Sign #115 - War Against God's People

Great Tribulation
Matthew 24:21-22, Mark 13:19-20, Luke 21:22-23

Sign #114 - Shocking Amount Of Destruction	Sign #136 - The Day Of The Lord
Sign #115 - War Against God's People	

Great Distress In The Land
Luke 21:23

Sign #136 - The Day Of The Lord	Sign #140 - Planet On Fire
Sign #138 - Earth Made Desolate	Sign #141 - Severe Storms

Wrath Upon This People
Luke 21:23

Sign #136 - The Day Of The Lord	Sign #143 - God's Wrath

Judeans Fall By The Sword
Luke 21:24

Sign #103 - Evil Leadership	Sign #115 - War Against God's People

Judeans Taken Captive Into All Nations
Luke 21:24

Sign #96 - Slavery	Sign #115 - War Against God's People

Jerusalem Trampled By Gentiles
Luke 21:24

Sign #92 - Anti-Semitism	Sign #112 - All Nations Against Israel
Sign #107 - Psalm 83 Allies	Sign #113 - Destruction Of Damascus
Sign #108 - Gog Of The Land Of Magog	Sign #115 - War Against God's People
Sign #109 - Gog's Allies	

Oblivious To The Signs When It's Obvious The King Is Coming

False Christs, False Prophets Show Signs And Wonders
Matthew 24:23-26, Mark 13:21-23

Sign #57 - False Prophets	Sign #60 - The Antichrist
Sign #58 - The False Prophet	Sign #61 - The Lie
Sign #59 - False Christs	Sign #63 - Lying Wonders

Signs In The Sun, Moon, Stars
Luke 21:25

| Sign #145 - Wonders In The Sun, Moon, Stars | Sign #147 - The Black Sun |
| Sign #146 - The Heavens Shake | Sign #148 - War In Heaven |

Distress Of Nations With Perplexity
Luke 21:25

| Sign #23 - Anxiety of Nations With Perplexity | Sign #103 - Evil Leadership |

Sea And Waves Roaring
Luke 21:25

| Sign #23 - Anxiety of Nations With Perplexity | Sign #103 - Evil Leadership |
| Sign #101 - Perilous Times | Sign #142 - Sea And Waves Roaring |

Men's Hearts Failing From Fear
Luke 21:26

Sign #13 - Great Fear

Coming Of The Son Of Man Like Lightning
Matthew 24:27

Sign #145 - Wonders In The Sun, Moon, Stars

Wherever The Carcass Is The Eagles Will Gather
Matthew 24:28

| Sign #116 - Gathered To Armageddon | Chapter 20 - Ready To Reign |
| Sign #126 - Israel's Birds Of Prey | |

After The Tribulation
Matthew 24:29, Mark 13:24

| Sign #116 - Gathered To Armageddon | Chapter 20 - Ready To Reign |

Sun Darkened
Matthew 24:29, Mark 13:24

| Sign #145 - Wonders In The Sun, Moon, Stars | Sign #147 - The Black Sun |

Moon No Light
Matthew 24:29, Mark 13:24

| Sign #145 - Wonders In The Sun, Moon, Stars | Sign #147 - The Black Sun |

Stars Fall From Heaven

Matthew 24:29, Mark 13:25

Sign #145 - Wonders In The Sun, Moon, Stars	Sign #146 - The Heavens Shake

Powers Of The Heavens Shaken

Matthew 24:29, Mark 13:25, Luke 21:26

Sign #64 - Polar Opposite - A Discerning Heart	Sign #146 - The Heavens Shake
Sign #145 - Wonders In The Sun, Moon, Stars	Sign #148 - War In Heaven

Sign Of The Son Of Man In Heaven

Matthew 24:30

Sign #145 - Wonders In The Sun, Moon, Stars

Tribes Mourn

Matthew 24:30

Sign #132 - Christian Revival	Chapter 20 - Ready To Reign

Son Of Man Coming On Clouds

Matthew 24:30, Mark 13:26, Luke 21:27

Sign #14 - Polar Opposite - A Seeking Heart	Chapter 20 - Ready To Reign
Sign #116 - Gathered To Armageddon	

Angels Gather The Elect

Matthew 24:31, Mark 13:27

Sign #150 - The Rapture	Chapter 17 - The Rapture

Parable Of The Fig Tree

Matthew 24:32-34, Mark 13:28-30, Luke 21:29-32

Sign #1 - Israel Is A Nation	Sign #150 - The Rapture
Sign #2 - The Timing Is Right	Chapter 17 - The Rapture
Sign #3 - When You See All These Things	

When These Things Begin To Happen, Jesus Is Near

Matthew 24:33, Mark 13:29, Luke 21:28

Chapter 1 - Watch	Sign #6 - The Point Of No Return
Sign #3 - When You See All These Things	Sign #150 - The Rapture
Sign #5 - Tribulation In View	Chapter 17 - The Rapture

Heaven And Earth Will Pass Away

Matthew 24:35, Mark 13:31, Luke 21:33

Sign #144 - Polar Opposite - Restored Earth	Sign #149 - Polar Opposite - New Heavens

Oblivious To The Signs When It's Obvious The King Is Coming

Jesus's Words Won't Pass Away
Matthew 24:35, Mark 13:31, Luke 21:33

Sign #119 - Prophets Warn About The Future	Sign #133 - The Gospel Preached Everywhere
Sign #122 - Prophecy Sealed Until End Times	

No One Knows The Day Or Hour, So Be Ready
Matthew 24:36, Mark 13:32

Chapter 1 - Watch	Sign #150 - The Rapture
Sign #3 - When You See All These Things	Chapter 17 - The Rapture
Sign #32 - Rapture 911	

Like Days Of Noah
Matthew 24:37-39

Sign #32 - Rapture 911	Sign #84 - Fading Of Normality
Sign #34 - God's Warnings Aren't Heeded	Sign #98 - Continually Only Evil
Sign #82 - Genetic Engineering	Sign #101 - Perilous Times
Sign #83 - Nephilim	Sign #150 - The Rapture

The People Didn't Know, They Were Oblivious
Matthew 24:39

Sign #32 - Rapture 911	Sign #84 - Fading Of Normality

One Will Be Taken, One Will Be Left
Matthew 24:40-41

Sign #150 - The Rapture	Chapter 17 - The Rapture

Watch, Or The Day Will Come On You Unexpectedly
Matthew 24:42-44, Mark 13:33-37, Luke 21:34-36

Chapter 1 - Watch	Sign #34 - God's Warnings Aren't Heeded
Sign #3 - When You See All These Things	Sign #75 - Drugs And Alcohol
Sign #5 - Tribulation In View	Sign #150 - The Rapture
Sign #32 - Rapture 911	Chapter 17 - The Rapture

Parable Of The Faithful And Evil Servant
Matthew 24:45-51

Sign #3 - When You See All These Things	Sign #65 - Hypocrisy
Sign #32 - Rapture 911	Sign #103 - Evil Leadership
Sign #38 - Rebellious	

Parable Of The 10 Virgins
Matthew 25:1-13

Sign #3 - When You See All These Things	Sign #150 - The Rapture
Sign #32 - Rapture 911	Chapter 17 - The Rapture

Parable Of The Talents

Matthew 25:14-30

| Sign #41 - Coveting | Sign #98 - Continually Only Evil |
| Sign #43 - Entitlement | Chapter 20 - Ready To Reign |

Parable Of The Sheep And Goats

Matthew 25:31-46

Sign #98 - Continually Only Evil	Sign #130 - The Accursed
Sign #116 - Gathered To Armageddon	Sign #149 - Polar Opposite - New Heavens
Sign #129 - The Blessed	Chapter 20 - Ready To Reign

SIGNS BY CATEGORY

Anti

Sign #3 - When You See All These Things
Sign #4 - Birth Pains
Sign #9 - Worshiping Other Gods
Sign #10 - Idolatry
Sign #12 - Satanism
Sign #15 - Puffed Up With Pride
Sign #16 - Lovers Of Ourselves
Sign #18 - Fortified Cities And High Towers
Sign #19 - Changing Times And Laws
Sign #29 - Despising God's Word
Sign #35 - Don't Endure Sound Doctrine
Sign #37 - Censorship
Sign #38 - Rebellious
Sign #41 - Coveting
Sign #42 - Jealousy
Sign #43 - Entitlement
Sign #44 - Lovers Of Pleasure
Sign #45 - Love Of Money
Sign #46 - Stealing
Sign #51 - Deception
Sign #53 - Conspiracy
Sign #54 - Blasphemy
Sign #55 - Assault On The Afterlife
Sign #60 - The Antichrist
Sign #61 - The Lie
Sign #62 - A Covenant With Death
Sign #63 - Lying Wonders
Sign #66 - Encouraging Sin
Sign #67 - Profane Worship
Sign #68 - Polluted Sanctuary
Sign #69 - One World Religion
Sign #70 - One World Currency
Sign #71 - Image Of The Beast
Sign #72 - Mark Of The Beast
Sign #73 - Forced Worship
Sign #80 - Attack On Marriage
Sign #86 - One World Government
Sign #88 - Hatred

Anti (Cont.)

Sign #91 - Betrayal
Sign #92 - Anti-Semitism
Sign #93 - Unholy People Celebrated
Sign #94 - God's Prophets Are Persecuted
Sign #95 - Oppression of God's People
Sign #96 - Slavery
Sign #98 - Continually Only Evil
Sign #100 - Cannibalism
Sign #101 - Perilous Times
Sign #102 - Evil Inventions
Sign #103 - Evil Leadership
Sign #104 - The Election Omen
Sign #105 - Kingdom Vs Kingdom
Sign #110 - The Antichrist Rules The World
Sign #112 - All Nations Against Israel
Sign #114 - Shocking Amount Of Destruction
Sign #115 - War Against God's People
Sign #116 - Gathered To Armageddon
Sign #130 - The Accursed
Sign #143 - God's Wrath
Sign #148 - War In Heaven

DD

Sign #3 - When You See All These Things
Sign #4 - Birth Pains
Sign #7 - Apostasy
Sign #9 - Worshiping Other Gods
Sign #10 - Idolatry
Sign #11 - The Occult
Sign #12 - Satanism
Sign #15 - Puffed Up With Pride
Sign #18 - Fortified Cities And High Towers
Sign #22 - Cancel Culture
Sign #26 - Refusal To Believe
Sign #29 - Despising God's Word
Sign #34 - God's Warnings Aren't Heeded
Sign #39 - No Apologies
Sign #44 - Lovers Of Pleasure
Sign #46 - Stealing

DD (Cont.)

Sign #54 - Blasphemy
Sign #67 - Profane Worship
Sign #75 - Drugs And Alcohol
Sign #79 - Sexual Perversion
Sign #80 - Attack On Marriage
Sign #98 - Continually Only Evil

Earth

Sign #3 - When You See All These Things
Sign #4 - Birth Pains
Sign #9 - Worshiping Other Gods
Sign #13 - Great Fear
Sign #14 - Polar Opposite - A Seeking Heart
Sign #18 - Fortified Cities And High Towers
Sign #20 - Polar Opposite - A Worshiping Heart
Sign #21 - Curses Are A Warning
Sign #49 - The Rise Of Babylon
Sign #63 - Lying Wonders
Sign #74 - Polar Opposite - A Steadfast Heart
Sign #77 - Abstain From Certain Foods
Sign #82 - Genetic Engineering
Sign #84 - Fading Of Normality
Sign #87 - Polar Opposite - An Upright Heart
Sign #108 - Gog Of The Land Of Magog
Sign #116 - Gathered To Armageddon
Sign #118 - God's Presence Is Obvious
Sign #120 - Many Run To And Fro
Sign #122 - Prophecy Sealed Until End Times
Sign #123 - Population Explosion
Sign #125 - Israel's Wealth
Sign #126 - Israel's Birds Of Prey
Sign #127 - Israel's Beasts
Sign #128 - The Third Temple
Sign #131 - Broken Pagan Altars
Sign #134 - A Place Prepared By God
Sign #135 - The Curse
Sign #136 - The Day Of The Lord
Sign #137 - Pestilences
Sign #138 - Earth Made Desolate
Sign #139 - Great Earthquakes
Sign #140 - Planet On Fire

Earth (Cont.)

Sign #141 - Severe Storms
Sign #142 - Sea And Waves Roaring
Sign #143 - God's Wrath
Sign #144 - Polar Opposite - Restored Earth
Sign #148 - War In Heaven
Sign #149 - Polar Opposite - New Heavens
Sign #150 - The Rapture

Gov

Sign #1 - Israel Is A Nation
Sign #2 - The Timing Is Right
Sign #3 - When You See All These Things
Sign #4 - Birth Pains
Sign #6 - The Point Of No Return
Sign #14 - Polar Opposite - A Seeking Heart
Sign #18 - Fortified Cities And High Towers
Sign #19 - Changing Times And Laws
Sign #20 - Polar Opposite - A Worshiping Heart
Sign #21 - Curses Are A Warning
Sign #22 - Cancel Culture
Sign #23 - Anxiety of Nations With Perplexity
Sign #33 - Polar Opposite - A Wise Heart
Sign #37 - Censorship
Sign #43 - Entitlement
Sign #45 - Love Of Money
Sign #47 - Destruction Of Wealth
Sign #48 - Wealth Gap
Sign #49 - The Rise Of Babylon
Sign #53 - Conspiracy
Sign #61 - The Lie
Sign #62 - A Covenant With Death
Sign #64 - Polar Opposite - A Discerning Heart
Sign #66 - Encouraging Sin
Sign #69 - One World Religion
Sign #70 - One World Currency
Sign #71 - Image Of The Beast
Sign #72 - Mark Of The Beast
Sign #73 - Forced Worship
Sign #75 - Drugs And Alcohol
Sign #80 - Attack On Marriage
Sign #82 - Genetic Engineering

Oblivious To The Signs When It's Obvious The King Is Coming

Gov (Cont.)
Sign #84 - Fading Of Normality
Sign #85 - Downfall Of The United States
Sign #86 - One World Government
Sign #92 - Anti-Semitism
Sign #93 - Unholy People Celebrated
Sign #95 - Oppression of God's People
Sign #96 - Slavery
Sign #97 - Polar Opposite - A Pure Heart
Sign #99 - Child Sacrifice
Sign #101 - Perilous Times
Sign #102 - Evil Inventions
Sign #103 - Evil Leadership
Sign #104 - The Election Omen
Sign #105 - Kingdom Vs Kingdom
Sign #106 - The Prince Of Persia
Sign #107 - Psalm 83 Allies
Sign #108 - Gog Of The Land Of Magog
Sign #109 - Gog's Allies
Sign #110 - The Antichrist Rules The World
Sign #111 - Nation Vs Nation
Sign #112 - All Nations Against Israel
Sign #113 - Destruction Of Damascus
Sign #114 - Shocking Amount Of Destruction
Sign #115 - War Against God's People
Sign #116 - Gathered To Armageddon
Sign #117 - Polar Opposite - A Good Heart
Sign #125 - Israel's Wealth
Sign #128 - The Third Temple
Sign #129 - The Blessed
Sign #130 - The Accursed
Sign #143 - God's Wrath

Israel
Sign #1 - Israel Is A Nation
Sign #2 - The Timing Is Right
Sign #3 - When You See All These Things
Sign #4 - Birth Pains
Sign #14 - Polar Opposite - A Seeking Heart
Sign #19 - Changing Times And Laws
Sign #20 - Polar Opposite - A Worshiping Heart
Sign #21 - Curses Are A Warning

Israel (Cont.)
Sign #33 - Polar Opposite - A Wise Heart
Sign #60 - The Antichrist
Sign #62 - A Covenant With Death
Sign #64 - Polar Opposite - A Discerning Heart
Sign #67 - Profane Worship
Sign #68 - Polluted Sanctuary
Sign #71 - Image Of The Beast
Sign #72 - Mark Of The Beast
Sign #74 - Polar Opposite - A Steadfast Heart
Sign #85 - Downfall Of The United States
Sign #92 - Anti-Semitism
Sign #94 - God's Prophets Are Persecuted
Sign #95 - Oppression of God's People
Sign #97 - Polar Opposite - A Pure Heart
Sign #106 - The Prince Of Persia
Sign #107 - Psalm 83 Allies
Sign #108 - Gog Of The Land Of Magog
Sign #109 - Gog's Allies
Sign #112 - All Nations Against Israel
Sign #113 - Destruction Of Damascus
Sign #115 - War Against God's People
Sign #116 - Gathered To Armageddon
Sign #117 - Polar Opposite - A Good Heart
Sign #122 - Prophecy Sealed Until End Times
Sign #125 - Israel's Wealth
Sign #126 - Israel's Birds Of Prey
Sign #127 - Israel's Beasts
Sign #128 - The Third Temple
Sign #129 - The Blessed
Sign #130 - The Accursed
Sign #134 - A Place Prepared By God
Sign #144 - Polar Opposite - Restored Earth

Jesus
Sign #7 - Apostasy
Sign #8 - Backsliding
Sign #9 - Worshiping Other Gods
Sign #10 - Idolatry
Sign #12 - Satanism
Sign #15 - Puffed Up With Pride
Sign #16 - Lovers Of Ourselves

Jesus (Cont.)

Sign #17 - Everyone Does Right In Own Eyes
Sign #24 - Always Learning But Never Know...
Sign #26 - Refusal To Believe
Sign #28 - Neither Hot Nor Cold
Sign #35 - Don't Endure Sound Doctrine
Sign #39 - No Apologies
Sign #42 - Jealousy
Sign #44 - Lovers Of Pleasure
Sign #45 - Love Of Money
Sign #46 - Stealing
Sign #50 - Polar Opposite - A Serving Heart
Sign #52 - Slander
Sign #55 - Assault On The Afterlife
Sign #56 - False Teachers
Sign #66 - Encouraging Sin
Sign #67 - Profane Worship
Sign #78 - Cussing
Sign #79 - Sexual Perversion
Sign #80 - Attack On Marriage
Sign #102 - Evil Inventions
Sign #110 - The Antichrist Rules The World
Sign #124 - Secrets Revealed

Jesus Olivet Discourse

Sign #1 - Israel Is A Nation
Sign #2 - The Timing Is Right
Sign #3 - When You See All These Things
Sign #4 - Birth Pains
Sign #5 - Tribulation In View
Sign #6 - The Point Of No Return
Sign #13 - Great Fear
Sign #14 - Polar Opposite - A Seeking Heart
Sign #23 - Anxiety of Nations With Perplexity
Sign #32 - Rapture 911
Sign #34 - God's Warnings Aren't Heeded
Sign #37 - Censorship
Sign #38 - Rebellious
Sign #41 - Coveting
Sign #43 - Entitlement
Sign #51 - Deception
Sign #53 - Conspiracy

Jesus Olivet Discourse (Cont.)

Sign #54 - Blasphemy
Sign #57 - False Prophets
Sign #58 - The False Prophet
Sign #59 - False Christs
Sign #60 - The Antichrist
Sign #61 - The Lie
Sign #63 - Lying Wonders
Sign #64 - Polar Opposite - A Discerning Heart
Sign #65 - Hypocrisy
Sign #68 - Polluted Sanctuary
Sign #71 - Image Of The Beast
Sign #75 - Drugs And Alcohol
Sign #81 - Without Natural Affection
Sign #82 - Genetic Engineering
Sign #83 - Nephilim
Sign #84 - Fading Of Normality
Sign #88 - Hatred
Sign #89 - Victimhood
Sign #91 - Betrayal
Sign #92 - Anti-Semitism
Sign #94 - God's Prophets Are Persecuted
Sign #95 - Oppression of God's People
Sign #96 - Slavery
Sign #98 - Continually Only Evil
Sign #100 - Cannibalism
Sign #101 - Perilous Times
Sign #103 - Evil Leadership
Sign #105 - Kingdom Vs Kingdom
Sign #107 - Psalm 83 Allies
Sign #108 - Gog Of The Land Of Magog
Sign #109 - Gog's Allies
Sign #111 - Nation Vs Nation
Sign #112 - All Nations Against Israel
Sign #113 - Destruction Of Damascus
Sign #114 - Shocking Amount Of Destruction
Sign #115 - War Against God's People
Sign #116 - Gathered To Armageddon
Sign #119 - Prophets Warn About The Future
Sign #122 - Prophecy Sealed Until End Times
Sign #126 - Israel's Birds Of Prey

Jesus Olivet Discourse (Cont.)

Sign #128 - The Third Temple
Sign #129 - The Blessed
Sign #130 - The Accursed
Sign #131 - Broken Pagan Altars
Sign #132 - Christian Revival
Sign #133 - The Gospel Preached Everywhere
Sign #134 - A Place Prepared By God
Sign #136 - The Day Of The Lord
Sign #137 - Pestilences
Sign #138 - Earth Made Desolate
Sign #139 - Great Earthquakes
Sign #140 - Planet On Fire
Sign #141 - Severe Storms
Sign #142 - Sea And Waves Roaring
Sign #143 - God's Wrath
Sign #144 - Polar Opposite - Restored Earth
Sign #145 - Wonders In The Sun, Moon, Stars
Sign #146 - The Heavens Shake
Sign #147 - The Black Sun
Sign #148 - War In Heaven
Sign #149 - Polar Opposite - New Heavens
Sign #150 - The Rapture
Chapter 17 - The Rapture
Chapter 20 - Ready To Reign

Leader

Sign #3 - When You See All These Things
Sign #4 - Birth Pains
Sign #6 - The Point Of No Return
Sign #8 - Backsliding
Sign #12 - Satanism
Sign #14 - Polar Opposite - A Seeking Heart
Sign #15 - Puffed Up With Pride
Sign #17 - Everyone Does Right In Own Eyes
Sign #19 - Changing Times And Laws
Sign #20 - Polar Opposite - A Worshiping Heart
Sign #21 - Curses Are A Warning
Sign #23 - Anxiety of Nations With Perplexity
Sign #33 - Polar Opposite - A Wise Heart
Sign #34 - God's Warnings Aren't Heeded
Sign #35 - Don't Endure Sound Doctrine

Leader (Cont.)

Sign #37 - Censorship
Sign #39 - No Apologies
Sign #40 - Polar Opposite - A Heart Of Flesh
Sign #41 - Coveting
Sign #44 - Lovers Of Pleasure
Sign #45 - Love Of Money
Sign #47 - Destruction Of Wealth
Sign #48 - Wealth Gap
Sign #50 - Polar Opposite - A Serving Heart
Sign #51 - Deception
Sign #52 - Slander
Sign #53 - Conspiracy
Sign #54 - Blasphemy
Sign #55 - Assault On The Afterlife
Sign #56 - False Teachers
Sign #57 - False Prophets
Sign #58 - The False Prophet
Sign #59 - False Christs
Sign #60 - The Antichrist
Sign #61 - The Lie
Sign #62 - A Covenant With Death
Sign #63 - Lying Wonders
Sign #64 - Polar Opposite - A Discerning Heart
Sign #65 - Hypocrisy
Sign #66 - Encouraging Sin
Sign #67 - Profane Worship
Sign #68 - Polluted Sanctuary
Sign #69 - One World Religion
Sign #70 - One World Currency
Sign #71 - Image Of The Beast
Sign #72 - Mark Of The Beast
Sign #73 - Forced Worship
Sign #74 - Polar Opposite - A Steadfast Heart
Sign #82 - Genetic Engineering
Sign #85 - Downfall Of The United States
Sign #86 - One World Government
Sign #87 - Polar Opposite - An Upright Heart
Sign #91 - Betrayal
Sign #92 - Anti-Semitism
Sign #94 - God's Prophets Are Persecuted

A. Signs By Categories

Leader (Cont.)
Sign #95 - Oppression of God's People
Sign #96 - Slavery
Sign #97 - Polar Opposite - A Pure Heart
Sign #100 - Cannibalism
Sign #102 - Evil Inventions
Sign #103 - Evil Leadership
Sign #104 - The Election Omen
Sign #105 - Kingdom Vs Kingdom
Sign #106 - The Prince Of Persia
Sign #108 - Gog Of The Land Of Magog
Sign #109 - Gog's Allies
Sign #110 - The Antichrist Rules The World
Sign #114 - Shocking Amount Of Destruction
Sign #115 - War Against God's People
Sign #116 - Gathered To Armageddon
Sign #117 - Polar Opposite - A Good Heart
Sign #119 - Prophets Warn About The Future
Sign #128 - The Third Temple
Sign #129 - The Blessed
Sign #130 - The Accursed
Sign #143 - God's Wrath
Sign #144 - Polar Opposite - Restored Earth
Sign #148 - War In Heaven
Sign #149 - Polar Opposite - New Heavens

Sky
Sign #3 - When You See All These Things
Sign #4 - Birth Pains
Sign #5 - Tribulation In View
Sign #13 - Great Fear
Sign #21 - Curses Are A Warning
Sign #61 - The Lie
Sign #63 - Lying Wonders
Sign #118 - God's Presence Is Obvious
Sign #120 - Many Run To And Fro
Sign #126 - Israel's Birds Of Prey
Sign #136 - The Day Of The Lord
Sign #137 - Pestilences
Sign #140 - Planet On Fire
Sign #141 - Severe Storms
Sign #142 - Sea And Waves Roaring

Sky (Cont.)
Sign #145 - Wonders In The Sun, Moon, Stars
Sign #146 - The Heavens Shake
Sign #147 - The Black Sun
Sign #148 - War In Heaven
Sign #149 - Polar Opposite - New Heavens
Sign #150 - The Rapture

Society
Sign #3 - When You See All These Things
Sign #4 - Birth Pains
Sign #6 - The Point Of No Return
Sign #7 - Apostasy
Sign #8 - Backsliding
Sign #9 - Worshiping Other Gods
Sign #10 - Idolatry
Sign #11 - The Occult
Sign #12 - Satanism
Sign #13 - Great Fear
Sign #14 - Polar Opposite - A Seeking Heart
Sign #15 - Puffed Up With Pride
Sign #16 - Lovers Of Ourselves
Sign #17 - Everyone Does Right In Own Eyes
Sign #20 - Polar Opposite - A Worshiping Heart
Sign #21 - Curses Are A Warning
Sign #22 - Cancel Culture
Sign #23 - Anxiety of Nations With Perplexity
Sign #24 - Always Learning But Never Know...
Sign #25 - Fake Bibles
Sign #26 - Refusal To Believe
Sign #27 - Scoffers
Sign #28 - Neither Hot Nor Cold
Sign #29 - Despising God's Word
Sign #30 - Atheism
Sign #31 - Hopelessness
Sign #32 - Rapture 911
Sign #33 - Polar Opposite - A Wise Heart
Sign #34 - God's Warnings Aren't Heeded
Sign #35 - Don't Endure Sound Doctrine
Sign #36 - Children Of Disobedience
Sign #37 - Censorship
Sign #38 - Rebellious

Oblivious To The Signs When It's Obvious The King Is Coming

Society (Cont.)

Sign #39 - No Apologies
Sign #40 - Polar Opposite - A Heart Of Flesh
Sign #41 - Coveting
Sign #42 - Jealousy
Sign #43 - Entitlement
Sign #44 - Lovers Of Pleasure
Sign #45 - Love Of Money
Sign #46 - Stealing
Sign #49 - The Rise Of Babylon
Sign #50 - Polar Opposite - A Serving Heart
Sign #51 - Deception
Sign #52 - Slander
Sign #53 - Conspiracy
Sign #54 - Blasphemy
Sign #55 - Assault On The Afterlife
Sign #64 - Polar Opposite - A Discerning Heart
Sign #65 - Hypocrisy
Sign #66 - Encouraging Sin
Sign #67 - Profane Worship
Sign #71 - Image Of The Beast
Sign #72 - Mark Of The Beast
Sign #73 - Forced Worship
Sign #74 - Polar Opposite - A Steadfast Heart
Sign #75 - Drugs And Alcohol
Sign #76 - Perverted Bodies
Sign #77 - Abstain From Certain Foods
Sign #78 - Cussing
Sign #79 - Sexual Perversion
Sign #80 - Attack On Marriage
Sign #81 - Without Natural Affection
Sign #82 - Genetic Engineering
Sign #83 - Nephilim
Sign #84 - Fading Of Normality
Sign #87 - Polar Opposite - An Upright Heart
Sign #88 - Hatred
Sign #89 - Victimhood
Sign #90 - Mocking
Sign #91 - Betrayal
Sign #92 - Anti-Semitism
Sign #93 - Unholy People Celebrated

Society (Cont.)

Sign #94 - God's Prophets Are Persecuted
Sign #95 - Oppression of God's People
Sign #96 - Slavery
Sign #97 - Polar Opposite - A Pure Heart
Sign #98 - Continually Only Evil
Sign #99 - Child Sacrifice
Sign #100 - Cannibalism
Sign #101 - Perilous Times
Sign #102 - Evil Inventions
Sign #104 - The Election Omen
Sign #116 - Gathered To Armageddon
Sign #117 - Polar Opposite - A Good Heart
Sign #120 - Many Run To And Fro
Sign #121 - Knowledge Shall Increase
Sign #122 - Prophecy Sealed Until End Times
Sign #123 - Population Explosion
Sign #124 - Secrets Revealed
Sign #129 - The Blessed
Sign #130 - The Accursed
Sign #131 - Broken Pagan Altars
Sign #132 - Christian Revival
Sign #133 - The Gospel Preached Everywhere
Sign #143 - God's Wrath

Tech

Sign #3 - When You See All These Things
Sign #4 - Birth Pains
Sign #5 - Tribulation In View
Sign #6 - The Point Of No Return
Sign #10 - Idolatry
Sign #11 - The Occult
Sign #13 - Great Fear
Sign #14 - Polar Opposite - A Seeking Heart
Sign #15 - Puffed Up With Pride
Sign #16 - Lovers Of Ourselves
Sign #18 - Fortified Cities And High Towers
Sign #22 - Cancel Culture
Sign #23 - Anxiety of Nations With Perplexity
Sign #24 - Always Learning But Never Know...
Sign #25 - Fake Bibles
Sign #28 - Neither Hot Nor Cold

A. Signs By Categories

Tech (Cont.)

Sign #30 - Atheism
Sign #31 - Hopelessness
Sign #32 - Rapture 911
Sign #33 - Polar Opposite - A Wise Heart
Sign #34 - God's Warnings Aren't Heeded
Sign #35 - Don't Endure Sound Doctrine
Sign #37 - Censorship
Sign #38 - Rebellious
Sign #42 - Jealousy
Sign #44 - Lovers Of Pleasure
Sign #46 - Stealing
Sign #47 - Destruction Of Wealth
Sign #48 - Wealth Gap
Sign #49 - The Rise Of Babylon
Sign #50 - Polar Opposite - A Serving Heart
Sign #51 - Deception
Sign #55 - Assault On The Afterlife
Sign #56 - False Teachers
Sign #57 - False Prophets
Sign #58 - The False Prophet
Sign #60 - The Antichrist
Sign #61 - The Lie
Sign #63 - Lying Wonders
Sign #66 - Encouraging Sin
Sign #68 - Polluted Sanctuary
Sign #69 - One World Religion
Sign #70 - One World Currency
Sign #71 - Image Of The Beast
Sign #72 - Mark Of The Beast
Sign #73 - Forced Worship
Sign #76 - Perverted Bodies
Sign #77 - Abstain From Certain Foods
Sign #78 - Cussing
Sign #79 - Sexual Perversion
Sign #81 - Without Natural Affection
Sign #82 - Genetic Engineering
Sign #83 - Nephilim
Sign #84 - Fading Of Normality
Sign #88 - Hatred
Sign #94 - God's Prophets Are Persecuted

Tech (Cont.)

Sign #95 - Oppression of God's People
Sign #96 - Slavery
Sign #99 - Child Sacrifice
Sign #102 - Evil Inventions
Sign #105 - Kingdom Vs Kingdom
Sign #106 - The Prince Of Persia
Sign #111 - Nation Vs Nation
Sign #113 - Destruction Of Damascus
Sign #114 - Shocking Amount Of Destruction
Sign #115 - War Against God's People
Sign #119 - Prophets Warn About The Future
Sign #120 - Many Run To And Fro
Sign #121 - Knowledge Shall Increase
Sign #122 - Prophecy Sealed Until End Times
Sign #123 - Population Explosion
Sign #124 - Secrets Revealed
Sign #125 - Israel's Wealth
Sign #129 - The Blessed
Sign #132 - Christian Revival
Sign #133 - The Gospel Preached Everywhere
Sign #137 - Pestilences
Sign #138 - Earth Made Desolate
Sign #139 - Great Earthquakes
Sign #140 - Planet On Fire
Sign #141 - Severe Storms
Sign #142 - Sea And Waves Roaring
Sign #143 - God's Wrath
Sign #145 - Wonders In The Sun, Moon, Stars
Sign #146 - The Heavens Shake
Sign #147 - The Black Sun
Sign #148 - War In Heaven

Trib

Sign #3 - When You See All These Things
Sign #4 - Birth Pains
Sign #5 - Tribulation In View
Sign #6 - The Point Of No Return
Sign #9 - Worshiping Other Gods
Sign #10 - Idolatry
Sign #11 - The Occult
Sign #12 - Satanism

Trib (Cont.)

Sign #13 - Great Fear
Sign #15 - Puffed Up With Pride
Sign #16 - Lovers Of Ourselves
Sign #18 - Fortified Cities And High Towers
Sign #19 - Changing Times And Laws
Sign #21 - Curses Are A Warning
Sign #23 - Anxiety of Nations With Perplexity
Sign #24 - Always Learning But Never Know...
Sign #25 - Fake Bibles
Sign #26 - Refusal To Believe
Sign #27 - Scoffers
Sign #28 - Neither Hot Nor Cold
Sign #29 - Despising God's Word
Sign #31 - Hopelessness
Sign #34 - God's Warnings Aren't Heeded
Sign #35 - Don't Endure Sound Doctrine
Sign #37 - Censorship
Sign #38 - Rebellious
Sign #39 - No Apologies
Sign #41 - Coveting
Sign #42 - Jealousy
Sign #43 - Entitlement
Sign #44 - Lovers Of Pleasure
Sign #45 - Love Of Money
Sign #46 - Stealing
Sign #47 - Destruction Of Wealth
Sign #48 - Wealth Gap
Sign #49 - The Rise Of Babylon
Sign #51 - Deception
Sign #52 - Slander
Sign #53 - Conspiracy
Sign #54 - Blasphemy
Sign #55 - Assault On The Afterlife
Sign #58 - The False Prophet
Sign #60 - The Antichrist
Sign #61 - The Lie
Sign #62 - A Covenant With Death
Sign #63 - Lying Wonders
Sign #66 - Encouraging Sin
Sign #67 - Profane Worship

Trib (Cont.)

Sign #68 - Polluted Sanctuary
Sign #69 - One World Religion
Sign #70 - One World Currency
Sign #71 - Image Of The Beast
Sign #72 - Mark Of The Beast
Sign #73 - Forced Worship
Sign #75 - Drugs And Alcohol
Sign #78 - Cussing
Sign #79 - Sexual Perversion
Sign #80 - Attack On Marriage
Sign #83 - Nephilim
Sign #84 - Fading Of Normality
Sign #85 - Downfall Of The United States
Sign #86 - One World Government
Sign #88 - Hatred
Sign #89 - Victimhood
Sign #90 - Mocking
Sign #91 - Betrayal
Sign #92 - Anti-Semitism
Sign #93 - Unholy People Celebrated
Sign #94 - God's Prophets Are Persecuted
Sign #96 - Slavery
Sign #98 - Continually Only Evil
Sign #100 - Cannibalism
Sign #101 - Perilous Times
Sign #102 - Evil Inventions
Sign #103 - Evil Leadership
Sign #104 - The Election Omen
Sign #105 - Kingdom Vs Kingdom
Sign #106 - The Prince Of Persia
Sign #108 - Gog Of The Land Of Magog
Sign #109 - Gog's Allies
Sign #110 - The Antichrist Rules The World
Sign #111 - Nation Vs Nation
Sign #112 - All Nations Against Israel
Sign #114 - Shocking Amount Of Destruction
Sign #115 - War Against God's People
Sign #116 - Gathered To Armageddon
Sign #118 - God's Presence Is Obvious
Sign #119 - Prophets Warn About The Future

A. Signs By Categories

Trib (Cont.)
Sign #122 - Prophecy Sealed Until End Times
Sign #123 - Population Explosion
Sign #125 - Israel's Wealth
Sign #126 - Israel's Birds Of Prey
Sign #127 - Israel's Beasts
Sign #128 - The Third Temple
Sign #130 - The Accursed
Sign #131 - Broken Pagan Altars
Sign #132 - Christian Revival
Sign #133 - The Gospel Preached Everywhere
Sign #134 - A Place Prepared By God
Sign #135 - The Curse

Trib (Cont.)
Sign #136 - The Day Of The Lord
Sign #137 - Pestilences
Sign #138 - Earth Made Desolate
Sign #139 - Great Earthquakes
Sign #140 - Planet On Fire
Sign #141 - Severe Storms
Sign #142 - Sea And Waves Roaring
Sign #143 - God's Wrath
Sign #145 - Wonders In The Sun, Moon, Stars
Sign #146 - The Heavens Shake
Sign #147 - The Black Sun
Sign #148 - War In Heaven

SIGNS IN DEUTERONOMY CURSES

Deuteronomy 28:15-68
Sign #6 - The Point Of No Return
Sign #7 - Apostasy
Sign #9 - Worshiping Other Gods
Sign #10 - Idolatry
Sign #13 - Great Fear
Sign #21 - Curses Are A Warning
Sign #23 - Anxiety Of Nations With Perplexity
Sign #24 - Always Learning But Never Know...
Sign #31 - Hopelessness
Sign #34 - God's Warnings Aren't Heeded
Sign #36 - Children Of Disobedience
Sign #43 - Entitlement
Sign #46 - Stealing
Sign #47 - Destruction Of Wealth
Sign #73 - Forced Worship
Sign #84 - Fading Of Normality

Deuteronomy 28:15-68 (Cont.)
Sign #85 - Downfall Of The United States
Sign #88 - Hatred
Sign #90 - Mocking
Sign #92 - Anti-Semitism
Sign #95 - Oppression of God's People
Sign #96 - Slavery
Sign #100 - Cannibalism
Sign #103 - Evil Leadership
Sign #111 - Nation Vs Nation
Sign #112 - All Nations Against Israel
Sign #135 - The Curse
Sign #137 - Pestilences
Sign #138 - Earth Made Desolate
Sign #141 - Severe Storms
Sign #143 - God's Wrath

SIGNS IN END TIMES NEW TESTAMENT SCRIPTURES

Romans 1:18-32
Sign #6 - The Point Of No Return
Sign #7 - Apostasy
Sign #9 - Worshiping Other Gods
Sign #10 - Idolatry
Sign #15 - Puffed Up With Pride
Sign #24 - Always Learning But Never Know...
Sign #30 - Atheism
Sign #37 - Censorship
Sign #38 - Rebellious
Sign #39 - No Apologies
Sign #41 - Coveting
Sign #42 - Jealousy
Sign #51 - Deception
Sign #52 - Slander
Sign #61 - The Lie
Sign #66 - Encouraging Sin
Sign #75 - Drugs And Alcohol
Sign #76 - Perverted Bodies
Sign #79 - Sexual Perversion
Sign #81 - Without Natural Affection
Sign #88 - Hatred
Sign #93 - Unholy People Celebrated
Sign #98 - Continually Only Evil
Sign #102 - Evil Inventions
Sign #104 - The Election Omen
Sign #118 - God's Presence Is Obvious
Sign #145 - Wonders In The Sun, Moon, Stars

Ephesians 5:3-6
Sign #6 - The Point Of No Return
Sign #10 - Idolatry
Sign #27 - Scoffers
Sign #36 - Children Of Disobedience
Sign #41 - Coveting
Sign #44 - Lovers Of Pleasure
Sign #51 - Deception
Sign #78 - Cussing
Sign #79 - Sexual Perversion

Colossians 3:5-10
Sign #10 - Idolatry
Sign #41 - Coveting
Sign #44 - Lovers Of Pleasure
Sign #51 - Deception
Sign #54 - Blasphemy
Sign #78 - Cussing
Sign #79 - Sexual Perversion
Sign #88 - Hatred
Sign #98 - Continually Only Evil

1 Timothy 4:1-3
Sign #7 - Apostasy
Sign #11 - The Occult
Sign #12 - Satanism
Sign #51 - Deception
Sign #65 - Hypocrisy
Sign #77 - Abstain From Certain Foods
Sign #79 - Sexual Perversion
Sign #80 - Attack On Marriage
Sign #98 - Continually Only Evil

2 Timothy 3:1-9, 13
Sign #4 - Birth Pains
Sign #6 - The Point Of No Return
Sign #15 - Puffed Up With Pride
Sign #16 - Lovers Of Ourselves
Sign #24 - Always Learning But Never Know...
Sign #29 - Despising God's Word
Sign #35 - Don't Endure Sound Doctrine
Sign #38 - Rebellious
Sign #43 - Entitlement
Sign #44 - Lovers Of Pleasure
Sign #45 - Love Of Money
Sign #51 - Deception
Sign #52 - Slander
Sign #54 - Blasphemy
Sign #56 - False Teachers
Sign #65 - Hypocrisy
Sign #75 - Drugs And Alcohol

2 Timothy 3:1-9, 13 (Cont.)
Sign #81 - Without Natural Affection
Sign #84 - Fading Of Normality
Sign #88 - Hatred

2 Timothy 3:1-9, 13 (Cont.)
Sign #91 - Betrayal
Sign #98 - Continually Only Evil
Sign #101 - Perilous Times

B. OBLIVIOUS SUMMARIES AND END TIMES NOTES

GOOD HEARTS AND BAD HEARTS

Good Hearts	Bad Hearts
A Seeking Heart Psalm 119:1-2	A Turned Away Heart 1 Kings 11:4
A Worshiping Heart Lamentations 3:41	A Prideful Heart Daniel 5:17-18, 20 NKJV
A Wise Heart Proverbs 16:23	A Foolish Heart Luke 24:13, 15, 25
A Flesh Heart Ezekiel 36:26	A Hardened Heart Exodus 7:13 NKJV
A Serving Heart Deuteronomy 10:12	A Coveting Heart 2 Peter 2:1, 14-15 NKJV
A Discerning Heart 1 Kings 3:9	A Deceiving Heart Jeremiah 14:14
A Steadfast Heart Psalm 112:7	A Discouraging Heart Deuteronomy 1:1, 22, 26-28 NKJV
An Upright Heart 1 Kings 3:6	A Perverse Heart Proverbs 6:12-14
A Pure Heart 1 Peter 1:22 NKJV	A Hateful Heart 1 Chronicles 15:29
A Good Heart Luke 6:45	An Evil Heart Jeremiah 11:6-8

PATTERNS IN THE PAST

Sign #119 - Prophets Warn About The Future
Sign #21 - Curses Are A Warning
Sign #34 - God's Warnings Aren't Heeded
Sign #57 - False Prophets
Sign #94 - God's Prophets Are Persecuted

END TIMES TIMELINE

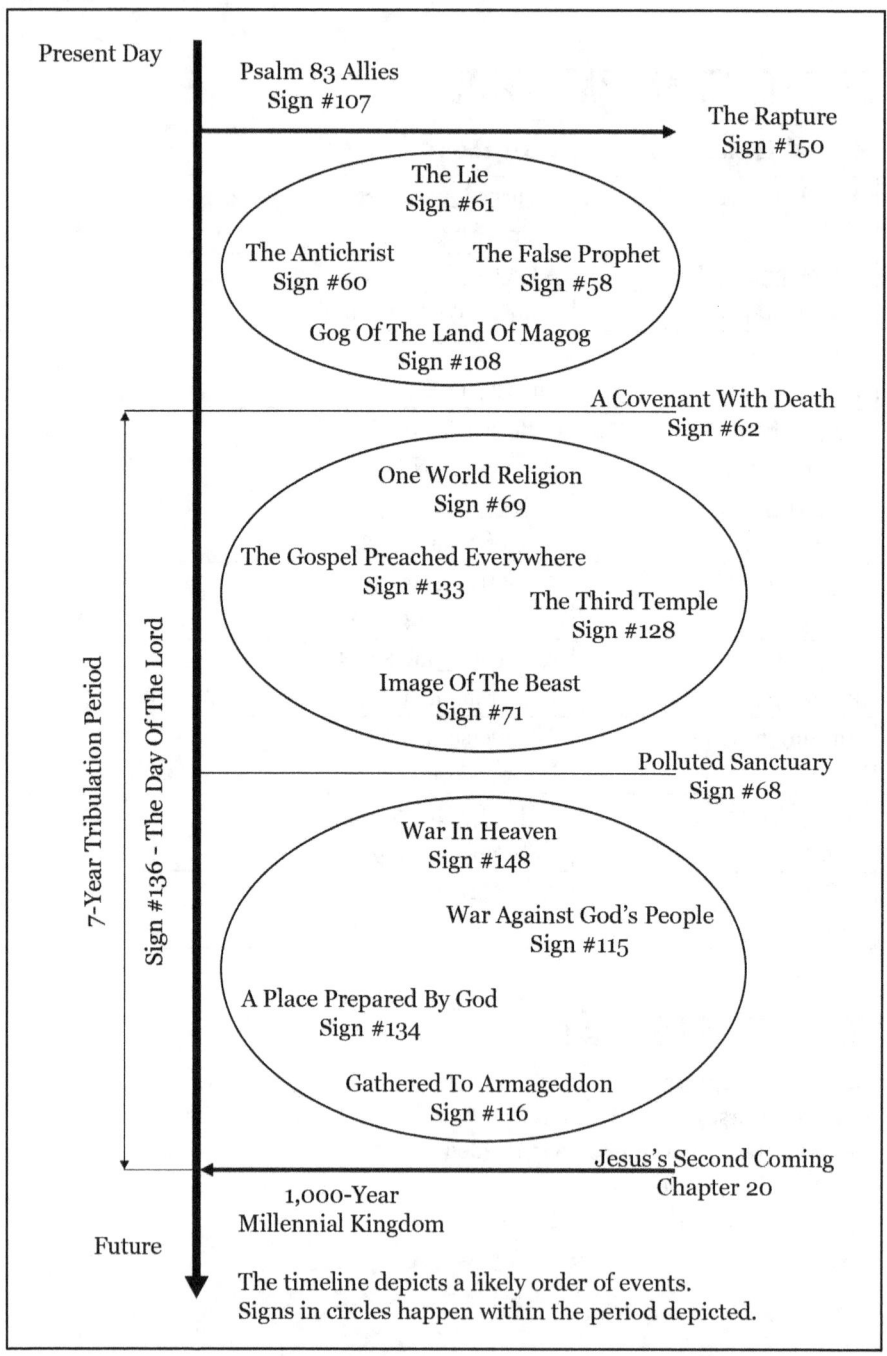

HEAVENLY REWARDS

Crowns Earned

Incorruptible Crown. (1 Corinthians 9:25)
Crown of Glory. (1 Peter 5:1-4)
Crown of Rejoicing. (1 Thessalonians 2:19-20)
Crown of Righteousness. (2 Timothy 4:7-8)
Crown of Life. (Revelation 2:10)
Cast crowns at Jesus's feet as a gift to him. (Revelation 4:10-11)

Rewards Inherited

- Eternal life. (John 3:16, Ephesians 2:8-9)
- Eat and drink at Jesus's table in his kingdom. (Luke 22:29-30)
- Shine like the sun. (Matthew 13:43)
- The kingdom of heaven is a treasure. (Matthew 13:44)
- Fruit from the tree of life in the paradise of God. (Revelation 2:7)
- Not harmed by the second death. (Revelation 2:11)
- Eat manna hidden in heaven. (Revelation 2:17)
- A white stone with a new name engraved on it. (Revelation 2:17)
- Clothed in white and walk with Jesus. (Revelation 3:5)
- Your name isn't erased from the Book of Life. (Revelation 3:5)
- Your name announced before God and his angels. (Revelation 3:5)
- Pillar in the temple of God. Like Solomon's Temple pillars that reflected the sun. (Revelation 3:12, 1 Kings 7:15-22, 2 Chronicles 3:15-17)
- The name of God written on you. (Revelation 3:12)
- The name of the city of God, New Jerusalem, written on you. Citizen of New Jerusalem. (Revelation 3:12)
- Jesus's new name written on you. (Revelation 3:12)
- Dine with Jesus. (Revelation 3:20)
- Sit with Jesus on his throne. (Revelation 3:21)

Rewards Earned
- Plant or water God's word in another. Earn a reward. (1 Corinthians 3:7-9)
- Fire will reveal if your work has value. If your work survives, earn a reward. (1 Corinthians 3:13-15)
- Disciple other believers. They will be your reward. (1 Thessalonians 2:19)
- Work willingly at whatever you do as though you're working for God. Earn an inheritance. (Colossians 3:23-25)
- Righteous behavior. Earn a reward. (Ezekiel 18:20)
- Sincerely seek God. Earn a reward. (Hebrews 11:6)
- Working when it seems useless. Trust God for your reward. (Isaiah 49:4)
- Earn a reward for your suffering. (Isaiah 61:8)
- Ready when Jesus arrives. Earn a meal served by Jesus. (Luke 12:35-37)
- Faithful and wise servant. Earn rulership. (Luke 12:41-48, Matthew 24:45-51)
- Invite the poor, lame, and blind to your feasts. Earn a blessing and be repaid. (Luke 14:12-14)
- Earn a great reward when people mock and persecute you for following Jesus. (Matthew 5:11-12)
- Love and pray for your enemies. Earn a reward. (Matthew 5:43-48)
- Pray privately to God. Earn a reward. (Matthew 6:6)
- Fast privately for God. Earn a reward. (Matthew 6:16-18)
- Receive a prophet as one who speaks for God. Earn the same reward the prophet gets. (Matthew 10:41)
- Receive a righteous person due to their righteousness. Earn a reward like theirs. (Matthew 10:41)
- Provide even a cup of water to a believer. Earn a reward. (Matthew 10:42)
- Sell what you have and give it to the poor. Earn treasure in heaven. (Matthew 19:16-22, Luke 12:33-34)
- Provide for needy believers and visit imprisoned believers. Earn a blessing and inherit the kingdom. (Matthew 25:31-46)
- Righteous living. Earn a reward. (Proverbs 23)
- Provide for your enemies. Earn a reward. (Proverbs 25:21-22)
- Be trustworthy. Earn a rich reward. (Proverbs 28:20)
- Read the book of Revelation and obey it. Earn a blessing. (Revelation 1:3)
- Obey God to the very end. Earn authority over the nations and the morning star. (Revelation 2:26-28)
- You're raptured. Earn protection from the great time of testing. (Revelation 3:10)
- You're invited to the marriage supper of Jesus (you're raptured). Earn a blessing. (Revelation 19:9)
- Earn a reward in accordance with your work. (Revelation 22:12)

ABOUT THE AUTHOR

Marsha Kuhnley is an American author of Christian non-fiction books. She has a passion for Bible prophecy, finance, and economics. You may have seen Marsha as a guest on the popular *Christ In Prophecy* TV program where she discusses her books, the Rapture, and End Times topics. She received her MBA in Finance and BA in Economics from the University of New Mexico. Prior to becoming an author, she enjoyed a career at Intel Corporation. She uses her education and career experience to take complex biblical information and present it in easily understandable concepts. You'll benefit from over 15 years of her research and study of the Bible, Bible prophecy, and Rapture theology. She lives in Albuquerque, NM with her husband where they attend Calvary Church with Pastor Skip Heitzig.

CONNECT WITH MARSHA

rapture911.com/connect

TESTIMONY OF MARSHA KUHNLEY

I was born and raised in Albuquerque, New Mexico. Like many of you reading this book, I didn't grow up knowing God or Jesus. As a young child, I was raised in a secular home. We didn't go to church. We didn't talk about faith or religion. I remember believing that God existed, but I often thought of him as a puppet master of sorts. Much like me playing with my dolls and orchestrating everything they did.

My first memorable encounter with someone religious happened when I was a first grader, six years old at the time. A mean boy in my class told me I was going to go to hell because I didn't go to church. I didn't really know what hell was, but I knew it wasn't good. After telling my mother about this, I learned it's the place bad people went when they died. I remember being so confused because I wasn't a bad person, and I didn't understand what being good had to do with going to church. So why did this mean boy tell me I was going to hell?

When I was a little older, middle school age, my mom and her friends were practicing new age spirituality. It didn't take long for this to influence my entire family. I attended psychic fairs, had tarot card readings, used a Ouija board with my friends, thought I had spirit guides, believed in past lives, and was even hypnotized several times so I could get a glimpse of those past lives. I grew up in a pagan, new age home. I thought I was enlightened. That I had a better understanding of the spirit realm and life after death than most people.

When I was in high school, I started dating my husband. He and his family were Christians. He did what any good Christian would do and invited his girlfriend to church with him. This was the first time anyone had ever invited me to church. I remember being excited because I was often curious about what church was like.

For many years, I attended church with my husband, but just on occasion. It's because I had a really hard time with it. I was still participating in new age activities during this time. I struggled to understand the songs they sang at church. I remember one song in particular with a verse, "nothing but the blood of Jesus."[1] Why were they singing about blood? It was gross. I also didn't understand what the preacher taught. I remember him talking about Jesus's death. But I didn't understand why it was important. I also didn't understand

Communion. They passed crackers and grape juice around during the service and then ate them after a prayer. My husband told me not to take it because I didn't believe. Believe what? That Jesus died? I didn't understand. I felt like I was the only person in the church who didn't participate in Communion. I felt like an outsider and like I was being judged during every service. I didn't fit in. I didn't understand why these Christians believed their way to heaven was the only way. I honestly believed that I would go to heaven because I was a good person.

I was also reading the Bible a little bit now and even had a difficult time understanding it. My husband even tried to explain these things to me. I wasn't struggling because I was incapable of learning. I had completed college and earned a couple degrees at this point. It's like I was up against an invisible wall preventing me from understanding, and I couldn't get past it. This is that veil I told you about in Chapter 19!

I remember one day during this time period. I was at my mother-in-law's house, and I read a note that was taped on my teenage brother-in-law's bathroom mirror. It was a simple note that read something like: "Pray for salvation for:" and then listed a couple names. My name was on his list! I was taken aback. I was shocked he was praying for me to be saved. This time was different than the little boy in first grade who told me I was going to hell. This time someone was praying for me. It filled me with wonder, and I felt special. It had an impact on me and, as you can tell, has stuck with me since.

When I was close to 30 years old, my mother-in-law invited me to a women's Bible study class at church. This was the first time I had been invited to a Bible study. Since I had struggled to read the Bible on my own and I really wondered what it said, I thought this class would help. So, I decided to go. I went through Beth Moore's book and class about Believing God.[2] I can't pinpoint what it was about this class, but this is when my understanding slowly started to improve. I learned a lot about God, the Bible and why we could trust it, and what some of God's promises were. I met God for the first time in this class.

A short time after finishing the Bible study, my husband and I moved to Los Angeles. Since we didn't know anyone there, we decided we should find a church to attend so that we could meet some people. We asked the only person we knew at the time, our realtor. Turns out he was a Christian and his brother-in-law was a preacher who had just helped start a new church in Hollywood.

The preacher, Tim Chaddick, had just started teaching through the book of John in the Bible.[3] He wasn't like any preacher I had ever heard before. He was immensely passionate about what he was teaching and that was infectious. I wanted to pay attention and learn where his passion came from. I learned that I was a sinner and why I needed a savior, that Jesus loves me, that Jesus died for me, and that I could be saved by believing in Jesus. I finally understood the meaning of Jesus's blood. This is when I met Jesus.

Fast forward a few months. I was by myself out of town flipping through channels on the TV in my hotel room trying to find something interesting to watch. I came across a couple women talking about the Bible and Jesus on one of the Christian channels. I listened for a while as they shared the gospel, and then the women said I could invite Jesus into my life and into my heart. I really wanted to, so I prayed right along with them. At the age of 30, I became a believer and put my faith in Jesus. I fell asleep that night with a sense of peace I can't explain.

A few months later, I had a strong desire to get baptized. My husband and I traveled back to Albuquerque so that I could get baptized in the church we were married in and where my faith journey started.

One of the first things I did after getting baptized was purge all of the new age stuff I had. I remembered reading about the people tearing down the altars of Baal in the Old Testament. I wanted to do that same thing in my life. I didn't want anything to do with new age practices or beliefs anymore. I gathered books, tarot cards, music, and pictures and threw it all away.

One of the first books I read after becoming a believer was Randy Alcorn's book *Heaven*.[4] I hadn't read the entire Bible at this point, and I didn't have a good understanding about heaven. I wanted to know what the Bible said about it now that I was certain I was going to live there forever. Looking back, I think one of the main reasons that God gave me a desire to learn about heaven after I was saved is because of my upbringing. God wanted me to understand His truth, so that I would no longer be deceived.

If you're not familiar with new age, it's kind of a buffet of religious practices. New agers essentially pick and choose what they want to believe. It's heavily influenced by some of the Eastern religions and the occult. They're into psychics, mediums, tarot, palm readers, past lives, healing power of crystals, and the list goes on. They believe that there are multiple paths to heaven. They believe that heaven is a spiritual state, not a real physical place. They believe that you evolve through multiple lives on earth and work your way to the heavenly state. They believe you can communicate with people who have died by using mediums. They believe you can communicate with spirit guides who teach the "real truth" about heaven and how to get there.

I don't remember any talk of Jesus. So, you see, just like Eve in the garden, the fallen angels and demons had deceived me and filled me with so many lies. In Randy's book, *Heaven*, I learned that God wasn't the one behind any of those new age practices because His word expressly forbids doing those things (Deuteronomy 18:9-14). It was the enemy masquerading as an angel of the light (2 Corinthians 11:14). God used Randy's book to correct all of those false beliefs that I had about heaven. It's hard to describe the peace I felt after learning God's truth.

This book also ended up steering my life in an unexpected new direction. In Randy's book he said some people wouldn't die. Instead, they would be taken to heaven in an event he called the rapture. I was completely fascinated with this and had to learn more. I read all sorts of books about the rapture, and that led to me reading books about Bible prophecy.

Soon afterwards, my husband and I moved back to Albuquerque and started attending the Calvary Church where pastor Skip Heitzig teaches.[5] He truly is one of the best Bible teachers on the planet. I've learned a ton in the time I've been attending his church. He helped instill a passion within me to study the Bible and share all the wonderful things I've learned about Jesus with all of you.

And here we are today. I'm so passionate about this topic that now I'm writing books about the rapture and Bible prophecy! Now that I know Jesus, I can't imagine life without him. I want everyone else to know what that's like too. I know that God will use the books I write to help people meet Jesus.

I often wish that I had grown up knowing Jesus, like my husband did. Before I met Jesus, I was so miserable, and life was so hard. I often felt alone, like no one cared, and that my life didn't have a purpose. I don't feel that way anymore. Life is still hard, but Jesus is with me every step. That gives me great comfort because I'm not alone and I know he completely understands everything I'm going through. I have someone to talk to now that truly gets me. He did create me after all! I know that growing up while having a relationship with Jesus would have given me that sense of peace that I have now. However, without my past, I wouldn't have the passion to help people who worship false gods and don't know or struggle to know God's Word, just as I did, come to see God's truth. God indeed works everything for good.

If you've put your faith in Jesus as a result of reading this book, that's absolutely fantastic! God is so good! I'd love to meet every single one of you, hear your story, and give you a big hug. If we don't get to meet while we're still on earth, I know we will in heaven.

ANSWERING GOD'S CALLING

I believe sharing this additional part of my testimony will help you realize what time it is. God has put a passion within me to deliver urgent messages regarding the rapture. He doesn't want anyone to be left behind!

After reading about and studying the rapture for years, I decided to create a binder full of information for someone left behind. This was the summer of 2012. I figured someone might come looking for me after the rapture and hopefully they'd find the binder. It would explain the rapture, where I had disappeared to, and how to be saved. The binder kept getting bigger and bigger because I kept coming up with more things the left behind person needed to know.

After some time, I realized that I should put all the information in a book and make it available for anyone. So, I started an outline of all the chapters and content the book would have. Fast forward one year. It's now the spring of 2018. I still hadn't started the book. I only had a really long outline. You know how it is. Life often gets in the way of things we hope to do one day. I couldn't seem to find the time to actually start writing.

Well, this is when God intervened.

I don't recall the actual day this happened. I only remember it was in the spring of 2018. So, I have a pretty even keel personality. I don't get easily agitated or fly off the handle at things. One day I woke up just not myself. I couldn't shake the feeling of frustration, anger, and irritation. I was short with my husband and people at work. I initially chalked it up to just being stressed from work. Yeah, that wasn't it.

This went on for a couple weeks. After not being able to get myself out of this funk, I reasoned that I was under a spiritual attack. And you know what, I could tell that it was indeed something spiritual. I can't easily explain this, but I could literally feel it. I called it my dark cloud. It was stuck to me.

So, I started praying specifically about my dark cloud. I asked God to remove the evil presence that was coming against me. No relief whatsoever.

On top of that, I started to get really frustrated with my job. The projects that I loved working on had all moved to a different campus in the company. I had absolutely no desire to move to a different state. Suddenly, I wasn't working on exciting projects anymore. All the opportunities that I once had at work, gone. I felt like my job wasn't a good fit for me anymore. That I needed to make a change and do something different.

Months have gone by. At this point the dark cloud has been with me for so long that my husband thinks I'm having some sort of a breakdown. I remember the day he told me that he thought I should see a doctor. I knew that wasn't going to solve my problem. I was absolutely convinced this was spiritual because I could feel my dark cloud still there. I asked him to pray that God would help me figure out what was going on.

In my daily Bible reading, I started to get the sense that God wanted me to quit my career. The more I prayed about that, the more confirmation I kept getting from God.

It all came to a head in the late summer of 2018. I was driving to work one morning with the Christian radio station on. I was talking to God, and I said something similar to this: "God, it seems like you want me to quit my job. Who walks away from a job like mine? That would be ridiculous!" Literally one second later, here's what I hear on the radio: "Sometimes you need to do the ridiculous in order to experience the miraculous."[1]

Yeah, that happened! So now on my drive to work I'm taken aback because God literally spoke to me through the radio. And then it hit me. God really did want me to quit my job. But he promised me a miracle if I did it!

So, I mustered up the courage to tell my husband about this experience. The very moment that I told my husband that I had decided to quit my job, my dark cloud went away. I could literally feel it lift off of me. I felt like myself. I knew all would be well once again.

My dark cloud is a mystery. The best example that I've found in the Bible is the distressing spirit that God sent to King Saul to trouble him (1 Samuel 16:14). Trouble me it did. Looking back, it seems I had been ignoring God's call on my life to start writing.

One month later and I was no longer employed. I started writing *Rapture 911* shortly afterwards.

Fast forward another year. It's now the winter of 2019, and I've just recently self-published *Rapture 911*. The very first person to contact me through my new website, rapture911.com, was Dr. David R. Reagan. He asked me to send him a copy of *Rapture 911*. So, I did. A couple weeks later he asked me to be a guest on his TV show *Christ In Prophecy* and talk about the rapture. God was the one who orchestrated all of this.

As for that miracle God promised me, I believe I'll see it on the other side of the rapture.

In these last days, what might God be calling you out to do? Don't wait to respond until you get a distressing dark cloud sent to stick to you. You know, Jesus called his disciples out of the life they were living because he had an extraordinary opportunity for them to partake in. They changed lives. So can you.

GET FREE BOOKS

rapture911.com/free

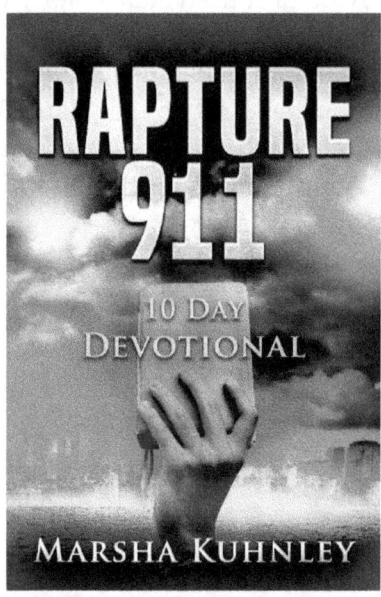

BOOKS BY MARSHA KUHNLEY

In English

Rapture 911 Series
* Rapture 911: What To Do If You're Left Behind
Rapture 911: What To Do If You're Left Behind (Pocket Edition)
Rapture 911: 10 Day Devotional
Rapture 911: Prophecy Reference Bible

End Times Armor Series
* The Election Omen: Your Vote Matters
* Assault On The Afterlife: Satan's War Against Heaven
Oblivious To The Signs When It's Obvious The King Is Coming
The Election Omen: 10 Day Devotional

Fiction
Kiara Kole And The Key Of Truth

Other Works
Seeing The Light In Dark Times: 10 Day Devotional

In Spanish

Serie Rapto 911
* Rapto 911: Qué hacer si eres dejado atrás
Rapto 911: Qué hacer si eres dejado atrás (Edición de Bolsillo)

Visit Marsha's website to find these books
rapture911.com

* - Also available as an audiobook

ENDNOTES

Chapter 1

1. Luke 12:37, 39; 21:34, 36. Mark 13:9, 23, 33-35, 37; 14:34, 37-38. Matthew 24:42-43; 25:13; 26:38, 40-41.
2. 483 years x 360 days = 173,880 days / 365 days = 476.4 years. Year difference = BC year + AD year - 1. 445 BC - 476.4 years -1 = AD 32.4.
3. Victor Kiprop, "Countries With The Most Protestant Christians," *WorldAtlas*, 6/21/2017, accessed 9/12/2024, https://www.worldatlas.com/articles/countries-with-the-most-protestant-christians.html.
4. Jonathan Cahn, *The Harbinger Companion With Study Guide*, eBook, (Lake Mary, FL: FrontLine, 2013), ch 1. Israel and America.

Chapter 2

1. "Ancient Jewish History: The Diaspora," JewishVirtualLibrary.org, accessed 6/26/2024, https://www.jewishvirtuallibrary.org/the-diaspora.
2. "What Was The Holocaust?," YadVashem.org, accessed 6/25/2024, https://www.yadvashem.org/holocaust/about.html.
3. "Israel," Wikipedia.org, accessed 6/25/2024, https://en.wikipedia.org/wiki/Israel.
4. "The Six-Day War," JewishVirtualLibrary.org, accessed 6/26/2024, https://www.jewishvirtuallibrary.org/background-and-overview-six-day-war.
5. "Demographics Of Israel," Wikipedia.org, accessed 6/25/2024, https://en.wikipedia.org/wiki/Demographics_of_Israel.
6. Aisha Majid, "Top 50 News Websites In The US," *Press Gazette*, 6/25/2024, accessed 6/25/2024, https://pressgazette.co.uk/media-audience-and-business-data/media_metrics/most-popular-websites-news-us-monthly-3/.
7. "The Prophecy Of The Week Of Millenniums," ChristInProphecy.org, accessed 6/26/2024, https://christinprophecy.org/articles/the-prophecy-of-the-week-of-millenniums/.
8. "Member States Of The United Nations," Wikipedia.org, accessed 6/26/2024, https://en.wikipedia.org/wiki/Member_states_of_the_United_Nations.
9. "Chapter 8: Messiah The Prince," BlueLetterBible.org, accessed 6/26/2024, https://www.blueletterbible.org/comm/anderson_robert/the-coming-prince/11-c08-messiah-the-prince.cfm.
10. "Rapture Ready Index," RaptureReady.com, accessed 6/27/2024, https://www.raptureready.com/rapture-ready-index/.
11. "Doomsday Clock," Wikipedia.org, accessed 6/27/2024, https://en.wikipedia.org/wiki/Doomsday_Clock.
John Mecklin, "2024 Doomsday Clock Statement," *Bulletin of the Atomic Scientists*, 1/23/2024, accessed 9/12/2024, https://thebulletin.org/doomsday-clock/current-time/.
12. "Hubble Space Telescope," Wikipedia.org, accessed 6/27/2024, https://en.wikipedia.org/wiki/Hubble_Space_Telescope.
"James Webb Space Telescope," Wikipedia.org, accessed 6/27/2024, https://en.wikipedia.org/wiki/James_Webb_Space_Telescope.
13. "Sputnik 1," Wikipedia.org, accessed 6/27/2024, https://en.wikipedia.org/wiki/Sputnik_1.
14. Therese Wood, "Who Owns Our Orbit," *World Economic Forum*, 10/23/2020, accessed 6/27/2024, https://www.weforum.org/agenda/2020/10/visualizing-easrth-satellites-sapce-spacex/.
15. Orbiting Now, Orbit.ing-now.com, accessed 6/27/2024.
16. "The Second Temple," JewishVirtualLibrary.org, accessed 6/27/2024, https://www.jewishvirtuallibrary.org/the-second-temple.
17. "War And Peace," OurWorldInData.org, accessed 6/27/2024, Combatant deaths in conventional wars 1800-2011, https://ourworldindata.org/war-and-peace?insight=some-conflicts-are-much-much-deadlier-than-most.
18. "Number Of Armed Conflicts, World," OurWorldInData.org, accessed 6/27/2024, https://ourworldindata.org/grapher/number-of-armed-conflicts.

19 "Peaceful And Hostile Relationships Between States, World," OurWorldInData.org, accessed 6/27/2024, https://ourworldindata.org/grapher/peaceful-and-hostile-relationships-between-states.
20 "Artemis III," NASA.gov, accessed 6/27/2024, https://www.nasa.gov/mission/artemis-iii/. "Mars," NASA.gov, accessed 6/27/2024, https://www.nasa.gov/humans-in-space/humans-to-mars/.
21 Andrea Vacchiano, "Elon Musk Predicts Crewed SpaceX Flights To Mars By 2028," *Fox Business*, 9/7/2024, accessed 9/17/2024, https://www.foxbusiness.com/technology/elon-musk-predicts-crewed-spacex-flights-mars-2028-hopes-self-sustaining-city-planet.
22 Michael Sheetz, "SpaceX Is Building A NASA Craft To Intentionally Destroy The International Space Station," *CNBC*, 6/24/2024, accessed 6/27/2024, https://www.cnbc.com/2024/06/26/spacex-wins-nasa-contract-for-iss-reentry-destruction.html.
23 "Abortion," *World Health Organization*, 5/17/2024, accessed 6/27/2024, https://www.who.int/news-room/fact-sheets/detail/abortion.
24 "Population By Country," WorldoMeters.info, accessed 6/27/2024, https://www.worldometers.info/world-population/population-by-country/.
25 "Population By Country," WorldoMeters.info (endnote 2.24).

Chapter 3
1 "If There Is Such Good Evidence For God, Why Don't More People Believe?," 3/7/2018, *Sean McDowell*, YouTube video, accessed 9/12/2024, https://www.youtube.com/watch?v=mPoIVirdU0o.

Chapter 4
1 Sam Hailes, "Deconstructing Faith: Meet The Evangelicals Who Are Questioning Everything," *Premier Christianity*, 3/17/2019, accessed 7/2/2024, https://www.premierchristianity.com/features/deconstructing-faith-meet-the-evangelicals-who-are-questioning-everything/267.article.
2 Alisa Childers, "Let's Deconstruct A Deconversion Story: The Case Of Rhett And Link," *Alisa Childers Blog*, 3/1/2020, accessed 7/2/2024, https://www.alisachildersblog.com/blog/lets-deconstruct-a-deconversion-story-the-case-of-rhett-and-link.
3 Good Mythical Morning, YouTube channel, accessed 7/2/2024, https://www.youtube.com/@GoodMythicalMorning.
4 "Religious Composition By Country, 2010-2050," *Pew Research Center*, 12/21/2022, accessed 7/2/2024, https://www.pewresearch.org/religion/feature/religious-composition-by-country-2010-2050/.
5 "How Religious Are Americans?," *Gallup*, 3/29/2024, accessed 7/2/2024, https://news.gallup.com/poll/358364/religious-americans.aspx.
6 "Signs Of Decline & Hope Among Key Metrics Of Faith," *Barna*, 3/4/2020, accessed 7/2/2024, https://www.barna.com/research/changing-state-of-the-church/.
7 Tracy Munsil, "Biblical Worldview Among U.S. Adults Drops," *Arizona Christian University*, 2/28/2023, accessed 7/2/2024, https://www.arizonachristian.edu/2023/02/28/biblical-worldview-among-u-s-adults-drops-33-since-start-of-covid-19-pandemic/.
8 "Israel: Population By Religion," JewishVirtualLibrary.org, accessed 7/2/2024, https://www.jewishvirtuallibrary.org/israel-population-by-religion.
9 "Religion In Israel," Wikipedia.org, accessed 7/2/2024, https://en.wikipedia.org/wiki/Religion_in_Israel.
10 "Biblical Worldview Among U.S. Adults Drops," *ACU* (endnote 4.7).
11 Dr. George Barna, "American Worldview Inventory 2024 (Release #3)," *Arizona Christian University*, 5/28/2024, accessed 7/2/2024, https://www.arizonachristian.edu/wp-content/uploads/2024/05/CRC-Release-AWVI-3-May-28-2024.pdf.
12 Dr. George Barna, "American Worldview Inventory 2022 (Release #5)," *Arizona Christian University*, 5/10/2022, accessed 7/2/2024, https://www.arizonachristian.edu/wp-content/uploads/2022/05/AWVI2022_Release05_Digital.pdf.
13 "Religious Composition By Country," *PRC* (endnote 4.4).
14 "Global Christianity," *Pew Research Center*, 12/19/2011, accessed 7/3/2024, https://www.pewresearch.org/religion/2011/12/19/global-christianity-exec/.
15 "The Global Catholic Population," *Pew Research Center*, 2/13/2013, accessed 7/4/2024, https://www.pewresearch.org/religion/2013/02/13/the-global-catholic-population/.
Fritz Ridenour, *So What's the Difference?*, eBook, (Bloomington, MN: Bethany House Publishers, 2013), ch 2.

16. "Eastern Orthodoxy," Britannica.com, accessed 7/4/2024, https://www.britannica.com/topic/Eastern-Orthodoxy.
17. Ridenour, *What's the Difference?*, ch 5-7 (endnote 4.15).
18. 31% Christian (see ch. 4 n. 13) x 37% Protestant (see ch. 4 n. 14) = 11.47%.
19. Emma Newburger, "Joe Biden Calls Climate Change The 'Number One Issue Facing Humanity'," *CNBC*, 10/24/2020, accessed 7/3/2024, https://www.cnbc.com/2020/10/24/joe-biden-climate-change-is-number-one-issue-facing-humanity.html.
20. "Greta Thunberg," Wikipedia.org, accessed 7/3/2024, https://en.wikipedia.org/wiki/Greta_Thunberg.
21. Josef Abramowitz, "Global Religious Leaders Promote Climate Action During UN Climate Conference COP 27," *PR Newswire*, 11/14/2022, accessed 7/3/2024, https://www.prnewswire.com/news-releases/global-religious-leaders-promote-climate-action-during-un-climate-conference-cop-27-301677245.html.
22. "Thirty New Honorary Doctorates To Be Conferred In The Conferment Jubilee," *University of Helsinki*, 3/20/2023, accessed 7/3/2024, https://www.helsinki.fi/en/news/science-policy/thirty-new-honorary-doctorates-be-conferred-conferment-jubilee.
23. "Climate Finance And The USD 100 Billion Goal," OECD.org, accessed 7/3/2024, https://www.oecd.org/en/topics/climate-finance-and-the-usd-100-billion-goal.html.
24. "From Billion To Trillions: Setting A New Goal On Climate Finance," *UNFCCC.int*, 4/29/2024, accessed 7/3/2024, https://unfccc.int/news/from-billions-to-trillions-setting-a-new-goal-on-climate-finance.
25. "Harry Potter," Wikipedia.org, accessed 7/4/2024, https://en.wikipedia.org/wiki/Harry_Potter.
26. "Top Lifetime Adjusted Grosses," BoxOfficeMojo.com, accessed 7/4/2024, https://www.boxofficemojo.com/chart/top_lifetime_gross_adjusted/?adjust_gross_to=2022. "The Exorcist," Wikipedia.org, accessed 7/4/2024, https://en.wikipedia.org/wiki/The_Exorcist.
27. "Stranger Things," Wikipedia.org, accessed 7/4/2024, https://en.wikipedia.org/wiki/Stranger_Things. "Most Popular TV Shows," IMDB, accessed 7/4/2024, https://www.imdb.com/chart/tvmeter/?sort=popularity%2Casc.
28. "Exploring Techno Witchcraft And Digital Paganism," LinkedIn post, 6/17/2024, accessed 8/7/2024, https://www.linkedin.com/pulse/exploring-techno-witchcraft-digital-paganism-deep-dive-emma-swailes-ua1re.
29. "#witchtok," TikTok hashtag, accessed 9/4/2024, https://www.tiktok.com/tag/witchtok?lang=en.
30. Claire Jones, "WitchTok: The Witchcraft Videos With Billions Of Views," *BBC*, 10/21/2022, accessed 9/4/2024, https://www.bbc.com/news/newsbeat-63403467.
31. Olivia Petter, "WitchTok: How Witchcraft Became The Latest Controversial Wellness Fad," *Independent*, 7/27/2024, accessed 9/4/2024, https://www.independent.co.uk/life-style/witchcraft-wellness-witchtok-kate-tomas-b2585162.html.
32. Tyler Kingkade, "As Conservatives Put Religion In Schools, Satanists Want In, Too," *NBC News*, 5/16/2024, accessed 9/4/2024, https://www.nbcnews.com/news/us-news/satanic-temple-christian-nationalism-school-chaplains-rcna151276.
33. "SatanCon," Wikipedia.org, accessed 9/4/2024, https://en.wikipedia.org/wiki/SatanCon.
34. "Lucifer (TV Series)," Wikipedia.org, accessed 7/4/2024, https://en.wikipedia.org/wiki/Lucifer_(TV_series).
35. "List Of Hazbin Hotel And Helluva Boss Characters," Wikipedia.org, accessed 7/4/2024, https://en.wikipedia.org/wiki/List_of_Hazbin_Hotel_and_Helluva_Boss_characters.
36. Daniel Kessel Odom, "Why This 6-Episode German Series Is Disney+'s Most Controversial Show Right Now," *Screen Rant*, 5/31/2024, accessed 7/4/2024, https://screenrant.com/pauline-disney-plus-show-controversy-devil-explained/.
37. Oscar Holland, "Lil Nas X's Unofficial 'Satan' Nikes Containing Human Blood Sell Out In Under A Minute," *CNN*, 3/29/2021, accessed 7/4/2024, https://www.cnn.com/style/article/lil-nas-x-mschf-satan-nike-shoes/index.html.
38. Nika Shakhnazarova, "Sam Smith, Kim Petras' 'Unholy' Grammy Performance Sparks FCC Complaints," *New York Post*, 5/19/2023, accessed 7/4/2024, https://nypost.com/2023/02/11/sam-smith-kim-petras-unholy-grammy-performance-sparks-fcc-complaints/.
39. Katelyn Webb, "Taylor Swift Is Engaging In Satanic Rituals In Live Shows," *The Christian Post*, 2/28/2024, accessed 7/4/2024, https://www.christianpost.com/news/taylor-swift-engaging-in-satanic-rituals-in-shows-musician-claims.html.

40 "Prepper Resources," Rapture911.com, accessed 7/4/2024, https://rapture911.com/prepper-resources/.
41 "Dogen City," N-Ark.jp, accessed 7/4/2024, https://www.n-ark.jp/en/dogen-city.
42 Ingrid Schmidt, "Billionaires' Survivalist Bunkers Go Absolutely Bonkers," *The Hollywood Reporter*, 2/12/2024, accessed 7/4/2024, https://www.hollywoodreporter.com/lifestyle/lifestyle-news/bunkers-billionaires-survive-apocalypse-cost-features-1235822762/.
43 "Doomsday Bunkers," Discovery.com, accessed 7/4/2024, https://www.discovery.com/shows/doomsday-bunkers.
44 Guthrie Scrimgeour, "Inside Mark Zuckerberg's Top-Secret Hawaii Compound," *Wired*, 12/14/2023, accessed 7/4/2024, https://www.wired.com/story/mark-zuckerberg-inside-hawaii-compound/.
45 D. Tighe, "Planned Annual Halloween Expenditure In The United States," *Statista*, 9/25/2023, accessed 8/31/2024, https://www.statista.com/statistics/275726/annual-halloween-expenditure-in-the-united-states/.

Chapter 5

1 "Best Sellers In Biographies," Amazon.com, accessed 7/5/2024, https://www.amazon.com/Best-Sellers-Books-Biographies/zgbs/books/2.
2 Nick Routley, "Visualizing The World's Top Social Media And Messaging Apps," *Visual Capitalist*, 11/18/2022, accessed 7/5/2024, https://www.visualcapitalist.com/social-media-universe-2022/.
3 "World Population," WorldoMeters.info, accessed 7/5/2024, https://www.worldometers.info/world-population/.
4 "Global Social Media Statistics," DataReportal.com, accessed 7/5/2024, https://datareportal.com/social-media-users.
5 Monica Anderson, "What Teens Post On Social Media," *Pew Research Center*, 11/16/2022, accessed 7/5/2024, https://www.pewresearch.org/internet/2022/11/16/1-what-teens-post-on-social-media/.
6 "Marriages And Divorces," OurWorldInData.org, accessed 7/5/2024, https://ourworldindata.org/marriages-and-divorces.
7 "Marriages And Divorces," OurWorldInData.org (endnote 5.6).
"Marriages Per 1,000 People," OurWorldInData.org, accessed 8/29/2024, https://ourworldindata.org/grapher/marriage-rate-per-1000-inhabitants.
8 Stacy Jo Dixon, "Daily Time Spent On Social Networking By Internet Users Worldwide," *Statista*, 4/10/2024, accessed 7/5/2024, https://www.statista.com/statistics/433871/daily-social-media-usage-worldwide/.
9 "Digital 2024: Global Overview Report," DataReportal.com, accessed 7/5/2024, Jan 2024 Daily Time Spent With Media graphic, https://datareportal.com/reports/digital-2024-global-overview-report.
10 "You Do You," Amazon.com, accessed 7/5/2024, https://www.amazon.com/dp/0316445126.
"Live Your Truth," Amazon.com, accessed 7/5/2024, https://www.amazon.com/dp/0989584992.
11 Colson Whitehead, "How 'You Do You' Perfectly Captures Our Narcissistic Culture," *The New York Times Magazine*, 3/31/2015, accessed 7/5/2024, https://www.nytimes.com/2015/04/05/magazine/how-you-do-you-perfectly-captures-our-narcissistic-culture.html.
12 John G. Matsusaka, "When Do Legislators Represent Their Constituents?," *USC Gould School of Law*, 7/22/2022, accessed 8/7/2024, p 26-27, https://dx.doi.org/10.2139/ssrn.2612342.
13 Ainhoa Ruiz Benedicto, "6 Out Of 10 People Worldwide Live In A Country That Has Built Border Walls," *TNI*, 11/18/2020, accessed 7/5/2024, https://www.tni.org/en/article/6-out-of-10-people-worldwide-live-in-a-country-that-has-built-border-walls.
14 Fernando de Querol Cumbrera, "Number Of Tall Buildings Completed," *Statista*, 2/8/2023, accessed 7/5/2024, https://www.statista.com/statistics/1069001/number-of-tall-building-completions-worldwide/.
15 Alan Bernau Jr, "The Tallest Buildings And Structures In The World Throughout History," *Alan's Factory Outlet*, 5/22/2024, accessed 7/5/2024, https://alansfactoryoutlet.com/the-tallest-buildings-and-structures-in-the-world-throughout-history/.
16 "9 Top Languages To Learn For International Business," *Rosetta Stone Enterprise*, 5/16/2024, accessed 7/5/2024, https://enterpriseblog.rosettastone.com/top-languages-for-international-business/.

17 "Official Languages Of The United Nations," Wikipedia.org, accessed 7/5/2024, https://en.wikipedia.org/wiki/Official_languages_of_the_United_Nations.
18 Judah Ari Gross, "Even Among Its Advocates, Changing The Law Of Return Proves Trickier Than Expected," *The Times Of Israel*, 1/27/2023, accessed 7/5/2024, https://www.timesofisrael.com/even-among-its-advocates-changing-the-law-of-return-proves-trickier-than-expected/.
Rafi Demogge, "The Looming War Over Israel's Law Of Return," *Mosaic*, 7/3/2023, accessed 7/5/2024, https://mosaicmagazine.com/essay/israel-zionism/2023/07/the-looming-war-over-israels-law-of-return/.
19 Toi Staff, "In Extraordinary Move, Trains Keep Running On Shabbat Amid War," *The Times Of Israel*, 10/13/2023, accessed 7/5/2024, https://www.timesofisrael.com/in-extraordinary-move-trains-to-keep-running-on-shabbat-amid-war/.
Jackie Hajdenberg, "Israeli Rabbis Are Issuing Guidance About How To Adjust Jewish Law During Wartime," *The Times Of Israel*, 10/23/2023, accessed 7/5/2024, https://www.timesofisrael.com/israeli-rabbis-are-issuing-guidance-about-how-to-adjust-jewish-law-during-wartime/.
20 "Basic Law: Israel As The Nation-State Of The Jewish People," Wikipedia.org, accessed 7/5/2024, https://en.wikipedia.org/wiki/Basic_Law:_Israel_as_the_Nation-State_of_the_Jewish_People.
21 Emanuel Fabian, "Gallant To Netanyahu: You Must Publicly Reject Israeli Civil Or Military Governance Of Gaza After Hamas," *The Times Of Israel*, 5/15/2024, accessed 7/5/2024, https://www.timesofisrael.com/liveblog_entry/gallant-to-netanyahu-you-must-publicly-reject-israeli-civil-or-military-governance-of-gaza-after-hamas-i-wont-allow-it/.
22 Jacob Magid, "Biden Calls For Netanyahu To Outline Plans For Post-War Governance In Gaza," *The Times Of Israel*, 5/9/2024, accessed 7/5/2024, https://www.timesofisrael.com/liveblog_entry/biden-calls-for-netanyahu-to-outline-plans-for-post-war-governance-in-gaza/.
23 Randy Alcorn, "What Are The New Jerusalem's Dimensions?," *Eternal Perspective Ministries*, 2/22/2010, accessed 7/5/2024, https://www.epm.org/resources/2010/Feb/22/what-are-new-jerusalems-dimensions/.
24 "A Bible For Every Believer," Persecution.com, accessed 7/5/2024, https://www.persecution.com/bibles/.
25 "Population By Country," WorldoMeters.info (endnote 2.24).

Chapter 6
1 "The Harbinger," Amazon.com, accessed 7/6/2024, https://www.amazon.com/dp/161638610X.
2 The Great State Of New California, NewCaliforniaState.com, accessed 7/6/2024.
3 James Bickerton, "Oregon Counties Voting To Join 'Greater Idaho'," *Newsweek*, 5/23/2024, accessed 7/6/2024, https://www.newsweek.com/oregon-counties-voting-join-greater-idaho-1904036.
4 Ivan Pereira, "Biden Disputed Diminishing Poll Numbers, Low Approval Rating After Debate," *ABC News*, 7/5/2024, accessed 7/6/2024, https://abcnews.go.com/Politics/biden-disputes-diminishing-poll-numbers-low-approval-rating/story?id=111695181.
5 "Americans' Feelings About Politics," *Pew Research Center*, 9/19/2023, accessed 7/6/2024, https://www.pewresearch.org/politics/2023/09/19/americans-feelings-about-politics-polarization-and-the-tone-of-political-discourse/.
6 "Israel's Gantz Challenges Netanyahu With Call For Election Amid Gaza War," *Al Jazeera*, 4/4/2024, accessed 7/6/2024, https://www.aljazeera.com/news/2024/4/4/israels-benny-gantz-pushes-for-september-election-amid-war-on-gaza.
7 "Elections In Israel," Wikipedia.org, accessed 7/6/2024, https://en.wikipedia.org/wiki/Elections_in_Israel.
8 "Population Having Attained At Least Some Formal Education," OurWorldInData.org, accessed 7/10/2024, https://ourworldindata.org/grapher/population-having-attained-at-least-basic-education.
9 Veera Korhonen, "Educational Attainment Distribution In The United States," *Statista*, 7/5/2024, accessed 7/10/2024, https://www.statista.com/statistics/184260/educational-attainment-in-the-us/.
10 "Global Education," OurWorldInData.org, accessed 7/10/2024, Key insights: Despite being in school, https://ourworldindata.org/global-education?insight=despite-being-in-school-many-children-learn-very-little#all-charts.

11. "Share In Poverty Relative To Different Poverty Thresholds," OurWorldInData.org, accessed 9/9/2024, https://ourworldindata.org/grapher/share-in-poverty-relative-to-different-poverty-thresholds.
12. Einar H. Dyvik, "Proportion Of Selected Age Groups Of World Population," *Statista*, 7/4/2024, accessed 7/10/2024, https://www.statista.com/statistics/265759/world-population-by-age-and-region/.
13. 8.12 billion people x 75% over age 15 (see ch. 6 n. 12) = 6 billion people x 89.2% attained a formal education (see ch. 6 n. 8) = 5.4 billion people. 8.12 billion people x 83.6% living in poverty (see ch 6. n. 11) = 6.8 billion people living in poverty.
14. "Best-Selling Book," GuinessWorldRecords.com, accessed 7/10/2024, https://www.guinnessworldrecords.com/world-records/best-selling-book-of-non-fiction.
15. Danny McLoughlin, "32 Bible Sales Statistics (2023)," *WordsRated*, 2/2/2022, accessed 7/10/2024, https://wordsrated.com/bible-sales-statistics/.
16. American Bible Society, *State of the Bible: USA 2024*, September 2024 Ed., (American Bible Society, 2024), ch 1 p 3, accessed 7/10/2024, https://1s712.americanbible.org/state-of-the-bible/stateofthebible/State_of_the_bible-2024.pdf.
17. David Brunn, "Gender In Bible Translation," *Themelios*, Volume 49 Issue 1, accessed 7/10/2024, https://www.thegospelcoalition.org/themelios/article/gender-in-bible-translation-a-crucial-issue-still-mired-in-misunderstanding/.
"The Inclusive Bible," Amazon.com, accessed 7/10/2024, https://www.amazon.com/dp/1580512135.
18. Methodist Voices, "Beware Liberal NRSVue Bible Translation Update," *Juicy Ecumenism*, 1/19/2022, accessed 7/10/2024, https://juicyecumenism.com/2022/01/19/liberal-nrsvue-bible-translation-update/.
19. Jackie Hajdenberg, "Backlash Over 'Gender-Sensitive' Hebrew Bible Translation," *The Times Of Israel*, 5/31/2023, accessed 7/10/2024, https://www.timesofisrael.com/backlash-over-gender-sensitive-hebrew-bible-translation-that-uses-god-not-he/.
20. The Holy Bible Feminine Translation Version, FTVbible.com, accessed 7/10/2024.
"The Divine Feminine Version Of The New Testament," Amazon.com, accessed 7/10/2024, https://www.amazon.com/dp/1545080852.
21. "The Vegan Bible," Amazon.com, accessed 7/10/2024, https://www.amazon.com/dp/1537260812.
22. "Chinese Communist Party Government Rewrites Portions Of The Bible," *International Christian Concern*, 7/21/2023, accessed 7/10/2024, https://www.persecution.org/2023/07/20/chinese-communist-party-government-rewrites-portions-of-the-bible/.
23. "The Queen James Bible," Amazon.com, accessed 7/10/2024, https://www.amazon.com/dp/0615724531.
"Modern Standard Version New Testament: Pride Pocket Edition," Amazon.com, accessed 7/10/2024, https://www.amazon.com/dp/B09SPC6BLY.
24. "Bible Translations Into English," Wikipedia.org, accessed 7/10/2024, https://en.wikipedia.org/wiki/Bible_translations_into_English.
25. "What Do Americans Believe About Jesus?," *Barna*, 4/1/2015, accessed 7/10/2024, https://www.barna.com/research/what-do-americans-believe-about-jesus-5-popular-beliefs/.
26. Aaron Earls, "The Most Common Lies People Believe About Jesus," *Lifeway Research*, 12/15/2022, accessed 7/10/2024, https://research.lifeway.com/2022/12/15/the-most-common-lies-people-believe-about-jesus/.
27. "Denial," PsychologyToday.com, accessed 7/10/2024, https://www.psychologytoday.com/us/basics/denial.
28. Roy Arad, "Earth Is Flat As A Pita," *Haaretz*, 9/5/2017, accessed 7/10/2024, https://www.haaretz.com/israel-news/2017-09-05/ty-article/earth-is-flat-as-a-pita-the-israelis-who-push-the-ultimate-conspiracy-theory/0000017f-db82-d856-a37f-ffc2505d0000.
29. Steve Mirsky, "Flat Earthers," *Scientific American*, 3/27/2020, accessed 7/10/2024, https://www.scientificamerican.com/podcast/episode/flat-earthers-what-they-believe-and-why/.
Rob Picheta, "The Flat-Earth Conspiracy Is Spreading Around The Globe.," *CNN*, 11/18/2019, accessed 7/10/2024, https://www.cnn.com/2019/11/16/us/flat-earth-conference-conspiracy-theories-scli-intl/index.html.
Darryl Fonseka, "I Watched Hundreds Of Flat-Earth Videos To Learn How Conspiracy Theories Spread," *The Conversation*, 6/27/2022, accessed 7/10/2024, https://theconversation.com/i-watched-hundreds-of-flat-earth-videos-to-learn-how-conspiracy-theories-spread-and-what-it-

could-mean-for-fighting-disinformation-184589.
Rachel Brazil, "Fighting Flat-Earth Theory," *Physics World*, 7/14/2020, accessed 7/10/2024, https://physicsworld.com/a/fighting-flat-earth-theory/.
Stephanie Pappas, "Flat Earth 'Theory'," *Live Science*, 1/27/2023, accessed 7/10/2024, https://www.livescience.com/24310-flat-earth-belief.html.

30. Mondo Gonzales, "Psalm 19 Project: Addressing Flat Earth Claims," *Prophecy Watchers*, 1/26/2023, accessed 7/10/2024, https://prophecywatchers.com/psalm-19-project-addressing-flat-earth-claims/.

31. Jeff Diamant, "About Four-In-Ten U.S. Adults Believe Humanity Is 'Living In The End Times'," *Pew Research Center*, 12/8/2022, accessed 7/10/2024, https://www.pewresearch.org/short-reads/2022/12/08/about-four-in-ten-u-s-adults-believe-humanity-is-living-in-the-end-times/.

32. Joel C. Rosenberg, "Giving Up On Messiah?," *All Israel News*, 5/21/2023, accessed 7/10/2024, https://allisrael.com/giving-up-on-messiah-shocking-new-survey-finds-nearly-half-of-israeli-jews-don-t-believe-messiah-will-ever-really-come-to-earth.

33. Joel Mathis, "Why U.S. Teens Aren't Getting Their Driver's Licenses," *The Week*, 2/16/2023, accessed 7/10/2024, https://theweek.com/travel/1020987/why-us-teens-arent-getting-their-drivers-licenses.

34. Daysia Tolentino, "Are Aliens Real?," *NBC News*, 7/27/2023, accessed 7/10/2024, https://www.nbcnews.com/tech/ufo-hearing-online-reactions-twitter-tiktok-rcna96664.

35. "Countries Where Christianity Is Illegal 2024," WorldPopulationReview.com, accessed 7/10/2024, https://worldpopulationreview.com/country-rankings/countries-where-christianity-is-illegal.

36. "Population By Country," WorldoMeters.info (endnote 2.24).
India (1,428,627,663) + Pakistan (240,485,658) + Nigeria (223,804,632) + Iran (89,172,767) + Afghanistan (42,239,854) + North Korea (26,160,821) + Somalia (18,143,378) + Libya (6,888,388) + Yemen (34,449,825) + Eritrea (3,748,901) + Saudi Arabia (36,947,025) = 2,150,668,912 people / World population 8,121,000,000 = 26.5%.

37. China (1,425,671,352) + Indonesia (277,534,122) + nations in prior endnote (2,150,668,912) = 3,853,874,386 people / World population 8,121,000,000 = 47.5%.

38. "List Of U.S. Jurisdictions Banning Conversion Therapy," Wikipedia.org, accessed 7/10/2024, https://en.wikipedia.org/wiki/List_of_U.S._jurisdictions_banning_conversion_therapy.

39. DCNF, "States Are Cracking Down On Therapists Who Don't Affirm Kids' Trans Identities," *Maine Wire*, 6/5/2023, accessed 7/10/2024, https://www.themainewire.com/2023/06/chilling-effect-states-are-cracking-down-on-therapists-who-dont-affirm-kids-trans-identities/.

40. Amy Howe, "Justices Side With High School Football Coach Who Prayed On The Field With Students," *SCOTUSblog*, 6/27/2022, accessed 7/10/2024, https://www.scotusblog.com/2022/06/justices-side-with-high-school-football-coach-who-prayed-on-the-field-with-students/.

41. Judah Ari Gross, "Half Of Jewish Israelis Back Prayer On Temple Mount, Mostly To 'Prove Sovereignty'," *The Times Of Israel*, 5/30/2022, accessed 7/10/2024, https://www.timesofisrael.com/half-of-jewish-israelis-back-prayer-on-temple-mount-mostly-to-prove-sovereignty/.
Josh Breiner, "Ben-Gvir Calls For Jews To Be Allowed To Pray On The Temple Mount," *Haaretz*, 6/5/2024, accessed 7/10/2024, https://www.haaretz.com/israel-news/2024-06-05/ty-article/.premium/ben-gvir-calls-for-jews-to-pray-on-temple-mount-netanyahu-status-quo-will-not-change/0000018f-e9af-d463-a19f-fdbffea90000.

42. Emma Camp, "In Britain, You Can Be Arrested For Silently Praying Outside An Abortion Clinic," *Reason*, 2/10/2023, accessed 7/11/2024, https://reason.com/2023/02/10/in-britain-you-can-be-arrested-for-silently-praying-outside-an-abortion-clinic/.
Jon Brown, "Woman Arrested For Silent Prayer Outside Abortion Clinic Notches Legal Win," *Fox News*, 6/14/2023, accessed 7/11/2024, https://www.foxnews.com/world/woman-arrested-silent-prayer-outside-abortion-clinic-notches-legal-win-but-still-faces-potential-charges.

43. Lauren Sforza, "Gaetz Dubs House Antisemitism Bill A 'Ridiculous Hate Speech Bill'," *The Hill*, 5/1/2024, accessed 7/10/2024, https://thehill.com/homenews/house/4637602-gaetz-dubs-house-antisemitism-bill-a-ridiculous-hate-speech-bill/.
Aneeta Mathur-Ashton, "The Controversy Surrounding The Antisemitism Bill," *U.S. News*, 5/7/2024, accessed 7/10/2024, https://www.usnews.com/news/national-news/articles/2024-05-07/explainer-the-controversy-surrounding-the-antisemitism-bill.

44. "How Religious Are Americans?," *Gallup* (endnote 4.5).

45 "Religion In Israel," Wikipedia.org (endnote 4.9).
46 "Religious 'Nones' In America," *Pew Research Center*, 1/24/2024, accessed 7/11/2024, https://www.pewresearch.org/religion/2024/01/24/religious-nones-in-america-who-they-are-and-what-they-believe/.
47 "Religious Composition By Country," *PRC* (endnote 4.4).
48 "How Do 'Nones' View Science?," *Pew Research Center*, 1/24/2024, accessed 7/11/2024, https://www.pewresearch.org/religion/2024/01/24/how-do-nones-view-science/.
49 Adriana Diaz, "Immortality Is Attainable By 2030," *New York Post*, 3/29/2023, accessed 7/11/2024, https://nypost.com/2023/03/29/immortality-is-attainable-by-2030-google-scientist/.
50 "Suicide Rate," OurWorldInData.org, accessed 7/11/2024, https://ourworldindata.org/grapher/death-rate-from-suicides-gho.
51 "Suicide Rate," OurWorldInData.org (endnote 6.50).
52 George Petras, "US Suicide Rate Reaches Highest Point In More Than 80 Years," *USA Today*, 11/29/2023, accessed 7/11/2024, https://www.usatoday.com/story/graphics/2023/11/29/2022-suicide-rate-historical-chart-comparison-graphic/71737857007/.
53 "Suicide," NIMH.NIH.gov, accessed 7/11/2024, https://www.nimh.nih.gov/health/statistics/suicide.
54 "Antidepressant Use Among Adults," CDC.gov, accessed 7/11/2024, Figure 4, https://www.cdc.gov/nchs/products/databriefs/db377.htm.
55 Kao-Ping Chua, MD, PhD, "Antidepressant Dispensing To US Adolescents And Young Adults," *American Academy of Pediatrics*, 2/26/2024, accessed 7/11/2024, https://publications.aap.org/pediatrics/article/153/3/e2023064245/196655.
56 "States With Legal Medical Aid In Dying (MAID)," ProCon.org, accessed 7/11/2024, https://euthanasia.procon.org/states-with-legal-physician-assisted-suicide/.
57 Katharina Buchholz, "Where Assisted Suicide Is Legal," *Statista*, 8/31/2022, accessed 7/11/2024, https://www.statista.com/chart/28133/assisted-dying-world-map/.
58 "Do You Consider Doctor-Assisted Suicide Morally Acceptable Or Morally Wrong?," *Statista*, 4/5/2024, accessed 7/11/2024, https://www.statista.com/statistics/225938/americans-moral-stance-towards-doctor-assisted-suicide/.
59 "Humanity Is 'Living In The End Times'," *PRC* (endnote 6.31).
60 "Giving Up On Messiah?," *AIN* (endnote 6.32).
61 AJ Willingham, "For Some Christians, 'Rapture Anxiety' Can Take A Lifetime To Heal," *CNN*, 9/27/2022, accessed 7/11/2024, https://www.cnn.com/2022/09/27/us/rapture-anxiety-evangelical-exvangelical-christianity-cec/index.html.
Kathryn Post, "Rapture Anxiety Is A Thing," *The Washington Post*, 4/21/2023, accessed 7/11/2024, https://www.washingtonpost.com/religion/2023/04/21/rapture-anxiety-is-thing/.
62 April Ajoy, TikTok channel, accessed 7/11/2024, https://www.tiktok.com/@aprilajoy.
63 Adam Cailler, "Elon Musk Is A 'Visionary Who Will Save All Of Humanity'," *Daily Star*, 11/1/2023, accessed 7/11/2024, https://www.dailystar.co.uk/news/world-news/elon-musk-visionary-who-save-31333955/.

Chapter 7
1 Sarah Melancon, "Frequency Of Sex Before Marriage," *Women's Health*, 12/2023, accessed 7/14/2024, https://www.womens-health.com/sex-before-marriage-statistics.
2 Helen Floersh, "First Live Birth Of A Chimeric Monkey Is A Technical Feat," *Fierce Biotech*, 11/10/2023, accessed 7/14/2024, https://www.fiercebiotech.com/research/first-live-birth-chimeric-monkey-technical-feat-pushes-ethical-boundaries.
3 Joy Allmond, "A Legacy Of Revival In The Nation's Capital," *Billy Graham Evangelistic Association*, 5/3/2010, accessed 7/14/2024, https://billygraham.org/story/a-legacy-of-revival-in-the-nations-capital/.
"National Day Of Prayer," Wikipedia.org, accessed 7/14/2024, https://en.wikipedia.org/wiki/National_Day_of_Prayer.
4 "Billy Graham," Wikipedia.org, accessed 7/14/2024, https://en.wikipedia.org/wiki/Billy_Graham.
5 Trevor Freeze, "Billy Graham Statue Unveiled At U.S. Capitol," *Billy Graham Evangelistic Association*, 5/16/2024, accessed 7/14/2024, https://billygraham.org/story/billy-graham-statue-unveiled-at-u-s-capitol-inviting-people-to-the-gospel/.
6 "Annual Statistics," GordonConwell.edu, accessed 7/14/2024, Status of Global Christianity 2024, https://www.gordonconwell.edu/center-for-global-christianity/resources/status-of-global-christianity/.

7. "Service Times & Speaking Schedule," LakewoodChurch.com, accessed 7/14/2024, https://www.lakewoodchurch.com/schedule.
8. "What Percentage Of Pastors Worldwide Have Theological Training?," GordonConwell.edu, accessed 7/14/2024, https://www.gordonconwell.edu/center-for-global-christianity/research/quick-facts/.
9. Alisa Childers, "5 Signs Your Church Might Be Heading Toward Progressive Christianity," *Alisa Childers Blog*, 5/8/2017, accessed 7/14/2024, https://www.alisachildersblog.com/blog/5-signs-your-church-might-be-heading-toward-progressive-christianity.
10. Maia Pandey, "Pope Removes Tyler's Bishop Joseph Strickland After Opposition To Church Reforms," *The Texas Tribune*, 11/11/2023, accessed 7/14/2024, https://www.texastribune.org/2023/11/11/new-article-Tyler-Bishop-Joseph-Strickland-removed/.
11. David Masci, "Where Christian Churches, Other Religions Stand On Gay Marriage," *Pew Research Center*, 12/21/2015, accessed 7/15/2024, https://www.pewresearch.org/short-reads/2015/12/21/where-christian-churches-stand-on-gay-marriage/.
12. Heather Hahn, "United Methodists Remove Same-Sex Wedding Ban," *UM News*, 5/3/2024, accessed 7/15/2024, https://www.umnews.org/en/news/united-methodists-remove-same-sex-wedding-ban.
James Farrell, "United Methodist Church Votes To Allow LGBTQ+ Clergy," *Forbes*, 5/1/2024, accessed 7/15/2024, https://www.forbes.com/sites/jamesfarrell/2024/05/01/united-methodist-church-votes-to-allow-lgbtq-clergy-amid-other-pro-lgbtq-efforts/.
13. Nicole Winfield, "Pope Approves Blessings For Same-Sex Couples," *AP News*, 12/19/2023, accessed 7/15/2024, https://apnews.com/article/vatican-lgbtq-pope-bfa5b71fa79055626e362936e739d1d8.
14. "The Global Catholic Population," *PRC* (endnote 4.15).
15. Mark Sandlin, "Ask A Progressive Christian - Q: Did The Resurrection Really Happen?," *Progressive Christianity*, 3/29/2024, accessed 7/14/2024, https://progressivechristianity.org/resource/ask-a-progressive-christian-q-did-the-resurrection-really-happen/.
16. Caleb J. Lines, "Ask A Progressive Christian - Q: Did Jesus Die For Our Sins?," *Progressive Christianity*, 3/12/2024, accessed 7/14/2024, https://progressivechristianity.org/resource/ask-a-progressive-christian-q-did-jesus-die-for-our-sins-2/.
17. Alisa Childers, AlisaChilders.com, accessed 7/14/2024.
Alisa Childers, YouTube channel, accessed 7/14/2024, https://www.youtube.com/user/alisachilders.
18. Pastor J.D., "Christianity Isn't Cussing Less And Giving More," *J.D. Greear Ministries*, 3/18/2019, accessed 7/15/2024, https://jdgreear.com/cussing-less-giving-more/.
19. "About Three-In-Ten U.S. Adults Are Now Religiously Unaffiliated," *Pew Research Center*, 12/14/2021, accessed 7/15/2024, https://www.pewresearch.org/religion/2021/12/14/about-three-in-ten-u-s-adults-are-now-religiously-unaffiliated/.
20. "Who Owns Your News?," TitleMax.com, accessed 7/15/2024, https://www.titlemax.com/discovery-center/who-owns-your-news-the-top-100-digital-news-outlets-and-their-ownership/.
Mira Nalbandian, "The Big Six's Big Media Game," *Pathfinder*, 5/9/2022, accessed 7/15/2024, https://pwestpathfinder.com/2022/05/09/the-big-sixs-big-media-game/.
21. "Tucker Carlson Tonight," Wikipedia.org, accessed 7/15/2024, https://en.wikipedia.org/wiki/Tucker_Carlson_Tonight.
22. Martin Pengelly, "Tucker Carlson Claims In Book Fox News Firing Was Part Of $787.5M Settlement," *The Guardian*, 7/26/2023, accessed 7/15/2024, https://www.theguardian.com/books/2023/jul/26/tucker-carlson-fox-news-firing-condition-dominion-settlement.
23. Melina Delkic, "Trump's Banishment From Facebook And Twitter," *The New York Times*, 5/10/2022, accessed 8/14/2024, https://www.nytimes.com/2022/05/10/technology/trump-social-media-ban-timeline.html.
24. Omri Wallach, "The World's Top 50 Influencers Across Social Media Platforms," *Visual Capitalist*, 5/14/2021, accessed 8/14/2024, https://www.visualcapitalist.com/worlds-top-50-influencers-across-social-media-platforms/.
25. "Musk Lifts Donald Trump's Twitter Ban," *BBC*, 11/19/2022, accessed 8/14/2024, https://www.bbc.com/news/world-us-canada-63692369.

26 Jim Hoft, "Former T-Mobile Agent Confirms Company's Censorship Of The Gateway Pundit," *The Gateway Pundit*, 1/13/2024, accessed 7/15/2024, https://www.thegatewaypundit.com/2024/01/former-t-mobile-agent-confirms-t-mobiles-censorship/.
27 Benjamin Goggin, "YouTubers Have Lost Thousands Of Dollars," *Business Insider*, 8/24/2019, accessed 7/15/2024, https://www.businessinsider.com/youtubers-entire-channels-can-get-mistakenly-demonetized-for-months-2019-8.
28 Tyler Durden, "Russell Brand Demonetized After Sexual Assault Claims," *Zero Hedge*, 9/20/2023, accessed 7/15/2024, https://www.zerohedge.com/political/russel-brand-demonetized-after-sexual-assault-claims.
Tyler Durden, "Britain's Parliament Demands That Rumble, X Deplatform Russell Brand," *Zero Hedge*, 9/22/2023, accessed 7/15/2024, https://www.zerohedge.com/political/britains-parliament-demands-rumble-x-deplatform-russell-brand.
29 "IVERIFY," UNDP.org, accessed 7/16/2024, https://www.undp.org/digital/iverify.
30 "Digital Services Coordinators," Digital-strategy.ec.europa.eu, accessed 7/16/2024, https://digital-strategy.ec.europa.eu/en/policies/dsa-dscs.
31 "Digital Services Act," Wikipedia.org, accessed 7/16/2024, https://en.wikipedia.org/wiki/Digital_Services_Act.
32 Ashley Belanger, "Robert F. Kennedy Jr. Sues Meta," *Ars Technica*, 5/16/2024, accessed 7/15/2024, https://arstechnica.com/tech-policy/2024/05/robert-f-kennedy-jr-sues-meta-citing-chatbots-reply-as-evidence-of-shadowban/.
33 John Fritze, "Supreme Court Allows White House To Press Social Media Companies To Remove Disinformation," *CNN*, 6/26/2024, accessed 7/15/2024, https://www.cnn.com/2024/06/26/politics/social-media-disinformation-supreme-court-ruling/index.html.
34 Leanne Delap, "John Fetterman Can't Wear Gym Short To Work Anymore," *Toronto Star*, 5/2/2024, accessed 7/16/2024, https://www.thestar.com/life/beauty-and-fashion/john-fetterman-can-t-wear-gym-shorts-to-work-anymore-thanks-to-a-historic-new/article_e164a58f-123b-5530-9aa1-d767ea455de6.html.
35 Leigh Boobyer, "Stonehenge Covered In Powder Paint By Just Stop Oil," *BBC*, 6/19/2024, accessed 7/16/2024, https://www.bbc.com/news/articles/cw44mdee0zzo.
36 Oliver Slow, "Mona Lisa: Protesters Throw Soup At Da Vinci Painting," *BBC*, 1/28/2024, accessed 7/16/2024, https://www.bbc.com/news/world-europe-68121654.
37 Nicholas Bloom, "The Great Resistance: Getting Employees Back To The Office," *Stanford Institute for Economic Policy Research*, 7/2022, accessed 7/16/2024, https://siepr.stanford.edu/publications/work/great-resistance-getting-employees-back-office.
38 Michael Torres, "Family Flees US After Teacher Spurs, Hides 10-Year-Old Daughter's Gender 'Transition'," *New York Post*, 2/1/2024, accessed 7/16/2024, https://nypost.com/2024/02/01/opinion/family-flees-us-after-teacher-spurs-hides-10-year-old-daughters-gender-transition/.
39 Joseph Figliolia, "Foster Children: The New Pawn In The Gender Wars," *City Journal*, 5/14/2024, accessed 7/16/2024, https://www.city-journal.org/article/foster-children-the-new-pawn-in-the-gender-wars.
40 Jaryn Crouson, "Parents Sue Governor Over New Law Allowing Schools To Secretly 'Transition' Kids," *World Net Daily*, 7/17/2024, accessed 8/14/2024, https://www.wnd.com/2024/07/potentially-devastating-parents-sue-governor-over-new-law-allowing-schools-to-secretly-transition-kids/.
41 Ben Weingarten, "The Durham Report Indicts The Deep State," *Newsweek*, 5/21/2023, accessed 7/16/2024, https://www.newsweek.com/durham-report-indicts-deep-state-media-opinion-1801198.
42 Miranda Devine, "It's Been Two Years Since 51 Intelligence Agents Interfered With An Election," *New York Post*, 10/20/2022, accessed 7/16/2024, https://nypost.com/2022/10/19/its-been-two-years-since-51-intelligence-agents-interfered-with-an-election-they-still-wont-apologize/.
43 "Countries With Freedom Of Speech 2024," WorldPopulationReview.com, accessed 7/16/2024, https://worldpopulationreview.com/country-rankings/countries-with-freedom-of-speech.

Chapter 8
1 "Hoarding Disorder," Wikipedia.org, accessed 7/23/2024, https://en.wikipedia.org/wiki/Hoarding_disorder.

2. David Mataix-Cols, "Hoarding Disorder Has Finally Arrived, But Many Challenges Lie Ahead," *National Library of Medicine*, 6/17/2018, accessed 7/23/2024, https://www.ncbi.nlm.nih.gov/pmc/articles/PMC5980544/.
3. "U.S. Self-Storage," *Statista*, 6/25/2024, accessed 7/23/2024, https://www.statista.com/topics/4922/self-storage-in-the-us.
4. "Vacancy Rate Of Self-Storage Space In The United States," *Statista*, 5/17/2024, accessed 7/23/2024, https://www.statista.com/statistics/914689/self-storage-vacancy-rate-usa/.
5. "Largest Non-U.S. Companies By Market Cap," TradingView.com, accessed 7/23/2024, https://www.tradingview.com/markets/world-stocks/worlds-non-us-companies/.
"US Companies With The Most Cash On Hand," TradingView.com, accessed 7/23/2024, https://www.tradingview.com/markets/stocks-usa/market-movers-highest-cash/.
6. Matt Krantz, "13 Firms Hoard $1 Trillion In Cash," *Investor's Business Daily*, 9/19/2023, accessed 7/23/2024, https://www.investors.com/etfs-and-funds/sectors/sp500-companies-stockpile-1-trillion-cash-investors-want-it/.
7. Catherine Stoddard, "Tonya Harding And Nancy Kerrigan: A Look Back," *LiveNOW*, 1/30/2024, accessed 7/24/2024, https://www.livenowfox.com/news/tonya-harding-nancy-kerrigan-1994-attack.
8. Christine Brennan, "Tonya Harding Movie Wants Your Sympathy," *USA Today*, 12/20/2017, accessed 7/24/2024, https://www.usatoday.com/story/sports/columnist/brennan/2017/12/20/tonya-harding-movie-wants-your-sympathy-but-lets-not-forget-facts/971183001/.
9. Emily A. Vogels, "Teens And Cyberbullying 2022," *Pew Research Center*, 12/15/2022, accessed 7/24/2024, https://www.pewresearch.org/internet/2022/12/15/teens-and-cyberbullying-2022/.
10. "Revenge Porn," Wikipedia.org, accessed 7/24/2024, https://en.wikipedia.org/wiki/Revenge_porn.
11. Tal Kopan, "States Criminalize 'Revenge Porn'," *Politico*, 10/30/2013, accessed 7/24/2024, https://www.politico.com/story/2013/10/states-criminalize-revenge-porn-099082.
12. The Associated Press, "Evanston, Illinois, Becomes First U.S. City To Pay Reparations To Black Residents," *NBC News*, 3/23/2021, accessed 7/24/2024, https://www.nbcnews.com/news/us-news/evanston-illinois-becomes-first-u-s-city-pay-reparations-blacks-n1261791.
13. Wendy Fry, "California Is The First State To Tackle Reparations For Black Residents," *CalMatters*, 6/19/2024, accessed 7/24/2024, https://calmatters.org/explainers/reparations-california/.
14. "Reparations Agreement Between Israel And The Federal Republic Of Germany," Wikipedia.org, accessed 7/24/2024, https://en.wikipedia.org/wiki/Reparations_Agreement_between_Israel_and_the_Federal_Republic_of_Germany.
Kirsten Grieshaber, "Germany Marks 70 Years Of Compensating Holocaust Survivors," *AP News*, 9/15/2022, accessed 7/24/2024, https://apnews.com/article/holocaust-survivor-compensation-fund-germany-0d35aa1cba7756d1b9b6008e9d7841b7.
15. Loveday Morris, "Israel Should Evacuate Settlements, Pay Reparations, ICJ Says," *The Washington Post*, 6/19/2024, accessed 7/24/2024, https://www.washingtonpost.com/world/2024/07/19/israel-icj-occupation-palestinian-territory/.
16. "Digital 2024: Global Overview," DataReportal.com (endnote 5.9).
17. Mike Snider, "Wayfair CEO Niraj Shah Tells Employees To 'Work Longer Hours' In Year-End Email," *USA Today*, 12/22/2023, accessed 9/4/2024, https://www.usatoday.com/story/money/business/2023/12/22/wayfair-ceo-niraj-shah-email-work-longer-hours/72010867007/.
18. Joshua Comins, "Mike Rowe Says 'The Days Are Gone' Where Work Ethic Used To Be A Virtue," *Fox News*, 12/30/2023, accessed 9/4/2024, https://www.foxnews.com/media/mike-rowe-says-days-gone-where-work-ethic-used-to-be-virtue.
19. "As The E&M Industry Grows To US $3.4 Trillion By 2028, Large New Revenue Pools Are Forming," *PwC*, 7/16/2024, accessed 7/24/2024, https://www.pwc.com/gx/en/issues/business-model-reinvention/outlook/insights-and-perspectives.html.
20. "Digital 2024: Global Overview Report," DataReportal.com, accessed 7/24/2024, Jan 2024 Top Websites: Semrush Ranking graphic, traffic between 09/01/2023 - 11/30/2023, https://datareportal.com/reports/digital-2024-global-overview-report.
21. Laura Ceci, "Market Size Of The Online Pornographic And Adult Content Industry In The United States," *Statista*, 4/15/2024, accessed 7/24/2024, https://www.statista.com/statistics/1371582/value-online-website-porn-market-us/.
22. "Digital 2024: Global Overview," DataReportal.com (endnote 8.20).
23. "2007-2008 Financial Crisis," Wikipedia.org, accessed 7/24/2024,

https://en.wikipedia.org/wiki/2007–2008_financial_crisis.

24 "Largest Bankruptcies In The United States," *Statista*, 2/29/2024, accessed 7/24/2024, https://www.statista.com/statistics/1096794/largest-bankruptcies-usa-by-assets/.

25 Around the Web, "Biden Implementing Radical Housing Policies," *World Net Daily*, 6/9/2024, accessed 7/24/2024, https://www.wnd.com/2024/06/bidens-radical-housing-policies-might-crash-whole-system/.

26 Kirsten Altus, "Mortgage Giant Gets Green Light From Biden Administration For Risky Pilot Program," *Fox Business*, 6/26/2024, accessed 7/24/2024, https://www.foxbusiness.com/media/mortgage-giant-gets-green-light-from-biden-administration-risky-pilot-program.

27 "Enron Scandal," Wikipedia.org, accessed 7/25/2024, https://en.wikipedia.org/wiki/Enron_scandal.

28 Brian O'Connell, "9 Of The Biggest Financial Fraud Cases In History," *U.S. News*, 5/21/2024, accessed 7/25/2024, https://money.usnews.com/investing/articles/biggest-corporate-frauds-in-history.

29 "Sam Bankman-Fried," Wikipedia.org, accessed 7/25/2024, https://en.wikipedia.org/wiki/Sam_Bankman-Fried.

30 Breck Dumas, "DOJ Charges Nearly 200 People Over $2.7 Billion In Health Care Fraud Schemes," *Fox Business*, 6/27/2024, accessed 7/25/2024, https://www.foxbusiness.com/politics/doj-charges-nearly-200-people-over-2-7-billion-health-care-fraud-schemes.

31 "Simon Leviev," Wikipedia.org, accessed 7/25/2024, https://en.wikipedia.org/wiki/Simon_Leviev.

32 Michael Horovitz, "Police Seek Charges In Cases Against Crypto Businessman," *The Times Of Israel*, 8/23/2023, accessed 7/25/2024, https://www.timesofisrael.com/police-seek-charges-in-fraud-case-against-crypto-businessman-moshe-hogeg/.

33 FBI Springfield, "How The FBI Is Combating Covid-19 Related Fraud," *FBI*, 1/12/2024, accessed 7/25/2024, https://www.fbi.gov/contact-us/field-offices/springfield/news/how-the-fbi-is-combatting-covid-19-related-fraud.
Ken Dilanian, "Biggest Fraud In A Generation," *NBC News*, 3/28/2022, accessed 7/25/2024, https://www.nbcnews.com/politics/justice-department/biggest-fraud-generation-looting-covid-relief-program-known-ppp-n1279664.

34 "2023 Official Cybercrime Report," eSentire.com, accessed 7/25/2024, https://www.esentire.com/resources/library/2023-official-cybercrime-report.

35 Darina L., "Rise Of Robots - Jobs Lost To Automation," *Leftronic*, 3/7/2023, accessed 7/24/2024, https://leftronic.com/blog/jobs-lost-to-automation-statistics.

36 "Real And Nominal Value Of The Federal Minimum Wage In The United States," *Statista*, 7/5/2024, accessed 7/24/2024, https://www.statista.com/statistics/1065466/real-nominal-value-minimum-wage-us/.

37 "TikTok Users Says Walmart Grocery Bill Nearly Quadrupled In Just Two Years," *PM.*, 6/27/2024, accessed 7/24/2024, https://thepostmillennial.com/tiktok-user-says-walmart-grocery-bill-nearly-quadrupled-in-just-two-years.

38 Megan Henney, "National Debt Tracker," *Fox Business*, 7/23/2024, accessed 7/24/2024, https://www.foxbusiness.com/economy/us-national-debt-tracker.

39 "US Population," WorldoMeters.info, accessed 7/24/2024, https://www.worldometers.info/world-population/us-population/.

40 $34.9 trillion US debt (see ch. 8 n. 38) / 342 million US population (see ch. 8 n. 39) = $102k per American.

41 Tyler Durden, "US GDP "Grew" $334 Billion In Q4," *Zero Hedge*, 2/28/2024, accessed 7/24/2024, https://www.zerohedge.com/markets/us-gdp-grew-334-billion-q4-growth-cost-834-billion-debt.

42 "General Government Debt," IMF.org, accessed 7/24/2024, https://www.imf.org/external/datamapper/GG_DEBT_GDP@GDD/CAN/FRA/DEU/ITA/JPN/GBR/USA/VEN.

43 Marcus Lu, "Visualizing Wealth Distribution In America," *Visual Capitalist*, 2/19/2024, accessed 7/23/2024, https://www.visualcapitalist.com/wealth-distribution-in-america.

44 "Wealth Share Of The Richest 10%," OurWorldInData.org, accessed 7/23/2024, https://ourworldindata.org/grapher/wealth-share-richest-10-percent.

45 Toi Staff, "Knesset Ups Tax Penalties For Extravagant Pay To Bank CEOs," *The Times of Israel*,

3/29/2016, accessed 9/15/2024, https://www.timesofisrael.com/knesset-ups-tax-penalties-for-extravagant-bank-ceo-pay/.

46 "Aggregated CEO-To-Worker Compensation Ration," *Statista*, 7/5/2024, accessed 7/23/2024, https://www.statista.com/statistics/261463/ceo-to-worker-compensation-ratio-of-top-firms-in-the-us.

47 "Company Pay Ratios," AFLCIO.org, accessed 7/23/2024, https://aflcio.org/paywatch/company-pay-ratios.

48 "S.3620 - Tax Excessive CEO Pay Act Of 2024," Congress.gov, accessed 7/23/2024, https://www.congress.gov/bill/118th-congress/senate-bill/3620/text.
"Sanders And Colleagues Introduce Legislation To Combat Corporate Greed," *Bernie Sanders*, 1/22/2024, accessed 7/23/2024, https://www.sanders.senate.gov/press-releases/news-sanders-and-colleagues-introduce-legislation-to-combat-corporate-greed-and-end-outrageous-ceo-pay-2/.

49 Niccolo Conte, "The World's Wealthiest Cities," *Visual Capitalist*, 6/27/2024, accessed 7/25/2024, https://www.visualcapitalist.com/cities-with-the-most-millionaires-and-billionaires/.

50 Jayna Locke, "Top 10 Most Futuristic Smart Cities In The World," *Digi*, 4/14/2023, accessed 7/25/2024, https://www.digi.com/blog/post/smart-cities-in-the-world.

51 Pansy Schulman, "Saudi Arabia's The Line Drastically Scales Back," *Architectural Record*, 4/17/2024, accessed 7/25/2024, https://www.architecturalrecord.com/articles/16851-saudi-arabias-the-line-drastically-scales-back-its-ambitions.

52 Kate Whiting, "This Is What The World's First Floating City Will Look Like," *World Economic Forum*, 4/29/2022, accessed 7/25/2024, https://www.weforum.org/agenda/2022/04/south-korea-floating-city-climate-change/.

53 "Babylon," WHC.UNESCO.org, accessed 7/25/2024, https://whc.unesco.org/en/list/278/.
"The Future Of Babylon," WMF.org, accessed 7/25/2024, https://www.wmf.org/project/future-babylon.

54 "Babylon Governorate," Wikipedia.org, accessed 7/25/2024, https://en.wikipedia.org/wiki/Babylon_Governorate.

55 "Iraq Population," WorldoMeters.info, accessed 7/25/2024, https://www.worldometers.info/world-population/iraq-population/.

56 "Embassy Of The United States, Baghdad," Wikipedia.org, accessed 7/25/2024, https://en.wikipedia.org/wiki/Embassy_of_the_United_States,_Baghdad.
Attiya Zainib, "5 Largest US Embassies In The World," *Insider Monkey*, 12/15/2023, accessed 7/25/2024, https://www.insidermonkey.com/blog/5-largest-us-embassies-in-the-world-1234751/?singlepage=1.

Chapter 9

1 Tyler Durden, "Forbes Censors Award-Winning Environmentalist's Apology Over Three-Decade 'Climate Scare'," *Zero Hedge*, 6/29/2020, accessed 7/30/2024, https://web.archive.org/web/20200705194535/https://www.zerohedge.com/political/forbes-censors-award-winning-environmentalists-apology-over-three-decade-climate-scare-so.
Christer Ericsson, "Climate Maps Manipulated To Mislead The Public," *Free West Media*, 7/7/2023, accessed 7/30/2024, https://freewestmedia.com/2023/07/07/climate-maps-manipulated-to-mislead-the-public/.

2 Tyler Durden, "Three Graphs That Show There Is No "Climate Crisis"," *Zero Hedge*, 11/27/2023, accessed 7/30/2024, https://www.zerohedge.com/geopolitical/three-graphs-show-there-no-climate-crisis.

3 Dr. Alan White, "The Globe Is Warming, But It's Not Your Fault!," *Answers In Genesis*, accessed 7/30/2024, https://answersingenesis.org/environmental-science/climate-change/globe-is-warming-but-its-not-your-fault/.

4 Tyler Durden, "Trust The "Science" … That Just Retracted 11,000 "Peer Reviewed" Papers," *Zero Hedge*, 5/27/2024, accessed 7/30/2024, https://www.zerohedge.com/markets/trust-sciencethat-just-retracted-11000-peer-reviewed-papers.

5 "Global Risks Report 2024," WEForum.org, accessed 7/30/2024, Figure 1.2, p 12-13, https://www.weforum.org/publications/global-risks-report-2024/.

6 Michelle Starr, "AI Has Already Become A Master Of Lies," *Science Alert*, 5/11/2024, accessed 7/30/2024, https://www.sciencealert.com/ai-has-already-become-a-master-of-lies-and-deception-scientists-warn.

7 "Basket Of Deplorables," Wikipedia.org, accessed 7/31/2024, https://en.wikipedia.org/wiki/Basket_of_deplorables.

8 Ben Shapiro, "The Worst Political Scandal In American History?," *The Daily Signal*, 5/17/2023,

accessed 7/31/2024, https://www.dailysignal.com/2023/05/17/the-worst-political-scandal-in-american-history.
9. Dennis Prager, "Why The Pope Is Wrong About An 'Empty' Hell," *World Net Daily*, 3/12/2024, accessed 7/31/2024, https://www.wnd.com/2024/03/pope-wrong-empty/.
10. "Religious Composition By Country," *PRC* (endnote 4.4).
11. Ridenour, *What's the Difference?*, ch 5 (endnote 4.15).
12. "Religious Composition By Country," *PRC* (endnote 4.4).
13. "Religious Composition By Country," *PRC* (endnote 4.4).
14. Ridenour, *What's the Difference?*, ch 6 (endnote 4.15).
15. "Religious Composition By Country," *PRC* (endnote 4.4).
16. Ridenour, *What's the Difference?*, ch 7 (endnote 4.15).
17. "'Imagine' Lyrics," AZLyrics.com, accessed 7/31/2024, https://www.azlyrics.com/lyrics/johnlennon/imagine.html.
18. Deepak Chopra, "Where Do We Go After We Die?," *Medium*, 5/13/2024, accessed 7/31/2024, https://deepakchopra.medium.com/where-do-we-go-after-we-die-957927200c98.
19. Michael Haynes, "Pope Francis Denies That Hell Is 'A Place'," *Life Site*, 3/16/2023, accessed 7/31/2024, https://www.lifesitenews.com/news/pope-francis-denies-that-hell-is-a-place-says-it-is-a-posture-towards-life.
20. "Immortality Is Attainable By 2030," *NYP* (endnote 6.49).
21. Fiona Jackson, "Could You Live Forever?," *Daily Mail*, 4/8/2023, accessed 7/31/2024, https://www.dailymail.co.uk/sciencetech/article-11938283/Could-live-forever-Experts-claim-humans-achieve-IMMORTALITY-2030.html.
22. "Prosperity Theology," Wikipedia.org, accessed 7/31/2024, https://en.wikipedia.org/wiki/Prosperity_theology.
23. "Prosperity Theology," Wikipedia.org (endnote 9.22).
    Joe Carter, "9 Things You Should Know About The Prosperity Gospel," *The Gospel Coalition*, 9/2/2023, accessed 7/31/2024, https://www.thegospelcoalition.org/article/9-things-prosperity-gospel/.
    Lisa Loraine Baker, "Who Is Steven Furtick?," *Christianity.com*, 2/26/2024, accessed 7/31/2024, https://www.christianity.com/wiki/people/steven-furtick.html.
    "Benny Hinn," Wikipedia.org, accessed 7/31/2024, https://en.wikipedia.org/wiki/Benny_Hinn.
    "Paula White," Wikipedia.org, accessed 7/31/2024, https://en.wikipedia.org/wiki/Paula_White.
    "Joel Osteen," Wikipedia.org, accessed 7/31/2024, https://en.wikipedia.org/wiki/Joel_Osteen.
    Leonardo Blair, "'If You Obey God, You Will Never Be Broke,' TD Jakes Says," *The Christian Post*, 9/28/2017, accessed 7/31/2024, https://www.christianpost.com/news/if-you-obey-god-you-will-never-be-broke-td-jakes-says.html.
24. Compiled from social media followers of the following pages on 7/31/2024. Joel Osteen: facebook.com/JoelOsteen; x.com/JoelOsteen; instagram.com/joelosteen; youtube.com/@joelosteen. Joyce Meyer: facebook.com/joycemeyerministries; x.com/JoyceMeyer; instagram.com/joycemeyer; youtube.com/@joycemeyer. TD Jakes: facebook.com/bishopjakes; x.com/BishopJakes; instagram.com/bishopjakes; youtube.com/@TDJakesOfficial. Steven Furtick: facebook.com/StevenFurtick; instagram.com/stevenfurtick; x.com/stevenfurtick; youtube.com/@stevenfurtick. Benny Hinn: facebook.com/BennyHinnMinistries; x.com/Benny_Hinn; instagram.com/pastorbennyhinn; youtube.com/@bennyhinnministries. Paula White: facebook.com/realpaulawhite; x.com/Paula_White; instagram.com/paulamichellewhite; youtube.com/@paulawhiteministries.
25. "Empty Out The Negative," 7/30/2016, *Joel Osteen*, YouTube video, accessed 7/31/2024, https://www.youtube.com/watch?v=gRmi3cQ2hBw.
26. "Pastor Joel Osteen's Full Sermon "The Power Of 'I Am'"," 10/28/2012, *OWN*, YouTube video, accessed 7/31/2024, https://www.youtube.com/watch?v=_kjSK-PcU9o.
27. "Timing Is Everything," 7/3/2022, *T.D. Jakes*, YouTube video, accessed 7/31/2024, https://www.youtube.com/watch?v=HrwtRU1vMC4.
28. "Predictions And Claims For The Second Coming," Wikipedia.org, accessed 8/1/2024, https://en.wikipedia.org/wiki/Predictions_and_claims_for_the_Second_Coming.
    "List Of Dates Predicted For Apocalyptic Events," Wikipedia.org, accessed 8/1/2024, https://en.wikipedia.org/wiki/List_of_dates_predicted_for_apocalyptic_events.
    "Rapture," Wikipedia.org, accessed 8/1/2024, https://en.wikipedia.org/wiki/Rapture.
29. "Religious Composition By Country," *PRC* (endnote 4.4).
30. Ruth Graham, "Christian Prophets Are On The Rise. What Happens When They're Wrong?," *The

New York Times, 2/11/2021, accessed 8/1/2024, https://www.nytimes.com/2021/02/11/us/christian-prophets-predictions.html.

31 Julia Duin, "The Christian Prophets Who Say Trump Is Coming Again," *Politico*, 2/18/2024, accessed 8/1/2024, https://www.politico.com/news/magazine/2021/02/18/how-christian-prophets-give-credence-to-trumps-election-fantasies-469598.
32 Sid Roth's It's Supernatural!, SidRoth.org, accessed 8/1/2024.
33 Sid Roth's It's Supernatural!, YouTube channel, accessed 8/1/2024, https://www.youtube.com/@sidroth.
34 Pope Francis, X.com profile, accessed 8/1/2024, https://x.com/Pontifex.
35 Philip Pullella, "Vatican Approves Blessings For Same-Sex Couples," *Reuters*, 12/18/2023, accessed 8/1/2024, https://www.reuters.com/world/vatican-approves-blessings-same-sex-couples-under-certain-conditions-2023-12-18/.
36 "Document On Human Fraternity," Wikipedia.org, accessed 8/1/2024, https://en.wikipedia.org/wiki/Document_on_Human_Fraternity.
37 "International Day Of Human Fraternity," Wikipedia.org, accessed 8/1/2024, https://en.wikipedia.org/wiki/International_Day_of_Human_Fraternity.
38 Shelley Walsh, "The Top 30 Social Media Influencers Worldwide," *Search Engine Journal*, 6/21/2024, accessed 8/1/2024, https://www.searchenginejournal.com/top-social-media-influencers/475776/.
39 MrBeast, YouTube channel, accessed 8/1/2024, https://www.youtube.com/@MrBeast.
40 "List Of Messiah Claimants," Wikipedia.org, accessed 8/1/2024, https://en.wikipedia.org/wiki/List_of_messiah_claimants.
"List Of People Claimed To Be Jesus," Wikipedia.org, accessed 8/1/2024, https://en.wikipedia.org/wiki/List_of_people_claimed_to_be_Jesus.
41 Ken Johnson, Th.D., *Ancient Paganism*, eBook, (USA: 2009), p 140. The coming of a new age, The Secret.
42 "Siege Of Jerusalem (70 CE)," Wikipedia.org, accessed 7/29/2024, https://en.wikipedia.org/wiki/Siege_of_Jerusalem_(70_CE).
43 "The History Of The Romans: Every Year," 12/31/2015, *EmperorTigerstar*, YouTube video, accessed 7/29/2024, https://www.youtube.com/watch?v=w5zYpWcz1-E.
Mark Milligan, "The Roman Empire - Interactive Map," *Heritage Daily*, 3/20/2020, accessed 7/29/2024, https://www.heritagedaily.com/2020/03/the-roman-world-interactive-map/110578.
44 "Hanukkah," Wikipedia.org, accessed 8/1/2024, https://en.wikipedia.org/wiki/Hanukkah.
45 Jonathan H. Kantor, "Top 10 Of History's Most Lethal Leaders," *ListVerse*, 3/12/2024, accessed 8/1/2024, https://listverse.com/2024/03/12/top-10-of-historys-most-lethal-leaders/.
46 Connor Sheppard, "The 10 Highest Grossing Movie Franchise Of All Time," *IGN*, 1/15/2024, accessed 8/1/2024, https://www.ign.com/articles/highest-grossing-movie-franchises.
47 "Introduction To The Holocaust," Encyclopedia.USHMM.org, accessed 8/1/2024, https://encyclopedia.ushmm.org/content/en/article/introduction-to-the-holocaust.
48 "Snap," MarvelCinematicUniverse.fandom.com, accessed 8/1/2024, https://marvelcinematicuniverse.fandom.com/wiki/Snap.
49 "Navy Pilot Recalls 'Out Of This World' Encounter," 12/20/2017, *Fox News*, YouTube video, accessed 8/1/2024, https://www.youtube.com/watch?v=EDj9ZZQY2kA.
50 "Are Aliens Real?," *NBC* (endnote 6.34).
51 Jay Peters, "Here's The Tech Behind The Carolina Panther's Giant AR Cat," *The Verge*, 9/15/2021, accessed 8/1/2024, https://www.theverge.com/2021/9/15/22672199/carolina-panthers-mixed-augmented-reality-viral-virtual-mascot.
"Carolina Panthers Debut Mixed-Reality Panther At Home Opener," 9/12/2021, *Carolina Panthers*, YouTube video, accessed 8/1/2024, https://www.youtube.com/watch?v=_XhgfnwVTts.
52 "Digital Twins And Holoportation With HoloLens 2," 6/13/2022, *Microsoft HoloLens*, YouTube video, accessed 8/2/2024, https://www.youtube.com/watch?v=SrH5LXB5uIE.
53 Debra Kaufman, ""Holography" At CES 2024," *Light Field Lab*, 3/25/2024, accessed 8/1/2024, https://www.lightfieldlab.com/blogposts/holography-at-ces-2024.
54 Sabrina Ortiz, "I Chatted With A Hologram At CES 2024," *ZDNET*, 1/8/2024, accessed 8/1/2024, https://www.zdnet.com/article/i-chatted-with-a-hologram-at-ces-2024-and-it-was-as-cool-as-it-sounds/.
55 "1948 Arab-Israeli War," Wikipedia.org, accessed 8/2/2024, https://en.wikipedia.org/wiki/1948_Arab–Israeli_War.
56 "Green Line (Israel)," Wikipedia.org, accessed 8/2/2024,

https://en.wikipedia.org/wiki/Green_Line_(Israel).
57 "Six-Day War," Wikipedia.org, accessed 8/2/2024, https://en.wikipedia.org/wiki/Six-Day_War.
58 "Abraham Accords," Wikipedia.org, accessed 8/2/2024, https://en.wikipedia.org/wiki/Abraham_Accords.
59 Seth J. Frantzman, "How The Israel-Hamas War Worsened Challenges Facing The Abraham Accords," *The Jerusalem Post*, 1/5/2024, accessed 8/2/2024, https://www.jpost.com/middle-east/abraham-accords/article-780928.
60 Dennis Ross, "Saudi-Israel Normalization Would Transform Middle East," *The Jerusalem Post*, 10/5/2023, accessed 8/2/2024, https://www.jpost.com/opinion/article-761683.
"America, Israel, And Saudi Are "At The Cusp Of A Deal"," *The Economist*, 9/24/2023, accessed 8/2/2024, https://web.archive.org/web/20230929152246/https://www.economist.com/middle-east-and-africa/2023/09/24/america-israel-and-saudi-are-at-the-cusp-of-a-deal.
61 Michael Schirber, "A Laser-Based "Lightning Rod"," *Physics Magazine*, 1/23/2023, accessed 8/2/2024, https://physics.aps.org/articles/v16/12.
Maria Temming, "A Powerful Laser Can Control The Paths That Lightning Takes," *Science News Explores*, 3/31/2023, accessed 8/2/2024, https://www.snexplores.org/article/laser-lightning-rod.
62 Will Bedingfield, "How Indiana Jones And The Dial Of Destiny De-Aged Harrison Ford," *Wired*, 7/7/2023, accessed 8/3/2024, https://www.wired.com/story/indiana-jones-and-the-dial-of-destiny-de-aging-tech/.
63 "Here - Official Trailer," 6/26/2024, *Sony Pictures Entertainment*, YouTube video, accessed 8/2/2024, https://www.youtube.com/watch?v=I_id-SkGU2k.
Sarah Novack, "These De-Aged Tom Hanks Images Really Unnerve Me," *Screen Rant*, 6/27/2024, accessed 8/2/2024, https://screenrant.com/here-movie-tom-hanks-robin-wright-deaged-images-weird-exciting/.
64 Nicholas Barber, "New Tom Hanks Film Here And The Unsettling 'De-Aging' Technology," *BBC*, 7/2/2024, accessed 8/2/2024, https://www.bbc.com/culture/article/20240701-new-tom-hanks-film-here-and-the-unsettling-new-de-aging-technology-keeping-stars-forever-young.
65 "United Nations Security Council Veto Power," Wikipedia.org, accessed 8/2/2024, https://en.wikipedia.org/wiki/United_Nations_Security_Council_veto_power.
66 "Bilderberg Meeting," Wikipedia.org, accessed 8/2/2024, https://en.wikipedia.org/wiki/Bilderberg_Meeting.

Chapter 10
1 "Covid Hypocrisy: Policymakers Breaking Their Own Rules," Heritage.org, accessed 8/5/2024, https://datavisualizations.heritage.org/public-health/covid-hypocrisy-policymakers-breaking-their-own-rules/.
2 "Arab And Muslim Nations Loudly Proclaim Their Support For Palestinian Cause," *All Arab News*, 10/19/2023, accessed 8/5/2024, https://allarab.news/arab-and-muslim-nations-loudly-proclaim-their-support-for-palestinian-cause-yet-refuse-to-accept-gaza-refugees/.
3 Elise Kaplan, "The Investigation Into Corruption In APD's DWI Unit," *City Desk ABQ*, 5/21/2024, accessed 8/5/2024, https://citydesk.org/2024/timeline-the-investigation-into-corruption-in-apds-dwi-unit/.
4 Lee Ohanian, "Why Shoplifting Is Now De Facto Legal In California," *Hoover Institution*, 8/3/2021, accessed 8/5/2024, https://www.hoover.org/research/why-shoplifting-now-de-facto-legal-california.
5 Around the Web, "U.S. Church Holds 'Drag Sunday'," *World Net Daily*, 9/18/2023, accessed 8/5/2024, https://www.wnd.com/2023/09/watch-u-s-church-holds-drag-sunday-bless-satanic-sisters-perpetual-indulgence/.
6 "Christian Movements And Denominations," *Pew Research Center*, 12/19/2011, accessed 8/5/2024, https://www.pewresearch.org/religion/2011/12/19/global-christianity-movements-and-denominations.
7 "Benny Hinn Historic Crusades: Atlanta (2010)," 5/29/2016, *BringBackTheCross*, YouTube video, accessed 8/5/2024, https://www.youtube.com/watch?v=8kkgccLG1Gg.
8 Caryle Murphy, "Interfaith Marriage Is Common In U.S.," *Pew Research Center*, 6/2/2015, accessed 8/5/2024, https://www.pewresearch.org/short-reads/2015/06/02/interfaith-marriage/.
9 Thomas D. Williams, PH.D., "Pope Francis: Christians, Jews, Muslims 'Worship The One God'," *Breitbart*, 6/28/2024, accessed 8/5/2024, https://www.breitbart.com/faith/2024/06/28/pope-francis-christians-jews-muslims-worship-the-one-god/.
10 "Top 10 Most Followed Accounts On Twitter/X," *Forbes India*, 7/15/2024, accessed 8/5/2024,

https://www.forbesindia.com/article/explainers/most-followed-accounts-twitter-x/88311/1.
11. Kate Gibson, "PayPal Bans Alex Jones, Infowars Website," *CBS News*, 9/21/2018, accessed 8/6/2024, https://www.cbsnews.com/news/paypal-bans-alex-jones-infowars-website-conspiracy-theories-from-processing-payments/.
12. Mike Elgan, "Uh-Oh: Silicon Valley Is Building A Chinese-Style Social Credit System," *Fast Company*, 8/26/2019, accessed 8/6/2024, https://www.fastcompany.com/90394048/uh-oh-silicon-valley-is-building-a-chinese-style-social-credit-system.
13. Tyler Durden, "The CrowdStrike Global Outage Show The Serious Dangers Of A Centralized, Digital World," *Zero Hedge*, 7/21/2024, accessed 8/6/2024, https://www.zerohedge.com/technology/crowdstrike-global-outage-shows-serious-dangers-centralized-digitized-world.
14. Tyler Durden, "CBDCs: The Ultimate Corruption Of Money," *Zero Hedge*, 8/14/2023, accessed 8/6/2024, https://www.zerohedge.com/crypto/cbdcs-ultimate-corruption-money.
  "IMF And DCMA Unveil Universal Monetary Unit," *Investing.com*, 4/17/2023, accessed 8/6/2024, https://www.investing.com/news/cryptocurrency-news/imf-and-dcma-unveil-universal-monetary-unit-to-reinforce-banking-3056611.
15. "Central Bank Digital Currency (CBDC)," FederalReserve.gov, accessed 8/6/2024, https://www.federalreserve.gov/cbdc-faqs.htm.
16. Tyler Durden, "Trump Vows To "Never Allow" A Central Band Digital Currency," *Zero Hedge*, 1/18/2024, accessed 9/4/2024, https://www.zerohedge.com/crypto/trump-vows-never-allow-central-bank-digital-currency.
17. Simon Torkington, "Quantum Computing Could Threaten Cybersecurity Measures," *World Economic Forum*, 8/23/2024, accessed 8/6/2024, https://www.weforum.org/agenda/2024/04/quantum-computing-cybersecurity-risks/.
18. Rebecca Hardy, "The Giant Company Announces Collaboration With America Dream Mall," *Blooloop*, 1/17/2024, accessed 8/6/2024, https://blooloop.com/immersive/news/the-giant-company-american-dream-mall/.
19. The Giant Company, TheGiantCompany.ie, accessed 8/6/2024.
20. Petroc Taylor, "Number Of Smartphone Mobile Network Subscriptions," *Statista*, 5/22/2024, accessed 8/6/2024, https://www.statista.com/statistics/330695/number-of-smartphone-users-worldwide/.
21. "World Population," WorldoMeters.info (endnote 5.3).
22. Zhanna L. Malekos Smith, "Human Microchip Implants Take Center Stage," *The Hill*, 1/23/2023, accessed 8/6/2024, https://thehill.com/opinion/technology/3817029-human-microchip-implants-take-center-stage/.
23. Tyler Durden, "Mastercard Launches It's Biometric Retail Payment System In Europe," *Zero Hedge*, 6/12/2024, accessed 8/6/2024, https://www.zerohedge.com/personal-finance/mastercard-launches-its-biometric-retail-payment-system-europe-using-poland.
24. "Elon Musk's Neuralink Implants Brain Chip In First Human," *Reuters*, 1/30/2024, accessed 8/6/2024, https://www.reuters.com/technology/neuralink-implants-brain-chip-first-human-musk-says-2024-01-29/.
25. Shannon Thaler, "Elon Musk's Neuralink Chip Suffers Unexpected Setback," *New York Post*, 5/9/2024, accessed 8/6/2024, https://nypost.com/2024/05/09/business/neuralink-says-its-first-in-human-brain-implant-malfunctioned/.
26. Ian Taylor, "The Injectable Nanosensor That Will One Day Read Your Thoughts," *BBC Science Focus*, 7/23/2021, accessed 8/6/2024, https://www.sciencefocus.com/news/the-injectable-nanosensor-that-will-one-day-read-your-thoughts/.
27. Masha Borak, "Iran Shares More On Using Facial Recognition To Police Hijabs," *Biometric Update*, 6/10/2024, accessed 8/6/2024, https://www.biometricupdate.com/202406/iran-shares-more-on-using-facial-recognition-to-police-hijabs.
  Maziar Motamedi, "Iran's Parliament Approves 'Hijab Bill'," *Al Jazeera*, 9/20/2023, accessed 8/6/2024, https://www.aljazeera.com/news/2023/9/20/irans-parliament-approves-hijab-bill-harsh-punishments-for-violations.

Chapter 11

1. Rick Nathanson, "Tiny Homes Village Still Has Tiny Occupancy," *Albuquerque Journal*, 7/20/2021, accessed 8/9/2024, https://www.abqjournal.com/news/local/tiny-homes-village-still-has-tiny-occupancy/article_c4c50fdf-5ec2-5008-b47e-cf0c84912d5d.html.
2. Cathy Cook, "Tiny Home Village Reaches 100% Occupancy For The First Time," *Albuquerque*

Journal, 7/8/2024, accessed 8/9/2024, https://www.abqjournal.com/news/tiny-home-village-reaches-100-occupancy-for-the-first-time/article_c4fd1f62-3b26-11ef-bc75-a370696ccae5.html.

3   "How Bad Is Addiction In The United States?," *Plan Street*, 9/1/2022, accessed 8/9/2024, https://www.planstreetinc.com/substance-abuse-how-bad-is-addiction-in-the-united-states/.
4   "Global Drug Use," *Statista*, 1/10/2024, accessed 8/9/2024, https://www.statista.com/topics/7786/global-drug-use/.
5   Ted Van Green, "Americans Overwhelmingly Say Marijuana Should Be Legal," *Pew Research Center*, 11/22/2022, accessed 8/9/2024, https://www.pewresearch.org/short-reads/2022/11/22/americans-overwhelmingly-say-marijuana-should-be-legal-for-medical-or-recreational-use/.
6   "Legality Of Cannabis By U.S. Jurisdiction," Wikipedia.org, accessed 8/9/2024, https://en.wikipedia.org/wiki/Legality_of_cannabis_by_U.S._jurisdiction.
7   The Associated Press, "Daily Marijuana Use Outpaces Daily Drinking In The U.S.," *NBC News*, 5/22/2024, accessed 8/9/2024, https://www.nbcnews.com/health/rcna153510.
8   Josh Aronson, "1 Out Of 4 Israelis Used Addictive Substances Since Oct. 7," *The Jerusalem Post*, 2/25/2024, accessed 8/9/2024, https://www.jpost.com/health-and-wellness/article-788660.
9   Renee Ghert-Zand, "Now World's No. 1 Opioid Consumer Per Capita, Israel Faces Addiction Epidemic," *The Times of Israel*, 4/30/2023, accessed 8/9/2024, https://www.timesofisrael.com/now-worlds-no-1-opioid-consumer-per-capita-israel-faces-addiction-epidemic/.
10 Tyler Durden, "Inside The Chinese Money-Laundering Network Fueling America's Fentanyl Crisis," *Zero Hedge*, 7/3/2024, accessed 8/9/2024, https://www.zerohedge.com/geopolitical/dark-chinese-laundering-network-fueling-americas-fentanyl-crisis.
11 Mattha Busby, "Inside The Megachurch Where Shrooms And Weed Are Religion," *Vice*, 6/5/2024, accessed 8/1/2024, https://www.vice.com/en/article/qjv53v/inside-the-megachurch-where-shrooms-and-weed-are-religion.
12 Katherine Schaeffer, "32% Of Americans Have A Tattoo," *Pew Research Center*, 8/15/2023, accessed 8/9/2024, https://www.pewresearch.org/short-reads/2023/08/15/32-of-americans-have-a-tattoo-including-22-who-have-more-than-one.
13 Gaby Wine, "Surge In Tattoos Since October 7," *The Jewish Chronicle*, 12/24/2023, accessed 8/9/2024, https://www.thejc.com/news/surge-in-tattoos-since-october-7-kmasnalc.
14 Tyler Durden, "Furries Are Infiltrating Our Schools," *Zero Hedge*, 1/20/2024, accessed 8/9/2024, https://www.zerohedge.com/political/furries-are-infiltrating-our-schools.
15 Jackie Cucco, "Mattel Launches Barbie Cutie Reveal Dolls," *The Toy Insider*, 2/17/2022, accessed 8/9/2024, https://thetoyinsider.com/barbie-cutie-reveal-launch/.
16 Isabel Keane, "Man Who Spent $14K On Hyper-Realistic Collie Costume," *New York Post*, 5/28/2024, accessed 8/9/2024, https://nypost.com/2024/05/28/world-news/man-who-spent-14k-to-become-a-dog-wants-to-be-new-animal/.
17 Azeen Ghorayshi, "Report Reveals Sharp Rise In Transgender Young People In The U.S.," *The New York Times*, 6/10/2022, accessed 8/9/2024, https://www.nytimes.com/2022/06/10/science/transgender-teenagers-national-survey.html.
18 Hannah Grossman, "Taxpayer-Funded Planned Parenthood Boasts About Being Leader In Transgender Medical Procedures," *Fox News*, 7/6/2024, accessed 8/9/2024, https://www.foxnews.com/media/taxpayer-funded-planned-parenthood-boasts-about-being-leader-transgender-medical-procedures.
19 Emily Baumgaertner, "Report Reveals Sharp Rise In Transgender Young People In The U.S.," *The New York Times*, 4/23/2023, accessed 8/9/2024, https://www.nytimes.com/2023/08/23/health/transgender-surgery.html.
20 "Food And Climate Change," UN.org, accessed 8/10/2024, Graph: Kilograms of greenhouse gas emissions per kilogram of food, https://www.un.org/en/climatechange/science/climate-issues/food.
21 Danielle Wiener-Bronner, "Tyson Foods, One Of The Biggest Meat Producers, Is Investing In Insect Protein," *CNN*, 10/20/2023, accessed 8/10/2024, https://www.cnn.com/2023/10/20/business/tyson-insect-ingredients/index.html.
22 Jonel Aleccia, "US Approves Chicken Made From Cultivated Cells," *AP News*, 1/21/2023, accessed 8/10/2024, https://apnews.com/article/cultivated-meat-lab-grown-cell-based-a88ab8e0241712b501aa191cdbf6b39a.
23 Toi Staff, "In World First, Israel Approves Cultured Beef For Sale," *The Times of Israel*,

1/17/2024, accessed 8/10/2024, https://www.timesofisrael.com/in-world-first-israel-approves-cultured-beef-for-sale-to-the-public/.

24 Around the Web, "Jeff Bezos's Charity Pours $100 Million In Developing Fake Meat," *World Net Daily*, 6/1/2024, accessed 9/4/2024, https://www.wnd.com/2024/06/jeff-bezos-charity-pours-100-million-developing-fake-meat/.

25 "The Finger," Wikipedia.org, accessed 9/16/2024, https://en.wikipedia.org/wiki/The_finger.

26 Constance Grady, "Why The **** Does Everyone Swear All The ******* Time?," *Vox*, 3/14/2024, accessed 8/10/2024, https://www.vox.com/culture/24098830/holy-shit-brief-history-profanity-melissa-mohr-what-the-f-benjamin-bergen-praise-michael-adams.

27 "Obscene, Indecent And Profane Broadcasts," FCC.gov, accessed 8/10/2024, https://www.fcc.gov/consumers/guides/obscene-indecent-and-profane-broadcasts.

28 The Conversation, "How The [Bleep] Changed Television," *Fast Company*, 5/7/2023, accessed 8/10/2024, https://www.fastcompany.com/90890708/how-the-bleep-changed-television.

29 "New Gadgets For Your TV," *CBS News*, 1/8/1999, accessed 8/10/2024, https://www.cbsnews.com/news/new-gadgets-for-your-tv/.

30 "List Of Films That Most Frequently Use The Word Fuck," Wikipedia.org, accessed 8/10/2024, https://en.wikipedia.org/wiki/List_of_films_that_most_frequently_use_the_word_fuck.

31 Beth DeCarbo, "What The %&#!?! Everyone Curses On The Screen Now," *The Wall Street Journal*, 12/18/2023, accessed 8/9/2024, https://www.wsj.com/arts-culture/film/movies-cursing-profane-language-8922aab7.

32 "Digital 2024: Global Overview," DataReportal.com (endnote 8.20).

33 Tyler Durden, "Outrage As Planned Parenthood Declares Virginity "A Social Construct"," *Zero Hedge*, 6/30/2023, accessed 8/9/2024, https://web.archive.org/web/20230630193802/https://www.zerohedge.com/political/outrage-planned-parenthood-declares-virginity-social-construct.

34 Lyman Stone, "Relationship Sequencing Preferences Of American Women," *Institute for Family Studies*, 3/9/2023, accessed 8/9/2024, https://ifstudies.org/blog/putting-things-in-order-relationship-sequencing-preferences-of-american-women.

35 Jeff Diamant, "Half Of U.S. Christians Say Casual Sex Between Consenting Adults Is Sometimes Or Always Acceptable," *Pew Research Center*, 8/31/2020, accessed 8/9/2024, https://www.pewresearch.org/short-reads/2020/08/31/half-of-u-s-christians-say-casual-sex-between-consenting-adults-is-sometimes-or-always-acceptable/.

36 "Share Of Respondents Who Identified As Lesbian, Gay, Bisexual, Or Transgender," *Statista*, 7/5/2024, accessed 8/9/2024, https://www.statista.com/statistics/719674/american-adults-who-identify-as-homosexual-bisexual-or-transgender/.

37 "Share Of Respondents Who Identified As Lesbian, Gay, Bisexual, Or Transgender By Generation," *Statista*, 7/5/2024, accessed 8/9/2024, https://www.statista.com/statistics/719685/american-adults-who-identify-as-homosexual-bisexual-transgender-by-generation/.

38 Tyler Durden, "Drag Queens Carry The Olympic Torch," *Zero Hedge*, 5/27/2024, accessed 8/9/2024, https://www.zerohedge.com/political/trans-sports-agenda-drag-queens-carry-olympic-torch-launch-summer-games.
Tyler Durden, "Olympics Opening Ceremony Features Dancing Drag Queens," *Zero Hedge*, 6/27/2024, accessed 8/9/2024, https://www.zerohedge.com/political/olympic-opening-ceremony-features-dancing-drag-queens-and-bizarre-symbology.
Tyler Durden, "After Failed 1984-Style Censorship-Crusade, Paris Olympics Forced To Apologize," *Zero Hedge*, 7/28/2024, accessed 8/9/2024, https://www.zerohedge.com/political/after-failed-1984-style-censorship-campaign-paris-olympics-forced-apologize-woke-opening.

39 Michael Snyder, "A Shocking UN Document Reveal The Sick Sexual Agenda," *End Of The American Dream*, 4/17/2023, accessed 9/4/2024, https://web.archive.org/web/20230522161604/https://endoftheamericandream.com/a-shocking-un-document-reveals-the-sick-sexual-agenda-that-the-globalists-plan-to-push-on-the-whole-world/.

40 "Parents Sue Governor," *WND* (endnote 7.40).

41 "Clerical Celibacy," Wikipedia.org, accessed 8/9/2024, https://en.wikipedia.org/wiki/Clerical_celibacy.

42 "Characteristics Of Same-Sex Couple Households," Census.gov, accessed 8/9/2024, 2005 file, https://www.census.gov/data/tables/time-series/demo/same-sex-couples/ssc-house-characteristics.html. Same sex 392,314 / (Opposite sex 55,224,773 + Same sex 392,314) = 0.71%.

43 "Same-Sex Households," 2022 file, Census.gov. Same sex 740,500 / (Opposite sex 60,180,000 +

Same sex 740,500) = 1.22% (endnote 11.42).
44 Daniel Estrin, "A Court In Israel Recognizes Online Civil Marriages As Valid," *NPR*, 9/30/2022, accessed 8/9/2024, https://www.npr.org/2022/09/30/1126083806/a-court-in-israel-recognizes-online-civil-marriages-as-valid.
45 "Share Of Respondents Who Reported To Have Cheated On Any Partner," *Statista*, 8/9/2024, accessed 8/9/2024, https://www.statista.com/statistics/1367073/us-reported-to-infidelity/.
46 "Marriages And Divorces," OurWorldInData.org (endnote 5.6).
47 Juliana Menasce Horowitz, "Marriage And Cohabitation In The U.S.," *Pew Research Center*, 11/6/2019, accessed 8/9/2024, https://www.pewresearch.org/social-trends/2019/11/06/marriage-and-cohabitation-in-the-u-s/.
48 Mark Travers, "A Psychologist Describes 7 Types Of Alternative Marriages," *Forbes*, 2/24/2024, accessed 8/9/2024, https://www.forbes.com/sites/traversmark/2024/02/24/a-psychologist-describes-7-types-of-non-traditional-marriages/.
49 Stephanie Kramer, "U.S. Has World's Highest Rate Of Children Living In Single-Parent Households," *Pew Research Center*, 12/12/2019, accessed 8/9/2024, https://www.pewresearch.org/short-reads/2019/12/12/u-s-children-more-likely-than-children-in-other-countries-to-live-with-just-one-parent/.
50 "The Two Extremes Of Fatherhood," Census.gov, accessed 8/9/2024, https://www.census.gov/library/stories/2019/11/the-two-extremes-of-fatherhood.html.
51 "Population Growth," OurWorldInData.org, accessed 8/9/2024, https://ourworldindata.org/population-growth?insight=population-growth-is-no-longer-exponential-it-peaked-decades-ago#key-insights.
52 "Sex Robot," Wikipedia.org, accessed 8/9/2024, https://en.wikipedia.org/wiki/Sex_robot. Zhang Tong, "China's Next-Gen Sexbots Powered By AI," *South China Morning Post*, 6/18/2024, accessed 8/9/2024, https://www.scmp.com/news/china/science/article/3266964/chinas-next-gen-sexbots-powered-ai-are-about-hit-shelves.
53 "Genetic Engineering," Wikipedia.org, accessed 8/10/2024, https://en.wikipedia.org/wiki/Genetic_engineering.
54 "Genetically Modified Food," Wikipedia.org, accessed 8/10/2024, https://en.wikipedia.org/wiki/Genetically_modified_food.
55 Amy Teibel, "Can Gene Editing Help Farmers Satisfy The Rising Demand For Food?," *The Times of Israel*, 5/4/2022, accessed 8/10/2024, https://www.timesofisrael.com/spotlight/can-gene-editing-help-farmers-satisfy-the-rising-demand-for-food/.
56 "Pharming (Genetics)," Wikipedia.org, accessed 8/10/2024, https://en.wikipedia.org/wiki/Pharming_(genetics).
57 Adam Rutherford, "Synthetic Biology And The Rise Of The 'Spider-Goats'," *The Guardian*, 1/14/2012, accessed 8/10/2024, https://www.theguardian.com/science/2012/jan/14/synthetic-biology-spider-goat-genetics.
Richard Martyn-Hemphill, "What Happened To Those Gm Spider Goats With The Silky Milk?," *AgFunderNews*, 9/12/2019, accessed 8/10/2024, https://agfundernews.com/what-happened-to-those-gm-spider-goats-with-the-silky-milk.
58 "GMO Crops, Animal Food, And Beyond," FDA.gov, accessed 8/10/2024, https://www.fda.gov/food/agricultural-biotechnology/gmo-crops-animal-food-and-beyond.
59 Ameya Paleja, "16 Lab-Grown Brains Run World's First 'Living Computer'," *Interesting Engineering*, 5/28/2024, accessed 8/10/2024, https://interestingengineering.com/innovation/worlds-first-living-computer-switzerland.
60 Bryan Lynn, "Scientists Create 'Biocomputer' With Lab-Grown Brain Tissue," *Voice of America News*, 12/17/2023, accessed 8/10/2024, https://learningenglish.voanews.com/a/scientists-create-biocomputer-with-lab-grown-brain-tissue/7399612.html.
61 Ken Johnson, Th.D., *Ancient Book of Jasher*, Biblefacts eBook, (USA: 2013), 4:18.
62 "Nephilim In Popular Culture," Wikipedia.org, accessed 8/10/2024, https://en.wikipedia.org/wiki/Nephilim_in_popular_culture.
63 Nathaniel Scharping, "Why Scientists Have Been Creating Chimeras," *Discover Magazine*, 3/21/2023, accessed 8/10/2024, https://www.discovermagazine.com/health/why-scientists-have-been-creating-chimeras-in-the-lab-for-decades.
64 Usha Lee McFarling, "International Team Creates First Chimeric Human-Monkey Embryos," *STAT*, 4/15/2021, accessed 8/10/2024, https://www.statnews.com/2021/04/15/international-team-creates-first-chimeric-human-monkey-embryos/.
65 Mass General Brigham Communications, "In A First, Genetically Edited Pig Kidney Is

Transplanted Into Human," *Harvard Medical School*, 3/21/2024, accessed 8/10/2024, https://hms.harvard.edu/news/first-genetically-edited-pig-kidney-transplanted-human.

66 Constance Grady, "Why The **** Does Everyone Swear All The ******* Time?," Vox, 3/14/2024, accessed 8/10/2024, https://www.vox.com/culture/24098830/holy-shit-brief-history-profanity-melissa-mohr-what-the-f-benjamin-bergen-praise-michael-adams.

Ken Johnson, Th.D., *Ancient Book of Enoch*, eBook, (USA: 2012), 6:1-2, 5; 7:1-2.

Ken Johnson, Th.D., *Ancient Book of Jubilees*, eBook, (USA: Biblefacts Ministries, 2013), 5:1, 6; 7:21.

67 "Greater Idaho Movement," Wikipedia.org, accessed 8/11/2024, https://en.wikipedia.org/wiki/Greater_Idaho_movement. NewCaliforniaState.com (endnote 6.2).

68 "United States Fed Funds Interest Rate," TradingEconomics.com, accessed 8/11/2024, https://tradingeconomics.com/united-states/interest-rate.

69 "Largest Bankruptcies In The United States," *Statista* (endnote 8.24).

70 "Funding The United Nations," *Council for Foreign Relations*, 2/29/2024, accessed 9/4/2024, https://www.cfr.org/article/funding-united-nations-what-impact-do-us-contributions-have-un-agencies-and-programs.

71 Office of the Prosecutor, "Applications For Arrest Warrants In The Situation In The State Of Palestine," *International Criminal Court*, 5/20/2024, accessed 9/4/2024, https://www.icc-cpi.int/news/statement-icc-prosecutor-karim-aa-khan-kc-applications-arrest-warrants-situation-state.

72 "The Federal Budget Impact Of The Disastrous Afghanistan Withdrawal," *Budget Committee*, 8/30/2023, accessed 8/11/2024, https://budget.house.gov/press-release/two-years-later-the-federal-budget-impact-of-the-disastrous-afghanistan-withdrawal.

73 "Congressionally Approved Ukraine Aid Totals $175 Billion," *Committee for a Responsible Federal Budget*, 5/10/2024, accessed 8/11/2024, https://www.crfb.org/blogs/congressionally-approved-ukraine-aid-totals-175-billion.

74 "Security Council Demands Immediate Ceasefire In Gaza For Month Of Ramadan," *United Nations*, 3/25/2024, accessed 8/11/2024, https://press.un.org/en/2024/sc15641.doc.htm.

75 Jacob Magid, "US Hasn't Withheld Weapons For Israel, But It's Done Fast-Tracking Them," *The Times of Israel*, 6/23/2024, accessed 8/11/2024, https://www.timesofisrael.com/us-hasnt-withheld-weapons-for-israel-but-its-done-fast-tracking-them-official/.

76 Andrew Solender, "Around Half Of Congress' Democrats Skip Netanyahu Speech," *Axios*, 7/24/2024, accessed 8/11/2024, https://www.axios.com/2024/07/24/half-house-senate-democrats-boycott-netanyahu.

77 "Kamala Harris's Absence From Netanyahu's Congressional Address," *The Jerusalem Post*, 7/25/2024, accessed 8/11/2024, https://www.jpost.com/opinion/article-811774.

78 "Member States Of The UN," Wikipedia.org (endnote 2.8).

79 "The United Nations & Its Legal Authority," Justia.com, accessed 8/11/2024, https://www.justia.com/international-law/the-united-nations/.

80 Michael Dorgan, "Disease X: Critics Say Biden Admin Selling Out US Sovereignty With WHO Treaty," *Fox News*, 3/28/2024, accessed 8/11/2024, https://www.foxnews.com/world/disease-x-critics-biden-admin-selling-us-sovereignty-who-treaty.

"Countries Agree On Efforts To Boost Pandemic Preparedness," *United Nations*, 6/2/2024, accessed 8/11/2024, https://news.un.org/en/story/2024/06/1150546.

81 "Summit Of The Future," UN.org, accessed 8/11/2024, https://www.un.org/en/summit-of-the-future.

82 Brett D. Schaefer, "The U.N.'s Latest Proposals Would Undermine U.S. Sovereignty," *The Heritage Foundation*, 7/17/2023, accessed 8/11/2024, https://www.heritage.org/global-politics/commentary/the-uns-latest-proposals-would-undermine-us-sovereignty.

Chapter 12

1 Josef Federman, "Israel's Military Will Begin Drafting Ultra-Orthodox Men," *AP News*, 7/16/2024, accessed 8/13/2024, https://apnews.com/article/israel-ultraorthodox-military-draft-gaza-war-c35b3a025da8cdd9b61f1c748a209419.

2 Katherine Schaeffer, "9 Facts About Bullying," *Pew Research Center*, 11/17/2023, accessed 8/13/2024, https://www.pewresearch.org/short-reads/2023/11/17/9-facts-about-bullying-in-the-us/.

3 Alba Cuebas-Fantauzzi, "In New Viral Trend, Women Spend Up To $8K On Rage Rituals," *Fox News*, 5/26/2024, accessed 8/13/2024, https://www.foxnews.com/media/new-viral-trend-women-spend-up-8k-rage-rituals-include-screaming-ceremonies-breaking-things.

4 "Cultural Issues And The 2024 Election," *Pew Research Center*, 6/6/2024, accessed 8/13/2024,

https://www.pewresearch.org/politics/2024/06/06/cultural-issues-and-the-2024-election/.
5. "Party Identification Among Religious Groups And Religiously Unaffiliated Voters," *Pew Research Center*, 4/9/2024, accessed 8/13/2024, https://www.pewresearch.org/politics/2024/04/09/party-identification-among-religious-groups-and-religiously-unaffiliated-voters/.
6. "Noah (2014 Film)," Wikipedia.org, accessed 8/13/2024, https://en.wikipedia.org/wiki/Noah_(2014_film).
7. "Olympics Opening Ceremony," *ZH* (endnote 11.38).
"Olympics Forced To Apologize," *ZH* (endnote 11.38).
8. "Dionysus," Wikipedia.org, accessed 8/13/2024, https://en.wikipedia.org/wiki/Dionysus#Identification_with_other_gods.
9. "Thirty Pieces Of Silver," Wikipedia.org, accessed 8/11/2024, https://en.wikipedia.org/wiki/Thirty_pieces_of_silver.
10. George Packer, "The Betrayal," *The Atlantic Magazine*, 1/31/2022, accessed 8/13/2024, https://web.archive.org/web/20220209230526/https://www.theatlantic.com/magazine/archive/2022/03/biden-afghanistan-exit-american-allies-abandoned/621307/.
11. Bob Unruh, "'Did We Just Witness A Coup?' Questions Swirl About Joe Biden's Departure Letter," *World Net Daily*, 7/22/2024, accessed 8/13/2024, https://www.wnd.com/2024/07/did-we-just-witness-a-coup-questions-swirl-about-joe-bidens-departure-letter/.
Edward Helmore, "Biden Continues To Resist Democratic Calls To End Re-Election Campaign," *The Guardian*, 7/20/2024, accessed 8/13/2024, https://www.theguardian.com/us-news/article/2024/jul/20/biden-resists-democratic-calls-step-down.
12. "Holocaust Denial," Wikipedia.org, accessed 8/14/2024, https://en.wikipedia.org/wiki/Holocaust_denial.
13. "UN Defines Holocaust Denial In New Resolution," *BBC*, 1/20/2022, accessed 8/14/2024, https://www.bbc.com/news/world-europe-60072506.
14. "Temple Denial," Wikipedia.org, accessed 8/14/2024, https://en.wikipedia.org/wiki/Temple_denial.
15. Ohad Merlin, "In Arab World, Many Still Refuse To Accept The Two Temples' Existence," *The Jerusalem Post*, 8/14/2024, accessed 8/14/2024, https://www.jpost.com/israel-news/article-814591.
16. "Boycott, Divestment And Sanctions," Wikipedia.org, accessed 8/14/2024, https://en.wikipedia.org/wiki/Boycott,_Divestment_and_Sanctions.
17. "Modest Warming In U.S. Views On Israel And Palestinians," *Pew Research Center*, 5/26/2022, accessed 8/14/2024, https://www.pewresearch.org/religion/2022/05/26/modest-warming-in-u-s-views-on-israel-and-palestinians/.
18. Dr. David R. Reagan, "Deceptive Slogans In The Propaganda War Against Israel," *Lamplighter*, Jan/Feb 2024, accessed 9/16/2024, https://christinprophecy.org/wp-content/uploads/Lamplighter_JanFeb24_War-Raging-Rulers-of-Darkness.pdf.
19. Haley Cohen, "Traditionally Quiet Campuses Now Face Widespread Anti-Israel Activity," *Jewish Insider*, 3/25/2024, accessed 8/14/2024, https://jewishinsider.com/2024/03/traditionally-quiet-campuses-now-face-widespread-anti-israel-activity/.
20. Fabiola Cineas, "The Failure Of The College President," *Vox*, 6/7/2024, accessed 8/14/2024, https://www.vox.com/politics/354208/college-presidents-resigned-israel-palestine.
21. Brianna Herlihy, "Federal Judge Rules Against UCLA In Lawsuit Over 'Jew Exclusion Zone'," *Fox News*, 8/15/2024, accessed 8/14/2024, https://www.foxnews.com/politics/so-abhorrent-federal-judge-rules-against-ucla-lawsuit-over-jew-exclusion-zone.
22. Margaret Flavin, "'Iran Paid Anti-Israel Protesters In America'," *The Gateway Pundit*, 6/10/2024, accessed 8/14/2024, https://www.thegatewaypundit.com/2024/07/director-national-intelligence-iran-paid-anti-israel-protesters/.
23. "Top 30 Social Media Influencers," *SEJ* (endnote 9.38).
24. "Brands (US & Canada)," BoxOfficeMojo.com, accessed 8/14/2024, https://www.boxofficemojo.com/brand/?sort=totalGross&ref_=bo_bns__resort#table.
25. Karlton Jahmal, "All Of The LGBTQ Characters In The MCU So Far," *BuzzFeed*, 7/28/2022, accessed 8/14/2024, https://www.buzzfeed.com/karltonjahmal/all-the-lgbtq-characters-in-the-mcu-so-far.
26. "Comics Code Authority," Wikipedia.org, accessed 8/14/2024, https://en.wikipedia.org/wiki/Comics_Code_Authority.
27. George Gene Gustines, "Superman Comes Out," *The New York Times*, 11/11/2021, accessed 8/14/2024, https://www.nytimes.com/2021/10/11/arts/superman-comes-out.html.
28. Tyler Durden, "Israel Fumin At UN's Moment Of Silence For Iran Leader," *Zero Hedge*,

5/21/2024, accessed 8/14/2024, https://www.zerohedge.com/geopolitical/iran-announces-interim-president-after-raisis-helicopter-hit-mountain-disintegrated.

29 Elizabeth Elkind, "Biden Admin Eviscerated For Response To 'Butcher Of Tehran' Raisi's Death," *Fox News*, 5/21/2024, accessed 8/14/2024, https://www.foxnews.com/politics/new-low-biden-admin-eviscerated-response-butcher-tehran-raisis-death.

30 "ICC Seeking Arrest Warrants For Hamas Leaders And Israel's Netanyahu," *United Nations*, 5/20/2024, accessed 8/14/2024, https://news.un.org/en/story/2024/05/1149966.

31 "List Of Black Lives Matter Street Murals," Wikipedia.org, accessed 8/14/2024, https://en.wikipedia.org/wiki/List_of_Black_Lives_Matter_street_murals.

32 Larry Buchanan, "Black Lives Matter May Be The Largest Movement In U.S. History," *The New York Times*, 7/3/2020, accessed 8/14/2024, https://www.nytimes.com/interactive/2020/07/03/us/george-floyd-protests-crowd-size.html.

33 "Pride Month," Wikipedia.org, accessed 8/14/2024, https://en.wikipedia.org/wiki/Pride_Month.

34 "Tel Aviv Pride," Wikipedia.org, accessed 8/14/2024, https://en.wikipedia.org/wiki/Tel_Aviv_Pride.

35 "International Transgender Day Of Visibility," Wikipedia.org, accessed 8/14/2024, https://en.wikipedia.org/wiki/International_Transgender_Day_of_Visibility.

36 Joseph R. Biden Jr., "A Proclamation On Transgender Day Of Visibility, 2024," *The White House*, 3/29/2024, accessed 8/14/2024, https://www.whitehouse.gov/briefing-room/presidential-actions/2024/03/29/a-proclamation-on-transgender-day-of-visibility-2024/.

37 "Johnson Amendment," Wikipedia.org, accessed 8/14/2024, https://en.wikipedia.org/wiki/Johnson_Amendment.

38 "Urgent-We Are Under Attack On YouTube," X.com post, 2/23/2023, accessed 8/14/2024, https://x.com/RealJackHibbs/status/1628859764896841729.

39 Samantha Kamman, "436 Acts Of Hostility Against US Churches Documented In 2023," *The Christian Post*, 2/22/2024, accessed 8/14/2024, https://www.christianpost.com/news/436-acts-of-hostility-against-us-churches-documented-in-2023.html.

40 Pastor Jack Hibbs, "Opening Prayer Given By The Guest Chaplain," *Office of the Chaplain*, 1/30/2024, accessed 8/14/2024, https://chaplain.house.gov/chaplaincy/display_gc.html?id=4734.

41 Ryan Foley, "Dems Upset Mike Johnson Selected Pastor Jack Hibbs To Serve As Guest Chaplain," *The Christian Post*, 2/21/2024, accessed 8/14/2024, https://www.christianpost.com/news/dem-lawmakers-upset-jack-hibbs-served-as-guest-chaplain.html.

42 Tim Dickinson, "MAGA Messianic Rabbi Blames Hamas Violence On Israeli Indifference To Jesus," *Rolling Stone*, 10/26/2023, accessed 8/14/2024, https://www.rollingstone.com/politics/politics-features/jonathan-cahn-messianic-rabbi-hamas-violence-israel-jesus-1234862172/.

43 "Special: Rolling Stone Attacks - Jonathan Cahn Responds," 11/6/2023, *Jonathan Cahn Official*, YouTube video, accessed 8/14/2024, https://www.youtube.com/watch?v=hAXCq3B5q3c.

44 "World Watch List 2024," OpenDoors.org, accessed 8/14/2024, https://www.opendoors.org/en-US/persecution/countries/.

45 Maya Zanger-Nadis, "Netanyahu Assures No Law Against Christians After Missionary Bill Outrage," *The Jerusalem Post*, 3/24/2023, accessed 8/14/2024, https://www.jpost.com/israel-news/politics-and-diplomacy/article-735162.

46 Michael Dorgan, "Vermont Christian Parents Say They Were Punished By Foster System," *Fox News*, 5/30/2024, accessed 8/14/2024, https://www.foxnews.com/politics/vermont-christian-parents-say-were-punished-foster-system-over-transgender-stance.

47 Brianna Herlihy, "GOP AGs Blast Biden Admin For Foster Care Plan," *Fox News*, 11/28/2023, accessed 8/14/2024, https://www.foxnews.com/politics/gop-ags-blast-biden-admin-foster-care-plan-they-say-would-effectively-ban-christians.

48 "U.S. Jurisdictions Banning Conversion Therapy," Wikipedia.org (endnote 6.38).

49 "Parents Sue Governor," *WND* (endnote 7.40).

50 "LGBTQ Curricular Laws," LGBTMap.org, accessed 8/14/2024, https://www.lgbtmap.org/equality-maps/curricular_laws.

51 S.A. McCarthy, "Federal Court Rules Maryland Parents Cannot Opt Children Out Of LGBT Lessons," *The Washington Stand*, 5/17/2024, accessed 8/14/2024, https://washingtonstand.com/news/federal-court-rules-maryland-parents-cannot-opt-children-out-of-lgbt-lessons.

52 "The Equality Act," Heritage.org, accessed 8/14/2024,

https://www.heritage.org/gender/heritage-explains/the-equality-act.
"Equality Act (United States)," Wikipedia.org, accessed 8/14/2024,
https://en.wikipedia.org/wiki/Equality_Act_(United_States).
53 Drew Desilver, "What The Data Says About Food Stamps In The U.S.," *Pew Research Center*, 7/19/2023, accessed 8/14/2024, https://www.pewresearch.org/short-reads/2023/07/19/what-the-data-says-about-food-stamps-in-the-u-s/.
54 "Human Trafficking Victims Identified Worldwide," *Statista*, 7/4/2024, accessed 8/14/2024, https://www.statista.com/statistics/459637/number-of-victims-identified-related-to-labor-trafficking-worldwide/.
55 "Trafficking In Persons," UNODC.org, accessed 8/14/2024, https://www.unodc.org/unodc/data-and-analysis/glotip.html.
United Nations, *Global Report on Trafficking in Persons*, 2022, p XV, 70, accessed 8/14/2024, https://www.unodc.org/documents/data-and-analysis/glotip/2022/GLOTiP_2022_web.pdf.
56 Karissa Hand, "Governor Healey Signs Parentage Act," *Mass.gov*, 8/9/2024, accessed 8/14/2024, https://www.mass.gov/news/governor-healey-signs-parentage-act-ensuring-equality-for-all-families-in-massachusetts.
Ken Ham, "Massachusetts Unanimously Passes Bill That Would Legalize Sale Of Babies," *Harbinger's Daily*, 6/21/2024, accessed 8/14/2024, https://harbingersdaily.com/massachusetts-unanimously-passes-bill-that-would-legalize-sale-of-babies-by-pregnant-mothers/.

Chapter 13
1 Tyler Durden, "Should You Believe Faulty U.S. Crime Stats?," *Zero Hedge*, 5/15/2024, accessed 8/21/2024, https://www.zerohedge.com/political/should-you-believe-faulty-us-crime-stats-or-your-own-lying-eyes.
2 Around the Web, "Dem-Run Cities See Police Forces Shrink As Crime Rages On," *World Net Daily*, 6/20/2024, accessed 8/21/2024, https://www.wnd.com/2024/06/dem-run-cities-see-police-forces-shrink-crime-rages/.
3 Steven Ross Johnson, "Rates Of Violent Death Up Among U.S. Youth," *U.S. News*, 6/15/2023, accessed 8/21/2024, https://www.usnews.com/news/health-news/articles/2023-06-15/cdc-study-shows-rise-in-violent-death-rates-among-u-s-youth.
4 "US Confirms Hamas HQ Under Shifa Hospital," *All Israel News*, 11/15/2023, accessed 8/21/2024, https://allisrael.com/us-confirms-hamas-hq-under-shifa-hospital-says-it-violates-law-of-war.
5 Felice Friedson, "In Gaza, 'Hardly A House That Doesn't Have An Entrance To A Tunnel, Shaft, Or Weapons'," *The Media Line*, 2/6/2024, accessed 8/21/2024, https://themedialine.org/top-stories/lt-col-conricus-to-tml-in-gaza-hardly-a-house-that-doesnt-have-an-entrance-to-a-tunnel-shaft-or-weapons/.
6 Toi Staff, "Releases Hostage Amit Soussana Recounts Sexual Assault At Hands Of Hamas Captor," *The Times of Israel*, 3/26/2024, accessed 8/21/2024, https://www.timesofisrael.com/released-hostage-amit-soussana-reveals-she-was-sexually-assaulted-by-hamas-captor/.
Rachel Clarke, "What Freed Israeli Hostages Are Saying About Being Held By Hamas," *CNN*, 12/20/2023, accessed 8/21/2024, https://www.cnn.com/2023/12/01/middleeast/israeli-hostages-released-accounts-hamas-intl-hnk/index.html.
7 "Abortion," *WHO* (endnote 2.23).
8 "World Population," WorldoMeters.info (endnote 5.3).
9 Isaac Maddow-Zimet, "Despite Bans, Number Of Abortions In The United States Increased In 2023," *Guttmacher*, 5/10/2024, accessed 8/21/2024, https://www.guttmacher.org/2024/03/despite-bans-number-abortions-united-states-increased-2023.
10 "Broad Public Support For Legal Abortion Persists," *Pew Research Center*, 5/13/2024, accessed 8/21/2024, https://www.pewresearch.org/politics/2024/05/13/broad-public-support-for-legal-abortion-persists-2-years-after-dobbs/.
11 Janell Fetterolf, "Support For Legal Abortion Is Widespread In Many Places," *Pew Research Center*, 5/15/2024, accessed 8/21/2024, https://www.pewresearch.org/short-reads/2024/05/15/support-for-legal-abortion-is-widespread-in-many-countries-especially-in-europe/.
12 "US Abortion Policies And Access After Roe," Guttmacher.org, accessed 8/21/2024, https://states.guttmacher.org/policies/.
Mary Kekatos, "A State-By-State Breakdown Of Abortion Laws," *ABC News*, 6/22/2024, accessed 8/21/2024, https://abcnews.go.com/US/state-state-breakdown-abortion-laws-2-years-after/story?id=111312220.
13 Holly, "There's No Such Thing As A "Late-Term Abortion"," *Planned Parenthood*, 10/13/2022,

accessed 8/21/2024, https://www.plannedparenthood.org/blog/theres-no-such-thing-as-a-late-term-abortion.

14 "'Micropreemie' Baby Who Weighed Just Over 1 Pound At Birth Goes Home From Illinois Hospital," *AP News*, 5/14/2024, accessed 8/21/2024, https://apnews.com/article/micropreemie-baby-girl-leaves-illinois-hospital-ff4a54895dd2e19a5ae9c0272f7e0e78.

15 Susan Berry, Ph.D., "Planned Parenthood Sold Aborted Baby Parts," *Life News*, 3/6/2024, accessed 8/21/2024, https://www.lifenews.com/2024/03/06/planned-parenthood-sold-aborted-baby-parts-in-exchange-for-intellectual-property/.

16 Natalia Mesa, PhD, "Scientists Consider How Overturning Roe Might Affect Research," *The Scientist*, 9/7/2022, accessed 8/21/2024, https://www.the-scientist.com/scientists-consider-how-overturning-roe-might-affect-research-70461.

17 "Born-Alive Abortion Survivors Protection Act," Wikipedia.org, accessed 8/21/2024, https://en.wikipedia.org/wiki/Born-Alive_Abortion_Survivors_Protection_Act.

18 Arielle Domb, "The Satanic Abortion Clinic That's Pissed Off Pretty Much Everyone," *Cosmopolitan*, 11/14/2023, accessed 8/21/2024, https://www.cosmopolitan.com/lifestyle/a45613416/satanic-group-abortion-clinic-samuel-alito-mom/.

19 "Is It Time For A More Subtle View On The Ultimate Taboo: Cannibalism?," *New Scientist*, 2/14/2024, accessed 8/18/2024, https://www.newscientist.com/article/mg26134783-600-is-it-time-for-a-more-subtle-view-on-the-ultimate-taboo-cannibalism/.
"About," NewScientist.com, accessed 8/18/2024, https://www.newscientist.com/about/.

20 Patricia Hartley, "Eating Cremated Human Remains," *Connecting Directors*, 7/3/2024, accessed 8/18/2024, https://connectingdirectors.com/68475-eating-human-cremated-remains.

21 Bruce Y. Lee, "If You Eat Your Placenta, This Can Happen," *Forbes*, 6/30/2017, accessed 8/18/2024, https://www.forbes.com/sites/brucelee/2017/06/30/cdc-if-you-eat-your-placenta-this-can-happen/.

22 John Edgar Browning, "Life Among The Vampires," *The Atlantic Magazine*, 10/31/2015, accessed 8/18/2024,
https://web.archive.org/web/20160211193729/https://www.theatlantic.com/health/archive/2015/10/life-among-the-vampires/413446/.
Scottie Andrew, "Inside The World Of Real-Life Vampires In New Orleans And Atlanta," *CNN*, 10/29/2022, accessed 8/18/2024, https://www.cnn.com/2022/10/29/us/real-vampires-new-orleans-atlanta-cec/index.html.
Linda Hall, "Inside The Life Of An Ohio Woman Who Identifies As A Vampire," *USA Today*, 10/31/2023, accessed 8/18/2024,
https://www.usatoday.com/story/news/nation/2023/10/31/hellen-schweizer-woman-identifies-as-vampire/71317120007/.

23 Myles Miller, "Suspect Arrested In Sucker-Punch Attacks," *NBC New York*, 4/24/2024, accessed 8/21/2024, https://www.nbcnewyork.com/news/local/crime-and-courts/suspect-arrested-sucker-punch-attacks-women-manhattan/5348231/.

24 Lisa Evers, "69-Year-Old Woman Punched In Apparent Random NYC Street Attack," *Fox 5 New York*, 5/21/2024, accessed 8/21/2024, https://www.fox5ny.com/news/nyc-crime-woman-punched-upper-east-side.

25 "Subway Shoves," NYPost.com, accessed 8/21/2024, https://nypost.com/tag/subway-shoves/.

26 Zoe Hussain, "Troubled Woman Accused Of Shoving Tourists Onto NYC Subway Tracks," *New York Post*, 8/8/2024, accessed 8/21/2024, https://nypost.com/2024/08/08/us-news/ebony-butts-accused-of-shoving-nyc-tourists-onto-subway-tracks-rants-in-court/.

27 Landon Mion, "Georgia Woman Intentionally Crashes Vehicle Into Popeyes," *New York Post*, 2/25/2023, accessed 8/21/2024, https://nypost.com/2023/02/25/georgia-woman-belinda-miller-crashes-suv-into-popeyes-over-missing-biscuits/.

28 Jessica Fu, "Fast Food Workers Are Using 911 Call Logs To Draw Attention To A Hidden "Crisis Of Violence"," *The Counter*, 12/14/2021, accessed 8/21/2024, https://thecounter.org/fast-food-workers-911-call-logs-workplace-customer-violence-mcdonalds-report/.

29 Petr Svab, "Crime Trends Have Been Tough To Track," *The Epoch Times*, 7/2/2024, accessed 8/21/2024, https://www.theepochtimes.com/article/crime-trends-have-been-tough-to-track-we-broke-down-the-10-biggest-cities-5675727.

30 Julia Frankel, "Lawlessness Is Blocking Aid Distribution After Israel's 'Tactical Pause' In Southern Gaza," *PBS*, 6/20/2024, accessed 8/21/2024, https://www.pbs.org/newshour/world/lawlessness-is-blocking-aid-distribution-after-israels-tactical-pause-in-southern-gaza-un-says.

31 "Attempted Assassination Of Donald Trump," Wikipedia.org, accessed 8/21/2024,

https://en.wikipedia.org/wiki/Attempted_assassination_of_Donald_Trump.

32 Brad Holden, "Capital Hill Autonomous Zone (CHAZ)," *History Link*, 12/30/2023, accessed 8/21/2024, https://www.historylink.org/File/22870.
Sam Spiegelman, "Seattle Pays The Price For CHAZ," *The Hill*, 3/20/2023, accessed 8/21/2024, https://thehill.com/opinion/judiciary/3905207-seattle-pays-the-price-for-chaz/.

33 "Nuclear Weapon," Wikipedia.org, accessed 8/21/2024, https://en.wikipedia.org/wiki/Nuclear_weapon.

34 "Atomic Bombings Of Hiroshima And Nagasaki," Wikipedia.org, accessed 8/21/2024, https://en.wikipedia.org/wiki/Atomic_bombings_of_Hiroshima_and_Nagasaki.

35 "Nuclear Weapons: Who Has What," ArmsControl.org, accessed 8/21/2024, https://www.armscontrol.org/factsheets/nuclear-weapons-who-has-what-glance.

36 Johnson, *Enoch*, 8:1-2 (endnote 11.66).

37 "Top 10 Most Lethal Leaders," ListVerse.com (endnote 9.45).

38 "Lobbying In The United States," Wikipedia.org, accessed 8/22/2024, https://en.wikipedia.org/wiki/Lobbying_in_the_United_States.

39 Joanne Haner, "Two Years After Dobbs, Lobbying Spending On Abortion Rights Neared $3.7 Million In 2023," *Open Secrets*, 2/1/2024, accessed 8/22/2024, https://www.opensecrets.org/news/2024/02/two-years-after-dobbs-lobbying-spending-on-abortion-rights-neared-3-7-million-in-2023/.

40 Hannah Fresques, "Doctors Prescribe More Of A Drug If They Receive Money From A Pharma Company Tied To It," *ProPublica*, 12/20/2019, accessed 8/22/2024, https://www.propublica.org/article/doctors-prescribe-more-of-a-drug-if-they-receive-money-from-a-pharma-company-tied-to-it.

41 "Supreme Court Of The United States," Wikipedia.org, accessed 8/22/2024, https://en.wikipedia.org/wiki/Supreme_Court_of_the_United_States.

42 Erica Orden, "Trump's Attempt To Remove Judge From Hush Money Case Fails," *Politico*, 8/14/2024, accessed 8/22/2024, https://www.politico.com/news/2024/08/14/trump-merchan-recusal-bid-fail-00173966.
Melissa Russo, "Judge Engoron Will Not Recuse Himself From Trump Civil Fraud Trial," *NBC New York*, 7/28/2024, accessed 8/22/2024, https://www.nbcnewyork.com/investigations/judge-engoron-not-recuse-himself-trump-civil-fraud-trial/5633242/.
Andrew Stanton, "Aileen Cannon 'Stunning' Refusal Of Judge Request To Recuse From Trump Case," *Newsweek*, 6/20/2024, accessed 8/22/2024, https://www.newsweek.com/aileen-cannon-refusal-recuse-trump-case-1915464.

43 Yana Gorokhovskaia, "Freedom In The World 2024," *Freedom House*, accessed 8/18/2024, https://freedomhouse.org/report/freedom-world/2024/mounting-damage-flawed-elections-and-armed-conflict.

44 "World Population," WorldoMeters.info, nations listed pop 4.65 billion / world pop 8.17 billion = 57% (endnote 5.3).

45 "Global Freedom Status," FreedomHouse.org, accessed 8/18/2024, https://freedomhouse.org/explore-the-map?type=fiw&year=2024.

46 "The World Has Recently Become Less Democratic," OurWorldInData.org, accessed 8/19/2024, https://ourworldindata.org/less-democratic.
"People Living In Democratizing And Autocratizing Countries," OurWorldInData.org, accessed 8/19/2024, https://ourworldindata.org/grapher/people-living-in-democratizing-autocratizing-countries-ert.

47 "World Less Democratic," OurWorldInData.org (endnote 13.46).
"People Living In Democracies And Autocracies," OurWorldInData.org, accessed 8/19/2024, https://ourworldindata.org/grapher/people-living-in-democracies-autocracies.

48 "The 'Regimes Of The World'," OurWorldInData.org, accessed 8/19/2024, https://ourworldindata.org/regimes-of-the-world-data.

49 "NATO," Wikipedia.org, accessed 8/22/2024, https://en.wikipedia.org/wiki/NATO.

50 "Shanghai Cooperation Organisation," Wikipedia.org, accessed 8/22/2024, https://en.wikipedia.org/wiki/Shanghai_Cooperation_Organisation.

51 "Islamic Military Counter Terrorism Coalition," Wikipedia.org, accessed 8/22/2024, https://en.wikipedia.org/wiki/Islamic_Military_Counter_Terrorism_Coalition.

52 "Russia-Syria-Iran-Iraq Coalition," Wikipedia.org, accessed 8/22/2024, https://en.wikipedia.org/wiki/Russia–Syria–Iran–Iraq_coalition.

53 "Space Race," Wikipedia.org, accessed 8/22/2024, https://en.wikipedia.org/wiki/Space_Race.

54 "Elon Musk," Wikipedia.org, accessed 8/22/2024, https://en.wikipedia.org/wiki/Elon_Musk.
55 "Jeff Bezos," Wikipedia.org, accessed 8/22/2024, https://en.wikipedia.org/wiki/Jeff_Bezos.
56 "Bill Gates," Wikipedia.org, accessed 8/22/2024, https://en.wikipedia.org/wiki/Bill_Gates.
"Bill & Melinda Gates Foundation," Wikipedia.org, accessed 8/22/2024, https://en.wikipedia.org/wiki/Bill_&_Melinda_Gates_Foundation.
57 Simon Constable, "Klaus Schwab's World Economic Forum In Davos Exposed," *Fox News*, 1/21/2024, accessed 8/22/2024, https://www.foxnews.com/world/klaus-schwabs-world-economic-forum-davos-exposed-place-cronyism-can-flourish.
58 Simon Tisdall, "The US Isn't The Biggest Power In The Middle East Any More. Iran Is.," *The Guardian*, 1/13/2024, accessed 8/20/2024, https://www.theguardian.com/commentisfree/2024/jan/13/iran-is-thwith-china-and-russia-behind-it-iran-is-the-big-kid-on-the-block.
59 Nik Martin, "Red Sea Shipping Crisis Worsens," *DW*, 7/24/2024, accessed 8/20/2024, https://www.dw.com/en/red-sea-shipping-crisis-worsens-after-israel-houthi-attacks/a-69738531.
"Red Sea Crisis," Wikipedia.org, accessed 8/20/2024, https://en.wikipedia.org/wiki/Red_Sea_crisis.
60 "Timeline Of Nuclear Diplomacy With Iran," ArmsControl.org, accessed 8/20/2024, https://www.armscontrol.org/factsheets/timeline-nuclear-diplomacy-iran-1967-2023.
61 "The Iran Primer," *US Institute of Peace*, 4/12/2024, accessed 8/20/2024, https://iranprimer.usip.org/blog/2021/feb/17/iran's-missiles-infographics-and-photos.
62 Josef Federman, "Israel Says Iran Launched More Than 300 Drones And Missiles," *AP News*, 4/13/2024, accessed 8/20/2024, https://apnews.com/article/strait-of-hormuz-vessel-33fcffde2d867380e98c89403776a8ac.
63 Dr. David R. Reagan, *The 9 Wars of the End-Times*, First Ed., (McKinney, TX: Lamb & Lion Ministries, 2023), p 28.
Todd Hampson, *The Non-Prophet's Guide to the End Times*, Paperback, (Eugene, OR: Harvest House Publishers, 2018), p 153.
64 "Religious Composition By Country," *PRC* (endnote 4.4).
"Gaza Strip," Wikipedia.org, accessed 8/20/2024, https://en.wikipedia.org/wiki/Gaza_Strip.
65 Bruce Scott, "The Land Of Israel Or Ishmael?," *Israel My Glory*, June/July 1993, accessed 8/20/2024, https://israelmyglory.org/article/the-land-of-israel-or-ishmael/.
66 Jean-Luc Mounier, "Qatar, Iran, Turkey, And Beyond: Hamas's Network Of Allies," *France 24*, 10/14/2023, accessed 8/20/2024, https://www.france24.com/en/middle-east/20231014-qatar-iran-turkey-and-beyond-the-galaxy-of-hamas-supporters.
Jim Zanotti, "Hamas: Background, Current Status, And U.S. Policy," *Congressional Research Service*, 8/7/2024, accessed 8/14/2024, https://crsreports.congress.gov/product/pdf/IF/IF12549.
67 Itamar Marcus, "Only 9% Of Palestinians Think Hamas Committed War Crimes," *Palestinian Media Watch*, 6/13/2024, accessed 8/20/2024, https://palwatch.org/page/35161.
68 "In Gaza, 'Hardly A House'," *TML* (endnote 13.5).
69 Reagan, *9 Wars*, p 28 (endnote 13.63).
Hampson, *Guide to the End Times*, p 156 (endnote 13.63).
Gary Stearman, "Sheba & Dedan," *The Prophecy Watcher*, April 2024.
70 "Annexation Of Crimea By The Russian Federation," Wikipedia.org, accessed 8/19/2024, https://en.wikipedia.org/wiki/Annexation_of_Crimea_by_the_Russian_Federation.
71 "Russian Invasion Of Ukraine," Wikipedia.org, accessed 8/19/2024, https://en.wikipedia.org/wiki/Russian_invasion_of_Ukraine.
72 "List Of Wars Involving Turkey," Wikipedia.org, accessed 8/19/2024, https://en.wikipedia.org/wiki/List_of_wars_involving_Turkey.
73 "2024 Military Strength Ranking," GlobalFirePower.com, accessed 8/19/2024, https://www.globalfirepower.com/countries-listing.php.
74 "Religious Composition By Country," *PRC* (endnote 4.4).
75 "How Is Eastern Orthodoxy Different?," AnswersInGenesis.org, accessed 8/19/2024, https://answersingenesis.org/world-religions/eastern-orthodoxy/.
76 "Religious Composition By Country," *PRC* (endnote 4.4).
77 Dr. David R. Reagan, *Islam and Christianity*, First Ed., (McKinney, TX: Lamb & Lion Ministries, 2022), p 28-29, 32-33. Sura 5 in Qur'an.
78 Ari Rabinovitch, "Israel Says Gas Exports To Egypt, Jordan Rose 25% In 2023," *Reuters*,

2/26/2024, accessed 8/19/2024, https://www.reuters.com/business/energy/israel-says-gas-exports-egypt-jordan-rose-25-2023-2024-02-26/.
79 Melissa Pistilli, "Top 10 Countries For Natural Gas Production," *Investing News Network*, 8/15/2024, accessed 8/19/2024, https://investingnews.com/top-natural-gas-producers/.
80 "Distribution Of Pipeline Natural Gas Export Volume From Russia," *Statista*, 7/1/2024, accessed 8/19/2024, https://www.statista.com/statistics/305394/russian-natural-gas-exports-by-destination/.
81 Soner Cagaptay, "Israel-Turkey Relations Nearing A Rupture," *The Washington Institute*, 8/9/2024, accessed 8/19/2024, https://www.washingtoninstitute.org/policy-analysis/israel-turkey-relations-nearing-rupture.
82 Reagan, *9 Wars*, p 28 (endnote 13.63).
Hampson, *Guide to the End Times*, p 156 (endnote 13.63).
Gary Stearman, "Sheba & Dedan," (endnote 13.69).
83 Tyler Durden, "Turkey Formally Requests To Join BRICS," *Zero Hedge*, 9/2/2024, accessed 9/4/2024, https://www.zerohedge.com/markets/turkey-formally-requests-join-brics-citing-frustration-eu-bid.
84 Enrique Fernandez, "Russia And Iran Try To Evade Sanctions," *Atalayar*, 5/30/2024, accessed 8/20/2024, https://www.atalayar.com/en/articulo/economy-and-business/russia-and-iran-try-to-evade-sanctions-through-oil-and-gas-corridors/20240530061000200620.html.
85 Merrill Matthews, "The New 'Axil Of Evil' Is Bigger," *Institute for Policy Innovation*, 4/16/2024, accessed 8/20/2024, https://www.ipi.org/ipi_issues/detail/the-new-axil-of-evil-is-bigger-better-armed-and-power-hungry.
86 Reuters, "Foreign Minister Urges NATO To Expel Turkey," *The Times of Israel*, 7/29/2024, accessed 8/20/2024, https://www.timesofisrael.com/foreign-minister-urges-nato-to-expel-turkey-over-threats-to-invade-israel/.
87 Kareem Chehayeb, "What Is Hezbollah, The Iranian-Backed Group," *AP News*, 6/24/2024, accessed 8/20/2024, https://apnews.com/article/hezbollah-israel-hamas-lebanon-gaza-62d6eb8831fbd871f862146add7970d9.
88 Jeremy Diamond, "Iran Launches Unprecedented Retaliatory Strikes On Israel," *CNN*, 4/14/2024, accessed 8/20/2024, https://www.cnn.com/2024/04/13/middleeast/iran-drones-attack-israel-intl-latam/index.html.
89 Abby Sewell, "Hamas' Top Political Leader Is Killed In Iran In Strike," *AP News*, 7/31/2024, accessed 9/16/2024, https://apnews.com/article/iran-hamas-israel-30968a7acb31cd8b259de9650014b779.
90 Bruno Venditti, "The World's Top 10 Billionaires," *Visual Capitalist*, 6/20/2024, accessed 8/22/2024, https://www.visualcapitalist.com/ranked-the-worlds-top-10-billionaires-in-2024/.
91 "The World's Most Powerful People," Forbes.com, accessed 8/22/2024, https://www.forbes.com/powerful-people/list/#tab:overall.
92 "United Nations Security Council," Wikipedia.org, accessed 8/23/2024, https://en.wikipedia.org/wiki/United_Nations_Security_Council.
93 "Secretary-General Of The United Nations," Wikipedia.org, accessed 8/23/2024, https://en.wikipedia.org/wiki/Secretary-General_of_the_United_Nations.
94 "Number Of State-Based Conflicts," OurWorldInData.org, accessed 8/22/2024, https://ourworldindata.org/grapher/number-of-state-based-conflicts.
95 "Nuclear Weapons: Who Has What," ArmsControl.org (endnote 13.35).
96 "2024 Military Strength Ranking," GlobalFirePower.com (endnote 13.73).
97 "Nuclear Weapons: Who Has What," ArmsControl.org (endnote 13.35).
98 "Israel Defense Forces," Wikipedia.org, accessed 8/20/2024, https://en.wikipedia.org/wiki/Israel_Defense_Forces.
99 "17 Miraculous Israeli Military Victories," JewishVirtualLibrary.org, accessed 8/20/2024, https://www.jewishvirtuallibrary.org/17-miraculous-israeli-military-victories.
Arlene Bridges Samuels, "The Miracles Of Israel's Six-Day War," *CBN Israel*, 6/9/2022, accessed 8/20/2024, https://cbnisrael.org/2022/06/09/fulfilling-gods-promises-the-miracles-of-israels-six-day-war/.
100 "2022 UNGA Resolutions On Israel Vs. Rest Of The World," *UN Watch*, 11/14/2022, accessed 8/20/2024, https://unwatch.org/2022-2023-unga-resolutions-on-israel-vs-rest-of-the-world/.
101 "UN General Assembly Condemns Israel 14 Times In 2023," *UN Watch*, 12/20/2023, accessed 8/20/2024, https://unwatch.org/un-general-assembly-condemns-israel-14-times-in-2023-rest-of-world-7/.
102 "Security Council Demands Immediate Ceasefire," *UN* (endnote 11.74).

103 "Netanyahu To Republicans: 'There's An Attempt To Ram A Palestinian State Down Our Throats'," *Israel National News*, 4/4/2024, accessed 8/20/2024, https://www.israelnationalnews.com/news/387951.
104 "Human Rights Council Resolution Urges Arms Embargo On Israel," *United Nations*, 4/5/2024, accessed 8/20/2024, https://news.un.org/en/story/2024/04/1148261.
105 "Arrest Warrants," *ICC* (endnote 11.71).
106 Greg Norman, "Netanyahu Compares ICC Arrest Warrant Request To Anti-Israel Protests," *Fox News*, 5/20/2024, accessed 8/20/2024, https://www.foxnews.com/world/netanyahu-compares-icc-arrest-warrant-request-anti-israel-protests-what-new-antisemitism-looks-like.
107 Jacob Magid, "Israel Livid As It's Added To UN 'List Of Shame'," *The Times of Israel*, 6/7/2024, accessed 8/20/2024, https://www.timesofisrael.com/israel-fumes-as-its-added-to-un-list-of-shame-for-wartime-childrens-rights-violations/.
108 Mike Corder, "Top UN Court Says Israel's Presence In Occupied Palestinian Territories Is Illegal," *AP News*, 7/19/2024, accessed 8/20/2024, https://apnews.com/article/icj-court-israel-palestinians-settlements-2d5178500c0410341b252335859f2316.
109 "UN Completes Investigation On UNRWA Staff," *United Nations*, 8/5/2024, accessed 8/20/2024, https://news.un.org/en/story/2024/08/1152841.
110 Tyler Durden, "UK Announces Partial Ban On Arms Exports To Israel," *Zero Hedge*, 9/2/2024, accessed 9/4/2024, https://www.zerohedge.com/geopolitical/uk-announces-partial-ban-arms-exports-israel.
111 "Damascus," Wikipedia.org, accessed 8/20/2024, https://en.wikipedia.org/wiki/Damascus.
112 "Syrian Civil War," Wikipedia.org, accessed 8/20/2024, https://en.wikipedia.org/wiki/Syrian_civil_war.
113 "Israel's Role In The Syrian Civil War," Wikipedia.org, accessed 8/20/2024, https://en.wikipedia.org/wiki/Israel's_role_in_the_Syrian_civil_war.
114 Albert Aji, "Israeli Airstrike Destroys Iran's Consulate In Damascus," *PBS*, 4/1/2024, accessed 8/20/2024, https://www.pbs.org/newshour/world/israeli-airstrike-destroys-irans-consulate-in-damascus-occupants-killed-or-wounded-syria-says.
115 "Nuclear Weapons: Who Has What," ArmsControl.org (endnote 13.35).
116 "Iranian Politician Says Tehran Might Already Have Nukes," *Iran International*, 5/10/2024, accessed 8/20/2024, https://www.iranintl.com/en/202405108870.
117 J.R. Wilson, "The New Era Of High-Power Electromagnetic Weapons," *Military+Aerospace Electronics*, 11/19/2019, accessed 8/21/2024, https://www.militaryaerospace.com/power/article/14072339/emp-high-power-electromagnetic-weapons-railguns-microwaves.
118 Richard Milner, "Disturbing Facts About The Most Powerful Nuclear Bomb," *Grunge*, 4/18/2024, accessed 8/21/2024, https://www.grunge.com/1557431/disturbing-facts-most-powerful-nuclear-bomb-ever-made/.
Richard Milner, "Here's Why A Hydrogen Bomb Is So Much More Devastating Than An Atomic Bomb," *Grunge*, 5/2/2024, accessed 8/21/2024, https://www.grunge.com/1565131/why-hydrogen-bomb-more-devastating-than-atomic-bomb/.
119 Alex Wellerstein, "The Untold Story Of The World's Biggest Nuclear Bomb," *Bulletin of the Atomic Scientists*, 10/29/2021, accessed 8/21/2024, https://thebulletin.org/2021/11/the-untold-story-of-the-worlds-biggest-nuclear-bomb/.
120 "What Was The Holocaust?," YadVashem.org (endnote 2.2).
121 "North Korea: Full Country Dossier, January 2024," OpenDoors.org, accessed 8/22/2024, p 3-4, https://www.opendoors.org/persecution/reports/North_Korea-Full_Country_Dossier-ODI-2024.pdf.
122 "Religious Composition By Country," *PRC* (endnote 4.4).
123 "North Korea," OpenDoors.org, p 3-4 (endnote 13.121).
124 "Religious Composition By Country," *PRC* (endnote 4.4).
125 "Trends," OpenDoors.org, accessed 8/22/2024, https://www.opendoorsus.org/en-US/persecution/persecution-trends/.
126 "Iran: Draconian Campaign To Enforce Compulsory Veiling Laws," *Amnesty International*, 3/6/2024, accessed 8/22/2024, https://www.amnesty.org/en/latest/news/2024/03/iran-draconian-campaign-to-enforce-compulsory-veiling-laws-through-surveillance-and-mass-car-confiscations.
Beth Bailey, "AI Enabling Iran's Crackdown On Women," *Fox News*, 6/8/2024, accessed 8/22/2024, https://www.foxnews.com/world/ai-enabling-irans-crackdown-on-women-authoritarian-regime-uses-tech-enforce-head-covering.
127 Drew Donnelly, PhD, "China Social Credit System Explained," *Horizons*, 2/11/2024, accessed

8/22/2024, https://joinhorizons.com/china-social-credit-system-explained.
"Chinese Surveillance State," *InfoWars*, 6/22/2023, accessed 9/4/2024, https://www.infowars.com/posts/chinese-surveillance-state-facial-recognition-and-social-credit-score-required-at-gas-stations/.

[128] Paul Mozur, "A.I., Brain Scans And Cameras," *The New York Times*, 3/30/2023, accessed 8/22/2024, https://www.nytimes.com/2023/03/30/technology/police-surveillance-tech-dubai.html.

[129] Sara Novak, "Is The Euphrates River Drying Up?," *Discover Magazine*, 2/8/2024, accessed 8/21/2024, https://www.discovermagazine.com/planet-earth/is-the-euphrates-river-drying-up.

[130] Pamela Weintraub, "Rewriting Tel Megiddo's Violent History," *Discover Magazine*, 5/21/2019, accessed 8/21/2024, https://www.discovermagazine.com/the-sciences/rewriting-tel-megiddos-violent-history.
"Megiddo, The Place Of Battles," BibleArchaeology.org, accessed 8/21/2024, https://biblearchaeology.org/research/conquest-of-canaan/3084-megiddo-the-place-of-battles.

[131] "World Population," WorldoMeters.info (endnote 5.3).
"Demographics Of India," Wikipedia.org, accessed 8/21/2024, https://en.wikipedia.org/wiki/Demographics_of_India.
1.45 billion India population x 67% age (15-64) x 51% male = 495 million males age 15-64 in India.

[132] "World Population," WorldoMeters.info (endnote 5.3).
"Demographics Of China," Wikipedia.org, accessed 8/21/2024, https://en.wikipedia.org/wiki/Demographics_of_China.
1.41 billion China population x 69% age (15-64) x 51% male = 496 million males age 15-64 in China.

Chapter 14

[1] Marsha Kuhnley, *Rapture 911: What To Do If You're Left Behind*, eBook, (Albuquerque, NM: Drezhn Publishing LLC, 2019), part 6.

[2] Peter W. Stoner, *Science Speaks: Scientific Proof Of The Accuracy Of Prophecy And The Bible*, Online Ed., (Chicago, IL: Moody Bible Institute of Chicago, 1976), ch 3, accessed 8/25/2024, https://sciencespeaks.dstoner.net/Christ_of_Prophecy.html#c9.

[3] Stoner, *Science Speaks*, ch 3 (endnote 14.2).

[4] Ted E. Bunch, "A Tunguska Sized Airburst Destroyed Tall El-Hammam," *Scientific Reports*, 9/20/2021, accessed 8/25/2024, https://www.nature.com/articles/s41598-021-97778-3.

[5] "Left Behind Series," Britannica.com, accessed 8/25/2024, https://www.britannica.com/topic/Left-Behind-book-series-by-Lahaye-and-Jenkins.

[6] "The Harbinger," Amazon.com (endnote 6.1).

[7] Lamb & Lion Ministries, ChristInProphecy.org, accessed 9/11/2024.
Prophecy Watchers, ProphecyWatchers.com, accessed 9/11/2024.
Olive Tree Ministries, OliveTreeViews.org, accessed 9/11/2024.
Behold Israel, BeholdIsrael.org, accessed 9/11/2024.
SkywatchTV, SkyWatchTV.com, accessed 9/11/2024.

[8] "Passenger Train," Wikipedia.org, accessed 8/25/2024, https://en.wikipedia.org/wiki/Passenger_train.
"Ocean Liner," Wikipedia.org, accessed 8/25/2024, https://en.wikipedia.org/wiki/Ocean_liner.

[9] "Car," Wikipedia.org, accessed 8/25/2024, https://en.wikipedia.org/wiki/Car.

[10] "Jet Airliner," Wikipedia.org, accessed 8/25/2024, https://en.wikipedia.org/wiki/Jet_airliner.

[11] Dorothy Neufeld, "Who Owns The Most Vehicles Per Capital?," *Visual Capitalist*, 2/21/2024, accessed 8/25/2024, https://www.visualcapitalist.com/vehicles-per-capita-by-country/.

[12] "Global Airline Passengers," OurWorldInData.org, accessed 8/25/2024, https://ourworldindata.org/grapher/number-airline-passengers.

[13] "William Shatner Goes To Space," *History*, 10/31/2021, accessed 8/25/2024, https://www.history.com/this-day-in-history/william-shatner-goes-to-space.

[14] "Space Tourism," Wikipedia.org, accessed 8/25/2024, https://en.wikipedia.org/wiki/Space_tourism.

[15] "SpaceX Mars Colonization Program," Wikipedia.org, accessed 8/25/2024, https://en.wikipedia.org/wiki/SpaceX_Mars_Colonization_Program.

[16] "Accelerating Change," Wikipedia.org, accessed 8/25/2024, https://en.wikipedia.org/wiki/Accelerating_change.
Marc Rosenberg, "The Coming Knowledge Tsunami," *Learning Guild*, 10/10/2017, accessed 8/25/2024, https://www.learningguild.com/articles/2468/marc-my-words-the-coming-knowledge-tsunami/.

[17] "Share Of The World's Population With Formal Basic Education," OurWorldInData.org, accessed

8/25/2024, https://ourworldindata.org/grapher/share-of-the-world-population-with-at-least-basic-education.

18. "Literate And Illiterate World Population," OurWorldInData.org, accessed 8/25/2024, https://ourworldindata.org/grapher/literate-and-illiterate-world-population.
19. "The Dead Sea Scrolls," IMJ.org.il, accessed 8/25/2024, https://www.imj.org.il/en/wings/shrine-book/dead-sea-scrolls.
20. "New Light On The Book Of Daniel From The Dead Sea Scrolls," BibleArchaeology.org, accessed 8/25/2024, https://biblearchaeology.org/research/divided-kingdom/3193-new-light-on-the-book-of-daniel-from-the-dead-sea-scrolls.
21. Jonathan Cahn, *The Oracle*, eBook, (Lake Mary, FL: FrontLine, 2019), ch 27.
22. Maya Margit, "How New Technologies Are Unraveling The Dead Sea Scrolls' Secrets," *The Jerusalem Post*, 6/29/2020, accessed 9/16/2024, https://www.jpost.com/israel-news/how-new-technologies-are-unraveling-the-dead-sea-scrolls-secrets-633151.
23. "Population," OurWorldInData.org, accessed 8/25/2024, https://ourworldindata.org/grapher/population.
24. "World Population," WorldoMeters.info (endnote 5.3).
25. "Population Growth," OurWorldInData.org (endnote 11.51).
26. "One-Child Policy," Britannica.com, accessed 8/25/2024, https://www.britannica.com/topic/one-child-policy.
27. "Are Aliens Real?," *NBC* (endnote 6.34).
Nomaan Merchant, "Whistleblower Tells Congress The US Is Concealing 'Multi-Decade' Program That Captures UFOs," *AP News*, 7/26/2023, accessed 8/26/2024, https://apnews.com/article/ufos-uaps-congress-whistleblower-spy-aliens-ba8a8cfba353d7b9de29c3d906a69ba7.
28. Jeff M. Smith, "The Lie Of The Century," *The Heritage Foundation*, 5/2/2024, accessed 8/26/2024, https://www.heritage.org/public-health/commentary/the-lie-the-century-the-origin-covid-19.
29. Greg Wehner, "Meta CEO Admits Biden-Harris Admin Pressured Company To Censor Americans," *Fox Business*, 8/27/2024, accessed 8/27/2024, https://www.foxbusiness.com/politics/meta-ceo-admits-biden-harris-admin-pressured-company-censor-americans.
30. Shannon Thaler, "Electric Vehicles Release More Toxic Emissions," *New York Post*, 3/5/2024, accessed 8/26/2024, https://nypost.com/2024/03/05/business/evs-release-more-toxic-emissions-are-worse-for-the-environment-study/.
31. "Julian Assange," Wikipedia.org, accessed 8/26/2024, https://en.wikipedia.org/wiki/Julian_Assange.
32. "Edward Snowden," Wikipedia.org, accessed 8/26/2024, https://en.wikipedia.org/wiki/Edward_Snowden.
33. "10 Most Famous Whistleblowers," *St Francis School of Law*, 11/21/2022, accessed 8/26/2024, https://stfrancislaw.com/blog/10-most-famous-whistleblowers/.
34. George Clooney, "George Clooney: I Love Joe Biden. But We Need A New Nominee.," *The New York Times*, 7/10/2024, accessed 8/26/2024, https://www.nytimes.com/2024/07/10/opinion/joe-biden-democratic-nominee.html.
35. Peter Nicholas, "President Joe Biden Drops Out Of 2024 Presidential Race," *NBC News*, 7/21/2024, accessed 8/26/2024, https://www.nbcnews.com/politics/2024-election/president-joe-biden-drops-2024-presidential-race-rcna159867.
36. Jonah Mandel, "Israeli Desalination, Wastewater Treatment Becomes Global Model," *The Times of Israel*, 8/10/2023, accessed 8/26/2024, https://www.timesofisrael.com/israeli-desalination-wastewater-treatment-becomes-global-model-for-water-scarcity/.
37. Rosella Tercatin, "Israeli Start-Up Enables Farmers To Grow Crops In Salty Water," *The Jerusalem Post*, 8/5/2020, accessed 8/26/2024, https://www.jpost.com/health-science/israeli-startup-enables-farmers-to-grow-crops-in-salty-water-637482.
38. "About Us," ShefaGems.com, accessed 8/26/2024, https://www.shefagems.com/about-us.
39. "Bible Comes To Life As Precious Gems Discovered For First Time In Israel," ShefaGems.com, accessed 8/26/2024, https://www.shefagems.com/shefa-gems-unearths-rare-mineral-copy.
40. "Diamond Industry In Israel," Wikipedia.org, accessed 8/26/2024, https://en.wikipedia.org/wiki/Diamond_industry_in_Israel.
41. "Diamonds In Israel," OEC.world, accessed 8/26/2024, https://oec.world/en/profile/bilateral-product/diamonds/reporter/isr.
42. "Natural Gas In Israel," Wikipedia.org, accessed 8/26/2024,

https://en.wikipedia.org/wiki/Natural_gas_in_Israel.
Sujata Ashwarya, "Natural Gas Discoveries And Israel's Energy Security," *Georgetown Journal of International Affairs*, 5/25/2020, accessed 8/26/2024, https://gjia.georgetown.edu/2020/05/25/natural-gas-discoveries-and-israels-energy-security/.

43 David Caploe, PhD, "Israel May Hold The World's Third Largest Reserve Of Shale Oil," *Oil Price*, 4/15/2011, accessed 8/26/2024, https://oilprice.com/Energy/Crude-Oil/Israel-May-Hold-The-Worlds-Third-Largest-Reserve-Of-Shale-Oil.html.

44 Menachem Bar-Shalom, "Israel Is An Annual Crossroads For 500 Million Birds," *All Israel News*, 12/10/2022, accessed 8/25/2024, https://allisrael.com/the-great-migration-israel-is-a-crossroads-for-500-million-birds-annually.

45 "Live From Hula Lake," KKL-JNF.org, accessed 8/25/2024, https://www.kkl-jnf.org/tourism-and-recreation/forests-and-parks/hula-lake-park/live_broadcast/.

46 Noa Fischer, "Hundreds Of Thousands Of Birds Arrive In Israel," *Ynet News*, 10/3/2022, accessed 8/25/2024, https://www.ynetnews.com/environment/article/sykkgzogj.

47 Sue Surkes, "Over Half Of The World's Lesser Spotted Eagle Population Set To Fly Over Israel," *The Times of Israel*, 10/4/2023, accessed 8/25/2024, https://www.timesofisrael.com/liveblog_entry/over-half-of-worlds-lesser-spotted-eagle-population-set-to-fly-over-israel/.

48 Assaf Golan, "IDF Uses Birds Of Prey To Locate Remains Of Massacre Victims," *Jewish News Syndicate*, 11/10/2023, accessed 8/25/2024, https://www.jns.org/idf-uses-birds-of-prey-to-locate-remains-of-massacre-victims/.

49 Anav Silverman Peretz, "Saving The Israeli Vulture," *Environment and Climate in the Middle East*, 5/5/2024, accessed 8/25/2024, https://mideastenvironment.apps01.yorku.ca/2024/05/saving-the-israeli-vulture-a-lifeline-for-the-biblical-bird-of-prey-jerusalem-post/.

50 "Arabian Leopard," Wikipedia.org, accessed 8/26/2024, https://en.wikipedia.org/wiki/Arabian_leopard.

51 "Wolf," Wikipedia.org, accessed 8/26/2024, https://en.wikipedia.org/wiki/Wolf.
"Arabian Wolf," Wikipedia.org, accessed 8/26/2024, https://en.wikipedia.org/wiki/Arabian_wolf.
"Golden Jackal," Wikipedia.org, accessed 8/26/2024, https://en.wikipedia.org/wiki/Golden_jackal.
"Caracal," Wikipedia.org, accessed 8/26/2024, https://en.wikipedia.org/wiki/Caracal.
"Striped Hyena," Wikipedia.org, accessed 8/26/2024, https://en.wikipedia.org/wiki/Striped_hyena.

52 "Syrian Brown Bear," Wikipedia.org, accessed 8/26/2024, https://en.wikipedia.org/wiki/Syrian_brown_bear.
Dave Garshelis, "Brown Bear(s) Do Exist In Syria," *International Bear News*, Spring 2015, accessed 8/26/2024, https://web.archive.org/web/20230411221415/https://www.bearbiology.org/fileadmin/tpl/Downloads/IBN_Newsletters/IBN_Spring_2015_Med.pdf.

53 "About The Temple Institute," TempleInstitute.org, accessed 8/26/2024, https://templeinstitute.org/about-us/.
"The Temple Institute: Building The Holy Temple!," 8/6/2024, *The Temple Institute*, YouTube video, accessed 8/26/2024, https://www.youtube.com/watch?v=rUbABhhBwoQ.

54 "The Red Heifer," TempleInstitute.org, accessed 8/26/2024, https://templeinstitute.org/para-aduma-the-red-heifer/.

55 Nicole Jansezian, "Does The Arrival Of Five Red Heifers In Israel Signal Third Temple, End Times?," *All Israel News*, 9/17/2022, accessed 8/26/2024, https://allisrael.com/does-the-arrival-of-five-red-heifers-in-israel-signal-third-temple-end-times.

56 Etgar Lefkovits, "An Indiana Farmer's Journey To Caring For Red Heifers Brought To Israel From Texas," *Jewish News Syndicate*, 5/20/2024, accessed 8/26/2024, https://www.jns.org/an-indiana-farmers-journey-to-caring-for-red-heifers-brought-to-israel-from-texas/.

57 "List Of Israeli Inventions And Discoveries," Wikipedia.org, accessed 8/26/2024, https://en.wikipedia.org/wiki/List_of_Israeli_inventions_and_discoveries.
Lior Bonfis, "Israeli Innovation Brings Life-Saving Services To Public," *Ynet News*, 7/31/2023, accessed 8/26/2024, https://www.ynetnews.com/health_science/article/bkahcxhoh.
Reuben Lewis, "Israeli Inventions That Changed The World," *Culture Trip*, 4/21/2021, accessed 8/26/2024, https://theculturetrip.com/middle-east/israel/articles/11-israeli-innovations-that-changed-the-world.

58 "List Of Israeli Nobel Laureates," Wikipedia.org, accessed 8/26/2024, https://en.wikipedia.org/wiki/List_of_Israeli_Nobel_laureates.

59 DenBerg, "The Inventions And Their Jewish Inventors That You Never Knew About," *Forward*,

5/23/2023, accessed 8/26/2024, https://forward.com/opinion/547927/jewish-inventions-inventors/.

60 Marnie Winston-Macauley, "Little Known Jewish Inventions," *Aish*, accessed 8/26/2024, https://aish.com/we-jews-little-known-jewish-inventions/.
Rivka Ronda Robinson, "10 Big Jewish Inventions," *Aish*, accessed 8/26/2024, https://aish.com/10-big-jewish-inventions/.

61 "Israel," Wikipedia.org (endnote 2.3).
"British Empire," Wikipedia.org, accessed 8/26/2024, https://en.wikipedia.org/wiki/British_Empire.

62 "Harry S. Truman," Wikipedia.org, accessed 8/26/2024, https://en.wikipedia.org/wiki/Harry_S._Truman.

63 "Israel-United States Relations," Wikipedia.org, accessed 8/26/2024, https://en.wikipedia.org/wiki/Israel–United_States_relations.

64 "United States," Wikipedia.org, accessed 8/26/2024, https://en.wikipedia.org/wiki/United_States.

65 "United Nations Security Council Resolution 242," Wikipedia.org, accessed 8/27/2024, https://en.wikipedia.org/wiki/United_Nations_Security_Council_Resolution_242.

66 "2000 Camp David Summit," Wikipedia.org, accessed 8/27/2024, https://en.wikipedia.org/wiki/2000_Camp_David_Summit.
"The Clinton Parameters," Wikipedia.org, accessed 8/27/2024, https://en.wikipedia.org/wiki/The_Clinton_Parameters.

67 "United Nations Security Council Resolution 1397," Wikipedia.org, accessed 8/27/2024, https://en.wikipedia.org/wiki/United_Nations_Security_Council_Resolution_1397.

68 "Turkish MP Who Suffered Heart Attack During Speech In Parliament Dies," *Al Jazeera*, 12/14/2023, accessed 8/27/2024, https://www.aljazeera.com/news/2023/12/14/turkish-mp-who-suffered-heart-attack-during-speech-in-parliament-dies.

69 "Iran's Raisi To Israel: 'Attack Could Lead To End Of Zionist Regime'," *The Jerusalem Post*, 4/24/2024, accessed 8/27/2024, https://www.jpost.com/middle-east/iran-news/irans-raisi-to-israel-attack-could-lead-to-end-of-zionist-regime-798399.

70 Parisa Hafezi, "Iranian President Ebrahim Raisi, Hardline Ally Of Khamenei, Killed In Helicopter Crash," *Reuters*, 5/20/2024, accessed 8/27/2024, https://www.reuters.com/world/middle-east/hopes-fade-wreckage-found-helicopter-carrying-iranian-president-raisi-2024-05-20/.

71 "The Iranian Mystery: 12 End-Time Signs!," 5/28/2024, *Jonathan Cahn Official*, YouTube video, accessed 8/27/2024, https://www.youtube.com/watch?v=hnxPRxEFEhg.

72 Brendan Pierson, "Christian Employers Do Not Have To Cover Gender Transition," *Reuters*, 3/5/2024, accessed 8/27/2024, https://www.reuters.com/legal/litigation/christian-employers-do-not-have-cover-gender-transition-judge-rules-2024-03-04/.

73 Thomas Fuller, "Oregon Decriminalizes Small Amounts Of Heroin And Cocaine," *The New York Times*, 11/4/2020, accessed 8/27/2024, https://www.nytimes.com/2020/11/04/us/ballot-measures-propositions-2020.html.

74 Mike Baker, "Oregon Is Recriminalizing Drugs," *The New York Times*, 4/1/2024, accessed 8/27/2024, https://www.nytimes.com/2024/04/01/us/oregon-drug-law-portland-mayor.html.

75 "Burning Man," Wikipedia.org, accessed 8/27/2024, https://en.wikipedia.org/wiki/Burning_Man.

76 Kiara Alfonseca, "Burning Man Flooded," *ABC News*, 9/4/2023, accessed 8/27/2024, https://abcnews.go.com/US/burning-man-flooding-happened-stranded-festivalgoers/story?id=102908331.

77 Adam Liptak, "In 6-To-3 Ruling, Supreme Court Ends Nearly 50 Years Of Abortion Rights," *The New York Times*, 6/24/2022, accessed 8/27/2024, https://www.nytimes.com/2022/06/24/us/roe-wade-overturned-supreme-court.html.

78 "State Laws And Policies," Guttmacher.org, accessed 8/27/2024, https://www.guttmacher.org/state-policy/explore/state-policies-abortion-bans.

79 "Jesus Movement," Wikipedia.org, accessed 8/27/2024, https://en.wikipedia.org/wiki/Jesus_movement.

80 "The Jesus Revolution," *TIME*, 6/21/1971, accessed 8/27/2024, https://time.com/vault/issue/1971-06-21/page/1/.

81 Billy Hallowell, "Satanist Accepts Jesus During History-Breaking Mass Baptism," *Faithwire*, 5/20/2024, accessed 9/4/2024, https://www.faithwire.com/2024/05/20/god-lit-a-match-satanist-accepts-jesus-during-history-breaking-mass-baptism-as-12000-people-immersed-in-california/.

82 "The Asbury Outpouring," Asbury.edu, accessed 8/27/2024, https://www.asbury.edu/outpouring/.

83 Talia Wise, "Hundreds Choose Christ At Auburn," *CBN*, 9/14/2023, accessed 8/27/2024,

https://www2.cbn.com/news/us/revival-happening-hundreds-choose-christ-auburn-get-spontaneously-baptized-lake.

84 Sanna Erela, "The Caspari Center Survey Released," *Caspari Center*, 2/7/2022, accessed 8/27/2024, https://www.caspari.com/2022/02/07/the-caspari-center-survey-released-the-israeli-messianic-movement-has-more-than-tripled-in-the-last-20-years/.

85 Adam Eliyahu Berkowitz, "Christian Revival In Iran," *World Net Daily*, 6/1/2024, accessed 8/27/2024, https://www.wnd.com/2024/06/christian-revival-iran-answer-todays-mideast-conflict/.

86 Michael Foust, "Muslims In Gaza Come To Christ After Seeing Jesus In Dreams," *Crosswalk*, 12/27/2023, accessed 8/27/2024, https://www.crosswalk.com/headlines/contributors/michael-foust/muslims-in-gaza-come-to-christ-after-seeing-jesus-in-dreams-report-says-it-was-a-miracle.html.

87 I Found the Truth, YouTube channel, accessed 8/27/2024, https://www.youtube.com/@IFoundTheTruth.

88 "Billy Graham," Wikipedia.org (endnote 7.4).

89 "List Of Megachurches In The United States," Wikipedia.org, accessed 8/27/2024, https://en.wikipedia.org/wiki/List_of_megachurches_in_the_United_States.

90 "Locations," CalvaryNM.church, accessed 8/27/2024, https://calvarynm.church/locations/#/.

91 Adam Macinnis, "'The Chosen' Breaks Record For Most-Translated TV Show," *Christianity Today*, 5/13/2024, accessed 8/27/2024, https://www.christianitytoday.com/news/2024/may/chosen-translation-dubbing-global-record.html.

92 "The History Of Jesus Film Project," JesusFilm.org, accessed 8/27/2024, https://www.jesusfilm.org/about/history/.

93 "State Of The Bible," *Wycliffe Bible Translators*, 2023, accessed 8/27/2024, https://cfbecdc18044a5f9a723.b-cdn.net/wp-content/uploads/2023/09/State-of-the-Bible-2023.pdf.
"Bible Translation Statistics," Wycliffe.org.uk, accessed 8/27/2024, https://wycliffe.org.uk/statistics.

94 "The Treasury," Maps.Google.com, accessed 8/27/2024, https://maps.app.goo.gl/NMH3Uo1yKto7UssS6.

95 "A Brief History Of Petra, Jordan," TheThrillOfPursuit.com, accessed 8/27/2024, https://thethrillofpursuit.com/world-wonder-petra-history/.
"Siq," Wikipedia.org, accessed 8/27/2024, https://en.wikipedia.org/wiki/Siq.
"Petra," Wikipedia.org, accessed 8/27/2024, https://en.wikipedia.org/wiki/Petra.

96 "Petra Water System," TravelTalesOfLife.com, accessed 8/27/2024, https://traveltalesoflife.com/petra-water-system/.

97 "Petra," Wikipedia.org (endnote 14.95).

Chapter 15

1 "Obesity And Overweight," *World Health Organization*, 3/1/2024, accessed 7/17/2024, https://www.who.int/news-room/fact-sheets/detail/obesity-and-overweight.

2 "World Life Expectancy," MacroTrends.net, accessed 7/17/2024, https://www.macrotrends.net/global-metrics/countries/WLD/world/life-expectancy.

3 "U.S. Life Expectancy," MacroTrends.net, accessed 7/17/2024, https://www.macrotrends.net/global-metrics/countries/USA/united-states/life-expectancy.
"Israel Life Expectancy," MacroTrends.net, accessed 7/17/2024, https://www.macrotrends.net/global-metrics/countries/ISR/israel/life-expectancy.

4 "Biodiversity," OurWorldInData.org, accessed 7/17/2024, https://ourworldindata.org/biodiversity.
"Living Planet Index," OurWorldInData.org, accessed 7/17/2024, https://ourworldindata.org/living-planet-index-decline.

5 Amanda Schupak, "Mass Animal Deaths On The Rise," *CBS News*, 1/16/2015, accessed 7/17/2024, https://www.cbsnews.com/news/mass-animal-deaths-on-the-rise-worldwide/.
Marion Renault, "Animals Are Dying In Droves," *The New Republic*, 5/3/2023, accessed 7/17/2024, https://newrepublic.com/article/172221/animals-dying-sea-lions.

6 Tia Ghose, "The 12 Biggest Volcanic Eruptions In Recorded History," *Live Science*, 6/10/2023, accessed 7/17/2024, https://www.livescience.com/planet-earth/volcanos/the-12-biggest-volcanic-eruptions-in-recorded-history.

7 Chelsea Thompson, "A Volcanic Eruption Sent Enough Water Vapor Into The Stratosphere To

Cause A Rapid Change In Chemistry," *NOAA*, 12/20/2023, accessed 7/17/2024, https://research.noaa.gov/2023/12/20/hunga-tonga-2022-eruption/.

8. "12 Biggest Volcanic Eruptions," *LS* (endnote 15.6).
9. Harry Baker, "Tonga Eruption's Towering Plume Was The Tallest In Recorded History," *Live Science*, 11/3/2022, accessed 7/17/2024, https://www.livescience.com/tonga-eruption-tallest-plume-ever.
Nicoletta Lanese, "Record-Breaking Tonga Volcano Generated The Fastest Atmospheric Waves," *Live Science*, 6/30/2022, accessed 7/17/2024, https://www.livescience.com/tonga-volcanic-eruption-fast-waves.
10. Kevin Hamilton, "Tonga Eruption Was So Intense, It Caused The Atmosphere To Ring Like A Bell," *Live Science*, 1/24/2022, accessed 7/17/2024, https://www.livescience.com/tonga-eruption-pressure-waves.
11. Nicholas LePan, "Visualizing The History Of Pandemics," *Visual Capitalist*, 3/14/2020, accessed 7/17/2024, https://www.visualcapitalist.com/history-of-pandemics-deadliest/.
"What Were The Death Tolls From Pandemics In History?," OurWorldInData.org, accessed 7/17/2024, https://ourworldindata.org/historical-pandemics.
12. "Autism Prevalence Is Now 1 In 36," *TACA*, 3/23/2023, accessed 7/17/2024, https://tacanow.org/press-release/autism-prevalence-is-now-1-in-36/.
13. Judy Siegel-Itzkovich, "Autism Spectrum Disorder Prevalence Nearly Doubles In Israel In Five Years," *The Jerusalem Post*, 1/31/2024, accessed 7/17/2024, https://www.jpost.com/health-and-wellness/article-784479.
14. "Influenza A Virus Subtype H5N1," Wikipedia.org, accessed 7/17/2024, https://en.wikipedia.org/wiki/Influenza_A_virus_subtype_H5N1.
15. Sue Surkes, "As Avian Flu Rises In Hula Valley Cranes, Authorities Spar Over Who Collects Carcasses," *The Times of Israel*, 2/15/2024, accessed 7/18/2024, https://www.timesofisrael.com/as-avian-flu-rises-in-hula-valley-cranes-authorities-spar-over-who-collects-carcasses/.
16. "H5N1 Bird Flu Detections Across The United States," CDC.gov, accessed 7/17/2024, https://www.cdc.gov/bird-flu/situation-summary/data-map-commercial.html.
17. India Bourke, "How Bird Flu Became An Animal Pandemic," *BBC*, 4/26/2024, accessed 7/17/2024, https://www.bbc.com/future/article/20240425-how-dangerous-is-bird-flu-spread-to-wildlife-and-humans.
18. Matej Mikulic, "Prescription Drug Expenditure," *Statista*, 1/18/2024, accessed 7/17/2024, https://www.statista.com/statistics/184914/prescription-drug-expenditures-in-the-us-since-1960/.
19. Matej Mikulic, "Global Spending On Medicines," *Statista*, 5/22/2024, accessed 7/17/2024, https://www.statista.com/statistics/280572/medicine-spending-worldwide/.
20. "China Created Covid-19 As A 'Bioweapon'," *The Jerusalem Post*, 6/28/2023, accessed 7/17/2024, https://www.jpost.com/health-and-wellness/coronavirus/article-748002.
21. "Famines," OurWorldInData.org, accessed 7/17/2024, https://ourworldindata.org/famines.
22. "Number Of Severely Food Insecure People," OurWorldInData.org, accessed 7/17/2024, https://ourworldindata.org/grapher/number-of-people-severely-food-insecure.
23. "Severely Food Insecure," OurWorldInData.org (endnote 15.22).
24. 892.7 million people severely food insecure (see ch. 15 n. 22) / 8,122 million World population = 10.99%.
25. "Food Security In The U.S.," ERS.USDA.gov, accessed 7/18/2024, https://www.ers.usda.gov/topics/food-nutrition-assistance/food-security-in-the-u-s/key-statistics-graphics/.
26. Daniel Dolev, "Hundreds Of Thousands Of Israeli Kids Go Hungry At School," *Shomrim*, 10/20/2022, accessed 7/18/2024, https://www.shomrim.news/eng/bottom-of-the-food-chain.
27. Gloria Dickie, "More Than Half Of The World's Large Lakes Are Drying Up," *Reuters*, 5/19/2023, accessed 7/18/2024, https://www.reuters.com/business/environment/more-than-half-worlds-large-lakes-are-drying-up-study-finds-2023-05-18/.
28. Shea Gunther, "8 Lakes And Rivers That Are Drying Up," *Treehugger*, 7/25/2022, accessed 7/18/2024, https://www.treehugger.com/lakes-and-rivers-that-are-drying-up-4869239.
29. "Euphrates River," *DM* (endnote 13.129).
30. Marianne Stein, "How The Russian Invasion Of Ukraine Has Impacted The Global Wheat Market," *ACES News*, 2/5/2024, accessed 7/18/2024, https://aces.illinois.edu/news/how-russian-invasion-ukraine-has-impacted-global-wheat-market.
31. Douglas Broom, "This Is How War In Europe Is Disrupting Fertilizer Supplies," *World Economic*

Forum, 3/1/2023, accessed 7/18/2024, https://www.weforum.org/agenda/2023/03/ukraine-fertilizer-food-security/.

32 Chris Hufstader, "How Will Climate Change Affect Agriculture?," *Oxfam*, 4/18/2024, accessed 7/18/2024, https://www.oxfamamerica.org/explore/stories/how-will-climate-change-affect-agriculture/.

33 Sybille De La Hamaide, "Why Are Farmers Protesting In Europe?," *Reuters*, 2/20/2024, accessed 7/18/2024, https://www.reuters.com/world/europe/why-farmers-are-protesting-europe-2024-02-01/.

34 "Deaths From Earthquakes," OurWorldInData.org, accessed 7/18/2024, https://ourworldindata.org/grapher/earthquake-deaths.

35 "Number Of Significant Earthquakes," OurWorldInData.org, accessed 7/18/2024, https://ourworldindata.org/grapher/significant-earthquakes.

36 "Significant Earthquakes," OurWorldInData.org (endnote 15.35).

37 "Earthquakes: Lists, Maps, And Statistics," USGS.gov, accessed 7/18/2024, World magnitude 7+ and 8+, https://www.usgs.gov/programs/earthquake-hazards/lists-maps-and-statistics.

38 Sarah Gibbens, "How Humans Are Causing Deadly Earthquakes," *National Geographic*, 10/2/2017, accessed 7/18/2024, https://www.nationalgeographic.com/science/article/human-induced-earthquakes-fracking-mining-video-spd.

39 "Climate Change Indicators: U.S. And Global Temperature," EPA.gov, accessed 7/19/2024, https://www.epa.gov/climate-indicators/climate-change-indicators-us-and-global-temperature.

40 Nuria Lopez, "June 2024 Marks 12th Month Of Global Temperature Reaching 1.5°C Above Pre-Industrial," *Copernicus*, 7/4/2024, accessed 7/19/2024, https://climate.copernicus.eu/copernicus-june-2024-marks-12th-month-global-temperature-reaching-15degc-above-pre-industrial.

41 "Weather Related Fatality And Injury Statistics," Weather.gov, accessed 7/19/2024, https://www.weather.gov/hazstat/.

42 "2003 European Heatwave," Wikipedia.org, accessed 7/19/2024, https://en.wikipedia.org/wiki/2003_European_heatwave.

43 "The Heatwave Of 2003," MetOffice.gov.uk, accessed 7/19/2024, https://www.metoffice.gov.uk/weather/learn-about/weather/case-studies/heatwave.

44 Bob Henson, "Record Heat Engulfs Both U.S. Coasts," *Yale Climate Connections*, 7/9/2024, accessed 7/19/2024, https://yaleclimateconnections.org/2024/07/record-heat-engulfs-both-u-s-coasts/.

45 Toi Staff, "Tel Aviv Temperatures Shatter 85-Year April Record," *The Times of Israel*, 4/25/2024, accessed 7/19/2024, https://www.timesofisrael.com/tel-aviv-temperatures-shatter-85-year-april-record-as-heatwave-scorches-country/.

46 Gloria Dickie, "Climate Change Boosted Deadly Saudi Haj Heat," *Reuters*, 6/27/2024, accessed 7/19/2024, https://www.reuters.com/business/environment/climate-change-boosted-deadly-saudi-haj-heat-by-25-c-scientists-say-2024-06-27/.

47 "Climate Change Indicators: Heat Waves," EPA.gov, accessed 7/19/2024, https://www.epa.gov/climate-indicators/climate-change-indicators-heat-waves.

48 "Basic Nuclear Physics And Weapons Effects," Acq.osd.mil, accessed 7/19/2024, https://www.acq.osd.mil/ncbdp/nm/NMHB2020rev/chapters/chapter13.html.

49 "Little Boy," Wikipedia.org, accessed 7/19/2024, https://en.wikipedia.org/wiki/Little_Boy.

50 "Firestorms," AtomicArchive.com, accessed 7/19/2024, https://www.atomicarchive.com/science/effects/firestorms.html.

51 "Talent (Measurement)," Wikipedia.org, accessed 7/17/2024, https://en.wikipedia.org/wiki/Talent_(measurement).

52 "What Countries Have Tornadoes?," WorldPopulationReview.com, accessed 7/19/2024, https://worldpopulationreview.com/country-rankings/what-countries-have-tornadoes.

53 Allison Chinchar, "Here's Why The US Has More Tornadoes Than Any Other Country," *CNN*, accessed 7/19/2024, https://www.cnn.com/weather/us-leads-tornado-numbers-tornado-alley-xpn/index.html.

54 "List Of Tornado Events By Year," Wikipedia.org, accessed 7/19/2024, US total tornadoes, https://en.wikipedia.org/wiki/List_of_tornado_events_by_year.

55 "Operation Popeye," Wikipedia.org, accessed 7/19/2024, https://en.wikipedia.org/wiki/Operation_Popeye.

56 Orkhan Huseynli, "Unleashing The Power Of Cloud Seeding," *Earth.org*, 4/18/2024, accessed 7/19/2024, https://earth.org/unleashing-the-power-of-cloud-seeding-navigating-potential-and-pitfalls/.

57 "Planned Weather Modification Through Cloud Seeding," AMetSoc.org, accessed 7/19/2024,

https://www.ametsoc.org/index.cfm/ams/about-ams/ams-statements/archive-statements-of-the-ams/planned-weather-modification-through-cloud-seeding/.

58 Laura Kuhl, "How Cloud Seeding Could Go Wrong," *Bulletin of the Atomic Scientists*, 8/11/2022, accessed 7/19/2024, https://thebulletin.org/2022/08/dodging-silver-bullets-how-cloud-seeding-could-go-wrong/.
59 "Hurricane Landfalls In The United States," OurWorldInData.org, accessed 7/19/2024, https://ourworldindata.org/grapher/hurricane-landfalls-us.
60 Jonathan Erdman, "The Staggering Cost Of U.S. Hurricanes," *The Weather Channel*, 5/5/2022, accessed 7/19/2024, https://weather.com/storms/hurricane/news/2022-05-05-us-hurricanes-tropical-storms-cost-half-trillion.
61 "Mediterranean Tropical-Like Cyclone," Wikipedia.org, accessed 7/19/2024, https://en.wikipedia.org/wiki/Mediterranean_tropical-like_cyclone.
62 "Storm Daniel," Wikipedia.org, accessed 7/19/2024, https://en.wikipedia.org/wiki/Storm_Daniel.
63 "Tsunamis," NOAA.gov, accessed 7/19/2024, https://www.noaa.gov/jetstream/tsunamis.
64 "Tsunamis Historical Context," NOAA.gov, accessed 7/19/2024, https://www.noaa.gov/jetstream/tsunamis/historical-context.
65 Caroline Reid, "What Would Happen If You Dropped A Nuclear Bomb Into A Volcano?," *IFLScience*, 8/28/2015, accessed 7/19/2024, https://www.iflscience.com/what-would-happen-if-you-dropped-bomb-volcano-30400.
66 Raul (Pete) Pedrozo, "Radioactive Tsunamis: Nuclear Torpedo Drones," *CIMSEC*, 9/4/2023, accessed 7/19/2024, https://cimsec.org/radioactive-tsunamis-nuclear-torpedo-drones-and-their-legality-in-war/.
67 Dave Mosher, "A New Russian Video May Show A 'Doomsday Machine' Able To Trigger 300 Foot Tsunamis," *Business Insider*, 7/24/2018, accessed 7/19/2024, https://www.businessinsider.com/russia-doomsday-weapon-submarine-nuke-2018-4.
68 Robert Lea, "Earth Is Safe From A Devastating Asteroid Impact For 1,000 Years," *Space.com*, 5/18/2023, accessed 7/19/2024, https://www.space.com/earth-probably-safe-devastating-asteroid-impact-thousand-years.
69 "Notable Asteroid Impacts In Earth's History," Planetary.org, accessed 7/19/2024, https://www.planetary.org/notable-asteroid-impacts-in-earths-history.
70 John Elflein, "Deadliest Animals Worldwide," *Statista*, 5/22/2024, accessed 7/20/2024, https://www.statista.com/statistics/448169/deadliest-creatures-in-the-world-by-number-of-human-deaths/.
71 "Animal Bites," *World Health Organization*, 1/12/2024, accessed 7/20/2024, https://www.who.int/news-room/fact-sheets/detail/animal-bites.
72 Nicholas L.S. Roberts, "Global Mortality Of Snakebite Envenoming," *Nature*, 10/25/2022, accessed 7/20/2024, https://www.nature.com/articles/s41467-022-33627-9.
73 Monika Martyn, "Dog Bite Statistics," *World Animal Foundation*, 8/24/2024, accessed 7/20/2024, https://worldanimalfoundation.org/advocate/dog-bite-statistics/.
74 "Killer Whales Are Attacking, Sinking Boats," *Fox KTVU*, 6/23/2023, accessed 7/20/2024, https://www.ktvu.com/news/killer-whales-are-attacking-sinking-boats-and-scientists-are-unsure-why.
Emma Beddington, "The Orca Uprising: Whales Are Ramming Boats," *The Guardian*, 7/11/2023, accessed 7/20/2024, https://www.theguardian.com/environment/2023/jul/11/the-orca-uprising-whales-are-ramming-boats-but-are-they-inspired-by-revenge-grief-or-memory.
75 "Global Risks Report 2024," WEForum.org (endnote 9.5).

Chapter 16

1 Joseph A. Seiss, *The Gospel In The Stars*, Paperback, (Mansfield Centre, CT: Martino Publishing, 2015). Free eBook at https://www.truthseekersministries.org/wp-content/uploads/seissgospelstars.pdf.
Ken Fleming, *God's Voice In The Stars*, First Ed., (Dubuque, IA: Emmaus Worldwide, 2012).
Joe Amaral, *Story In The Stars*, First Ed., (New York, NY: FaithWords, 2018).
2 "Story In The Stars," 8/29/2022, *Joe Amaral*, YouTube video, accessed 9/10/2024, https://www.youtube.com/watch?v=O68gs8ueSAw.
3 "The Revelation 12 Sign In 3 Minutes!!," 6/29/2017, *Parable of the Vineyard*, YouTube video, accessed 9/10/2024, https://www.youtube.com/watch?v=0jYg0X4NL7g.
Stellarium, Stellarium-web.org, accessed 9/11/2024.
4 Michael Snyder, "This Is The Eclipse "Conspiracy Theory" That The Mainstream Media Doesn't

Want To Talk About," *The Economic Collapse*, 4/4/2024, accessed 7/12/2024, https://theeconomiccollapseblog.com/this-is-the-eclipse-conspiracy-theory-that-the-mainstream-media-doesnt-want-to-talk-about/.

5. Michael Snyder, "Have You Heard About The 2 Gigantic Crosses That Stand At The Intersections Of The Eclipses?," *End Of The American Dream*, 4/4/2024, accessed 7/12/2024, https://endoftheamericandream.com/have-you-heard-about-the-2-gigantic-crosses-that-stand-at-the-intersections-of-the-eclipses/.

6. Miles Hatfield, "NASA Rockets Will Fly Into Oct. Eclipse's Shadow," *NASA*, 9/29/2023, accessed 7/12/2024, https://science.nasa.gov/solar-system/skywatching/eclipses/solar-eclipses/2023-solar-eclipse/to-study-atmosphere-nasa-rockets-will-fly-into-oct-eclipses-shadow/.

7. "Planetary Alignment 2024," *Star Walk*, 6/5/2024, accessed 7/12/2024, https://starwalk.space/en/news/what-is-planet-parade.

8. Eric Ralls, "Cryovolcanic "Mother Of Dragons" Devil Comet Is Now Visible From Earth," *Earth.com*, 4/6/2024, accessed 7/12/2024, https://www.earth.com/news/devil-comet-is-visible-in-the-northern-hemisphere/.

9. "The 2024 Eclipse In Enoch, Texas, USA," Eclipse2024.org, accessed 7/12/2024, https://eclipse2024.org/eclipse-cities/city/38588.html.
"The 2024 Eclipse In Elijah, Missouri, USA," Eclipse2024.org, accessed 7/12/2024, https://eclipse2024.org/eclipse-cities/city/23494.html.

10. AC Katz, *The Great American Writing On The Wall*, eBook, (Meadville, PA: Christian Faith Publishing, Inc., 2023).

11. Max Obeidin, "A Biblical Framework For Understanding The 2017 And 2024 Total Solar Eclipses," *Koenig World Watch Daily*, 4/6/2024, accessed 7/12/2024, https://watch.org/node/111110.

12. Jamie Carter, "A 'New Star' Will Appear In The Sky Any Night Now," *Live Science*, 6/20/2024, accessed 7/12/2024, https://www.livescience.com/space/astronomy/a-new-star-could-appear-in-the-sky-any-night-now-heres-how-to-see-the-blaze-star-ignite.

13. Elisha Sauers, "Astronomers Just Witnessed A Whole Galaxy 'Turn On The Lights'," *Mashable*, 6/18/2024, accessed 7/12/2024, https://mashable.com/article/space-galaxy-black-hole-activation.

14. Keith Cooper, "Rare 'Polar Rain' Aurora Seen From Earth For First Time," *Space.com*, 7/5/2024, accessed 7/12/2024, https://www.space.com/rare-smooth-aurora-north-pole-explained.

15. "Radio Astronomy," Wikipedia.org, accessed 7/12/2024, https://en.wikipedia.org/wiki/Radio_astronomy.
"Radio Waves," Science.NASA.gov, accessed 7/12/2024, https://science.nasa.gov/ems/05_radiowaves/.

16. "Sonifications," Science.NASA.gov, accessed 7/12/2024, https://science.nasa.gov/mission/hubble/multimedia/sonifications/.

17. Lee Mohon, "New NASA Black Hole Sonifications With A Remix," *NASA*, 5/4/2022, accessed 7/12/2024, https://www.nasa.gov/universe/new-nasa-black-hole-sonifications-with-a-remix/.

18. Alejandro Vigna-Gomez, "Constraints On Neutrino Natal Kicks From Black-Hole Binary VFTS 243," *American Physical Society*, 5/9/2024, accessed 7/12/2024, https://journals.aps.org/prl/abstract/10.1103/PhysRevLett.132.191403.

19. Frank Landymore, "Scientists Attempt To Explain Why Hundreds Of Stars Disappeared," *Futurism*, 5/23/2024, accessed 7/12/2024, https://futurism.com/the-byte/scientists-explain-stars-disappear-sky.

20. Michelle Starr, "Hundreds Of Huge Stars Disappeared From The Sky," *Science Alert*, 5/24/2024, accessed 7/12/2024, https://www.sciencealert.com/hundreds-of-huge-stars-disappeared-from-the-sky-we-may-finally-know-why.

21. Caroline Delbert, "The World's Scientists Are Arguing About Whether Or Not To Block The Sun," *Popular Mechanics*, 3/18/2024, accessed 7/12/2024, https://www.popularmechanics.com/science/a60189547/the-worlds-scientists-are-arguing-about-whether-or-not-to-block-the-sun/.

22. Duncan McLaren, "The Global Conversation About Solar Geoengineering," *Legal Planet*, 3/8/2024, accessed 7/12/2024, https://legal-planet.org/2024/03/08/the-global-conversation-about-solar-geoengineering-just-changed/.

23. Corbin Hiar, "Solar Geoengineering Looks To Silicon Valley For New Wave Of Funding," *Scientific American*, 2/25/2024, accessed 7/12/2024, https://www.scientificamerican.com/article/solar-geoengineering-looks-to-silicon-valley-for-new-wave-of-funding/.

24. "National UFO Reporting Center," NUFORC.org, accessed 7/12/2024, https://nuforc.org/about-us/.

[25] Katharina Buchholz, "Are UFO Sightings Taking Off Again?," *Statista*, 6/30/2023, accessed 7/12/2024, https://www.statista.com/chart/8452/ufo-sightings-are-at-record-heights/.
[26] Bill Chappell, "The Pentagon Got Hundreds Of New Reports Of UFOs In 2022," *NPR*, 1/13/2023, accessed 7/12/2024, https://www.npr.org/2023/01/13/1149019140/ufo-report.
[27] Tyler Durden, "Non-Human 'Biologics' Recovered From UFOs," *Zero Hedge*, 7/29/2023, accessed 7/12/2024, https://www.zerohedge.com/political/non-human-biologics-recovered-ufos-whistleblower-testifies.
Tyler Durden, "Air Force Whistleblower's Concerns "Legit" Over US Govt UFO Program Cover-Up," *Zero Hedge*, 1/14/2024, accessed 7/12/2024, https://www.zerohedge.com/political/air-force-whistleblowers-concerns-legit-over-us-govt-ufo-program-cover-house-oversight.
[28] Lucy Sarret, "Tucker Carlson Claims He's Seen Evidence Of 'Underwater' UFOs On Joe Rogan's Podcast," *Daily Express US*, 4/20/2024, accessed 7/12/2024, https://www.the-express.com/news/weird-news/135019/tucker-carlson-joe-rogan-podcast-UFO.
"Joe Rogan Experience #2138 - Tucker Carlson," 4/18/2024, *PowerfulJRE*, YouTube video, accessed 9/10/2024, https://www.youtube.com/watch?v=DfTU5LA_kw8.
[29] Jonathan Cahn, *The Return Of The Gods*, Hardback, (Lake Mary, FL: FrontLine, 2022).
[30] "New Jerusalem," Wikipedia.org, accessed 7/12/2024, https://en.wikipedia.org/wiki/New_Jerusalem.

Chapter 17
[1] Maria Temming, "How Many Stars Are There In The Universe?," *Sky & Telescope*, 7/15/2014, accessed 9/17/2024, https://skyandtelescope.org/astronomy-resources/how-many-stars-are-there/.
[2] Jeff Van Hatten, "Parallels Of Prophetic Significance," *The Prophecy Watcher*, July 2023.
[3] Elijah resurrected a widow's son (1 Kings 17:21-22). Elisha resurrected a widow's son (2 Kings 4:18-35). Elisha's bones resurrected a dead man (2 Kings 13:20-21). Jonah resurrected (Jonah 2:1-10). Jesus resurrected Jairus's daughter (Luke 8:54-55), a widow's son (Luke 7:11-15), Lazarus (John 11:11-44). Peter resurrected Tabitha (Acts 9:36-42). Paul resurrected Eutychus (Acts 20:9-10). Two witnesses resurrected (Revelation 11:11-12).
[4] "The Rapture - Part Seventeen - Gone In A Time," *Rapture Party*, 11/11/2022, accessed 9/17/2024, https://raptureparty.net/2022/11/11/the-rapture-part-seventeen/.

Chapter 19
[1] "Ancient Egyptian Religion," Wikipedia.org, accessed 9/17/2024, https://en.wikipedia.org/wiki/Ancient_Egyptian_religion.
[2] "Jesus Revolution," IMDB.com, accessed 9/17/2024, https://www.imdb.com/title/tt10098448.
"Risen," IMDB.com, accessed 9/17/2024, https://www.imdb.com/title/tt3231054.
"The Chosen," TheChosen.TV, accessed 9/17/2024, https://www.thechosen.tv/en-us.

Chapter 20
[1] Ron Rhodes, *The Topical Handbook of Bible Prophecy*, eBook, (Eugene, OR: Harvest House Publishers, 2010), see Scriptures for Day Of The Lord and Tribulation Period.

Appendix - Testimony
[1] "Nothing But The Blood Of Jesus," Hymnary.org, accessed 9/17/2024, https://hymnary.org/text/what_can_wash_away_my_sin.
[2] Beth Moore, *Believing God: Experiencing A Fresh Explosion of Faith - Bible Study Book*, (Nashville, TX: LifeWay Press, 2006).
[3] "Tim Chaddick Sermons," RealityLA.com, accessed 9/17/2024, referenced teachings through the book of John are sermons dated 06/04/2006 - 11/18/2007, https://realityla.com/tag/tim-chaddick/.
[4] Randy C. Alcorn, *Heaven*, (Carol Stream, IL: Tyndale House Publishers, 2004).
[5] Connect With Skip Heitzig, ConnectWithSkip.com, accessed 9/11/2024.

Appendix – Answering God's Calling
[1] "Francis Anfuso - June 2018 - Ridiculous Leads To Miraculous," SoundCloud.com, accessed 9/17/2024, https://soundcloud.com/klove-radio/francis-anfuso-june-2018-ridiculous-leads-to-miraculous.